Second edition

Global Marketing

A market-responsive approach

Svend Hollensen

FINANCIAL TIMES
Prentice Hall

An imprint of **Pearson Education**

Harlow, England · London · New York · Reading, Massachusetts · San Francisco
Toronto · Don Mills, Ontario · Sydney · Tokyo · Singapore · Hong Kong · Seoul
Taipei · Cape Town · Madrid · Mexico City · Amsterdam · Munich · Paris · Milan

Pearson Education Limited
Edinburgh Gate
Harlow
Essex CM20 2JE
England

and Associated Companies throughout the world

Visit us on the World Wide Web at:
www.pearsoneduc.com

First published 1998 by Prentice Hall
Second edition 2001

© Prentice Hall Europe 1998
© Pearson Education Limited 2001

ISBN 0-273-64644-3

British Library Cataloguing-in-Publication Data
A catalogue record for this book can be obtained from the British Library

Library of Congress Cataloging-in-Publication Data
Hollensen, Svend.
  Global marketing : a market-responsive approach / Svend Hollensen.-- 2nd ed.
    p. cm.
  Includes bibliographical references and index.
  ISBN 0-273-64644-3 (alk. paper)
    1. Export marketing. I. Title

  HF1416 .H65 2000
  658.8'48--dc21

                                        00-047695

10 9 8 7 6 5 4 3 2
06 05 04 03 02

Designed by Claire Brodmann, Book Designs

Typeset by 25
Printed by Ashford Colour Press Ltd., Gosport

Short Contents

A Companion Web site accompanies

GLOBAL MARKETING:
A market-responsive approach

by **Svend Hollensen**

Visit the Global Marketing Companion Web site at

www.booksites.net/hollensen

where you will find valuable teaching and learning material including:

For Students
- Study material designed to help you improve your results.
- A web link database containing the most valuable resources on the Internet.
- A search facility to locate specific information on the site.

For Lecturers
- A secure, password-protected site with teaching material.
- A downloadable version of the full instructor's manual.
- Extra case studies to enhance your teaching.
- Extra Internet exercises to make full use of the web's resources.
- A syllabus manager that will build and host a course web page.

Contents

Part I The decision whether to internationalize

Part III   Market entry strategies   227

Part IV Cases 556

Part V

Implementing and coordinating the global marketing programme 573

18 International sales negotiations 575

19 Organization and control of the global marketing programme 590

Part V Cases 610

Preface

For many years the globalization of markets, caused by the convergence of tastes across borders, was thought to result in very large multinational enterprises, which could use their advantages in scale economies to introduce world-standardized products successfully.

In his famous book from 1994, *The Global Paradox*, John Naisbitt has contradicted especially the last part of this myth:[1]

> The mindset that in a huge global economy the multinationals dominate world business couldn't have been more wrong. The bigger and more open the world economy becomes, the more small and middle sized companies will dominate. In one of the major turnarounds in my lifetime, we have moved from 'economies of scale' to 'diseconomies of scale'; from bigger is better to bigger is inefficient, costly and wastefully bureaucratic, inflexible, and, now, disastrous. And the paradox that has occurred is, as we move to the global context: The smaller and speedier players will prevail on a much expanded field.

When the largest corporations (e.g. IBM, ABB) downsize, they are seeking to emulate the entrepreneurial behaviour of successful SMEs (small and medium-sized enterprises) where the implementation phase plays a more important role than in large companies. Since the behaviours of smaller and (divisions of) larger firms (according to the above quotation) are convergent, the differences in the global marketing behaviour between SMEs and LSEs (large-scale enterprises) are slowly disappearing. What is happening is that the LSEs are downsizing and decentralizing their decision-making process. The result will be a more action-oriented approach to global marketing. This approach will also characterize this book.

The primary role of marketing management, in any organization, is to design and execute effective marketing programmes that will pay off. Companies can do this in their home market or they can do it in one or more international markets. Going international is an enormously expensive exercise, in terms of both money and, especially, top management time and commitment. Due to the high cost, going international must generate added value for the company beyond extra sales. In other words, the company needs to gain a competitive advantage by going international. So, unless the company gains by going international, it should probably stay at home.

The task of global marketing management is complex enough when the company operates in one foreign national market. It is much more complex when the company starts operations in several countries. Marketing programmes must, in

[1] Naisbitt, J. (1994) *The Global Paradox*, Nicholas Brealey Publishing, London p.17.

these situations, adapt to the needs and preferences of customers that have different levels of purchasing power as well as different climates, languages and cultures. Moreover, patterns of competition and methods of doing business differ between nations and sometimes also within regions of the same nation. In spite of the many differences, however, it is important to hold on to similarities across borders. Some coordination of international activities will be required, but at the same time the company will gain some synergy across borders, in the way that experience and learning acquired in one country can be transferred to another.

Objectives

The book's value chain offers the reader an analytic framework for the development and implementation of global marketing programmes. Consequently, the reader should be able to analyze, select and evaluate the appropriate conceptual frameworks for approaching the five main management decisions connected with the global marketing process: (1) whether to internationalize, (2) deciding which markets to enter, (3) deciding how to enter the foreign market, (4) designing the global marketing programme and (5) implementing and coordinating the global marketing programme.

Having studied this book, the reader should be better equipped to understand how the firm can achieve global competitiveness through the design and implementation of market-responsive programmes.

Target audience

This book is written for people who want to develop effective and efficient market-responsive global marketing programmes. It can be used as a textbook for undergraduate or graduate courses in global/international marketing. A second audience is the large group of people joining 'global marketing' or 'export' courses on non-university programmes. The book is of special interest to the manager who wishes to keep abreast of the most recent developments in the global marketing field.

Prerequisites

An introductory course in marketing.

Special features

The book has been written from the perspective of the firm competing in international markets, irrespective of its country of origin. The book has the following key features:

- Market-responsive approach.
- e-commerce approach.
- Decision/'action'-oriented approach.
- Value chain approach.
- Buyer/seller relations.

● Focus on SMEs as subsuppliers on the global market.
● Use of Internet in global marketing research.
● Focus on global marketing in Far East countries (especially China).
● Many illustrative examples and cases.

Outline

As the book has a clear decision-oriented approach, it is structured according to the five main decisions which marketing people in companies face in connection with the global marketing process. The seventeen chapters are divided into five parts. The schematic outline of the book in Figure 1 shows how the different parts fit together. As is seen in the figure, global marketing research will be regarded as a support system for all five phases of the decision process. Therefore this section of the book is placed as an appendix. Examples of the practice of global marketing by actual companies are used throughout the book, in the form of exhibits. Furthermore, each part ends with several cases, including questions for the students.

Figure 1   **Structure of the book**

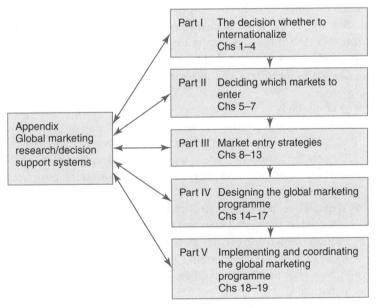

Preface to the second edition

As this book goes to press we face an environment in which global marketing has become the norm for most companies, big and small, rather than the exception. The main reason for this is the ongoing development of information technology which now allows even small companies to promote and sell their products globally through the Internet.

This second edition contains a number of important changes which update and improve the content and structure of the book. I have maintained the same five-part structure which follows the decision process regarding internationalization in small and medium-sized enterprises. This structure provides a strong pedagogic support but there have been many important changes made to individual chapters, some of which have been completely rewritten.

Because of the rapid development of electronic commerce (e-commerce) on the Internet, the most significant improvement to this edition is the integration of Internet concepts and global e-commerce strategies in several chapters.

The more important changes for this edition are as follows:

- A completely new chapter on e-commerce strategies (Chapter 13). Because of the comprehensive character of e-commerce strategies I could have included a chapter on e-commerce strategies in all five parts of the book. Instead I have chosen to create a new main e-commerce chapter in Part III ('How to enter international markets') and then integrate e-commerce perspectives into the rest of the book.
- Though we are in the Information Age, cultural differences should still be reflected in the global strategy, therefore I have introduced a separate chapter on cultural dimensions (Chapter 6). The subtitle 'A market-responsive approach' is more important than ever. In Chapter 6 ethical issues have also been emphasized.
- A new chapter on the political and economic environment has been included (Chapter 5).
- Chapter 3 (Export behaviour theories) has been completely rewritten, with the explanation of the 'Transaction cost analysis model' being strengthened. Furthermore, a new group of internationalized firms has been introduced: the 'Born Globals'.
- As an illustration to each chapter in the book, 19 case studies have been added. These cases range from international distribution of erotic videos to internationalization of funeral services.
- Internet exercises for each of the 19 chapters have also been added.

In the revision and improvement of the text a number of reviewers have been involved, whom I would like to thank for their important and valuable contribution. I also thank Dr Mohan Lal Agrawal, XLRI Jamshedpur (India) for his contributions to two new end-of-part cases (Titan Industries Ltd and Timex watches).

I am grateful to my publisher, Pearson Education. Throughout the revision, I had the pleasure of working with two editors who have seen this project through to its completion. I would therefore like to thank Development Editor, Jacqueline Senior, Acquisition Editor, Liz Sproat and Editor, Magda Robson (and the team behind them) for their encouragement and professionalism in transforming the manuscript into the final book.

I also extend my greatest gratitude to my colleagues at the University of Southern Denmark for their constant help and inspiration.

Finally, I thank my family for their support through the revision process. I am pleased to dedicate this version to Jonna, Nanna and Julie.

Svend Hollensen
Sønderborg, Denmark
November 2000

svend@sam.sdu.dk
http://www.sb.sdu.dk/~svend/

Acknowledgements

Writing any book is a long-term commitment and involves time-consuming effort. The successful completion of a book depends on the support and generosity of many people. The realization of this book is certainly no exception.

I wish to thank the many scholars whose articles, books and other materials I have cited or quoted. However, in this preface it is not possible to acknowledge everyone by name. In particular I am deeply indebted to the following individuals and organizations. I thank you all for your help and contribution:

Organization/name	Contribution
University of Southern Denmark	
Management at University of Southern Denmark	The best possible environment for writing and completing this project.
Colleagues	Encouragement and support during the writing process.
Charlotte Hansen and Aase Simonsen	Together with Michala Prip, Charlotte and Aase took care of word processing and translation of my drafts in a highly efficient manner.
Benthe Heldbjerg Hansen	Benthe provided useful www-addresses for the Appendix: Global marketing research.
The Library, Ole Krogh and the team behind him	Provided articles and books from different world-wide sources.
Reviewers	Provided suggestions which were useful in improving many parts of the text.
Case contributors	
Lars Tvede, The Fantastic Corporation, Baar, Switzerland	Case I.1 The Fantastic Corporation
Dr. Mohan Lal Agrawal, XLRI Jamshedpur, (India)	Case I.5 Titan Industries Ltd and III.5 Timex watches

Bill Merrilees and Dale Miller, Marketing Group, Department of Management, University of Newcastle, Australia	Case II.1 CarLovers
Neil C. Macpherson, Napier Marketing Group, Napier University, Edinburgh, Scotland	Case II.2 Automobile Citroën
Benjamin Tan Lin Boon, Nanyang Technological University, Singapore	Case III.1 Hong Guan Technologies

I also wish to acknowledge the help from the following firms whose managers have provided valuable material that has enabled me to write the following cases. I have been in direct personal contact with most of the companies and I thank the managers involved for their very useful comments.

Bridgestone/Firestone, Bruxelles, Belgium/Tokyo, Japan	Case I.2 Bridgestone Tyres
Oticon, Copenhagen, Denmark	Case I.3 Oticon
HSUs Ginseng Enterprises, Inc., Wausau, Wisconsin, USA	Case I.4 HSU's Ginseng Enterprises
Bertelsmann Music Group (BMG), Gütersloh, Germany	Cases III.2 and IV.3 Bertelsmann Music Group (BMG)
Autoliv AB, Stockholm, Sweden	Case III.3 Autoliv Air Bags
Imax Corporation, Toronto, Canada	Case III.4 Imax Corporation
The Absolut Company, a division of Vin & Sprit AB, Stockholm, Sweden	Case IV.1 Absolut Vodka
Dandy Chewing Gum, Vejle, Denmark	Cases IV.2 and V.3 Dandy
Tytex, a division of Thygesen Group, Herning, Denmark	Case IV.4 Tytex
3B Scientific, Poul Binhold, Lehrmittelfabrik, GmbH, Hamburg, Germany	Case V.2 3B Scientific
SKF, Göteborg, Sweden	Case V.4 SKF Rolling Bearings

I am also grateful to the following international advertising agencies, which have provided me with examples of standardized and/or localized advertising campaigns:

McCann-Erickson Advertising Ltd, London, England
   Contributed with international ads for Cathay Pacific (Plate 12)
Dentsu, Young & Rubicann, Seoul, Korea
   Contributed with an ad for Motorola's Star TAC (Plate 8)

J. Walter Thompson (JWT Europe), London
  Contributed with a European ad for LUX soap (Plate 16a)

Hindustan Thompson (HTA), Bombay, India
  Contributed with an ad for Kellogg's Basmati Flakes in India (Plate 9) and an ad for LUX soap in India (Plate 16b)

J. Walter Thompson Argentina SA, Buenos Aires, Argentina
  Contributed with two ads for Organics (Unilever) in Argentina (Plate 7)

Ammirati Puris Lintas, Hamburg, Germany
  Contributed with an ad from the 'Me and my Magnum' campaign (Plate 11)

I would also like to thank Danfoss Wärme- und Kältetechnik GmbH, LEGO and Langnese (special thanks to Silke for her efforts to get the Magnum ad) for their contributions to different examples in the book.

I would especially like to thank Universal McCann Worldwide, London, and Fiona Bristow and Mike Longhurst in particular, for their valuable contribution to Case V.1, 'Implementation of international advertising strategies – Martini versus Eurocard'.

We are grateful to the following for permission to reproduce copyright material:

Figure 1.4 from Mintzberg, H. (1987) 'The strategy concept I: Five Ps for strategy' from *California Management Review* Vol. 30 (1), copyright © 1987 by The Regents of the University of California and an extract from Lovelock, C. and Yip, G. S. (1996) 'Developing global strategies for service business' from *California Management Review* Vol. 38 (2), copyright © 1996, by The Regents of the University of California, reprinted by permission of The Regents; Figure 1.5 from Johnson, G. (1988) 'Rethinking incrementalism' from *Strategic Management Journal* Vol. 9, reproduced by permission of John Wiley & Sons, Ltd; Figure 1.7 from Peters, T. J. and Waterman, R. H. (1982) *In Search of Excellence*, copyright © 1982 by Thomas J. Peters and Robert H. Waterman, Jr., reprinted with permission of HarperCollins Publishers, Inc; Figure 1.8 adapted from Porter, M. E. (1985) *Competitive Advantage: Creating and Sustaining Superior Performance* adapted with permission from The Free Press, a Division of Simon & Schuster, Inc., copyright © 1985, 1998 by Michael E. Porter; Figure 3 adapted from Kreutzer, R. (1988) 'Standardisation: an integrated approach in global marketing' from *European Journal of Marketing* Vol. 22 (10), Figure 11.3 from Raffée, H. and Kreutzer, R. (1989) 'Organizational dimensions of global marketing' from *European Journal of Marketing* Vol. 23 (5), Figure 12.6 and Table 12.1 from Jüttner, U. and Wehrli, H. P. (1994) 'Relationship marketing from a value system perspective' from *International Journal of Service Industry Management* No. 5, Figure 14.19 adapted from Wu, H. J. and Dunn, S. C. (1995) 'Environmentally responsible logistics systems' from *International Journal of Physical Distribution and Logistics Management* Vol. 25 (2), Figure 16.4 adapted from Pirog III, S. F. and Lancioni, R. (1997) 'US-Japan distribution channel cost structures: is there a significant difference?' from *International Journal of Physical Distribution and Logistics Management* Vol. 27 (1), Table 14.3 adapted from Onkvisit, S. and Shaw, J. J. (1989) 'The international dimension of branding: strategic considerations and decisions' from *International Marketing Review* Vol. 6 (3) and Table 14.4 from Boze, B. V. and Patton, C. R. (1995) 'The future of consumer branding as seen from the picture today' from *Journal of Consumer Marketing* Vol. 12 (4), reproduced with permission from MCB University Press; Figure 3.2 and 3.3 from Welch, L. S. and Loustarinen, R. (1988) 'Internationalization: evolution of a concept' from *Journal of General Management* Vol. 14 (2), Figure 12.5 from Turnbull, P. W. and Valla, J. P. (1986) 'Internalization: evolution of a concept' from *Journal of General Management* Vol. 14 (2) and Table 4.3 adapted from Burton, J. (1995) 'Composite strategy: the combination of collaboration and competition' from *Journal of General Management* Vol. 21 (1), reproduced with permission from The Braybrooke Press Ltd; Figure 3.9 from Johnson, J. and Mattson, L. G. (1988) 'Internationalization in industrial systems' in Hood, N. and Vahlne, M. E. (eds) *Strategies in Global Competition* (pub Croom Helm), Figure 15.9 and Figure 17.3 from Phillips, C. *et al.* (1994) *International Marketing Strategy Analysis, Development and Implementation* (pub Routledge), reproduced with permission from International Thomson Publishing Services Ltd; Figure 4.5 from Tampoe, M. (1994) 'Exploiting the core competences of your organization' from *Long Range Planning* Vol. 27 (4), Figure 11.4 from Lasserre, P. (1996) 'Regional headquarters – the spearhead for Asian Pacific markets' from *Long Range Planning* Vol. 29 (1), Exhibit 11.1 from Schütte, H. (1995) 'Henkel's strategy for Asia Pacific' from *Long Range Planning* Vol. 28 (1), Figure 13.6 from Butler, P. and Peppard, J. (1998) 'Consumer purchasing on the Internet: process and prospects' from *European Management Journal* Vol. 16 (5), Figure 14.5 from MacNamee, P. (1984) 'Competitive analysis using matrix displays' from *Long Range Planning* Vol. 17 (3), Table 14.2, Figure 14.9 and Figure 14.10 from Topfer, A. (1995) 'New products – cutting the time to market' from *Long Range Planning* Vol. 28 (2), Figure 15.5 from Shibata, T. (1993) 'Sony's successful strategy for compact discs' from *Long Range Planning* Vol. 26 (4), Figure 15.6 and Table 15.3 from Diller, H. and Bhukari, I. (1994) 'Pricing conditions in the European Common Market' from *European Management Journal* Vol. 12 (2), Table 17.5 from Honeycutt, E. D. and Ford, J. B. (1995) 'Guidelines for managing an international sales force' from *Industrial Marketing Management* Vol. 24, and Exhibit 14.10 adapted from Preece, S. *et al.* (1995) 'Building a reputation along the value chain at Levi Strauss' from *Long Range Planning* Vol. 28 (6), all reproduced with permission of Elsevier Science; Figure 6.3 from Usunier, J.-C. (2000) *International Marketing*, Figure 7.7 and Table 14.5 from Welford, R. and Prescott, K. (1996) *European Business: An issue-based approach*, Figure 7.10 from Keegan, W. (1995) *Global Marketing Management*, Figure 7.11 from Bradley, F. (1995) *International Marketing Strategy*, Figure 16.2 from Chee, H. and Harris, R. (1994) *Marketing: A global perspective*, Figure 16.10 and Table 16.5 from McGoldrick, P.J. and Davies, G. *International Retailing: Trends and Strategies*, reproduced by permission of Pearson Education Limited; Figure 6.4 from Askegaard, S. and Masden, T. K. 'European food cultures: an exploratory analysis of food related preferences and behaviour in European regions' from *MAPP Working Paper No. 26*, reproduced with permission from The MAPP Centre; Figure 6.5 from Hofstede, G. (1980) *Culture's Consequences: International Differences in Work-Related Values*, reproduced with permission from Sage Publications, Inc; Figure 7.12 from Ayal, I. and Zif, J. (1979) 'Market expansion strategies in multinational marketing' from *Journal of Marketing*

Vol. 43, Spring and Figure 12.7 from Dwyer, R. F., Schurr, P. H. and Oh, S. (1987) 'Developing buyer-seller relationships' from *Journal of Marketing*, Vol. 51, April, reproduced with permission from the American Marketing Association; Figure 10.5 and Figure 10.6 from Harrigan, K. R. (1985) *Strategies for Joint Ventures*, reproduced with permission from Jossey-Bass Publishers, Inc and the author; Figure 11.2 from Oviatt, B. M. and McDougall, P. P. 'Toward a theory of international new ventures' from *Journal of International Business Studies* (First Quarter 1994) Vol. 25 (1), pp.45–64, reprinted with permission; Figure 11.5 from Bartlett, C. A. and Ghoshal, S. (1989) *Managing Across Borders: The Transnational Solution*, reprinted by permission of Harvard Business School Press, copyright © 1989 by the President and Fellows of Harvard College, all rights reserved; Figure 11.6 from Benito, G. (1996) 'Why are subsidiaries divested? A conceptual framework' *Working Paper No. 3–93*, reproduced with permission from Department of International Economics and Management, Copenhagen Business School; Figure 14.6, Figure 14.13 and Table 15.6 from Onkvisit, S. and Shaw, J. J. (1997) from *International Marketing, Third Edition* © 1997, Figure 14.12 adapted from Keegan, W. J. (1996) *Global Marketing Management, Fifth Edition*, © 1996, Figure 15.3 and Figure 15.4 from Czepiel, J. A. (1992) *Competitive Marketing Strategy*, © 1992, Figure 16.8 and an extract from Albaum, G. *et al.* (1994) *International Marketing and Export Management*, © 1994, and Table 16.2 from Toyne, B. and Walters, P. G. P. (1993) *Global Marketing Management: A Strategic Perspective, Second Edition*, © 1993, reprinted by permission of Prentice-Hall, Inc., Upper Saddle River, NJ; Figure 14.8 from Zikmund, W. and D'Amico, M. (1989) *Marketing, Third Edition*, reprinted by permission from John Wiley & Sons, Inc; Figure 14.16 'Danfoss Cool Quality Label' reproduced with permission from Danfoss Wärme- und Kältetechnik GmbH; Figure 15.7 from Simon, H. and Kucher, E. (1993) 'The European pricing bomb – and how to cope with it' from *Marketing and Research Today* February and Table from Chapter 6 Case study from Carey, G. *et al.* (1997) 'Is there one global village for our future generation?' from *Marketing and Research Today* February, reproduced with permission from European Society for Opinion and Marketing Research; Figure 15.8 from Chase Manhattan Bank (1984) *Dynamics of Trade Finance*, reproduced with permission; Figure 16.3 from Cateora, P. R. (1993) *International Marketing, Eighth Edition*, reproduced with permission from The McGraw-Hill Companies; Figure 16.12 from Paliwoda, S. (1993) *International Marketing*, reprinted with permission of Butterworth-Heinemann Publishers, a division of Reed Educational & Professional Publishing Ltd; Figure 17.5 from Rossen, J. R. and Seringhaus, F. H. R. (1996) 'Trade fairs as international marketing venues: a case study' paper presented at the Twelfth IMP Conference, University of Karlsruhe, reproduced by permission of Dalhousie University; Figure 19.7 and Table 19.2 from Samli, A. C. *et al.* (1993) *International Marketing: Planning and Practice*, reproduced with permission of Macmillan Publishers Ltd; Figure A.5 from McDaniel, C. Jr. and Gates, R. (1993) *Contemporary Marketing Research, Second Edition* (pub West Group), reproduced with permission; Table 5.1 from 'The Big Mac Index' from *The Economist* 29.4.00; Table 13.6 from Lohse, G. L. and Spiller, P. (1999) 'Internet retail store design: How the user interface influences traffic and sales' from *Journal of Computer-Mediated Communication* Vol. 5 (2) December, reproduced with permission; Table 15.5 from Cavusgil, S. T.

(1988) 'Unravelling the mystique of export pricing' from *Business Horizons* Vol. 31 (3); Exhibit 1.3 from Katayama, O. (1996) 'Flour power' from *Look Japan* March, Exhibit 2.1 adapted from Kato, K. (1995) 'The president's office is outside' from *Look Japan* January, Exhibit 14.5 adapted from Katayama, O. (1995) 'Life is a ball' from *Look Japan* December, Exhibit 19.1 adapted from Katayama, O. (1994) 'Not toying around' from *Look Japan* November, reproduced with kind permission from the authors and *Look Japan*; Exhibit 2.3 and Exhibit 5.1 from Waters, P. G. P. and Zhu, M. (1995) 'International marketing in Chinese enterprises: some evidence from the PRC' from *Management International Review* Vol. 35 (3), reproduced by permission of Management International Review; Exhibit 7.2 from Mazur, L. and Lannon, J. (1993) 'Crossborder marketing lessons from 25 European success stories' *EIU Research Report*, reproduced with permission; Exhibit 12.1 from Hines, P. (1995) 'Network sourcing: a hybrid approach' from *International Journal of Purchasing and Materials Management* Spring, Vol. 31 (2), pp. 18–24, reproduced with permission from the publisher, The National Association of Purchasing Management; Exhibit 13.3 from 'Web cuts out entire order of middlemen: 'Information technology in Japan: B-t-B e-commerce is threatening the livelihoods of thousands of inter-mediaries'' by A. Nausbaum from *Financial Times* 11.1.00 and Exhibit 14.9 adapted from 'Internet distribution strategies: Dilemmas for the incumbent' by N. Kumar from *Financial Times* 15.3.99, reproduced with permission from Financial Times; Exhibit 13.4 from 'Gucci doubles its net profit for third quarter' from *Financial Times* 11.12.99, reproduced with permission from Associated Press; Exhibit 13.5 from Jardine, A. (1999) 'Laura Ashley site to offer net sales' from *Marketing* 9 December, reproduced with permission of the copyright owner, Haymarket Business Publications Ltd; Exhibit 14.1 from Tomesco, F. (1995) 'Central Europeans in North America: pioneering spirit' from *Business Central Europe* September, reproduced with permission from Business Central Europe; Exhibit 16.3 from Spegel, R. (2000) 'Sony shocks Japanese dealers with direct sales web site' from *E-Commerce Times* 1 February, *www.EcommerceTimes.com*, reproduced with permission from NewsFactor Network; Headline 'New Hefner at the helm is trying fresh focus – the famous bunny is going global' from *USA Today* 6.10.99, reproduced with permission.

Plate 8, Motorola Star TAC advertisement reproduced with permission from Motorola Korea; Plates 9 and 16b, Kellogg's and Lux Soap advertisements reproduced with permission from Hindustan Thompsn Associates Ltd; Plate 15, Gammel Dansk advertisements reproduced with permission from Danisco Distillers Berlin GmbH and DDSF Copenhagen; Plate 21, Martini advertisements supplied and reproduced with permission from McCann-Erickson, from a campaign developed by Amster Yard, New York.

While every effort has been made to trace the owners of copyright material, in a few cases this has proved impossible and we take this opportunity to offer our apologies to any copyright holders whose rights we have unwittingly infringed.

About the author

Svend Hollensen is an Associate Professor of International Marketing at Southern Denmark Business School. He holds an M.Sc. (Business Administration) from Aarhus Business School. He has practical experience from a job as International Marketing Coordinator in a large Danish multinational enterprise as well as from being International Marketing Manager in a company producing agricultural machinery.

After working in industry he received his Ph.D. in 1992 from Copenhagen Business School.

He has published articles in journals and is the author of two case books which focus on general marketing and international marketing (published by Copenhagen Business School Press).

The author may be contacted via:

University of Southern Denmark
Grundtvigs Allé 150
DK-6400 Sønderborg
Denmark

Fax: +45 65 50 12 92
e-mail: svend@sam.sdu.dk
www-homepage: http://www.sb.sdu.dk/~svend/

Case studies

(Where available, WWW addresses have been given for further company information; these Web sites can also be accessed via **http://www.booksites.net/hollensen**, and the author's homepage at **http://www.sb.sdu.dk/~svend/**)

Case V.3   Dandy

Part B: The corporate organizational structure of the Dandy group
http://www.stimorol.com

Case V.4   SKF Rolling Bearings

Asia: the great challenge
http://skfwww01.skf.se/index.html

Colour plates

Abbreviations

CIF   Cost, Insurance and Freight: the seller quotes a price including insurance, all transportation and miscellaneous charges to the point of debarkation.

ECO   Ecology

EU   European Union: title for the former EEC used since the ratification of the Maastricht Treaty in 1992.

EXW   Ex-Works: the seller quotes a price that applies only at the point of origin: the seller agrees to place the goods at the disposal of the buyer at the specified place on the date or within the fixed period.

FDI   Foreign Direct Investment: a market entry strategy in which a company invests in a subsidiary or partnership in a foreign market (joint venture).

FMCG   Fast Moving Consumer Goods

FOB   Free On Board: the seller quotes a price covering all expenses up to the point of shipment.

GNP   Gross National Product: the total 'gross value' of all goods and services produced in the economy in one year.

HQ   Headquarters

IMF   International Monetary Fund: a group of countries that has agreed to place reserves with the IMF to support the value of their currency relative to that of other members, thus diminishing the variations in exchange rates.

JV   Joint Venture: an agreement in which a company joins forces with a local partner to enter a particular market.

LDCs   Less Developed Countries

LSEs   Large-Scale Enterprises

MNCs   Multinational Companies

MNE   Multinational Enterprise

NAFTA   North American Free Trade Agreement: a free trade agreement to establish an open market between the United States, Canada and Mexico.

OECD   Organization for Economic Cooperation and Development: a multi-national forum that allows the major industrialized nations to discuss economic policies and events.

OEM   Original Equipment Manufacturer (outsourcer)

PLC   Product Life Cycle: a theory that characterizes the sales history of products as passing through four stages: introduction, growth, maturity, decline.

R&D   Research and Development

RHQ   Regional Headquarters

SBU   Strategic Business Unit: a single business or a collection of related businesses that can be planned separately from the rest of the company.

SMEs   Small and Medium-sized Enterprises

TFs   Trade Fairs

Part I

The decision whether to internationalize

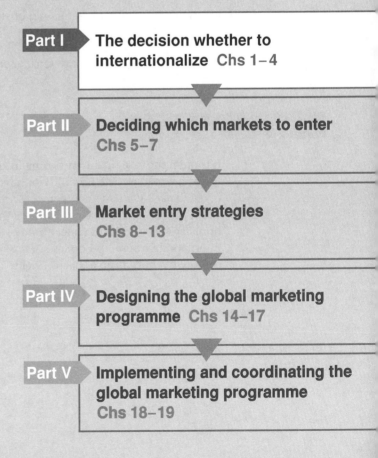

Introduction

It is often the case that a firm going into an export adventure should have stayed in the home market. The firm did not have the necessary competences to start exporting. *Chapter 1* discusses competences and global marketing strategies from the value chain perspective. *Chapter 2* discusses the major motivations of the firm to internationalize. *Chapter 3* will concentrate on some central theories which explain firms' internationalization processes. *Chapter 4* discusses the concept of 'international competitiveness' from a macro level to a micro level.

1

Global marketing in the firm

After studying this chapter you should be able to do the following:

- Characterize and compare the management style in SMEs (small and medium-sized enterprises) and LSEs (large-scale enterprises).

- Explain the role of global marketing in the firm from a holistic perspective.

- Describe and understand the concept of the value chain.

- Identify and discuss different ways of internationalizing the value chain.

1.1 Introduction

In the global/international marketing literature, the 'staying at home' alternative is not discussed thoroughly. However, Solberg (1997) argues that with limited international experience and a weak position in the home market there is little reason for a firm to engage in international markets. Instead the firm should try to improve its performance in its home market. This alternative is window no. 1 in Figure 1.1.

If the firm finds itself in a global industry as a dwarf among large multinational firms, then Solberg (1997) argues that the firm may seek ways to increase its net worth so as to attract partners for a future buy-out bid. This alternative (window no. 7 in Figure 1.1) may be relevant to SMEs selling advanced hi-tech components (as subsuppliers) to large industrial companies with a global network. In situations with fluctuations in the global demand, the SME (with limited financial resources) will often be financially vulnerable. If the firm has already acquired some competences in international business operations, it can overcome some of its competitive disadvantages by going into alliances with firms representing complementary competences (window no. 8). The other windows in Figure 1.1 are further discussed by Solberg (1997).

| Figure 1.1 | **The nine strategic windows** |

Preparedness for internationalization	*Mature*	3. Enter new business	6. Prepare for globalization	9. Strengthen your global position
	Adolescent	2. Consolidate your export markets	5. Consider expansion in international markets	8. Seek global alliances
	Immature	1. Stay at home	4. Seek niches in international markets	7. Prepare for a buy-out
		Local	*Potentially global*	*Global*
		Industry globalism		

(Source: Solberg, 1997, p. 11. Reprinted with kind permission)

1.2 Comparison of the global marketing and management style of SMEs and LSEs

In the preface, a change towards a 'convergence of orientation' in LSEs (large scale enterprises) and SMEs (small and medium-size enterprises) was indicated. This 'convergence' is shown in Figure 1.2.

| Figure 1.2 | **The 'convergence of orientation' in LSEs and SMEs** |

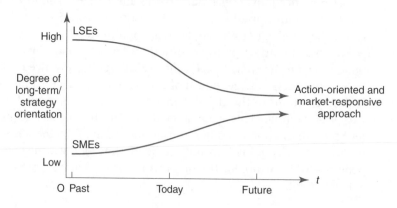

The reason underlying this 'convergence' is that many large multinationals (like IBM, Philips, GM and ABB) have begun downsizing operations, so in reality many LSEs act like a confederation of small, autonomous, entrepreneurial and action-oriented companies. One can always question the change in orientation of SMEs. Some studies (e.g. Bonaccorsi, 1992) have rejected the widely accepted proposition that firm size is positively related to export intensity. Furthermore, many researchers (e.g. Julien *et al.*, 1997) have found that SMEs as exporters do not behave as a homogeneous group. In Figure 1.2 it is assumed that SMEs and LSEs are learning from each other.

The consequence of both movements may be an action-oriented approach, where firms use the strengths of both orientations. The following section will discuss the differences in the starting points of LSEs and SMEs in Figure 1.2. The rest of the book will concentrate on a common 'action-oriented' and market-responsive approach. The result of the convergence movement of LSEs and SMEs can be illustrated by Figure 1.3.

As a reaction to pressures from international markets, both LSEs and SMEs evolve towards a globally integrated but market-responsive strategy. However, the starting points of the two firm types are different (see Figure 1.3). The huge global companies have traditionally based their strategy on taking advantage of 'economies of scale' by launching standardized products on a world-wide basis. These companies have realized that a higher degree of market responsiveness is necessary to maintain competitiveness on national markets. On the other side, SMEs have traditionally regarded national markets as independent of each other. But as international competences evolve, they have begun to realize that there is interconnectedness between their different international markets. They recognize the benefits of co-ordinating the different national marketing strategies in order to utilize economies of scale in R & D, production and marketing.

Exhibit 1.1 is an example of a LSE (McDonalds) which has also moved from the left to the right in Figure 1.3, towards a higher degree of market responsiveness.

Figure 1.3   **The global integration/market responsiveness grid: the future orientation of LSEs and SMEs**

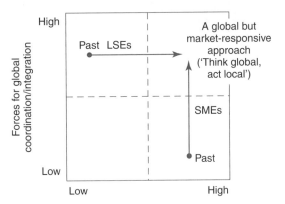

| Exhibit 1.1 | McDonald's is moving towards a higher degree of market responsiveness |

McDonald's (www.mcdonalds.com) has now expanded to about 20,000 restaurants in over 100 countries. Executives at the headquarters of the McDonald's Corp. in Oak Brook, Illinois, have learned that despite the cost/savings inherent in standardization, success is often about being able to adapt to the local environment.

Examples:

Japan

McDonald's first restaurant in Japan opened during 1971. At the time, fast food here was either a bowl of noodles or miso soup.

With its first mover advantage, McDonald's kept its lead in Japan. By 1997, McDonald's had over 1,000 outlets across that nation, and these sold more food in Japan than any other restaurant company. This includes an annual 500 million burgers.

Among the offerings of McDonald's Co. (Japan) Ltd are chicken tatsuta, teriyaki chicken, and the Teriyaki McBurger. Burgers are garnished with a fried egg. Beverages include iced coffee and corn soup.

McDonald's in Japan imports about 70 per cent of its food needs, including pickles from the USA and beef patties from Australia. High volumes facilitate bargaining with suppliers, in order to guarantee sourcing at a low cost.

India

McDonald's, which now has seven restaurants in India, was launched there in 1996. It has had to deal with a market that is 40 per cent vegetarian; with the aversion to either beef or pork among meateaters; with a hostility to frozen meat and fish; with the general Indian fondness for spice with everything.

The Big Mac was replaced by the Maharaja Mac, made from mutton, and offered vegetarian rice-patties flavoured with vegetables and spice.

Other countries

In tropical markets, guava juice was added to the McDonald's product line. In Germany, McDonald's did well selling beer as well as McCroissants. Bananafruit pies became popular in Latin America and McSpaghetti noddles became a favourite in the Philippines. In Thailand, McDonald's introduced the Samurai Pork Burger with sweet sauce. Meanwhile, McDonald's in New Zealand launched the Kiwiburger served with beetroot sauce and optional apricot pie.

In Singapore, where fries came to be served with chilli sauce, the Kiasuburger chicken breakfast became a bestseller. Singapore was among the first markets in which McDonald's introduced delivery service.

McDonald's also experimented with vegetarian needs. Its first meatless burger was the 'Hula Burger', consisting of grilled pineapple with cheese on a bun. This product was a failure, but in The Netherlands, during 1992, McDonald's tried to launch another vegetarian item, the Dutch veggie burger, made of spiced potatoes, peas, carrots and onions.

Despite success in many key markets, McDonald's also encountered difficulties marketing abroad. In October 1991, a poster illustrating the French celebrity Paul Bocuse was displayed in 66 outlets across The Netherlands; the problem was that it showed him with four other French chefs, examining a batch of dressed chickens, while the caption indicated that the chefs were dreaming of Big Macs. This was interpreted as an insult to French *haute cuisine*. Then, McDonald's aggravated the situation with a letter of apology, in which it was claimed that the internationally reputed chef was not well known in The Netherlands.

Source: Adapted from a variety of public media.

Qualitative characteristics of SMEs and LSEs

Despite the convergence of behaviour in SMEs and LSEs, there are still some differences. Table 1.1 gives an overview of the main qualitative differences between

Table 1.1　　The characteristics of LSEs and SMEs

	LSEs	SMEs
Resources	Many resources Internalization of resources Coordination of 　personnel 　financing 　market knowledge, etc.	Limited resources Externalization of resources (outsourcing of resources)
Formation of strategy/decision-making processes	Deliberate strategy formation (Mintzberg, 1987; Mintzberg and Waters, 1985) (see Figure 1.4) Adaptive decision-making mode in small incremental steps (logical incrementalism) (e.g. each new product: small innovation for the LSE) (see Figure 1.5)	Emergent strategy formation (Mintzberg, 1987; Mintzberg and Waters, 1985) (see Figure 1.4) The entrepreneurial decision-making model (e.g. each new product: considerable innovation for the SME) The owner/manager is directly and personally involved and will dominate all decision making throughout the enterprise
Organization	Formal/hierarchical Independent of one person	Informal The owner/entrepreneur usually has the power/ charisma to inspire/control a total organization
Risk taking	Mainly risk averse Focus on long-term opportunities	Sometimes risk taking/sometimes risk averse Focus on short-term opportunities
Flexibility	Low	High
Take advantage of economies of scale and economies of scope	Yes	Only limited
Use of information sources	Use of 'advanced' techniques: 　Databases 　External consultancy 　Internet	Information gathering in an informal manner and an inexpensive way: 　Internal sources 　Face-to-face communication

Figure 1.4

The intended and emergent strategy

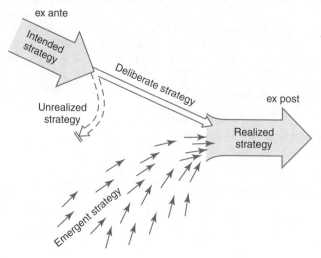

(Source: Mintzberg, 1987, p. 14. Copyright © 1987 by the Regents of the University of California. Reprinted from the *California Management Review*, vol. 30, no. 1. By permission of the Regents.)

Figure 1.5

Incremental change and strategic drift

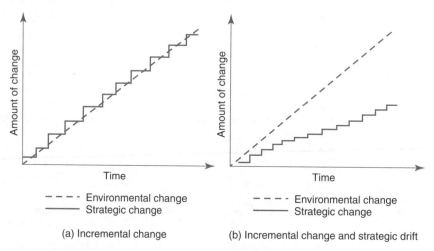

(Source: Johnson, 1988. Reproduced by permission of John Wiley & Sons Ltd.)

management and marketing styles in SMEs and LSEs. We will discuss each of the headings in turn.

Resources

● *Financial.* A well-documented characteristic of the SMEs is the lack of financial resources due to a limited equity base. The owners put only a limited amount of capital into the business, which quickly becomes exhausted.

● *Business education/specialist expertise.* Contrary to LSEs, a characteristic of SME managers is their limited formal business education. Traditionally, the SME owner/manager is a technical or craft expert, and is unlikely to be trained in any of the major business disciplines. Therefore specialist expertise is often a constraint because managers in small businesses tend to be generalists rather than specialists. In addition, global marketing expertise is often the last of the business disciplines to be acquired by an expanding SME. Finance and production experts usually precede the acquisition of a marketing counterpart. Therefore, it is not unusual to see owners of SMEs closely involved in sales, distribution, price setting and especially product development.

Formation of strategy/decision-making processes

As is seen in Figure 1.4, the realized strategy (the observable output of an organization's activity) is a result of the mix between the intended ('planned') strategy and the emergent ('not planned') strategy. No companies form a purely deliberate or intended strategy. In practice, all enterprises will have some elements of both intended and emergent strategy.

In the case of the deliberate ('planned') strategy (mainly LSEs), managers try to formulate their intentions as precisely as possible and then strive to implement these with a minimum of distortion.

This planning approach 'assumes a progressive series of steps of goal setting, analysis, evaluation, selection and planning of implementation to achieve an optimal long-term direction for the organization' (Johnson, 1988). Another approach for the process of strategic management is so-called *logical incrementalism* (Quinn, 1980), where continual adjustments in strategy proceed flexibly and experimentally. If such small movements in strategy prove successful, then further development of the strategy can take place. According to Johnson (1988), managers may well see themselves as managing incrementally, but this does not mean that they succeed in keeping pace with environmental change. Sometimes the incrementally adjusted strategic changes and the environmental market changes move apart and a *strategic drift* arises (Figure 1.5).

Exhibit 1.2 gives an example of strategic drift (LEGO).

Exhibit 1.2	**LEGO's strategic drift**

The Danish family owned LEGO group (www.lego.com) is today the world's fifth largest toy producer after Mattel (known for the Barbie doll), Hasbro (known for Trivial Pursuit and Disney figures, via a licensing agreement with Disney), Nintendo (computer games) and SEGA (computer games).

Until now LEGO has strongly believed that its unique concept was superior to other products, but today LEGO feels pressured into competing for children's time. The famous LEGO bricks receive increasing competition from TV, video, CD-ROM games and the Internet. It seems that in LEGO's case a 'strategic drift' has arisen, where LEGO management's blind faith in its unique and pedagogical toys has not been harmonized with the way in which the world has developed. Many working parents have less and less time to 'control' children's play habits. Spectacular computer games win over 'healthy' and pedagogical toys which LEGO represents. This development has accelerated and has forced LEGO to re-evaluate its present strategy regarding product programmes and marketing. One result is a cooperation with the American partner Mindscape (one of the world's leading producers of consumer software) on the development of the first LEGO CD-ROM ('Adventures on LEGO Island') which is to be followed by others. Among other things, future manuals to LEGO building sets will be replaced by a CD-ROM. This gives new possibilities of exploiting synergy effects between LEGO's core product programme and new technology. Furthermore, negotiations are taking place in the USA with several TV production companies about producing children's programmes in the category of 'edutainment', which combines education and entertainment. As there is a lack of this type of children's programmes in the USA, it is a possibility for LEGO to supply educational material. LEGO has no plans, though, to establish its own TV production.

LEGO is now (year 2000) trying to extend their traditional concepts and values into media products for children aged between two and 16. These new categories – including PC and console software, books, magazines, TV, film and music – aim to replicate the same feelings of confidence and trust already long-established amongst children and their parents.

Whether it is programmable robots from the LEGO Mindstorms division, inspiring clothing and accessories from LEGO Lifestyle, or the famous LEGOland parks, these operations complement the traditional play materials business in symbiotic fashion.

Launched Christmas 1998, LEGO Creator, LEGO Loco and LEGO Chess were the first of a whole stream of new software titles. LEGO Creator held several record retail chart positions in the run up to the festive season.

On the other hand, the SME is characterized by the entrepreneurial decision-making model (Figure 1.6). Here more drastic changes in strategy are possible because decision making is intuitive, loose and unstructured. In Figure 1.6 the range of possible realized strategies is determined by an interval of possible outcomes. SME entrepreneurs are noted for their propensity to seek new opportunities. This

Figure 1.6   The entrepreneurial decision-making model

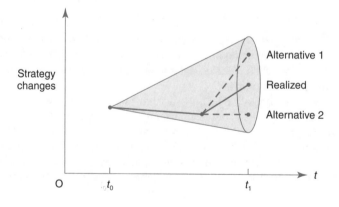

natural propensity for change inherent in entrepreneurs can lead to considerable changes in the enterprise's growth direction. Because the entrepreneur changes focus, this growth is not planned or coordinated and can therefore be characterized by sporadic decisions that have an impact on the overall direction in which the enterprise is going.

Organization

Compared to LSEs the employees in SMEs are usually closer to the entrepreneur, and because of the entrepreneur's influence these employees must conform to his or her personality and style characteristics if they are to remain employees.

Risk taking

There are, of course, different degrees of risk. Normally the LSEs will be risk averse because of their use of a decision-making model which emphasizes small incremental steps with a focus on long-term opportunities.

In SMEs risk taking depends on the circumstances. Risk taking can occur in situations where the survival of the enterprise may be under threat, or where a major competitor is undermining the activities of the enterprise. The entrepreneur may also be taking risks when he or she has not gathered all the relevant information, and thus has ignored some important facts in the decision-making process.

On the other hand, there are, of course, some circumstances in which an SME will be risk averse. This can often occur when an enterprise has been damaged by previous risk taking and the entrepreneur is therefore reluctant to take any kind of risk until confidence returns.

Flexibility

Because of the shorter communication lines between the enterprise and its customers, the SMEs can react in a quicker and more flexible way to customer enquiries.

Economies of scale and economies of scope

- *Economies of scale.* Accumulated volume in production and sales will result in lower cost price per unit due to 'experience curve effects' and increased efficiency in production, marketing, etc. Because of size (bigger market share) and accumulated experience, the LSEs will normally take advantage of this. SMEs tend to concentrate on lucrative small market segments. Such market segments are often too insignificant for LSEs to target, but can be substantial and viable in respect to the SME. However, they will only result in a very limited market share of a given industry.

- *Economies of scope.* Synergy effects can occur when the firm is serving more international markets. The LSEs often serve many different markets (countries) on more continents and are thereby able to transfer experience acquired in one country to another country. Typically, SMEs serve only a very limited number of international markets outside their home market. Sometimes the SME can make use of economies of scope when it goes into an alliance or a joint venture with a partner which has what the particular SME is missing on the international market in question: a complementary product programme or local market knowledge.

Use of information sources

Typically, LSEs rely on commissioned market reports made by well-reputed (and well-paid!) international consultancy firms as their source of vital global marketing information.

The SMEs usually gather information in an informal manner by use of face-to-face communication. The entrepreneur is able unconsciously to synthesize this information and use it to make decisions. The acquired information is mostly incomplete and fragmented, and evaluations are based on intuition and often guesswork. The whole process is dominated by the desire to find a circumstance which is ripe for exploitation.

Furthermore, the demand for complex information grows as the SME selects a more and more explicit orientation toward the international market and as the firm evolves from a production-oriented ('upstream') to a more marketing-oriented ('downstream') firm (Cafferata and Mensi, 1995).

1.3 The role of global marketing in the firm: a holistic approach

Some firms are successful without having a complex marketing organization. Other firms have a lot of subactivities belonging to the global marketing function, and yet fail to achieve success. However, marketing is not simply a structural matter that can be isolated from the firm's culture and its shared value system. A firm and a marketing infrastructure will have better chances of success if they operate in a corporate culture where the employees see their basic task as satisfying customers and their expectations. Every firm exists to satisfy the needs of its customers. The firm stands to win or lose by its ability to attain such a goal. This approach requires one to view the firm as a total system. Peters and Waterman's book, *In Search of Excellence* (1982) views the firm from a holistic point of view by forcing managers to ask themselves many questions about the main elements of corporate excellence. The model, which is referred to as the 7-S framework for effective organizations, is based on the thesis that organizational effectiveness stems from the interaction of seven factors: structure, systems, style, staff, skills, strategy and shared values. Figure 1.7 shows the seven Ss and highlights their interconnectedness.

According to the model, strategy is viewed as only one of seven elements typical of best-managed firms. Each of the seven Ss can be the driving force of change at a given point in time. Shared values are the centrepiece of the paradigm. A company has shared values when the employees share the same guiding values and missions. These are often unwritten and go beyond the conventional formal statement of corporate objectives. They are based on the firm's corporate philosophy and attitudes. The drive for their accomplishment pulls the firm's organization together; it provides the engine that pulls the firm in a desired direction.

Figure 1.7   **The 7-S framework**

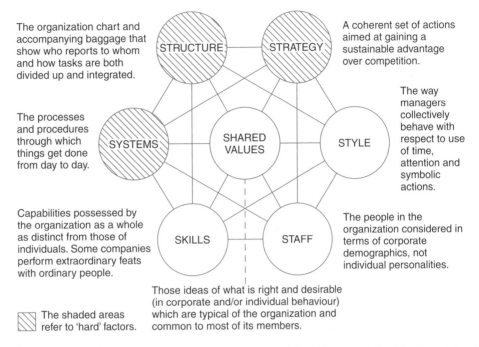

The organization chart and accompanying baggage that show who reports to whom and how tasks are both divided up and integrated.

A coherent set of actions aimed at gaining a sustainable advantage over competition.

The processes and procedures through which things get done from day to day.

The way managers collectively behave with respect to use of time, attention and symbolic actions.

Capabilities possessed by the organization as a whole as distinct from those of individuals. Some companies perform extraordinary feats with ordinary people.

The people in the organization considered in terms of corporate demographics, not individual personalities.

Those ideas of what is right and desirable (in corporate and/or individual behaviour) which are typical of the organization and common to most of its members.

The shaded areas refer to 'hard' factors.

(Source: Majaro, 1993, p. 4. Copyright © 1982 by Thomas J. Peters and Robert H. Waterman, Jr. Reprinted by permission of HarperCollins Publishers, Inc.)

One of the important features of the 7-S framework is the interconnectedness of the seven Ss. They must all work in harmony within the firm's changing international environment, with a view to creating and developing satisfied customers ('keeping the customers happy').

1.4 The value chain as a framework for identifying international competitive advantage

The 7-S framework studied in section 1.3 can be regarded as the roots from which the firm's different activities come. In particular, shared values should be a main determinant of the configuration of the value chain.

The concept of the value chain

The value chain shown in Figure 1.8 provides a systematic means of displaying and categorizing activities. The activities performed by a firm in any industry can be grouped into the nine generic categories shown.

At each stage of the value chain there exists an opportunity to contribute positively to the firm's competitive strategy by performing some activity or process in a way that is better than the competitors, and so providing some uniqueness or

Figure 1.8   **The value chain**

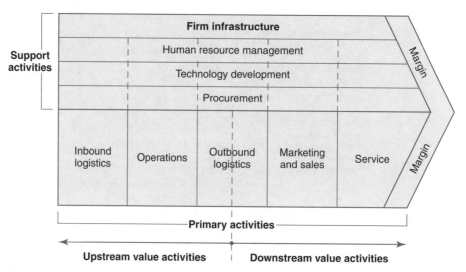

(Source: Adapted from Porter, 1985, pp. 21, 24. Reprinted with the permission of The Free Press, a division of Simon & Schuster, from *Competitive Advantage: Creating and Sustaining Superior Performance* by Michael E. Porter. Copyright © Michael E. Porter)

advantage. If a firm attains such a competitive advantage, which is sustainable, defensible, profitable and valued by the market, then it may earn high rates of return, even though the industry structure may be unfavourable and the average profitability of the industry modest.

In competitive terms, value is the amount that buyers are willing to pay for what a firm provides them (perceived value). A firm is profitable if the value it commands exceeds the costs involved in creating the product. Creating value for buyers that exceeds the cost of doing so is the goal of any generic strategy. Value, instead of cost, must be used in analyzing competitive position, since firms often deliberately raise their costs in order to command a premium price via differentiation. The concept of buyers' perceived value will be discussed further in Chapter 4.

The value chain displays total value and consists of value activities and margin. Value activities are the physically and technologically distinct activities that a firm performs. These are the building blocks by which a firm creates a product valuable to its buyers. Margin is the difference between total value (price) and the collective cost of performing the value activities.

Competitive advantage is a function of either providing comparable buyer value more efficiently than competitors (lower cost), or performing activities at comparable cost but in unique ways that create more customer value than the competitors are able to offer, and, hence, command a premium price (differentiation). The firm might be able to identify elements of the value chain that are not worth the costs. These can then be unbundled and produced outside the firm (outsourced) at a lower price.

Value activities can be divided into two broad types, primary activities and support activities. *Primary activities*, listed along the bottom of Figure 1.8, are the activities involved in the physical creation of the product, its sale and transfer to the buyer, as well as after-sale assistance. In any firm, primary activities can be divided into the five generic categories shown in the figure. *Support activities* support the primary activities and each other by providing purchased inputs, technology, human resources and various firm-wide functions. The dotted lines reflect the fact that procurement, technology development and human resource management can be associated with specific primary activities as well as supporting the entire chain. Firm infrastructure is not associated with particular primary activities, but supports the entire chain.

Primary activities

The primary activities of the organization are grouped into five main areas: inbound logistics, operations, outbound logistics, marketing and sales, and service.

- *Inbound logistics* are the activities concerned with receiving, storing and distributing the inputs to the product/service. These include materials, handling, stock control, transport, etc.
- *Operations* transform these various inputs into the final product or service: machining, packaging, assembly, testing, etc.
- *Outbound logistics* collect, store and distribute the product to customers. For tangible products this would involve warehousing, material handling, transport, etc.; in the case of services it may be more concerned with arrangements for bringing customers to the service if it is in a fixed location (e.g. sports events).
- *Marketing and sales* provide the means whereby consumers/users are made aware of the product/service and are able to purchase it. This would include sales administration, advertising, selling, etc. In public services, communication networks which help users access a particular service are often important.
- *Services* cover all the activities which enhance or maintain the value of a product/service. Asugman *et al.* (1997) have defined after-sales service as 'those activities in which a firm engages after purchase of its product that minimize potential problems related to product use, and maximize the value of the consumption experience'. After-sales service consists of the following: the installation and start-up of the purchased product, the provision of spare parts for products, the provision of repair services, technical advice regarding the product, and the provision and support of warranties.

Each of these groups of primary activities is linked to support activities.

Support activities

These can be divided into four areas:

- *Procurement*. This refers to the process of acquiring the various resource inputs to the primary activities (not to the resources themselves). As such, it occurs in many parts of the organization.
- *Technology development*. All value activities have a 'technology', even if it is simply 'know-how'. The key technologies may be concerned directly with the

product (e.g. R & D, product design) or with processes (e.g. process development) or with a particular resource (e.g. raw material improvements).

● *Human resource management.* This is a particularly important area which transcends all primary activities. It is concerned with the activities involved in recruiting, training, developing and rewarding people within the organization.

● *Infrastructure.* The systems of planning, finance, quality control, etc. are crucially important to an organization's strategic capability in all primary activities. Infrastructure also consists of the structures and routines of the organization which sustain its culture.

As indicated in Figure 1.8, a distinction is also made between the production-oriented, 'upstream' activities and the more marketing-oriented, 'downstream' activities.

Having looked at Porter's original value chain model, a simplified version will be used in most parts of this book (Figure 1.9). This simplified version of the value chain is characterized by the fact that it contains only the primary activities of the firm.

Although value activities are the building blocks of competitive advantage, the value chain is not a collection of independent activities, but a system of interdependent activities. Value activity is related by linkages within the value chain. Linkages are relationships between the way in which one value activity is performed and the cost or performance of another.

In understanding the competitive advantage of an organization, the strategic importance of the following types of linkage should be analyzed in order to assess

Figure 1.9   A 'simplified' version of the value chain

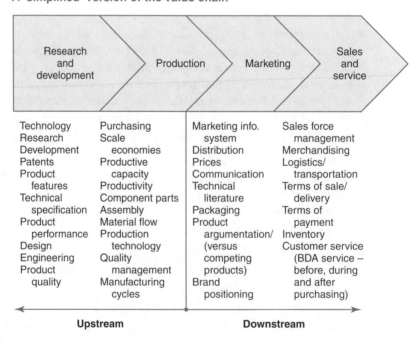

how they contribute to cost reduction or value added. There are two kinds of linkage:

- *Internal linkages* between activities within the same value chain, but perhaps on different planning levels within the firm.
- *External linkages* between different value chains 'owned' by the different actors in the total value system.

Internal linkages

There may be important links between the primary activities. In particular, choices will have been made about these relationships and how they influence value creation and strategic capability. For example, a decision to hold high levels of finished stock might ease production scheduling problems and provide a faster response time to the customer. However, it will probably add to the overall cost of operations. An assessment needs to be made of whether the added value of 'stocking' is greater than the added cost. Suboptimization of the single value chain activities should be avoided. It is easy to miss this point in an analysis if, for example, the marketing activities and operations are assessed separately. The operations may look good because they are geared to high-volume, low-variety, low-unit-cost production. However, at the same time the marketing team may be selling quickness, flexibility and variety to the customers. When put together these two potential strengths are weaknesses because they are not in harmony, which is what a value chain requires. The link between a primary activity and a support activity may be the basis of competitive advantage. For example, an organization may have a unique system for procuring materials. Many international hotels and travel companies use their computer systems to provide immediate 'real-time' quotations and bookings world-wide from local access points.

As a supplement to comments about the linkages between the different activities, it is also relevant to regard the value chain (illustrated in Figure 1.9 in the simplified form) as a thoroughgoing model on all three planning levels in the organization.

In purely conceptual terms, a firm can be described as a pyramid as illustrated in Figure 1.10. It consists of an intricate conglomeration of decision and activity levels. It consists of three distinct levels, but the main value chain activities are connected to all three strategic levels in the firm.

- The *strategic level* is responsible for formulation of the firm's mission statement, determining objectives, identifying the resources that will be required if the firm is to attain its objectives, and selecting the most appropriate corporate strategy for the firm to pursue.
- The *managerial level* has the task of translating corporate objectives into functional and/or unit objectives and ensuring that resources placed at its disposal (e.g. in the marketing department) are used effectively in the pursuit of those activities that will make the achievement of the firm's goals possible.
- The *operational level* is responsible for the effective performance of the tasks which underlie the achievement of unit/functional objectives. The achievement of operational objectives is what enables the firm to achieve its managerial and

Figure 1.10 **The value chain in relation to the strategic pyramid**

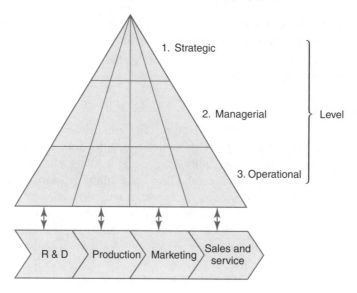

strategic aims. All three levels are interdependent, and clarity of purpose from the top enables everybody in the firm to work in an integrated fashion towards a common aim.

External linkages

One of the key features of most industries is that a single organization rarely undertakes all value activities from product design to distribution to the final consumer. There is usually a specialization of roles, and any single organization usually participates in the wider value system which creates a product or service. In understanding how value is created, it is not enough to look at the firm's internal value chain alone. Much of the value creation will occur in the supply and distribution chains, and this whole process needs to be analyzed and understood.

Suppliers have value chains (upstream value) that create and deliver the purchased inputs used in a firm's chain. Suppliers not only deliver a product, but also can influence a firm's performance in many other ways. For example, Benetton, the Italian fashion company, managed to sustain and elaborate networks of suppliers, agents and independent retail outlets as the basis of its rapid and successful international development during the 1970s and 1980s.

In addition, products pass through the value chain channels (channel value) on their way to the buyer. Channels perform additional activities that affect the buyer and influence the firm's own activities. A firm's product eventually becomes part of its buyer's value chain. The ultimate basis for differentiation is a firm and its product's role in the buyer's value chain, which is determined by buyer needs. Gaining and sustaining competitive advantage depends on understanding not only a firm's value chain, but how the firm fits into the overall value system.

Exhibit 1.3 shows an example of a Japanese manufacturer of rice-milling machines moving into 'downstream' activities.

Exhibit 1.3	## Satake Corporation: A specialist in machines for rice milling

Satake Corporation of Higashi Hiroshima is a pioneer in the manufacture of power rice-whitening machines, with its home base in Japan. It has developed a full line of machinery for harvesting and processing rice: dryers (to prepare freshly harvested paddy rice for storage), separators (to eliminate straws and foreign objects like stones), huskers (to remove the bran) and packaging machines.

The company is the world leader in the market for large-scale rice mills. However, the problem is that rice mills buy machinery only once every fifteen or twenty years. Therefore, Satake have sought ways of expanding their business and in the 1990s they have exploited two opportunities:

● In 1991 Satake purchased the UK company Robinson Milling Systems, the second largest manufacturer of flour-milling equipment in the world, and established Satake UK Ltd. Working from that base, it applied to wheat flour milling the technology that it had gained in rice whitening.

● Satake's downstream strategy has led it into such areas as 'instant' rice that can be cooked in a microwave, and emergency-preparedness kits containing 'alpha rice', mineral water, trivets and solid fuel.

The dream of Satoru Satake, president of Satake Corporation, is to set up joint ventures with partners so that together they can have an entire value chain system that goes from rice production through rice milling and all the way to sales.

Source: Katayama (1996). With kind permission from O. Katayama/*Look Japan*.

There are often circumstances where the overall cost can be reduced (or the value increased) by collaborative arrangements between different organizations in the value system. It will be seen in Chapter 10 that this is often the rationale behind joint ventures (e.g. sharing technology in the international motor manufacture and electronics industries).

Internationalizing the value chain

International configuration and coordination of activities

All internationally oriented firms must consider an eventual internationalization of the value chain's functions. The firm must decide whether the responsibility for the single value chain function is to be moved to the export markets, or is best handled centrally from head office. Principally, the value chain function should be carried out where there is the highest competence (and the most cost effectiveness), and this is not necessarily at head office.

A distinction immediately arises between the activities labelled downstream on Figure 1.9 and those labelled upstream activities. The location of downstream activities, those more related to the buyer, is usually tied to where the buyer is located. If a firm is going to sell in Australia, for example, it must usually provide service in Australia, and it must have salespeople stationed in Australia. In some industries it is possible to have a single sales force that travels to the buyer's country and back again; other specific downstream activities, such as the production of advertising copy, can sometimes also be performed centrally. More typically, however, the firm must locate the capability to perform downstream activities in each of the countries in which it operates. In contrast, upstream activities and support activities are more independent of where the buyer is located (Figure 1.11). However, if the export markets are culturally close to the home market, it may be relevant to control the entire value chain from head office (home market).

This distinction carries some interesting implications. First, downstream activities create competitive advantages that are largely country specific: a firm's reputation, brand name and service network in a country grow largely out of its activities and create entry/mobility barriers largely in that country alone. Competitive advantage in upstream and support activities often grows more out of the entire system of countries in which a firm competes than from its position in any single country.

Second, in industries where downstream activities or other buyer-tied activities are vital to competitive advantage, there tends to be a more multidomestic pattern of international competition. In many service industries, for example, not only downstream activities but frequently upstream activities are tied to buyer location, and global strategies are comparatively less common. In industries where upstream and support activities such as technology development and operations are crucial to competitive advantage, global competition is more common.

For example, there may be a large need in firms to centralize and coordinate the production function world-wide to be able to create rational production units that are able to exploit economies of scale.

Furthermore, as customers increasingly join regional cooperative buying organizations, it is becoming more and more difficult to sustain a price differentiation across markets. This will put pressure on the firm to coordinate a European price policy. This will be discussed further in Chapter 15.

Figure 1.11   **Centralizing the upstream activities and decentralizing the downstream activities**

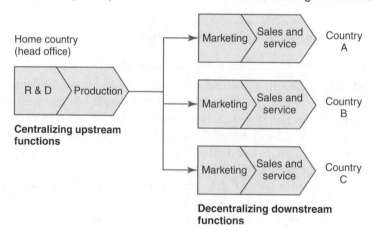

The distinctive issues of international strategies, in contrast to domestic, can be summarized in two key dimensions of how a firm competes internationally. The first is called the *configuration* of a firm's world-wide activities, or the location in the world where each activity in the value chain is performed, including the number of places. The second dimension is called *coordination*, which refers to how identical or linked activities performed in different countries are coordinated with each other (Porter, 1986).

1.5 Information business and the virtual value chain

Most business managers would agree that we have recently entered a new era, 'The Information Age', which differs markedly from the industrial age. What have been the driving forces for these changes?

The consensus has shifted over time. To begin with, it was thought to be the automation power of computers and computation. Then it was the ability to collapse time and space through telecommunications. More recently it has been seen as the value-creating power of information, a resource which can be reused, shared, distributed or exchanged without any inevitable loss of value; indeed, value is sometimes multiplied. Today's fascination with competing on invisible assets means that people now see knowledge and its relationship with intellectual capital as the critical resource, because it underpins innovation and renewal.

One way of understanding the strategic opportunities and threats of information is to consider the 'virtual value chain' as a supplement to the 'physical value chain' (Figure 1.12).

By introducing the *virtual value chain*, Rayport and Sviokla (1996) have made an extension of the conventional value chain model, which treats information as a supporting element in the value-adding process. Rayport and Sviokla (1996) show how information in itself can be used to create value (see Exhibit 1.4).

Exhibit 1.4 | **Geffen Records (a unit of MCA's music division): An example of the 'virtual value chain'**

The traditional product of a record label is a package of pre-recorded music captured on an audiocassette or compact disc. This 'physical' value-adding process consists of discovering new musicians, screening them for marketability, recording their work in a studio, editing and selecting their music, creating master tapes, producing CDs or cassettes, and finally packaging, promoting and distributing the product.

Today, new competitors for Geffen's business are emerging in the market space (Internet). Musicians can record and edit material inexpensively themselves, and distribute and promote it over the World Wide Web.

To counter these competitive moves, Geffen Records has made a site on the World Wide Web where it can test consumers' reactions to its music and build an audience for its recorded performances. The Web page in the market space has become a showroom for its bands and the company uses it to distribute digital audio and video samples and to provide information about the bands' tours. The Web page can even be used as a potential new retail channel, where consumers can buy the CDs of the bands. Thus, the 'virtual value chain' in the market space is a mirror of activities that have traditionally taken place in the physical world.

Source: Rayport and Sviokla (1996), pp. 23–4.

Fundamentally, there are four ways of using information to create business value (Marchand, 1999):

1. *Managing risks.* In the 20th century, the evolution of risk management has stimulated the growth of functions and professions such as finance, accounting, auditing and controlling. These information-intensive functions tend to be major consumers of IT resources and people's time.

2. *Reducing costs.* Here the focus is on using information as efficiently as possible to achieve the outputs required from business processes and transactions. This process view of information management is closely linked with the re-engineering and continuous improvement movements of the 1990s. The common elements are focused on eliminating unnecessary and wasteful steps and activities, especially paperwork and information movements, and then simplifying and, if possible, automating the remaining processes.

3. *Offering products and services.* Here the focus is on knowing one's customers, and sharing information with partners and suppliers to enhance customer satisfaction. Many service and manufacturing companies focus on building relationships with customers and on demand management as ways of using information. Such strategies have led companies to invest in point-of-sale systems, account management, customer profiling and service management systems.

4. *Inventing new products.* Finally, companies can use information to innovate – to invent new products, provide different services and use emerging technologies. Companies such as Intel and Microsoft are learning to operate in 'continuous discovery mode', inventing new products more quickly and using market intelligence to retain a competitive edge. Here, information management is about mobilizing people and collaborative work processes to share information and promote discovery throughout the company.

Every company pursues some combination of the above strategies.

In relation to Figure 1.12 information can be captured at all stages of the physical value chain. Obviously such information can be used to improve performance at each stage of the physical value chain and to coordinate across it. However, it can also be analyzed and repackaged to build content-based products or to create new lines of businesses.

A company can use its information to reach out to other companies' customers or operations, thereby rearranging the value system of an industry. The result might be that traditional industry sector boundaries disappear. The CEO of Amazon.com, Bezos, clearly sees his business as not in the book-selling business, but in the information-broker business.

Figure 1.12 The virtual value chain in relation to the physical value chain

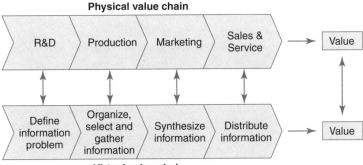

1.6 Summary

SMEs are often characterized by an entrepreneurial and action-oriented decision-making model, where drastic changes in strategy are possible because decision making is intuitive, sporadic and unstructured. On the other hand, SMEs are more flexible than LSEs and are able to react more quickly to sudden changes in the international environment.

However, as a consequence of LSEs often acting like a confederation of SMEs, there seems to be a convergence of the marketing behaviour in SMEs and LSEs towards a market-responsiveness approach.

On the basis of the 7-S framework, a simplified version of Porter's original value chain model was introduced, as a framework model for major parts of this book. In understanding how value is created, it is not enough to look at the firm's internal value chain alone. In most cases the supply and distribution value chains are interconnected, and this whole process needs to be analyzed and understood before considering an eventual internationalization of value chain activities. This also involves decisions about configuration and coordination of the world-wide value chain activities.

At the end of this chapter the 'virtual value chain' was introduced as a supplement to the 'physical value chain', in that way using information to create further business value.

Case study Vermont Teddy bear

Should the Vermont Teddy Bear go abroad?

As Elisabeth B. Robert, CEO of the Vermont Teddy Bear Company (www.vtbear.com), leaves the annual meeting of the Vermont Teddy Bear Company on 2 December 1999 she can look back on the best year in the history of the company:

	1998/99
Net revenues:	$21.6 million
Net profit:	$1.8 million

(Number of employees as of 30 June 1999: 223 of whom 112 were employed in sales and marketing positions.)

But Elisabeth has further ambitions for the company:

My longer-term vision for the company is to leverage our marketing and operational strengths with a sound brand strategy to grow our company with teddy bears and other products in the gift delivery service industry. Unlike other Internet companies, we have proven our ability to profitably market a gift delivery service using radio and the Internet. Unlike other Internet companies, we have an established, state-of-the-art, cost-effective fulfilment operation with integrated systems to customize, personalize, pick, pack, and ship and provide superior customer service. And, the people of The Vermont Teddy Bear Company are not only persistent and smart, they have become over the past several years extremely good at what they do. Why shouldn't we aspire to be one of the premier gift delivery services in the world?'

(Source: Annual Report 1999)

The company

The Vermont Teddy Bear Company® is the USA's largest maker of handcrafted teddy bears, sewing and assembling more than 350,000 bears a year out of its northern Vermont factory. The largest of the company's business segments is the Bear-Gram gift delivery service comprising 84 per cent of the company's total business for the fiscal year ended 30 June 1999. The company's Bear-Gram segment sales are heavily seasonal, with Valentine's Day, Christmas, and Mother's Day as its largest sales seasons. The company primarily uses the direct response radio distribution channel supported visually by the Internet to market its Bear-Gram gift delivery service.

Late in 1999 the company made a co-promotion for Seagram's Ginger Ale. Across the country, 20 million litre bottles of Seagram's Ginger Ale will be labelled with a chance to win a Vermont Teddy Bear and a coupon for a 20 per cent discount on any of the Vermont-made bears offered through the Bear-Gram gift delivery service.

The company began taking orders on its Website in March 1997, recognizing that the Website provided visual support to the Company's radio advertising campaign across the country and a convenient way for customers to place orders. In December 1997, online orders represented 7 per cent of total Bear-Gram orders. In April 2000 approximately 35 per cent of the Bear-Gram orders are received via the Company's Website, triple the level of the prior year.

The company competes with a number of sellers of flowers, balloons, candy, cakes and other gift items, which can be ordered by telephone for special occasions and delivered by express service in a manner similar to Bear-Gram gifts. The company also competes to a lesser degree with a number of companies that sell teddy bears in the United States, including, but not limited to, Steiff of Germany, Dakin, North American Bear, and Gund. Many of these competitors have greater financial, sales, and marketing resources than Vermont Teddy Bear.

There are no material barriers to entry into this market, and accordingly, there can be no assurance that additional companies will not seek to compete directly with the company, including those with greater resources than the company.

Approximately 100 different bear outfits are manufactured, including ballerina bears, birthday bears, bride and groom bears, business bears, nurse bears, and sports bears. More than 50 per cent of this production is outsourced to overseas manufacturers, mainly in Asia. Until now the company has only been selling to American customers. However, the management is exploring some opportunities in other parts of the world.

As Elisabeth Robert says: 'Gift giving is a deeply rooted tradition in many foreign cultures. Using common carriers such as FedEx and taking orders on the Internet, we avoid setting up an international distribution infrastructure. Handling an order from Tokyo is now no different than handling one from St Louis.'

Questions

1. What kind of difficulties would the company meet, if it were to internationalize its business?
2. In what part of the world should the company start its internationalization?
3. How should the company penetrate the foreign markets
   (a) by Internet?
   (b) by physical stores?
   (c) by a combination of the two?
4. Would some kind of product line extension be relevant for the company to explore?

Questions for discussion

1. What is the reason for the 'convergence of orientation' in LSEs and SMEs?
2. How can an SME compensate for its lack of resources and expertise in global marketing when trying to enter export markets?
3. What are the main differences between global marketing and marketing in the domestic context?
4. In Exhibit 1.3 the Satake Corporation tries to control the entire value chain system by setting up joint ventures with partners. Explain the main risks of following such a strategy.
5. Explain the main advantages of centralizing upstream activities and decentralizing downstream activities.
6. How is the 'virtual value chain' different from the 'conventional value chain'? (Use Exhibit 1.4 as a starting point.)

Internet exercise

Playboy Enterprises
Internationalization of the Playboy Business

Please go to:

www.playboy.com/corporate/

www.britannica.com (use the search function for downloading some interesting articles about Playboy Enterprises)

Playboy Enterprises Inc. (PEI) is an international multimedia entertainment company that sells and markets branded products and services in almost 200 countries worldwide. The Company's six business groups (SBUs) are Publishing, Entertainment, Product Marketing, Catalog, Casino Gaming and Playboy.com, Inc.

'We're going from a domestic print-oriented magazine to a global entertainment company. This has been the vision that I had since becoming CEO', Christie Hefner, chairman and CEO of PBE and PEI. ('New Hefner at helm is trying fresh focus – The famous bunny is going global', *USA Today*, 6 October 1999)

Christie Hefner adds: 'To have long-term survivability, brands shouldn't be identified in the consumer's mind with a single product. They should reflect a point of view that you can own and adapt what products will best express it, given trends, lifestyle, and technology. What we've done is extract from the magazine the essence of what the brand stands for as a lifestyle, and a sense of fun, sexy entertainment and then marry that with the right content of the right product to represent the brand in a different format, whether that be Playboy Television or Playboy Online'. ('Pulling rabbits out of hats', *Chief Executive*, New York, September 1999)

Although most analysts have been impressed by Ms Hefner's approach to the business, there are also some who remain critical about the future value of PBE: '… Playboy is no longer unique. Each one of these magazines has taken on a part of Playboy's niche. It is hard to find a way to grow'. (Magazine industry analyst Samir Husni, 'New Hefner at helm is trying fresh focus – The famous bunny is going global', *USA Today*, 6 October 1999)

Questions

1. Make an evaluation of the internationalization potential of the Playboy brand compared to its competitors such as Hustler (www.hustler.com).

2. Playboy would like to have a larger market share in Europe: which of the six SBUs in the product portfolio should it focus on?

3. Should PBE try to transfer its brand image to other product areas? Which ones and how?

For further exercises and cases, see this book's website at *www.booksites.net/hollensen*

References

Asugman, G., Johnson, J.L. and McCullough, J. (1997) 'The role of after-sales service in international marketing', *Journal of International Marketing*, vol. 5, no. 4, pp. 11–28.

Bonaccorsi, A. (1992) 'On the relationship between firm size and export intensity', *Journal of International Business Studies*, Fourth Quarter, pp. 605–35.

Cafferata, R. and Mensi, R. (1995) 'The role of information in the internationalisation of SMEs: a typological approach', *International Small Business Journal*, vol. 13, no. 3, pp. 35–46.

Johnson, G. (1988) 'Rethinking incrementalism', *Strategic Management Journal*, vol. 9, pp. 75–91.

Julien, P.E., Joyal, A., Deshaies, L. and Ramangalahy, C. (1997) 'A typology of strategic behaviour among small and medium-sized exporting businesses – a case study', *International Small Business Journal*, vol. 15, no. 2, pp. 33–49.

Katayama, O. (1996) 'Flour power', *Look Japan*, March, pp. 26–7.

Marchand, D.A. (1999) 'Hard IM choices for senior managers'. Part 10 of 'Your guide to mastering information management', *Financial Times*, 5 April.

Majaro, S. (1993) *The Essence of Marketing*, Prentice Hall, London.

Mintzberg, H. (1987) 'The strategy concept 1: five Ps for strategy', *California Management Review*, Fall, pp. 11–24.

Mintzberg, H. and Waters, A. (1985) 'Of strategies, deliberate and emergent', *Strategic Management Journal*, vol. 6, pp. 257–72.

Peters, T.J. and Waterman, R.H. (1982) *In Search of Excellence*, Harper and Row, New York.

Porter, M.E. (1985) *Competitive Advantage*, The Free Press, New York.

Porter, M.E. (1986) 'Competition in global industries: a conceptual framework', in Porter, M.E. (ed.), *Competition in Global Industries*, Harvard Business School Press, Boston, MA.

Quinn, J.B. (1980) 'Strategies for change – logical incrementalism', *Sloan Management Review*, vol. 20, no. 1, pp. 7–21.

Rayport, J.F. and Sviokla, J.J. (1996) 'Exploiting the virtual value chain', *McKinsey Quarterly*, no. 1, pp. 21–36.

Solberg, C.A. (1997) 'A framework for analysis of strategy development in globalizing markets', *Journal of International Marketing*, vol. 5, no. 1, pp. 9–30.

2

Initiation of internationalization

After studying this chapter you should be able to do the following:

● Discuss the reason (motives) why firms go international.

● Explain the difference between proactive and reactive motives.

● Analyze the triggers of export initiation.

● Explain the difference between internal and external triggers of export initiation.

● Describe different factors hindering export initiation.

● Discuss the critical barriers in the process of exporting.

2.1 Export motives

The fundamental reason for exporting, in most firms, is to make money. But as in most business activities, one factor alone rarely accounts for any given action. Usually a mixture of factors results in firms taking steps in a given direction.

Table 2.1 provides an overview of the major motivations to internationalize. They are differentiated into proactive and reactive motives. *Proactive* motives represent stimuli to attempt strategy change, based on the firm's interest in exploiting unique competences (e.g. a special technological knowledge) or market possibilities. *Reactive* motives indicate that the firm reacts to pressures or threats in its home market or in foreign markets and adjusts passively to them by changing its activities over time.

Let us take a closer look at each export motive.

Proactive motives

Profit and growth goals

The desire for short-term profit is especially important to SMEs which are at a stage of initial interest in exporting. The motivation for growth may also be of particular importance for the firm's export start.

Table 2.1	Major motives for starting export	
	Proactive motives	**Reactive motives**
	● Profit and growth goals	● Competitive pressures
	● Managerial urge	● Domestic market: small and saturated
	● Technology competence/unique product	● Overproduction/excess capacity
	● Foreign market opportunities/ market information	● Unsolicited foreign orders
	● Economies of scale	● Extend sales of seasonal products
	● Tax benefits	● Proximity to international customers/psychological distance

Source: Adapted from Albaum *et al.*, 1994, p. 31

Over time, the firm's attitude towards growth will be influenced by the type of feedback received from past efforts. For example, the profitability of exporting may determine management's attitude towards it. Of course, the perceived profitability, when planning to enter international markets, is often quite different from profitability actually attained. Initial profitability may be quite low, particularly in international start-up operations. The gap between perception and reality may be particularly large when the firm has not previously engaged in international market activities. Despite thorough planning, sudden influences often shift the profit picture substantially. For example, a sudden shift in exchange rates may drastically alter profit forecasts even though they were based on careful market evaluation.

The stronger the firm's motivation to grow, the greater will be the activities it generates, including search activity for new possibilities, in order to find means of fulfilling growth and profit ambitions.

Managerial urge

Managerial urge is a motivation that reflects the desire, drive and enthusiasm of management towards global marketing activities. This enthusiasm can exist simply because managers like to be part of a firm that operates internationally. Further, it can often provide a good reason for international travel. Often, however, the managerial urge to internationalize is simply a reflection of general entrepreneurial motivation – of a desire for continuous growth and market expansion.

Exhibit 2.1 shows a Japanese manager with an entrepreneurial attitude towards global marketing (Mont-bell).

Exhibit 2.1	**Mont-bell president Isamu Tatsuno, a true entrepreneur**

During junior high school, Isamu Tatsuno was more interested in climbing mountains than going to school. In 1975, at the age of 28, he established a company in the city of Osaka, Japan. He called the company 'Mont-bell', taking the name from the French 'Mont Belle' or beautiful mountain.

The Du Pont company of the USA was marketing new synthetic fibers at the time, and Tatsuno spent a year developing them into a new sleeping bag. It sold fairly well on the Japanese market even though it was more expensive than conventional sleeping bags. Tatsuno would go on to use high-function Du Pont textiles to create rain gear, tents, rucksacks and winter gear. All were hits and all aimed at the highest quality in the world. These five products (sleeping bags included) constitute Mont-bell's entire line.

In 1978, three years after he had set up his company, Isamu Tatsuno knocked without appointment on the door of Sport Schuster, a famous sporting goods store in Munich. He was trying to sell the sleeping bag that he had developed himself. The manager was not interested – that is, until Tatsuno mentioned that he had climbed the north face of the Eiger in 1969. It turned out that the manager was also a mountaineer. Four months later, Sport Schuster sent Tatsuno an order. He was finally doing business in Europe.

Today sales to Europe and North America are handled under an arrangement with Land's End, the largest mail-order company in North America. Mont-bell provides designs and expertise to the company in return for royalties. In 1995 the Mont-bell group posted current profits of Y900 million ($9 million) on sales of Y9 billion ($90 million). Even today Mont-bell's equipment is tested personally by the president, Isamu Tatsuno.

Source: Adapted from Kato (1995). With kind permission from K. Kato/*Look Japan*.

Managerial attitudes play a critical role in determining the exporting activities of the firm. In SMEs export decisions may be the province of a single decision maker; in LSEs they can be made by a decision-making unit. Irrespective of the number of people involved in the export decision-making process, the choice of a foreign market entry strategy is still dependent on the decision-maker's perceptions of foreign markets, expectations concerning these markets and the company's capability of entering them.

The internationalization process may also be encouraged by the cultural social-ization of the managers. Managers who either were born or have the experience of living or travelling abroad may be expected to be more internationally minded than other managers. Prior occupation in exporting companies, or membership in trade and professional associations, may also reinforce key decision-makers' perceptions and evaluations of foreign environments. See also Case I.4 (HSU's Ginseng Enterprises) as an example of this phenomenon.

Technology competence/unique product

A firm may produce goods or services that are not widely available from interna-tional competitors or may have made technological advances in a specialized field. Again, real and perceived advantages should be differentiated. Many firms believe that theirs are unique products or services, even though this may not be the case in the international market. If products or technology are unique, however, they can certainly provide a competitive edge and result in major business success abroad. One issue to consider is how long such a technological or product advantage will continue. Historically, a firm with a competitive edge could count on being the sole supplier to foreign markets for years to come. This type of advantage, however, has shrunk dramatically because of competing technologies and a frequent lack of international patent protection.

However, a firm producing superior products is more likely to receive enquiries from foreign markets because of perceived competence of its offerings. Several dimensions in the product offering affect the probability that a potential buyer will be exposed to export stimuli. Furthermore, if a company has developed unique competences in its domestic market, the possibilities of spreading unique assets to overseas markets may be very high because the opportunity costs of exploiting these assets in other markets will be very low.

Foreign market opportunities/market information

It is evident that market opportunities act as stimuli only if the firm has or is capable of securing those resources necessary to respond to the opportunities. In general, decision-makers are likely to consider a rather limited number of foreign market opportunities in planning their foreign entry. Moreover, such decision-makers are likely to explore first those overseas market opportunities perceived as having some similarity with the opportunities in their home market.

From time to time certain overseas markets grow spectacularly, providing tempting opportunities for expansion-minded firms. The attraction of the south-east Asian markets is based on their economic successes, while the attraction of the eastern European markets is rooted in their new-found political freedoms and desire to develop trade and economic relationships with countries in western Europe, North America and Japan. Other countries that are likely to increase in market attractiveness as key internal changes occur include the People's Republic of China and the Republic of South Africa.

Specialized marketing knowledge or access to information can distinguish an exporting firm from its competitors. This includes knowledge about foreign customers, marketplaces or market situations that is not widely shared by other firms. Such special knowledge may result from particular insights based on a firm's international research, special contacts a firm may have, or simply being in the right place at the right time (for example, recognizing a good business situation during a vacation trip). Past marketing success can be a strong motivator for future marketing behaviour ('logical incrementalism' – see discussion in section 1.2). Competence in one or more of the major marketing activities will often be a sufficient catalyst for a company to begin or expand exports.

Economies of scale

Becoming a participant in global marketing activities may enable the firm to increase its output and therefore climb more rapidly on the learning curve. Ever since the Boston Consulting Group showed that a doubling of output can reduce production costs by up to 30 per cent, this effect has been very much sought. Increased production for the international market can therefore also help in reducing the cost of production for domestic sales and make the firm more competitive domestically as well. This effect often results in seeking market share as a primary objective of firms. (See Exhibit 2.2 as an example of this.) At an initial level of internationalization, it may mean an increased search for export markets; later on, it can result in opening foreign subsidiaries and foreign production facilities.

Through exporting, fixed costs arising from administration, facilities, equipment, staff work, and R & D can be spread over more units. For some companies a condition for exploiting scale effects on foreign markets to the fullest extent is the possibility of standardizing the marketing mix internationally. For others, however, standardized marketing is not necessary for scale economies.

Exhibit 2.2

Global marketing and economies of scale in Japanese firms

Japanese firms exploit foreign market opportunities by using a penetration pricing strategy – a low entry price to build up market share and establish a long-run dominant market position. They do accept losses in early years, as they view it as an investment in long-run market development. This can be achieved because much of Japanese industry is supported or owned by banks or other financial institutions with a much lower cost of capital. Furthermore, because of the lifetime employment system, labour cost is regarded as a fixed expense, not a variable as it is in the West. Since all marginal labour cost will be at the entry salary level, raising volume is the only way to increase productivity rapidly. As a result, market share, not profitability, is the primary concept in Japanese firms, where scale of operation and experience allows *economies of scale*, which also help to reduce distribution costs. The international trading companies typically take care of international sales and marketing, allowing the Japanese firm to concentrate on economies of scale and resulting in lower cost per unit.

Source: Genestre *et al.* (1995).

Tax benefits

Tax benefits can also play a major motivating role. In the United States, a tax mechanism called the Foreign Sales Corporation (FSC) has been instituted to assist exporters. It is in conformity with international agreements and provides firms with certain tax deferrals. Tax benefits allow the firm either to offer its products at a lower cost in foreign markets or to accumulate a higher profit. This may therefore tie in closely with the profit motivation.

Reactive motives

Competitive pressures

A prime form of reactive motivation is reaction to competitive pressures. A firm may fear losing domestic market share to competing firms that have benefited from economies of scale gained by global marketing activities. Further, it may fear losing foreign markets permanently to domestic competitors that decide to focus on these markets, knowing that market share is most easily retained by the firm that obtains it initially. Quick entry may result in similarly quick withdrawal once the firm recognizes that its preparations have been insufficient. In addition to this, knowing that other firms, particularly competitors, are internationalizing provides a strong incentive to internationalize. Competitors are an important external factor stimulating internationalization. Coca-Cola became international much earlier than Pepsi did, but there is no doubt whatever that Coca-Cola's move into overseas markets influenced Pepsi to move in the same direction.

Domestic market: small and saturated

A company may be pushed into exporting because of a small home market potential. For some firms, domestic markets may be unable to sustain sufficient economies of scale and scope, and these companies automatically include export markets as part of their market entry strategy. This type of behaviour is likely for industrial products that have few, easily identified customers located throughout the world, or for producers of specialized consumer goods with small national segments in many countries.

A saturated domestic market, whether measured in sales volume or market share, has a similar motivating effect. Products marketed domestically by the firm may be at the declining stage of the product life cycle. Instead of attempting a push-back of the life cycle process, or in addition to such an effort, firms may opt to prolong the product life cycle by expanding the market. In the past, such efforts were often met with success as customers in many developing countries only gradually reached a level of need and sophistication already attained by customers in industrialized nations. Some developing nations are still often in need of products for which the demand in the industrialized world is already on the decline. In this way, firms can use the international market to prolong the life cycle of their product. (See also section 14.4, 'The product life cycle', for further discussion.)

Many US appliance and car manufacturers initially entered international markets because of what they viewed as near-saturated domestic markets. US producers of asbestos products found the domestic market legally closed to them, but because some overseas markets had more lenient consumer protection laws, they continued to produce for overseas markets.

Another perspective on market saturation is also relevant for understanding why firms may expand overseas. Home market saturation suggests that unused productive resources (such as production and managerial slack) exist within the firm. Production slack is a stimulus for securing new market opportunities, and managerial slack can provide those knowledge resources required for collecting, interpreting and using market information.

Overproduction/excess capacity

If a firm's domestic sales of a product are below expectation, the inventory can be above desired levels. This situation can be the trigger for starting export sales via short-term price cuts on inventory products. As soon as the domestic market demand returns to previous levels, global marketing activities are curtailed or even terminated. Firms that have used such a strategy may encounter difficulties when trying to employ it again because many foreign customers are not interested in temporary or sporadic business relationships. This reaction from abroad may well lead to a decrease in the importance of this motivation over time.

In some situations, however, excess capacity can be a powerful motivation. If equipment for production is not fully utilized, firms may see expansion into the international market as an ideal possibility for achieving broader distribution of fixed costs. Alternatively, if all fixed costs are assigned to domestic production, the firm can penetrate international markets with a pricing scheme that focuses mainly on variable costs. Although such a strategy may be useful in the short term, it may result in the offering of products abroad at a lower cost than at home, which in turn may stimulate parallel importing. In the long run, fixed costs have to be recovered to ensure replacement of production equipment. A market penetration strategy based on variable cost alone is therefore not feasible over the long term.

Sometimes excess production capacity arises because of changing demand in the domestic market. As domestic markets switch to new and substitute products, companies making older product versions develop excess capacity and look for overseas market opportunities.

Unsolicited foreign orders

Many small companies have become aware of opportunities in export markets because their products generated enquiries from overseas. These enquiries can result from advertising in trade journals which have a world-wide circulation, through exhibitions and by other means. As a result, a large percentage of exporting firms' initial orders were unsolicited.

Extend sales of seasonal products

Seasonality in demand conditions may be different in the domestic market from other international markets. This can act as a persistent stimulus for foreign market exploration that may result in a more stable demand over the year.

A producer of agricultural machinery in Europe had demand from its domestic market primarily in the spring months of the year. In an attempt to achieve a more stable demand over the year, it directed its market orientation towards the southern hemisphere (e.g. Australia, South Africa), where it is summer when the northern hemisphere has winter and vice versa.

Proximity to international customers/psychological distance

Physical and psychological closeness to the international market can often play a major role in the export activities of a firm. For example, German firms established near the Austrian border may not even perceive their market activities in Austria as global marketing. Rather, they are simply an extension of domestic activities, without any particular attention being paid to the fact that some of the products go abroad.

Unlike American firms, most European firms automatically become international marketers simply because their neighbours are so close. As an example, a European firm operating in Belgium needs to go only 100 km to be in multiple foreign markets. Geographic closeness to foreign markets may not necessarily translate into real or perceived closeness to the foreign customer. Sometimes cultural variables, legal factors and other societal norms make a foreign market that is geographically close seem psychologically distant. For example, research has shown that US firms perceive Canada as psychologically much closer than Mexico. Even England, mainly because of similarity in language, is perceived by many US firms as much closer than Mexico or other Latin American countries, despite the geographic distances.

2.2 ❘ Triggers of export initiation (change agents)

For internationalization to take place, someone or something within or outside the firm (so-called change agents) must initiate it and carry it through to implementation (see Table 2.2).

Internal triggers

Perceptive management

Perceptive managements gain early awareness of developing opportunities in overseas markets. They make it their business to become knowledgeable about these markets, and maintain a sense of open-mindedness about where and when their companies should expand overseas. Perceptive managements include many cosmopolites in their ranks.

A trigger factor is frequently foreign travel, during which new business opportunities are discovered, or information received that makes management believe that such opportunities exist. Managers who have lived abroad, have learned foreign languages or are particularly interested in foreign cultures are likely, sooner rather than later, to investigate whether global marketing opportunities would be appropriate for their firm.

Often, managers enter a firm having already had some global marketing experience in previous jobs and try to use this experience to further the business activities of their new firm. In developing their goals in the new job, managers frequently consider an entirely new set of options, one of which may be global marketing activities.

Specific internal event

A significant event can be another major change agent. A new employee who firmly believes that the firm should undertake global marketing may find ways to motivate management. Overproduction or a reduction in domestic market size can serve as such an event, as can the receipt of new information about current product uses. For instance, a company's research activity may develop a by-product suitable for sale overseas, as happened with a food-processing firm that discovered a low-cost protein ideal for helping to relieve food shortages in some parts of Africa.

Research has shown that in SMEs the initial decision to export is usually made by the president, with substantial input provided by the marketing department. The carrying out of the decision – that is, the initiation of actual global marketing activities and the implementation of these activities – is then primarily the

Table 2.2	Triggers of export initiation	

Internal triggers	External triggers
● Perceptive management	● Market demand
● Specific internal event	● Competing firms
● Importing as inward internationalization	● Trade associations
	● Outside experts

responsibility of marketing personnel. Only in the final decision stage of evaluating global marketing activities does the major emphasis rest again with the president of the firm. In order to influence a firm internally, it therefore appears that the major emphasis should be placed first on convincing the president to enter the international marketplace and then on convincing the marketing department that global marketing is an important activity. Conversely, the marketing department is a good place to be if one wants to become active in international business.

| Exhibit 2.3 | Beijing Broadcast Equipment Factory (BBEF): export motives and triggers of export initiation in a Chinese enterprise |

Founded in 1950, BBEF is a manufacturer of broadcasting and TV equipment with over 4,500 employees. Primary product lines include broadcasting equipment, TV transmitting products, microwave relay equipment, radar systems and video recording products. Exports account for around 13 per cent of sales.

The permission to engage in exporting was given to BBEF by the Chinese government in 1987 and BBEF established its own Foreign Trade Corporation (FTC), Beijing Yanjing United Electronic Import and Export Corporation, which has some 90 employees and is the export trading arm for BBEF and ten other enterprises in the group. Most overseas business is done in Asia and key markets include North Korea, Singapore and Burma. Some business is also done in eastern Europe and the United States.

Principal motives for BBEF's export involvement include market diversification, competitive benefits and promotional reasons. Overseas operations stimulate efficiency, and export earnings can be used for the importation of foreign technology and equipment necessary for modernization. There is also a domestic prestige associated with exporting, and direct exporters are often viewed in a better light in China.

Source: Waters and Zhu (1995). Reproduced by permission of Management International Review.

Inward internationalization (importing)

Welch and Loustarinen (1993) claim that inward internationalization (importing) may precede and influence outward internationalization (international market entry and marketing activities) – see Figure 2.1.

A direct relationship exists between inward and outward internationalization in the way that effective inward activities can determine the success of outward activities, especially in the early stages of internationalization. The inward internationalization may be initiated by:

● The buyer: active international search of different foreign sources (buyer initiative = reverse marketing).

● The seller: initiation by the foreign supplier (traditional seller perspective).

During the process from inward to outward internationalization, the buyer's role (in country A) shifts to seller, both to domestic customers (in country A) and to foreign customers. Through interaction with the foreign supplier, the buyer (importer) gets access to the network of the supplier, so that at some later time there

Figure 2.1   **Inward/outward internationalization: a network example**

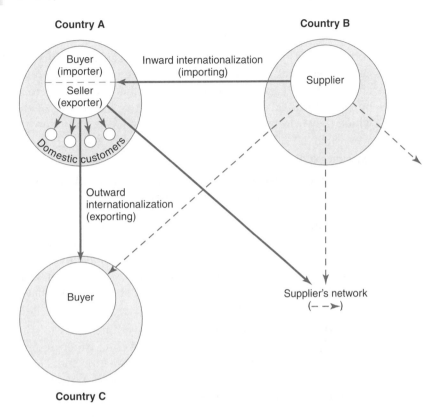

may be an outward export to members of this network. In some cases, inward foreign licensing may be followed by outward technology sales.

External triggers

Market demand

Growth in international markets causes the demand for the products of some companies also to grow, pushing the makers of these products into internationalization. Many pharmaceutical companies entered international markets when growth in the international demand for their products was first getting under way. The US-based company Squibb entered the Turkish market before it was large enough to be profitable. But the market was growing rapidly, which encouraged Squibb to internationalize further.

Competing firms

Information that an executive in a competing firm considers certain international markets to be valuable and worthwhile to develop captures the attention of management. Such statements not only have source credibility, but are also viewed with a certain amount of fear because the competitor may eventually infringe on the firm's business.

Trade associations

Formal and informal meetings among managers from different firms at trade association meetings, conventions or business round tables often serve as a major change agent. It has even been suggested that the decision to export may be made by small firms on the basis of the collective experience of the group of firms to which they belong.

Outside experts

Several outside experts encourage internationalization. Among them are export agents, governments, chambers of commerce and banks.

- *Export agents.* Export agents as well as export trading companies and export management firms generally qualify as experts in global marketing. They are already dealing internationally with other products, have overseas contacts and are set up to handle other exportable products. Many of these trade intermediaries approach prospective exporters directly if they think that their products have potential markets overseas.

- *Governments.* In nearly all countries, governments try to stimulate international business through providing global marketing expertise (export assistance programmes). For example, government stimulation measures can have a positive influence not only in terms of any direct financial effects that they may have, but also in relation to the provision of information.

- *Chambers of commerce.* Chambers of commerce and similar export production organizations are interested in stimulating international business, both exports and imports. These organizations seek to motivate individual companies to get involved in global marketing and provide incentives for them to do so. These incentives include putting the prospective exporter or importer in touch with overseas business, providing overseas market information, and referring the prospective exporter or importer to financial institutions capable of financing global marketing activity.

- *Banks.* Banks and other financial institutions are often instrumental in getting companies to internationalize. They alert their domestic clients to international opportunities and help them to capitalize on these opportunities. Of course, they look forward to their services being used more extensively as domestic clients expand internationally.

2.3　Export barriers/risks

A wide variety of barriers to successful export operations can be identified. Some problems mainly affect the export start; others are encountered in the process of exporting.

Barriers hindering export initiation

Critical factors hindering *export initiation* include the following (mainly internal) barriers:

- Insufficient finances.
- Insufficient knowledge.
- Lack of foreign market connections.
- Lack of export commitment.
- Lack of capital to finance expansion into foreign markets.
- Lack of productive capacity to dedicate to foreign markets.
- Lack of foreign channels of distribution.
- Management emphasis on developing domestic markets.
- Cost escalation due to high export manufacturing, distribution and financing expenditures.

Inadequate information on potential foreign customers, competition and foreign business practices are key barriers facing active and prospective exporters. Obtaining adequate representation for overseas distribution and service, ensuring payment, import tariffs and quotas, and difficulties in communicating with foreign distributors and customers are also major concerns. Serious problems can also arise from production disruptions resulting from a requirement for non-standard export products. This will increase the cost of manufacturing and distribution.

Barriers hindering the process of exporting

Critical barriers in the *process of exporting* may be divided into three groups: general market risks, commercial risks and political risks.

General market risks

- Comparative market distance.
- Competition from other firms in foreign markets.
- Differences in product usage in foreign markets.
- Language and cultural differences.
- Differences in product specifications in foreign markets.
- Complexity of shipping services to overseas buyers.

Commercial risks

- Exchange rate fluctuations when contracts are made in a foreign currency.
- Failure of export customers to pay due to contract dispute, bankruptcy, refusal to accept the product and fraud.
- Delays and damage in the export shipment and distribution process.
- Difficulties in obtaining export financing.

Political risks

Among the political risks resulting from intervention by home and host country governments are the following:

● Foreign government restrictions.
● National export policy.
● Foreign exchange controls imposed by host governments that limit the opportunities for foreign customers to make payment.
● Lack of governmental assistance in overcoming export barriers.
● Lack of tax incentives for companies that export.
● High value of the domestic currency relative to those in export markets.
● High foreign tariffs on imported products.
● Confusing foreign import regulations and procedures.
● Complexity of trade documentation.
● Enforcement of national legal codes regulating exports.
● Civil strife, revolution and wars disrupting foreign markets.

The importance of these risks must not be overemphasized and various risk management strategies are open to exporters. These include the following:

● Avoid exporting to high-risk markets.
● Diversify overseas markets and ensure that the firm is not overdependent on any single country.
● Insure risks when possible. Government schemes are particularly attractive.
● Structure export business so that the buyer bears most of the risk. For example, price in a hard currency and demand cash in advance.

2.4 Summary

This chapter provides an overview of the major motives for firms to internationalize. They are differentiated into proactive and reactive motives. Proactive motives represent internal stimuli to attempt strategy change, based on the firm's interest in exploiting unique competences or market possibilities. Reactive motives indicate that the firm reacts to pressures or threats in its home market or in foreign markets and adjusts passively to them.

For internationalization to take place, someone or something ('triggers') inside or outside the firm must initiate it and carry it through implementation. To succeed in global marketing the firm has to overcome export barriers. Some barriers mainly affect the export initiation and others are encountered in the process of exporting.

Case study   Blooming Clothing

A bumpy path to exports

It was nine o'clock on a misty morning in February 1995. Martha O'Byrne cycled down the narrow avenue to the clothing factory of which she was managing director and the main shareholder. Wheeling her bicycle into her small office, she wondered if Janet Evans had called yet. Janet, the chief buyer with the Mothercare chain of stores in the UK, had promised to phone her that morning, to let her know if she would be placing a further order with her company. Listening to the messages on her answering machine, Martha remembered the path that she had taken to establish her own enterprise.

Blooming Clothing, the small company that Martha O'Byrne owns and manages, is situated in the Liberties, an old and historic part of Dublin, Ireland. Established in 1985, the firm employs 80 people manufacturing maternity wear for the Irish and export markets.

Martha O'Byrne had come to this business by an unusual route. Having established herself as a successful merchant banker, she had been considering setting up her own busines for some time. 'Women, I think, can have a mid-life crisis at the menopause, but I got mine when I was 28', she recalls. In 1984, a shopping trip with her pregnant sister-in-law revealed that the maternity wear available on the Irish market was dowdy and depressing. In that moment, the idea for Blooming Clothing was conceived. Martha resigned from her position in the investment bank in 1985, and set up in business with two partners as a retailer of maternity wear. Her shop, called 'Blooming', was located on South Leinster Street, on the fringes of Dublin's most prestigous shopping district. It quickly won recognition and sales for its more modern clothes, which proved particularly popular with working women. 'There was a need for a new, more vibrant look', comments Martha, 'while still retaining the femininity and mystique of the pregnant woman.' The emphasis of the 'Blooming' label is on softly tailored separates – jackets, trousers, skirts and dresses – for office wear and special occasions (see Plate 1). Having experienced problems with outsourcing garments, Martha and her team started to manufacture their own lines in 1986.

By 1987, Blooming Clothing had a turnover of IR£250,000. The company built up further sales in Ireland through concession outlets in department stores and through a range of independent outlets. The break into exporting also came in 1987. Martha O'Byrne, herself six months pregnant at the time, made a presentation to a buyer from Harrods, the well-known department store in London. The store agreed to carry the Blooming label in its maternity wear section, and has been a good customer since. Arising out of this success, Blooming appointed agent, Favoro & Co., to build up further business in the UK.

By 1992, the firm had a turnover of IR£1.1m and had moved manufacturing to the current premises at Carman's Hall, Francis Street. It had established a good sales base in Ireland and was selling in the UK to such prestigious retailers as Harrods, John Lewis and Selfridges. The firm depended heavily on a personal approach to secure orders. It did not have a full-time salesperson as such or attend trade fairs. Would-be buyers would receive a presentation on the Blooming range from Martha O'Byrne herself or from Barbara Connolly, the firm's part owner and chief designer.

However, 1992 saw the UK economy go into deep recession, and clothing was one of the first industries to feel the pain. As if this was not enough, 1992/3 also saw the development of a major currency crisis for the Irish pound *vis-à-vis* the pound sterling. The Irish pound, which had been trading at a rate of 96–8 pence to the pound sterling, rapidly appreciated in value, eventually trading at IR£1.10 = £1 sterling. Irish exporters, for whom the UK is the single most important market, found their prices increased and their customers falling away. Blooming Clothing was not alone in experiencing these trends, and along with other companies received financial assistance from a state-funded scheme designed to help exporters through this crisis. In the meantime, cash flow was squeezed and the aftermath was felt for two years. The management of Blooming spent 1993 trying to generate orders to make up for the business it had lost. Martha O'Byrne remained optimistic. 'There may be peaks and troughs in a business, but there are always opportunities in any market if you look', she remarked.

In 1994, Blooming appointed an agent in Belgium. The agreement was signed just in time for the onset of a recession, and sales did not materialize. A foray into the Swedish market proved disappointing. The agent selected by the firm did not generate worthwhile orders and the relationship gradually faded away.

1995 marked a new departure. The firm began to build up increased sales through the appointment of new retail outlets. The the British chain store Mothercare, part of the Storehouse group, agree to stock a range of Blooming lines. Mothercare stores offer a range of nursery goods, children's clothes and associated items, through a network of over 330 outlets in the UK and international franchise operations in 25 countries with nearly 130 outlets. The order, woth £100,000 initially, would give both parties a chance to evaluate the success of the label and the fit with Mothercare's existing range of maternity wear. If the Blooming range was a success, a partnership with Mothercare would allow Blooming the opportunity to penetrate the European market, with access to a broad range of outlets.

Martha O'Byrne gazed out the window of her office, taking in the view of St Patrick's Cathedral, a famous local landmark. As she waited in anticipation for a telephone call, she wondered what the future held for Blooming and more particularly the company's export sales.

Questions

1. What criteria do you think Blooming Clothing has used in selecting export markets?

2. Analyze and evaluate the modes of export market entry used by Blooming.

3. Draft an outline sales presentation, to be used by Martha O'Byrne at her next meeting with a UK chain store buyer who is interested in stocking a new range of maternity wear.

4. The telephone rings. Janet Evans is on the line. What do you think is the outcome of the call?

Prepared by Edel Foley and Eibhlin Curley, College of Marketing and Design, Dublin Institute of Technology, Ireland. Information from company interviews and C. Flynn, 'A 40-something crisis', *Irish Independent*, 5 October 1995.

Questions for discussion

1. Export motives can be classified as reactive or proactive. Give examples of each group of export motives. How would you prioritize these motives? Can you think of motives other than those mentioned in the chapter? What are they?

2. What is meant by 'change agents' in global marketing? Give examples of different types of change agent.

3. Discuss the most critical barriers in the process of exporting.

4. What were the most important change agents in Mont-bell (Exhibit 2.1) and Beijing Broadcast Equipment Factory (BBEF) (Exhibit 2.3)?

5. What were the most important export motives in Japanese firms (Exhibit 2.2)?

Internet exercise

Eurovision Song Contest 2000/Olsen Brothers

Please go to the official website of Swedish Television: *http://www.eurosong2000.com/* or to the unofficial:

http://www.irj1307.freeserve.co.uk/

http://www.torget.se/users/e/Euro/esc2000.htm

http://eurosong.net/years/2000/2000_start.htm

The 2000 Eurovision Song Contest (ESC) was held at The Stockholm Globen Arena in Stockholm, Sweden, on Saturday 13 May 2000. Each of the participants from 24 countries could sing in any language they liked, but 14 countries chose to sing in English.

Eurovision is actually the name given to the Europe-wide TV distribution network run by the European Broadcasting Union. It was set up in the mid-1950s, and continues to supply news and sports material across the continent and beyond.

Denmark surprised everyone but themselves when they walked their way to winning the first Eurovision Song Contest of the Millennium. With three juries left to vote the contest was over; Denmark had won and only two other acts reached three figures. The title of the winning Danish contribution at ESC 2000 was 'Fly on the Wings of Love' by the Olsen Brothers (or Brødrene Olsen in Danish), Jørgen (49) and Niels (45), or 'Noller' as he is commonly called. This year's entry was written by Jørgen in protest of a prejudice he had come across in newspapers and magazines, that the beauty of a woman would vanish with increasing age. They have been performing together for over 20 years now, mostly with songs written by Jørgen. Their breakthrough came with the musical Hair, in which they both performed. Nowadays, music is just a part-time job and Jørgen earns his living as a teacher, whereas Noller is involved in a cultural project on a local basis. However, this will probably change now.

Jørgen and Niels are more or less veterans in the Danish Song Contest. They participated in 1978, 1979, 1980 and 1982 together, whereafter Jørgen gave a couple of solo performances (1989, 1990). Now, 22 years after their first participation, they have once again given their best shot and this time actually won for the first time.

Question

1. If you were the manager for the Olsen Brothers, how would you use the victory in the Eurovision Song Contest to market the Olsen Brothers internationally?

For further exercises and cases, see this book's website at *www.booksites.net/hollensen*

References

Albaum, G., Strandskov, J., Duerr, E. and Dowd, L. (1994) *International Marketing and Export Management* (2nd edn), Addison-Wesley, Reading, Massachusetts.

Genestre, A., Herbig, D. and Shao, A.T. (1995) 'What does marketing really mean to the Japanese?', *Marketing Intelligence and Planning*, vol. 13, no. 9, pp. 16–27.

Kato, K. (1995) 'The president's office is outside', *Look Japan*, January, pp. 22–3.

Waters, P.G.P. and Zhu, M. (1995) 'International marketing in Chinese enterprises: some evidence from the PRC', *Management International Review*, vol. 35, no. 3, pp. 265–77.

Welch, L.S. and Loustarinen, R.K. (1993) 'Inward–outward connections in internationalization', *Journal of International Marketing*, vol. 1, no. 1, pp. 44–56.

3

Internationalization theories

After studying this chapter you should be able to do the following:

● Analyze the three theories explaining firms' internationalization process:
  the Uppsala internationalization model;
  the transaction cost theory; and
  the network model.

● Compare and contrast the three internationalization theories in order to find differences.

● Distinguish between four different situations characterized by the degree of the firm's and the market's internationalization (four cases of internationalization).

● Explain and discuss the relevance of the network model for an SME serving as a subcontractor.

● Explain the term 'Born Global' and its connection to internet marketing.

3.1 Introduction

Having discussed the barriers to starting internationalization in Chapter 2, we will start with presenting the different theoretical approaches to international marketing and then we will choose three models for further discussion in sections 3.2, 3.3 and 3.4.

Historical development of internationalization

Much of the early literature in internationalization was inspired by general marketing theories. Later on, internationalization dealt with the choice between exporting and FDI (Foreign Direct Investment). During the last 10–15 years, there has been much focus on internationalization in networks, by which the firm has different relationships not only to customers but also to other actors in the environment.

The traditional marketing approach

The Penrosian tradition (Penrose, 1959 Prahalad and Hamel, 1990) reflects the traditional marketing focus on the firm's core competences combined with opportunities in the foreign environment.

The cost-based view of this tradition suggested that the firm must possess a 'compensating advantage' in order to overcome the 'cost of foreignness' (Hymer, 1976; Kindleberger, 1969). This led to the identification of technological and marketing skills as the key elements in successful foreign entry.

'Life cycle' concept for international trade

Sequential modes of internationalization were introduced by Vernon's 'Product Cycle Hypothesis' (1966), in which firms go through an exporting phase before switching first to market-seeking FDI, and then to cost-orientated FDI. Technology and marketing factors combine to explain standardization, which drives location decisions.

Vernon's hypothesis is that producers in advanced countries (ACs) are 'closer' to the markets than producers elsewhere; consequently, the first production facilities for these products will be in the ACs. As demand expands a certain degree of standardization usually takes place. 'Economies of scale', through mass production, become more important. Concern about production cost replaces concern about product adaptations. With standardized products the less developed countries (LDCs) may offer competitive advantages as production locations. One example of this is the movement of production locations for personal computers from ACs to LDCs. The 'life cycle' concept is illustrated in Figure 14.6.

The Uppsala School approach

The Scandinavian 'stages' models of entry suggest a sequential pattern of entry into successive foreign markets, coupled with a progressive deepening of commitment to each market. Increasing commitment is particularly important in the thinking of the Uppsala School (Johanson and Wiedersheim-Paul, 1975; Johanson and Vahlne, 1977). The main consequence of this model is that firms tend to intensify their commitment towards foreign markets as their experience grows. Closely associated with the stages models is the notion of 'psychic distance', which attempts to conceptualize and, to some degree, measure the cultural distance between countries and markets (Hallen and Wiedersheim-Paul, 1979).

The internationalization/transaction cost approach

In the early 1970s intermediate forms of internationalization such as licensing were not considered to be interesting. Buckley and Casson (1976) expanded the choice to include licensing as a means of reaching customers abroad. But in their perspective, the multinational firm would usually prefer to 'internalize' transactions via direct equity investment rather than license its capability. Joint ventures were not explicitly considered to be in the spectrum of governance choices until the mid-1980s (Kogut, 1988; Contractor and Lorange, 1988).

Buckley and Casson's focus on market-based (externalization) versus firm-based (internalization) solutions highlighted the strategic significance of licensing in market entry. Internationalization involves two interdependent decisions – regarding location and mode of control.

The internalization perspective is closely related to the transaction cost (TC) theory (Williamson, 1975). The paradigmatic question in internalization theory is that, upon deciding to enter a foreign market, should a firm do so through internalization within its own boundaries (a subsidiary) or through some form of collaboration with an external partner (externalization)? The internalization and TC perspectives are both concerned with the minimization of TC and the conditions underlying market failure. The intention is to analyze the characteristics of a transaction in order to decide on the most efficient, i.e. TC minimizing, governance mode. The internalization theory can be considered to be the TC theory of the multinational corporation (Rugman, 1986; Madhok, 1997, 1998).

Dunning's eclectic approach

In his eclectic Ownership–Location–Internalization (OLI) framework Dunning (1988) has discussed the importance of locational variables in foreign investment decisions. The word 'eclectic' represents the idea that a full explanation of the transnational activities of firms needs to draw on several strands of economic theory. According to Dunning the propensity of a firm to engage itself in international production increases if the following three conditions are being satisfied:

- *Ownership advantages*: a firm which owns foreign production facilities has bigger ownership advantages compared to firms of other nationalities. These 'advantages' may consist of intangible assets.
- *Locational advantages*: it must be profitable for the firm to continue these assets with factor endowments (labour, energy, materials, components, transport and communication channels) in the foreign markets. If not, the foreign markets would be served by exports.
- *Internalization advantages*: it must be more profitable for the firm to use its advantages rather than selling them, or the right to use them, to a foreign firm.

The network approach

The basic assumption in the network approach is that the international firm cannot be analyzed as an isolated actor but has to be viewed in relation to other actors in the international environment. Thus, the individual firm is dependent on resources controlled by others. The relationships of a firm within a domestic network can be used as connections to other networks in other countries (Johanson and Mattson, 1988).

In the following three sections we will concentrate on three of the approaches presented above.

3.2 The Uppsala internationalization model

The stage model

During the 1970s, a number of Swedish researchers at the University of Uppsala (Johanson and Wiedersheim-Paul, 1975; Johanson and Vahlne, 1977) focused their interest on the internationalization process. Studying the internationalization of

Swedish manufacturing firms, they developed a model of the firm's choice of market and form of entry when going abroad. Their work was influenced by Aharoni's seminal (1966) study.

With these basic assumptions in mind, the Uppsala researchers interpreted the patterns in the internationalization process they had observed in Swedish manufacturing firms. They had noted, first of all, that companies appeared to begin their operations abroad in fairly nearby markets and only gradually penetrated more far-flung markets. Second, it appeared that companies entered new markets through exports. It was very rare for companies to enter new markets with sales organizations or manufacturing subsidiaries of their own. Wholly owned or majority-owned operations were established only after several years of exports to the same market.

Johanson and Wiedersheim-Paul (1975) distinguish between four different modes of entering an international market, where the successive stages represent higher degrees of international involvement/market commitment:

● Stage 1. No regular export activities (sporadic export).
● Stage 2. Export via independent representatives (export modes).
● Stage 3. Establishment of a foreign sales subsidiary.
● Stage 4. Foreign production/manufacturing units.

The assumption that the internationalization of a firm develops step by step was originally supported by evidence from a case study of four Swedish firms. The sequence of stages was restricted to a specific country market. This market commitment dimension is shown in Figure 3.1.

The concept of market commitment is assumed to contain two factors – the

Figure 3.1   **Internationalization of the firm: an incremental approach**

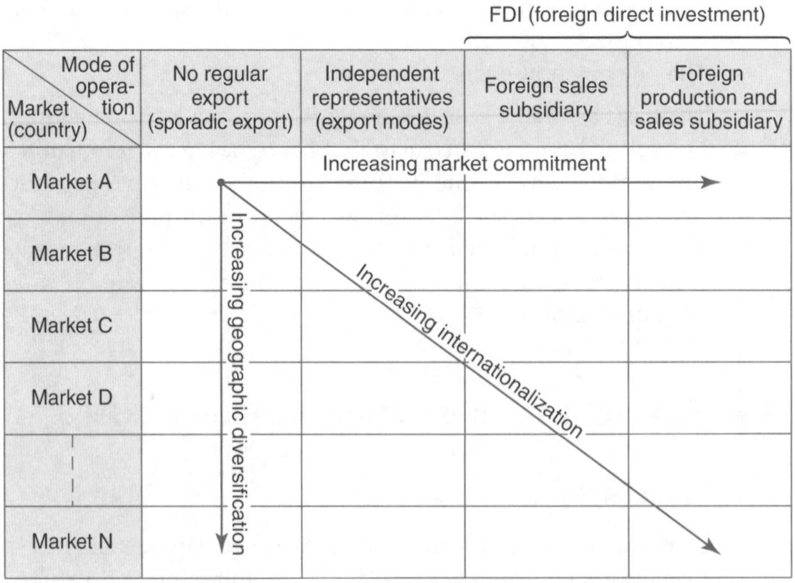

(Source: Adapted from Forsgren and Johanson, 1975, p. 16.)

amount of resources committed and the degree of commitment. The amount of resources could be operationalized to the size of investment in the market (marketing, organization, personnel, etc.), while the degree of commitment refers to the difficulty of finding an alternative use for the resources and transferring them to the alternative use.

International activities require both general knowledge and market-specific knowledge. Market-specific knowledge is assumed to be gained mainly through experience in the market, whereas knowledge of the operations can be transferred from one country to another; the latter will thus facilitate the geographic diversification in Figure 3.1. A direct relation between market knowledge and market commitment is postulated: knowledge can be considered as a dimension of human resources. Consequently, the better knowledge about a market, the more valuable are the resources and the stronger the commitment to the market.

Figure 3.1 implies that additional market commitment as a rule will be made in small incremental steps, both in the market commitment dimension and in the geographical dimension. There are, however, three exceptions. First, firms that have large resources experience small consequences of their commitments and can take larger internationalization steps. Second, when market conditions are stable and homogeneous, relevant market knowledge can be gained in ways other than experience. Third, when the firm has considerable experience from markets with similar conditions, it may be able to generalize this experience to any specific market (Johanson and Vahlne, 1990).

The geographical dimension in Figure 3.1 shows that firms enter new markets with successively greater psychic distance. Psychic distance is defined in terms of factors such as differences in language, culture and political systems, which disturb the flow of information between the firm and the market. Thus firms start internationalization by going to those markets they can most easily understand. There they will see opportunities, and there the perceived market uncertainty is low.

The original stage model has been extended by Welch and Loustarinen (1988), who operate with six dimensions of internationalization (see Figure 3.2).

- Sales objects (what?): goods, services, know-how and systems.
- Operations methods (how?): agents, subsidiaries, licensing, franchising management contracts.
- Markets (where?): political/cultural/psychic/physical distance differences between markets.
- Organizational structure: export department, international division.
- Finance: availability of international finance sources to support the international activities.
- Personnel: international skills, experience and training.

Critical views of the original Uppsala model

Various criticisms have been put forward. One criticism is that the model is too deterministic (Reid, 1983; Turnbull, 1987).

It has also been argued that the model does not take into account interdepen-

Figure 3.2 **Dimensions of internationalization**

(Source: Welch and Loustarinen, 1988. Reproduced with permission from The Braybrooke Press Ltd.)

dencies between different country markets (Johanson and Mattson, 1986). It seems reasonable to consider a firm more internationalized if it views and handles different country markets as interdependent than if it views them as completely separate entities.

Studies have shown that the internationalization process model is not valid for service industries. In research into the internationalization of Swedish technical consultants – a typical service industry – it has been demonstrated that the cumulative reinforcement of foreign commitments implied by the process model is absent (Sharma and Johanson, 1987).

The criticism has been supported by the fact that the internationalization process of new entrants in certain industries has recently become more spectacular. Firms have lately seemed prone to *leap-frog* stages in the establishment chain, entering 'distant' markets in terms of psychic distance at an early stage, and the pace of the internationalization process generally seems to have speeded up.

Nordström's preliminary (1990) results seem to confirm this argument. The UK, Germany and the USA have become a more common target for the very first establishment of sales subsidiaries by Swedish firms than their Scandinavian neighbours.

The leap-frogging tendency not only involves entering distant markets. We can also expect a company to leap-frog some intermediate entry modes (foreign operation methods) in order to move away from the sequentialist pattern and more directly to some kind of foreign investment (Figure 3.3).

In market no. 1 the firm follows the mainstream evolutionary pattern, but in market no. 6 the firm has learned from the use of different operation methods on previous markets, and therefore chooses to leap-frog some stages and go directly to foreign investment.

Others have claimed that the Uppsala school is not valid in situations of highly internationalized firms and industries. In these cases, competitive forces and factors override psychic distance as the principal explanatory factor for the firm's process of internationalization. Furthermore, if knowledge of transactions can be transferred from one country to another, firms with extensive international experience are likely to perceive the psychic distance to a new country as shorter than firms with little international experience.

Nordström (1990) argues that the world has become much more homogeneous and that consequently psychic distance has decreased. He expects that recent starters are willing and able to enter directly into large markets as some of these are

Figure 3.3   **Internationalization pattern of the firm as a sum of target country patterns**

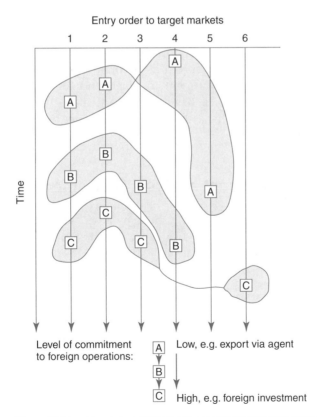

(Source: Welch and Loustarinen, 1988. Reproduced with permission from The Braybrooke Press Ltd.)

now as close to Sweden in a cultural sense as are other Scandinavian countries. Hence, the explanatory value of psychic distance has decreased.

A similar way of reducing uncertainty is offered by international consulting firms. The consulting industry has experienced tremendous growth during the last twenty years. It is possible to buy knowledge about legal and financial standards from international accounting firms and investment banks. Local and international consulting firms offer information about competitors, market potential, distribution systems, local buying standards, possible entry modes, etc. Thus, there is a well-developed market for knowledge about foreign markets.

Firms today also have quicker and easier access to knowledge about doing business abroad. It is no longer necessary to build up knowledge in-house in a slow and gradual trial-and-error process. Several factors contribute to this. For example, universities, business schools and management training centres all over the world are putting more and more emphasis on international business.

Probably even more important, the absolute number of people with experience of doing business abroad has increased. Hence, it has become easier to hire people with the experience and knowledge needed, rather than develop it in-house. The number of people with experience of doing business abroad has increased over time as an effect of continuous growth in world trade and foreign direct investment.

The spectacular development of information technologies, in terms of both absolute performance and diminishing price/performance ratios, has made it easier for a firm to become acquainted with foreign markets, thus making a 'leap-frog' strategy more realistic (see also section 3.5 about internet-based 'Born Globals').

In spite of the criticisms put forward, the Uppsala model has gained strong support in studies of a wide spectrum of countries and situations. The empirical research confirms that commitment and experience are important factors explaining international business behaviour. In particular, the model receives strong support regarding export behaviour, and the relevance of cultural distance has also been confirmed.

3.3 The transaction cost analysis (TCA) model

The foundation for this model was made by R. Coase. He argued that 'a firm will tend to expand until the cost of organizing an extra transaction within the firm will become equal to the cost of carrying out the same transaction by means of an exchange on the open market' (Coase, 1937, p. 395). It is a theory which predicts that a firm will perform internally those activities it can undertake at lower cost through establishing an internal ('hierarchical') management control and implementation system while relying on the market for activities in which independent outsiders (such as export intermediaries, agents or distributors) have a cost advantage.

Transaction costs emerge when markets fail to operate under the requirements of perfect competition ('friction free'); the cost of operating in such markets (i.e. the transaction cost) would be zero, and there would be little or no incentive to impose any impediments to free market exchange. However, in the real world there is always some kind of 'friction' between buyer and seller, resulting in transaction costs (see Figure 3.4).

The transaction cost analysis (TCA) framework argues that cost minimization explains structural decisions. Firms internalize, that is, integrate vertically, to reduce transaction costs.

Transaction costs can be divided into *different forms of costs* related to the transactional relationship between buyer and seller. The underlying condition for the following description of the cost elements is this equation:

$$\text{Transaction cost} = \text{Ex ante costs} + \text{Ex post costs} = (\text{search costs} + \text{contracting costs}) + (\text{monitoring costs} + \text{enforcement costs})$$

Ex ante costs

● *Search costs*: include the cost of gathering information to identify and evaluate potential export intermediaries. Although such costs can be prohibitive to many exporters, knowledge about foreign markets is critical to export success. The search costs for distant, unfamiliar markets, where available (published) market information is lacking and organizational forms are different, can be especially prohibitive (e.g. exports from the UK to China). In comparison, the search costs for nearby, familiar markets may be more acceptable (e.g. export from UK to Germany).

Figure 3.4   **The principles of the TCA model**

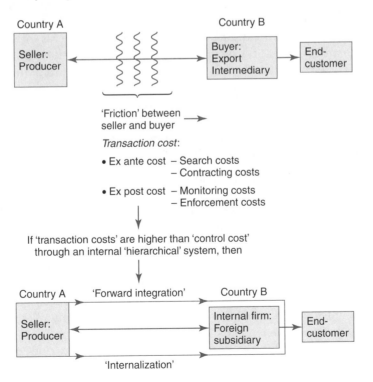

● *Contracting costs*: refer to the costs associated with negotiating and writing an agreement between seller (producer) and buyer (export intermediary).

Ex post costs

● *Monitoring costs*: refer to the costs associated with monitoring the agreement to ensure that both seller and buyer fulfil the predetermined set of obligations.

● *Enforcement costs*: refer to the costs associated with the sanctioning of a trading partner who does not perform in accordance with the agreement.

A fundamental assumption of transaction cost theory is that firms will attempt to minimize the combination of these costs when undertaking transactions. Thus, when considering the most efficient form of organizing export functions, transaction cost theory suggests that firms will choose the solution which minimizes the sum of ex ante and ex post costs.

Williamson (1975) based his analysis on the assumption of transaction costs and the different forms of governance structure under which transactions take place. In his original work, Williamson identified two main alternatives of governance markets: externalization and internalization ('hierarchies'). In the case of externalization, market transactions are by definition external to the firm and the price mechanism conveys all the necessary governance information. In the case of internalization, the international firm creates a kind of internal market in which the hierarchical governance is defined by a set of 'internal' contracts.

Externalization and internalization of transactions are equated with intermediaries (agents, distributors) and sales subsidiaries (or other governance structures involving ownership control) respectively.

In this way, Williamson's framework provides the basis for a variety of research into the organization of international activity and the choice of international market entry mode. We will return to this issue in Part III of this book.

In Figure 3.5 all the transaction cost variables are shown together with their correlation (plus or minus) on the transaction costs and in the end, on the internationalization mode.

Let us start with the variables under the head of '*underlying conditions*' (all with positive correlation with transaction costs).

● *Bounded rationality*: the rationality of human behaviour is limited by the actor's ability to process information. If one of the parties (seller and buyer) does not have complete information, the situation will be open for opportunistic behaviour, thus increasing transaction costs.

● *Small number bargaining*: in a situation with very intensive competition on the foreign market (the opposite of 'small number bargaining') the threat of replacement can restrain the opportunistic behaviour of the export intermediary. This would reduce transaction costs for the seller (producer). Conversely, if only a limited number of export intermediaries (i.e. 'small number bargaining') is available on the foreign market the export intermediary would be tempted to behave in an opportunistic way, thus increasing transaction costs for the seller (producer). The same would happen for the buyer (export intermediary) if there

Figure 3.5 The TCA model for choice of 'internationalization mode'

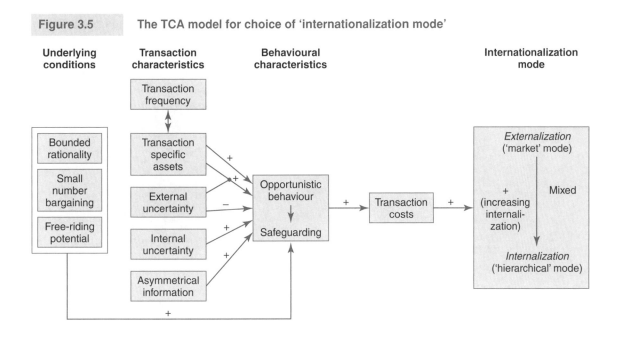

were only a small number of producers within a specific product area. In short, 'small number bargaining' is like a kind of an oligopoly; in the real world, 'small number' trading relationships are frequently found.

● *Free-riding potential*: this last construct concerns the idea that firms which invest in brand promotion are more exposed to 'free riding', either through damaging the entrant's brand in favour of another brand, or through capitalizing on the reputation of the brand without incurring the costs of maintaining it. See one extreme example of 'free-riding' in Figure 3.6.

If 'free riding' happens frequently, the seller (producer) has to set up some control mechanisms to prevent this behaviour. This 'safeguarding' (see the connection to the 'behavioural characteristics' box in Figure 3.5) would then automatically result in transaction costs for the seller.

Now, let us continue with *transaction characteristics* (variables).

Transaction-specific assets (TSA)

A transaction-specific asset (TSA) is one which is capable of severely limited use outside of the transaction for which it was designed/acquired. TSAs involve investments in human and physical capital that cannot be redeployed without losing productive value. These assets may be in plant and equipment uniquely suited to producing a specific product or serving a particular customer, in brand name capital, or in terms of specific knowledge and expertise.

A transaction-specific asset (or asset specificity) is the core determinant in the transaction cost logic developed by Williamson. Partners signing a contract that requires investments specific to a transaction enter a relationship of mutual dependence. Market forces will no longer be readily able to punish opportunism. To

Figure 3.6

One extreme form of 'free-riding': A brand pirate copy of 'Levi's' jeans (the pirate copy, 'Live's', has been bought in Poland)

Source: M. Gezelius (1998), Piratkopier er en stigende trussel, *Signature*, no. 3, p. 26.

minimize contracting hazards due to opportunistic exploitation, safeguard mechanisms have to be employed. The problem arises from the difficulty in transmitting tacit or proprietary knowledge to another partner and in the small numbers bargaining hazard. The latter refers to the situation where a partner with limited exchange alternatives is required to invest in transaction-specific assets and is, therefore, locked into this relationship. This party may be subject to exploitation by the stronger partner.

Closely connected to TSA is the tacitness of the firm's offerings. Know-how is often tacit as the firm is unable to articulate all the knowledge it possesses. Tacitness results in difficulties (transaction costs) both in the pricing of know-how and in its transferring through the contractual process. It is very difficult to set a fair price for both partners and the relationship is therefore open to opportunistic behaviour.

Transaction frequency

Transaction frequency relates to the frequency with which transactions involved in sourcing the same service recur. Under different levels of transaction frequency, whether a firm should rely on market governance or vertically integrate is contingent upon the level of asset specificity (see Figure 3.7).

In the matrix of Figure 3.7 investment specificity is one element governing the choice of degree of vertical linkage. Investment specificity increases as we move from left to right. The greater the asset specificity, the tighter the buyer–supplier link will be. The closest buyer–seller relationship is complete owner integration (internalization). We see that vertical integration is most common when transactions between the two parties are frequent and the optimal investment strategy involves highly specific assets.

For low-specificity firms (producers/sellers) externalization is appropriate under both occasional (low frequency) and recurrent transaction (high frequency) as the market for the transaction is competitive and the party is not required to make specialized investments.

| Figure 3.7 | The characteristics of the transaction determine the international governance structure |

		Asset / investment specificity		
		Low	*Medium*	*High*
Frequency of transaction	*Low*	Externalization: occasional transactions	Contracts	Contracts/ turnkey projects
	High	Externalization (market transactions = distributor/importer)	Bilateral agreement (joint ventures)	Internationalization (vertical integration = 100% owned subsidiaries)

The three remaining cells represent more a mix of externalization and internalization.

Joint ventures are a less bonded mode of integration and more like bilateral contracts.

External uncertainty

External uncertainty can be caused by demand and/or supply instability, political risks, competitive pressures, etc.

This construct addresses the fluctuation and unpredictability of the firm's environment. While search costs to locate unfamiliar markets are high, negotiations to secure export contracts with end-buyers from these markets may also be very costly due to cultural and language barriers. As a result, manufacturers may be more likely to use export intermediaries to enter distant, unfamiliar markets in order to save on export-related search and negotiation costs. Hence, in markets characterized by a high degree of external uncertainty, firms are, ceteris paribus, expected to shift the burden of risk to outsiders: that is, to use externalization (therefore minus).

However, in cases where asset specificity is involved, flexibility is lost and the unpredictability of the environment increases intermediaries' opportunities to behave opportunistically. In such cases, the propensity to internalize (higher degree of control) increases (Anderson and Gatignon, 1986). Put another way: when 'transaction-specific assets' and 'external uncertainty' are combined (see Figure 3.5), transaction-specific assets will win, because they are the most important single factor in the TSA approach.

Internal uncertainty

This behavioural uncertainty refers to the difficulty in measuring the performance of the contractual parties. It represents especially the producer's difficulty in monitoring the behaviour of an export intermediary to which the task has been allocated, and in measuring and evaluating its outputs. First, monitoring difficulty is problematic because it raises the potential for an opportunistic partner to shirk contractually assigned responsibilities. Second, evaluation difficulties complicate attempts to write contracts that provide compatible incentives to both parties. Hence, in the case of high internal uncertainty, the propensity to internalize increases.

Asymmetrical information

Information pertaining to a transaction, or sets of transactions, is often asymmetrically distributed between the parties to an exchange. Consequently, the party with more knowledge would be tempted to behave opportunistically, thus increasing transaction costs.

The transformation (in Figure 3.5) from *opportunistic behaviour* to *safeguarding* to *transaction costs* can be explained as follows. Human beings are prone to *opportunistic behaviour*. Williamson (1985) defines it as 'self-interest seeking with guile'. It includes not only the more obvious forms of cheating, but also clearly calculated methods of misleading, distortion, disguise, and confusion. To protect against the hazards of opportunism, the parties may employ a variety of safeguards or governance structures. The term '*safeguard*' (or alternatively 'governance structure') as used here can be defined as a control mechanism which has the objective of bringing about the perception of fairness or equity among transactors. The purpose of safeguards is to provide, at minimum cost, the control and 'trust' that is necessary for transactors to believe that engaging in the exchange will make them better off. The most prominent safeguard employed in Western economies is the legal contract.

The '*safeguarding*' could take place in the following way. For simple transactions, when asset specificity is low, a classical contract is typically employed. The costs of writing a classical contract are relatively low since the entire obligations of each party are explicitly written. A legal contract specifies the obligations of each party and allows a transactor to go to a third party (i.e. court/state) to sanction an opportunistic trading partner. As asset specificity increases, the parties will attempt to write a more complex contract with contingency clauses which allow for equitable adjustment as market conditions change. In theory, and practice, writing such a contract is more costly than writing a classical contract. Thus, as asset specificity increases, so does the full array of transaction costs (i.e. contracting, monitoring, and enforcement costs). In short, writing 'complex' contracts increases transaction costs.

Exhibit 3.1	TCA used on the German software giant SAP

SAP AG (www.sap.com) is the fourth largest software company in the world. Founded in 1972 by five former IBM systems engineers, SAP now employs more than 21,700 people in more than 50 countries. SAP software is deployed at more than 25,000 business installations in more than 110 countries and is currently used by companies of all sizes, including more than half of the world's 500 top companies.

SAP not only clearly leads the market for business applications software (IDC reports that SAP's share is 36 per cent); the company has also become the top supplier of end-to-end inter-enterprise solutions for the collaborative business processes that enable customers to profit from the new economy, the virtual economy of the Internet.

The primary ambition of SAP is to simplify day-to-day work for its customers' employees in their different roles, making a sustained contribution to value creation. This is being achieved through in-depth knowledge of business processes and their optimization, and by thorough and continuous customer relationship management.

On the different international markets SAP has got its own sales subsidiaries; however, to take care of the sales and implementation of its EPR (Enterprise Resource Planning) software in local companies, it has contracts with independent consultancy firms (partner strategy).

Questions

1. What is the degree of 'tacit' knowledge, TSA and 'free riding' that SAP face?
2. What would be the implications of (1) for the choice of 'internalization' or 'externalization' on international markets for SAP? (Use Figure 3.5.)
3. Do you agree with SAP's partner strategy with local consultancy firms?

Limitations of the TCA framework

Narrow assumptions of human nature

Ghoshal and Moran (1996) have criticized the original work of Williamson as having too narrow assumptions of human nature (opportunism and its equally narrow interpretation of economic objectives). They also wonder why the theory's mainstream development has remained immune to such important contributions as Ouchi's (1980) insight on social control. Ouchi (1980) points to the relevance of intermediate forms (between markets and hierarchies), such as the clan, where governance is based on a win–win situation (in contrast to a zero-sum game situation).

Excluding 'internal' transaction costs

The TCA framework also seems to ignore the 'internal' transaction cost, assuming zero friction within a multinational firm. One can imagine severe friction (resulting in transaction cost) between the head office of a firm and its sales subsidiaries when internal transfer prices have to be settled (see Part III introduction, Figure 3).

Relevance of 'intermediate' forms for SMEs

One can also question the relevance of the TCA framework to the internationalization process of the SMEs (Christensen and Lindmark, 1993). The lack of resources and knowledge in SMEs is a major force for the externalization of activities. But since the use of markets often raises contractual problems, markets in many instances are not real alternatives to hierarchies for SMEs. Instead, the SMEs have to rely on intermediate forms of governance, such as contractual relations and relations based on clan-like systems created by a mutual orientation of investments, skills and trust building. Therefore, SMEs are often highly dependent on the cooperative environment available. Such an approach will be presented and discussed in the next section.

Importance of 'production cost' is understated

It can be argued that the importance of transaction cost is overstated and that the importance of production cost has not been taken into consideration. Production cost is the cost of performing a particular task/function in the value chain, such as R&D costs, manufacturing costs and marketing costs. According to Williamson (1985), the most efficient choice of internationalization mode is one that will help *minimize the sum of production and transaction costs*. If, as suggested by transaction cost analysis, minimization of transaction costs alone was sufficient to guide choice of internalization mode, more firms would be totally vertically integrated in the current uncertain environment in which the firms routinely incur substantial transaction specific investments. Especially in SMEs, the use of internalization (i.e. own subsidiaries) is very limited. In many cases you will see market failures, but in few cases will internalization be the result. Why? From a transaction-cost point of view, it can be explained in the following way:

● In SMEs the investment (production cost) associated with the establishment of an own subsidiary cannot be spread over a sufficiently large sales volume, and it is therefore not possible to reap the economies-of-scale benefits of a foreign marketing and sales function.

● If channel volume for a SME product line is relatively low, the firm is likely to prefer externalization where an export intermediary can handle the product line of the firm together with complementary product lines from other firms.

● An LSE, on the other hand, with bigger sales volume in a foreign market, achieves economies of scale in utilizing management skills, enabling it to get more mileage out of the subsidiary investments in a local sales force and other marketing instruments.

3.4 ❙ The network model

Basic concept

Business networks are a mode of handling activity interdependences between several business actors. As we have seen, other modes of handling or governing interdependences in a business field are markets and hierarchies.

The network differs from the market with regard to relations between actors. In a market model, actors have no specific relations to each other. The interdependences are regulated through the market price mechanism. In contrast, in the business network the actors are linked to each other through exchange relationships, and their needs and capabilities are mediated through the interaction taking place in the relationships.

The industrial network differs from the hierarchy in the way that the actors are autonomous and handle their interdependences bilaterally rather than via a coordinating unit on a higher level. Whereas a hierarchy is organized and controlled as one unit from the top, the business network is organized by each actor's willingness to engage in exchange relationships with some of the other actors in the network.

The networks are more loosely coupled than are hierarchies; they can change shape more easily. Any actor in the network can engage in new relationships or break old, thereby modifying its structure. Thus business networks can be expected to be more flexible in response to changing conditions in turbulent business fields, such as those where technical change is very rapid.

It can be concluded that business networks will emerge in fields where coordination between specific actors can give strong gains and where conditions are changing rapidly. Thus, the network approach implies a move away from the firm as the unit of analysis, towards exchange between firms and between a group of firms and other groups of firms as the main object of study. However, it also implies a move away from transactions towards more lasting exchange relationships constituting a structure within which international business takes place and evolves.

Evidently, business relationships and consequently industrial networks are subtle phenomena, which cannot easily be observed by an outside observer: that is, a potential entrant. The actors are tied to each other through a number of different bonds: technical, social, cognitive, administrative, legal, economic, etc.

A basic assumption in the network model is that the individual firm is dependent on resources controlled by other firms. The companies get access to these external resources through their network positions. Since the development of positions takes time and depends on resource accumulations, a firm must establish and develop positions in relation to counterparts in foreign networks.

To enter a network from outside requires that other actors be motivated to engage in interaction, something which is resource demanding and may require several firms to make adaptions in their ways of performing business. Thus, foreign market or network entry of the firm may very well be the result of interaction initiatives taken by other firms which are insiders in the network in the specific country. However, the chances of being the object of such initiatives are much greater for an insider.

The networks in a country may well extend far beyond country borders. In relation to the internationalization of the firm, the network view argues that the internationalizing firm is initially engaged in a network which is primarily domestic.

The relationships of a firm in a domestic network can be used as bridges to other networks in other countries. In some cases, the customer demands that the supplier follows it abroad if the supplier wants to keep the business at home. An example of an international network is shown in Figure 3.8. It appears that one of the subsuppliers established a subsidiary in Country B. Here the production subsidiary is served by the local company of the subsupplier. Countries E and F, and partly Country C, are sourced from the production subsidiary in Country B. Generally, it can be assumed that direct or indirect bridges exist between firms and different country networks. Such bridges can be important both in the initial steps abroad and in the subsequent entry of new markets.

The character of the ties in a network is partly a matter of the firms involved. This is primarily the case with technical, economic and legal ties. To an important extent, however, the ties are formed between the persons engaged in the business relationships. This is the case with social and cognitive ties. Industries as well as countries may differ with regard to the relative importance of firm and personal

| Figure 3.8 | An example of an international network |

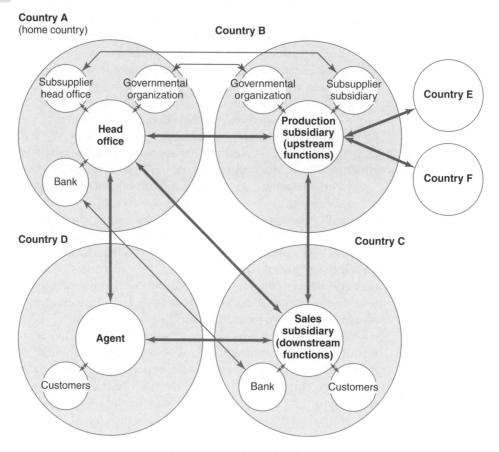

relationships. But it can be expected that the personal influence on relationships is strongest in the early establishment of relationships. Later in the process, routines and systems will become more important.

When entering a network, the internationalization process of the firm will often proceed more quickly. In particular, SMEs in high-tech industries tend to go directly to more distant markets and to set up their own subsidiaries more rapidly. One reason seems to be that the entrepreneurs behind those companies have networks of colleagues dealing with the new technology. Internationalization, in these cases, is an exploitation of the advantage that this network constitutes.

Four cases of internationalization

The Uppsala internationalization model treated internationalization independently of the situation and the competition in the market. In the following we will try to combine these two important aspects. A 'production net' contains relationships between those firms whose activities together produce functions linked to a specific area. The firm's degree of internationalization shows the extent to which the firm has positions in different national nets, how strong those positions are, and how integrated they are.

The network model also has consequences for the meaning of internationalization of the market. A production net can be more or less internationalized. A high degree of internationalization of a production net implies that there are many and strong relationships between the different national sections of the global production net. A low degree of internationalization means that the national nets have few relationships with each other.

We will distinguish between four different situations, characterized by, on the one hand, a low or a high degree of internationalization of the firm and, on the other, a low or high degree of internationalization of the market (the production network) (Figure 3.9).

The early starter

In this situation, competitors, customers, suppliers and other firms in the domestic market as well as in foreign markets have no important international relationships.

The people behind the Uppsala internationalization model have described this situation and its transition to the lonely international (section 3.2). Gradual and slow involvement in the market via an agent, leading to a sales subsidiary and then a manufacturing subsidiary, is primarily a process by which market knowledge gives the basis for stronger commitments.

The lonely international

In this situation, the firm has experience of relationships with and in foreign countries. It has acquired knowledge and means to handle environments which differ with respect to culture, institutions and so on. The knowledge situation is also more favourable when establishing the firm in a new national net.

Initiatives to further internationalization do not come from other parties in the production nets, as the firm's suppliers, customers and competitors are less inter-

Figure 3.9   **Four cases of internationalization of a firm**

| | | Degree of internationalization of the market | |
		Low	High
Degree of internationalization of the firm	Low	The early starter	The late starter
	High	The lonely international	The international among others

(Source: Johanson and Mattson, 1988 p. 298.)

nationalized. On the contrary, the lonely international has the competences to promote internationalization of its production net and, consequently, the firms engaged in it. The firm's relationships with, and in, other national nets may function as a bridge to those nets for its suppliers and customers.

The late starter

In a situation with international customers and competitors, the less internationalized firm can be 'pulled out' of the domestic market by its customers or complementary suppliers to the customers. Sometimes the step abroad can be rather large in the beginning.

How will the firm go abroad in this situation? Here we will differentiate between the SMEs and the LSEs.

SMEs going abroad in an internationalized world probably have to be highly specialized and adjusted to solutions in specific sections of the production nets. Starting production abroad is probably a question of what bonds are important to the customers, and in this matter SMEs are very flexible.

LSEs which have become large in the domestic market are often less specialized than small firms, and their situation is often more complex than that of the small firm. One possibility is to get established in a foreign production net through acquisition or joint venture.

In general, it is probably more difficult for a firm which has become large at home to find a niche in highly internationalized nets. It cannot, as the small firm can, adjust in the flexible way which may be necessary in such a net.

Compared to the early starter, the late starter often finds it difficult to establish new positions in a tightly structured net. The best distributors are already linked to competitors. Competitors can, more or less legally, make the late newcomer unprofitable by predatory pricing. When we compare early and late starters we can see how important timing is in global marketing.

The international among others

In this situation the firm has the possibility of using positions in one net to bridge over to other nets, with regard to both extensions and penetration. There is a strong need for coordination of the international activities along the value chain (e.g. R & D, production and marketing/sales). Operations in one market may make it possible to utilize production capacity for sales in other markets. This may lead to production coordination by product specialization and increased intra-firm trade across borders.

Establishment of sales subsidiaries is probably speeded up by high internationalization because the international knowledge level is higher and there is a stronger need to coordinate sales and marketing activities in different markets.

The relevance of the network model for the SME serving as a subcontractor

Until now a network has been connected with development of mutual trust and interests between firms in the network. In the following, domination and control characteristics will form the starting point for the formation of a more power-balanced network.

In the SME context, it is clear that where, for example, a small firm derives a significant proportion of its turnover and profits from acting as a subcontractor to another, often larger firm, the small firm becomes dependent on the latter. In turn, the large firm may acquire power over its subcontractor. This power can be measured in terms of the larger company's influence on decision making within the smaller firm in areas such as pricing and investment.

Exchange networks are based on control, coordination and cooperation. By 'control' is understood quasi-hierarchical relationships allowing one company to dominate another: for example, the relationship that traditionally obtains in the car industry between the major manufacturers and their subcontractors. By 'coordination' is understood a situation in which a 'leading' or 'hub' firm in the network orchestrates the value-adding chain. This allows firms to specialize in those components of the value chain in which they have competitive advantage, abandoning and farming out those activities in which they are disadvantaged to network partners that do have strengths in these areas.

'Cooperation' is the result of increasing specialization in small market niches, which has tended to encourage interdependency between firms in the value-added chain. Whereas in many subcontracting relationships in the past, the subcontractor simply followed instructions of the dominating firm on design and manufacture, the need to adjust to ever-quicker changes in the market-place can have the effect of making the subcontractor a more equal partner in the whole design to production process. The nature of the relationship between subcontractor and buyer thereby changes. Greater trust is required to make the partnership a success. Greater coordination is also required, creating a role for companies who simply 'manage' the value chain. In order to meet the pressures of these new circumstances, the small firm will depend on the nature and number of its links to other firms. As a result, the need for and value of networking have increased.

Where the network is dominated by a single firm and relationships are of the 'traditional' subcontracting kind, competition on price (or prices simply being imposed by the dominating firm) is the rule. Also, cooperating firms know that, while optimal networking is an effective strategy to reduce risk, less optimal networking will increase risk by increasing their dependence on, for example, a potentially unreliable supplier. To overcome the danger of dependence, 'traditional' risk reduction strategies can be implemented, such as the implementation of multiple sourcing by the purchasing company, or client diversification by the selling company.

3.5 Born Globals

Introduction

In recent years research has identified an increasing number of firms which certainly do not follow the traditional stages pattern in their internationalization process. In contrast, they aim at international markets or maybe even the global market right from their birth. Such firms have been named 'Born Globals'. 'Born Globals' are typically characterized by being SMEs with less than 500 employees and annual sales under $100 million – and reliance on cutting-edge technology in the development of relatively unique product or process innovations. But the most distinguishing feature of 'Born Global' firms is that they tend to be managed by entrepreneurial visionaries, who view the world as a single, borderless marketplace from the time of the firm's founding. 'Born Globals' are small, technology-oriented companies that operate in international markets from the earliest days of their establishment. There is a growing evidence of the emergence of 'Born Globals' in numerous countries of the developed world. The 'Born Global' phenomenon suggests a new challenge to traditional theories of internationalization.

Born Globals are challenging traditional theories

The case of Born Globals may be similar to the situation of the 'Late Starter' or the 'International Among Others' (Johanson and Mattson, 1988). In the latter situation both the environment and the firm are highly internationalized. Johanson and Mattson (1988) point out that internationalization processes of firms will be much faster in internationalized market conditions, among other reasons because the need for coordination and integration across borders is high. Since relevant partners/distributors will often be occupied in neighbouring markets, firms do not necessarily follow a 'rings in the water' approach to market selection. In the same vein their 'establishment chain' need not follow the traditional picture because strategic alliances, joint ventures, etc. are much more prevalent; firms seek partners with supplementary skills and resources. In other words, internationalization processes of firms will be much more individual and situation specific in internationalized markets.

Many industries are characterized by *global sourcing activities* and also by networks across borders. The consequence is that innovative products can very quickly spread to new markets all over the world – because the needs and wants of buyers become more homogeneous. Hence, the internationalization process of subcontractors may be quite diverse and different from the stages models. In other words, the new market conditions pull the firms into many markets very fast. Finally, financial markets have also become international which means that an entrepreneur in any country may seek financial sources all over the world (Madsen *et al.*, 1999).

In the case of Born Globals we may assume that the background of the decision-maker (founder) has a large influence on the internationalization path followed. Market knowledge, personal networking of the entrepreneur, or international contacts and experience transmitted from former occupations, relations, and education are examples of such international skills obtained prior to the birth of the firm. Factors like education, experience from living abroad, experience of other internationally oriented jobs etc. mould the mind of the founder and decrease the psychic distances to specific product-markets significantly; the previous experience and knowledge of the founder extends the network across national borders, opening possibilities for new business ventures. Often Born Globals govern their sales and marketing activities through a specialized network in which they seek partners who complement their own competences; this is necessary because of their limited resources.

Most often, Born Globals must choose a business area with homogeneous and minimal adaptation of the marketing mix. The argument is that these small firms cannot take a multi-domestic approach like large firms, simply because they do not have sufficient scale in operations worldwide. They are vulnerable because they are dependent on a single product which they have to commercialize in lead markets first, no matter where such markets are situated geographically. The reason is that such markets are the key to broad and rapid market access which is important because the fixed costs in these firms are relatively high. Since this is the key factor influencing the choice of the initial market, the importance of psychic distance as market selection criteria is reduced.

Factors giving rise to the emergence of Born Globals

Several trends may explain the increasing importance of Born Globals and help explain why such companies can successfully enter international markets:

Increasing role of niche markets

There is a growing demand among customers in mature economies for specialized or customized products. With the globalization of markets and increasing world-wide competition from large multinationals, many smaller firms may have no choice but to specialize in the supplying of products that occupy a relatively narrow global niche.

Advances in process/technology production

Improvements in microprocessor-based technology imply that low-scale, batch-type production can be economical. New machine tools now permit the manufacture of complex, non-standard parts and components with relative ease. New technologies allow small companies to achieve comparable footing with large multinationals in the production of sophisticated products for sale around the world. Technology allows small importers to streamline production in ways that make their products highly competitive in the global marketplace. Furthermore, technology is facilitating the production of widely diverse products on an ever smaller scale. The consequence of this is increasing specialization in many industries – more and more consumer goods will likely be tailor-made to fit ever more diverse preferences.

Flexibility of SMEs/Born Globals

The advantages of small companies – quicker response time, *flexibility*, adaptability, and so on – facilitate the international endeavours of Born Globals. SMEs are more flexible and quicker to adapt to foreign tastes and international standards.

Global networks

Successful international commerce today is increasingly facilitated through partnerships with foreign businesses – distributors, trading companies, subcontractors, as well as more traditional buyers and sellers. Inexperienced managers can improve their chances for succeeding in international business if they take the time to build mutually beneficial, long-term alliances with foreign partners.

Advances in information technology

A very important trend in favour of Born Globals is the recent advance in *communications technology*. Gone are the days of large, vertically integrated firms where information flows were expensive and took a considerable time to be shared. With the invention of the Internet and other telecommunication aids such as mobile/WAP phones, email and other computer-supported technologies such as electronic data interchange (EDI), managers even in small firms can efficiently manage operations across borders. Information is now readily and more quickly accessible to everyone.

Another important trend is the *globalization of technology*. Joint research and development platforms, international technology transfers, and the cross-border education of students in science and engineering have all exploded in recent years. As such, new and better approaches to manufacturing, product innovation, and general operations have become much more readily available to smaller firms.

Internet-based Born Globals

The Internet revolution offers new opportunities for young SMEs to establish a global sales platform by developing e-commerce websites. Today many new and small firms are Born Globals in the way that they are 'start-ups' on the Internet and they sell to a global audience via a centralized e-commerce website. However, after some time many of these firms realize they cannot expand global sales to the next level without having some 'localized e-commerce Websites'. If we compare the flow of financial results in physical ('bricks and mortar') companies with Internet-based companies we will often see a result such as that shown in Figure 3.10.

In the 'physical' companies we will often see the 'law of diminishing returns to scale' in function. This happens where the variable costs are relatively high compared to fixed costs of the company. We are learning that the law of diminishing returns does not always apply. In many cases, the optimal production point is no longer determined by factory size, but by the point at which total market demand is satisfied. This occurs in markets in which fixed costs are much higher than variable costs. This is the case for products in digital form, where a single copy (of software, for instance) can satisfy total market needs, and for products with very high investment in intellectual content, like pharmaceuticals.

In the successful internet companies, gains associated with increasing shares of markets do not diminish with time but actually increase. This increase creates 'increasing returns to scale'. In this environment, companies must *win market shares rapidly*, which has driven many companies to create new strategies for market share capture. America Online (AOL) distributed diskettes of its software in everything from magazine inserts to fast-food giveaways, making its trial offer almost irresistible to millions of networks users. Netscape's strategy was to give its product away, with the intent of drawing revenues from associated business opportunities.

Figure 3.10   **Models of economic efficiency**

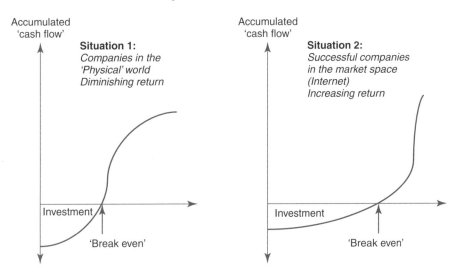

Funding the large investments required to capture significant market share in the internet economy does not come cheaply, especially if many companies are competing for the same market space. A substantial part of the investment must be made up front, sometimes years before revenues begin to outpace operating cost.

In a global economy, companies must also be prepared, almost from the start, to serve larger market segments. Neither proposition is cheap. America Online and Amazon.com have achieved market dominance, but not without investing a half-billion dollars a year in sales and marketing.

Amazon.com is perhaps an example of Situation 2 in Figure 3.10 but, despite considerably increasing sales, they have not yet reached break-even. Many companies must also rethink their alliance strategies. No longer are alliances primarily about efficiency: 'How can I outsource certain functions to improve performance?' Now the emphasis is on gaining access to markets to exploit network effects, and on creating product and service synergies in aligning with larger, already-dominant companies. For example, companies like American Broadcasting Company (ABC) are partnering with America Online for access to its customer base and expected synergies with its offerings. Access has proven to be so valuable that companies are now paying America Online more than a billion dollars for the ability to reach its customers.

As economic fundamentals that have held true for decades begin to change, many traditional business strategies are becoming obsolete. In the electronic company now taking shape, companies are spending multiples of their revenues on marketing and sales just to garner a few more share points. In this game, share must be defended vigorously to sustain leadership positions in markets that ultimately will support only a few dominant players. The perfect profit formula for this new business environment is not yet clear. What is clear, however, is that new business theories (along with new markets, services and companies) have emerged.

Electronic commerce is changing the rules, and every business, even the most successful, needs a new business plan.

3.6 ▌ Summary

The main conclusions of this chapter are summarized in Table 3.1

Table 3.1	Summary of the three models for explaining the internationalization process of the firm		
	Uppsala internationalization model	**Transaction cost analysis (TCA) model**	**Network model**
Unit of analysis	The firm	The transaction or set of transactions	Multiple interorganizational relationships between firms Relationships between one group of firms and other groups of firms
Basic assumptions about firms' behaviour	The model is based on behavioural theories and an incremental decision-making process with little influence from competitive market factors. A gradual learning-by-doing process.	In the real world there is 'friction'/transactional difficulties between buyer and seller. This friction is mainly caused by opportunistic behaviour: the self-conscious attention of the single manager (i.e. seeking of self-interest with guile).	The 'glue' that keeps the network (relationships) together is based on technical, economic, legal and especially personal ties. Managers' personal influence on relationships is strongest in the early phases of the establishments of relationships. Later in the process, routines and systems will become more important.
Explanatory variables affecting the process development	The firm's knowledge/market commitment Psychic distance between home country and the firm's international markets	Transactional difficulties and transaction costs increase when transactions are characterized by: ● asset specificity ● uncertainty (internal and external) ● frequency of transaction.	The individual firms are autonomous. The individual firm is dependent on resources controlled by other firms. Business networks will emerge in fields where there is frequent coordination between specific actors and where conditions are changing rapidly.
Normative implications for international marketers	Additional market commitments should be made in small incremental steps: ● Choose new geographic markets with small psychic distances from existing markets ● Choose an 'entry mode' with few marginal risks.	Under the above-mentioned conditions (i.e. prohibitively high transaction costs), firms should seek internalization of activities (i.e. implement the global marketing strategy in wholly owned subsidiaries).	The relationships of a firm in a domestic network can be used as bridges to other networks in other countries. Such direct or indirect bridges to different country networks can be important in the initial steps abroad and in the subsequent entry of new markets. Sometimes an SME can be forced to enter foreign networks: for example, if a customer requires that the subsupplier (an SME) follows it abroad. As an example see the Case Study in Chapter 12, LM Glasfiber.

Case study   LetsBuyIt.com

A 'Born Global'

Not many people can claim to have built a business from a standing start to a global brand with a $100m-plus marketing budget within a year. Even fewer would dare to launch a business when it is not (entirely) ready in order to get the feedback needed to help its evolution. But John Palmer is on his way to achieving this with e-commerce operation LetsBuyIt.com (LetsBuyIt), already in Europe and set to extend its reach to America and Australia.

Palmer, 39, is co-founder of the Swedish-based company and responsible for its strategic direction, setting up alliances with brand manufacturers and helping to secure finance. It works through consumers joining together to drive down the price of products through the benefit of bulk buying. A consumer becomes a member, identifies a product and then joins a co-buy. Graphics show a recommended retail price, the guaranteed reduced start price and the potential final price plus where the price currently stands. The more who join the lower the price goes until it reaches the final point.

When buying from a street store, the price that one typically pays includes the overheads of the manufacturer, distributors, suppliers and so on, plus a healthy mark-up margin by the retailer. LetsBuyIt.com, on the other hand, sources directly with suppliers, thus eliminating many intermediary costs and so enabling it to deliver brand-name merchandise at lower prices. More traditional online e-commerce sites may offer discounted prices, but they often don't reflect the power of joining in numbers and driving down prices to the lowest possible level.

The key to LetsBuyIt's success is selling the concept to global brand manufacturers. The company establishes pre-arranged frame agreements with manufacturers who deliver the products at a discounted price to a logistics partner. Members can also suggest merchandise and services and what price they would be willing to pay, and LetsBuyIt will approach manufacturers to source the product and secure preferential terms.

LetsBuyIt takes a small commission of each transaction. The plan is that the scale of the operation will turn this small cut into a handsome revenue stream. Palmer is confident this will happen, predicting that the company will turn in profit in three and a half years from now. Certainly costs are kept to a minimum as the goods never pass through LetsBuyIt's hands while its American logistics partner Sykes manages that side of the business plus the call centres across Europe.

Securing investment and manufacturer deals were the first hurdles to overcome. 'We had to develop a step-by-step demonstration because at that time there was really only Amazon around in terms of e-commerce,' Palmer explains. 'It was important that we convinced the suppliers that we would take care when presenting their products so as not to damage their brands.'

Initial backing came from German TV company ProSieben, which has a 25 per cent stake. At the end of January the company secured a further 49m Euros from venture capitalists including Gilde IT Find, NeSBIC Cte Fund and Sofinnova

Partners. This round of funding will be used to expand its product offerings, improve customer experience and enhance its customer support functions. Palmer says: 'We've got a big job ahead of us as we build this business into a global power-house.'

The UK launch in October followed the blueprint of other local launches, or as Palmer says: 'Build the site in three months, launch it when it is not ready, get feedback and evolve.' This soft launch approach helps the company to feel its way in each locality but as the word gets out it can prove a problem. Certainly LetsBuyIt did not escape the 1999 pre-Christmas delivery problems and customer disappointment that has dogged e-commerce operations. Palmer blames its UK logistics operation, which has since been revamped.

LetsBuyIt.com is fuelling the massive $100m into its global marketing expansion. The Scandinavian-based business is already operating in 14 European countries, and part of this marketing budget will go into launching the project in Latin America, USA, and Asia.

In February 2000 the first phase of a worldwide marketing campaign was unveiled as troops of funky cartoon ants took to our TV screens to promote the brand and its proposition – a member-driven, pan-European buying collective.

The group's global marketing director, Soame Hines, said that the spend will focus on traditional media. The TV campaign launches at the end of January, and although the brand across the globe will be universal, Hines said: 'To market on a pan-European basis is very different. Buying habits in different places vary enormously.'

Question

1. Discuss the further internationalization strategy of LetsBuyIt.com.

Source: Adapted from Harrigan, S. (2000) 'The world in his web', *In-Store Marketing*, 1 March.
New Media Age (2000) 'Big spend from LetsBuyIt', *New Media Age*, 8 March.
http://LetsBuyIt.com/.

Questions for discussion

1. Explain why internationalization is an ongoing process in constant need of evaluation.

2. Explain the main differences between the three theories of internationalization: the Uppsala internationalization model; the transaction cost theory; and the network model.

3. What is meant by the concept of 'psychological' or 'psychic distance'?

Internet exercise

Fox Kids Europe

Please go to: http://www.euromheg.org/reference/company_briefs/fox_kids.htm

Early in 1997, a young Israeli television executive called Ynon Kreiz left the US, heading for London. The task he had been given was to set up a pan-European children's television business from scratch. At the time he had less than two years' experience of full-time work in the entertainment business.

Three years later the company he set up, Fox Kids Europe, has a presence in 30 countries in Europe and the Middle East, broadcasts in 11 different languages, and reaches 17m households. It controls the European rights to a range of children's programmes including Spiderman, Teenage Mutant Ninja Turtles and Pokemon, and has become a credible competitor to more established rivals such as Viacom's Nickelodeon and Time Warner's Cartoon Network.

Question

1. Which internationalization theory has the best match with the internationalization of Fox Kids Europe?

For further exercises and cases, see this book's website at *www.booksites.net/hollensen*

References

Aharoni, Y. (1966) *The Foreign Investment Decision Process*, Harvard Business School, Boston, MA.

Anderson, E. and Gatignon, H. (1986) 'Modes of foreign entry: a transaction cost analysis and propositions', *Journal of International Business Studies*, vol. 17, no. 3, pp. 1–26.

Buckley, P.J. and Casson, M. (1976) *The Future of the Multinational Enterprise*. Holmes and Meier, New York.

Christensen, P.R. and Lindmark, L.L. (1993) 'Location and internationalisation of small firms', in Lindquist, L. and L.O. (eds.) *Visions and Strategies in European Integration*, Springer Verlag, Berlin and Heidelberg.

Coase, R.H. (1937) 'The nature of the firm', *Economica*, pp. 386–405.

Contractor, F.J. and Lorange, P. (eds.) (1998) *Cooperative Strategies in International Business*. Lexington Books, Lexington, MA.

Dunning, J.H. (1988) *Explaining International Production*. Unwin, London.

Forsgren, M. and Johanson, J. (1975) *International företagsekonomi*, Norstedts, Stockholm.

Ghoshal, S. and Moran, P. (1996) 'Bad for practice: a critique of the transaction cost theory', *Academy of Management Review*, vol. 21, no. 1, pp. 13–47.

Hallen, L. and Wiedersheim-Paul, F. (1979) 'Physical distance and buyer-seller interaction. *Organisasjon, Marknad och Samhalle*, vol. 16, no. 5, pp. 308–24.

Hymer, S.H. (1976) *The International Operations of National Firms: A study of direct foreign investment*. Unpublished 1960 PhD thesis, MIT Press, Cambridge, MA.

Johanson, J. and Mattson, L.G. (1986) 'International marketing and internationalization processes – some perspectives on current and future research', in Paliwoda, S. and Turnbull, P. (eds.), *Research in Developments in International Marketing*, Croom Helm, Beckenham (UK).

Johanson, J. and Mattson, L.G. (1988) 'Internationalization in industrial systems', in Hood, N. and Vahlne, J.E. (eds.), *Strategies in Global Competition*, Croom Helm, Beckenham (UK).

Johanson, J. and Vahlne, J.E. (1977) 'The internationalization process of the firm – a model of knowledge development and increasing foreign market commitment', *Journal of International Business Studies*, vol. 8, no. 1, pp. 23–32.

Johanson, J. and Vahlne, J.E. (1990) 'The mechanism of internationalization', *International Marketing Review*, vol. 7, no. 4, pp. 11–24.

Johanson, J. and Wiedersheim-Paul, F. (1975) 'The internationalization of the firm – four Swedish cases', *Journal of Management Studies*, October, pp. 305–22.

Kindleberger, C.P. (1969) *American Business Abroad*. Yale University Press, New Haven, CT.

Kogut, B. (1988) 'Joint ventures: theoretical and empirical perspective'. *Strategic Management Journal*, vol. 9, pp. 319–32.

Madhok, A. (1997) 'Cost, value and foreign market entry mode: The transaction and the firm'. *Strategic Management Journal*, vol. 18, pp. 39–61.

Madhok, A. (1998) 'The nature of multinational firm boundaries: Transaction cost, firm capabilities and foreign market entry mode'. *International Business Review*, vol. 7, pp. 259–90.

Madsen, T.K., Rasmussen, E. and Servais, P. (1999) 'Differences and similarities between Born Globals and other types of exporters', *Working Papers in Marketing*, no. 22, University of Southern Denmark-Odense.

Nordström, K.A. (1990) *The Internationalization Process of the Firm: Searching for new patterns and explanations*, Stockholm School of Economics, Stockholm.

Ouchi, W.G. (1980) 'Markets, bureaucracies and clans', *Administrative Science Quarterly*, vol. 25, pp. 129–42.

Penrose, E. (1959) *The Theory of the Growth of the Firm*. Basil Blackwell, London.

Prahalad, C.K. and Hamel, G. (1990) 'The core competence and the corporation'. *Harvard Business Review*, May, pp. 71–97.

Reid, S.D. (1983) 'Firm internationalization, transaction costs and strategic choice', *International Marketing*, vol. 1, no. 2, p. 44.

Rugman, A.M. (1986) 'New theories of the multinational enterprise: An assessment of internationalization theory'. *Bulletin of Economic Research*, vol. 38, no. 2, pp. 101–18.

Sharma, D.D. and Johanson, J. (1987) 'Technical consultancy in internationalization', *International Marketing Review*, Winter, pp. 20–9.

Turnbull, P.N. (1987) 'Interaction and international marketing: an investment process', *International Marketing Review*, Winter, pp. 7–19.

Vernon, R. (1966) 'International investment and international trade in the product cycle'. *Quarterly Journal of Economics*, vol. 80, pp. 190–207.

Welch, L.S. and Loustarinen, R. (1988) 'Internationalization: evolution of a concept', *Journal of General Management*, vol. 14, no. 2, pp. 36–64.

Williamson, O.E. (1975) *Markets and Hierarchies: Analysis and antitrust implications*, The Free Press, New York.

Williamson, O.E. (1985) *The Economic Institutions of Capitalisation*, The Free Press, New York.

4

Development of the firm's international competitiveness

Learning objectives

After studying this chapter you should be able to do the following:

● Define the concept 'international competitiveness' in a broader perspective from a macro level to a micro level.

● Discuss the factors influencing the firm's international competitiveness.

● Explain how Porter's traditional competitive-based five forces model can be extended to a collaborative (five sources) model.

● Explore the idea behind the 'competitive triangle'.

● Analyze the basic sources of competitive advantage.

● Explain the steps in competitive benchmarking.

4.1 Introduction

The topic of this chapter is how the firm creates and develops competitive advantages in the international market. Development of a firm's international competitiveness takes place interactively with the environment. The firm must be able to adjust to customers, competitors and public authorities. To be able to participate in the international competitive arena, the firm must have established a competitive basis consisting of resources, competences and relations to others in the international arena.

To enable an understanding of the development of a firm's international competitiveness in a broader perspective, a model in three stages (see Figure 4.1) will be presented:

1. Analysis of national competitiveness (the Porter diamond).

2. Competition analysis in an industry (Porter's five forces).

3. Value chain analysis:
     (a) competitive triangle;
     (b) benchmarking.

Figure 4.1 Development of a firm's international competitiveness

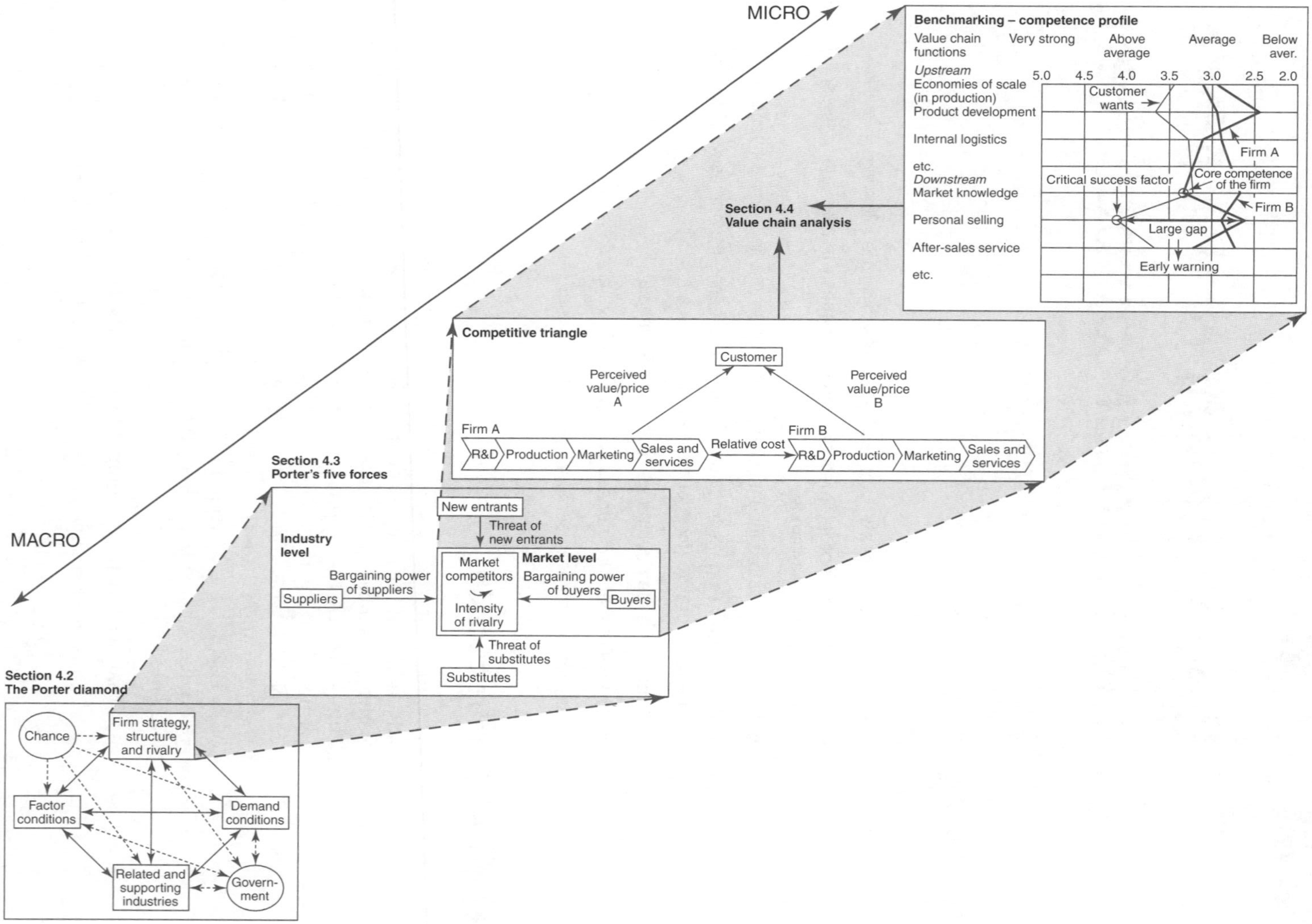

The analysis starts at the macro level and then moves into the firm's competitive arena through Porter's five forces framework. Based on the firm's value chain, the analysis is concluded with a discussion of which activities/functions in the value chain are the firm's core competences (and must be developed internally in the firm) and which competences must be placed with others through alliances and market relations.

The graphical system used in Figure 4.1 (which will be referred to throughout this chapter) places the models after each other in a hierarchical windows logic, where you get from stage 1 to stage 2 by clicking on the icon box: 'Firm strategy, structure and rivalry'. Here Porter's five forces model appears. From stage 2 to 3 we click the middle box called 'Market competitors/buyers' and the model for a value chain analysis/competitive triangle appears.

4.2 Analysis of national competitiveness (the Porter diamond)

Analysis of national competitiveness represents the highest level in the entire model (Figure 4.1). Michael Porter called his work *The Competitive Advantage of Nations* (1990), but as a starting point it is important to say that it is firms which are competing in the international arena not nations. Yet the characteristics of the home nation play a central role in a firm's international success. The home base shapes a company's capacity to innovate rapidly in technology and methods, and to do so in the proper directions. It is the place from which competitive advantage ultimately emanates and from which it must be sustained. Competitive advantage ultimately results from an effective combination of national circumstances and company strategy. Conditions in a nation may create an environment in which firms can attain international competitive advantage, but it is up to a company to seize the opportunity. The national diamond becomes central to choosing the industries to compete with, as well as the appropriate strategy. The home base is an important determinant of a firm's strengths and weaknesses relative to foreign rivals.

Understanding the home base of foreign competitors is essential in analyzing them. Their home nation yields them advantages and disadvantages. It also shapes their likely future strategies.

Porter (1990) describes a concentration of firms within a certain industry as industrial clusters. Within such industrial clusters, firms have a network of relations to other firms in the industry: customers (including firms which work on semi-manufactured goods), suppliers and competitors. These industrial clusters may go world-wide, but they will usually have their starting point and location in a certain country or region of a country.

A firm gains important competitive advantages from the presence in its home nation of world-class buyers, suppliers and related industries. They provide insight into future market needs and technological developments. They contribute to a climate for change and improvement, and become partners and allies in the innovation process. Having a strong cluster at home unblocks the flow of information and allows deeper and more open contact than is possible when dealing with foreign firms. Being part of a cluster localized in a small geographic area can be even more valuable, so the central question we can ask is: what accounts for the national location of a particular global industry? The answer begins, as does all classical trade theory, with the match between the factor endowments of the country and the needs of the industry.

Let us now take a closer look at the different elements in Porter's diamond, beginning with the factor conditions.

Factor conditions

In this connection it is important to mention that the most enduring competitive advantages for nations are created by those factors that have the least degree of mobility. Table 4.1 lists the various factors of production and indicates the mobility of each.

At one extreme, we have climate with no mobility. Finland will never be a major producer of citrus fruit, no matter what government and industry do to try to change the rest of the national diamond.

At the other end of the mobility scale we have capital, probably the most mobile of the factors of production. Over the years we have seen enormous increases in the inflow and outflow of foreign investment capital in the industrialized and developing countries of the world. This can be seen as part of the process of global economic integration. Technology and the loosening of currency restrictions throughout the world have improved the flow of capital across nations and suggest that differences in capital availability are no longer likely to constitute a very stable competitive advantage for an area.

Demand conditions

The nature and size of home demand is represented in the right-hand box of Porter's diamond (Figure 4.1). There exists an interaction between scale economies, transportation costs and the size of the home market. Given sufficiently strong economies of scale, each producer wants to serve a geographically extensive market from a single location. To minimize transportation costs, the producer chooses a location with large local demand. When scale economies limit the number of production locations, the size of a market will be an important determinant of its attractiveness. Large home markets will also ensure that firms located at that site develop a cost advantage based on scale and often on experience as well.

Table 4.1	Factor conditions and their degree of mobility

Factor	Degree of mobility
Climate	Low
Physical infrastructure (transport, etc.)	↑
Natural resources (minerals, oil)	
Educational system	
Human resources (movement of labour)	
Technological infrastructure (software, communication network)	↓
Capital	High

An interesting pattern is that an early large home market which has become saturated forces efficient firms to look abroad for new business. For example, the Japanese motorcycle industry with its large home market used its scale advantages in the global marketplace after an early start in Japan. The composition of demand also plays an important role.

A product's fundamental or core design nearly always reflects home market needs. In electrical transmission equipment, for example, Sweden dominates the world in the high-voltage distribution market. In Sweden there is a relatively large demand for transporting high voltage over long distances, as a consequence of the location of population and industry clusters. Here the needs of the home market shaped the industry that was later able to respond to global markets (with ABB as one of the leading producers on the world market).

The sophistication of the buyer is also important. The US government was the first buyer of chips and remained the only customer for many years. The price inelasticity of government encouraged firms to develop technically advanced products without worrying too much about costs. Under these conditions, the technological frontier was clearly pushed much further and much faster than it would have been had the buyer been either less sophisticated or more price sensitive. Today the Japanese, who dominate the market for semiconductors, are influencing the shape of the industry and price issues have become more salient.

Related and supporting industries

In part, the advantages of clustering come from a reduction in the transportation costs for intermediate goods. In many other cases, advantages come from being able to use labour which is attracted to an area to serve the core industry, but which is available and skilled for supporting industries. Coordination of technology is also eased by geographic proximity. Porter argues that Italian world leadership in gold and silver jewellery has been sustained in part by the local presence of manufacturers of jewellery-making machinery. Here the advantage of clustering is not so much transportation cost reductions, but technical and marketing cooperation. In the semiconductor industry, the strength of the electronics industry in Japan (which buys the semiconductors) is a strong incentive to the location of semiconductors in the same area. It should be noted that clustering is not independent of scale economies. If there were no scale economies in the production of intermediate inputs, then the small-scale centres of production could rival the large-scale centres. It is the fact that there are scale economies in both semiconductors and electronics, coupled with the technological and marketing connections between the two, that give rise to clustering advantages.

Firm strategy, structure and rivalry

One of the most compelling results of Porter's study of successful industries in ten different nations is the powerful and positive effect that domestic competition has on the ability to compete in the global marketplace. In Germany, the fierce domestic rivalry among BASF, Hoechst and Bayer in the pharmaceutical industry is well known. Furthermore, the process of competition weeds out inferior technologies, products and management practices, and leaves as survivors only the most efficient firms. When domestic competition is vigorous, firms are forced to become more efficient, adopt new cost-saving technologies, reduce product development time, and learn to motivate and control workers more effectively. Domestic rivalry is especially important in stimulating technological developments among global firms.

The small country of Denmark has three producers of hearing-aids (Oticon (see case I.3), Widex and Danavox), which are all among the top ten of the world's largest producers of hearing-aids. In 1996 Oticon and Widex fought a violent technological fight to be the first in the world to launch a 100 per cent digitalized hearing-aid. Widex (the smaller of the two producers) won, but forced Oticon at the same time to keep a leading edge in technological development.

Chance

When we look at the history of most industries, we also see the role played by chance. Perhaps the most important instance of chance involves the question of who comes up with a major new idea first. For reasons having little to do with economics, entrepreneurs will typically start their new operations in their home countries. Once the industry begins in a given country, scale and clustering effects can cement the industry's position in that country.

Government

Governments play a powerful role in encouraging the development of industries within their own borders that will assume global positions. One way governments do this is through their effect on other elements of the national diamond. Governments finance and construct infrastructure, providing roads, airports, education and health care, and can support use of alternative energy (e.g. windmills) or other environmental systems that affect factors of production.

From the firm's point of view the last two variables, chance and government, can be regarded as exogenous variables which the firm must adjust to. Alternatively, the government may be considered susceptible through lobbying, interest organizations and mass media.

In summary, we have identified six factors that influence the location of global industries: factors of production, home demand, the location of supporting industries, the internal structure of the domestic industry, chance and government. We have also suggested that these factors are interconnected. As industries evolve, their dependence on particular locations may also change. For example, the shift in users of semiconductors from the military to the electronics industry has had a profound effect on the shape of the national diamond in that industry. To the extent that governments and firms recognize the source of any locational advantages that they have, they will be better able to both exploit those differences and anticipate their shifts.

4.3 Competition analysis in an industry

The next step in understanding the firm's competitiveness is to look at the competitive arena in an industry, which is the top box in the diamond model (see Figure 4.1).

One of the most useful frameworks for analyzing the competitive structure has been developed by Michael E. Porter. Porter (1980) suggests that competition in an industry is rooted in its underlying economic structure and goes beyond the behaviour of current competitors. The state of competition depends upon five basic competitive forces, as shown in Figure 4.1. Together, these factors determine the ultimate profit potential in an industry, where profit is measured in terms of long-run return on invested capital. The profit potential will differ from industry to industry.

To make things clearer, we need to define a number of key terms. An *industry* is a group of firms that offer a product or class of products that are close substitutes for each other. Examples are the car industry and the pharmaceutical industry (Kotler, 1997, p. 230). A *market* is a set of actual and potential buyers of a product and sellers. A distinction will be made between industry and market level, as we assume that the industry may contain several different markets. This is why the outer box in Figure 4.1 is designated 'industry level' and the inner box 'market level'.

Thus the *industry level* consists of all types of actors (new entrants, suppliers, substitutes, buyers and market competitors) which have a potential or current interest in the industry.

The *market level* consists of actors with a current interest in the market: that is, buyers and sellers (market competitors). In section 4.4 (value chain analysis) this market level will be further elaborated as the buyers' perceived value of different competitor offerings will be discussed.

Although division into the above-mentioned two levels is appropriate for this approach, Levitt (1960) pointed out the danger of 'marketing myopia', where the seller defines the competition field (i.e. the market) too narrowly. For example, the European luxury car manufacturers showed this myopia with their focus on each other rather than on the Japanese mass manufacturers, who were new entrants into the luxury car market.

The goal of competition analysis is to find a position in industry where the company can best defend itself against the five forces, or can influence them in its favour. Knowledge of these underlying pressures highlights the critical strengths and weaknesses of the company, shows its position in the industry, and clarifies areas where strategy changes yield the greatest pay-off. Structure analysis is fundamental for formulating competitive strategy.

Each of the five forces in the Porter model in turn comprises a number of elements that combine to determine the strength of each force, and its effect on the degree of competition. Each force is now discussed.

Market competitors

The intensity of rivalry between existing competitors in the market depends on a number of factors:

- *The concentration of the industry.* Numerous competitors of equal size will lead to more intense rivalry. There will be less rivalry when a clear leader (at least 50 per cent larger than the second) exists with a large cost advantage.
- *Rate of market growth.* Slow growth will tend towards greater rivalry.
- *Structure of costs.* High fixed costs encourage price cutting to fill capacity.
- *Degree of differentiation.* Commodity products encourage rivalry, while highly differentiated products, which are hard to copy, are associated with less intense rivalry.
- *Switching costs.* When switching costs are high because the product is specialized, the customer has invested a lot of resources in learning how to use the product or has made tailor-made investments that are worthless with other products and suppliers (high asset specificity), rivalry is reduced.
- *Exit barriers.* When barriers to leaving a market are high due to such factors as lack of opportunities elsewhere, high vertical integration, emotional barriers or the high cost of closing down plant, rivalry will be more intense than when exit barriers are low.

Firms need to be careful not to spoil a situation of competitive stability. They need to balance their own position against the well-being of the industry as a whole. For example, an intense price or promotional war may gain a few percentage points in market share, but lead to an overall fall in long-run industry profitability as competitors respond to these moves. It is sometimes better to protect industry structure than to follow short-term self-interest.

Exhibit 4.1 shows an example of the intensive global competition between two sellers in the alkaline battery market.

Exhibit 4.1	**The battle of the alkaline battery world market**

Two American companies fight on the world market for alkaline batteries: Duracell and Ever Ready (marketer of, among others, Energizer batteries). Despite the fact that Duracell typically sells at a 5–10 per cent premium to Energizer, Duracell is in the lead world-wide, with 42 per cent of the global alkaline battery market compared with Ever Ready's 24 per cent share (see Table 4.2). The famous Duracell rabbit has been widely used in the company's TV advertising.

The world market for alkaline batteries is approximately 7 billion units, but alkaline batteries only account for approximately one-third of the 20 billion unit world-wide market for batteries.

Table 4.2   **Market shares in the alkaline battery market, 1995 (%)**

	USA	World market
Duracell	44	42
Every Ready (Energizer)	37	24
Others	19	34
Total	100	100

Duracell's operating margins are higher (20 per cent) than Ever Ready's (12 per cent). What caused this big gap has mainly to do with the overseas strategies of the two companies. In essence, Duracell chose to go with a global brand, setting up its own European manufacturing centres and using offshore acquisitions only to improve distribution. Ever Ready, on the other hand, initially elected to keep local brands and production lines rather than consolidate all of its European alkaline brands under the Energizer brand name. This did not work because Ever Ready also had to combat declining sales of its zinc carbon batteries while trying to support the myriad of different alkaline brands that competed with the zinc carbon batteries.

Realizing its mistake in relying on local European brands and manufacturing, Ever Ready has been struggling to catch up with Duracell by consolidating all of its alkaline brands under the Energizer name over the past two years.

The most lucrative market of all foreign markets is China, where many consumers are now buying high-powered electronic devices. In China, Duracell has already built an alkaline plant. This will give Duracell a huge cost advantage, since the heavy tariffs ordinarily imposed on imported batteries will be eliminated by producing locally. And the first two years of Duracell's profits in China will be tax exempted there.

Although Duracell's main challenger is Ever Ready, other companies have also tried making headway in the alkaline battery market. Consider Kodak's entrance into the market in 1986. Armed with its powerful brand name, its unique gold-tipped batteries and flashy commercials featuring a jingle sung by Stevie Wonder, Kodak seemed poised to threaten the market leaders. But today Kodak has less than a 1 per cent share of the alkaline battery market. What happened?

Kodak may be known as a quality brand for film and cameras, but that does not necessarily mean that customers will automatically assume that Kodak batteries are just as good as Duracell's. Another US company, Rayovac, has tried to enter the market via its rechargeable alkaline battery, Renewal, but until now without success.

Source: LaMonica (1996).

Suppliers

The cost of raw materials and components can have a major bearing on a firm's profitability. The higher the bargaining power of suppliers, the higher the costs. The bargaining power of suppliers will be higher in the following circumstances:

● Supply is dominated by few companies and they are more concentrated than the industry they sell to.

● Their products are unique or differentiated, or they have built up switching costs.

● They are not obliged to contend with other products for sale to the industry.

● They pose a credible threat of integrating forwards into the industry's business.

● Buyers do not threaten to integrate backwards into supply.

● The market is not an important customer to the supplier group.

A firm can reduce the bargaining power of suppliers by seeking new sources of supply, threatening to integrate backwards into supply, and designing standardized components so that many suppliers are capable of producing them.

Buyers

The bargaining power of buyers is higher in the following circumstances:

● Buyers are concentrated and/or purchase in large volumes.
● Buyers pose a credible threat of integrating backwards to manufacture the industry's product.
● Products they purchase are standard or undifferentiated.
● There are many suppliers (sellers) of the product.
● Buyers earn low profits, which create a great incentive to lower purchasing costs.
● The industry's product is unimportant to the quality of the buyer's products, but price is very important.

Firms in the industry can attempt to lower buyer power by increasing the number of buyers they sell to, threatening to integrate forward into the buyer's industry, and producing highly valued, differentiated products. In supermarket retailing, the brand leader normally achieves the highest profitability partially because being number one means that supermarkets need to stock the brand, thereby reducing buyer power in price negotiations.

Substitutes

The presence of substitute products can reduce industry attractiveness and profitability because they put a constraint on price levels.

If the industry is successful and earning high profits, it is more likely that competitors will enter the market via substitute products in order to obtain a share of the potential profits available. If there are high prices for coffee, for example, tea will become more attractive.

The threat of substitute products depends on the following factors:

● The buyer's willingness to substitute.
● The relative price and performance of substitutes.
● The costs of switching to substitutes.

The threat of substitute products can be lowered by building up switching costs. These costs may be psychological. Examples are the creation of strong, distinctive brand personalities, and maintaining a price differential commensurate with perceived customer values.

New entrants

New entrants can serve to increase the degree of competition in an industry. In turn, the threat of new entrants is largely a function of the extent to which barriers to entry exist in the market. Some key factors affecting these entry barriers include the following:

● Economies of scale.

● Product differentiation and brand identity, which give existing firms customer loyalty.

● Capital requirements in production.

● Switching costs – the cost of switching from one supplier to another.

● Access to distribution channels.

Because high barriers to entry can make even a potentially lucrative market unattractive (or even impossible) to enter for new competitors, the marketing planner should not take a passive approach but should actively pursue ways of raising barriers to new competitors.

High promotional and R & D expenditures and clearly communicated retaliatory actions to entry are some methods of raising barriers. Some managerial actions can unwittingly lower barriers. For example, new product designs that dramatically lower manufacturing costs can make entry by newcomers easier.

The collaborative 'five sources' model

Porter's original model is based on the hypothesis that the competitive advantage of the firm is best developed in a very competitive market with intense rivalry relations.

The five forces framework thus provides an analysis for considering how to squeeze the maximum competitive gain out of the context in which the business is located – or how to minimize the prospect of being squeezed by it – on the five competitive dimensions that it confronts.

Over the last decade, however, an alternative school (e.g. Reve, 1990; Kanter, 1994; Burton, 1995) has emerged which emphasizes the positive role of cooperative (rather than competitive) arrangements between industry participants, and the consequent importance of what Kanter (1994) has termed 'collaborative advantage' as a foundation of superior business performance.

An all-or-nothing choice between a single-minded striving for either competitive or collaborative advantage would, however, be a false one. The real strategic choice problem that all businesses face is where (and how much) to collaborate, and where (and how intensely) to act competitively.

Put another way, the basic questions that firms must deal with in respect of these matters are as follows:

● Choosing the combination of competitive and collaborative strategies that are appropriate in the various dimensions of the industry environment of the firm.

● Blending the two elements together so that they interact in a mutually consistent and reinforcing, and not counterproductive, manner.

● In this way, optimizing the firm's overall position, drawing upon the foundation and utilization of both collaborative and competitive advantage.

This points to the imperative in the contemporary context of complementing the competitive strategy model with a sister framework that focuses on the assessment of collaborative advantage and strategy. Such a complementary analysis, which is called the *five sources framework* (Burton, 1995), is outlined below.

Corresponding to the array of five competitive forces that surround a company – as elaborated in Porter's treatment – there are also five potential sources for the building of collaborative advantage in the industrial environments of the firm. These sources are listed in Table 4.3.

In order to forge an effective and coherent business strategy, a firm must evaluate and formulate its collaborative and competitive policies side by side. It should do this for two purposes:

● To achieve the appropriate balance between collaboration and competition in each dimension of its industry environment (e.g. relations with suppliers, policies towards customers/channels).

● To integrate them in a way that avoids potential clashes and possibly destructive inconsistencies between them.

This is the terrain of composite strategy, which concerns the bringing together of competitive and collaborative endeavours.

Table 4.3   **The five sources model and the corresponding five forces in the Porter model**

Porter's five forces model	The five sources model
Market competitors	Horizontal collaborations with other enterprises operating at the same stage of the production process/producing the same group of closely related products (e.g. contemporary global partnering arrangements among car manufacturers).
Suppliers	Vertical collaborations with suppliers of components or services to the firm – sometimes termed vertical quasi-integration arrangements (e.g. the *keiretsu* formations between suppliers and assemblers that typify the car, electronics and other industries in Japan).
Buyers	Selective partnering arrangements with specific channels or customers (e.g. lead users) that involve collaboration extending beyond standard, purely transactional relationships.
Substitutes	Related diversification alliances with producers of both complements and substitutes. Producers of substitutes are not 'natural allies', but such alliances are not inconceivable (e.g. collaborations between fixed-wire and mobile telephone firms in order to grow their joint network size).
New entrants	Diversification alliances with firms based in previously unrelated sectors, but between which a 'blurring' of industry borders is potentially occurring, or a process (commonly due to new technological possibilities) that opens up the prospect of cross-industry fertilization of technologies/business that did not exist before (e.g. the collaborations in the emerging multimedia field).

Source: From Burton (1995). Reproduced with permission from The Braybrooke Press Ltd.

4.4　Value chain analysis

Until now we have discussed the firm's international competitiveness from a strategic point of view. To get closer to the firm's core competences, we will now look at the market-level box in Porter's five forces model, which treats buyers and sellers (market competitors). Here we will look closer at what creates a competitive advantage among market competitors towards customers at the same competitive level.

The competitive triangle

Success in the marketplace is dependent not only upon identifying and responding to customer needs, but also upon our ability to ensure that our response is judged by customers to be superior to that of competitors (i.e. high perceived value). Several writers (e.g. Day and Wensley, 1988; Porter, 1980) have argued that causes of difference in performance within a market can be analyzed at various levels. The immediate causes of differences in the performance of different firms, these writers argue, can be reduced to two basic factors:

● The *perceived value* of the product/services offered, compared to the perceived sacrifice. The *perceived sacrifice* includes all the 'costs' the buyer faces when making a purchase, primarily the *purchase price*, but also acquisition costs, transportation, installation, handling, repairs and maintenance (Ravald and Grönroos, 1996). In the models presented, the (purchase) price will be used as a representative of the perceived sacrifice.

● The firm-related *costs* incurred in creating this perceived value.

These two basic factors will be further discussed later in this section.

The more value customers perceive in a market offering relative to competing offerings, and the lower the costs in producing the value relative to competing producers, the higher the performance of the business. Hence, firms producing offerings with a higher perceived value and/or lower relative costs than competing firms are said to have a competitive advantage in that market.

This can be illustrated by the 'competitive triangle' (see Figure 4.1). There is no one-dimensional measure of competitive advantage, and perceived value (compared to the price) and relative costs have to be assessed simultaneously. Given this two-dimensional nature of competitive advantage, it will not always be clear which of the two businesses will have a competitive advantage over the other.

Looking at Figure 4.2, firm A will clearly have an advantage over firm B in case I, and clearly have a disadvantage in case IV, while cases II and III do not immediately allow such a conclusion. Firm B may have an advantage in case II, if customers in the market are highly quality conscious and have differentiated needs and low price elasticity, while firm A may have a similar advantage in case II when customers have homogeneous needs and high price elasticity. The opposite will take place in case III.

Even if firm A has a clear competitive advantage over firm B, this may not necessarily result in a higher return on investment for A, if A has a growth and B a hold policy. Thus performance would have to be measured by a combination of return

Figure 4.2 **Perceived value, relative costs and competitive advantage**

		Perceived value (compared to the purchase price)	
		Higher for A	*Higher for B*
Relative costs	*Lower for A*	I	II
	Lower for B	III	IV

on investment and capacity expansion, which can be regarded as postponed return on investment.

While the relationship between perceived value, relative costs and performance is rather intricate, we can retain the basic statement that these two variables are the cornerstone of competitive advantage. Let us take a closer look at these two fundamental sources of competitive advantage.

Perceived value advantage

We have already observed that customers do not buy products, they buy benefits. Put another way, the product is purchased not for itself but for the promise of what it will 'deliver'. These benefits may be intangible: that is, they may relate not to specific product features but rather to such things as image or reputation. Alternatively, the delivered offering may be seen to outperform its rivals in some functional aspect.

Perceived value is the customer's overall evaluation of the product/service offered. So, establishing what value the customer is actually seeking from the firm's offering (value chain) is the starting point for being able to deliver the correct mix of value-providing activities. It may be some combination of physical attributes, service attributes and technical support available in relation to the particular use of the product. This also requires an understanding of the activities which constitute the customer's value chain.

Unless the product or service we offer can be distinguished in some way from its competitors, there is a strong likelihood that the marketplace will view it as a 'commodity', and so the sale will tend to go to the cheapest supplier. Hence the importance of seeking to attach additional values to our offering to mark it out from the competition.

What are the means by which such value differentiation may be gained?

If we start in the value chain perspective (see section 1.4), we can say that each activity in the business system adds perceived value to the product or service. Value, for the customer, is the perceived stream of benefits that accrue from obtaining the product or service. Price is what the customer is willing to pay for that stream of benefits. If the price of a good or service is high, it must provide high value, otherwise it is driven out of the market. If the value of a good or service is low, its price must be low, otherwise it is also driven out of the market. Hence, in a competitive situation, and over a period of time, the price that customers are willing to pay for a good or service is a good proxy measure of its value.

If we look especially at the downstream functions of the value chain, a differential advantage can be created with any aspect of the traditional 4-P marketing mix: product, distribution, promotion and price are all capable of creating added customer perceived value. The key to whether improving an aspect of marketing is worth while is to know if the potential benefit provides value to the customer.

If we extend this model, particular emphasis must be placed upon the following (see Booms and Bitner, 1981; Magrath, 1986; Rafiq and Ahmed, 1995):

- *People*. These include both consumers, who must be educated to participate in the service, and employees (personnel), who must be motivated and well trained in order to ensure that high standards of service are maintained. Customers identify and associate the traits of service personnel with the firms they work for.

- *Physical aspects*. These include the appearance of the delivery location and the elements provided to make the service more tangible. For example, visitors experience Disneyland by what they see, but the hidden, below-ground support machinery is essential for the park's fantasy fulfilment.

- *Process*. The service is dependent on a well-designed method of delivery. Process management assures service availability and consistent quality in the face of simultaneous consumption and production of the service offered. Without sound process management, balancing service demand with service supply is extremely difficult.

Of these three additional Ps, the firm's *personnel* occupy a key position in influencing customer perception of product quality. As a consequence, the *image* of the firm is very much influenced by the personnel. It is therefore important to pay particular attention to the quality of employees and to monitor their performance. Marketing managers need to manage not only the service provider–customer interface, but also the actions of other customers. For example, the number, type and behaviour of other people will influence a meal at a restaurant.

Relative cost advantage

Each activity in the value chain is performed at a cost. Getting the stream of benefits that accrue from the good or service to the customer is thus done at a certain 'delivered cost' which sets a lower limit to the price of the good or service if the business system is to remain profitable. Decreasing the price will thus imply that the delivered cost be first decreased by adjusting the business system. As mentioned earlier, the rules of the game may be described as *providing the highest possible perceived value to the final customer, at the lowest possible delivered cost*.

A firm's cost position depends on the configuration of the activities in its value chain versus that of competitors and its relative location on the cost drivers of each activity. A cost advantage is gained when the cumulative cost of performing all the activities is lower than competitors' costs. This evaluation of the relative cost position requires an identification of each important competitor's value chain. In practice, this step is extremely difficult because the firm does not have direct information on the costs of competitors' value activities. However, some costs can be estimated from public data or interviews with suppliers and distributors.

Creating a relative cost advantage requires an understanding of the factors that affect costs. It is often said that 'big is beautiful'. This is partly due to economies of scale, which enable fixed costs to be spread over a greater output, but more particularly it is due to the impact of the *experience curve*.

The experience curve is a phenomenon that has its roots in the earlier notion of the learning curve. The effects of learning on costs were seen in the manufacture of fighter planes for the Second World War. The time taken to produce each plane gradually fell as learning took place. The combined effect of economies of scale and learning on cumulative output has been termed the experience curve. The Boston Consulting Group estimated that costs reduced on average by approximately 15–20 per cent each time cumulative output doubled.

Subsequent work by Bruce Henderson, founder of the Boston Consulting Group, extended this concept by demonstrating that all costs, not just production costs, would decline at a given rate as volume increased. In fact, to be precise, the relationship that the experience curve describes is between real unit costs and cumulative volume.

This suggests that firms with greater market share will have a cost advantage through the experience curve effect, assuming that all companies are operating on the same curve. However, a move towards a new manufacturing technology can lower the experience curve for adopting companies, allowing them to leap-frog more traditional firms and thereby gain a cost advantage even though cumulative output may be lower.

The general form of the experience curve and the above-mentioned leap-frogging to another curve are shown in Figure 4.3.

Leap-frogging the experience curve by investing in new technology is a special

Figure 4.3   **Leap-frogging the experience curve**

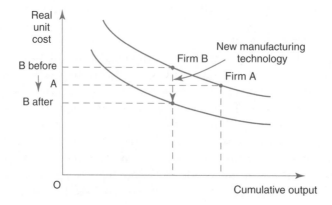

opportunity for SMEs and newcomers to a market, since they will (as a starting point) have only a small market share and thereby a small cumulative output.

The implications of the experience curve for the pricing strategy will be discussed further in Chapter 15. According to Porter (1980), there are other cost drivers that determine the costs in value chains:

● *Capacity utilization*. Underutilization incurs costs.

● *Linkages*. Costs of activities are affected by how other activities are performed. For example, improving quality assurance can reduce after-sales service costs.

● *Interrelationships*. For example, different SBUs' sharing of R & D, purchasing and marketing will lower costs.

● *Integration*. For example, deintegration (outsourcing) of activities to subsuppliers can lower costs and raise flexibility.

● *Timing*. For example, first movers in a market can gain cost advantage. It is cheaper to establish a brand name in the minds of the customers if there are no competitors.

● *Policy decisions*. Product width, level of service and channel decisions are examples of policy decisions that affect costs.

● *Location*. Locating near suppliers reduces in-bound distribution costs. Locating near customers can lower out-bound distribution costs. Some producers locate their production activities in eastern Europe or the Far East to take advantage of low wage costs.

● *Institutional factors*. Government regulations, tariffs, local content rules, etc. will affect costs.

The basic sources of competitive advantage

The perceived value created and the costs incurred will depend on the firm's *resources* and its *competences* (see Figure 4.4).

Resources

Resources are the basic units of analysis. They include all inputs into the business processes – that is, financial, technological, human and organizational resources. Although resources provide the basis for competence building, on their own they are barely productive.

Resources are necessary in order to participate in the market. The competitors in a market will thus not usually be very different with regard to these skills and resources, and the latter will not explain differences in created perceived value, relative costs and the resulting performance. They are failure preventers, but not success producers. They may, however, act as barriers to entry for potential new competitors, and hence raise the average level of performance in the market.

Competences

Competences – being components of a higher level – result from a combination of the various resources. Their formation and quality depend on two factors. The first factor is the specific capabilities of the firm in integrating resources. These

Figure 4.4   **The roots of performance and competitive advantage**

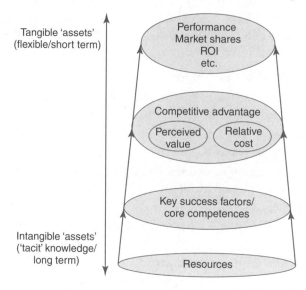

(Source: Adapted from Jüttner and Wehrli, 1994)

capabilities are developed and improved in a collective learning process. On the other hand, the basis for the quality of a competence is the resource assortment. This forms a potential for competences, which should be exploited to the maximum extent.

A firm can have a lot of competences but only a few of them are core competences: that is, a value chain activity in which the firm is regarded as a better performer than any of its competitors (see Figure 4.5).

In Figure 4.5 a core competence is represented by a strategic resource (asset) which competitors cannot easily imitate and which has the potential to earn long-term profit. The objective of the firm will be to place products and services at the top-right corner. The top-left corner also represents profit possibilities, but the competitive advantage is easier to imitate, so the high profit will only be short term. The bottom-left corner represents the position of the price-sensitive commodity supplier. Here the profits are likely to be low because the product is primarily differentiated by place (distribution) and especially price.

Competitive benchmarking

The ultimate test of the efficiency of any marketing strategy has to be in terms of profit. Those companies that strive for market share, but measure market share in terms of volume sales, may be deluding themselves to the extent that volume is bought at the expense of profit.

Because market share is an 'after the event' measure, we need to utilize continuing indicators of competitive performance. This will highlight areas where improvements in the marketing mix can be made.

Figure 4.5   **Illustration of the core competence**

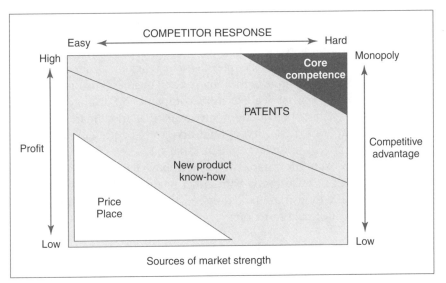

(Source: Tampoe, 1994, p. 413. Reprinted with permission from Elsevier Science Ltd, The Boulevard, Langford Lane, Kidlington, OX5 1GB, UK)

In recent years a number of companies have developed a technique for assessing relative marketplace performance, which has come to be known as *competitive benchmarking*. Originally, the idea of competitive benchmarking was literally to take apart a competitor's product, component by component, and to compare its performance in a value engineering sense with your own product. This approach has often been attributed to the Japanese, but many western companies have also found the value of such detailed comparisons.

The concept of competitive benchmarking is similar to what Porter (1996) calls operational effectiveness (OE), meaning performing similar activities better than competitors perform them. However, Porter (1996) also thinks that OE is a necessary but not a sufficient condition for outperforming rivals. Firms also have to consider strategic (or market) positioning, meaning the performance of *different* activities from rivals or performing similar activities in different ways. Only a few firms have competed successfully on the basis of OE over a long period. The main reason is the rapid diffusion of best practices. Competitors can rapidly imitate management techniques and new technologies with support from consultants.

However, the idea of benchmarking is capable of extension beyond this simple comparison of technology and cost effectiveness. Because the battle in the marketplace is for 'share of mind', it is customers' perceptions that we must measure.

The measures that can be used in this type of benchmarking programme include delivery reliability, ease of ordering, after-sales service, the quality of sales representation and the accuracy of invoices and other documentation. These measures are not chosen at random, but are selected because of their importance to the customer. Market research, often based on in-depth interviews, would typically be employed to identify what these 'key success factors' are. The elements that customers identify as being the most important (see Table 4.4) then form the basis for the benchmark questionnaire. This questionnaire is administered to a sample of customers on a regular basis: for example, German Telecom carries out a daily telephone survey of a random sample of its domestic and business customers to measure customers' perceptions of service. For most companies an annual survey might suffice; in other cases, perhaps a quarterly survey, particularly if market conditions are dynamic. The output of these surveys might typically be presented in the form of a competitive profile, as in the example in Table 4.4.

Most of the criteria mentioned above relate to downstream functions in the value chain. Concurrently with closer relations between buyers and suppliers, especially in the industrial market, there will be more focus on the supplier's competences in the upstream functions.

Table 4.4　　Competitive benchmarking (examples with only few criteria)

Examples of value chain functions (mainly downstream functions)	Customer					Own firm (Firm A)					Key competitor (Firm B)				
	Importance to customer (*key success factors*)					How do customers rate performance of our firm?					How do customers rate performance of key competitor?				
	High importance		Low importance			Good				Bad	Good				Bad
	5	4	3	2	1	5	4	3	2	1	5	4	3	2	1
Uses new technology															
High technical quality and competence															
Uses proved technology															
Easy to buy from															
Understands what customers want															
Low price															
Delivery on schedule															
Accessible for enquiries															
Takes full responsibility															
Flexible and quick															
Known contact person															
Provides customer training															
Takes account of future requirements															
Courteous and helpful															
Specified invoices															
Gives guarantees															
ISO 9000 certified															
Right first time															
Can give references															
Environment conscious															

Development of a dynamic benchmarking model

On the basis of the value chain's functions, we will suggest a model for the development of a firm's competitiveness in a defined market. The model will be based on a specific market as the market demands are assumed to differ from market to market, and from country to country.

Before presenting the basic model for development of international competitiveness I will first define two key terms:

● *Critical success factors*. Those value chain functions where the customer demands/expects the supplier (firm X) to have a strong competence.

● *Core competences*. Those value chain functions where firm X has a strong competitive position.

The strategy process

The model for the strategy process is shown in Figure 4.6.

Stage 1: Analysis of situation (identification of competence gaps)

We will not go into details here about the problems there have been in measuring the value chain functions. The measurements cannot be objective in the traditional way of thinking, but must rely on internal assessments from firm representatives (interviews with relevant managers) supplemented by external experts ('key informants') who are able to judge the market's (customers') demand now and in the future.

The competence profile for firm A in Figure 4.1 (top-right diagram) is an example of how a firm is not in accordance with the market (= customer) demand. The company has its core competences in parts of the value chain's functions where customers place little importance (market knowledge in Figure 4.1).

Figure 4.6   Model for development of core competences

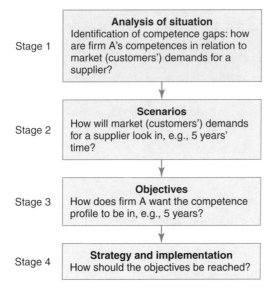

If there is a generally good match between the critical success factors and firm A's initial position, it is important to concentrate resources and improve this core competence to create sustainable competitive advantages.

If, on the other hand, there is a large gap between customers' demands and the firm's initial position in critical success factors in Figure 4.1 (as with the personal selling functions), it may give rise to the following alternatives:

● Improve the position of the critical success factor(s).
● Find business areas where firm A's competence profile better suits the market demand and expectations.

As a new business area involves risk, it is often important to identify an eventual gap in a critical success factor as early as possible. In other words, an 'early warning' system must be established that continuously monitors the critical competitive factors so that it is possible to start initiatives that limit an eventual gap as early as possible.

In Figure 4.1 the competence profile of firm B is also shown.

Stages 2 and 3: Scenarios and objectives

To be able to estimate future market demand, different scenarios are made of the possible future development. These trends are first described generally, then the effect of the market's future demand/expectations on a supplier's value chain function is concretized.

By this procedure the described 'gap' between market expectations and firm A's initial position becomes more clear. At the same time, the biggest gap for firm A may have moved from personal sales to, for example, product development. From knowledge of the market leader's strategy it is possible to complete scenarios of the market leader's future competence profile.

These scenarios may be the foundation for a discussion of objectives and of which competence profile the company wants in, say, five years' time. Objectives must be set realistically and with due consideration of the organization's resources (the scenarios are not shown in Figure 4.1).

Stage 4: Strategy and implementation

Depending on which of firm A's value chain functions are to be developed, a strategy is prepared. This results in implementation plans which include the adjustment of the organization's current competence level.

4.5 Summary

The main issue of this chapter is how the firm creates and develops competitive advantages in the international marketplace. A three-stage model allows us to understand the development of a firm's international competitiveness in a broader perspective:

1. Analysis of national competitiveness (the Porter diamond).

2. Competition analysis (Porter's five forces).
3. Value chain analysis:
   (a) competitive triangle;
   (b) benchmarking.

Analysis of national competitiveness

The analysis starts at the macro level, where the Porter diamond indicates that the characteristics of the home nation play a central role in the firm's international success.

Competition analysis

The next stage is to move to the competitive arena where the firm is the unit of analysis. Porter's five forces model suggests that competition in an industry is rooted in its underlying economic structure and goes beyond the behaviour of current competitors. The state of competition depends upon five basic competitive forces, which determine the profit potential in an industry.

Value chain analysis

Here we look at what creates a competitive advantage at the same competitive level (among industry competitors). According to the *competitive triangle*, it can be concluded that firms have a competitive advantage in a market if they offer products with the following:

● A higher perceived value to the customers.
● Lower relative costs than competing firms.

A firm can find out its competitive advantages or core competences by using *competitive benchmarking*, which is a technique where customers measure marketplace performance of the firm compared to a 'first-class' competitor. The measures in the value chain that can be used include delivery reliability, ease of ordering, after-sales service and quality of sales representation. These value chain activities are chosen on the basis of their importance to the customer. As customers' perceptions change over time, it may be relevant to try and estimate customers' future demands on a supplier of particular products.

Case study   Microsoft X-box

Will Microsoft's X-box beat Sega, Nintendo and Sony's Playstation?

In the video game market, leadership has changed with each new generation of consoles, which comes along every five years or so.

In a challenge that could have come from a 'beat-'em-up' computer game, Microsoft – the world's biggest software company – has announced plans to take on the mighty trio of Sony, Nintendo and Sega by launching its own games console. But the Seattle company's attempts to muscle into a market that is worth £10bn worldwide will meet stiff opposition from its rivals, which already have new, faster machines either released or planned. Microsoft's product, dubbed the 'X-box', will not be launched before autumn 2001.

The X-box will be based on a 600MHz microprocessor that is expected to be supplied by Advanced Micro Devices. It will also incorporate a custom-designed high-performance graphics chip from Nvidea, a Silicon Valley chip designer. The console will include a DVD player, which can also be used to watch movies, and a high-capacity hard-disc drive which could be used to save game sessions as well as to bring full speech to video games. A sports game, for example, might include running commentary.

Like the Playstation 2, the X-box will link to the Internet to enable multi player games and downloadable games. However, Microsoft is gearing the X-box to 'broadband' high-speed connections; unlike today's video game machines, the X-box will enable Internet chat among players, with voice communications rather than typed messages.

Microsoft will subcontract production of the X-box to an unnamed third party, but will market and sell the games console under its own name. Like other video games companies, Microsoft will 'certify' games software and take a royalty charge on each game sold. Microsoft has yet to set a price for the X-box, but analysts suggest the price will be around $300.

'We welcome competition,' said Shelly Field at Nintendo, which intends to launch its next-generation 'Dolphin' machine early next year. 'But you don't really make your profit on the hardware, it's in the games software. And Microsoft does not have a big games division.'

After sinking into the doldrums of the mid-1990s, the games console market has exploded in the past few years, spurred on by the Sony Playstation, launched in 1995. An estimated five million Playstations have been sold in the UK alone. Sony will thus be Microsoft's biggest rival, having already sold nearly a million units of its new PlayStation2 model (whose high-speed 128-bit processor is more powerful than most PCs) in the six days since its launch in Japan.

In Japan Sony had to admit it had received 'thousands' of service calls from new customers. Some were having problems with the inbuilt DVD player failing to play discs, while others had problems with a memory chip. But Sony added that 26 per cent of the calls were from people who were simply befuddled by their new gadget.

Predictions for the future of gaming

In the US and Western Europe, the online gaming market is set to be worth $4.9bn, with 31m gamers in Europe by 2004.

Datamonitor claims from its research that there is substantial consumer demand for online gaming and surf and play solutions. This will be met by two principal growth factors – games consoles and online gaming.

The introduction of better bandwidth – broadband – will increase popularity and consumer awareness, with the console gradually phasing out the PC as the main gaming device.

Questions

1. What could be the motives for Microsoft to enter this market?

2. What are the chances that Microsoft will beat the other games console suppliers?

(Sources: *Financial Times* (2000) 'Companies & Markets: Microsoft to take on video game leaders', 10 March; *New Media Age* (2000) 'Let the games begin', 8 March)

Questions for discussion

1. How can analysis of national competitiveness explain the competitive advantage of the single firm?

2. Identify the major dimensions used to analyze a competitor's strengths and weaknesses profile. Do local, regional and global competitors need to be analyzed separately?

3. How can a country with high labour costs improve its national competitiveness?

4. As the global marketing manager for Coca-Cola, how would you monitor reactions around the world of a major competitor such as Pepsi?

Internet exercise

NTT Mobile Communications Network (Japan)

Please go to:

http://www.lookjapan.com/Jan00/Jan00_costrats1.html

http://www.lookjapan.com/oct99/oct99_cover_story.html

http://www.motorola.com/

NTT Mobile Communications Network is the major player in the fast-growing Japanese mobile telephone market.

Questions

1. Characterize the Japanese mobile telephone market.

2. Should NTT Mobile Communications Network go international (outside Japan)?

3. Would a Western company like Motorola be able to reach a position in Japan where they could threaten NTT Mobile Communications Network?

For further exercises and cases, see this book's website at *www.booksites.net/hollensen*

References

Booms, B.H. and Bitner, M.J. (1981) 'Marketing strategies and organization structures for service firms', in Donnelly, J.H. and George, W.R. (eds), *Marketing of Services*, American Marketing Association, Chicago, IL.

Burton, J. (1995) 'Composite strategy: the combination of collaboration and competition', *Journal of General Management*, vol. 21, no. 1, pp. 1–23.

Day, G.S. and Wensley, R. (1988) 'Assessing advantage: a framework for diagnosing competitive superiority', *Journal of Marketing*, vol. 52, no. 2, pp. 1–20.

Jüttner, U. and Wehrli, H.P. (1994) 'Competitive advantage: merging marketing and the competence-based perspective', *Journal of Business and Industrial Marketing*, vol. 9, no. 4, pp. 42–53.

Kanter, R.M. (1994) 'Collaborative advantage: the art of alliances', *Harvard Business Review*, July–August, pp. 96–108.

Kotler, P. (1997) *Marketing Management: Analysis, planning, implementation, and control* (9th edn), Prentice Hall, Englewood Cliffs, NJ.

LaMonica, Paul R. (1996) 'Battling batteries – why Duracell and Ever Ready are neck and neck in market share, but not in brand value', *Financial World*, 30 January.

Levitt, T. (1960) 'Marketing myopia', *Harvard Business Review*, July–August, pp. 45–56.

Magrath, A.J. (1986) 'When marketing service's 4 Ps are not enough', *Business Horizons*, May–June, pp. 44–50.

Porter, M.E. (1980) *Competitive Strategy*, The Free Press, New York.

Porter, M.E. (1990) *The Competitive Advantage of Nations*, The Free Press, New York.

Porter, M.E. (1996) 'What is strategy?', *Harvard Business Review*, November–December, pp. 61–78.

Rafiq, M. and Ahmed, P.K. (1995) 'Using the 7Ps as a generic marketing mix', *Marketing Intelligence and Planning*, vol. 13, no. 9, pp. 4–15.

Ravald, A. and Grönroos, C. (1996) 'The value concept and relationship marketing', *European Journal of Marketing*, vol. 30, no. 2, pp. 19–30.

Reve, T. (1990) 'The firm as a nexus of internal and external contracts', in Aoki, M., Gustafsson, M. and Williamson, O.E. (eds), *The Firm as a Nexus of Treaties*, Sage, London.

Tampoe, M. (1994) 'Exploiting the core competences of your organization', *Long Range Planning*, vol. 27, no. 4, pp. 66–77.

Case **I.1** The Fantastic Corporation

From start-up to global player in eighteen months

At the beginning of January 1996, two Danish nationals living in Zug, Switzerland, met to discuss an idea. Their idea was to create the next generation of computer on-line technology.

Their idea had been generated through personal experience. They were both eager users of the Internet, but had also seen its limitations. People were increasingly using it for multimedia applications, but the result was just network congestion, failed dial-ups and what was termed the 'World Wide Wait'.

The names of the two Danes were Lars Tvede and Frank Ewald. Their concept was to transmit multimedia content to PCs via television networks instead of telephone lines. Television networks operated via satellite and cable, which could transmit data more than 1,000 times faster than a telephone line.

They agreed to go ahead and found the company, which they named The Fantastic Corporation. It was a fairly ambitious name for a company operated by two people from their respective home offices. The mission statement of the company is simple: 'The internet is slow; we are going to speed it up.' (Peter Ohnemus, President & CEO of the The Fantastic Corporation). See also Plate 2.

The speed you need

Lars Tvede and Frank Ewald were sure that their idea had great market potential. They were also sure that they could find the people needed to create the technology. But they had a basic problem, which is typical of small high-tech start-ups: the company would have to grow to a critical mass before much larger companies woke up and created competition. The challenge was to get big very fast, or die. They would probably have to be employing 50 people within a year and more than 100 within two years.

The solution was to find a senior investor who could provide sufficient additional financing and at the same time open more doors for the company.

They divided the task between them. Lars Tvede was a former investment banker and as such was used to presenting concepts and plans in writing. Frank Ewald was a former sales director and knew how to approach people and sell them an idea. So they agreed that Lars should write the business plans and budgets, and Frank should arrange the presentations.

Within a week they had the written business plan, and by the end of January they had already made a number of presentations to investors. In early February they received a confirmation of interest from Giorgio Ronchi, who was former president and chief executive officer of Memorex/Telex. He would invest enough to take the company through the first eighteen months.

Armed with this commitment, they started recruiting software developers and signing outsourcing agreements with external software houses. They also produced an interactive demo of how the final product would appear to the end user. This was done with software that can create the impression of a fully functional multimedia experience, even when there is not yet a real functionality behind it.

During the spring and summer they met one of their friends, Peter Ohnemus, at several social gatherings. Each time they dragged him aside and told him the latest news about their expansion. Peter, who had build up Sybase in most of Europe, was known to be an eminent motivator and he had an impressive social network. His motto was: 'Software business is people business.' During the summer, Frank and Lars decided to ask him if he would head the company, so that Frank could focus fully on sales and Lars on business development – the two areas they did best and liked most. Peter agreed and joined the company as president and chief executive in October.

The first, still somewhat unstable, version of The Fantastic Corporation's software was ready for presentation at an exhibition in Cannes, where the product was presented at a press conference.

Several journalists described it as the most interesting product at the exhibition that year.

Key to success

How did the company grow from two people's idea to a global player within eighteen months? Lars Tvede comments:

> There were a number of factors. The first was of course that we had a very good idea in the first place, and there were not a lot of other people talking about the same idea.
>
> The second is about sequence. We didn't develop anything but concepts until we had ensured the financing. If you start developing the product and then look for external financing before it is finished, then the potential investors will take you apart, because everything you have done will at that stage look messy and unfinished. I think it is much easier to defend an idea.
>
> A third factor was that we built a great team. You need a great team to build a great company. Frank and I are each good at doing some things, but we swallowed our pride and let in people that could take some of the roles – even eventually to take over the top management position. There is always somebody who is better at some of the things you do, and you should accept that.

Demonstration product

Another element that proved to be key for us was that we built a mock-up of our final product as one of the first things after we had raised the first capital. After that, we went out to a lot of TV companies and said, 'Would you like to send Internet services via your network without having to invest massively?' Most said yes. Then we asked what they would expect from such a service, and they listed some features. And then we said: 'Should we create a demonstration for you that shows how it may look?' They couldn't say no to that either, so we went back, modified our mock-up demo a bit so that it had their branding and so on, and presented it to them. That presentation made it to many board meetings, and from then on there were many companies waiting for our launch of the real software.

Simplicity

A key to our success was also the partnership philosophy. What we proposed to a TV network was a com-pletely new technology for them, which meant that if we tried to explain how complicated the technology really was, then we would just get bogged down in ever finer technical discussions. So instead we had to reduce it to a commercial decision at a high level. We should talk with people who didn't bother about the details of the product at all, and we should make sure that they didn't have to. It had to be really simple, which meant a turn-key solution. So we asked our-selves: 'Which parts should we not produce our-selves?' We concluded that we would not make hardware and electronic contents. So we wrote into our presentation material that we, as a matter of policy, would not be in those businesses but were looking for partners in these areas. This made part-ners comfortable with working with us, and we were soon able to close a number of partnership agreements that made our total offering a turn-key solution.

Setting up mirrors

That leads me to what was perhaps the most impor-tant success factor of all. I think that business-to-business marketing for a start-up company is largely about putting up mirrors, so to speak. You can be a small company with the greatest idea in the world. You present to potential customers. They cannot think of any important arguments against what you say. But they turn you down anyway because they are just basically feeling uncomfortable. Why? They have no way of knowing whether there is a snag hidden somewhere and they haven't got the time to investigate thoroughly. So what you need to do is find a way to make somebody who is generally trusted show that they trust you. Everybody else will now see you through this trusted company, which is where the mirror comes in. This starts a positive feedback loop, where you get trust from more and more partners. The best way to create this approval effect is to look for partnerships with credible companies that sell com-plementary products, gain their trust, make it visible, and then live fully up to it.

During the spring of 1997 the company made trial installation agreements with TV networks in Europe, Asia/Pacific, USA and Africa.

In April 1997 The Fantastic Corporation pre-sented its product at a large convention in Las

Vegas. A few weeks later it was able to announce in a press release that it had entered into a commercial agreement with ESM (European Satellite Multimedia Services), which is a joint venture between Intel (the world's largest computer chip manufacturer), Astra (the world's largest direct broadcasting satellite network), Deutsche Telekom (the world's largest cable television network), Hughes Network Services (one of the world's largest satellite companies) and Luxembourg Telecom.

The Fantastic Corporation will assist in delivering multimedia content directly to PCs in businesses and households via broadband satellite at increased speed compared to standard telephone lines. The system requires a single, fixed satellite dish of a diameter of 50 cm or larger pointed at the Astra satellite system and a high-performance (pentium) PC equipped with a DVB (Digital Video Broadcasting)-compliant PC card.

Questions

1. What are the success criteria in the multimedia business?

2. Discuss the contents of the value chain for The Fantastic Corporation.

3. Which international market possibilities do you see from the agreement with ESM?

Case 1.2 Bridgestone Tyres

European marketing strategy

It is a lovely spring morning in central Tokyo in 1996. Although the city is just awakening with all its noise and stress, it does not bother the president of Bridgestone Corporation, Yoichiro Kaizaki, as he is on his way to work. The Annual Report 1995 for Bridgestone has just been publicized, and shows an increase in net earnings of nearly 70 per cent (compared to 1994), a record level of ¥54 billion (US$526 million).

The prospects look good. On his way into his office, Yoichiro Kaizaki asks his assistant to give him a copy of Bridgestone's 1995 market shares in the most important tyre markets in the world. Yoichiro is having a meeting with the board of directors the next day. Here they will discuss Bridgestone's strategies in Europe, Asia and North America.

The market shares are shown in Table 1. Together with Goodyear and Michelin, Bridgestone is among the world's largest manufacturers of tyres. But it has a comparatively low market share and low brand awareness in Europe. The question for Yoichiro Kaizaki is: how can Bridgestone increase its market share for tyres in Europe? The following is a concentrated report on the market conditions for tyres in Europe.

The European tyre market

The European market for car tyres (including commercial vehicles) fell slightly from 1992 to 1994, but in the past two years the market has risen again, primarily due to increasing car sales. Competition

among tyre producers is very heavy and tyre prices in real terms have fallen over the last few years.

In 1994 the total European market for tyres was 229.8 million tyres, which corresponds to a value of some DKK70 billion (in ex works prices). A breakdown of the total market is shown in Table 2. This table shows sales of new tyres for entirely new cars (= new sales) or as replacement of worn-down tyres (= replacement sales). Table 3 shows the total European tyre market broken down into countries, together with the market shares of the most important producers in the individual markets. On the basis of Table 3 the Boston Consulting Group (BCG) charts of the individual producers have been prepared (Figure 1). In this connection, it should be noted that the areas of the circles show total sales in the respective countries and not the sales of the individual companies in the markets in question, which is normally the case in BCG charts.

Retreaded tyres

So far the markets have been described on the assumption that only production and sales of new tyres were involved. For many years, consumers have considered the retreaded tyre one of low price and low quality. In consequence, European consumers have been rather reluctant to buy retreaded tyres.

Over the past few years, however, sales of retreaded tyres have grown, primarily for two reasons:

● Waste problems in connection with the accumulation of used tyres have made retreaded tyres an environmentally correct recycling solution.

Table 1	Bridgestone's market share for tyres in the most important markets, 1995
Market area	**Bridgestone market share (%)**
Asia	29
Europe	8
USA	22
World total	19

Table 2	The European tyre market, 1994		
Million units	**Car tyres**	**Truck tyres**	**Total**
New sales	65.4	9.3	74.7
Replacement sales	131.8	23.3	155.1
Total	197.2	32.6	229.8

Table 3   The European market for tyres (cars and trucks)

	France	Germany	Italy	Spain	UK	Other markets	Total
Million units							
New sales	13.2	22.7	7.0	9.1	8.7	14.0	74.7
Replacement sales	24.2	36.7	15.8	8.9	22.0	47.5	155.1
Total	37.4	59.4	22.8	18.0	30.7	61.5	229.8
Producers' market shares (%)							
Michelin	55	24	31	44	30	—	35.1
Continental	4	26	8	7	13	—	14.4
Goodyear	7	16	11	4	16	—	11.3
Pirelli	5	6	23	13	11	—	10.4
SP (Dunlop)	10	10	4	4	14	—	8.9
Bridgestone/ Firestone	7	5	8	18	7	—	7.2
Others	12	13	15	10	9	—	12.7
Total	100	100	100	100	100	—	100.0

Note: 'Other markets' include eastern Europe and Scandinavia, for which market shares are not available.

Figure 1   BCG charts for leading tyre producers

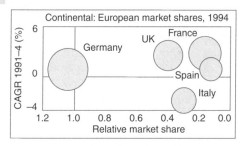

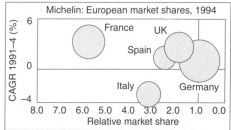

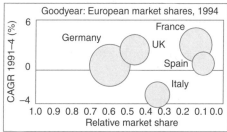

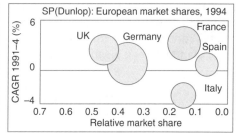

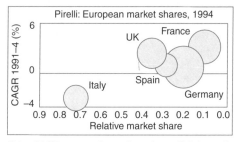

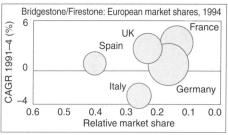

Notes: CAGR: compound annual growth rate. Relative market share: the market share of the individual producer in relation to the largest producer on the market.
(Source: MarketLine)

<table>
<tr><td>Table 4</td><td colspan="6">Sales of retreaded tyres in main European markets, 1994 (million units)</td></tr>
</table>

	France	Germany	Italy	Spain	UK
Cars	2.30	3.50	2.70	0.03	4.80
Trucks	0.85	1.40	0.95	0.44	0.95
Total	3.15	4.90	3.65	0.47	5.75

● The use of retreaded tyres reduces consumption of natural rubber, natural minerals, metal wire, oil and other chemicals that are normally used in the production of new tyres.

In 1994 sales of retreaded tyres were distributed as shown in Table 4. Currently, the production of retreaded tyres accounts for 10–15 per cent of the replacement market, but the European Commission encourages and recommends the increased use of retreaded tyres (rising to approximately 30 per cent of total sales).

One threat against a development like this is, however, that the price of new imported tyres from the Far East is sometimes lower than that of retreaded tyres.

Characterization of the leading producers (mentioned in Table 3)

In many countries the producers use several different brands to appeal to a larger clientele who have different preferences for different brands of tyres. A list of brand names is given in Table 5.

Europe's leading tyre suppliers may be briefly characterized as follows.

Michelin

Michelin is the world's largest tyre producer. Since 1989 it has had a share of 18–19 per cent of the world tyre market, closely followed by Bridgestone/Firestone (18 per cent) and Goodyear (17 per cent). In Europe, Michelin is a clear market leader with a market share of 32 per cent, well ahead of Continental and Goodyear.

Michelin produces 3,500 different types of tyre, and its brand names include Michelin, Kléber, Goodrich, Laurent and Wolber. These are produced at 67 factories in 13 countries. The total number of employees in the Michelin group is over 100,000.

Michelin's largest market is North America, which takes about 45 per cent of the tyre production, followed by Europe with 40 per cent and Asia with 5 per cent. The rest is sold in other parts of the world.

In 1993 Michelin registered a loss of nearly FRF4 billion. This led to widespread rationalization: for example, the staff were reduced by 10,000. As early as 1994 the Michelin group was back in the black. A turnover of some FRF67 billion resulted in a profit of FRF1.4 billion. This positive trend continued in 1995 and 1996.

Bridgestone/Firestone

Bridgestone was founded by Shojiro Ishibashi in 1931. The English translation of his surname Ishibashi is 'stone bridge'. Firestone was acquired

<table>
<tr><td>Table 5</td><td colspan="2">Producers' nationality and different brand names</td></tr>
</table>

Producer	Nationality (ownership)	Brands
Michelin	France	Michelin, Kléber, Tyremaster
Continental	Germany	Continental, Uniroyal, Semperit, Barum, Viking, Gislaved, Mabor, Sava
Bridgestone/Firestone	Japan	Bridgestone, Firestone, Dayton, Europa, First Stop
Pirelli	Italy	Pirelli, Curier
Goodyear	USA	Goodyear, Kelly, Fulda
Dunlop/SP	Japan	Dunlop, Pneumant, India
Others		Stomil, Tigar, Komho, Lassa, Marshal, Toyo

by the Japanese-owned Bridgestone Corporation in 1988. Traditionally, Bridgestone has targeted the upper 'price–quality' segment, while Firestone rather appeals to the 'mid-range' segment. Firestone has in particular contributed to strengthening the group's sales to car producers (new sales) in Europe (primarily Ford, Opel/Vauxhall, VW/Audi and Fiat).

There are 92,000 employees of the Bridgestone Corporation around the world. Of the total turnover around 25 per cent comes from non-tyre products, including conveyor belts, rubber crawlers, construction materials and vibration isolation parts (for vehicles). In Europe, Brussels-based Bridgestone/Firestone Europe SA oversees local production and R & D at the European facilities. There are five European tyre plants: one in France, one in Italy and three in Spain. Bridgestone's European sales subsidiaries are located in Austria, Benelux, Denmark, Finland, France, Germany, Italy, Portugal, Spain, Sweden, Switzerland and the UK.

However, brand awareness is still lower for Bridgestone than its competitors, as shown in Table 6. As a consequence, Bridgestone began sponsoring Bridgestone tyres to Formula One teams in 1996.

Continental

Continental produces tyres for all forms of vehicles: cars, trucks, heavy vehicles, agricultural machinery, bicycles, motor cycles, etc. Continental bought (from Michelin) the rights to use the Uniroyal brand all over Europe. In return, Michelin undertook to buy low-price tyres from Continental's overseas 'low-cost' production sites. Continental is very dependent on the German market, which accounts for 33 per cent of its world-wide sales.

Goodyear

Goodyear has 86 factories in 26 different countries. The world-wide staff total more than 100,000, of which 20,000 are employed in Europe. Some 55 per cent of the group's sales relate to the US market, where Goodyear is the market leader.

Dunlop/SRI

Japan's Sumitomo Rubber Industries (SRI) acquired the rights to produce and market the Dunlop brand in western Europe in 1984. Today the tyre group is the world's fifth largest tyre producer.

Pirelli

The Italian Pirelli group has two main activities: tyres and cables. The group employs 3,800 employees world-wide. Pirelli has the best market position in Italy, where it is second to Michelin. In 1992 Pirelli tried in vain to acquire its German competitor, Continental.

The distribution of tyres in Europe

The majority of replacement sales (replacement of tyres) take place through specialized tyre distributors:

● Independent chains.

Table 6		Brand awareness in the major European markets: spontaneous (unaided) awareness (%)					

Brand	UK	Germany	France	Italy	Spain	Total
Michelin	73	78	98	92	90	85
Pirelli	51	45	40	91	66	57
Goodyear	52	48	56	70	41	54
Dunlop	60	53	48	25	25	44
Firestone	**32**	**25**	**40**	**37**	**69**	**38**
Continental	12	65	15	26	20	31
Bridgestone	**10**	**26**	**7**	**17**	**9**	**15**
Population (million)	58	81	58	57	39	223

Source: Market survey by Brigestone/Firestone Europe.

- Producer-owned chains (e.g. in Germany, Continental owns the Vergös chain and Michelin owns the Euromaster chain).
- Franchise-based chains.

In addition, service stations have a certain share of replacement sales. This share is highest in newly developed east European markets, while it is decreasing in western Europe.

As a consultant for president Yoichiro Kaizaki, you are required to answer the following questions.

Questions

1. Make an assessment of the competitive strategies that Michelin, Continental and Goodyear, respectively, may pursue to strengthen their European market positions.

2. Make an assessment of the alternative competitive strategies that Bridgestone can pursue to strengthen its European market position.

3. Give a well-reasoned proposal for criteria to be used by Bridgestone when choosing a market (country) that requires a larger marketing effort.

4. Give a well-reasoned proposal for Bridgestone's distribution and communication strategies in a market chosen by you.

Sources: EIU, 'The European market for car and truck tyres', *Europe's Automotive Components Business*, 2nd quarter, 1995, pp. 14–26; MarketLine, 'German vehicle tyres', 1996, pp. 193–327; EIU, 'Strategic profile of Michelin', *Europe's Automotive Components Business*, 3rd quarter, 1995, pp. 45–51; material from Bridgestone/Firestone Europe SA.

Developing international competitiveness for hearing aids

Oticon is one of the world's largest manufacturers of hearing aids. Still, Oticon's aim is broader than just manufacturing and selling hearing aids. It wishes to supply a combination of hardware, software and knowledge which will result not only in hearing aids being sold, but in a higher quality of life for users.

Oticon was founded in 1904 as a commercial business. The company's own production of hearing aids was established in Denmark in 1944. From the 1950s to the 1970s a network of sales companies was established in foreign countries, and Oticon was the leading firm in a transition from pocket hearing aids to behind-the-ear hearing aids. In the late 1970s Oticon was the largest company in this trade with a world-wide market share of above 15 per cent.

In the 1980s Oticon underestimated the significance of custom-made in-the-ear hearing aids, which caused the company to lose approximately half of its market share over a ten-year period. Furthermore, due to the instability of the foreign exchange market, Oticon experienced a sudden reduction in profitability in 1986 and 1987, which resulted in a considerable loss. The negative development reached its peak in 1987 when Oticon had a deficit of DKK41 million before taxes, corresponding to 11 per cent of the turnover.

After a management shift in 1988 the company has experienced considerable rationalization in expenditures as well as the introduction of a new and very flexible company structure. During recent years there has been a significant increase in both turnover and profits due to this rationalization as well as to the new company structure, the strongly increased research and development costs, and the thorough renewal of control and information systems.

In the beginning of 1995 Oticon took over the Swiss hearing aid company Ascom Audiosys AG, which has an annual turnover of DKK235 million.

The global market situation

Introduction

The need for hearing aids has increased. The number of elderly people increases every year, and with them also the need for hearing aids. There is also an increasing understanding in society that a hearing aid is a very valuable aid to a person suffering from a hearing deficiency. Although the need for hearing aids is rising, however, this has, in recent years, not meant a similar increase in the overall market for hearing aids. There may be many reasons for this, but the three most important factors are believed to be as follows:

● The *stigma* of hearing loss:

World-wide there are approximately 300 million people with some degree of hearing loss. Approximately 270 million of them have done nothing about it. The stigma means that the impaired persons are reluctant to accept their hearing loss, so they will wait an estimated period of 5 to 15 years before seeking professional help. Also the stigma is expressed in the reluctance to adopt and use hearing aids.

● The economic limitations of elderly people and of the public authorities providing subsidies.

● The technical limitations of the hearing aids.

Trade structure

The hearing aid trade can be divided functionally into component suppliers, hearing aid manufacturers and retail businesses/clinics.

The most important components (microphones, telephones, loudspeakers, switches, volume controls, trimmers, tele coils and printed circuit boards) are supplied by approximately ten component manufacturers with well-established client relations towards a broad section of the companies within the trade. The number of suppliers of certain components is fairly small. At least two-thirds of the microphones and loudspeakers used in hearing aids are supplied by Knowles Electronics Inc. in the

USA. Knowles has had this position for a considerable number of years. The Danish company Microtronic A/S has a leading position as regards supply of a number of micromechanic components for the hearing aid trade, and the Canadian company Gennum Corporation is the dominating supplier of chips. These companies all have good earnings and a stable supplier relationship towards their customers.

Market size

There is no generally accepted survey of the size of the market for hearing aids. Based on reports from Oticon's sales companies around the world, Oticon has estimated the total sale in the world market in 1994 to be 4.5 million hearing aids, divided into regions and main types as shown in Tables 1 and 2.

In the American market, which constitutes about one-third of the world market, in-the-ear hearing aids are dominant, whereas behind-the-ear hearing aids are dominant in the rest of the world. Pocket hearing aids have a very limited market in the USA and Europe, but are quite popular in Japan and the developing countries.

In the 1980s the market share of in-the-ear hearing aids saw a constant increase, but this development has ceased in the 1990s because new and advanced signal-processing methods are always being introduced in behind-the-ear hearing aids, the size of which allows more complex aids with a higher efficiency and better sound quality.

Still, Oticon expects that the share of the in-the-ear hearing aids in the long run will rise to about 60 per cent of the total market.

It is assumed that those who are hearing impaired constitute a minimum of 5 per cent of the world population, corresponding to about 300 million people. Furthermore, it is assumed that 30 per cent of this group's hearing loss can be helped by hearing aids (potential market = 100%). The penetration of hearing aids varies greatly from market to market. The penetration in Scandinavia is greatest (about 30–40 per cent), followed by Great Britain and Australia (both 25–30 per cent). The high level of penetration in these countries can be explained by the fact that the largest part of the costs of hearing aid treatment are paid by public authorities. The rest of Europe, the USA and Japan have a lower level of penetration, typically 10–25 per cent. France is a country with a comparatively low penetration (15 per cent) as the use of hearing aids is associated with being old. In less developed countries such as India and China the penetration level is under 1 per cent. Apart from their economic limitations, there is no infrastructure in these countries within which people can be examined for hearing loss and have a hearing aid adjusted to their needs.

Distribution

The majority of sales are effected through retail stores. In Scandinavia, Great Britain and Australia things are organized differently. In these countries most hearing aids are distributed through public hearing care clinics, where the hearing aids are distributed without any charge except, in some cases, a possible extra fee to be paid by the client. Thus, most hearing aids sales are effected through a specialized distribution system concerned solely with the field of hearing care.

Table 1	Number of sold hearing aids in 1994, divided into regions (1,000 pcs.)	
	Total market (000 pcs.)	Market share (%)
Europe	1,900	42
USA	1,500	33
Japan	350	8
Rest	750	17
Total	4,500	100

Source: Oticon's stock prospectus, 1995.

Table 2	Number of sold hearing aids in 1994, divided into types (1,000 pcs.)	
	Total market (000 pcs.)	Market share (%)
Pocket hearing aids	200	4
Behind-the-ear hearing aids	2,250	50
In-the-ear hearing aids	2,050	46
Total	4,500	100

Source: Oticon's stock prospectus, 1995.

In some countries, including Japan and some central and southern European countries, sales also take place through opticians' shops, which cover both eye care and hearing care. Oticon estimates that the joint sales of hearing aids and glasses will not increase significantly in the near future, so most hearing aids will continue to be sold through a specialized distribution system.

During the last decade there has been a concentration in the retail trade whereby wholesale chains and chains with joint marketing have become very significant. This gives the distributors a position of power in relation to the manufacturer. The manufacturer's risk is that its product is reduced to a standard product marketed under the chain's own name, thus reducing the manufacturer's contact with the end user.

Competition

It is estimated that the ten largest producers of hearing aids cover about 80 per cent of the world market, while about 100 smaller producers cover the rest. The Siemens hearing aids division and the American hearing aids company Starkey each have a market share of 15–20 per cent, while Oticon (including Audiosys) covers 10–15 per cent of the market. In addition to this there are five or six companies with a market share between 3 and 6 per cent. Three of the ten largest companies are Danish – Oticon, Widex (Tøpholm & Westermann Aps) and GN Danavox A/S, which is part of the GN Store Nord concern. It is estimated that these three Danish producers together have 25 per cent of the world market for hearing aids.

Oticon positions itself, compared to Siemens and Starkey, through a more extensive audiologically based knowledge. Oticon sells a higher proportion of behind-the-ear hearing aids, which reflects the fact that Oticon to a greater extent than the other two market leaders deals with the severely hearing impaired and the experienced users of hearing aids. Furthermore, Oticon differentiates itself from competitors by having a distribution system which is considered to be more international. Oticon's sales cover all continents and are divided into more markets than the sales of the competitors.

Despite the tradition of high loyalty between the distributor and manufacturer, the experience of the last three years has shown that unique products combined with an extensive marketing effort can move market shares considerably, even in a stagnant market.

Both Siemens and Starkey have over the last decade participated in the structural rationalization that has taken place in the trade. During this period Siemens has taken over two large competitors and Starkey has taken over a large number of smaller competitors. Neither of the two companies has made any significant takeovers during the last three years.

The profits in the trade are very modest, taken as a whole, because of intense price competition. However, Oticon has been able to increase its price level and profits by differentiating its offering from that of others through its high knowledge content and greater user satisfaction. This means that Oticon's products will, generally, be among the most expensive on the market.

Development of the Danish hearing aid industry

The Danish hearing aid industry has obtained an international position since the Second World War. The achievement of this position has to a high degree been attached to the following factors:

● The existence of a company-based electronic competence in the Danish electronic industry from the first half of the twentieth century.

● Contacts to Danish research.

● Utilization of the early demand for advanced equipment by hospitals, generated by high-quality health policies during the 1960s.

Furthermore, the hearing aid industry's early high product quality is also the result of the Danish government's regulations when establishing public hearing care clinics and minimum requirements for the products supplied. The flourishing hearing aid industry in Denmark has thus been attached to the knowledge-intensive end user (the hearing care clinic). This has created the basis for the development of the domestic market and later export markets. Denmark was the first country in the world to give free hearing aids to the public (1951). The intense competition since the 1950s between the three hearing aid producers Widex, Danavox and Oticon has also promoted technological development.

The Oticon concern today

Oticon's objective is to help people with hearing deficiencies lead the life they wish with the hearing they have. Hearing is fundamental to the interplay between people and therefore to the quality of life for each individual.

Oticon is a niche company focusing on one single business area, unlike a number of competitors where hearing aids are a department/division of a very large company involved in a broader business area (e.g. Siemens). In the line of hearing aids, Oticon's production strategy focuses on innovative high-efficiency products which can be sold at relatively high prices and with high contributions. The product line is completed by more traditional products giving the end user a satisfactory solution at a lower price level. Oticon's general product strategy is to be market leader in the three areas which experience has shown are the most important to people with hearing deficiencies:

● Reliability.

● Sound quality.

● Size and design.

Oticon's latest product is the fully digitalized 'DigiFocus', shown in Plate 3.

Organization

Oticon's organization form varies according to function and geography. In Denmark the central office is constructed as a flexible project organization where many employees carry out several functions. The traditional organization has been replaced by a network in which there are no traditional offices and where the majority of communications are informal or electronic.

Oticon has chosen this organization form in order to release its employees' creative resources, who thus work faster and more efficiently than the employees of competitors. Specialists with completely different backgrounds work together in project groups, and the composition and physical location of these groups change with the ongoing projects.

The basis for this knowledge-based organization is an electronic infrastructure comprising all functions in the company and linking the main office to the sales companies.

Oticon abolished job titles and introduced flexible work teams, resulting in what is known as the 'spaghetti organization', which is not a matrix organization. The only structure within the spaghetti organization is provided by the projects, with the additional dimension that the staff is multiskilled. Furthermore, each employee rotates from project to project, almost always working on two or more projects simultaneously. As a result, not only has Oticon eliminated the organization chart, but its employees also no longer have traditional offices (i.e. there are no walls). In this way, project teams can sit together, enabling decisions to be taken instantly rather than waiting for a meeting.

Production

Today Oticon has a lower degree of automation and therefore higher production costs than many of its competitors, but the plan is to change this through an intense effort over the next three years.

The production of hearing aids takes place at factories in Thisted, Denmark and in Hamilton, Scotland. The production capacity at the factories is presently fully utilized in one full day shift and a smaller evening shift. A full utilization of the factories in two shifts would increase production volume by about 50 per cent.

Since July 1993 Oticon's quality control system has been certified according to the ISO 9001 standards, despite the fact that in principle the flexible organization is opposed to the quality certification of the ISO 9001. But it has turned out that the very discipline and systemization required by the ISO 9001 certification balances the creative and informal structure at Oticon very well.

Oticon has realized that it can no longer master all technologies and competences at the highest level. An increasing number of functions are transferred to subsuppliers. Through outsourcing the manufacturing of all metal parts and the production of coils, switches and other electromechanical components, etc., Oticon has lowered its production costs and simplified its company structure. Outsourcing has also helped create new companies, such as Estron ApS in Jutland. Estron took over Oticon's production equipment with a view to operating as an independent subsupplier, and now employs sixteen people.

Table 3	The economic development of the Oticon concern, 1992–6				
	1992	**1993**	**1994**	**1995**	**1996**
Turnover (DKK m)	539	661	750	940	1,087
Gross profits (DKK m)	18	84	135	136	160
Net capital (DKK m)	146	192	273	449	539
Number of employees	1,069	1,073	1,192	1,485	1,443

Economic development

The economic development of the Oticon concern over the last five years is shown in Table 3.

Distribution of the market

Oticon's sales are concentrated in the highly developed markets, primarily in western Europe and Japan. Its three largest single markets are the USA, Japan and Germany. Oticon's turnover divided into single regions is shown in Table 4.

Sales take place in 80–100 markets and in 1994 about 93 per cent of the production was sold outside Denmark. The market shares are highest in close markets. Oticon's share has increased in the three largest markets in recent years.

The increase in turnover which Oticon has experienced in a stagnant market over the last three years has primarily occurred in western Europe and Japan. This indicates that the advanced hearing aids have gained a foothold in these markets. This is despite the fact that, especially in western Europe, there has been a considerable tightening of public subsidies for hearing aid treatment, so that the price of hearing aids has become even more important. It is Oticon's experience that even in this situation there is a substantial market for innovative, high-efficiency products sold at a high price.

By setting up an agency in Moscow, Russia, and founding a sales company in Poland, Oticon has begun to strengthen its distribution in the eastern European markets. Extensive growth is expected over the next couple of years in this part of the world.

The geographic distribution of Audiosys' sales is quite different from Oticon's, since more than one-third of its retail sales (but a considerably smaller part of its turnover) is effected in Australia in connection with a contract that the company has with the Australian state. A part of the contract is that the state will support in different ways the export of Audiosys' hearing aids to the Asian region. Audiosys' other main markets are Germany, the USA and France. Audiosys has sales companies in these markets as well as in Great Britain and Italy, while about 40 other markets are covered by independent distributors.

The international sales organization and distribution

Distribution to the various markets is via 15 subsidiary companies in the primary markets. Apart from this there are about 80 independent distributors in the remaining markets.

In the Danish market, Oticon, Widex and Danavox have established a joint sales company, Otwidan, through which the sales of all Danish hearing aids are invoiced, as a service to the Danish hearing care centres. The three companies are separate actors in the Danish market and thus compete within the framework of Otwidan. The cooperation in Otwidan results in lower distribution costs in the Danish market, which benefits the hearing care system through lower prices.

The core of Oticon's distribution strategy in individual countries is to build up long-term cooperation with the most professional distributors of hearing aids – those with the necessary education for the custom fitting of hearing aids and who have the equipment required for doing this.

Table 4	Oticon's turnover (1994) divided into markets (%)
Scandinavia	14
The rest of Europe	38
North America	17
Asia	16
The rest of the world	15
Total	100

Furthermore, the distributors must have a concept focusing on achieving long-term user satisfaction.

The precise form of cooperation varies from country to country. In some countries (e.g. Germany), the parties enter into a yearly contract in which their mutual obligations are stated.

Market communication

Oticon's marketing strategy is a combination of influencing both the distributor and the end user. It seeks to motivate the distributor to try out an Oticon hearing aid on all users and thereby give the user a choice between hearing aids of different quality and price levels. This effort is supplemented by information given to the user, making him or her aware of the fact that hearing aids are not standard products and that it is of great importance to choose a high-quality aid with a high degree of service.

The formation of marketing concepts takes place concurrently with product development and is an integral part of the project group's work. The introduction of new products in most cases includes a considerable training effort directed towards the distributor fitting the hearing aids according to users' needs. Oticon thereby ensures that new hearing aids are used correctly. The introduction of still more complex hearing aids increases the significance of this part of the marketing strategy, and Oticon therefore seeks to extend the training and information functions considerably.

Along with the marketing of the individual products, Oticon carries out campaigns with the aim of extending the use of hearing aids in certain segments. The latest example of this is Otikids, the children's programme. The Otikids programme includes an audiological part where the most recent knowledge concerning the fitting of hearing aids for children is transferred to audiologists all over the world. In addition there is a design programme directed towards the child, where child-orientated materials as well as choice of colours and packaging can change the child's conception of the hearing aid. The aim is for the child to see the hearing aid not as an aid for the physically impaired, but as a modern, technological and attractive system of communication. The programme is supported by information to parents and teachers.

Normally the direct contact with the end user is in the hands of the distributor, but in a few markets Oticon has private hearing care clinics, primarily with the aim of testing concepts of marketing and maintaining a direct contact with the user. In connection with its takeover of its former distributor in Australia, Oticon also took over a nationwide network of hearing care clinics. These clinics are now used for company development work regarding the optimization of market communication to the user.

Questions

1. Assess the determinants of the development of Oticon's international competitiveness. Base your assessment on Figure 4.1:
   (a) Porter's diamond model (national competitiveness).
   (b) Porter's five forces model.
   (c) The value chain model (competitor triangle and benchmarking).

2. What implications will the heterogeneous markets have for Oticon's international marketing strategy?

3. What can a hearing aid manufacturer like Oticon do about the stigma problem? Approximately 300 million people in the world have some degree of hearing loss but only 30 million of them seek professional advice.

Source: Some of the information in this case is taken from Oticon's stock prospectus before its introduction on the stock exchange in May 1995.

Case I.4 Hsu's Ginseng Enterprises

Internationalization of the ginseng business

As always, Paul Hsu, president of Hsu's Ginseng Enterprises Inc., is concerned about the publicity of the company. One day at the end of 1996 a journalist from the *Journal of Business Strategy* is visiting him. Paul Hsu says:

Small and medium-sized companies, like mine, have manoeuvrability, persistence, and creative vision, but, unfortunately, they don't have the capital or the people power that big companies have. It is important for them, however, to not let these factors hold them back by not experimenting with overseas markets. In order to grow, a firm must expand its product lines and markets. And a great way to do this is by pursuing customers overseas.

The world-wide production of ginseng is 8–9 million pounds. After China (3.5 million pounds) and Korea (2.5 million pounds) the USA is the world's third largest ginseng producer (1 million pounds) and Hong Kong provides its biggest market, buying US$35 million worth of the American medical herb a year. The price is about $50 per pound.

There is a wide range of ginseng products in the American market, including capsules and tonics, but Hong Kong consumers prefer it in its root form, cut up and made into tea. The small county of Marahton in Wisconsin, with over a thousand ginseng growers, produces 75 per cent of the nation's ginseng, worth an estimated $70 million. But the American preference for its Asian cousins means that nearly all domestically grown ginseng is exported. Of the $60 million in exports, the leading US exporter Hsu's Ginseng Enterprises accounts for 20 per cent.

Americans mainly buy Korean and Chinese ginseng. They think it is steeped in Asian mystique and so regard it as better than American ginseng.

What is ginseng?

It is the most valued, revered and legendary medicinal plant, found growing wild only in northern Manchuria and the north-eastern United States. It is a perennial plant which stands about 10–20 inches high with 2–5 clusters of a group of five leaves and a spindle-shaped root. Small white flowers in summer are followed by red berries (bearing seed) in the autumn. Two varieties are generally regarded as 'ginseng', American ginseng and Chinese/Korean ginseng. Ginseng is consumed in natural form and also in tablets and in liquid/beverage form.

American ginseng is commonly used to balance and tone the body's chemistry, enhance the immune system, provide energy, improve physical strength and endurance, reduce fatigue, increase overall vitality and stimulate circulation. American ginseng is considered by Chinese herbalists to be 'cooling' to the body. Therefore, it is recommended to reduce stress and fatigue instead of the more stimulating Chinese and Korean ginsengs.

Ginseng is not a cheap crop. It is a long-term investment like a vineyard. American ginseng needs about four years to mature before the first crop can be harvested. It involves an investment of about $30,000 to harvest just one acre. Hsu credits the soil, climate and available technology as being the key components in his success as an agricultural exporter.

The internationalization of Hsu's Ginseng Enterprises

Hsu started his business as a sideline in 1974 while he was employed by the State of Wisconsin as a social worker. Born in Pescadores, Taiwan, Hsu came to the USA in 1968 for graduate studies at the University of Denver. He began as a distributor, using his personal network of family and acquaintances in Taiwan, and expanded to cultivating ginseng four years later, in 1978. He bought a 160-acre farm in Wausau, Wisconsin and began growing the crop himself. Then, in 1981, he started working on exporting his product to the then-closed People's Republic of China.

Early development

1974   Mail order business established.

1975–6 Began export trade with Taiwan and Hong Kong. Hsu's ginseng roots and products available in Chinese herbal stores in the USA and Canada.

1978   160-acre farm was purchased and Paul Hsu became the first Chinese ginseng grower in America.

1981   Moved into 5,000 square feet office building. President Paul Hsu appointed to the Wisconsin Governor's Advisory Committee on International Trade. Participated in Wisconsin Governor's Trade Delegation to the People's Republic of China.

Development of world market

1983   Took part in Halumi Food Show in Japan to develop the Far East markets.

1984   Completed major expansion of ginseng farming operation. Participated in Helfex Health Food Show in England to develop the European markets. Company was fully computerized.

1985   West coast branch office was established in Los Angeles to strengthen the wholesale services. Took part in International Health Food Show in Australia to develop the Australian market.

1986   Received the Wisconsin Governor's Award for Export Excellence.

1987   Acquired new plant with 7,500 square feet.

1988   Participated in Helfex International Health Food Show in England to further expand the European markets. East coast office in New York established. Exclusive distributor in the UK appointed.

1989   Over 300 acres of prime ginseng land was purchased.

1990   Developed American Ginseng Tea and Candy. Also new PVC plastic 10-cc vials of Fresh Royal Jelly were added to the product line. An additional 4,500 square feet area was constructed to join the two plants together.

1991   Hong Kong (Asia) regional office was established. President Paul Hsu was honoured as the Small Business Person of the Year (1991) in the Greater Wausau Area, Wisconsin, USA.

1992   President Paul Hsu named National Small Business Exporter of the Year (1992) by the US Small Business Administration. Built 9,100 square feet agricultural drying and storage facility.

1993   Hsu's Ginseng Joint Venture Company was established at Zangjiagang, Jiang Su, China. Canada branch office opened in Toronto.

1994   Second Joint Venture Company in China was established at Ning Bo.

1995   Third Joint Venture Company in Pu Ning was established. China office in Nanjing was established. President Paul Hsu was given the 'Award for distinguished achievement as an Asian farmer' by US Department of Agriculture.

1996   Chinese Herbal Health Supplement added to product line. Several hundred acres added to Hsu's prime ginseng land. Indonesia 'Bird's Nest' sources purchased for product line. Became US distributor for Japanese Dried Scallops. Korean toll-free number added to serve US Korean market.

Since 1981 Hsu has diligently attended state trade missions and participated in world-wide trade shows to cultivate Chinese contacts – even though China was not open to American commerce and foreign investors until around 1988.

During the 1980s, he was appointed by the governor of Wisconsin to serve on the Wisconsin Governor's Advisory Committee on International Trade. The company was also selected to be a participant in the Wisconsin Governor's Trade Delegation to the People's Republic of China. A decade after he started out, his plan began to pay off.

Hsu attributes his success to his persistence, not his native language abilities. 'You have to develop trust and build relationships with customers overseas. You have to establish common bonds and understand their cultures.' Hsu also has a bachelor's degree in sociology from the University of Taiwan and believes this background helped him to form interpersonal contacts with different types of people.

Hsu's Ginseng Enterprises today

Hsu is obviously doing something right. In 1995 the company had revenues of more than $20 million, half of which came from export markets: Hong Kong, Taiwan, Singapore, Malaysia, China and Canada.

In addition to the headquarters office in Wisconsin, the company has ten offices including branch offices, wholly owned subsidiaries and joint ventures outside the United States. There are about 210 employees all together, with eight dialects and ethnic groups involved in the business. Hsu's Ginseng Enterprises employs many facets of advertisement, such as trade magazines, catalogues, calendars, giveaways, newspapers, radio, TV and Internet.

The company has attained vertical integration from growing the products, manufacturing the finished products, exporting, brokering, wholesale and mail order. In September 1997 it plans to launch an international mail order programme with five shipping locations for its main international markets. The company is also using horizontal integration by including other products.

You have been contacted by Paul Hsu concerning consultancy on the company's future internationalization strategy.

Questions

1. Characterize the present internationalization strategy of Hsu's Ginseng Enterprises.

2. What are the reasons for the present and past course of the internationalization process?

3. What is your assessment of the involvement of Hsu's Ginseng Enterprises in so many functions in the value chain (in both vertical and horizontal integration)?

Case I.5 Titan Industries Ltd

Is Titan Watches ready for globalization?

Titan Industries Ltd

Titan Industries Ltd (Titan) came into being in 1986, as a venture of TATA, the leading business group of companies in India. The US$10 billion TATA group is a highly diversified group with business interests in automobiles, steel, power, engineering services and goods, chemicals, telecommunications, information technology, plantations, agro-industries, hotels and consumer goods. The TATA group is internationally known and respected for its ethical business practices – a reputation that has helped the group to forge and cement international business partnerships in all sectors of industry.

Titan has its head office in Bangalore, a city known as the home of multiple computer software companies. The Titan plant is one of the most sophisticated watchmaking plants in India – costing over US$100 million in 1986. It now employs more than 2,500 employees. The plant has five extremely modern and well-equipped factories. The manufacturing of quartz watches and standard of quality inspection are very stringent and world-class. Titan claims that its watches are 'guaranteed to gain/lose no more than 30 seconds in a month'.

Producing around 6 million units of watches and clocks, Titan is presently one of the largest integrated watch and jewelry manufacturers in the world. It also produces over 1,500,000 pieces of jewelry annually in the brand name of Tanishq. Though Titan began with the objective of catering to the Indian markets, it has now become international. It has offices in Australia, Singapore, London and Dubai. The Singapore office handles sales and marketing for countries in the Asia Pacific region while the London office coordinates the pan-European management, marketing and distribution. The Middle East and Africa is centrally managed from Dubai. Titan continues the traditions of the TATA group, its promoters. Like its parents, Titan has transformed itself into a model corporate citizen. For six years, from 1992–99, it kept its place as India's most admired company in consumer durables. The zenith of the Titan was in

year 2000 when it was voted the most respected brand in India, ahead of such international names as Coca-Cola, P&G and Pepsi, etc. The most liked attributes of Titan are its quality and brand image.

India: an evolving nation

Indian provides a curious mix of good and bad as far as global business is concerned. India is now ranked as the seventh largest country in the world. It has a continuous and documented history from about 2000 BC. Internationally, India has of late been growing in importance. It is not only a profitable destination for many items from the West but it is also now considered a low-cost manufacturing base by MNCs. This has all become possible since 1991, when the Narasimha Rao government pursued a programme of market reforms and economic liberalization programmes. Now the annual growth rate of India ranges from 5 to 6 per cent. There has been a steady increase in foreign investment, joint ventures, partnerships, and direct ownership by American, Japanese, and European businesses in India since then. The Clinton administration recognized these changes and designated India as one of the world's 10 big emerging markets. India is a favourable location for establishing low-wage manufacturing units and an inexpensive source of developing sophisticated world-class software. It is also an attractive market for banking, chemicals, telecommunications, entertainment

| Table 1 | A financial snapshot of Titan |

Major indicators	1997–98 (Rs million)	1996–97 (Rs million)	1995–96 (Rs million)
Value of assets	5,773	5,610	4,670
Gross block	3,388	3,150	2,950
Total income	4,452	4,210	3,540
Sales	4,420.6	4,090	3,510
PBT	162.4	280	280
Exports	358	560	370

Note: US$1 = Rs 44 (March 2000)

services, automobiles, and power generation industries. India is expanding its ties with the US, Japan, and Western Europe. The Indian government promotes Indian exports aggressively and assists its exporters through a variety of incentives, finances and tax concessions.

Indian watch market

The Indian watch market has traditionally been a functional market for wristwatches. As a developing country where 40 per cent of the population lives in poverty, owning a wristwatch itself is a luxury and they have in the past been bought as timekeeping, functional devices. Until the arrival of Titan, watches were not considered at all to be a fashion accessory. Naturally, the buying attributes for wristwatches were quality and functionality. For most Indians, wristwatches have been regarded as a durable item which, once bought, would be good for another 10 years or until they were beyond repair. Price has been a major buying consideration in the Indian markets. For instance, in 1999, watches costing less than Rs 450 constituted half of the watch market. Those between Rs 450 and Rs 1,000 constituted another 30 per cent, leaving only a fifth of the market for watches above Rs 1,000.

In 1987, Titan changed the watch market for good. Offering premium quartz watches in a variety of styles, Titan succeeded in turning the watch buyers into a style-conscious segment. Since then, variety and designs have become the buying attributes of Indians. Of course, all this has had to come at a reasonable price. It has been the only way to make Indian buyers buy more watches and to make them replace old pieces more frequently and as and when fashion changed.

A major segment of Indian watches is Indian Made Foreign Quartz (IMFQ). Mostly operated by the unorganized sector, the IMFQ watches are stylish, fashionable, cheap and disposable. The IMFQ category is driven solely by price, with most of the watches falling in the Rs 200–400 price band. Mostly they are bought by children and youngsters as well as by low-income group consumers. Estimated at 18 million pieces a year, this segment has often grown at the expense of the organized quartz watch market. In the last five years, the organized quartz market in which Titan and Timex,

the US watch maker which was a partner of Titan until 1999, has shrunk by nearly 17 per cent.

The domestic marketing of Titan

Titan began with an undifferentiated marketing strategy in domestic markets of India. Its main aim was to sell to anyone who had an interest in buying quality and design together in wristwatches. Before Titan, Indian consumers could not get quality and design simultaneously in a wristwatch at a reasonable price. Titan's main competitor was HMT, a public sector enterprise also located in Bangalore. HMT no doubt provided quality in wristwatches, but it did not have a marketing drive, or the designs and interest in its customers. The Japanese and Swiss-made watches provided styles and designs but their quality was suspect as most of them entered India through the grey channels. Titan marketing changed all that. It provided a huge competition to both HMT and global brands of watches in India. In fact Titan dwarfed both in a very short time and grew to be the first choice of Indian wristwatch customers.

The brands–segments matrix

Initially, Titan sold watches without knowing who was buying them or who wanted more specific features. Later it graduated to the segmented marketing framework in the mid-1990s. It designed watches for specific segments and created a marketing pull for them through persuasive marketing efforts. It used a broad spectrum of segmentation variables and zeroed in on such demographic segments as male, female, children, businessmen and executives. It then identified segments based on functional as well as lifestyle reasons, marriage, seasonal gifts, multiunit ownership, occasion-matching and suiting different seasons etc.

The modular approach

By the end of 1998, the marketing strategy had the following goals in the Indian market:

- make Titan a mother brand and move it up the value chain
- align with international brands
- enrich the choice range with low-end independent brands

- create specific segment sub-brands to attract fast-rising kids, businessmen, women etc.
- re-launch existing brands (Royal, Exacta, Raga, etc.),
- create leverage on the Titan brand names for other products including jewelry

Sensing a huge potential in the Indian Made Foreign Quartz (IMFQ) segment, Titan decided to align with a global brand. The IMFQ players offered flashy watches and more variety at a much lower price to Indian consumers. As per some estimates, the segment accounted for as high as 75 per cent of the product category in India in 1999. Thus, assuming the total market size to be 40 million units, the IMFQ watch segment accounted for to 20–30 million pieces. The IMFQ players imported watch movements and dials at very cheap prices. With a low-cost, low-overhead operation, they were able to sell for as low as Rs 350. Titan, due to its own movements manufacturing, was no match in the IMFQ segment. Therefore, in 1995–96, Titan forged a joint venture with the American firm, Timex. This joint venture continued for two years but ended in 1998. The lack of success has not deterred Titan, however, from pursuing the same path again as better opportunities and options presented themselves. In 1999, the Indian Government removed quantitative restrictions on imports. It encouraged Titan to take advantage of this opportunity by either aligning with global brands for distribution or by supplying its own brands or by even marketing global brands via its own vast network of retailing.

Retailing power

Right from the beginning, Titan made it a point of its marketing initiatives that its brands were available in as many locations and outlets as possible in India. The result was a vast retail network for Titan, which also included, as Titan claimed, the world's largest chain of exclusive showrooms for watches and jewelry. In 1999, the number of outlets where Titan could be bought exceeded over 5,500 in more than 1,500 cities in 33 countries.

The exclusive retail network of Titan consisted of two forms of outlets. The first was the World of Titan (WoT) which, up to the end of 1999 existed at 107 locations across 68 towns in India. Each shopper visiting and buying at the WoT became entitled to join the Signet Club, a customer loyalty plan offering additional privileges and benefits. The other retailing outlet of Titan was Time Zone. All Titan showrooms were artistically designed and they offered courteous service in a spacious and stylish retail ambience. By 1999, the Time Zone outlets were found in 52 Indian cities. Since Titan also sold branded jewelry (Tanishq), it set up exclusive Tanishq outlets. These were more exclusive and up-market premium showrooms and provided a rich ethnic Indian buying experience. The network of Tanishq showrooms covered almost every capital and major town in India. The Titan retailing network was strongly supplemented by the bigger but very traditional independent watch retailers.

Titan was fairly successful in roping in the independent retailing network in India. In fact, Titan was credited with having broken several traditions in Indian watch retailing. Before Titan's arrival, wristwatches in India were never sold in high street shops. Interested buyers had to search for specialized watch shops. These shops were poorly styled and lit and had virtually no retailing infrastructure or ambience to retain the customers. Customers wanted to get out of the shop the moment they completed their purchase. Titan revolutionized this by bringing watch retailing in India to the high streets and introduceing lifestyle buying. Titan also made its brands available in all those shops where customer traffic was expected to be higher and more frequent (like general provision stores, clothes shops, electronics shops etc.). These shops were fresh, younger looking and were also visited more by younger customers. Titan has also made its brands available in gift stores and departmental stores to position them as gift items and encourage impulse purchases. To provide its customers easy access to enhanced after-sales service, Titan has a network of watch care centres numbering over 350 in India and around the world.

Going global

TATA group, the promoter of Titan, always believed in global markets and in global alliances. This was necessary partly to be in tune with the changing global business environment and partly for business reasons in India. The demand pattern and growth in Indian markets began to mature. In keeping with TATA philosophy, Titan too initiated international forays in the mid-1990s. Titan has segmented its overseas world into four markets: the Middle East and Africa, Europe, the Far East and Australia. In each of these places, Titan has an office that coordinates its international operations and promotes the brand image. These offices are also on the look-out to identify international partners and brand alliances. In May 1999, Titan was permitted to participate in the 1999 Basel Fair. It was the first time that Indian exhibitors had been allowed free and unfettered display of their products in the fair. Once in the Fair, Titan tried to make the most of the opportunity and put on display its new range of jewelry and watches: Criterion, Concert, Chronata and Fastrack. The visitors, media and, of course, the watch connoisseurs visited the Titan stall and showed an appreciation of its designs and product range. Some retailers who visited the Titan showroom at the Fair also showed their interest in retailing Titan watches in new markets and/or stocking it in more shops in the existing markets.

The global competition

After lording it over the Indian market with no meaningful competition for a decade, the year 1999 was altogether different. In this year, the government of India removed quantitative restrictions on the import of watches, movements and parts, which meant that global majors like Swatch, Citizen, Casio and Seiko could again enter Indian markets and pose a bigger challenge to Titan. Titan termed this as a positive development: in reality, the new policy means both opportunity and challenge to Titan. For instance, in the open era of global competition, Titan too will not be shackled by the need to first create an assembly before launching a product. If it spots an opportunity, it can buy the products and put them on the market. On the other hand, the challenge is that the new global entrants might encourage brand switching; this would be at Titan's expense. A positive outcome of this new competition may be that the Indian market itself might grow. More players will create more interest in the product category by their physical presence and their communication. To date, Titan's had been the lone voice; the watch product category was overshadowed by colour televisions, garments and other consumer durables. The collective voice of Titan and global brands like Swatch and Citizen may excite a new consumer interest in watches.

The new dreams

By 1999, Titan had begun to envision itself in the business of personal adornment and as a global brand. It proclaimed in its media interactions that it was ready to move on beyond just wristwatches and jewelry (Tanishq). Its vision was to introduce Titan pens, sunglasses, leather products and more. Titan believed that, for instance, its watch brands for segments such as youth, children and women afforded it a unique opportunity to launch a whole new range of product categories for these segments. For instance, Dash!, the wristwatch for the youngsters, had entrenched itself as a fun children's brand. In other words, Titan could leverage in the kids' market, extend itself and offer Dash! books, Dash! electronic toys, Dash! writing materials etc. Titan officials are confident that they can use their marketing and distribution to sell other products in the personal adornment segment and a whole range of products related to youth – like music. Four streams are on the agenda in this direction: brand extensions, leveraging Titan's expertise in marketing, retailing and skills in precision engineering areas.

The other dream of Titan is to be a global brand. Having defeated domestic competition and having become the most respected brand in India, Titan believes that it is ready to take on the world.

Questions

1. Is Titan ready to launch a global brand?

2. What will be the criteria to examine its preparedness as a global brand?

3. In what ways does a national brand differ from a global brand?

Prepared by Dr Mohan Lal Agrawal, Professor of Marketing, XLRI Jamshedpur (India) and Associate Professor Svend Hollensen. Inputs for the case were sourced from a variety of public media.

Part II

Deciding which markets to enter

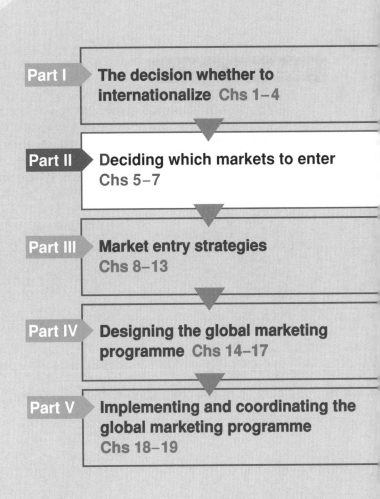

Part I	The decision whether to internationalize Chs 1–4
Part II	Deciding which markets to enter Chs 5–7
Part III	Market entry strategies Chs 8–13
Part IV	Designing the global marketing programme Chs 14–17
Part V	Implementing and coordinating the global marketing programme Chs 18–19

Chapter 5   The political and economic environment

Chapter 6   The sociocultural environment

Chapter 7   The international market selection (IMS) process

Part II Cases

Introduction

After considering the initial phase (Part I, The decision whether to internationalize) the structure of this part follows the process of selecting the 'right' international market. The political economic environment (*Chapter 5*) and the sociocultural environment (*Chapter 6*) are used as inputs to the process from which the output is the target market(s) that the firm should select as a basis for development of the international marketing mix (Part IV of this book). The structure of Part II is shown in Figure 1.

Figure 1   **The structure and process of Part II**

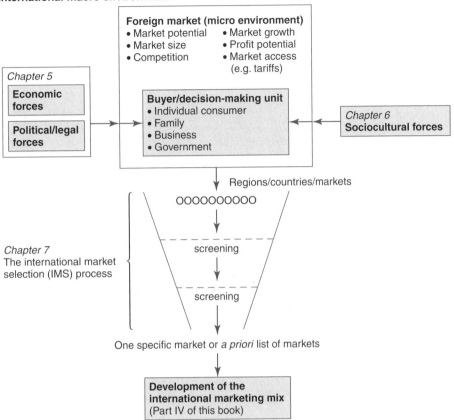

As Figure 1 shows, the forces in Chapters 5 and 6 provide the environmental framework that is necessary for the following:

● The subsequent description of the foreign market/buyer behaviour.

● The discussion and development of the global marketing mix.

The discussion following chapters 5 and 6 will be limited to the major macro environmental dimensions affecting market and buyer behaviour and thus the global marketing mix of the firm.

The political and economic environment

After studying this chapter you should be able to do the following:

- Discuss how the political/legal environment will affect the attractiveness of a potential foreign market.
- Distinguish between political factors in the home country environment and the host country environment.
- Explain the steps in a political risk analysis procedure.
- Distinguish between tariff barriers and non-tariff barriers.
- Describe the major trading blocs.
- Explore why the structure of consumption is different from country to country.
- Explain how managers can influence local politics.
- Define regional economic integration and identify different levels of integration.
- Discuss the benefits and drawbacks associated with regional economic integration.

5.1 Introduction

This chapter is devoted to macro environmental factors that explain the many forces to which a firm is exposed. The marketer has to adapt to a more or less uncontrollable environment within which he or she plans to operate. In this chapter the environmental factors in the foreign environment are limited to the political/legal forces, and the economic forces.

5.2 ❚ The political/legal environment

This section will concentrate mainly on the political issues. The political/legal environment comprises primarily two dimensions:

● The home country environment.

● The host country environment.

Besides these two dimensions there is also a third dimension:

● The general international environment (see Figure 5.1).

Home country environment

A firm's home country political environment can constrain its international operations as well as its domestic operations. It can limit the countries that the international firm may enter.

The best-known example of the home country political environment affecting international operations has been South Africa. Home country political pressures induced firms to leave the country altogether.

After US companies left South Africa, the Germans and the Japanese remained as the major foreign presence. German firms did not face the same political pressures at home that US firms had. However, the Japanese government was embarrassed when Japan became South Africa's leading trading partner. As a result, some Japanese companies reduced their South African activity.

One challenge facing multinationals is the triple-threat political environment. Even if the home country and the host country do not give them problems, they may face threats in third markets. Firms that did not have problems with their home government or the South African government, for example, could be bothered or boycotted about their South African operations in third countries, like the United States. Today European firms face problems in the United States if they do business in Cuba. Nestlé's problems with its infant formula controversy were most serious not at home in Switzerland, or in African host countries, but in a third market – the United States.

| Figure 5.1 | **Barriers in the political/legal environment** |

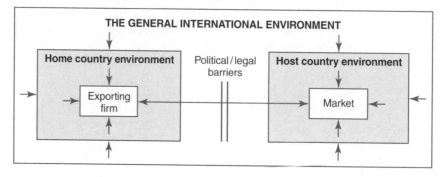

A third area in which some governments regulate global marketing concerns bribery and corruption. In many countries, payments or favours are a way of life, and an 'oiling of the wheels' is expected in return for government services. In the past, many companies doing business internationally, routinely paid bribes or did favours for foreign officials in order to gain contracts.

Many business managers argue that their home country should not apply its moral principles to other societies and cultures in which bribery and corruption are endemic. If they are to compete globally, these managers argue, they must be free to use the most common methods of competition in the host country. Particularly in industries that face limited or even shrinking markets, such stiff competition forces firms to find any edge possible to obtain a contract.

On the other hand, applying different standards to management and firms, depending on whether they do business abroad or domestically, is difficult to envisage. Also, bribes may open the way for shoddy performance and loose moral standards among managers and employees, and may result in a concentration on how best to bribe rather than on how best to produce and market products.

The global marketer must carefully distinguish between reasonable ways of doing business internationally – including compliance with foreign expectations – and outright bribery and corruption.

Promotional activities (sponsored by governmental organizations)

The programmes adopted by governmental organizations to promote exporting are an increasingly important force in the international environment. Many of the activities involve implementation and sponsorship by government alone, while others are the results of the joint efforts of government and business.

Furthermore, so-called regulatory supportive activities are direct government attempts to make its country's products more competitive in world markets. Also, there are attempts to encourage greater participation in exporting, particularly by smaller companies.

The granting of subsidies is of special interest: export subsidies are to the export industries what tariffs are to domestic industries. In both cases, the aim is to ensure the profitability of industries and individual firms that might well succumb if exposed to the full force of competition. For export industries, revenue is supplemented by subsidies, or costs are reduced by subsidies to certain input factors. Subsidies can be given through lower taxes on profits attributable to export sales, refunding of various indirect taxes, etc. Furthermore, a subsidy may take the form of a direct grant, which enables the recipient to compete against companies from other countries that enjoy cost advantages, or may be used for special promotion by recipient companies.

In a broader sense, government export promotion programmes, and programmes for global marketing activities in general, are designed to deal with the following internal barriers (Albaum *et al.*, 1994):

- Lack of motivation, as global marketing is viewed as more time consuming, costly and risky, and less profitable, than domestic business.
- Lack of adequate information.

● Operational/resource-based limitations.

Some of these programmes are quite popular in developing countries, especially if they enjoy the support of the business community.

Financial activities

Through the membership of international financial organizations such as the International Monetary Fund and the World Bank, the national government can assume its role as an international banker. The granting of subsidies is another financially based promotional activity of national governments.

One of the most vital determinants of the results of a company's export marketing programme is its credit policy. The supplier that can offer better payment terms and financing conditions may make a sale, even though its price may be higher or the quality of its product inferior to that of its competitors.

If the credit terms are extended, the risks of non-payment increase, and many exporters are reluctant to assume the risks. Consequently, it may be necessary to offer exporters the opportunity of transferring some of the risk to governmental organizations through credit insurance. *Export credit insurance* and guarantees cover certain commercial and political risks that might be associated with any given export transaction.

Information services

Many large companies can collect the information they need themselves. Other firms, even if they do not possess the expertise to do their own research, can afford to hire outside research agencies to do the necessary research. However, a large number of companies are not in a position to take either of these approaches. For these firms, generally smaller companies or newcomers to global marketing, their national government is the major source of basic marketing information.

Although the information relevant for international/export marketers varies from country to country, the following kinds are typically available (Albaum *et al.*, 1994, p. 68):

● Economic, social and political data on individual countries, including their infrastructure.

● Summary and detailed information on aggregate global marketing transactions.

● Individual reports on foreign firms.

● Specific export opportunities.

● Lists of potential overseas buyers, distributors and agents for various products in different countries.

● Information on relevant government regulations both at home and abroad.

● Sources of various kinds of information not always available from the government: for example, foreign credit information.

● Information that will help the company manage its operation: for example, information on export procedures and techniques.

Most types of information are made available to firms through published reports or through the Internet (www). Appendix A lists some relevant data sources and corresponding www addresses. In addition, government officials often participate in seminars and workshops aimed at helping the international marketer.

Export-facilitating activities

A number of national government activities can stimulate export activities. These include the following (Albaum *et al.*, 1994, p. 69):

● Trade development offices abroad, either as a separate entity or as part of the normal operations of an embassy or consulate.

● Government-sponsored trade fairs and exhibitions. A trade fair is a convenient marketplace in which buyers and sellers can meet, and in which an exporter can display products.

● Sponsoring trade missions of businesspeople who go abroad for the purpose of making sales and/or establishing agencies and other foreign representation.

● Operating permanent trade centres in foreign market areas, which run trade shows often concentrating on a single industry.

From the national government's point of view, each of these activities represents a different approach to stimulating the growth of exports. From the point of view of an individual company, these activities provide relatively low-cost ways of making direct contact with potential buyers in overseas markets.

Promotion by private organizations

Various non-governmental organizations play a role in the promotion of global marketing. These include the following (Albaum *et al.*, 1994, p. 70):

● Industry and trade associations, national, regional and sectoral industry associations, associations of trading houses, mixed associations of manufacturers and traders, and other bodies.

● Chambers of commerce: local chambers of commerce, national chambers, national and international associations of chambers, national chambers abroad and binational chambers.

● Other organizations concerned with trade promotion: organizations carrying out export research, regional export promotion organizations, world trade centres, geographically oriented trade promotion organizations, export associations and clubs, international business associations, world trade clubs and organizations concerned with commercial arbitration.

● Export service organizations, banks, transport companies, freight forwarders, export merchants and trading companies.

The type of assistance available to firms includes information and publications, education and assistance in 'technical' details, and promotion in foreign countries.

State trading

Many of the former communist countries are now allowing some private trading activities either through joint ventures or as a result of privatization of state-owned enterprises. However, there are still countries with active state trading, such as Cuba and to some extent China.

Private businesses are concerned about state trading for two reasons. First, the establishment of import monopolies means that exporters have to make substantial adjustments in their export marketing programmes. Second, if state traders wish to utilize the monopolistic power they possess, private international marketers will have a difficult time.

Exhibit 5.1

Global marketing in Chinese-owned companies

Since economic reforms started in 1978, China's exports have increased dramatically. In the pre-reform era, monolithic national foreign trade corporations (FTCs) were the exclusive channels through which business with the rest of the world was managed. However, the reforms of the 1980s have resulted in alternative routes for entering overseas markets, such as joint ventures with western partners. The export success of these firms is typically based on China's comparative advantage in labour-intensive products and easy access to the global networks of the foreign partners, which are primarily responsible for overseas business.

However, the situation of wholly owned Chinese companies is different. To be involved in indirect exporting, the enterprise must have permission. Key conditions for receiving direct export authority, meaning a status as an FTC, include critical mass in terms of size and the manufacture of products which are perceived to meet appropriate quality standards for foreign market sales. Management must also commit itself to using a proportion of foreign currency earnings to import technology and equipment which will strengthen the firm's competitive position.

Government-specified sales quotas, for both the Chinese and export markets, have to be met in order to maintain direct export rights. For sales in excess of the export quota, the FTC keeps more export revenue and there is greater flexibility in the use of the foreign funds generated. In case of unfulfilled export quotas, the FTC has to buy foreign exchange to meet the shortfall in remittances to the government. If export quotas are not met for three years, then direct export rights can be withdrawn.

In 1979, twelve national FTCs controlled all foreign trade in and out of China. Today thousands of enterprises have status as FTCs and are permitted to be engaged in overseas trade. Many larger enterprises are permitted to set up their own FTC, but the dispersion of foreign trade authority has mainly been accomplished through local FTCs at the provincial and city level. In these cases each FTC manages and takes care of the export activities of many SMEs with complementary products.

Source: From Walters and Zhu (1995). Adapted by permission of Management International Review.

Host country environment

Managers must continually monitor the government, its policies and its stability to determine the potential for political change that could adversely affect operations of the firm.

Political risks

There is political risk in every nation, but the range of risks varies widely from country to country. In general, political risk is lowest in countries that have a history of stability and consistency. Three major types of political risk can be encountered:

● *Ownership risk*, which exposes property and life.

● *Operating risk*, which refers to interference with the ongoing operations of a firm.

● *Transfer risk*, which is mainly encountered when companies want to transfer capital between countries.

Political risk can be the result of government action, but it can also be outside the control of government. The types of action and their effects can be classified as follows:

● *Import restrictions.* Selective restrictions on the import of raw materials, machines and spare parts are fairly common strategies to force foreign industry to purchase more supplies within the host country and thereby create markets for local industry. Although this is done in an attempt to support the development of domestic industry, the result is often to hamstring and sometimes interrupt the operations of established industries. The problem then becomes critical when there are no adequately developed sources of supply within the country.

● *Local-content laws.* In addition to restricting imports of essential supplies to force local purchase, countries often require a portion of any product sold within the country to have local content: that is, to contain locally made parts. This requirement is often imposed on foreign companies that assemble products from foreign-made components. Local-content requirements are not restricted to Third World countries. The European Union has a 45 per cent local-content requirement for foreign-owned assemblers. This requirement has been important for Far East car producers.

● *Exchange controls.* Exchange controls stem from shortages of foreign exchange held by a country. When a nation faces shortages of foreign exchange, controls may be levied over all movements of capital or, selectively, against the most politically vulnerable companies to conserve the supply of foreign exchange for the most essential uses. A problem for the foreign investor is getting profits and investments into the currency of the home country (transfer risks).

● *Market control.* The government of a country sometimes imposes control to prevent foreign companies from competing in certain markets. Recently the US government has threatened to boycott foreign firms trading with Cuba. The EU countries have protested against this threat.

● *Price controls.* Essential products that command considerable public interest, such as pharmaceuticals, food, petrol and cars, are often subjected to price controls. Such controls can be used by a government during inflationary periods to control the environmental behaviour of consumers or the cost of living.

● *Tax controls.* Taxes must be classified as a political risk when used as a means of controlling foreign investments. In many cases, they are raised without warning and in violation of formal agreements. In underdeveloped countries where the economy is constantly threatened with a shortage of funds, unreasonable taxation of successful foreign investments appeals to some governments as the most convenient and quickest means of finding operating funds.

● *Labour restrictions.* In many nations, labour unions are very strong and have great political influence. Using its strength, labour may be able to persuade the government to pass very restrictive laws that support labour at heavy cost to business. Traditionally, labour unions in Latin America have been able to prevent lay-offs and plant shutdowns. Labour unions are gradually becoming strong in western Europe as well. For example, Germany and a number of other European nations require labour representation on boards of directors.

● *Expropriation.* Defined as official seizure of foreign property, this is the ultimate government tool for controlling foreign firms. This most drastic action against foreign firms is fortunately occurring less often as developing countries begin to see foreign direct investment as desirable.

● *Domestication.* This can be thought of as creeping expropriation and is a process by which controls and restrictions placed on the foreign firm gradually reduce the control of the owners. The firm continues to operate in the country while the host government is able to maintain leverage on the foreign firm through imposing different controls. These controls include: greater decision-making powers accorded to nationals; more products produced locally rather than imported for assembly; gradual transfer of ownership to nationals (demand for local participation in joint ventures); and promotion of a large number of nationals to higher levels of management. Domestication provides the host country with enough control to regulate the activities of the foreign firm carefully. In this way, any truly negative effects of the firm's operations in the country are discovered and prompt corrective action may be taken.

Trade barriers from home country to host country

Free trade between nations permits international specialization. It also enables efficient firms to increase output to levels far greater than would be possible if sales were limited to their own domestic markets, thus permitting significant economies of scale. Competition increases, prices of goods in importing countries fall, while profits increase in the exporting country.

While countries have many reasons for wishing to trade with each other, it is also true to say that all too frequently an importing nation will take steps to inhibit the inward flow of goods and services.

One of the reasons why international trade is different from domestic trade is that it is carried on between different political units, each one a sovereign nation exercising control over its own trade. Although all nations control their foreign trade, they vary in the degree of control. Each nation or trading bloc invariably establishes trade laws that favour its indigenous companies and discriminate against foreign ones.

There are two main reasons why countries levy tariffs.

● *To protect domestic producers*. First, tariffs are a way of protecting domestic producers of a product. Because import tariffs raise the effective cost of an imported good, domestically produced goods can appear more attractive to buyers. In this way, domestic producers gain a protective barrier against imports. Although producers receiving tariff protection can gain a price advantage, protection can keep them from increasing efficiency in the long run. A protected industry can be destroyed if protection encourages complacency and inefficiency when it is later thrown into the lion's den of international competition.

● *To generate revenue*. Second, tariffs are a source of government revenue. Using tariffs to generate government revenue is most common among relatively less developed nations. The main reason is that less developed nations tend to have less formal domestic economies that presently lack the capability to record domestic transactions accurately. The lack of accurate record keeping makes the collection of sales taxes within the country extremely difficult. Nations solve the problem by simply raising their needed revenue through import and export tariffs. Those nations obtaining a greater portion of their total revenue from taxes on international trade are mainly the poorer nations.

Trade distortion practices can be grouped into two basic categories: tariff and non-tariff barriers.

Tariff barriers

Tariffs are direct taxes and charges imposed on imports. They are generally simple, straightforward and easy for the country to administer. While they are a barrier to trade, they are a visible and known quantity and so can be accounted for by companies when developing their marketing strategies.

Tariffs are used by poorer nations as the easiest means of collecting revenue and protecting certain home industries. They are a useful tool for politicians to show indigenous manufacturers that they are actively trying to protect their home markets.

The most common forms of tariffs are as follows:

● *Specific*. Charges are imposed on particular products, by either weight or volume, and usually stated in the local currency.

● *Ad valorem*. The charge is a straight percentage of the value of the goods (the import price).

● *Discriminatory*. In this case the tariff is charged against goods coming from a particular country, either where there is a trade imbalance or for political purposes.

Non-tariff barriers

In the last 40 years the world has seen a gradual reduction in tariff barriers in most developed nations. However, in parallel to this, non-tariff barriers have substantially increased. Non-tariff barriers are much more elusive and can be more easily disguised. However, in some ways the effect can be more devastating because they are an unknown quantity and are much less predictable.

Among non-tariff barriers the most important (not earlier mentioned) are as follows.

Quotas

A restriction on the amount (measured in units or weight) of a good that can enter or leave a country during a certain period of time is called *a quota*. After tariffs, a quota is the second most common type of trade barrier. Governments typically administer their quota systems by granting quota licenses to the companies or governments of other nations (in the case of import quotas), and domestic producers (in the case of exports quotas). Governments normally grant such licenses on a year-by-year basis.

● *Reasons for import quotas*. There are two reasons why a government imposes *import quotas*. First, it may wish to protect its domestic producers by placing a limit on the amount of goods allowed to enter the country. This helps domestic producers maintain their market shares and prices because competitive forces are restrained. In this case, domestic producers win because of the protection of their markets. Consumers lose because of higher prices and less selection due to lower competition. Other losers include domestic producers whose own production requires the import slapped with a quota. Companies relying on the importation of so-called 'intermediate' goods will find the final cost of their own products increase.

Second, a government may impose import quotas to force the companies of other nations to compete against one another for the limited amount of imports allowed.

Thus those wishing to get a piece of the action will likely lower the price that they are asking for their goods. In this case, consumers win from the resulting lower prices. Domestic producers of competing goods win if external producers do not undercut their prices, but lose if they do.

● *Reasons for export quotas*. There are at least two reasons why a country imposes *export quotas* on its domestic producers. First, it may wish to maintain adequate supplies of a product in the home market. This motive is most common among countries exporting natural resources that are essential to domestic business or the long-term survival of a nation.

Second, a country may restrict exports to restrict supply on world markets, thereby increasing the international price of the good. This is the motive behind the formation and activities of the Organization of Petroleum Exporting Countries (OPEC). This group of nations from the Middle East and Latin America attempts to restrict the world's supply of crude oil to earn greater profits.

● *Voluntary export restraints*. A unique version of the export quota is called a voluntary export restraint (VER) – a quota that a nation imposes on its exports usually at the request of another nation. Countries normally self-impose a voluntary export restraint in response to the threat of an import quota or total ban on the product by an importing nation. The classic example of the use of a voluntary export restraint is the automobile industry in the 1980s. Japanese carmakers were making significant market share gains in the US market. The closing of US carmakers' production facilities in the United States was creating a volatile anti-Japan sentiment among the population and the US Congress. Fearing punitive legislation in Congress if Japan did not limit its auto exports to the United States, the Japanese government and its carmakers self-imposed a voluntary export restraint on cars headed for the United States.

Consumers in the country that imposes an export quota benefit from greater supply and the resulting lower prices if domestic producers do not curtail production. Producers in an importing country benefit because the goods of producers from the exporting country are restrained, which may allow them to increase prices. Export quotas hurt consumers in the importing nation because of reduced selection and perhaps higher prices. However, export quotas might allow these same consumers to retain their jobs if imports were threatening to put domestic producers out of business. Again, detailed economic studies are needed to determine the winners and losers in any particular export quota case.

Embargoes

A complete ban on trade (imports and exports) in one or more products with a particular country is called an embargo. An embargo may be placed on one or a few goods or completely ban trade in all goods. It is the most restrictive non-tariff trade barrier available and is typically applied to accomplish political goals. Embargoes can be decreed by individual nations or by supranational organizations such as the United Nations. Because they can be very difficult to enforce, embargoes are used less today than in the past. One example of a total ban on trade with another country is the United States' embargo on trade with Cuba. In fact, US tourists are not even allowed to vacation in Cuba.

Administrative delays

Regulatory controls or bureaucratic rules designed to impair the rapid flow of imports into a country are called administrative delays. This non-tariff barrier includes a wide range of government actions such as requiring international air carriers to land at inconvenient airports; requiring product inspections that damage the product itself; purposely understaffing customs offices to cause unusual time delays; and requiring special licenses that take a long time to obtain. The objective of such administrative delays for a country is to discriminate against imported products – in a word, it is protectionism.

Although Japan has removed some of its trade barriers, many subtle obstacles to imports remain. Products ranging from cold pills and vitamins to farm products and building materials find it hard to penetrate the Japanese market.

Local content requirements

Laws stipulating that a specified amount of a good or service be supplied by producers in the domestic market are called local content requirements. These requirements can state that a certain portion of the end product consist of domestically produced goods, or that a certain portion of the final cost of a product have domestic sources.

The purpose of local content requirements is to force companies from other nations to employ local resources in their production processes – particularly labour. Similar to other restraints on imports, such requirements help protect domestic producers from the price advantage of companies based in other, low-wage countries. Today, companies can circumvent local content requirements by locating production facilities inside the nation stipulating such restrictions.

Historical development of barriers

Non-tariff barriers become much more prevalent in times of recession. In the USA and Europe we have witnessed the mobilization of quite strong political lobby groups as indigenous industries, which have come under threat, lobby their governments to take measures to protect them from international competition. The last major era of protectionism was in the 1930s. During that decade, under the impact of the most disastrous trade depression in history, most countries of the world adopted high tariffs.

After the Second World War there was a reaction against the high tariff policy of the 1930s and significant efforts were made to move the world back to free trade. World organizations (like GATT and its successor, WTO) have been developed to foster international trade and provide a trade climate in which such barriers can be reduced.

The general international environment

In addition to the politics and laws of both the home and the host countries, the marketer must consider the overall international political and legal environment. Relations between countries can have a profound impact on firms trying to do business internationally.

The international political environment involves political relations between two or more countries. This is in contrast to our previous concern for what happens only within a given foreign country. The international firm almost inevitably becomes somewhat involved with the host country's international relations, no matter how neutral it may try to be. It does so because its operations in a country are frequently related to operations in other countries, either on the supply or the demand side or both. East–West relations are a good example of a situation in the international political environment that is continually evolving.

The effect of politics on global marketing is determined by both the bilateral political relations between home and host countries and the multilateral agreements governing the relations among groups of countries. One aspect of a country's international relations is its relationship with the firm's home country.

A second critical element affecting the political environment is the host country's relations with other nations. If a country is a member of a regional group, such as the EU or ASEAN, this influences the firm's evaluation of the country. If a nation has particular friends or enemies among other nations, the firm must modify its international logistics to comply with how that market is supplied and to whom it can sell.

Another clue to a nation's international behaviour is its membership of international organizations. Membership of the IMF or the World Bank may aid a country's financial situation, but it also puts constraints on the country's behaviour. Many other international agreements impose rules on their members. These agreements may affect, for example, patents, communication, transportation and other items of interest to the international marketer. As a rule, the more international organizations a country belongs to, the more regulations it accepts, and the more dependable is its behaviour.

The political risk analysis procedure

We now outline in general terms a procedure for analyzing political risk and avoiding the common error of over- or underestimating such risk at the firm level. The goal of this procedure is to help firms make informed decisions based on the ratio of the return to risk, so that firms can enter or stay in a country when the ratio is favourable and avoid or leave a country when the ratio for them is poor. This procedure involves three major steps (Figure 5.2).

Step 1: Assessing issues of relevance to the firm

Clearly, the relevant issues and the magnitude of their importance will vary by firm even within a given country. For one firm the repatriation of profits (and therefore policies and changes that affect that issue) could be the most important. For another firm in the same country, repatriation of profits may be less of a concern,

| Figure 5.2 | Three-step process of political risk analysis |

Step 1: Issues of relevance to the firm
Determine critical economic/business issues relevant to the firm. Assess the relative importance of these issues.

Step 2: Potential political events
Determine the relevant political events.
Determine their probability of occurring.
Determine the cause and effect relationships.
Determine the government's ability and willingness to respond.

Step 3: Probable impacts and responses
Determine the initial impact of probable scenarios.
Determine possible responses to initial impacts.
Determine initial and ultimate political risk.

but product quality (and therefore policies and changes that affect labour, material or technology) may be of the highest concern.

Step 2: Assessing potential political events

In general, political instability is more likely during greater periods of economic depression. However, the more the event is controllable and the more government is able and willing to exercise control, the lower the probability that the event will have a direct impact on foreign firms.

It is important to estimate not only the probability of a single political event occurring or the confidence with which that prediction is made, but also the sequence of related events. For example, suppose it was highly likely that Russian president Vladimir Putin was going to be replaced by a new president. Would this have any effect on policies on the repatriation of profits, the regulations of exports and other related issues?

Step 3: Assessing probable impacts and responses

Step 3 is really where 'political risk' for the particular firm is assessed. Because political instability in a country does not equal political risk for a firm, the same scenario of politically destabilizing events could have very different associated risks for different firms in the same industry or for firms in different industries. The fact that firms can be differentially affected by political events because of their unique mix of inputs, outputs and goals reinforces the usefulness of constructing political scenarios rather than single-item forecasts.

Influencing local politics

Managers must be able to deal with the political risks, rules and regulations that apply in each national business environment. Moreover, laws in many nations are susceptible to frequent change, with new laws continually being enacted and existing ones modified. To influence local politics in their favour, managers can propose changes that positively affect their local activities.

● *Lobbying*. Influencing local politics always involves dealing with local lawmakers and politicians, either directly or through lobbyists. Lobbying is the policy of hiring people to represent a company's views on political matters. Lobbyists meet with local public officials and try to influence their position on issues relevant to the company. They describe the benefits that a company brings to the local economy, natural environment, infrastructure, and workforce. Their ultimate goal is getting favourable legislation passed and unfavourable legislation rejected.

● *Corruption*. Bribes are one method of gaining political influence. They are routinely used in some countries to get distributors and retailers to push a firm's products through distribution channels. Sometimes they mean the difference between obtaining important contracts and being completely shut out of certain markets.

In summary, the political risk perspective of a nation can be studied using factors such as those in the following list:

● Change in government policy.
● Stability of government.
● Quality of host government's economic management.
● Host country's attitude towards foreign investment.
● Host country's relationship with the rest of the world.
● Host country's relationship with the parent company's home government.
● Attitude towards the assignment of foreign personnel.
● Closeness between government and people.
● Fairness and honesty of administrative procedures.

The importance of these factors varies from country to country and from firm to firm. Nevertheless, it is desirable to consider them all to ensure a complete knowledge of the political outlook for doing business in a particular country.

5.3 The economic environment

Market size and growth are influenced by many forces, but the total buying power in the country and the availability or non-availability of electricity, telephone systems, modern roads and other types of infrastructure will influence the direction of that spending.

Economic development results from one of three types of economic activity:

● *Primary*. These activities are concerned with agriculture and extractive processes (e.g. coal, iron ore, gold, fishing).
● *Secondary*. These are manufacturing activities. There are several evolutions. Typically countries will start manufacturing through processing the output of primary products.
● *Tertiary*. These activities are based upon *services* – for example, tourism, insurance and health care. As the average family income in a country rises, the percentage of income spent on food declines, the percentage spent on housing and household activities remains constant, and the percentage spent on service activities (e.g. education, transport and leisure) will increase.

How exchange rates influence business activities

Times of crisis are not the only occasions during which companies are affected by exchange rates. In fact, movement in a currency's exchange rate affects the activities of both domestic and international companies. Let's now examine how exchange rate changes affect the business decisions of companies, and why stable and predictable rates are desirable.

Exchange rates affect demand for a company's products in the global marketplace. When a country's currency is *weak* (valued low relative to other currencies), the price of its exports on world markets declines and the price of imports increases. Lower prices make the country's exports more appealing on world markets. They also give companies the opportunity to take market share away from companies whose products are highly priced in comparison.

Furthermore, a company selling in a country with a *strong* currency (one that is valued high relative to other currencies) while paying workers in a country with a weak currency improves its profits.

The international lowering of the value of a currency by the nation's government is called devaluation. The reverse, the intentional raising of its value by the nation's government, is called revaluation. These concepts are not to be confused with the terms *weak* and *strong* currencies, although their effects are similar.

Devaluation lowers the price of a country's exports on world markets and increases the price of imports because the country's currency is now worth less on world markets. Thus, a government might devalue its currency to give its domestic companies an edge over competition from other countries. It might also devalue to boost exports so that a trade deficit can be eliminated. However, such a policy is not wise because devaluation reduces consumers' buying power. It also allows inefficiencies to persist in domestic companies because there is now less pressure to be concerned with production costs. In such a case, increasing inflation may be the result. Revaluation has the opposite effect: it increases the price of exports and reduces the price of imports.

As we have seen, unfavourable movements in exchange rates can be costly for both domestic and international companies. Therefore, managers prefer that exchange rates be *stable*. Stable exchange rates improve the accuracy of financial planning, including cash flow forecasts. Although methods do exist for insuring against potentially adverse exchange rate movements, most of these are too expensive for small and medium-sized businesses. Moreover, as the unpredictability of exchange rates increases, so too does the cost of insuring against the accompanying risk.

Law of one price

An exchange rate tells us how much of one currency we must pay to receive a certain amount of another. But it does not tell us whether a specific product will actually cost us more or less in a particular country (as measured in our own currency). When we travel to another country, we discover that our own currency buys more or less than it does at home. In other words, we quickly learn that exchange rates do not guarantee or stabilize the buying power of our currency. Thus, we can lose purchasing power in some countries while gaining it in others.

The law of one price stipulates that an identical product must have an identical price in all countries when price is expressed in a common-denominator currency. For this principle to apply, products must be identical in quality and content in all countries, and must be entirely produced within each particular country.

Big Mac Index/Big MacCurrencies

The usefulness of the law of one price is that it helps us determine whether a currency is overvalued or undervalued. Each year *The Economist* magazine publishes what it calls its 'Big MacCurrencies' exchange-rate index (see Table 5.1). This index uses the law of one price to determine the exchange rate that should exist between the US dollar and other major currencies. It employs the McDonald's Big Mac as its single product to test the law of one price. Why the Big Mac? Because each Big Mac is fairly identical in quality and content across national markets and almost entirely produced within the nation in which it is sold. The underlying assumption is that the price of a Big Mac in any world currency should, after being converted to dollars, equal the price of a Big Mac in the United States. A country's currency

| Table 5.1 | The Big Mac index: April–May 2000 |

	Big Mac prices		Implied PPP* of the dollar	Actual $ exchange rate 25/04/00	Under(−)/ over (+) valuation against the dollar, %
	in local currency	in dollars			
United States†	$2.51	2.51	—	—	—
Argentina	Peso2.50	2.50	1.00	1.00	0
Australia	A$2.59	1.54	1.03	1.68	−38
Brazil	Real2.95	1.65	1.18	1.79	−34
Britain	£1.90	3.00	1.32‡	1.58‡	+20
Canada	C$2.85	1.94	1.14	1.47	−23
Chile	Peso1,260	2.45	502.00	514.00	−2
China	Yuan9.90	1.20	3.94	8.28	−52
Czech Rep	Koruna54.37	1.39	21.70	39.10	−45
Denmark	DKr24.75	3.08	9.86	8.04	+23
Euro area	€2.56	2.37	0.98§	0.93§	−5
France	FFr18.50	2.62	7.37	7.07	+4
Germany	DM4.99	2.37	1.99	2.11	−6
Italy	Lire4,500	2.16	1,793.00	2,088.00	−14
Spain	Pta375	2.09	149.00	179.00	−17
Hong Kong	HK$10.20	1.31	4.06	7.79	−48
Hungary	Forint339	1.21	135.00	279.00	−52
Indonesia	Rupiah14,500	1.83	5,777.00	7,945.00	−27
Israel	Shekel14.5	3.58	5.78	4.05	+43
Japan	¥294	2.78	117.00	106.00	+11
Malaysia	M$4.52	1.19	1.80	3.80	−53
Mexico	Peso20.90	2.22	8.33	9.41	−11
New Zealand	NZ$3.40	1.69	1.35	2.01	−33
Poland	Zloty5.50	1.28	2.19	4.30	−49
Russia	Rouble39.50	1.39	15.70	28.50	−45
Singapore	S$3.20	1.88	1.27	1.70	−25
South Africa	Rand9.00	1.34	3.59	6.72	−47
South Korea	Won3,000	2.71	1,195.00	1,108.00	+8
Sweden	SKr24.00	2.71	9.56	8.84	+8
Switzerland	SFr5.90	3.48	2.35	1.70	+39
Taiwan	NT$70.00	2.29	27.90	30.60	−9
Thailand	Baht55.00	1.45	21.90	38.00	−42

* Purchasing-power parity: local price divided by price in United States
† Average of New York, Chicago, San Francisco and Atlanta
‡ Dollars per pound
§ Dollars per euro
Source: The Economist, 29 April 2000

would be overvalued if the Big Mac price (converted to dollars) is higher than the US price. Conversely, a country's currency would be undervalued if the converted Big Mac price was lower than the US price. According to the Big Mac index, the average price of a Big Mac was $2.51 in the United States. The cheapest Big Macs were found in China and Malaysia at a dollar-equivalent price of $1.19–1.20, the most expensive in Israel at $3.58. According to the Big Mac index, therefore, the Malaysian ringgit is undervalued by 53 per cent. On the other hand, the Israeli shekel is overvalued by 43 per cent.

Such large discrepancies between a currency's exchange rate on currency markets and the rate predicted by the Big Mac index are not surprising for several reasons. For one thing, the selling price of food is affected by subsidies for agricultural products in most countries. Also, the Big Mac is not a 'traded' product in the sense that one can buy Big Macs in low-priced countries and sell them in high-priced countries. Prices can also be affected because Big Macs are subject to different marketing strategies in different countries. Finally, countries impose different levels of sales tax on restaurant meals.

The drawbacks of the Big Mac index reflect the fact that applying the law of one price to a single product is too simplistic a method for estimation of exchange rates. Nonetheless, a recent study finds that currency values in eight out of twelve industrial countries do tend to change in the direction suggested by the Big Mac index. And for six out of seven currencies that change more than 10 per cent, the Big Mac index was as good a predictor as more sophisticated methods.

Table 5.1 also uses the concept of purchasing power parity (PPP), which economists use when adjusting national income data (GNP etc.) to improve comparability. PPPs are the rates of currency conversion that equalize the purchasing power of different currencies by eliminating the differences in price levels between countries. In their simplest form, PPPs are simply price relatives which show the ratio of the prices in national currencies of the same good or service in different countries.

The easiest way to see how a PPP is calculated is to consider Table 5.1 for a product which is identical in several countries. For example, a Big Mac costs CAD2.85 in Canada. If we divide 2.85 with the price in USA, USD2.51, the result will be the PPP of the dollar = 1.14 (the 'theoretical' exchange rate of CAD). Then if we divide 1.14 with the actual exchange rate, 1.47, we find that the CAD is undervalued by $1 - (1.14/1.47) \times 100 = 23\%$.

PPPs are not only calculated for individual products; they are calculated for a 'basket' of products, and PPP is meaningful only when applied to such a 'basket' of products.

Classification by income

Countries can be classified in a variety of ways. Most classifications are based on national income (GDP or GNP per capita) and the degree of industrialization. The broadcast measure of economic development is *gross national product* (GNP) – the value of all goods and services produced by a country during a one-year period. This figure includes income generated both by domestic production and by the country's international activities. *Gross domestic product* (GDP) is the value of all goods and services produced by the domestic economy over a one-year period. In other words, when we add to GDP the income generated from exports, imports, and the international operations of a nation's companies, we get GNP. A country's GNP per capita is simply its GNP divided by its population. GDP per capita is calculated similarly.

Both GNP per capita and GDP per capita measure a nation's income per person.

Less developed countries (LDCs)

This group includes underdeveloped countries and developing countries. The main features are a low GDP per capita (less than $3,000), limited amount of manufacturing activity and a very poor and fragmented infrastructure. Typical infrastructure weaknesses are in transport, communications, education and health care. In addition, the public sector is often slow moving and bureaucratic.

It is common to find that LDCs are heavily reliant on one product and often on one trading partner. The typical pattern for single-product dependence is the reliance on one agricultural crop, or on mining. Colombia (coffee) and Cuba (sugar) are examples of extreme dependence upon agriculture. The risks posed to the LDC by changing patterns of supply and demand are great. Falling commodity prices can result in large decreases in earnings for the whole country. The resultant economic and political adjustments may affect exporters to that country through possible changes in tariff and non-tariff barriers.

A wide range of economic circumstances influences the development of the less developed countries in the world. Without real prospects for rapid economic development, private sources of capital are reluctant to invest in such countries. This is particularly the case for long-term infrastructure projects. As a result, important capital spending projects rely heavily on world aid programmes.

The quality of distribution channels varies considerably between countries. There are often great differences between the small-scale, undercapitalized distribution intermediaries in LDCs and the distributors in more advanced countries. Retailers, for example, are more likely to be market traders. The incidence of large-scale self-service outlets will be comparatively low.

Newly industrialized countries (NICs)

NICs are countries with an emerging industrial base: one that is capable of exporting. Examples of NICs are the 'tigers' of south-east Asia: Hong Kong, Singapore, South Korea and Taiwan. Brazil and Mexico are examples of NICs from South America. In NICs, although the infrastructure shows considerable development, high growth in the economy results in difficulties with producing what is demanded by domestic and foreign customers.

Advanced industrialized countries (ACs)

These countries have considerable GDP per capita, a wide industrial base, considerable development in the services sector and substantial investment in the infrastructure of the country.

This attempt to classify the economies of the world into neat divisions is not completely successful. For example, some of the advanced industrialized countries (e.g. the USA and France) have important agricultural sectors.

Regional economic integration

Economic integration has been one of the main economic developments affecting world markets since the Second World War. Countries have wanted to engage in economic cooperation to use their respective resources more effectively and to provide large markets for member-country producers.

Some integration efforts have had quite ambitious goals, such as political integration; some have failed as a result of perceptions of unequal benefits from the arrangement or a parting of ways politically. Figure 5.3, a summary of the major forms of economic cooperation in regional markets, shows the varying degrees of formality with which integration can take place. These economic integration efforts are dividing the world into trading blocs.

The levels of economic integration will now be described.

Free trade area

The free trade area is the least restrictive and loosest form of economic integration among nations. In a free trade area, all barriers to trade among member countries are removed. Each member country maintains its own trade barriers *vis-à-vis* non-members.

The European Free Trade Area (EFTA) was formed in 1960 with an agreement by eight European countries. Since that time, EFTA has lost much of its original

Figure 5.3   Forms of economic integration in regional markets

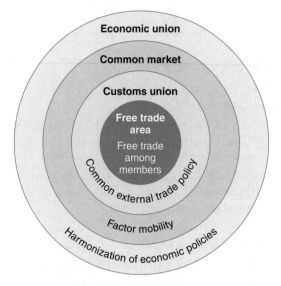

(Source: Czinkota and Ronkainen, 1996, p. 112)

significance due to its members joining the European Union (EU) (Denmark and the United Kingdom in 1973, Portugal in 1986, and Austria, Finland and Sweden in 1995). All EFTA countries have cooperated with the EU through bilateral free trade agreements, and since 1994 through the European Economic Area (EEA) arrangement that allows for free movement of people, products, services and capital within the combined area of the EU and EFTA. Of the EFTA countries, Iceland and Liechtenstein have decided not to apply for membership of the EU and Norway turned down membership after a referendum in 1994. Switzerland also decided to stay out of the EU.

After three failed tries during this century, the United States and Canada signed a free trade agreement that went into effect in 1989. North American free trade expanded in 1994 by the inclusion of Mexico in the North American Free Trade Agreement (NAFTA).

Customs union

The customs union is one step further along the spectrum of economic integration. As in the free trade area, goods and services are freely traded among members of the customs union. In addition, however, the customs union establishes a common trade policy with respect to non-members. Typically, this takes the form of a common external tariff, whereby imports from non-members are subject to the same tariff when sold to any member country. The Benelux countries formed a customs union in 1921 that later became part of wider European economic integration.

Common market

The common market has the same features as a customs union. In addition, factors of production (labour, capital and technology) are mobile among members. Restrictions on immigration and cross-border investment are abolished. When factors of production are mobile, capital, labour and technology may be employed in their most productive uses.

The removal of barriers to the free movement of goods, services, capital and people in Europe was ratified by the passing of the Single European Act in 1987 with the target date of 31 December 1992 to complete the internal market. In December 1991 the EC agreed in Maastricht that the so-called 1992 process would be a step towards cooperation beyond the economic dimension. While many of the directives aimed at opening borders and markets were completed on schedule, some sectors, such as cars, will take longer to open up.

Economic union

The creation of true economic union requires integration of economic policies in addition to the free movement of goods, services and factors of production across borders. Under an economic union, members harmonize monetary policies, taxation and government spending. In addition, a common currency is used by members and this could involve a system of fixed exchange rates. The ratification of the Maastricht Treaty in late 1993 resulted in the European Union (EU) being effective from 1 January 1994. Clearly the formation of a full economic union requires the surrender of a large measure of national sovereignty to a supranational body. Such a union is only a short step away from political unification, but many countries in the EU (especially in the northern part of Europe) are sceptical about this development because they feel a loss of national identity.

Benefits of regional integration

Nations engage in specialization and trade because of the gains in output and consumption, and higher standards of living for all should result from higher levels of trade between nations.

Trade creation

As we have seen, economic integration removes barriers to trade and/or investment for nations belonging to a trading bloc. The increase in the level of trade between nations that results from regional economic integration is called trade creation. One result of trade creation is that consumers and industrial buyers in member nations are faced with a wider selection of goods and services not available before.

Another result of trade creation is that buyers can acquire goods and services at less cost following the lowering of trade barriers such as tariffs. Furthermore, lower costs tend to lead to higher demand for goods because people have more money left over after a purchase to buy other products.

Greater consensus

The World Trade Organization (WTO) works to lower barriers on a global scale. Efforts at regional economic integration differ in that they comprise smaller groups of nations – ranging anywhere from several countries to as many as 30 or more nations. The benefit of trying to eliminate trade barriers in smaller groups of counties is that it can be easier to gain consensus from fewer members as opposed to, say, the 133 countries that comprise the WTO.

Political cooperation

There can also be political benefits from efforts at regional integration. A group of nations can have significantly greater political weight in the world than the nations have individually. Thus nations can have more say when negotiating with other countries. Moreover, integration involving political cooperation can reduce the potential for military conflict between member nations.

Drawbacks of regional integration

Although trade tends to benefit countries, it can also have substantial negative effects. Let's now examine the more important of these.

Trade diversion

The flip side of trade creation is trade diversion – the diversion of trade away from nations not belonging to a trading bloc and toward member nations. Trade diversion can occur after formation of a trading bloc because of the lower tariffs charged between member nations. It can actually result in reduced trade with a more efficient non-member producer and increased trade with a less efficient producer within the trading bloc. In this sense, economic integration can unintentionally reward a less efficient producer within the trading bloc. Unless there is other internal competition for the producer's good or service, buyers will be paying more after trade diversion due to the inefficient production methods of the producer.

Shifts in employment

Perhaps the most controversial aspect of regional economic integration is how people's jobs are affected. Because the formation of trading blocs significantly reduces or eliminates barriers to trade among members, the producer of a particular good or service is more likely to be the most productive producer. Industries requiring mostly unskilled labour, for example, will tend to shift production to low-wage nations within a trading bloc.

Thus trade agreements do cause dislocations in labour markets – some jobs are lost while others are gained.

It is highly likely that countries protecting low-wage domestic industries from competition will see these jobs move to the country where wages are lower once trade and investment barriers are removed. But this is also an opportunity for workers to upgrade their skills and gain more advanced job training. This can help nations increase their competitiveness because a better educated and more skilled workforce attracts higher paying jobs than does a less skilled workforce. However, an opportunity for a nation to improve some abstract 'factors of production' is little consolation to people finding themselves suddenly without work.

Loss of national sovereignty

Successive levels of integration require that nations surrender more of their national sovereignty. A certain amount of sovereignty has to be surrendered to the trading bloc.

Major trading blocs

Table 5.2 shows the major trading blocs together with their population, GNP and GNP per capita. The size and economic importance of the USA and Japan stand out. The affluence of Luxembourg and Switzerland – both small countries – is marked by high values of GNP per head.

Besides the major trading blocs mentioned in Table 5.2 the most important global market will be the Triad.

The triad of Europe, North America and Japan

The global economic size of these three, Europe, USA and Japan, is disproportionate to their actual number of physical size. Ohmae (1985) cites Japan and the USA alone as accounting for 30 per cent of the Free World Total and that with the addition of UK, West Germany, France and Italy this increases to 45 per cent. Aside from

Table 5.2	Major trading blocs

Organization	Type	Members	Population (million)	GNP (US$bn)	GNP per capita (US$)
European Union	Political and economic union	Belgium	10.2	259.0	25,380
		Luxembourg	0.4	19.2	45,100
		Denmark	5.3	175.2	33,040
		France	58.8	1,465.4	24,210
		Germany	82.0	2,179.8	26,570
		Ireland	3.7	69.3	18,710
		Italy	57.6	1,157.0	20,090
		UK	59.1	1,264.3	21,410
		Netherlands	15.7	389.1	24,780
		Greece	10.5	123.4	11,740
		Portugal	10.0	106.4	10,670
		Spain	39.4	555.2	14,100
		Sweden	8.9	226.5	25,580
		Austria	8.1	216.7	26,830
		Finland	5.2	125.1	24,280
		Total	374.9	8,331.6	22,224
Association of South East Asian Nations (ASEAN)	Limited trade and cooperation agreement	Indonesia	203.7	130.6	640
		Brunei	n.a.	n.a.	n.a.
		Vietnam	76.5	26.5	350
		Malaysia	22.2	81.3	3,670
		Singapore	3.2	95.5	30,170
		Philippines	75.2	78.9	1,050
		Thailand	61.2	131.9	2,160
		Total	442.0	414.1	937
Asia Pacific Economic Cooperation (APEC, excl. ASEAN, USA and Canada)	Formal institution	China	1,238.6	923.6	750
		Japan	126.4	4,089.1	32,350
		South Korea	46.4	398.8	8,600
		Taiwan[a]	21.8	261.6	12,000
		Australia	18.8	387.0	20,640
		New Zealand	3.8	55.4	14,600
		Total	1,455.8	6,115.5	4,201
North American Free Trade Area (NAFTA)	Free trade area	USA	270.3	7,903.0	29,240
		Canada	30.3	580.9	19,170
		Mexico	95.8	368.1	3,840
		Total	396.4	8,852.0	22,331

[a] Estimated from different sources as Taiwan is not in the World Bank statistics.
Source: Adapted from World Bank Atlas (2000).

economic wealth, these countries share other similarities as well: mature stagnant economies, ageing populations, dynamic technological developments taking place, costs of research and development constantly escalating as are production facilities. This is all part of the new reality as Ohmae sees it.

This triad creates a market of 600 million with marked demographic similarities and levels of purchasing power as a result of:

● growth of capital intensive manufacturing,

● accelerated tempo of new technology,

● concentrated pattern of consumption.

A reaction to any of those forces above is protectionism. Ohmae shows that industries critical to wealth generation in the 1980s were all concentrated in Japan, USA and Europe, constituting more than 80 per cent of global production and consumption. The implication of the triad is that these 600 million consumers share the same desires for the same goods: Gucci bags, Sony Walkmans, McDonald's hamburgers, etc. While there is an international youth market for denims, CDs and tapes, tastes are not the same nor is purchasing power equal either. Psychographic segmentation based on values and attitudes which may also be shared across national boundaries is what is important.

The answer to market entry in each of the triad regions comes through consortia and joint ventures which pose a new challenge for the corporation, as Ohmae points out, of learning how to communicate institutionally with the very different corporate cultures and languages of other companies. This ties in with the networking approach of the IMP research group.

Per capita income

The statistic most frequently used to describe a country economically is its per capita income. This figure is used as a shorthand expression for a country's level of economic development as well as its degree of modernization and progress in health, education and welfare. Partial justification for using this figure in evaluating a foreign economy lies in the fact that it is commonly available and widely accepted. A more pertinent justification is that it is, in fact, a good indicator of the size or quality of a market.

The per capita income figures vary widely among the countries of the world. The World Bank finds over half the world's population living in countries with an average per capita income of only $330.

However, a number of criticisms can be made of per capita income figures:

● *Purchasing power is not reflected.* Per capita income comparisons are expressed in a common currency – usually US dollars – through an exchange rate conversion. The dollar figure for a country is derived by dividing its per capita income figure in national currency by its rate of exchange against the dollar. The resulting dollar statistic for a country's per capita income is accurate only if the exchange rate reflects the relative domestic purchasing power of the two currencies. There is often reason for doubting that it does. For example, the impact of speculation can pull a currency away from its 'true' value.

● *Lack of comparability.* Another limitation to the use of per capita income figures is that there is a twofold lack of comparability in the income figures themselves. Goods entering into the national income totals of the developed economies are only partially in the money economy in less developed countries. A large part of a European's budget, for example, goes for food, clothing and shelter. In many less developed nations, these items may be largely self-provided and are therefore not reflected in national income totals.

● *Sales are not related to per capita income.* Another limitation to using per capita income figures to indicate market potential is that the sales of many goods show little correlation with per capita income. Many consumer goods sales correlate more closely with population or household figures than with per capita income. Some examples might be Coca-Cola, ballpoint pens, bicycles, sewing machines and transistor radios. Industrial goods and capital equipment sales generally correlate better with industrial structure or total national income than with per capita income.

● *Uneven income distribution.* Finally, per capita figures are less meaningful if there is great unevenness of income distribution in the country. This has already been discussed. Per capita income figures are averages and are meaningful if most people of the country are near the average. Frequently, however, this is not the case. Among world nations, the Scandinavian countries have a relatively equal distribution of income among people. Even here, however, marketers are very attentive to differences in income levels when studying potential for their product if the product is at all income sensitive. Many countries have a relatively uneven distribution of income. An extreme example is Brazil, where the lowest 20 per cent of the population receive less than 3 per cent of the national income, whereas the highest 20 per cent receive 63 per cent of that income.

| Table 5.3 | Consumption expenditures of selected countries |

Country	Food and beverages	Clothing and footwear	Housing and operations	Household furnishing	Medical care and health	Transportation	Recreation	Other
Industrial market economies								
Belgium	19.7	6.8	17.7	10.7	10.6	13.1	6.6	14.8
Canada	16.2	5.7	22.4	9.7	4.2	15.8	11.3	14.7
France	19.4	6.2	17.8	8.2	10.5	6.8	8.1	13.0
Japan	20.8	6.1	18.6	6.3	10.4	10.7	10.6	16.5
Sweden	22.3	8.4	23.5	6.8	2.7	17.9	10.5	8.0
UK	21.1	6.7	18.4	7.2	1.3	18.3	10.1	17.0
USA	13.3	7.7	17.4	6.3	12.4	16.4	11.7	14.8
Middle-income countries								
Mexico	37.4	8.2	12.6	12.4	4.0	9.1	5.6	10.8
Philippines	60.0	5.3	3.1	13.5	n.a.	2.3	n.a.	15.8
Republic of Korea	36.8	4.7	9.9	6.1	7.2	11.2	11.9	12.3
Low-income countries								
India	53.5	13.1	11.1	4.9	2.4	7.5	3.2	4.3
Sri Lanka	52.7	10.1	4.2	5.5	1.3	18.3	4.1	3.9

Note: The expenditures are expressed as percentages of total consumption in constant prices. 'Other' includes expenditures for personal care, restaurants and hotels. n.a. indicates that data are not available.
Source: Jain (1996), p. 192.

Structure of consumption

While it is important to measure the volume of consumption among various cultures, nations and societies, the characteristics of that consumption reveal its structure. Depending on economic factors, a country may have to emphasize producer goods over consumer goods. Moreover, what are considered necessities in one economy may be luxuries in another. In addition, consumption in most advanced countries is characterized by a higher proportion of expenditures devoted to capital goods than in poor countries, where substantially more is spent on consumer goods.

The structural differences with regard to expenditures among nations can be explained by a theory propounded by the German statistician Engel. The law of consumption (Engel's law) states that poorer families and societies spend a greater proportion of their income on food than well-to-do people. Housing, in particular, receives a much smaller share of income in underdeveloped countries than in the advanced nations (Table 5.3).

The structure of consumption varies among developed countries. While the average person in England eats 13 pounds of cereal a year, per capita consumption in France is just 1 pound, and in Japan less than one-quarter of a pound. Americans eat about 10 pounds of cereal each per year (Jain, 1996, p. 193).

5.4 Summary

In this chapter concern has rested on analyzing the political/legal and the economic environment as it affects the firm in international markets. Most companies are unable to influence the environment of their markets directly but their opportunities for successful business conduct largely depend on the structure and content of that environment. A marketer serving international markets or planning to do so, therefore, has to assess carefully the political and legal environments of the markets served or under consideration to draw the appropriate managerial consequences.

Political environment

The international marketer's political environment is complex because of the interaction among domestic, foreign and international politics. When investing in a foreign country, firms have to be sensitive to that country's political concerns. The firm should prepare a monitoring system that allows it to systematically evaluate the political risks – such as expropriation, nationalization and restrictions against exports and/or imports. Through skilful adaptation and control, political risks can be reduced or neutralized.

Tariffs have traditionally been used as barriers to international trade. International trade liberalization during the last decade of the twentieth century has led to a significant reduction of tariff barriers. Therefore, governments have been increasingly using non-tariff barriers to protect some of their countries' industries which they think are unable to sustain free international competition. A government may also support or deter international business through its investment policy, that is, the general rules governing legislation concerning domestic as well as foreign participation in the equity or ownership of businesses and other organizations of the country.

There are various trade barriers that can inhibit global marketing. Although nations have used the WTO (the former GATT) to lessen many of the restrictions, many of these barriers will undoubtedly remain.

Economic environment

The economic environment is a major determinant of market potential and opportunity. Significant variations in national markets originate in economic differences. Population characteristics, of course, represent one major dimension. The income and wealth of the nation's people are also extremely important because these key figures determine people's purchasing power. Countries and markets may be at different stages of economic development, each stage having different characteristics.

Formal methods for gauging economic development in other nations include (a) national production, such measures as *gross national product (GNP)* and *gross domestic product (GDP)*; (b) *purchasing power parity (PPP)*, or the relative ability of two countries' currencies to buy the same 'basket' of goods in those two countries. This index is used to correct comparisons that are made.

Case study | World Bank and the IMF

What on earth is globalization about? Massive protests during a meeting in Washington

The Internet may be spearheading a global communications revolution; fashion designers may embrace 'ethnic' hues and styles; McDonald's may spread its restaurants across the globe. Globalization is a reality that, for better or worse, touches our lives in ways most us never stop to think about. Many would certainly say it was a good thing. Increased international trade has made us wealthier and allowed us to lead more diverse lifestyles.

But the legions of demonstrators now amassing in Washington for the spring 2000 meetings of the International Monetary Fund and the World Bank disagree. The coalition of environmentalists, anti-poverty campaigners, trade unionists and anti-capitalist groups see the growth of global companies as raising more problems than it solves.

Some would say the world was as globalized 100 years ago as it is today, with international trade and migration. But the 1930s depression put paid to that. Nation states drew back into their shell on realizing that international markets could deliver untold misery in the form of poverty and unemployment. The resolve of Western states to build and strengthen international ties in the aftermath of the Second World War laid the groundwork for today's globalization. It has brought diminishing national borders and the fusing of individual national markets. The fall of protectionist barriers has stimulated free movement of capital and paved the way for companies to set up several bases around the world. The rise of the Internet and recent advances in telecommunications have boosted the already surging train.

For consumers and avowed capitalists, this is largely a good thing. Vigorous trade has made for more choice in the high street, greater spending, rising living standards and a growth in international travel. Supporters of globalization say it has promoted information exchange, led to a greater understanding of other cultures and allowed democracy to triumph in most countries.

But as the street protests against the November 1999 World Trade Organisation conference in Seattle proved, there is a growing opposition to the forces of globalization. Critics say the West's gain has been at the expense of developing countries. The already meagre share of the global income of the poorest people in the world has dropped from 2.3 per cent to 1.4 per cent in the last decade. But even in the developed world, not everyone has been a winner. The freedoms granted by globalization are leading to increased insecurity in the workplace. Manual workers in particular are under threat as companies shift their production lines overseas to low-wage economies.

At the heart of the demonstrators' concerns is the fact that huge transnational companies are becoming more powerful and influential than democratically elected governments, putting shareholder interests above those of communities and even customers. Ecological campaigners say corporations are disregarding the environment in the stampede for worldwide mega-profits. Human rights groups say corporate power is restricting individual freedom. Even business people behind small firms have sympathy for the movement, afraid as they are that global economies of scale will put them out of work.

The mere fact the debate can take place simultaneously across countries and continents, however, may well show that the celebrated global village is already here.

Questions

1. What are the the the key arguments of the demonstrators at the annual meeting of the IMF and World Bank?

2. How could these massive protests affect the operations of multinational companies?

3. How could the IMF and World Bank do a better marketing job in communicating their views to the global audience?

(Source: Adapted from BBC News, 14 April 2000, http://news.bbc.co.uk/hi/english/special_report/1999/02/99/ e-cyclopedia/newsid_711000/711906.stm)

Questions for discussion

1. Identify different types of barrier to the free movement of goods and services.

2. Explain the importance of a common European currency to firms selling goods to the European market.

3. How useful is GNP when undertaking a comparative analysis of world markets? What other approaches would you recommend?

4. Discuss the limitations of per capita income in evaluating market potential.

5. Distinguish among (a) free trade area, (b) customs union, (c) common market, (d) economic and monetary union and (e) political union.

6. Why is the international marketer interested in the age distribution of the population in a market?

7. Describe the ways in which foreign exchange fluctuations affect (1) trade, (2) investments, (3) tourism.

8. Why is political stability so important for international marketers? Find some recent examples from the press to underline your points.

9. How can the change of major political goals in a country have an impact on the potential for success of an international marketer?

10. A country's natural environment influences its attractiveness to an international marketer of industrial products. Discuss.

11. Explain why a country's balance of trade may be of interest to an international marketer.

Internet exercise

Caterpillar and John Deere

Please go to:

http://www.cat.com/

http://www.deere.com/ (Latest annual report of John Deere:

http://www.deere.com/deerecom/Investors+and+Stockholders/default.htm)

Question

1. Which political and economic factors in the global environment would have the biggest effect on:

   (a) The global sales of Caterpillar construction and mining equipment?

   (b) The global sales of John Deere agricultural machinery?

For further exercises and cases, see this book's website at *www.booksites.net/hollensen*

References

Albaum, G., Strandskov, J., Duerr, E. and Dowd, L. (1994) *International Marketing and Export Management* (2nd edn), Addison Wesley, Reading, MA.

Czinkota, M.R. and Ronkainen, I.A. (1996) *Global Marketing*, The Dryden Press, Fort Worth.

Jain, S.C. (1996) *International Marketing Managment*, South-Western College Publishing, Cincinnati, OH.

Ohmae, K. (1985) *Triad Power: The coming shape of global competition*, Free Press, New York.

Walters, P.G.P and Zhu, Z. (1995) 'International marketing in Chinese enterprises: some evidence from the PRC', *Management International Review*, vol. 35, no. 3, pp. 265–77.

World Bank (2000) *World Bank Atlas*, Washington, DC.

6

The sociocultural environment

Learning objectives

After studying this chapter you should be able to do the following

- Discuss how the sociocultural environment will affect the attractiveness of a potential market.

- Define culture and name some of its elements.

- Explain the '4 + 1' dimensions in Hofstede's model.

- Discuss the strengths and weaknesses of Hofstede's model.

- Discuss whether the world's cultures are converging or diverging.

6.1 Introduction

Culture as a concept is very difficult to define. Every author who has dealt with culture has given a different definition. Hofstede's (1980) definition is perhaps the best known to management scholars and is used here. *Culture is the collective programming of the mind which distinguishes the members of one human group from another. … Culture, in this sense, includes systems of values; and values are among the building blocks of culture* (p. 21).

The importance of culture to the international marketer is profound. It is an obvious source of difference. Some cultural differences are easier to manage than others. In tackling markets in which buyers speak different languages or follow other religions, for instance, the international marketer can plan in advance to manage specific points of difference. Often a greater problem is to understand the underlying attitudes and values of buyers in different countries.

The concept of culture is broad and extremely complex. It encompasses virtually every part of a person's life. The way in which people live together in a society is influenced by religion, education, family and reference groups. It is also influenced by legal, economic, political and technological forces. There are various interactions between these influences. We can look for cultural differences in the ways different societies communicate: different spoken languages are used, and the importance of spoken and other methods of communication (e.g. the use of space between people) will vary. The importance of work, the use of leisure, and the types of reward and recognition that people value vary from culture to culture. In some countries, people are highly motivated by monetary rewards, while in other countries and cultures social position and recognition are more important.

Culture develops through recurrent social relationships which form patterns that are eventually internalized by members of the entire group. In other words, a culture does not stand still, but changes slowly over time. Finally, cultural differences are not necessarily visible but can be quite subtle, and can surface in situations where one would never notice them.

It is commonly agreed that a culture must have these three characteristics:

- It is learned: that is, acquired by people over time through their membership of a group that transmits culture from generation to generation. In the case of a national culture, you learn most intensively in the early years of life. By the age of five you are already an expert in using your language. You have internalized values associated with such functions as

  - interacting with other members of your family,

  - eliciting rewards and avoiding punishments,

  - negotiation for what you wanted,

  - causing and avoiding conflict.

- It is interrelated: that is, one part of the culture is deeply connected with another part such as religion and marriage, business and social status.

- It is shared: that is, tenets of a culture extend to other members of the group. The cultural values are passed on to an individual by other members of the culture group. These include parents, other adults, family, institutions such as schools, and friends.

Culture can be thought of as having three other levels (Figure 6.1). The tangible aspects of a culture – things you can see, hear, smell, taste or touch – are artefacts or manifestations of underlying values and assumptions that a group of people share. The structure of these elements is like that of an iceberg, as in Figure 6.1.

The part of the iceberg that you see above the water is only a small fraction of what is there. What you cannot see are the values and assumptions that can sink your ship if you mistakenly run into them. Daily behaviour is influenced by values and social morals which work closer to the surface than the basic cultural assumptions. The values and social norms help people to make adjustments to their short-term daily behaviour; these standards change over shorter periods of time (ten or twenty years) whereas the basic cultural assumptions are probably formed over centuries.

For the purposes of this book we will define culture as the learned ways in which a society understands, decides and communicates.

One way to approach the analysis of cultural influences is to examine cultures by means of a high context/low context analysis. Because languages are an important component of culture and an important means of communication, we will look at spoken languages and silent languages.

| Figure 6.1 | The visible and invisible parts of culture |

The visible daily behaviour
e.g. – body language
– clothing
– lifestyle
– drinking and eating habits

Values and social morals
e.g. – family values
– sex roles
– friendship patterns

Basic cultural assumptions
e.g. – national identity
– ethnic culture
– religion

The differences between some cultures may be large. Language and value differences between the Swiss and Chinese cultures, for instance, are considerable. There are also differences between the Spanish and Italian cultures, but they are much less. Both have languages based on Latin, they use the same written form of communication and they have similar, although not identical, values and norms.

| Exhibit 6.1 | Scotch whisky crossing international borders |

Scotch whisky is consumed globally but bought for many different reasons. The right image has to be communicated for each culture, without of course losing any of the product's core brand values. The key value for Scotch generally is status.

In the UK this tends to be underplayed, never brash or 'in-your-face'. In Italy the image is more tied to machismo and any Scotch ad would have to show a man with a woman on his arm, and flaunting the status the drink confers. In Japan, however, the status value is all about going with the majority. It is not aspirational to be individualistic in Japan.

Thus the understated drinker image that might work in the UK is inappropriate in other countries.

(Source: Adapted from Boundary Commission, *Marketing Week*, London, 29 January 1998; Sophie MacKenzie)

In different cultures, the use of communication techniques varies. In some languages, communication is based strictly on the words that are said or written; in others, the more ambiguous elements such as surroundings or the social status of the message-giver are important variables in the transmission of understanding. Hall (1960) used this finding to make a generalized division between what he referred to as 'low-context cultures' and 'high-context cultures'.

6.2] Layers of culture

The norms of behaviour accepted by the members of the company organization becomes increasingly important with the company's internationalization. When people with increasingly diverse national cultural backgrounds are hired by international firms, the layers of culture can provide a common framework to understand the various individuals' behaviour and their decision-making process of how to do business.

The behaviour of the individual person is influenced by different layers of culture. The national culture determines the values that influence business/industry culture which then determines the culture of the individual company.

Figure 6.2 illustrates a typical negotiation situation between a seller in one country and a buyer in another country. The behaviour of the individual buyer or seller is influenced by cultural aspects on different levels, which are interrelated in a complex way. Each of the different levels influences the individual's probable behaviour.

In Figure 6.2 the different levels are looked at from a 'nesting' perspective, where the different culture levels are nested into each other in order to grasp the cultural interplay between the levels. The total nest consists of the following levels:

- *National culture*. This gives the overall framework of cultural concepts and legislation for business activities.

- *Business/industry culture*. Every business is conducted within a certain competitive framework and within a specific industry (or service sector). Sometimes these

| Figure 6.2 | The different layers of culture |

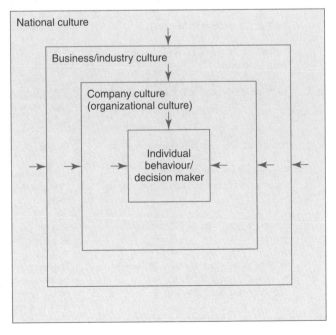

may overlap but, in general, a firm should be able to articulate quite clearly what business it is in. This level has its own cultural roots and history, and the players within this level know the rules of the game. Industry culture is very much related to a branch of industry, and this culture of business behaviour and ethics is similar across borders. For example, shipping, the oil business, international trading and electronics have similar characteristics across national borders.

● *Company culture (organizational culture).* The total organization often contains subcultures of various functions. Functional culture is expressed through the shared values, beliefs, meanings and behaviours of the members of a function within an organization (e.g. marketing, finance, shipping, purchasing, top management and blue-collar workers).

● *Individual behaviour.* The individual is affected by the other cultural levels. In the interaction environment, the individual becomes the core person who 'interacts' with the other actors in industrial marketing settings. The individual is seen as important because there are individual differences in perceiving

Table 6.1   General comparative characteristics of cultures

Characteristic	Low-context/individualistic (e.g. western Europe, USA)	High-context/collectivistic (e.g. Japan, China, Saudi Arabia)
Communication and language	Explicit, direct	Implicit, indirect
Sense of self and space	Informal handshakes	Formal hugs, bows and handshakes
Dress and appearance	Dress for individual success, wide variety	Indication of position in society, religious rule
Food and eating habits	Eating is a necessity, fast food	Eating is social event
Time consciousness	Linear, exact, promptness is valued, time = money	Elastic, relative, time spent on enjoyment, time = relationships
Family and friends	Nuclear family, self oriented, value youth	Extended family, other oriented, loyalty and responsibility, respect for old age
Values and norms	Independence, confrontation of conflict	Group conformity, harmony
Beliefs and attitudes	Egalitarian, challenge authority, individuals control destiny, gender equity	Hierarchical, respect for authority, individuals accept destiny, gender roles
Mental process and learning	Linear, logical, sequential, problem solving	Lateral, holistic, simultaneous, accepting life's difficulties
Business/work habits	Deal oriented ('Quickly getting down to business'), rewards based on achievement, work has value	Relationship oriented ('First you make a friend, then you make a deal'), rewards based on seniority, work is a necessity

the world. Culture is learned; it is not innate. The learning process creates individuals due to different environments in learning and different individual characteristics.

6.3 High- and low-context cultures

Edward T. Hall (1960) introduced the concept of high and low contexts as a way of understanding different cultural orientation. Table 6.1 summarizes some of the ways in which high- and low-context cultures differ.

● *Low-context cultures* rely on spoken and written language for meaning. Senders of messages encode their messages, expecting that the receivers will accurately decode the words used to gain a good understanding of the intended message.

● *High-context cultures* use and interpret more of the elements surrounding the message to develop their understanding of the message. In high-context cultures, the social importance and knowledge of the person and the social setting add extra information, and will be perceived by the message-receiver.

Figure 6.3 shows the contextual differences in the cultures around the world. At one extreme are the low-context cultures of northern Europe. At the other extreme are the high-context cultures. The Japanese and Arabs have a complex way of communicating with people according to their sociodemographic background.

The greater the context difference between those trying to communicate, the greater the difficulty in achieving accurate communication.

Figure 6.3 **The contextual continuum of differing cultures**

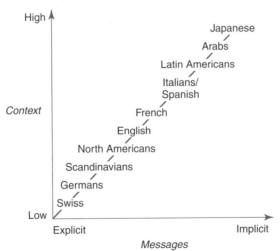

(Source: Usunier, J.-C. (2000). *International Marketing*, Pearson Education Limited.

6.4 ▌ Elements of culture

There are varying definitions of the elements of culture, including one (Murdoch, 1945) that counts 73 'cultural universals'.

The following elements are usually included in the concept of culture:

Language

A country's language is the key to its culture and can be described as the mirror of the culture. Thus, if one is to work extensively with any one culture, it is imperative to learn the language. Learning a language well means learning the culture because the words of the language are merely concepts reflecting the culture from which it derives.

Language can be divided into two major elements. The verbal language of vocal sounds in patterns that have meaning is the obvious element. Non-verbal language is less obvious, but it is a powerful communicator through body language, silences and social distance.

Verbal language

Verbal language is an important means of communication. In various forms, such as plays and poetry, the written word is regarded as part of the culture of a group of people. In the spoken form, the actual words spoken and the ways in which the words are pronounced provide clues to the receiver about the type of person who is speaking.

Language capability plays four distinct roles in global marketing:

● Language is important in information-gathering and evaluation efforts. Rather than rely completely on the opinions of others, the manager is able to see and hear personally what is going on. People are far more comfortable speaking their own language, and this should be treated as an advantage. The best intelligence is gathered on a market by becoming part of the market rather than observing it from the outside. For example, local managers of a global corporation should be the firm's primary source of political information to assess potential risk.

● Language provides access to local society. Although English may be widely spoken, and may even be the official company language, speaking the local language may make a dramatic difference. For example, firms that translate promotional materials and information are seen as being serious about doing business in the country.

● Language capability is increasingly important in company communications, whether within the corporate family or with channel members. Imagine the difficulties encountered by a country manager who must communicate with employees through an interpreter.

● Language provides more than the ability to communicate; it extends beyond mechanics to the interpretation of contexts.

A very important dimension of the language that can vary by culture is the extent to which communication is explicit or implicit. In explicit-language cultures, managers are taught that to communicate effectively you should 'say what you mean, and mean what you say'. Vague directives and instructions are seen as a sign of poor communication abilities. The assumption in explicit-language cultures is that the burden of effective communication is on the speaker. In contrast, in implicit-language cultures (mostly high context) the assumption is that the speaker and listener both share the burden of effective communication. Implicit communication also helps avoid unpleasant and direct confrontations and disagreements.

Estimates of the main spoken languages around the world are given in Table 6.2. Chinese is spoken as the mother tongue (or first language) by three times more people than the next largest language, English. However, Chinese is overtaken by English when spoken business-language population numbers are taken into account.

It should be noted that official languages are not always spoken by the whole population of a country. For example, French is an official language in Canada, but many Canadians have little or no fluency in French.

Hence, English is often, but by no means always, the common language between businesspeople of different nationalities. The figures presented in Table 6.3 highlight the popularity of the English language across European countries. They show how different the spoken languages are from one European country to another.

Non-verbal language

Non-verbal language is a powerful means of communication. The importance of non-verbal communication is greater in high-context countries. In these cultures, people are more sensitive to a variety of different message systems, while in the low-context Anglo-Germanic cultures, many of these non-verbal language messages would not be noticed.

Non-verbal language messages, according to Hall (1960), communicate up to 90 per cent of the meaning in high-context cultures. Table 6.4 describes some of the main non-verbal languages.

| Table 6.2 | Official languages and spoken languages in the world |

Mother tongue (first language)	No. of speakers (m)
Chinese	1,000
English	350
Spanish	250
Hindi	200
Arabic	150
Bengali	150
Russian	150
Portuguese	135
Japanese	120
German	100
French	70
Punjabi	70

Note: Chinese is composed of a number of dialects of which Mandarin is the largest.
Source: Adapted from Phillips *et al.* (1994), p. 97.

Table 6.3	Foreign languages spoken by European businesspeople (%)

Language	All	UK	France	Germany	Italy	Spain	Netherlands	Denmark
English	53	100	28	32	23	21	78	36
French	34	8	100	15	21	19	22	3
German	29	4	6	100	4	3	41	13
Italian	16	1	3	4	100	3	2	—
Spanish	12	2	3	3	2	100	3	1
Dutch	7	1	1	2	—	—	100	—
Danish	8	—	—	2	—	—	1	100
Any foreign language	46	12	39	50	35	43	90	40

— denotes less than 1%.
Source: Adapted from Ogilvy and Mather (1988), pp. 22–3.

Manners and customs

Changes occurring in manners and customs must be carefully monitored, especially in cases that seem to indicate a narrowing of cultural differences between peoples. Phenomena such as McDonald's and Coca-Cola have met with success around the world, but Exhibit 6.2 indicates that there are still differences in the European food culture.

Understanding manners and customs is especially important in negotiations because interpretations based on one's own frame of reference may lead to a totally incorrect conclusion. To negotiate effectively abroad, one needs to read correctly all types of communication.

In many cultures, certain basic customs must be observed by the foreign businessperson. One of them concerns the use of the right and left hands. In so-called right-hand societies, the left hand is the 'toilet hand' and using it to eat, for example, is considered impolite.

Technology and material culture

Material culture results from technology and is directly related to how a society organizes its economic activity. It is manifested in the availability and adequacy of the basic economic, social, financial and marketing infrastructures.

With technological advancement comes cultural convergence. Black-and-white television sets extensively penetrated the US market more than a decade before they reached similar levels in Europe and Japan. With colour television, the lag was reduced to five years. With videocassette recorders, the difference was only three years, but this time the Europeans and the Japanese led the way, while Americans concentrated on cable systems. With the compact disc, penetration rates were even after only one year. Today, with Internet or MTV available by satellite across Europe, no lag exists at all.

Social institutions

Social institutions – business, political, family or class related – influence the behaviour of people and the ways in which people relate to each other. In some

Table 6.4   The main non-verbal languages in international business

Non-verbal language	Implications for global marketing and business
Time	The importance of being 'on time'. In the high-context cultures (Middle East, Latin America), time is flexible and not seen as a limited commodity.
Space	Conversational distance between people. *Example:* Individuals vary in the amount of space they want separating them from others. Arabs and Latin Americans like to stand close to people they are talking with. If an American, who may not be comfortable with such close range, backs away from an Arab, this might be taken incorrectly as a negative reaction.
Material possessions	The relevance of material possessions and interest in latest technology. This can have a certain importance in both low-context and high-context countries.
Friendship patterns	The significance of trusted friends as a social insurance in times of stress and emergency. *Example:* In high-context countries, extended social acquaintance and the establishment of appropriate personal relations are essential to conducting business. The feeling is that one should often know one's business partner on a personal level before transactions occur.
Business agreements	Rules of negotiations based on laws, moral practices or informal customs. *Example:* Rushing straight to business will not be rewarded in high-context cultures because deals are made not only on the basis of the best product or price, but also on the entity or person deemed most trustworthy. Contracts may be bound by handshakes, not complex agreements – a fact that makes some, especially western, businesspeople uneasy.

countries, for example, the family is the most important social group, and family relationships sometimes influence the work environment and employment practices.

In Latin America and the Arab world, a manager who gives special treatment to a relative is considered to be fulfilling an obligation. From the Latin point of view, it makes sense only to hire someone you can trust. In the United States and Europe, however, it is considered favouritism and nepotism. In India there is a fair amount of nepotism. But there too it is consistent with the norms of the culture. By knowing the importance of family relationships in the workplace and in business transactions, embarrassing questions about nepotism can be avoided.

An important part of the socialization process of consumers world-wide is *reference groups*. These groups provide the values and attitudes that become influential

| Exhibit 6.2 | **An example of one element of the European food culture** |

In a European lifestyle survey conducted in 1989, one particular question dealt with binary choice of a preference for either a meal consisting of one proper dish with meat and accompanying vegetables or a 'composite meal' consisting of many small dishes. The response pattern to this question is depicted in Figure 6.4.

By analyzing the variations in terms of a 10 per cent divergence from the European average percentage, a border between Latin European and Anglo-Saxon and Germanic food cultures becomes clearly visible. It runs between Germany and France, through the southern part of Belgium, northern France and western Switzerland. North of this line, there is an overwhelming preference for the 'single dish' meal, whereas south of the line there is a general majority in favour of the 'composite meal'. One can also note the apparent existence of a more 'Latin European' preference pattern in three capitals of central and northern Europe: Vienna, Brussels and Copenhagen. This could be interpreted as a sign of a more 'cosmopolitan' food culture in these highly urbanized regions compared to their respective countries.

The case of northern Norway does not constitute an exception in the same way, since the percentage 'for' the proper meal was 68 per cent, thus slightly under what was required to join the rest of the northern and central European regions, whereas the percentages in favour of the proper meal were below the European average in the three urban cases.

Source: Askegaard and Madsen (1995).

in shaping behaviour. Primary reference groups include the family, co-workers and other intimate groupings, whereas secondary groups are social organizations in which less continuous interaction takes place, such as professional associations and trade organizations.

Social organizations also determine the roles of managers and subordinates and how they relate to one another. In some cultures, managers and subordinates are separated. In other cultures, managers and subordinates are on a more common level, and work together in teams.

Education

Education includes the process of transmitting skills, ideas and attitudes, as well as training in particular disciplines. Even primitive peoples have been educated in this broader sense. For example, the Bushmen of South Africa are well educated for the culture in which they live.

One function of education is the transmission of the existing culture and traditions to the new generation. However, education can also be used for cultural change. The promotion of a communist culture in the People's Republic of China is a notable example, but this, too, is an aspect of education in most nations. Educational levels will have an impact on various business functions. Training programmes for a production facility will have to take the educational backgrounds of trainees into account.

Figure 6.4

Preferences in Europe for one proper dish with vegetables versus many small dishes

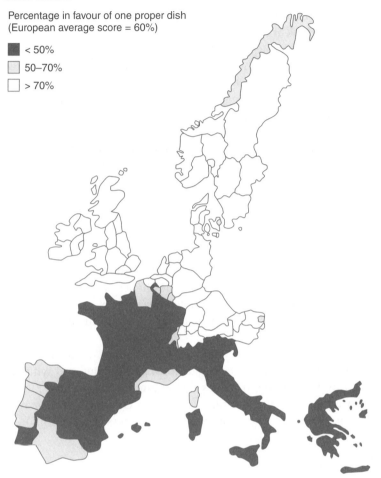

Percentage in favour of one proper dish
(European average score = 60%)

■ < 50%
□ 50–70%
□ > 70%

(Source: Askegaard and Madsen, 1995. Reprinted by permission)

The global marketing manager may also have to be prepared to overcome obstacles in recruiting a suitable sales force or support personnel. For example, the Japanese culture places a premium on loyalty, and employees consider themselves to be members of the corporate family. If a foreign firm decides to leave Japan, employees may find themselves stranded in mid-career, unable to find a place in the Japanese business system. University graduates are therefore reluctant to join all but the largest and most well known of foreign firms.

If technology is marketed, the level of sophistication of the product will depend on the educational level of future users. Product adaptation decisions are often influenced by the extent to which targeted customers are able to use the product or service properly.

Values and attitudes

Our attitudes and values help determine what we think is right or appropriate, what is important, and what is desirable. Some relate to marketing, and these are the ones we will look at here.

The more rooted values and attitudes are in central beliefs (such as religion), the more cautiously the global marketing manager has to move. Attitude towards change is basically positive in industrialized countries, whereas in more tradition-bound societies, change is viewed with great suspicion, especially when it comes from a foreign entity.

In a conservative society, there is generally a greater reluctance to take such risks. Therefore, the marketer must also seek to reduce the risk involved in trying a new product as perceived by customers or distributors. In part, this can be accomplished through education; guarantees, consignment selling or other marketing techniques can also be used.

Aesthetics

Aesthetics refers to attitudes towards beauty and good taste in the art, music, folklore and drama of a culture. The aesthetics of a particular culture can be important in the interpretation of symbolic meanings of various artistic expressions. What is and what is not acceptable may vary dramatically even in otherwise highly similar markets. Sex in advertising is an example.

It is important for companies to evaluate in depth such aesthetic factors as product and package design, colour, brand name and symbols. For instance, some conventional brand names that communicate positive messages in America have a totally different meaning in another country, which may substantially damage corporate image and marketing effectiveness (see Table 6.5).

Religion

The major religions are shared by a number of national cultures:

● Christianity is the most widely practised. The majority of Christians live in Europe and the Americas, and numbers are growing rapidly in Africa.

Table 6.5	American brand names and slogans with offensive foreign translations

Company	Product	Brand name or slogan	Country	Meaning
ENCO	Petroleum	Former name of EXXON	Japan	'Stalled car'
American Motors	Automobile	Matador	Spain	'Killer'
Ford	Truck	Fiera	Spain	'Ugly old woman'
Pepsi	Soft drink	'Come alive with Pepsi'	Germany	'Come out of the grave'

Source: Copeland and Griggs (1985), p. 62.

| Exhibit 6.3 | Sensuality and touch culture in Saudi Arabian versus European advertising |

Although Saudi Arabia has a population of only about 9 million people (including 2 million immigrants) the country is the sixth biggest fragrance market in the world behind the USA, Japan, Germany, France and Italy. Saudi Arabia also has the world's highest per capita consumption of fragrance, leaving all other countries far behind.

In promoting perfumes the big importers generally use the same advertising materials used by marketers in Europe. What is specifically Arabian in the campaigns is often dictated by Arabian morals.

Normally Saudi Arabia is a high-touch culture, but inappropriate use of touch in advertising messages may cause problems. Plate 4, shows two advertisements for the men's perfume Drakkar Noir, in which Guy Laroche (via the advertising agency Mirabelle) tones down the sensuality for the Arab version. The European ad (left) shows a man's hand clutching the perfume bottle and a woman's hand seizing his bare forearm. In the Saudi version (right), the man's arm is clothed in a dark jacket sleeve, and the woman is touching the man's hand only with her fingertip.

Source: Field (1986).

- Islam is practised mainly in Africa, the Arab counties and around the Mediterranean, and in Indonesia. There has been a recent rise in Islamic fundamentalism in Iran, Pakistan, Algeria, and elsewhere.

- Hinduism is most common in India. Beliefs emphasize the spiritual progress of each person's soul rather than hard work and wealth creation.

- Buddism has adherents in Central and South-East Asia, China, Korea and Japan. Like Hinduism it stresses spiritual achievement rather than wealth although the continuing development of these regions shows that it does not necessarily impede economic activity.

- Confucianism has adherents mainly in China, Korea, and Japan. The emphasis on loyalty and obligation between superiors and subordinates has influenced the development of family companies in these regions.

Religion can provide the basis for transcultural similarities under shared beliefs in Islam, Buddhism or Christianity, for example. Religion is of utmost importance in many countries. In America and Europe substantial efforts are made to keep government and church matters separate. Nevertheless, there remains a healthy respect for individual religious differences. In some countries, such as Lebanon and Iran, religion may be the very foundation of the government and a dominant factor in business, political and educational decisions.

Religion may affect the global marketing strategy directly in the following ways:

- Religious holidays vary greatly among countries, not only from Christian to Muslim, but even from one Christian country to another. In general, Sundays are a religious holiday in all nations where Christianity is an important religion. In the Muslim world, however, the entire month of Ramadan is a religious holiday for all practical purposes.

In Saudi Arabia, for example, during the month of Ramadan, Muslims fast from sunrise to sunset. As a consequence, worker production drops. Many Muslims rise earlier in the morning to eat before sunrise and may eat what they perceive to be enough to last until sunset. This affects their strength and stamina during the working day. An effort by management to maintain normal productivity levels will probably be rejected, so managers must learn to be sensitive to this custom and to others like it.

● Consumption patterns may be affected by religious requirements or taboos. Fish on Friday for Catholics used to be the classic example. Taboos against beef for Hindus and pork for Muslims and Jews are other examples. The pork restriction exists in Israel as well as in Islamic countries in the Middle East, such as Saudi Arabia, Iraq and Iran, and south-east Asian countries, such as Indonesia and Malaysia.

● Islamic worshippers pray facing the holy city of Mecca five times each day. Visiting westerners must be aware of this religious ritual. In Saudi Arabia and Iran, it is not unusual for managers and workers to place carpets on the floor and kneel to pray several times during the day.

● The economic role of women varies from culture to culture, and religious beliefs are an important cause. In the Middle East women may be restricted in their capacity as consumers, as workers or as respondents in a marketing study. These differences can require major adjustments in the approach of a management conditioned in the western markets. Women are, among other things, required to dress in such a way that their arms, legs, torso, and faces are concealed. An American female would be expected to honour this dress code while in the host country.

Exhibit 6.4	**Polaroid's success in Muslim markets**

During the past 30 years Polaroid's instant photography has been largely responsible for breaking down taboos against picture taking in the Arab world, especially those concerning women revealing their faces.

When Polaroid entered the market in the mid-1960s, it discovered that instant photography had a special appeal. Because of religious constraints, there were only a few photo-processing laboratories. But with Polaroid's instant cameras, Arab men were able to photograph their wives and daughters without fear of a stranger in a film laboratory seeing the women unveiled and without the risk of someone making duplicates.

Source: Harper (1986).

6.5] Hofstede's original work on national cultures the '4+1' dimensions model

While an international manager may have neither the time nor the resources to obtain a comprehensive knowledge of a particular culture, a familiarity with the most pervasive cultural 'differentiators' can provide useful guidance for corporate strategy development. One approach to identifying these pervasive fundamental differences of national cultures is provided by Hofstede (1983). Geert Hofstede tried to find an explanation for the fact that some concepts of motivation did not work in the same way in all countries. Hofstede based his research on an extensive IBM database from which – between 1967 and 1973 – 116,000 questionnaires (from IBM employees) were used in 72 countries and in 20 languages.

According to Hofstede, the way people in different countries perceive and interpret their world varies along four dimensions (the 4-D model): power distance, uncertainty avoidance, individualism and masculinity.

1. *Power distance* refers to the degree of inequality between people in physical and educational terms (i.e. from relatively equal to extremely unequal). In high power distance societies, power is concentrated among a few people at the top who make all the decisions. People at the other end simply carry these decisions out. They accept differences in power and wealth more readily. In low power distance societies, on the other hand, power is widely dispersed and relations among people are more egalitarian. The lower the power distance, the more individuals will expect to participate in the organizational decision-making process. A high power distance score was observed in Japan. The USA and Canada record a middle-level rating on power distance, but countries such as Denmark, Austria and Israel exhibit much lower ratings.

2. *Uncertainty avoidance* concerns the degree to which people in a country prefer formal rules and fixed patterns of life, such as career structures and laws, as means of enhancing security. Another important dimension of uncertainty avoidance is risk taking. High uncertainty avoidance is probably associated with risk aversion. Organization personnel in low uncertainty avoidance societies face the future as it takes shape without experiencing undue stress. In high uncertainty avoidance cultures, managers engage in activities like long-range planning to establish protective barriers to minimize the anxiety associated with future events. On uncertainty avoidance, the USA and Canada score quite low, indicating an ability to be more responsive in coping with future changes. But Japan, Greece, Portugal and Belgium score high, indicating their desire to meet the future in a more structured and planned fashion (see Figure 6.5).

3. *Individualism* denotes the degree to which people in a country learn to act as individuals rather than as members of groups. In individualistic societies, people are self-centred and feel little need for dependency on others. They seek fulfilment of their own goals over the group's. In collectivistic societies, members have a group mentality. They are interdependent on each other and seek mutual accommodation to maintain group harmony. Collectivistic managers have high loyalty to their organizations, and subscribe to joint decision making. The UK, Australia, Canada and the USA show very similar high ratings on individualism, while Japan, Brazil, Colombia, Chile and Venezuela exhibit very low ratings.

4. *Masculinity* relates to the degree to which 'masculine' values, such as achievement, performance, success, money and competition, prevail over 'feminine' values, such as the quality of life, maintaining warm personal relationships, service, care for the weak, preserving the environment, and solidarity. Masculine

Figure 6.5 Uncertainty avoidance versus power distance

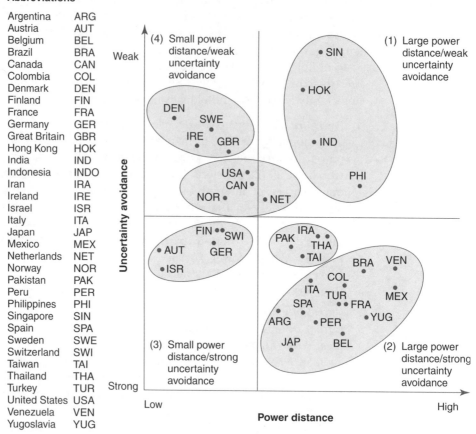

Abbreviations

Argentina	ARG
Austria	AUT
Belgium	BEL
Brazil	BRA
Canada	CAN
Colombia	COL
Denmark	DEN
Finland	FIN
France	FRA
Germany	GER
Great Britain	GBR
Hong Kong	HOK
India	IND
Indonesia	INDO
Iran	IRA
Ireland	IRE
Israel	ISR
Italy	ITA
Japan	JAP
Mexico	MEX
Netherlands	NET
Norway	NOR
Pakistan	PAK
Peru	PER
Philippines	PHI
Singapore	SIN
Spain	SPA
Sweden	SWE
Switzerland	SWI
Taiwan	TAI
Thailand	THA
Turkey	TUR
United States	USA
Venezuela	VEN
Yugoslavia	YUG

(Source: Hofstede, 1980, p. 316. Reprinted by permission of Sage Publications, Inc.)

cultures exhibit different roles for men and women, and perceive anything big as important. The feminine cultures value 'small as beautiful', and stress quality of life and environment over materialistic ends. A relatively high masculinity index was observed for the USA, Italy and Japan. In low-masculinity societies such as Denmark and Sweden people are basically motivated by a more qualitative goal set as a means to job enrichment. Differences on masculinity scores are also reflected in the types of career opportunity available in organizations and associated job mobility.

5. *Time perspective* In a 23-country study, some years after Hofstede's original work, Hofstede and Bond (1988) identified a fifth dimension which they first termed Confucian Dynamism and then renamed 'time orientation'. This 'time orientation' is defined as the way members in an organization exhibit a pragmatic future-oriented perspective rather than a conventional history or short-term point of view. The consequences of a high score on the long-term orientation (LTO) index are: persistence, ordering relationships by status and

| Exhibit 6.5 | **Global entertainment companies are getting local** |

TV-series/motion pictures

The last year's television sales in Cannes have shown that American TV series are being pushed out of prime time by local programmes. English-language pictures still command nearly 80 per cent of the world's box office market – but for how long?

Blockbuster Hollywood movies are still a huge draw world-wide but most audiences prefer local TV shows. This is bad news for the Hollywood studios, which have been relying on international sales to make up the difference between the $1.5 million or so that it costs to produce an hour-long drama episode and the $1 million the US networks will typically pay for it. But in the emerging markets of Asia and Latin America, where the big media conglomerates own channels instead of just selling to them, they try to give the audience the local programmes that they want.

Music industry

In some countries, as much as 70 per cent of CD sales come from local performers, yet five global companies – Sony, Warner, Universal, Bertelsmann and EMI – dominate the local scene as effectively as they deliver the international hits. That gives them two revenue streams – exports and local artists.

Examples of countries with mainly local music are:

- Brazil: 60 per cent local (pop, hard rock, reggae), 40 per cent imports (Hanson).
- India: 70 per cent local (mostly Hindi film music, some middle-aged crooners set to dance beats), 30 per cent imports (Bryan Adams-style American rock).
- Taiwan: 70 per cent local (primarily weepy ballads), 30 per cent imports (groups featuring young boys).

Whereas Japan has 20 per cent local, 80 per cent imports. 'The key to making a hit,' says an MTV Japan executive, 'is a song that can be sung by karaoke.'

(Source: Adapted from a variety of public media.)

observing this order. The opposite is short-term orientation, which includes personal steadiness and stability.

Most South-East Asian markets, such as China, Hong Kong, Taiwan and South Korea, score high on the LTO index. This tendency has something to do with the Confucian traditions prevalent there. On the other hand many European countries are short-term oriented. They believe in preserving history and continuing past traditions.

6.6 The strengths and weaknesses of Hofstede's model

The strengths are:

- Though the data are 30 years old, no study since then has been based on such a large sample (116,000 respondents).

- The *information population* (IBM employees) is *controlled* across countries which means comparisons can be made. This is a strength despite the difficulties of generalizing to other occupational groups within the same national culture.

- The *four dimensions* tap into deep cultural values and make significant comparisons between national cultures.

- The connotations of each dimension are highly *relevant*. The questions asked of the respondents relate to issues of importance to the international managers.

- No other study compares so many other national cultures in so much detail. Simply, this is *the best there is*.

The weaknesses are:

- Like all national cultural studies, it assumes that *national territory* and the limits of the culture correspond. But cultural homogeneity cannot be taken for granted in countries which include a range of culture groups or with socially dominant and inferior culture groups, like the United States, Italy (North/South debate), Belgium (French and Flemish cultures) and Spain (Basque, Catalan, and Castillian). The break-up of Yugoslavia during the 1990s demonstrates the futility of trying to create tight political units from disparate national cultures.

- Hofstede's respondents worked within a *single industry* (the computer industry) and a single multinational. This is misleading for two reasons. In any one country the values of IBM employees are typical only to a small group (educated generally middle class, city-dwelling); other social groups (for instance unskilled manual workers, public sector employees, family entrepreneurs, etc.) are more or less unrepresented. This problem of representation would occur whichever single company provided respondents.

- There may be technical difficulties in Hofstede's research due to an overlap between the four dimensions, e.g. small power distance/feminine and large power distance/masculine.

- Likewise the definition of the dimensions may be different from culture to culture, e.g. collectivist behaviour in one context might have different connotations elsewhere. For instance, Japanese collectivism is organization based but Chinese collectivism is family based. In Japanese terms, a Taiwanese employee who places his family interests above the interests of the Japanese-owned multinational is disloyal and cannot be fully trusted.

6.7　Managing cultural differences

Having identified the most important factors of influence from the cultural environment on the firm's business and having analyzed those factors, the international marketer is able to take decisions about how to react to the results of the analysis.

In accordance with Chapter 7 (The international market selection process) less attractive markets will not be considered further. On the other hand, in the more attractive markets, marketing management must decide to what extent adaptions to the given cultural specifics are needed.

For example, consider *punctuality*. In the most low-context cultures – the Germans, Swiss, and Austrians, for example – punctuality is considered extremely important. If you have a meeting scheduled for 9:00 and you arrive at 9:07 a.m., you are considered 'late'. Punctuality is highly valued within these cultures, and to arrive late for a meeting (thus 'wasting' the time of those forced to wait for you) is not appreciated.

By contrast, in some southern European nations, and within Latin America, a somewhat 'looser' approach to time may pertain. This does not imply that one group is 'wrong' and the other 'right'. It simply illustrates that different approaches to the concept of time have evolved for a variety of reasons, over many centuries, within different cultural groups. Culture can and does influence the business sector in different parts of the world to function in distinct ways.

Another example of how cultural differences influence the business sector concerns the presentation of business cards. Within the United States – which has a very 'informal' culture – business cards are typically presented in a very casual manner. Cards are often handed out quickly and are just as quickly placed into the recipient's pocket or wallet for future reference.

In Japan, however – which has a comparatively 'formal' culture – the presentation of a business card is a more carefully orchestrated event. There, business cards are presented by holding the card up with two hands while the recipient carefully scrutinizes the information it contains. This procedure ensures that one's title is clearly understood: an important factor for the Japanese, where one's official position within one's organizational 'hierarchy' is of great significance.

To simply take the card of a Japanese and to immediately place it into one's card holder could well be viewed (from a Japanese perspective) in a negative light. However, within the United States, to take several moments to carefully and deliberately scrutinize an American's business card might also be taken in a negative way, perhaps suggesting that one's credibility is in doubt.

These examples – the sense of time/punctuality and the presentation of the business card – illustrate just two of the many ways in which cultural factors can influence business relationships.

In attempting to understand another culture, we inevitably interpret our new cultural surroundings on the basis of our existing knowledge of our own culture.

In global marketing it is particularly important to understand new markets in the same terms as buyers or potential buyers in that marketplace. For the marketing concept to be truly operational, the international marketer needs to understand buyers in each marketplace and to be able to use marketing research in an effective way.

James Lee (1966) used the term *self-reference criterion* (SRC) to characterize our unconscious reference to our own cultural values. He suggested a four-step approach to eliminate SRC:

1. Define the problem or goal in terms of home country culture, traits, habits and norms.

2. Define the problems or goals in terms of the foreign culture, traits, habits and norms.

3. Isolate the SRC influence in the problem and examine it carefully to see how it complicates the problem.

4. Redefine the problem without the SRC influence and solve for the foreign market situation.

It is therefore of crucial importance that the culture of the country is seen in the context of that country. It is better to regard the culture as different from, rather than better or worse than, the home culture. In this way, differences and similarities can be explored and the reasons for differences can be sought and explained.

6.8 Convergence or divergence of the world's cultures

As we have seen earlier in this book the right mix between local knowledge of different cultures and globalization/integration of national marketing strategies is the key to success in global marketing.

There seems to be a great difference in attitude towards the globalization of cultures among different age groups, the youth culture being more international/global than other age groups (Smith, 2000).

Youth culture

Countries may be at different stages in the evolution of particular product and service categories, but in most cases youth is becoming more homogeneous across national markets. Youth cultures are more international than national. There are still some strong national characteristics and beliefs, but they are being eroded. The McDonald's culture is spreading into southern Europe, and at the same time we can see satellite TV taking the values of MTV, The Simpsons, and Ricky Lake all over the world with English language culture in their wake.

Differences between youth and adult markets are changing in several key respects, the professionals agree. Younger consumers differ from adults in emphasizing quality and being both discerning and technically literate. Younger consumers are now much more self-reliant and take responsibility far earlier. They are sensible, sophisticated and grown-up at an early age.

Generational barriers are now very blurred. The style leaders for many young people – musicians, sports stars and so on – are often in their 30s and 40s. Cultural and family influences remain very strong throughout Europe and the rest of the world. Few young people have 'role models', but they respects achievers particularly in music and sport – and their parents, particularly if their parents have succeeded from humble beginnings.

The lack of clarity age-group targeting has to be weighed against a growth in cross-border consistencies. But marketers should beware of strategies aimed too blatantly at younger consumers. Young people tend to reject marketing and promotions which are obviously targeted at 'youth'. They perceive it to be false and hypocritical (Smith, 1998).

Today's youth have greater freedom than previous generations had. They are more culturally aware and are reluctant to take anything – or anyone – at face value. Pasco (2000) argues that getting youngsters to relate to celebrities is increasingly difficult. Celebrities often fail or disappoint young people, too often succumbing to the rustle of the greenback. Time and again they 'sell out', giving up the integrity for which they were admired in the first place.

Disillusion with celebrities has led youth to look elsewhere for inspiration. They select values from a range of individuals rather than buy wholesale into one. Despite their mistrust of corporations, youth increasingly aspire to, and engage with brands. It appears safer to invest emotionally in brands than in celebrities.

6.9 | The effects of cultural dimensions on ethical decision making

As more and more firms operate globally, an understanding of the effects of cultural differences on ethical decision making becomes increasingly important for avoiding potential business pitfalls and for designing effective *international marketing* management programmes.

Culture is a fundamental determinant of ethical decision making. It directly affects how an individual perceives ethical problems, alternatives, and consequences. In order to succeed in today's international markets, managers must recognize and understand how ideas, values, and moral standards differ across cultures, and how these in turn influence marketing decision making.

Some countries, such as India, are well known for 'requiring' small payments if customs officials are to allow goods to enter the country. While this may indeed be a bribe and illegal, the ethics of that country seem to allow it (at least to a certain extent). The company is then left with a problem: does it bribe the official, or does it wait for normal clearance and let its products sit in the customs warehouse for a considerably longer time?

Fees and commissions paid to a firm's foreign intermediate or to consultant firms for their services are a particular problem – when does the legal fee become a bribe? One reason for employing a foreign representative or consultants is to benefit from his or her contacts with decision makers, especially in a foreign administration. If the export intermediary uses part of the fee to bribe administrators, there is little that the firm can do.

Thus, every culture – national, industry, organizational or professional – establishes a set of moral standards for business behaviour, that is, a code of business ethics. This set of standards influences all decisions and actions in a company, including, for example, what and how to manufacture (or not), what wages are appropriate to pay, how many hours personnel should work under what conditions, how to compete, and what communication guidelines to follow. Which actions are considered right or wrong, fair or unfair, in the conduct of business and which are particularly susceptible to ethical norms is heavily influenced by the culture in which they take place (the bribery theme is further discussed in Chapter 18).

The ethical commitment of an international company is illustrated in Figure 6.6 as a continuum from unacceptable ethical behaviour to most ethical decision making.

The adherence only to the letter of law reflects minimally acceptable ethical behaviour. A classification of a company as a 'most ethical' company requires that the firm's code of ethics should address the following six major issues:

● *Organizational relations*, including competition, strategic alliances, and local sourcing.

● *Economic relations*, including financing, taxation, transfer prices, local reinvestment, equity participation.

| Figure 6.6 | Ethical decision making |

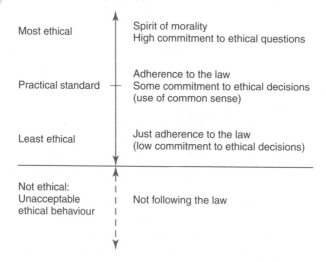

Exhibit 6.6

Levi Strauss: An example of a multinational company's ethics code

Levi Strauss, the American jeans manufacturer then operating in 40 countries, announced in May 1993 that it planned to end most of its business in the People's Republic of China. This meant phasing out the use of Chinese subcontractors, which at that time accounted for about 2 per cent of total production (approximately $50 million a year). The reason given was China's record of 'pervasive human rights abuses'.

The decision to leave China reflected principles embodied in the company's organizational culture. This culture was expressed in sets of standards for doing business abroad, which emphasized a commitment to fair working conditions. If the company could not operate in a country without compromising its principles, it should withdraw – as it had done in Myanmar and had threatened in Bangladesh.

Source: Various public media.

| Exhibit 6.7 | **Have the US tobacco companies got a different 'code of ethics' abroad?** |

Big Tobacco companies may be adhering to a voluntary 'code of ethics' in marketing to smokers at home, but when it comes to selling products overseas, US cigarette makers subscribe to an altogether different set of standards. The international sales of cigarettes are booming even as the US market shrinks. While cigarette consumption here declined by 4.5 per cent between 1990 and 1995, it rose 5.6 per cent in Eastern Europe and 8 per cent in Asia. In fact, the world's largest tobacco company, Philip Morris, now sells nearly three times as many cigarettes abroad as it does in the United States. After all, Americans now account for only 4 per cent of smokers worldwide.

In the latest threat to Big Tobacco, anti-smoking activists have begun attacking brand stretching and weak package warnings on exports as examples of an unacceptable double standard. And their arguments are getting a good hearing as warnings about the global public health costs become more urgent.

American tobacco companies are unapologetic about their international marketing practices. 'We advertise in an ethical and legal manner everywhere we operate', says Adam Bryan-Brown of R. J. Reynolds International. The industry's own documents show that products like the Salem Attitude clothing line were established precisely 'to extend the trademark beyond tobacco category restrictions'. And in some cases, the tobacco companies distance themselves from the promotions by allowing a separate corporate entity to purchase the licensing rights to a brand.

But critics also charge – and the industry denies – that many international promotions target teenagers. Philip Morris's Marlboro brand, for example, features athletic bags popular with kids in Beijing and child-size T-shirts in Kenya. In Kiev, Ukraine, where tobacco ads are banned on television, a local station airs a musical programme for young people called Camel Rock.

Tobacco manufacturers have long insisted that cigarette advertising only encourages current smokers to switch from domestic brands, which dominate in most foreign countries, to Western imports. And they link the rise in female smokers simply to greater freedom and higher incomes. Yet independent academic studies have also indicated that advertising creates new smokers.

Source: Headden, S. (1998): 'The Marlboro man lives', *US News and World Report*, Washington, 21 September.

- *Employee relations*, including compensation, safety, human rights, nondiscrimination, collective bargaining, training, and sexual harassment.
- *Customer relations*, including pricing, quality, and advertising.
- *Industrial relations*, including technology transfer, research and development, infrastructure development, and organizational stability/longevity.
- *Political relations*, including legal compliance, bribery and other corrupt activities, subsidies, tax incentives, environmental protection, and political involvement.

It is easy to generalize about the ethics of political payoffs and other types of payments; it is much more difficult to make the decision to withhold payment of money when the consequences of not making the payment may affect the company's ability to do business profitably at all. With the variety of ethical standards and levels of morality that exist in different cultures, the dilemma of ethics and pragmatism that faces international business cannot be resolved until more countries decide to deal effectively with the issue.

6.10 Summary

For international marketers, it is important to understand their customers' personal values and accepted norms of behaviour in order to market to them properly. At the same time, marketers must search for groups with shared cognitions that result in shared views of the marketer's offerings and in similar product-related behaviour, to simplify their task. Such groups may even exist across country borders.

How we perceive other cultures is from our own cultural mind-set, and it is very difficult not to take the ethnocentric point of view when classifying other cultures. Classification of cultures is necessary to develop marketing and advertising strategies in the global marketplace. Classifying cultures on dimensions has proved to be the most constructive method. It helps in vocalizing and labelling cultural differences and similarities. Many of the cultural differences are reflected in the type of communication culture used. In this chapter different models for classification have been discussed.

High/low context cultures

The difference between high- and low-context communication cultures helps us understand why, for example, Asian (high context) and Western (low context) styles are so different, why the Asians prefer indirect verbal communication and symbolism over the direct assertive communication approaches used by Western people. Other dimensions, such as different concepts of time, can also explain major differences between East and West.

Hofstede's model

In order to construct a more refined classification system, Geert Hofstede developed a model of '4 + 1' dimensions for comparing work-related values, based on data collected in an extensive study. This model also proves to be useful for comparing cultures with respect to consumption-related values. As a result, it can explain the variety of values and motivations used in marketing and advertising across cultures.

It can also explain differences in actual consumption behaviour and product use and thus can assist in predicting consumer behaviour or effectiveness of marketing strategies for cultures other than one's own. This will be particularly useful for companies that want to develop global marketing and advertising strategies.

The problem of business ethics is infinitely more complex in the international marketplace because value judgements differ widely among culturally diverse groups. What is commonly accepted as right in one country may be completely unacceptable in another. Giving business gifts of high value, for example, is generally condemned in the Western countries, but in many countries of the world, gifts are not only accepted but expected.

Case study   Teenage culture

Is there one global village for kids and teenagers?

Hassan and Katsanis (1991) claimed that the 'teenage culture' on a global scale shares a youthful lifestyle that values growth and learning with appreciation for future trends, fashion, and music. Teenagers are very self-conscious about the way they look, and role models play an important influence on their choices. For example, MTV Network, the cable company for youth, broadcasts its English-language programming in 25 countries. Music is becoming an effective tool in communication globally with teenagers and the Coca-Cola Company responded to that by introducing its first global advertising campaign, 'You Can't Beat the Feeling'.

Are the teenagers and kids really so similar from country to country?

A Global Kids Study was conducted in the spring of 1996 among 2,400 children aged 7 to 12 years and their mothers, in China, Japan, France, the United Kingdom, Germany, and the United States.

Here are some of the important findings from that survey:

	United States	United Kingdom	France	Germany	Japan	China
Snack and beverage consumption by kids aged 7–12 years (% using 3+ times per week)						
Potato chips	62	88	38	31	45	38
Carbonated beverages	59	68	74	50	23	27
Kid purchase influence – fast food for kids						
Child decides	34	56	70	40	68	44
Child decides/conferred	91	89	91	91	96	82
Television usage by kids aged 7–12 years (hours per day)						
Non-school days	3.7	3.6	3.0	2.6	3.4	3.2
School days	2.0	2.0	1.3	1.2	2.3	1.0
What kids think/daydream about (%)						
Helping other people	80	76	77	73	84	90
Being smarter	79	68	54	62	91	87
Being rich	80	59	63	61	64	47
Being a famous actor/actress or singer	53	38	41	35	19	29
Travelling in outer space	36	29	41	37	34	61
Being President/Prime Minister/ Chancellor Premier	23	8	9	4	7	24

Source: Carey et al., (1997)

When it comes to carbonated beverages, Asian kids show a significantly lower frequency, with below three in ten reporting three or more times per week, compared to at least half in Germany, six in ten in the United States, and approximately seven in ten in the United Kingdom and France. For the Chinese and Japanese children, it is possible that tea, water (hot or cold), and juices still play a much bigger role than carbonated drinks.

Quantifying the size of the kid business opportunity: kids as an influence market

Children do hold considerable decision-making power in making purchases of various products. The following are examples in the fast food category. Autonomous decision-making varies, with France and Japan leading the group, and the United States bringing up the rear. But when we combine the answers of 'Child decides and child is conferred with', nine in ten children participate in the decision making in all countries except China where the number is eight in ten, still an overwhelming majority.

Marketers need to understand children's interests and concerns and know where and how children spend their time. Children spend an average of 3.2 hours per day watching television when they are not in school (i.e. during weekends and holidays). The frequency is highest in the United States and the United Kingdom – 3.7 and 3.6 respectively – and lowest in Germany, 2.6.

During schooldays the hours are reduced by more than half in China, France and Germany to around one hour per day. The discipline is less severe in the other three countries, but the hours are also reduced significantly.

Are there value differences for our future generation? It is comforting that overwhelming majorities of children have altruistic thoughts. The Asian kids appear to place more importance on being smart than being rich, whereas kids in the United States, France, and Germany place at least equal importance on these two thoughts. The percentage of children dreaming of being rich is the highest in the United States – eight in ten – and the next closest is about six in ten among the rest of the developed countries. Less than half of the Chinese kids dream about being rich.

Question

1. What are the managerial implications of the survey results for an international marketer of:

    (a) potato chips?

    (b) soft drinks?

    (c) fast food restaurants?

    (d) chart shows like the Pepsi Chart Show and BBC's 'Top of the Pops?

(Sources: Adapted from:

Hassan, S.S. and Katsanis, L.P. (1991) 'Identification of global consumer segments: a behavioural framework'. *Journal of International Consumer Marketing*, vol. 3, no. 2, pp. 11–28.

Carey, G. Zhao, X., Chiaramonte, J. and Eden, D. (1997) 'Is there one global village for our future generation? Talking to 7–12 year olds around the world'. *Marketing and Research Today*, February, pp. 12–16.

Questions for discussion

1. Because English is the world language of business, is it necessary for UK managers to learn a foreign language?

2. According to Hofstede and Hall, Asians are (1) more group oriented, (2) more family oriented and (3) more concerned with social status. How might such orientations affect the way you market your product to Asian consumers?

3. Do you think that cultural differences between nations are more or less important than cultural variations within nations? Under what circumstances is each important?

4. Identify some constraints in marketing to a traditional Muslim society. Use some of the examples in the chapter.

5. What layers of culture have the strongest influence on business people's behaviour?

6. The focus of this chapter has mainly been the influence of culture on international marketing strategies. Try also to discuss the potential influences of marketing on cultures.

7. What role does the self-reference criterion play in international business ethics?

8. Compare the role of women in your country to their role in other cultures. How do the different roles affect women's behaviour as consumers and as business people?

Internet exercise

Coca-Cola in the Middle East

Please visit:
http://news.bbc.co.uk/hi/english/world/middle_east/newsid_747000/747575.stm

www.cocacola.com

In May 2000 rumours circulated that if the Coca-Cola logo is viewed in a mirror or upside down, it appears to read in Arabic: 'No to Mohammed' or 'No to Mecca'.

It does require a leap of the imagination, but Coca-Cola, which has huge sales in the Middle East, has apparently been sufficiently alarmed by the possible consequences of the perceived insult to seek help from Egypt's mufti.

According to the weekly magazine *Rose Al-Yousef*, Coca-Cola contacted the mufti after pamphlets appeared calling on Egyptians to boycott the drink on the grounds it is destroying their religion.

Questions

1. Which kind of cultural context does this case belong to?

2. If you were responsible for Coca-Cola's sales in the Middle East, what would you do?

For further exercises and cases, see this book's website at *www.booksites.net/hollensen*

References

Askegaard, S. and Madsen, T.K. (1995) 'European food cultures: an exploratory analysis of food related preferences and behaviour in European regions', MAPP working paper no. 26, Århus, Denmark.

Copeland, L. and Griggs, L. (1985) *Going International*, Random House, New York.

Field, M. (1986) 'Fragrance marketers sniff out rich aroma', *Advertising Age* (special report on 'Marketing to the Arab world'), 30 January, p. 10.

Hall, E.T. (1960) 'The silent language in overseas business', *Harvard Business Review*, May–June, pp. 87–96.

Harper, T. (1986) 'Polaroid clicks instantly in Moslem market', *Advertising Age* (special report on 'Marketing to the Arab world'), 30 January, p. 12.

Headden, S. (1998) 'The Marlboro man lives', *US News and World Report*, Washington, 21 September.

Hofstede, G. (1980) *Culture's Consequences: International differences in work-related values*, Sage, Beverly Hills, CA, and London.

Hofstede, G. (1983) 'The cultural relativity of organizational practices and theories', *Journal of International Business Studies*, Fall, pp. 75–89.

Hofstede, G. and Bond, M.R. (1988) 'The Confucius connection: from cultural roots to economic growth', *Organizational Dynamics*, vol. 16, no. 4, pp. 4–21.

Lee, J. (1966) 'Cultural analysis in overseas operations', *Harvard Business Review*, March–April, pp. 106–14.

Murdoch, G.P. (1945) 'The common denominator of cultures', in Linton, R. (ed.), *The Science of Man in the World Crises*, Columbia University Press, New York.

Ogilvy and Mather (1988) *Marketing to Europe*, Brethlenholm Print, London.

Phillips, C., Doole, I. and Lowe, R. (1994) *International Marketing Strategy: Analysis, development and implementation*, Routledge, London.

Pasco, M. (2000) 'Brands are replacing celebrities as role models for today's youth', *Kids Marketing Report*, 27 January.

Smith, D.S. (1998) 'Europe's youth is our future', *Marketing*, London, 22 January.

Smith, K.V. (2000) 'Why SFA is a tough sell in Latin America', *Marketing News*, Chicago, 3 January.

Usunier, J.C. (1993) *International Marketing: A cultural approach*, Prentice Hall, Hemel Hempstead.

7

The international market selection process

After studying this chapter you should be able to do the following:

● Define international market selection and identify the problems in achieving it.

● Explore how international marketers screen potential markets/countries using secondary and primary data (criteria).

● Distinguish between preliminary and 'fine-grained' screening.

● Realize the importance of segmentation in the formulation of the global marketing strategy.

● Choose among alternative market expansion strategies.

● Distinguish between concentration and diversification in market expansion.

7.1　Introduction

Identifying the 'right' market(s) to enter is important for a number of reasons:

● It can be a major determinant of success or failure, especially in the early stages of internationalization.

● This decision influences the nature of foreign marketing programmes in the selected countries.

● The nature of geographic location of selected markets affects the firm's ability to coordinate foreign operations.

7.2　International market selection: SMEs versus LSEs

The international market selection (IMS) process seems different in small and medium-sized enterprises (SMEs) and large-scale enterprises (LSEs).

In the SME, the IMS is often simply a reaction to a stimulus provided by a change agent. This agent can appear in the form of an unsolicited order. Government agencies, chambers of commerce and other change agents may also bring foreign opportunities to the firm's attention. Such cases constitute an externally driven decision in which the exporter simply responds to an opportunity in a given market.

In other cases the IMS of SMEs is based on the following criteria (Johanson and Vahlne, 1977):

● Low 'psychic' distance: low uncertainty about foreign markets and low perceived difficulty of acquiring information about them.

● Low 'cultural' distance: low perceived differences between the home and destination cultures.

● Low geographic distance.

Using any one of these criteria often results in targeting the same foreign market. The choice is often limited to the SMEs' immediate neighbours, since geographic proximity is likely to reflect cultural similarity, more knowledge about foreign markets and greater ease in obtaining information.

By limiting their consideration to a nearby country the SMEs effectively narrow the IMS into one decision: to go or not to go to a nearby country. The reason for this behaviour can be that SME executives, usually being short of human and financial resources, find it hard to resist the temptation of selecting target markets intuitively.

In a study of internationalization in Danish SMEs, Sylvest and Lindholm (1997) found that the IMS process was very different in 'old' SMEs (established before 1960) from in 'young' SMEs (established in 1989 or later). The young SMEs entered more distant markets much earlier than the older SMEs, which followed the more traditional 'step-by-step' IMS process. The reason for a more rapid internationalization of young SMEs may be their status as subsuppliers to larger firms, where they are 'pulled out' to international markets by their large customers and their international networks.

While SMEs must make first entry decisions by selecting targets among largely unknown markets, LSEs with existing operations in many countries have to decide in which of them to introduce new products. By drawing on existing operations LSEs have easier access to product-specific data in the form of primary information that is more accurate than any secondary database. As a result of this the LSEs can be more proactive. Although selecting markets based on intuition and pragmatism can be a satisfying way for SMEs (see, e.g., Case II.1), the following will be based on a more proactive IMS process, organized in a systematic and step-by-step analysis.

However, in 'real life' the IMS process will not always be a logical and gradual sequence of activities, but an iterative process involving multiple feed back loops (Andersen and Strandskov, 1998).

7.3 ▌ Building a model for international market selection

Research from the Uppsala school on the internationalization process of the firm has suggested several potential determinants of the firm's choice of foreign markets.

These can be classified into two groups: (1) environmental and (2) firm characteristics (see Figure 7.1).

Let us look first at the environment. How do we define 'international markets'? The following approach suggests two dimensions:

● The international market as a country or a group of countries.

● The international market as a group of customers with nearly the same characteristics. According to this latter definition, a market can consist of customers from several countries.

Most books and studies in global marketing have attempted to segment the world market into the different countries or groups of countries. This has been done for two principal reasons:

● International data are more easily (and sometimes exclusively) available on a nation-by-nation basis. It is very difficult to acquire accurate cross-national statistical data.

● Distribution management and media have also been organized on a nation-by-nation basis. Most agents/distributors still represent their manufacturers only in one single country. Few agents are selling their products on a cross-national basis.

However, country markets or multicountry markets are not quite adequate. In many cases, boundary lines are the result of political agreement or war and do not reflect a similar separation in buyer characteristics among people on either side of the border.

Figure 7.1   **Potential determinants of the firm's choice of foreign markets**

Presentation of a market-screening model

In Figure 7.1 an outline model for IMS was presented. In the following we will look in more detail at the box labelled 'international market segmentation'. The elements of IMS are shown in Figure 7.2.

Steps 1 and 2: Defining criteria

In general, the criteria for effective segmentation are as follows:

- *Measurability*: the degree to which the size and purchasing power of resulting segments can be measured.
- *Accessibility*: the degree to which the resulting segments can be effectively reached and served.
- *Substantiality/profitability*: the degree to which segments are sufficiently large and/or profitable.
- *Actionability*: the degree to which the organization has sufficient resources to formulate effective marketing programmes and 'make things happen'.

A high degree of measurability and accessibility indicates more general characteristics as criteria (at the top of Figure 7.3) and vice versa.

It is important to realize that more than one measure can be used simultaneously in the segmentation process.

Figure 7.2   **International market segmentation**

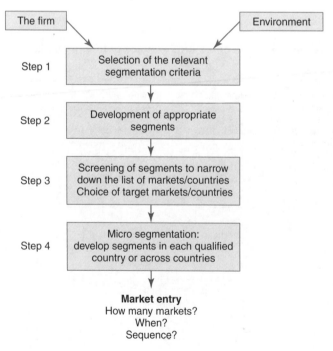

| Figure 7.3 | The basis of international market segmentation |

General characteristics
Geographic
Language
Political factors
Demography
Economy
Industrial structure
Technology
Social organization
Religion
Education

High degree of measurability,
accessibility, and actionability

↑

↓

Specific characteristics
Cultural characteristics
Lifestyle
Personality
Attitudes and tastes

Low degree of measurability,
accessibility, and actionability
(however, high degree of
relevance in specific situations)

In Chapters 5 and 6 the different segmentation criteria in the international environment were discussed and structured according to the following PEST approach:

● Political/legal.

● Economic.

● Social/cultural.

● Technological.

We will now describe in more detail the general and specific criteria mentioned in Figure 7.3.

General characteristics

Geographic location

The location of the market can be critical in terms of segmenting world markets. Scandinavian countries or Middle Eastern countries may be clustered not only according to their geographic proximity, but also according to other types of similarity as well. However, the geographic location alone could be a critical factor. For instance, air-conditioning needs in some of the Arab countries could make a manufacturer consider these countries as specific clusters.

Language

Language has been described as the mirror of the culture. On one level, its implications for the international marketer are self-evident: advertising must be translated; brand names must be vetted for international acceptability; business negotiations must often be conducted through expensive interpreters or through the yet more expensive acquisition of a foreign translator. In the latter case, genuine fluency is essential; persuasion and contract negotiation present enough difficulties even in a mother tongue.

Less obvious is the fact that foreign language may imply different patterns of thought and different customer motivations. In such cases a knowledge – again, a good knowledge – of the language will do more than facilitate communication; it provides automatic insight into the relevant culture.

Political factors

Countries may be grouped and world markets segmented according to broad political characteristics. Until recently the Iron Curtain was the basis of one such division. In general terms, the degree of power that the central government has may be the general criterion for segmentation. It is possible, for instance, that a company is producing certain chemicals but that, due to government regulations, many of the world markets may be considered too difficult to enter.

Demography

Demographics is a critical basis for segmentation. For instance, it is often necessary to analyze population characteristics in terms of the proportion of elderly people or children in the total population.

If the country's population is getting older and the number of infants per thousand is declining, which is the case in some European countries, a baby food company would not consider entering that country. In Europe birth rates are tumbling and life spans lengthening. Baby-based industries from toys to foods and nappies face sharp competition. Consumer electronics and housing may also be affected.

Economy

As the earlier studies have indicated, economic development level could be a critical variable for international market segmentation. Electric dishwashers or washer-dryers require a certain level of economic development. There is not a good market for these products in India. However, in western European countries, these products are becoming almost a basic necessity. On the basis of the level of economic development, certain specific consumption patterns emerge. Societies with high personal income spend more time and money on services, education and recreation. Thus, it may be possible to arrange certain income groups from different countries into certain clusters.

Industrial structure

A country's industrial structure is depicted by the characteristics of its business population. One country may have many small retailers; another country may rely on a large number of department stores for retail distribution. One country may be thriving on small manufacturers; another may have very concentrated and large-scale manufacturing activity. The type of competition that exists at the wholesale level may be the critical specific factor for clustering international markets. The international marketer may wish to work with a series of strong wholesalers.

Technology

The degree of technological advancement or the degree of agricultural technology may easily be the basis for segmentation. A software company planning to enter international markets may wish to segment them on the basis of the number of PCs per thousand of the population. It may not be worthwhile for this company to enter markets below a certain number of PCs per thousand of the population. For example, it may find Pakistan, Iran and most Arab countries, all of Africa and all of eastern Europe less than satisfactory for entry.

Social organization

The family is an important purchasing group in any society. In Europe marketers are accustomed to either the so-called nuclear family, with father, mother and children all living together under one roof, or, increasingly as society changes, the single-parent family. In other countries the key unit is the extended family, with three or four generations all in the same house.

In the USA, for instance, socioeconomic groupings have been used extensively as segmentation tools. A six-category classification is used: upper upper class, lower upper, upper middle, lower middle, upper lower and lower lower. The US high-income professionals are relegated to the lower upper class, described as those 'who have earned their position rather than inherited it', the *nouveaux riches*.

In contrast, it would have been hard to find useful socioeconomic groupings in Russia beyond white-collar worker, blue-collar worker and farm worker.

Religion

Religious customs are a major factor in marketing. The most obvious example, perhaps, is the Christian tradition of present giving at Christmas, yet even in this simple matter pitfalls lie in wait for the international marketer: in some Christian countries the traditional exchange of presents takes place not on Christmas Day but on other days in December or early January.

The impact of religion on marketing becomes most evident in the case of Islam. Islamic laws, based on the Koran, provide guidance for a whole range of human activities, including economic activity.

Education

Educational levels are of importance to the international marketer from two main standpoints: the economic potential of the youth market and, in developing countries, the level of literacy.

Educational systems vary a lot from country to country. The compensation for on-the-job training also varies a great deal. As a result, the economic potential of the youth market is very different from country to country.

In most industrialized countries, literacy levels are close to 100 per cent and the whole range of communications media is open to the marketer. In developing countries, literacy rates can be as low as 25 per cent, and in one or two 15 per cent or less, although at such low levels the figures can be no more than estimates. In those same countries television sets and even radios are economically beyond the reach of most of the population, although communal television sets are sometimes available. The consumer marketer faces a real challenge in deciding on promotional policies in these countries, and the use of visual material is more relevant.

Specific characteristics

Cultural characteristics

Cultural characteristics may play a significant role in segmenting world markets. To take advantage of global markets or global segments, firms require a thorough understanding of what drives customer behaviour in different markets. They must learn to detect the extent to which similarities exist or can be achieved through marketing activities. The cultural behaviour of the members of a given society is constantly shaped by a set of dynamic variables which can also be used as segmentation criteria: language, religion, values and attitudes, material elements and technology, aesthetics, education and social institutions. These different elements were dealt with more extensively in Chapters 5 and 6.

Lifestyles

Typically, activity, interest and opinion research is used as the tool for analyzing lifestyles. However, such a research tool has not quite been developed for international purposes. Perhaps certain consumption habits or practices may be used as an indication of the lifestyle that is being studied. Food consumption habits can be used as one such general indicator. Types of food eaten can easily indicate lifestyles which an international food company should be ready to consider. For example, Indian-style hot curries are not likely to be very popular in the rather bland cooking of Germany. Very hot Arab dishes are not likely to be very popular in western Europe.

Personality

Personality is reflected in certain types of behaviour. A general characteristic may be temper, so that segmentation may be based on the general temper of people. Latin Americans or Mediterranean people are known to have certain personality traits. Perhaps those traits are a suitable basis for the segmentation of world markets. One example is the tendency to haggle. In pricing, for instance, the international firm will have to use a substantial degree of flexibility where haggling is widespread. Haggling in a country such as Turkey is almost a national pastime. In the underground bazaars of Istanbul, the vendor would be almost offended if the customer accepted the first asking price.

Attitudes, tastes or predispositions

These are all complex concepts, but it is reasonable to say that they can be utilized for segmentation. Status symbols can be used as indicators of what some people in a culture consider would enhance their own self-concept as well as their perception among other people.

Step 3: Screening of markets/countries

This screening process can be divided in two:

● *Preliminary screening.* This is where markets/countries are screened primarily according to external screening criteria (the state of the market). In the case of the SMEs, the limited internal resources (e.g. financial resources) must also be taken into account. There will be a number of countries which can be excluded in advance as potential markets.

● *Fine-grained screening.* This is where the firm's competitive power (and special competences) in the different markets can be taken into account.

Preliminary screening

The number of markets is reduced by 'coarse-grained', macro-oriented screening methods based on criteria such as the following:

● Restrictions in the export of goods from one country to another.
● Gross national product (GNP) per capita.
● Cars owned per 1,000 of the population.
● Government spending as a percentage of GNP.
● Population per hospital bed.

When screening countries it is particularly important to assess the political risk of entering a country. Over recent years, marketers have developed various indices to help assess the risk factors in the evaluation of the potential market opportunities. One of these indices is the *Business Environment Risk Index (BERI)*.

BERI measures the general quality of a country's business climate. Launched in 1972, it was developed by Frederich Haner of the University of Delaware, USA. It has

Table 7.1 Criteria included in the overall BERI index

Criteria	Weights	Multiplied with the score (rating) on a scale of 0 – 4[a]	Overall BERI index[b]
Political stability	3		
Economic growth	2.5		
Currency convertibility	2.5		
Labour cost/productivity	2		
Short-term credit	2		
Long-term loans/venture capital	2		
Attitude towards the foreign investor and profits	1.5		
Nationalization	1.5		
Monetary inflation	1.5		
Balance of payments	1.5		
Enforceability of contracts	1.5		
Bureaucratic delays	1		
Communications: telex, telephone	1		
Local management and partner	1		
Professional services and contractors	0.5		
Total	25	× 4 (max.)	= Max. 100

[a] 0 unacceptable; 1 poor; 2 average conditions; 3 above average conditions; 4 superior conditions.
[b] Total points: >80 favourable environment for investors, advanced economy. 70–79 not so favourable, but still an advanced economy. 55/69 an immature economy with investment potential, probably an NIC. 40/54 a high-risk country, probably an LDC. Quality of management has to be superior to realize potential. <40 very high risk. Would only commit capital if some extraordinary justification

since expanded into country-specific forecasts and country risk forecasts for international lenders, but its basic service is the Global Subscription Service. This assesses 48 countries four times a year on fifteen economic, political and financial factors on a scale from 0 to 4. The overall index ranges from 0 to 100 (see Table 7.1).

The BERI index has been questioned as a general management decision tool and should therefore be supplemented by in-depth country reports before final market entry decisions are made.

Among other macro-oriented screening methods is the *shift-share approach* (Green and Allaway, 1985; Papadopoulos and Denis, 1988). This approach is based upon the identification of relative changes in international import shares among various countries. The average growth rate of imports for a particular product for a 'basket' of countries is calculated and then each country's actual growth rate is compared with the average growth rate. The difference, called the 'net shift', identifies growing or declining markets. This procedure has the advantage that it takes into account both the absolute level of a country's imports and their relative growth rate. On the other hand, it examines only those criteria and does not take into account other macro-oriented criteria.

| Figure 7.4 | The market attractiveness/competitive strength matrix |

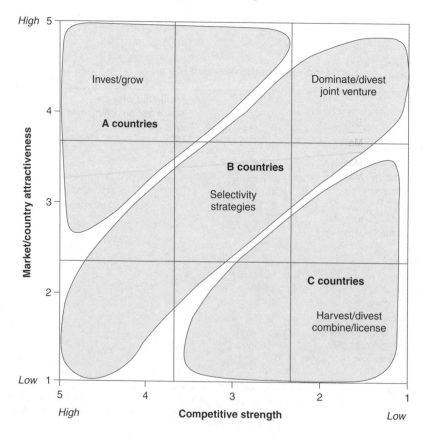

'Fine-grained' screening

As the BERI index focuses only on the political risk of entering new markets, a broader approach that includes the competences of the firm is often needed.

For this purpose a powerful aid to the identification of the 'best opportunity' target countries is the application of the market attractiveness/competitive strength matrix (Figure 7.4). This market portfolio model replaces the two single dimensions in the BCG growth–share matrix with two composite dimensions applied to global marketing issues. Measures on these two dimensions are built up from a large number of possible variables as listed in Table 7.2. In the following, one of the important dimensions will be described and commented upon.

Market size

The total market volume per year for a certain country/market can be calculated as:

Production (of a product in a country)

+import

−export
= theoretical market size

+/−changes in stocks at distributors
= effective market size

Production, import and export figures can usually be found in the specific country's statistics, if it is a standardized product with an identifiable customs position.

A more precise location of a particular country (in Figure 7.4) may be determined by using the questionnaire in Figure 7.5.

| Table 7.2 | **Dimensions of market/country attractiveness and competitive strength** |

Market/country attractiveness	Competitive strength
Market size (total and segments)	Market share
Market growth (total and segments)	Marketing ability and capacity (country-specific know-how)
Buying power of customers	Product fit to market demands
Market seasons and fluctuations	Price
Average industry margin	Contribution margin
Competitive conditions (concentration, intensity, entry barriers, etc.)	Image
Market prohibitive conditions (tariff/non tariff barriers, import restrictions, etc.)	Technology position
Government regulations (price controls, local content, compensatory exports, etc.)	Product quality
Infrastructure	Market support
Economic and political stability	Quality of distributors and service
Psychic distance (from home base to foreign market)	Financial resources
	Access to distribution channels

Figure 7.5 **Underlying questionnaire for locating countries on a market attractiveness/competitive strength matrix**

Time of analysis:
Analysis of product area:
in country:

A. Market attractiveness

	1 Very poor	2 Poor	3 Medium	4 Good	5 Very good	% Weight factor	Result (grading × weight)
Market size							
Market growth							
Buying structure							
Prices							
Buying power							
Market access							
Competitive intensity							
Political/economical risks							
etc.							
Total						100	

Market attractiveness = Result : 100 = ...

B. Relative competitive strength
with regard to the strongest competitor = ...

	1 Very poor	2 Poor	3 Medium	4 Good	5 Very good	% Weight factor	Result (grading × weight)
Products fit to market demands							
Prices and conditions							
Market presence							
Marketing							
Communication							
Obtainable market share							
Financial results							
etc.							
Total						100	

Relative competitive strength = Result : 100 = ...

As seen from Figure 7.4 one of the results of this process is a prioritized classification of countries/markets into distinct categories:

- *A countries.* These are the primary markets (i.e. the key markets), which offer the best opportunities for long-term strategic development. Here companies may want to establish a permanent presence and should therefore embark on a thorough research programme.

- *B countries.* These are the secondary markets, where opportunities are identified but political or economic risk is perceived as being too high to make long-term irrevocable commitments. These markets would be handled in a more pragmatic way due to the potential risks identified. A comprehensive marketing information system would be needed.

- *C countries.* These are the tertiary or 'catch what you can' markets. They will be perceived as high risk, and so the allocation of resources will be minimal. Objectives in such countries would be short term and opportunistic; companies would give no real commitment. No significant research would be carried out.

| Exhibit 7.1 | **Market assessment for Ford Tractors** |

The large multinational company Ford Tractors used a lot of market analysis responses to produce the matrix shown in Figure 7.6. The information inputs required may sometimes be beyond the reach of an SME. In such cases there is still value in using this approach as a framework for identifying key markets; however, the analysis will then have to be based on more subjectively assessed criteria.

Source: Harrell and Kiefer (1995), p. 97.

| Figure 7.6 | **Country attractiveness: the example of Ford Tractors** |

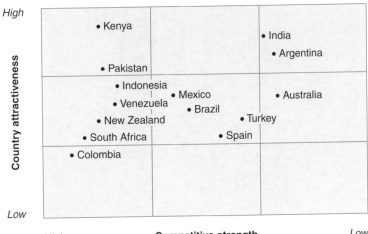

Step 4: Develop subsegments in each qualified country and across countries

Once the prime markets have been identified, firms then use standard techniques to segment markets within countries, using variables such as the following:

● Demographic/economic factors.
● Lifestyles.
● Consumer motivations.
● Geography.
● Buyer behaviour.
● Psychographics, etc.

Thus, the prime segmentation basis is geographic (by country) and the secondary is within countries. The problem here is that, depending on the information basis, it may be difficult fully to formulate secondary segmentation bases. Furthermore, such an approach can run the risk of leading to a differentiated marketing approach, which may leave the company with a very fragmented international strategy.

| Figure 7.7 | Transnational clustering of the western European market |

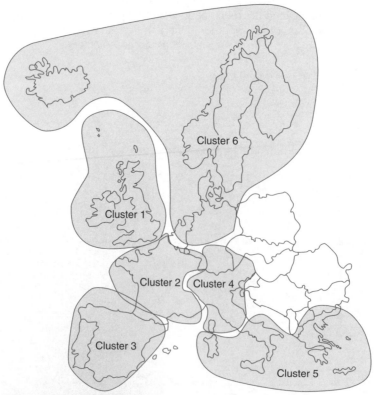

(Source: Welford, R. and Prescott, K. (1996), *European Business: An issue-based approach*, Pearson Education Limited.)

The drawback of traditional approaches lies in the difficulty of applying them consistently across markets. If a company is to try to achieve a consistent and controlled marketing strategy across all its markets, it needs a transnational approach to its segmentation strategy.

It can be argued that companies competing internationally should segment markets on the basis of consumers, not countries. Segmentation by purely geographical factors leads to national stereotyping. It ignores the differences between customers within a nation and ignores similarities across boundaries.

Cluster analysis can be used to identify meaningful cross-national segments, each of which is expected to evoke a similar response to any marketing mix strategy. Figure 7.7 shows an attempt to segment the western European market into six clusters.

Once the firm has chosen a certain country as a target market, the next stage in the micro segmentation process is to decide with which products or services the company wishes to become active in the individual countries. Here it is necessary to make a careful market segmentation, especially in the larger and more important foreign markets, in order to be in a position to exhaust the market potential in a differentiated manner (Figure 7.8).

In this context it is necessary to draw attention to a specific strategic procedure, which is oriented world-wide towards similar market segments. Here it is not the country-specific market attractiveness which influences the decision on specific markets, but the recognition of the existence of similar structures of demand and similar consumer habits in segments (and perhaps only in small segments) of different markets.

| **Figure 7.8** | **Micro market segmentation** |

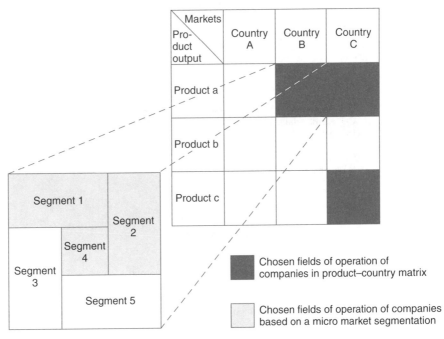

An illustration of the whole international market segmentation/screening process (steps 1–4 in Figure 7.2) is seen in Figure 7.9.

The model in Figure 7.9 begins by regarding the world market as the potential market for a firm's product. However, if the firm only regards western Europe as a

Figure 7.9   The international market segmentation/screening process: an example of the proactive and systematic approach

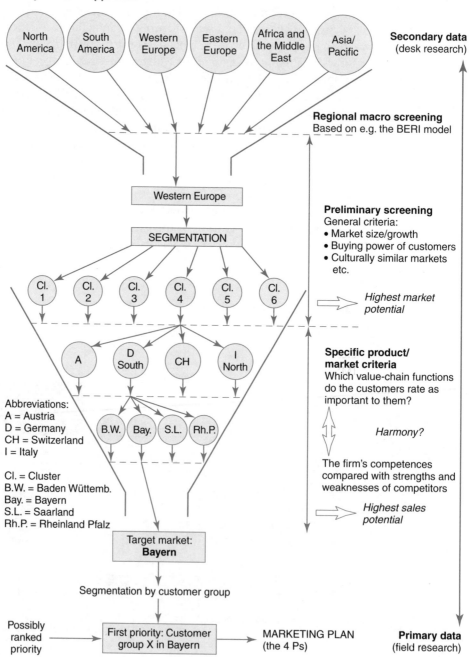

possible market, then the firm may start the screening process at this lower level. The six western European clusters are based on the transnational clustering in Figure 7.7. The further down in the model, the greater the use of primary data (personal interviews, field research, etc.), as well as screening from internal criteria. Furthermore, the firm may discover a *high market potential* in some geographic segments. However, this is not the same as a *high sales potential* for the firm's product. There may be some restrictions (e.g. trade barriers) on the exporting of products to a particular country. Also the management of the company may have a certain policy only to select markets which are culturally similar to the home market. This may exclude far distant countries from being selected as target markets, though they may have a high market potential. Furthermore, to be able to transform a high market potential into a high sales potential, there must be a harmony between the firm's competences (internal criteria) and the value-chain functions that customers rate as important to them. Only in this situation will a customer regard the firm as a possible supplier, equal to other possible suppliers.

In general, Figure 7.9 is based on proactive and systematic decision-making behaviour by the firm. This is not always a realistic condition, especially not in SMEs, where a *pragmatic approach* is required. Often, firms are not able to segment from own criteria but must expect to be evaluated and chosen (as subsuppliers) by much larger firms. The pragmatic approach to IMS can also give rise to the firm choosing customers and markets with a background similar to the managers' own personal network and cultural background. In Case I.4 (Hsu's Ginseng Enterprises) the owner chose China as the first export market due to his Chinese background. Crick and Chaudhry (1995) studied the export practices of ethnic minority-owned SMEs in the UK and found that ethnic minorities are potentially more likely to start exporting to countries psychologically close to their cultural roots. Also contingencies and the serendipity of the top manager play a large role in the early phases of IMS (see, e.g., Case II.1).

7.4 ▌ Market expansion strategies

The choice of a market expansion strategy is a key decision in export marketing. First, different patterns are likely to cause development of different competitive conditions in different markets over time. For example, a fast rate of growth into new markets characterized by short product life cycles can create entry barriers towards competitors and give rise to higher profitability. On the other hand, a purposeful selection of relatively few markets for more intensive development can create higher market shares, implying stronger competitive positions.

In designing their strategy, firms have to answer two underlying questions:

● Will they enter markets incrementally (the waterfall approach) or simultaneously (the shower approach) (see Figure 7.10)?

● Will entry be concentrated or diversified across international markets?

| Figure 7.10 | The incremental strategy (waterfall approach) and simulataneous strategy (the shower approach in an LSE with a global presence): sales in advanced countries, developing countries and less developed countries |

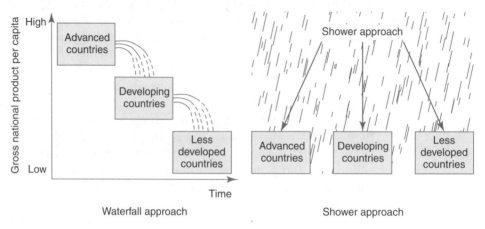

Waterfall approach   Shower approach

(Source: Keegan, W. (1995) *Global Marketing Management*, Pearson Education Limited.)

Incremental versus simultaneous entry

A firm may decide to enter international markets on an incremental or experimental basis, entering first a single key market in order to build up experience in international operations, and then subsequently entering other markets one after the other. Alternatively, a firm may decide to enter a number of markets simultaneously in order to leverage its core competence and resources rapidly across a broader market base. (Read about Sanex's shower approach in Exhibit 7.2.)

For the big global company, the two strategies can be translated into the concept of the *international product life cycle* (Vernon, 1966), as illustrated in Figure 7.10. See also Figure 14.6, p. 402.

Entry on an incremental basis, especially into small markets, may be preferred where a firm lacks experience in foreign markets and wishes to edge gradually into international operations. Information about, and familiarity with, operating in foreign markets are thus acquired step by step. This strategy may be preferable if a company is entering international markets late and faces entrenched local competition. Equally, if a firm is small and has limited resources, or is highly risk averse, it may prefer to enter a single or a limited number of markets and gradually expand in a series of incremental moves rather than making a major commitment to international expansion immediately.

Some companies prefer a rapid entry into world markets in order to seize an emerging opportunity or forestall competition. Rapid entry facilitates early market penetration across a number of markets and enables the firm to build up experience rapidly. It also enables a firm to achieve economies of scale in production and marketing by integrating and consolidating operations across these markets. This may be especially desirable if the product or service involved is innovative or represents a significant technological advance, in order to forestall pre-emption or limitation by other competitors. While increasingly feasible due to developments in global information technology, simultaneous entry into multiple markets typically requires substantial financial and management resources and entails higher operating risk.

The appropriate expansion strategy for the SME

The SME often exploits domestic market opportunities to build up company resources, which later may be used in international markets (Figure 7.11)

The company strategy for market expansion should be concentrated on the product-market segment where the core competences of the company give it a competitive advantage (here product A, B, C and market 1, 2).

The process might evolve step by step, taking one market at a time, market 1, niche 1, learning from it, and then using it as a bridgehead to transfer that competence to the same niche in the next market (market 2, niche 1). The company may develop its international operations by continuing to develop new markets in a step-by-step process, ensuring consolidation and profitability before moving on.

Concentration versus diversification

The firm must also decide whether to concentrate resources on a limited number of similar markets, or alternatively to diversify across a number of different markets. A company may concentrate its efforts by entering countries that are highly similar in terms of market characteristics and infrastructure to the domestic market. Management could also focus on a group of proximate countries. Alternatively, a company may prefer to diversify risk by entering countries that differ in terms of environmental or market characteristics. An economic recession in one

| Figure 7.11 | Appropriate global marketing strategies for SMEs |

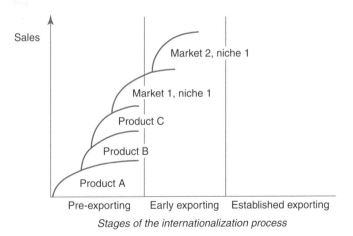

(Source: Bradley, F. (1995) *International Marketing Strategy*, Pearson Education Limited.)

country could be counterbalanced by growth in another market. The strength of competition also often varies from one market to another, and profits in a relatively protected or less competitive market may be funnelled into more fiercely competitive markets. Spreading out operations over a broader geographic base, and investing in different regions throughout the world, may also diversify risk, since in some industries, markets in different regions are not interdependent (i.e. trends in one region will not spill over into another).

The question of concentrating or diversifying on the country level can be combined with concentration or diversification on the customer (segment) level. The resulting matrix (Figure 7.12) illustrates the four possible strategies.

From Figure 7.12 four expansion alternatives can be identified:

1. Few customer groups/segments in few countries.
2. Many customer groups/segments in few countries.
3. Few customer groups/segments in many countries.
4. Many customer groups/segments in many countries.

A company can calculate its degree of export concentration and compare it over time or with other firms, using the Herfindahl index. This index is defined as the sum of the squares of the percentage of sales in each foreign country.

$$C = \sum S_i^2 \qquad i = 1, 2, 3, 4 \dots n \quad \text{countries}$$

Figure 7.12 **The market expansion matrix**

	Market/customer target group	
	Concentration	*Diversification*
Country *Concentration*	1	2
Country *Diversification*	3	4

(Source: Ayal and Zif, 1979, p. 84)

where C = the export concentration index of the firm
           S_i = exports to country i as a percentage (measured in decimal numbers from 0 to 1) of the firm's total exports

$$\sum S_i = 1$$

Maximum concentration ($C = 1$) occurs when all the export is made to one country only, and minimum concentration ($C = 1/n$) exists when exports are equally distributed over a large number of countries.

Exhibit 7.2

Sanex's aggressive search for cross-border niches: an example of the diversification approach

Sanex was developed as a liquid personal soap in 1984. Its success was established quickly – within a year it had gained market leadership in Spain. Soon afterwards it was bought by the American consumer giant Sara Lee, which has four main product sectors:

● Packaged meats and bakery products.

● Personal products.

● Coffee and groceries.

● Household and personal care products.

The market basis for Sanex was the growing shower gel market in Europe. Consumers were moving from the ritual of bathing to the more hygienic routine of showering. The Sanex concept of healthy skin fitted perfectly into this trend. The word 'Sanex' is derived from *sano*, which is Spanish for 'healthy'. The idea behind the positioning was to build up a cross-border (European) concept of health in consumers' minds. This positioning strategy was in contrast to the positioning of the established players like Procter & Gamble, Unilever, Colgate-Palmolive and Henkel. They were marketing their products under the cosmetic umbrella with strong perfume and colours, and high levels of detergents, supported by the sort of advertising familiar in the cosmetic industry, using beautiful women and exotic surroundings.

The market expansion strategy of Sanex was to launch the product simultaneously on a number of European markets (the 'shower approach' in Figure 7.10). The idea behind this strategy was that Sanex should obtain a 'first-mover advantage', which meant that the big competitors did not have time to copy the product concept before Sanex had product extensions ready for international market launching. The concept of Sanex's shower gel was well understood in most countries, but the potential for the brand would be different. If the habit of showering was well established, the opportunity for Sanex would be better. But in the UK, for example, baths are still very important, although the frequency of showering has increased. In another big potential market, the USA, people use bars of soap, although they have recently begun to switch to liquid soap.

In a relatively short time Sanex succeeded in developing and launching a broad range of products, including deodorants, colognes and body milk. With 1995 revenues of almost $100 million a year, Sanex is now marketed throughout Europe and the Far East.

Sources: Mazur and Lannon (1993); p.23 Crossborder Marketing, the Economist Intelligence Unit Limited.

Table 7.3	International market diversification versus market concentration

Factors favouring country diversification	Factors favouring country concentration
Company factors	
High management risk consciousness	Low management risk consciousness
Objective of growth through market development	Objective of growth through market penetration
Little market knowledge	Ability to pick 'best' markets
Product factors	
Limited specialist uses	General uses
Low volume	High volume
Non-repeat	Repeat-purchase product
Early or late in product life cycle	Middle of product life cycle
Standard product saleable in many markets	Product requires adaptation to different markets
Market factors	
Small markets – specialized segments	Large markets – high-volume segments
Unstable markets	Stable markets
Many similar markets	Limited number of markets
New or declining markets	Mature markets
Low growth rate in each market	High growth rate in each market
Large markets are very competitive	Large markets are not excessively competitive
Established competitors have large share of key markets	Key markets are divided among many competitors
Low customer loyalty	High customer loyalty
High synergy effects between countries	Low synergy effect between countries
Short competitive lead time	Long competitive lead time
Marketing factors	
Low communication costs for additional markets	High communication costs for additional markets
Low order-handling costs for additional markets	High order-handling costs for additional markets
Low physical distribution costs for additional markets	High physical distribution costs for additional markets
Standardized communication in many markets	Communication requires adaptation to different markets

Source: Adapted from Piercy (1981) and Ayal and Zif (1979).

7.5 The global product/market portfolio

The corporate portfolio analysis provides an important tool to assess how to allocate resources not only across geographic areas, but also across the different product business (Douglas and Craig, 1995). The global corporate portfolio represents the most aggregate level of analysis and it might consist of operations by product businesses or by geographic areas.

As illustrated in Figure 7.13 (based on the market attractiveness/competitive strength matrix of Figure 7.4), Unilever's most aggregate level of analysis is its different product businesses. With this global corporate portfolio as a starting point,

Figure 7.13 Unilever's global portfolio

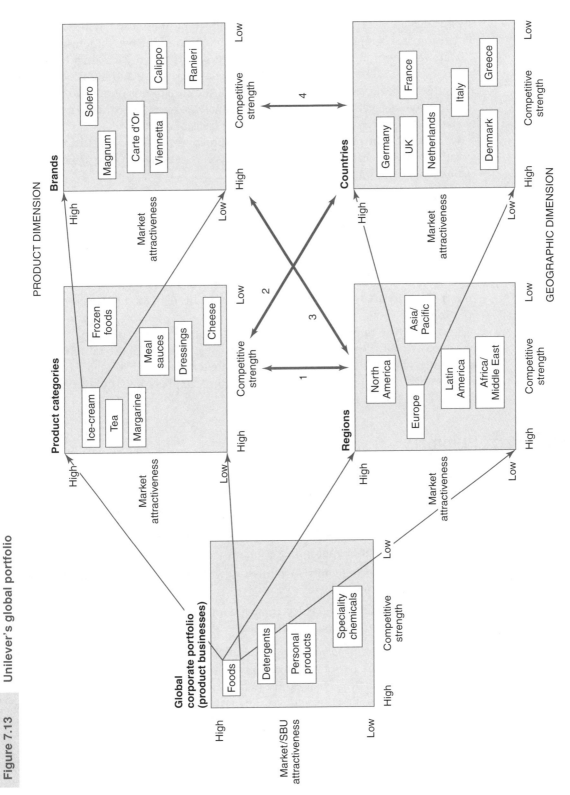

the further analysis of single corporate product business can go in a product dimension, a geographic dimension or a combination of the two dimensions.

It appears from the global corporate portfolio in Figure 7.13 that Unilever's 'foods' business is characterized by high market attractiveness and high competitive strengths. However, a more distinct picture of the situation is obtained by analyzing underlying levels. This more detailed analysis is often required to give an operational input to specific market-planning decisions.

By combining the product and geographic dimensions it is possible to analyze the global corporate portfolio at the following levels (indicated by the arrows in the example of Figure 7.13):

1. Product categories by regions (or vice versa).
2. Product categories by countries (or vice versa).
3. Regions by brands (or vice versa).
4. Countries by brands (or vice versa).

Of course, it is possible to make further detailed analysis of, for example, the country level by analyzing different customer groups (e.g. food retailers) in certain countries.

Thus it may be important to assess the interconnectedness of various portfolio units across countries or regions. A customer (e.g. a large food retail chain) may have outlets in other countries, or the large retailers may have formed cross-border alliances in retailing with central purchasing from suppliers (e.g. Unilever) – see also section 16.7 on international retailing.

7.6 ▎ Summary

Especially in SMEs, international market selection (IMS) is simply a reaction to a stimulus provided by a change agent, in the form of an unsolicited order.

A more proactive and systematic approach to IMS entails the following steps:

Step 1. Selection of relevant segmentation criteria.

Step 2. Development of appropriate segments.

Step 3. Screening of segments to narrow down the list of appropriate countries (choice of target).

Step 4. Micro segmentation: development of subsegments in each qualified country or across countries.

However, the *pragmatic approach* to IMS is often used successfully by firms. Often coincidences and the personal network of top managers play an important role in the 'selection' of the firm's first export market.

After the four steps described above, the market expansion strategy of the chosen market is a key decision. In designing this strategy, the firm has to answer two underlying questions:

● Will it enter markets incrementally (the waterfall approach) or simultaneously (the shower approach)?

● Will entry be concentrated or diversified across international markets?

Corporate portfolio analysis represents an excellent way of combining the international market selection (the geographic dimension) with the product dimension. It is important to assess how to allocate resources across geographic areas/product businesses. However, it is also important to evaluate the interconnectedness of various portfolio units across geographic borders. For example, a particular customer (located in a certain country) may have business in several countries.

Case study   The Loewen Group Inc.

International market selection for one of the world's biggest suppliers of funeral services

What is a funeral?

A funeral is similar to other ceremonies in our lives. Like a graduation ceremony, or a wedding, a funeral is a rite of passage by which we recognize an important event that distinguishes our lives.

The funeral declares that a death has occurred. It celebrates the life that has been lived, and offers family and friends the opportunity to pay tribute to their loved one. The gathering of family and friends for a time of sharing and funeral service helps to provide emotional support so needed at that time. This will help those who grieve to face the reality of death and, consequently, to take the first step toward a healthy emotional adjustment.

The funeral can and does take many varied forms. Funerals can last from minutes to months and are usually influenced by the religion, lifestyle and values of the bereaved family and friends. If the dead person has had some special wishes for the funeral, this would also be followed in most cultures.

In our society, two basic forms of disposal of the dead are practised:

1. *Earth burial*, which continues to be the most frequently chosen method.

2. *Cremation*, whereby the body is reduced by intense heat over several hours to a few ounces of small fragments. These cremated remains are usually placed in an urn which may be buried, placed in a memorial niche, or kept in some other location. Cremated remains may also be scattered where permitted by law.

Entombment in a crypt is also a choice and is one of the oldest forms of burial. Today many cemeteries maintain crypts for entombment which may be in a mausoleum or in an outdoor garden. This form is not very often used.

Though earth burial is still the most used option, cremation is getting more and more popular. According to the Cremation Association of North America, cremation accounted for 21 per cent of death arrangements in 1986, and is forecasted to account for 26 per cent in 2000 and 40 per cent in 2010. Cremation costs less compared to a traditional funeral and burial; the cost difference is up to 50 per cent. There is a similar development in the European funeral market.

The Loewen Group (LG)

Based in Vancouver, The Loewen Group Inc. owns or operates more than 1,100 funeral homes and more than 400 cemeteries across the United States, Canada, and the United Kingdom. The Company employs approximately 13,000 people and derives approximately 90 per cent of its revenue from its US operations.

LG has just started international activities by acquiring a few funeral homes and cemeteries in the UK in 1997. However, international activities only account for a small fraction of its total revenue.

LG is the second largest funeral home and cemetery operator in North America and in the whole world after SCI, which is also the main competitor for LG. Revenues for 1999 were $1,030.4 million, compared with $1,136.2 million in 1998. Including non-operating charges during 1999, the net loss for 1999 was $465.2 million ($6.40 per share).

Service Corporation International (SCI)

Service Corporation International (SCI) is the world's largest provider of death care services, with nearly 4,500 funeral service locations and crematoria in North America, South America, Europe and the Pacific Rim. Its 40,000 professionals help families in 20 countries with funeral, burial and cremation services and associated merchandise, prearranged funeral plans, and pre-need cemetery property and merchandise. Since the company's founding in 1962, SCI's annual revenues have grown to nearly $3.3 billion.

During the 1980s, the company briefly experimented with operating a casket manufacturing and distribution division. By the end of the decade, however, SCI decided to refocus all of its efforts on its core businesses – funeral homes and cemeteries – and to explore the possibilities of new international markets.

In 1993, SCI boldly stepped beyond the bounds of North America and astonished the funeral industry when it acquired the Pine Grove Funeral Group of Australia. This purchase and the subsequent acquisition of Melbourne's Le Pine Holdings Proprietary Limited in 1994 added some 100 funeral homes and resulted in the creation of a new subsidiary, SCI-Australia.

During 1994, SCI looked toward Europe with its entry into Great Britain. The company acquired 154 funeral homes, 2 cemeteries and 13 crematoriums owned by Great Southern Group plc, and 380 funeral homes held by Plantsbrook Group plc, gaining SCI approximately 15 per cent of the British market. However SCI's experience in Britain has been uncomfortable, and has caused some to question its ability to expand elsewhere in Europe. The takeovers were hostile (subsequent acquisitions have been by consent), and created a vocal opposition.

In July 1995, SCI announced the acquisition of two divisions of the French conglomerate Lyonnaise des Eaux, which included Pompes Funebres Generales S.A. (PFG) the largest death care organization in Europe. This purchase added some 950 funeral homes in France and additional facilities in Switzerland, Italy, Belgium, the Czech Republic, and Singapore. In France, where SCI has around 20–25% of the market, it is trying hard to sell more tombstones, which the French spend far more on than other Europeans.

SCI has thus become one of the world's largest providers of death care services.

SCI expanded successfully into Australia in the early 1990s, and found that rationalisation, consolidation and better marketing worked as well there as in America.

The international market for funeral services

The funeral industry in the western world has yearly sales of something like $20 billion. A trend is towards cremation, which is almost always cheaper and saves land. It is prohibited by Islam and Orthodox Christianity, but in much of the rest of the world (especially northern Europe and eastern Asia) it is already the preferred option.

A weakening of organised religion, coupled with the breakdown of the traditional family, means that the 'traditional' funeral faces a decline.

One important characteristic of the funeral industry is the vertical integration of the functions in the value chain: combining several or even all elements of the funeral package under one roof. This enables, for example, an undertaker to sell a gravestone at the same time as he sells the coffin and funeral.

Also, funeral services need some kind of marketing activities. Whether the selling is done by letter, telephone call or personal visit, some customers inevitably find it distressing – and are liable to complain. The worst of SCI's bad publicity in the British media arose from some high-pressure selling of funeral services in Southern England.

The consolidation of the industry also raises issues of competition: a funeral provider owning its local crematorium is like an airline that owns a hub airport. Even if prices are nominally the same for all, such a provider can easily favour the in-house customer – for example, by keeping competitors out of the prime-time weekend and midday slots. SCI insists it never does this.

As the competition in the funeral industry has increased there have appeared several ways of boosting revenues. This can reach an extent which defies parody. One American undertaker, for example, apparently offers a coffin fitted with a mobile telephone, air conditioning, a light and a computer toy, in case the corpse revives.

Another way of boosting revenues is the pre-planned funeral, in which the funeral home gets customers, and their money, in advance. The number of funerals bought in advance varies sharply from country to country. In the Netherlands and Belgium, for example, 70 per cent of the population have a pre-paid funeral plan; in Spain the figure is 50 per cent. In Britain, barely 2 per cent of funerals are now pre-paid, although the figure is increasing sharply. In America, the sums involved are in the billion-dollar range.

American funeral market

The American funeral market is the most developed and most lucrative in the world, particularly for big companies like SCI and LG. Anyone planning to organize a funeral in the developed world has to ask himself whether the American companies will succeed in dominating the business.

The trend toward higher funeral prices has gained momentum with the continued consolidation in the industry. Today, five big corporations, including the Loewen Group and Service Corp. International, own nearly 20 per cent of the nations's 22,200 funeral homes. It now costs more than ever to die, reflecting the high price the large chains have paid to acquire funeral homes. An average funeral in 1996 (the most recent year for which figures are available) cost $4,782, up 17 per cent since 1993, according to the National Funeral Directors Association.

The latest development

For those whose wiring has lost its earthly current, a multimedia Web site obituary is the latest trend in the funeral process. Non-commercial tributes have been around for some time, but the funeral industry is catching on to the potential profit. For around $1,000, an American company (accessible at www.memorials.com) offers a dedicated page on its Web site. Rather than physically visiting the family tomb, relatives and friends can refresh their memories of a loved one at the click of a mouse.

The Web site can offer video and audio clips (for example of the deceased and the funeral), as well as a family tree that may in future be linked by hypertext to other obituary sites.

In the late 1980s, Wall Street started paying attention to the industry. Funeral homes became an attractive investment as statistics demonstrated that the absolute number of deaths in North America would nearly double by 2040. In the beginning of the 1990s, consolidators (the big companies) typically saw a 25 per cent operating profit margin, while independents barely squeezed out 10 per cent.

However, in the year 2000 the trend towards the low-cost cremation plus the increased competition in the US market has lowered the market prices and has also resulted in lower profit margins (and lower stock prices) for LG. SCI is not doing too well either but the top management in LG has heard that SCI is still making money on its international operations (outside USA).

Therefore LG has asked you to make an evaluation of the possible new international markets which LG could enter in future.

Questions

1. Discuss which criteria LG should use in its market screening process?
2. Are there any relevant alternatives for LG to 'acquisitions' of foreign funeral homes?
3. How do you think the internet development in funeral services will affect LG's international business activities?

Sources: Adapted from:
Anon. (1997) 'An expensive way to go', *The Economist*, 4 January.
Manus, P. (1998) 'Death's future', *Marketing News*, (2), 19 January, pp. 15–17.
Sharke, S. (1999) 'The eternal when', *Target Marketing*, December, pp. 40–2.
Websites of funeral services suppliers.

Questions for discussion

1. Why is screening of foreign markets important? Outline the reasons why many firms do not systematically screen countries/markets.

2. Explore the factors which influence the international market selection process.

3. Discuss the advantages and disadvantages of using only secondary data as screening criteria in the IMS process.

4. What are the advantages and disadvantages of an opportunistic selection of international markets?

5. What are the differences between a global market segment and a national market segment? What are the marketing implications of these differences for a firm serving segments on a world-wide basis?

6. Discuss the possible implications that the firm's choice of geographic expansion strategy may have on the ability of a local marketing manager of a foreign subsidiary to develop and implement marketing programmes.

Internet exercise

Durex Global Sex Survey

Please go to:
http://www.durex.com (please click on Global Sex survey 2000)

www.condomi.com (Condomi AG is a competitor to Durex/SSL International)

The Durex Global Sex Survey focuses exclusively on the sexual attitudes and behaviour of today's youth in 20 countries around the world. The survey is sponsored by SSL International, manufacturers of Durex, the world's largest condom brand.

Questions

1. Which sociocultural factors are important to consider in the global marketing of condoms?

2. How could the German condom manufacturer Condomi AG use the survey in their international market selection?

3. Which of the 14 markets in the survey would you recommend Condomi to concentrate on?

For further exercises and cases, see this book's website at *www.booksites.net/hollensen*

References

Anderson, P. H. and Strandskov, J. (1998) 'International market selection', *Journal of Global Marketing*, vol. 11, no. 3, pp. 65–84.

Ayal, I. and Zif, J. (1979) 'Market expansion strategies in multinational marketing', *Journal of Marketing*, vol. 43, Spring, pp. 84–94.

Bradley, F. (1995) *International Marketing Strategy*, Prentice Hall, London.

Crick, D. and Chaudhry, S. (1995) 'Export practices of Asian SMEs: some preliminary findings', *Marketing Intelligence and Planning*, vol. 13, no. 11, pp. 13–21.

Douglas, S. and Craig, C.A. (1995) *Global Marketing Strategy*, McGraw-Hill, New York.

Green, R.T. and Allaway, A.W. (1985) 'Identification of export opportunities: a shift-share approach', *Journal of Marketing*, vol. 49, Winter, pp. 83–8.

Harrell, G.D. and Kiefer, R.O. (1995) 'Multinational market portfolios' in Paliwoda, S.J. and Ryans Jr, J.K., *International Marketing Reader*, Routledge, London/New York.

Johanson, J. and Vahlne, J.E. (1977) 'The internationalization process of the firm – a model of knowledge development and increasing foreign market commitment', *Journal of International Business Studies*, vol. 8, no. 1, pp. 23–32.

Keegan, W. (1995) *Global Marketing Management*, Prentice Hall, Englewood Cliffs, NJ.

Mazur, Laura and Lannon, Judie (1993) 'Crossborder marketing lessons from 25 European success stories', *EIU Research Report*, the Economist Intelligence Unit Limited, London, pp. 17–19.

Papadopoulos, N. and Denis, J.E. (1988) 'Inventory, taxonomy and assessment of methods for international market selection', *International Marketing Review*, Autumn, pp. 38–51.

Piercy, N. (1981) 'Company internationalisation: active and reactive exporting', *European Journal of Marketing*, vol. 15, no. 3, pp. 26–40.

Sylvest, J. and Lindholm, C. (1997) 'Små globale virksomheder', *Ledelse & Erhvervsøkonomi*, vol. 61, April, pp. 131–43.

Vernon, R. (1966) 'International investment and international trade in product cycle', *Quarterly Journal of Economics*, vol. 80, pp. 190–207.

Welford, R. and Prescott, K. (1996) *European Business*, Pitman, London.

Case II.1 CarLovers

Serendipity as a factor in foreign market selection: the case of CarLovers from Australia

The CarLovers brand was introduced into the Australian market in March 1989 by three Australian and two American businessmen, and was incorporatized and fully Australianized in December 1990. The concept was to revolutionize the car-washing industry, which is dominated in most countries by the major petrol companies. The brand is strong on environmental considerations, with less polluting grease and chemicals being released into public drains, and 80 per cent reclaiming and recycling of all water used in the car-washing process. These public benefits are supplemented by private benefits to consumers, since the laser technology also results in less damage to cars when they are washed. Additionally the facility is easy to use in a bright, clean retailing atmosphere, as opposed to the often greasy facilities and low service priority offered at petrol stations. An example of CarLovers' facilities is shown in Figure 1.

Business activities initially gave emphasis to the Australian operations, resulting in 48 car washes by 1995, 14 of them company owned and 34 of them franchised. Franchising was seen as an important way to grow the business in the first five years. Since 1995 the number of car washes has increased to about 80, with all additions being company owned.

The original strategy was to develop the concept, prove that it could be multiplied in the mode of McDonald's, and then take it to other countries. *The decision to internationalize* was therefore present at the beginning of the company's life. However, it was more of 'a dream, rather than a grand plan', according to Mr Steve Spencer, managing director of CarLovers International, in an interview for this case study. The McDonald's experience was always an inspirational factor, providing a lesson in developing a good concept, proving it domestically and then going international.

The success of the concept relative to the offer of competitors is clearly evident in the rapid and sustained growth of car washes. Within a few years it would have been clear that the concept was ready for internationalization. The focus of this case study is the selection of country markets: that is, *which countries to enter in what order*. The managing director of CarLovers made it quite clear that the standard textbook model of market selection (see Figure 7.2) was *not* used. Business does not work that way, says Steve Spencer. Instead he gives emphasis to opportunities, chance meetings, rejecting the less viable options, and seizing the best opportunities as they present themselves. This is the way business works in practice. The textbook model may be appropriate for larger firms, but for small and medium-sized firms in general, and certainly for the case of CarLovers, the pragmatic model better describes the internationalization process.

To illustrate this process in more detail, here are five steps taken by CarLovers to enter foreign markets:

1. In mid-1993 executives of CarLovers were in the USA holding discussions with their equipment suppliers. This led to a chance meeting with some Mexican businessmen visiting the same supplier. Following discussions with the Mexicans, agreement was reached for them to start a Mexican franchise of the business. One could say that the choice of country (Mexico) and partners was based on chance.

2. A year later, further discussions with business contacts in the USA led to an American franchise being established in Grand Rapids. To avoid council red tape, an existing car wash site was used and 'retrofitted' to the CarLovers design. The success of this operation can be seen in the tripling of turnover at the site. A second American site has been retrofitted.

3. In late 1994 an executive from CarLovers held discussions with the Malaysian manager of Caltex and this led to CarLovers introducing

Figure 1   **Facilities at a CarLovers car wash**

two outlets *within* Caltex service stations. The CarLovers brand was not prominent in this arrangement. In any case, a particular friendship and business contact in Malaysia determined both the second foreign market to be entered and the partner involved.

4. Later in 1994, further business contacts led to meetings in Kuala Lumpur with representatives from a Malaysian conglomerate called the Berjaya group. These discussions were so fruitful that the Berjaya group purchased 24 per cent of the equity of CarLovers. Further equity and more planning led to the January 1997 go-ahead to build four new CarLover car washes in Malaysia in 1997 and more later.

5. The January 1997 decision also flagged Kuala Lumpur as the training centre for all of the Asian operations. Three countries, Indonesia, the Philippines and Korea, are the priority target markets, followed by China. Formal planning is greater for this next (fifth) wave of foreign entry, perhaps a reflection that CarLovers is now a bigger operation (though still a medium-sized company) and needs to satisfy a large conglomerate partner. The factors leading to the selection of the top three target markets included size of market, degree of development, cost of land, opportunity and the emerging mass of middle-class consumers. These factors are closer to the textbook model of market selection.

These five phases of foreign market selection provide great insight into the actual process used by a service-based exporter (though CarLovers also sells some manufactured products as well). *The pragmatic model*, reflecting the cut and thrust of seeking business opportunities, plays an important role in the selection of country, partner, distributor and distribution system (company owned, franchised or concession arrangement). Business contacts and networking are at the heart of this cut and thrust. In many cases, the business relationships were determined first and the choice of target markets was determined second. However, as a small business gets larger, although serendipity may continue to play a part, it is a smaller part of the target market selection process.

The CarLovers case study is also a good example of the need to be flexible in terms of both entry modes and international marketing programmes. The entry mode for Mexico was less restricted than for the USA, which was strongly influenced by local government regulations. Two different entry modes were used in Malaysia, initially a concession approach and then a fully branded franchised system, to reflect the different nature of the distributors. Slightly different marketing programmes are needed across countries. Although the basic concept of less damage to cars, a clean and pleasant retailing environment and environmental care holds true in most countries, there can be subtle differences which need to be taken into account at the specific country level. For example, the benefit of water conservation is more important in a low-rainfall country like Australia than in tropical Malaysia.

Questions

1. How would you characterize the IMS process in this case compared to the textbook model?

2. What are the general differences in the IMS process between LSEs and SMEs?

3. In this case the management implicitly have some criteria in the IMS process. Could there be other relevant screening criteria?

Prepared by Bill Merrilees and Dale Miller, Marketing Group, Department of Management, University of Newcastle, Australia.

Case II.2   Automobile Citroën

Marketing strategy for the Far Eastern market

You will be expected to update information where you think necessary and to source additional information to enable you to tackle the questions, and to suggest a strategy for the next millennium.

Background

Citroën is now part of the PSA group, which is a global player in the automotive and associated industries. Citroën cars are sold in over 170 countries world-wide. The company currently operates in two main business streams, Peugeot and Citroën, which are very closely related in that most components and parts are common, and each manufacturer has a 'paired model' in the range (e.g. the Citroën Saxo is paired with the older but highly successful Peugeot 106, the ZX with the 306, and the Xantia with the 406). However, brand identity is still very individual, even to the extent of having different selling outlets and servicing arrangements.

Brands are managed on a global basis, although each regional market is considered. Citroën has been increasing its presence in the emerging markets of Asia and the Pacific rim, under the leadership of a specific Far East management team. This is viewed as an important opportunity for substantial growth. For example, the Malaysian company Proton will be building a version of the AX for the Far East market and a Proton-bodied version of the new Saxo for the European market (to be on sale in the UK in 1998). The old and outmoded Lada taxis in China are now being replaced by Chinese-built ZXs (Daihatsu also has a share of this market). This version of the ZX, known as 'Happiness and Prosperity', is the first European car to be built in China (at Wuhan) that is not based on a discontinued model. 'China is incontestably the market of the future,' according to Jacques Calvet, PSA chairman. Sister brand Peugeot is also built in China.

The group is committed to 'growing through profitability, volume and brand strength on an international basis to maintain a presence as a global player'.

The Rennes la Janais plant in the north-west of France produces the Xantia and is reckoned to be one of the most sophisticated production lines in the world. The plant is supplied by more than 30 local suppliers, integrated into the production process on a just-in-time basis. The aim of the plant is to achieve a zero technical default rate and a tolerance of less than 1 mm on all opening parts. A high level of training is undertaken and some 4 per cent of the budget is spent on training activities.

The influential consumer satisfaction studies by the American J.D. Power and Associates have found that PSA now outranks VW, Fiat and Renault, confirming the progress it has made in quality.

Product range

One of the key reasons behind this success is the introduction of a brand new model in all five major European segments over just six years, ensuring a modern vehicle for every type of driver. Each model has been developed in response to researched customer needs, and there is continuing investment and development to try and ensure that Citroën has a competitive advantage in terms of design, performance, reliability, economy, safety and overall marketplace acceptance.

The Citroën product range is shaped by its marque identity and corporate culture. The company tailors its products and communications to a very wide but carefully targeted audience. Table 1 gives details of the range.

Table 1   The Citroën models

Model	Sector	Peugeot equivalent	Joint with
AX	Compact	n.a.	n.a.
Saxo	Small	106, 205	n.a.
ZX	Small/family/fleet	306	n.a.
Xantia	Family/fleet	406	n.a.
XM	Large/executive	605	n.a.
Synergie	MPV	n.a.	Fiat

New product development strategy

Decisions to achieve a high degree of commonality between the Citroën and Peugeot product lines have meant that sister models share the same engines, drivetrains, suspension components, electrics, switchgear and even body parts, including the expensive floorpan (some 50 per cent of components are common). The overall aim is to reduce development timescales down to the average achieved by the leading Japanese manufacturers, $3\frac{1}{2}$ years. The decision was also taken to introduce eight new models every six years. This concentration on product development has been a key factor in the recent success of the marque.

The outlook: The Antares Project

The Antares Project is an ambitious five-year programme designed to bring Citroën up to and beyond Japanese manufacturers such as Toyota and Honda in terms of build quality, reliability and costs of manufacture. The aims are straightforward and involve manufacturing practices of both Citroën and its suppliers.

Much of the future revolves around the impending environmental legislation issues not only for Citroën, but for all motor manufacturers. However, the following developments have been prioritized by Citroën:

- *Clean-running cars* by reducing exhaust emissions. Research is being conducted using existing technologies such as the catalytic converter and diesel, but work is also underway on two-stroke and hydrogen engines as well as alternative fuels.

- *Fuel-efficient cars* by reducing average fuel consumption (the now elderly AX is a world leader for a production car).

- *Quiet-running cars* by reducing powerplant noise and road noise. A goal of 50 per cent reduction in both has been set in the next five years.

- *Electric cars* initially for commercial vehicles, then passenger cars for city use.

- *Smart cars* using the ISIS interactive road signs systems. The Japanese appear to have a substantial lead in this technology.

- *Recyclable cars* in the short term by rebuilding certain mechanical components and recovering

raw materials. Improved steels for body parts and major advances in corrosion protection should ensure a considerably longer life for the vehicle, enabling savings in replacements to be made. However, this will have a knock-on effect on new car sales.

Questions

If possible, make use of Tables 2–4.

Table 2 — Demand for cars and small utility vehicles by geographic zone, 1990

Zone	No. of vehicles (m)	%
USA and Canada	15.5	32
Western Europe	15.3	32
Eastern Europe	3.2	7
Middle East	0.4	1
Latin America	1.7	3
Africa	0.6	1
Asia	11.8	24
Total	48.5	100

Table 3 — Asian car sales by country

	1995 (000)	2000 (000)	Top brand
Japan	6,387	7,120	Toyota
South Korea	1,536	1,640	Hyundai
Thailand	572	915	Toyota
Malaysia	286	420	Proton
China	1,415	2,210	VW
Vietnam	12	55	Kia
Philippines	129	280	Toyota
Indonesia	384	675	Toyota
Australia	637	675	Ford
Singapore	47	n.a.	Mercedes
Taiwan	573	598	Ford/Mazda

You should also specify any areas where you require further information, although you should spend a limited amount of your study time conducting your own market research – say, a couple of hours. If you have access to the Internet this will not take long, and if you have a good library close by, an hour will generate a wealth of

Table 4	Asian car sales by brand (total SE Asia sales: 1,332,807)

Brand	Market share (%)
Toyota	22.1
Isuzu	12.6
Mitsubishi	12.2
Nissan	9.9
Proton	8.5
Suzuki	5.8
Daihatsu	5.6
Honda	4.2
Mazda	2.5
Mercedes	1.9
Others	14.7

Source: EIU, *Automotive Resources Asia*, 1996.

information. If this is not possible, a scan of current relevant motor magazines will be useful, as will cutting out Citroën advertising.

1. As newly appointed marketing director of Citroën, briefly assess the current range of models available, and then outline the key points of a global marketing strategy for the next ten years.

2. You have been given particular responsibility for the Far Eastern market. Briefly outline the information that you require to enable you to conduct an analysis of these markets. How would you propose to screen these markets and what criteria would you use?

3. Develop marketing strategies for the chosen Far Eastern markets.

Prepared by Neil C. Macpherson, Napier Marketing Group, Edinburgh.

Case II.3 Tipperary Mineral Water Company

Market selection inside/outside Europe

The Irish firm Tipperary Mineral Water Company (TMWC) was founded in 1986 by Patrick and Nicholas Cooney. It has since developed into a major national brand in the £40 million Irish mineral water market, with about 15 per cent market share there. The market share outside Ireland is very small.

The 60 employees in the company generated in 1998 a total turnover of about £7 million Irish (IEP). The net profit was 0.3 million IEP (1 IEP = 1.2 US$).

TMWC is a part of the Gleeson Group which has a solid base in the Irish drinks market. The Gleeson Group ranks amongst the top 200 companies in Ireland. As a consequence, TMWC has a solid and sound financial background.

Tipperary mineral water (sparkling and still water) is available in a range of packaging options including 200 ml, 500 ml, 1 litre, 1.5 litre and 2 litre bottles. All bottles are recyclable and all labels bear the recyclable symbol. The product range has been extended into the office and leisure market with its 19 litre Tipperary Cooler Dispensers for offices (see also a picture of the product range at *http://www.tipperary-water.ie/products.html/*).

Mineral water in Ireland

General acceptance of bottled water as an alternative to alcohol when socializing is a relatively recent phenomenon in Ireland and Britain. However, it has long been a way of life in Continental Europe and the United States. This has as much to do with historical traditions as the quality of tap water. France has a tradition of drinking bottled water going back to Roman times. French consumers today use different brands on different occasions and have a highly developed palate for water, which could be said for most Continental countries.

Ireland is therefore at an early stage of development as regards the consumption of bottled waters. Few consumers can distinguish between alternative brands and sales of sparkling water are greater than still water. In Europe and the US, bottled water is part of the way of life and sales of still water greatly outweigh sales of sparkling water, with much substitution of bottled for tap water.

Consumption per capita of bottled water in Ireland is perhaps 5 litres per capita per annum, and Britain is at 8 litres. However, consumption per capita in France is in excess of 80 litres per capita per annum, with Germany averaging 80, and the US over 60.

Tipperary as a brand name abroad gains instant recognition from the song 'It's a long way from Tipperary' which is one of the most international of songs. It was particularly popular during the First and Second World Wars as a marching song and was broadcast to a world-wide cinema audience through Movietone news reports.

The location of Ireland to source bottled water is a good idea in that Ireland is generally perceived as green, unspoiled and lacking in industrialization or pollution.

The European market for mineral water

The following examines the retail market for mineral waters in six major markets: France, Italy, the UK, Germany, Spain and Benelux (Belgium, the Netherlands and Luxembourg). Sales through 'horeca' (hotels, restaurants and catering establishments) are for the main part excluded.

Mineral water originates from a pure earth source and contains healthy constituents like minerals and trace elements. It must be bottled at source and must not undergo any form of treatment except that of separating the iron from sulphur to avoid any discoloration or smell. Nothing may be added or taken away from the water, except carbon dioxide to make sparkling water. Mineral water has benefited from the shift away from alcohol consumption due to stricter drink-drive laws and health awareness generally. Greater concern over the quality of municipal tap water supplies has also underpinned rising demand for mineral waters.

| Table 1 | Value sales of mineral waters in US dollars by country 1997 |

Country	US$ m 1997
Germany	3,491
Italy	2,421
France	2,087
UK	657
Spain	415
Benelux	354

Source: *Euromonitor*

Table 1 shows the total market values of mineral water in the major European markets. The mineral waters market is broken down into the following sectors (Table 2):

● still

● sparkling

● flavoured

Still water is the dominant sector in the mineral waters market, offering a direct, healthy alternative to tap water. Sparkling water demand is more meal/occasion-specific, and the digestive properties on offer mean that sparkling water tends to attract a higher margin. Flavoured water remains a negligible influence on most markets, but is the most dynamic sector where sales exist.

An increased spread of distribution outlets and wider availability have exposed mineral waters to a greater audience. So mineral waters have established a commodity status in several countries and this is increasingly affecting trends apparent in the market. As a consequence the mineral waters market is characterized by high levels of private label penetration.

| Table 2 | Volume sales of mineral waters by sector and by country: percentage analysis 1997 |

% volume	France	Italy	UK	Germany	Spain	Benelux
Still	80.9	64.3	62.7	36.2	93.7	58.5
Sparkling	16.7	35.7	37.3	62.6	6.3	34.2
Flavoured	2.4	—	—	1.2	—	7.3
Total	100.0	100.0	100.0	100.0		100.0

Source: *Euromonitor*

| Table 3 | Volume of manufacturer shares of mineral waters by country 1997 |

% volume	France	Italy	UK	Germany	Spain	Benelux
Nestlé	29.5	34.5	10.8	—	3.1	10.0
Danone	26.4	15.0	17.6	—	17.4	8.0
Castel	14.2	—	—	—	—	—
San Benedetto	—	17.0	—	—	—	—
Gerolsteiner	—	—	—	9.5	—	—
Apollinarls	—	—	—	5.3	—	—
Vilsa	—	—	—	2.9	—	—
Fürst Bismarck	—	—	—	2.9	—	—
Spadel	—	—	—	—	—	29.0
Vichy Catalán	—	—	—	—	14.8	—
Private label	10.8	—	40.0	—	2.8	43.0
Others	19.1	33.5	31.6	79.4	61.9	10.0
Total	100.0	100.0	100.0	100.0	100.0	100.0

Source: *Euromonitor*

Competitive situation on the European mineral water market

The global bottled waters market underwent dramatic changes in terms of brand ownership in 1992, when the Swiss food giant Nestlé bought all Perrier's mineral water brands except Volvic, which was sold to BSN (now known as Groupe Danone). Today Nestlé (with brands like Perrier and Vittel) and Danone (with brands like Evian and Volvic) are the leading mineral water producers, both in Europe and in the whole world. The market shares of the manufacturers are shown in Table 3.

Domestic producers continue to have a significant presence, despite increasing consolidation, in France (Groupe Neptune with Castel), Italy (San Benedetto), Spain (Vichy Catlan) and Benelux (Spadel from Belgium is the market leader with 29 per cent of total value sales in 1997).

As an international marketing consultant you are contacted by the management group of TMWC. They want you to prepare a report in which you give well-founded solutions to the following tasks.

Questions

1. Which country or countries in Europe (outside Ireland) would you recommend TMWC to concentrate on?

2. Which country or countries outside Europe would you recommend TMWC to concentrate on (use Table 4)?

Table 4	Volume and value of all mineral waters by country			
	Per capita volume 1997 (litres)	Total value 1997 (US$ m)	% change 1993/1997 (US$ value)	Per capita value 1997 (US$)
Argentina	13.1	300	46.6	8.40
Australia	8.4	133	48.6	7.20
Brazil	8.9	1,244	219.9	7.78
Canada	18.6	436	44.6	14.39
Chile	5.2	46	33.3	3.13
China	0.4	447	48.9	0.36
Columbia	14.2	755	92.5	20.87
Hong Kong, China	7.1	47	40.5	7.21
India	0.0	12	923.6	0.01
Indonesia	4.1	270	52.9	1.34
Israel	22.8	117	71.0	20.13
Japan	5.4	757	60.3	6.01
Malaysia	1.2	28	28.0	1.30
Mexico	4.6	365	39.3	3.79
New Zealand	2.3	9	53.7	2.46
Philippines	3.3	136	170.8	1.85
Singapore	7.0	47	97.1	15.16
South Africa	0.3	17	165.6	0.38
South Korea	11.5	408	48.5	8.87
Taiwan	7.6	149	83.7	6.95
Thailand	0.0	1	54.1	0.01
Turkey	2.6	165	56.0	2.59
USA	44.7	8,567	48.8	31.98
Venezuela	5.7	86	88.2	3.72
Vietnam	0.5	26	991.9	0.33

Source: *Consumer International*, 1999

Part III

Market entry strategies

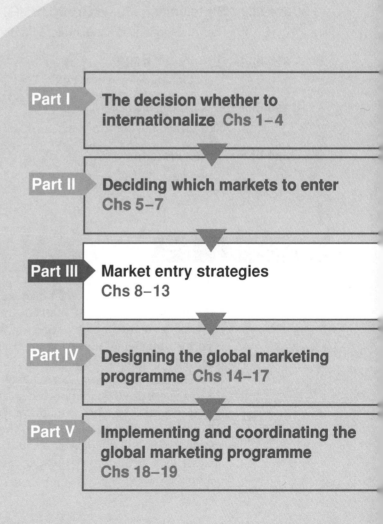

Part III Cases

Introduction

Once the firm has chosen target markets abroad (see Part II) the question arises as to the best way to enter those markets. In Part III we will consider the major market entry modes and criteria for selecting them. An international market entry mode is an institutional arrangement necessary for the entry of a company's products, technology and human capital into a foreign country/market.

To separate Part III from later chapters, let us take a look at Figure 1. The figure shows the classical distribution systems in a national consumer market.

In this context the chosen market entry mode (here, own sales subsidiary) can be regarded as the first decision level in the vertical chain that will provide marketing and distribution to the next actors in the vertical chain. In Chapter 16 we will take a closer look at the choice between alternative distribution systems at the single national level.

Figure 1 **Examples of different market entry modes and the distribution decision**

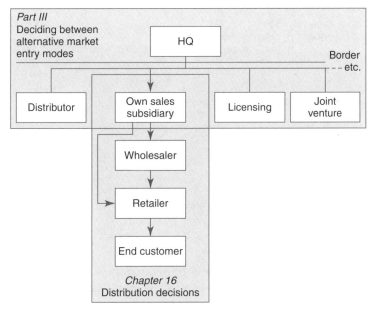

Some firms have discovered that an ill-judged market entry selection in the initial stages of a firm's internationalization can threaten the firm's future market entry and expansion activities. Since it is common for firms to have their initial mode choice institutionalized over time, as new products are sold through the same established channels and new markets are entered using the same entry method, a problematic initial entry mode choice can survive through the institutionalization of this mode. The inertia in the shift process of entry modes delays the transition to a new entry mode. The reluctance of firms to change entry modes once they are in place, and the difficulty involved in so doing, makes the mode of entry decision a key strategic issue for firms operating in today's rapidly internationalizing marketplace (Hollensen, 1991).

For most SMEs the market entry represents a critical first step, but for established companies the problem is not how to enter new emerging markets, but how to exploit opportunities more effectively within the context of their existing network of international operations.

There is, however, no ideal market entry strategy, and different market entry methods might be adopted by different firms entering the same market and/or by the same firm in different markets.

As shown in Figure 2, three broad groupings emerge when one looks at the assortment of entry modes available to the firm when entering international markets. There are different degrees of control, risk and flexibility associated with each of these different market entry modes. For example, the use of hierarchical modes (investment modes) gives the firm ownership and thereby high control, but committing heavy resources to foreign markets also represents a higher potential risk. At the same time, heavy resource commitment creates exit barriers, which diminish

Figure 2 | **Classification of market entry nodes**

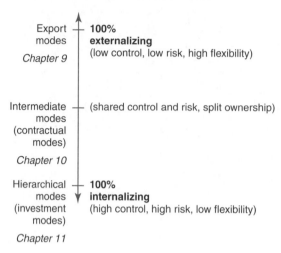

the firm's ability to change the chosen entry mode in a quick and easy way. So the entry mode decision involves trade-offs, as the firm cannot have both high control and high flexibility.

Figure 3 shows three examples representing the main types of market entry mode. By using hierarchical modes, transactions between independent actors are substituted by intra-firm transactions, and market prices are substituted by internal transfer prices.

Many factors should be considered in deciding on the appropriate market entry mode. These factors (criteria) vary with the market situation and the firm in

Figure 3 | **Examples of the different market entry modes in the consumer market**

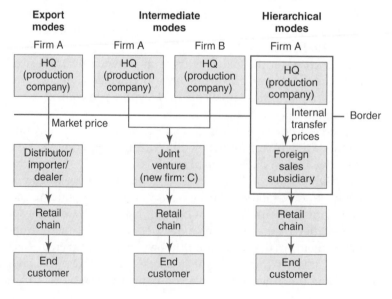

question. *Chapter 8* will examine the different decision criteria and how they influence the choice among the three main groupings of market entry modes.

Chapter 9 (Export modes), *Chapter 10* (Intermediate modes) and *Chapter 11* (Hierarchical modes) will discuss in more detail the three main types of entry mode. A special issue for SMEs is how their internationalization process is related to their much bigger customers and their sourcing and entry mode decisions. This will be discussed further in *Chapter 12*.

The simple version of the value chain (see Figure 1.9) will be used to structure the different entry modes in Chapters 9, 10 and 11.

References

Hollensen, S. (1991) 'Shift of market servicing organization in international markets: a Danish case study', in Vestergaard, H. (ed.), *An Enlarged Europe in the Global Economy*, EIBA's 17th Annual Conference, Copenhagen.

Plate 1 Blooming Clothing (Case Study Chapter 2)

Plate 2 Mission of the Fantastic Corporation (Case I.1)

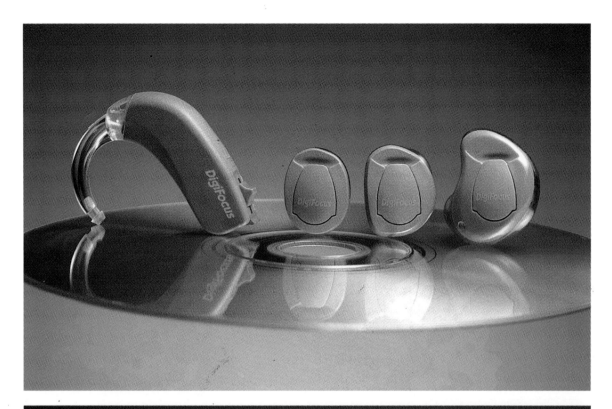

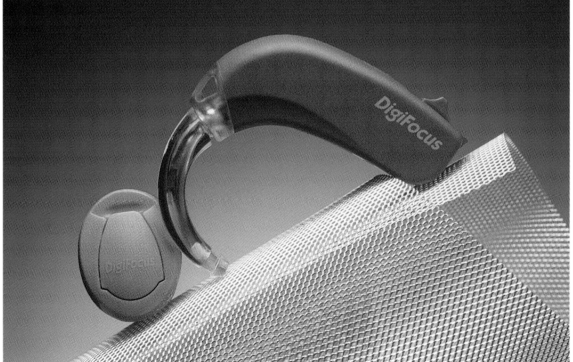

Plate 3 Oticon's fully digitalized 'DigiFocus' hearing aid (Case I.3)

Plate 4 Drakkar Noir: Sensuality and touch culture in Europe and Saudi Arabia (Exhibit 6.3)

Plate 5 Children in Ka-Boo-Ki clothes (LEGO licence) (Case Study Chapter 10)

Plate 6 Two of BMG's top artists: Toni Braxton and David Bowie (Case III.2 and IV.3)

NUEVO
ORGANICS
SHAMPOO
NUTRIENTE DE LA RAIZ
con Glucasil®

CABELLO FUERTE
Y SALUDABLE
DESDE LA
RAIZ

EXTRA CUERPO
PARA CABELLO FINO/SIN VIDA
para uso frecuente

E L I D A
HAIR INSTITUTE

INDUSTRIA ARGENTINA

ORGANICS

EL PRIMER SHAMPOO NUTRIENTE DE LA RAIZ

Organics es la primera línea para el cuidado del pelo con Glucasil, el nutriente natural del pelo que actúa en lo más profundo: la raíz. Organics fortalece todo tu pelo llenándolo de vida, dejándolo más sano y hermoso cada día.

ELIDA
HAIR
INSTITUTE
PARIS

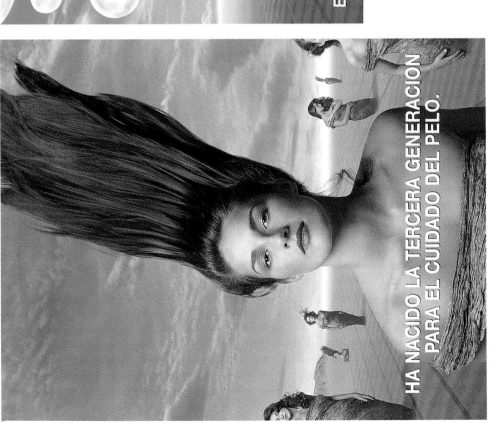

HA NACIDO LA TERCERA GENERACION PARA EL CUIDADO DEL PELO.

Plate 7 Unilever's introduction of Organics in Argentina (Chapter 14)

Plate 8 An advertisement for Motorola's Star TAC in the Korean market (Chapter 14)

Plate 9 An advertisement for Kellogg's Basmati Flakes in the Bombay area (Chapter 14)

(a)

Plate 10 Danish Klassic (Case Study Chapter 14)

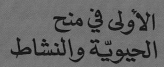

(b)

Plate 10 (continued)

(c)

Plate 10 (continued)

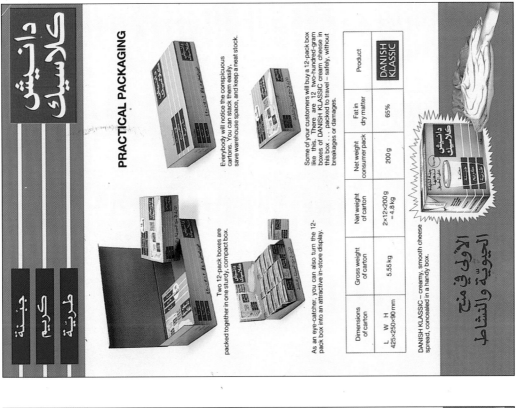

(e)

(d)

Plate 10 (continued)

(f)

Plate 10 (continued)

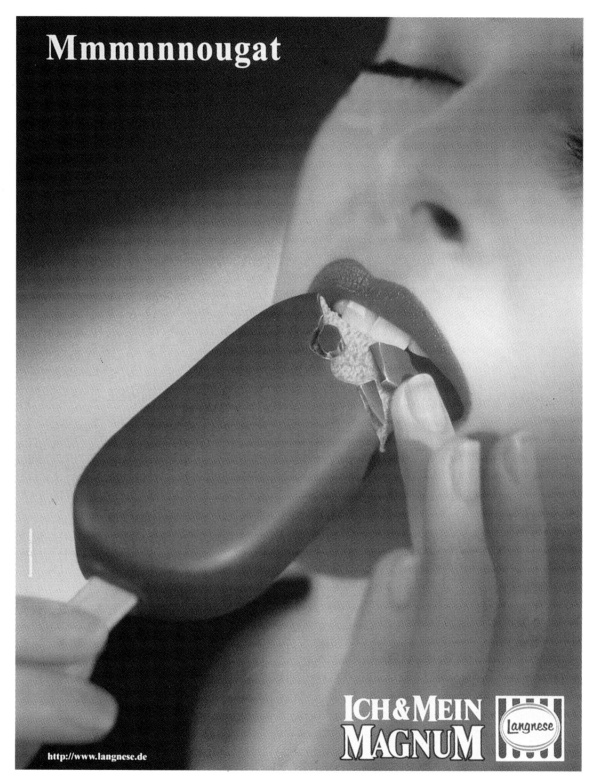

Plate 11 'Me and my Magnum' advertisement German version (Exhibits 17.2 and 19.2)

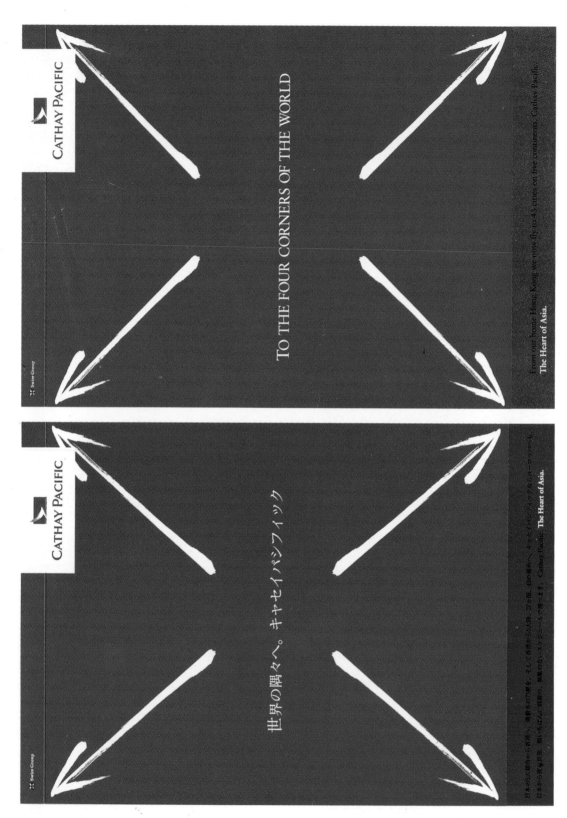

Plate 12 Standardized advertisements from Cathay Pacific (Chapter 17)

8

Some approaches to the choice of entry mode

Learning objectives

After studying this chapter you should be able to do the following:

● Identify and classify different market entry modes.

● Explore different approaches to the choice of entry mode.

● Explain how opportunistic behaviour affects the manufacturer/intermediary relationship.

● Identify the factors to consider when choosing a market entry strategy.

8.1 Introduction

We have seen the main groupings of entry modes that are available to companies that wish to take advantage of foreign market opportunities. At this point we are concerned with the question: what kind of strategy should be used for the entry mode selection?

According to Root (1994) there are three different rules:

● *Naive rule*. The decision-maker uses the same entry mode for all foreign markets. This rule ignores the heterogeneity of the individual foreign markets.
● *Pragmatic rule*. The decision-maker uses a workable entry mode for each foreign market. In the early stages of exporting, the firm typically starts doing business with a low-risk entry mode. Only if the particular initial mode is not feasible or profitable will the firm look for another workable entry mode. In this case not all potential alternatives are investigated, and the workable entry may not be the 'best' entry mode.
● *Strategy rules*. This approach requires that all alternative entry modes are systematically compared and evaluated before any choice is made. An application of

this decision rule would be to choose the entry mode that maximizes the profit contribution over the strategic planning period subject to (1) the availability of company resources, (2) risk and (3) non-profit objectives.

Although many SMEs probably use the pragmatic or even the naive rule, this chapter is mainly inspired by an analytical approach, which is the main principle behind the strategy rule.

8.2 ▌ The transaction cost approach

The principles of transaction cost analysis have already been presented in Chapter 3 (section 3.3). This chapter will go into further details about 'friction' and opportunism.

The unit of analysis is the transaction rather than the firm. The basic idea behind this approach is that in the real world there is always some friction between the buyer and seller in connection with market transactions. This friction is mainly caused by opportunistic behaviour in the relation between a producer and an export intermediary.

In the case of an agent, the producer specifies sales-promoting tasks which the export intermediary is to solve in order to receive a reward in the shape of commission.

In the case of an importer, the export intermediary has a higher degree of freedom as the intermediary itself, to a certain extent, can fix sales prices and thus base its earnings on the profit between the producer's sales price (the importer's buying price) and the importer's sales price.

No matter who the export intermediary may be, there will be some recurrent questions that may result in conflicts and opportunistic actions:

- Stock size of the export intermediary.
- Extent of technical and commercial service that the export intermediary is to carry out for its customers.
- Division of marketing costs (advertising, exhibition activities, etc.) between producer and export intermediary.
- Fixing of prices: from producer to export intermediary, and from the export intermediary to its customers.
- Fixing of commission to agents.

Opportunistic behaviour from the export intermediary

In this connection the export intermediary's opportunistic behaviour may be reflected in two activities:

- In most producer–export intermediary relations a split of the sales promoting costs has been fixed. Thus, statements by the export intermediary of too high sales promotion activities (e.g. by manipulating invoices) may form the basis of a higher payment from producer to export intermediary.

- The export intermediary may manipulate information on market size and competitor prices in order to obtain lower ex works prices from the producer. Of course, this kind of opportunism can be avoided if the export intermediary is paid a commission of realized turnover (the agency case).

Opportunistic behaviour from the producer

In this chapter we have until now presumed that the export intermediary is the one who has behaved opportunistically. The producer may, however, also behave in an opportunistic way, as the export intermediary must also use resources (time and money) on building up the market for the producer's product programme. This is especially the case if the producer wants to sell expensive and technically complicated products.

Thus, the export intermediary carries a great part of the economic risk, and will always have the threat of the producer's change of entry mode hanging over its head. If the export intermediary does not live up to the producer's expectations, it risks being replaced by another export intermediary, or the producer may change to its own export organization (sales subsidiary), as the increased transaction frequency (market size) can obviously bear the increased costs.

The last case may also be part of a deliberate strategy from the producer: namely, to tap the export intermediary for market knowledge and customer contacts in order to establish a sales organization itself.

What can the export intermediary do to meet this situation?

Heide and John (1988) suggest that the agent should make a number of further 'offsetting' investments in order to counterbalance the relation between the two parties. These investments create bonds that make it costly for the producer to leave the relationship: that is, the agent creates 'exit barriers' for the producer (the principal). Examples of such investments are as follows:

- Establish personal relations with the producer's key employees.
- Create an independent identity (image) in connection with selling the producer's products.
- Add further value to the product, such as BDA service (before–during–after service), which creates bonds in the agent's customer relations.

If it is impossible to make such offsetting investments, Heide and John (1988) suggest that the agent reduces its risk by representing more producers.

These are the conditions that the producer is up against, and when several of these factors appear at the same time, the theory recommends that the company (the producer) internalizes rather than externalizes.

8.3　Factors influencing the choice of entry mode

A firm's choice of its entry mode for a given product/target country is the net result of several, often conflicting forces. The need to anticipate the strength and direction of these forces makes the entry mode decision a complex process with numerous trade-offs among alternative entry modes.

Generally speaking, the choice of entry mode should be based on the expected contribution to profit. This may be easier said than done, particularly for those foreign markets where relevant data are lacking. Most of the selection criteria are qualitative in nature, and a quantification is very difficult.

As shown in Figure 8.1, four groups of factors are believed to influence the entry mode decision:

● Internal factors.

● External factors.

● Desired mode characteristics.

● Transaction-specific behaviour.

In what follows a proposition is formulated for each factor: how is each factor supposed to affect the choice of foreign entry mode? The direction of influence is also indicated both in the text and in Figure 8.1. Because of the complexity of the entry

Figure 8.1   **Factors affecting the foreign market entry mode decision**

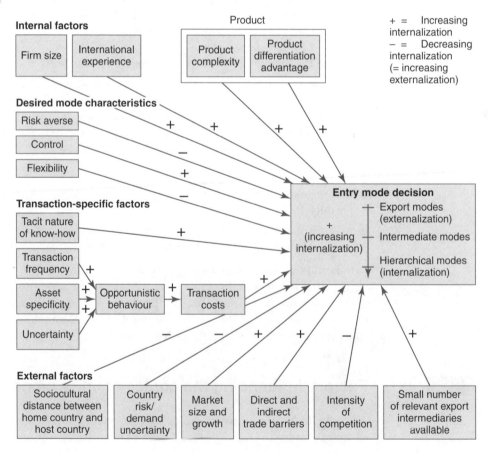

mode decision, the propositions are made under the condition of other factors being equal.

Internal factors

Firm size

Size is an indicator of the firm's resource availability; increasing resource availability provides the basis for increased international involvement over time. Although SMEs may desire a high level of control over international operations and wish to make heavy resource commitments to foreign markets, they are more likely to enter foreign markets using export modes because they do not have the resources necessary to achieve a high degree of control or to make these resource commitments. Export entry modes (market modes), with their lower resource commitment, may therefore be more suitable for SMEs. As the firm grows, it will increasingly use the hierarchical model.

International experience

Another firm-specific factor influencing mode choice is the international experience of managers and thus of the firm. Experience, which refers to the extent to which a firm has been involved in operating internationally, can be gained from operating either in a particular country or in the general international environment. International experience reduces the cost and uncertainty of serving a market, and in turn increases the probability of firms committing resources to foreign markets.

In developing their theory of internationalization, Johanson and Vahlne (1977) assert that uncertainty in international markets is reduced through actual operations in foreign markets (experiential knowledge) rather than through the acquisition of objective knowledge. They suggest that it is direct experience with international markets that increases the likelihood of committing extra resources to foreign markets.

Product

The physical characteristics of the product or service, such as its value/weight ratio, perishability and composition, are important in determining where production is located. Products with high value/weight ratios, such as expensive watches, are typically used for direct exporting, especially where there are significant production economies of scale, or if management wishes to retain control over production. Conversely, in the soft drinks and beer industry, companies typically establish licensing agreements, or invest in local bottling or production facilities, because shipment costs, particularly to distant markets, are prohibitive.

The nature of the product affects channel selection because products vary so widely in their characteristics and use, and because the selling job may also vary markedly. For instance, the technical nature of a product (high complexity) may require service both before and after sale. In many foreign market areas, marketing intermediaries may not be able to handle such work. Instead firms will use one of the hierarchical modes.

Products distinguished by physical variations, brand name, advertising and after-sales service (e.g. warranties, repair and replacement policies) which promote preference for one product over another may allow a firm to absorb the higher costs of being in a foreign market. Product differentiation advantages give firms a certain amount of impulse in raising prices to exceed costs by more than normal profits (quasi rent). They also allow firms to limit competition through the development of entry barriers, which are fundamental in the competitive strategy of the firm, as well as serving customer needs better and thereby strengthening the competitive position of the firm compared to other firms. Because these product differentiation advantages represent a 'natural monopoly', firms seek to protect their competitive advantages from dissemination through the use of hierarchical modes of entry.

External factors

Sociocultural distance between home country and host country

Socioculturally similar countries are those that have similar business and industrial practices, a common or similar language, and comparable educational levels and cultural characteristics.

Sociocultural differences between a firm's home country and its host country can create internal uncertainty for the firm, which influences the mode of entry desired by that firm.

The greater the perceived distance between the home and host country in terms of culture, economic systems and business practices, the more likely it is that the firm will shy away from direct investment in favour of joint venture agreements. This is because the latter institutional modes enhance firms' flexibility to withdraw from the host market, if they should be unable to acclimatize themselves comfortably to the unfamiliar setting. To summarize, other things being equal, when the perceived distance between the home and host country is great, firms will favour entry modes that involve relatively low resource commitments and high flexibility.

Country risk/demand uncertainty

Foreign markets are usually perceived as riskier than the domestic market. The amount of risk the firm faces is a function not only of the market itself, but also of its method of involvement there. In addition to its investment, the firm risks inventories and receivables. When planning its method of entry, the firm must do a risk analysis of both the market and its method of entry. Exchange rate risk is another variable. Moreover, risks are not only economic; there are also political risks.

When country risk is high, a firm will do well to limit its exposure to such risk by restricting its resource commitments in that particular national domain. That is, other things being equal, when country risk is high, firms will favour entry modes that involve relatively low resource commitments (export modes).

Unpredictability in the political and economic environment of the host market increases the perceived risk and demand uncertainty experienced by the firm. In turn, this disinclines firms to enter the market with entry modes requiring heavy resource commitments; on the other hand, flexibility is highly desired.

Market size and growth

Country size and rate of market growth are key parameters in determining the mode of entry. The larger the country and the size of its market, and the higher the growth rate, the more likely management will be to commit resources to its development, and to consider establishing a wholly owned sales subsidiary or to participate in a majority-owned joint venture. Retaining control over operations provides management with direct contact and allows it to plan and direct market development more effectively.

Small markets, on the other hand, especially if they are geographically isolated and cannot be serviced efficiently from a neighbouring country, may not warrant significant attention or resources. Consequently, they may be best supplied via exporting or a licensing agreement. While unlikely to stimulate market development or maximize market penetration, this approach enables the firm to enter the market with minimal resource commitment, and frees resources for potentially more lucrative markets.

Direct and indirect trade barriers

Tariffs or quotas on the import of foreign goods and components favour the establishment of local production or assembly operations (hierarchical modes).

Product or trade regulations and standards, as well as preferences for local suppliers, also have an impact on mode of entry and operation decisions. Preferences for local suppliers, or tendencies to 'buy national', often encourage a company to consider a joint venture or other contractual arrangements with a local company (intermediate modes). The local partner helps in developing local contacts, negotiating sales and establishing distribution channels, as well as in diffusing the foreign image.

Product and trade regulations and customs formalities similarly encourage modes involving local companies, which can provide information about and contacts in local markets, and can ease access. In some instances, where product regulations and standards necessitate significant adaptation and modification, the firm may establish local production, assembly or finishing facilities (hierarchical modes).

The net impact of both direct and indirect trade barriers is thus likely to be a shift towards performing various functions such as sourcing, production and developing marketing tactics in the local market.

Intensity of competition

When the intensity of competition is high in a host market, firms will do well to avoid internalization, as such markets tend to be less profitable and therefore do not justify heavy resource commitments. Hence, other things being equal, the greater the intensity of competition in the host market, the more the firm will favour entry modes that involve low resource commitments (export modes).

Small number of relevant intermediaries available

In such a case the market field is subject to the opportunistic behaviour of the few export intermediaries, and this will favour the use of hierarchical modes in order to reduce the scope for opportunistic behaviour.

Desired mode characteristics

Risk averse

If the decision-maker is risk averse, he or she will prefer export modes (e.g. indirect and direct exporting) or licensing (an intermediate mode) because they typically entail low levels of financial and management resource commitment. A joint venture provides a way of sharing risk, financial exposure and the cost of establishing local distribution networks and hiring local personnel, although negotiating and managing joint ventures often absorb considerable management time and effort. However, modes of entry that entail minimal levels of resource commitment and hence minimal risks are unlikely to foster the development of international operations and may result in significant loss of opportunity.

Control

Mode-of-entry decisions also need to consider the degree of control that management requires over operations in international markets. Control is often closely linked to the level of resource commitment. Modes of entry with minimal resource commitment, such as indirect exporting, provide little or no control over the conditions under which the product or service is marketed abroad. In the case of licensing and contract manufacturing, management needs to ensure that production meets its quality standards. Joint ventures also limit the degree of management control over international operations and can be a source of considerable conflict where the goals and objectives of partners diverge. Wholly owned subsidiaries (hierarchical mode) provide the most control, but also require a substantial commitment of resources.

Flexibility

Management must also weigh up the flexibility associated with a given mode of entry. The hierarchical modes (involving substantial equity investment) are typically the most costly but the least flexible and most difficult to change in the short run. Intermediate modes (contractual agreements and joint ventures) limit the firm's ability to adapt or change strategy when market conditions are changing rapidly.

Transaction-specific factors

The transaction cost analysis approach was discussed in Chapter 3 (section 3.3) and earlier in this chapter. We will therefore refer to only one of the factors here.

Tacit nature of know-how

When the nature of the firm-specific know-how transferred is tacit, it is by definition difficult to articulate. This makes the drafting of a contract (to transfer such complex know-how) very problematic. The difficulties and costs involved in transferring tacit know-how provide an incentive for firms to use hierarchical modes. Investment modes are better able to facilitate the intra-organizational transfer of tacit know-how. By using a hierarchical mode, the firm can utilize human capital, drawing upon its organizational routines to structure the transfer problem. Hence, the greater the tacit component of firm-specific know-how, the more a firm will favour hierarchical modes.

8.4 Summary

Seen from the perspective of the manufacturer (international marketer), market entry modes can be classified into three groups:

● Export modes: low control, low risk, high flexibility.

● Intermediate modes (contractual modes): shared control and risk, split owner-ship.

● Hierarchical modes (investment modes): high control, high risk, low flexibility.

It cannot be stated categorically which alternative mode is the best. There are many internal and external conditions which affect this choice and it should be empha-sized that a manufacturer wanting to engage in global marketing may use more than one of these methods at the same time. There may be different product lines, each requiring a different entry mode.

Case study ## Condomi AG

Germany's Condomi forms a condom factory joint venture in Kenya

Africa is to get its first condom factory to cope with an expected boom in demand for this product. The joint venture between Germany's specialist condom manufac-turer, Condomi, and Kenya's Olagi Enterprises will open in Nairobi by the end of the year 2000.

The $2.5m factory is initially expected to produce 100m condoms every year. Currently, Kenyans use 120m condoms a year, a figure expected to rise to 650m by the end of 2003.

High demand

The German company says that demand for condoms has grown by 250 per cent in Kenya over the past three years because of a recent change in the government's atti-tude towards preventing the spread of the HIV virus. In November 1999, the Kenyan President Daniel arap Moi declared Aids a national disaster. He also reversed his opinion on condoms, saying he did not oppose their use to prevent Aids.

At least 760,000 Kenyans have died of the disease. The HIV virus that can lead to Aids has infected at least two million people in Kenya's population of three million. The infection rate doubles every month.

'The future venture will manufacture condoms that are affordable, accessible, suitable and acceptable to the local population,' Condomi said in a statement.

The new company, Condomi Health Kenya, also plans to launch an intensive education drive since safer sex is the only known prevention against the HIV virus.

Questions

1. What could be the motives for Condomi to use this kind of entry mode in Kenya?

2. Evaluate some other alternative 'entry modes' for Condomi in Kenya.

(Source: BBC Business, 12 February 2000;
http://news2.thls.bbc.co.uk/hi/english/world/africa/newsid%5F640000/640853.stm)

Questions for discussion

1. Why is choosing the most appropriate market entry and development strategy one of the most difficult decisions for the international marketer?

2. Do you agree with the view that LSEs use a 'rational analytic' approach ('strategy rule') to the entry mode decision, while SMEs use a more pragmatic/opportunistic approach?

3. Use Figure 8.1 to identify the most important factors affecting the choice of foreign entry mode. Prioritize the factors.

Internet exercise

Ford India

Please go to:

http://www.india.ford.com/index2.htm

One company, a joint venture between Suzuki of Japan and the Indian government, controls most of the Indian car market. The many other international firms that have entered the market in recent years are still selling relatively tiny numbers of cars. However, in November 1999 American motor giant Ford (through their own Indian subsidiary) launched the first car (Ford Ikon) designed specifically for India, in an effort to grab a major share of the country s growing auto market.

Questions

1. What are the advantages and disadvantages of launching cars for the Indian market

    (a) through an own subsidiary?
    (b) through a joint venture with an Indian partner?

2. Regarding the 'entry mode': what recommendation would you make for Ford?

For further exercises and cases, see the book's website at *www.booksites.net/hollensen*

References

Heide, J.B. and John, G. (1988) 'The role of dependence balancing in safeguarding transaction-specific assets in conventional channels', *Journal of Marketing*, vol. 52, January, pp. 20–35.

Johanson, J. and Vahlne, J.E. (1977) 'The internationalization process of the firm – a model of knowledge', *Journal of International Business Studies*, vol. 8, no. 1, pp. 23–32.

Root, F.R. (1994) *Entry Strategies for International Markets: Revised and Expanded Edition*, The New Lexington Press, Lexington, MA.

Export modes

After studying this chapter you should be able to do the following:

● Distinguish between indirect, direct and cooperative export modes.

● Describe and understand the five main entry modes of indirect exporting:
   export buying agent;
   broker;
   export management company (EMC)/export house (EH);
   trading company; and
   piggyback.

● Describe the two main entry modes of direct exporting:
   distributor;
   agent.

● Discuss the advantages and disadvantages of the main export modes.

● Discuss how manufacturers can influence intermediaries to be effective marketing partners.

9.1 Introduction

With export entry modes, a firm's products are manufactured in the domestic market or a third country, and then transferred either directly or indirectly to the host market.

Export is the most common mode for initial entry into international markets. Sometimes, an unsolicited order is received from a buyer in a foreign country, or a domestic customer expands internationally and places an order for its international operations. This prompts the firm to consider international markets and to investigate their growth potential.

Exporting is thus typically used in initial entry and gradually evolves towards foreign-based operations. In some cases where there are substantial scale economies

Figure 9.1 Export modes

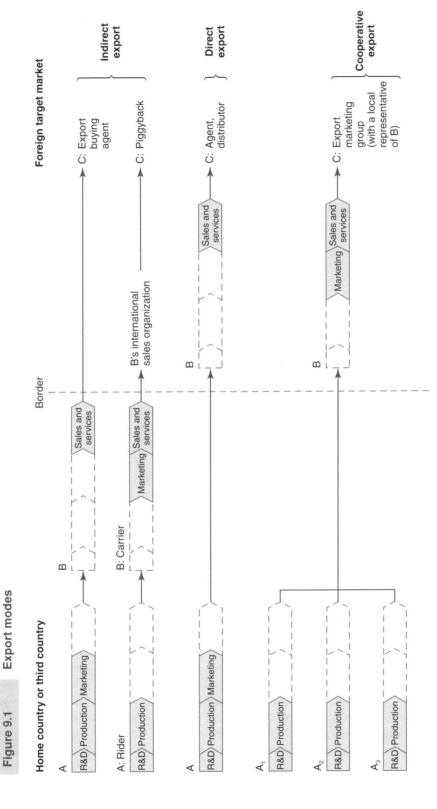

Note: A, A_1, A_2 and A_3 are manufacturers of products/services.
B is an independent intermediary.
C is the customer.

or a limited number of buyers in the market world-wide (for example, aerospace), production may be concentrated in a single or a limited number of locations, and the goods then exported to other markets.

Exporting can be organized in a variety of ways, depending on the number and type of intermediaries. As in the case of wholesaling, export and import agents vary considerably in the range of functions performed. Some, such as export management companies, are the equivalent of full-service wholesalers and perform all functions relating to export. Others are highly specialized and handle only freight forwarding, billing or clearing goods through customs.

In establishing export channels, a firm has to decide which functions will be the responsibility of external agents, and which will be handled by the firm itself. While export channels may take many different forms, for the purposes of simplicity three major types may be identified: indirect, direct and cooperative export marketing groups.

● *Indirect export*. This is when the manufacturing firm is not taking direct care of exporting activities. Instead another domestic company, such as an export house or trading company, performs these activities, often without the manufacturing firm's involvement in the foreign sales of its products.

● *Direct export*. This usually occurs when the producing firm takes care of exporting activities and is in direct contact with the first intermediary in the foreign target market. The firm is typically involved in handling documentation, physical delivery and pricing policies, with the product being sold to the agents and distributors.

● *Cooperative export*. This involves collaborative agreements with other firms (export marketing groups) concerning the performance of exporting functions.

In Figure 9.1 the different export modes are illustrated in a value chain.

9.2 Indirect export modes

Indirect export occurs when the exporting manufacturer uses independent organizations *located in the producer's country*. In indirect exporting, the sale is like a domestic sale. In fact, the firm is not really engaging in global marketing, because its products are carried abroad by others. Such an approach to exporting is most likely to be appropriate for a firm with limited international expansion objectives. If international sales are viewed primarily as a means of disposing of surplus production, or as a marginal, use of indirect export modes may be appropriate. This method may also be adopted by a firm with minimal resources to devote to international expansion, which wants to enter international markets gradually, testing out markets before committing major resources and effort to developing an export organization.

It is important for a firm to recognize, however, that the use of agents or export management companies carries a number of risks. In the first place, the firm has little or no control over the way the product or service is marketed in other countries. Products may be sold through inappropriate channels, with poor servicing or sales support and inadequate promotion, or be under- or overpriced. This can damage the reputation or image of the product or service in foreign markets. Limited effort may be devoted to developing the market, resulting in lost potential opportunities.

Particularly significant for the firm interested in gradually edging into international markets is that, with indirect exporting, the firm establishes little or no contact with markets abroad. Consequently, the firm has limited information about foreign market potential, and obtains little input to develop a plan for international expansion. The firm will have no means to identify potential sales agents or distributors for its products.

While exporting has the advantage of the least cost and risk of any entry method, it allows the firm little control over how, when, where and by whom the products are sold. In some cases the domestic company may even be unaware that its products are being exported.

Moreover, an SME which is already experienced in traditional exporting may have resources that are too limited to open up a great number of export markets by itself. Thus, through indirect export modes the SME is able to utilize the resources of other experienced exporters and to expand its business to many countries.

There are five main entry modes of indirect exporting:

● Export buying agent.
● Broker.
● Export management company (EMC)/export house (EH).
● Trading company.
● Piggyback (shown as a special case of indirect exporting in Figure 9.1).

Export buying agent (export commission house)

Some firms or individuals do not realize that their products or services have potential export value until they are approached by a buyer from a foreign organization, which might make the initial approach, purchase the product at the factory gate and take on the task of exporting, marketing and distributing the product in one or more overseas markets.

The export buying agent is a representative of foreign buyers who resides in the exporter's home country. As such, this type of agent is essentially the overseas customer's hired purchasing agent in the exporter's domestic market, operating on the basis of orders received from these buyers. Since the export buying agent acts in the interests of the buyer, it is the buyer that pays a commission. The exporting manufacturer is not directly involved in determining the terms of purchase; these are worked out between the export buying agent and the overseas buyer.

The export commission house essentially becomes a domestic buyer. It scans the market for the particular merchandise it has been requested to buy. It sends out specifications to manufacturers inviting bids. Other conditions being equal, the lowest bidder gets the order and there is no sentimentality, friendship or sales talk involved.

From the exporter's point of view, selling to export commission houses represents an easy way to export. Prompt payment is usually guaranteed in the exporter's home country, and the problems of physical movement of the goods are generally taken completely out of its hands. There is very little credit risk and the exporter has only to fulfil the order, according to specifications. A major problem is that the exporter has little direct control over the global marketing of products.

Small firms find that this is the easiest method of obtaining foreign sales, but being totally dependent on the purchaser, they are unlikely to be aware of a change in consumer behaviour and competitor activity, or of the purchasing firm's intention to terminate the arrangement. If a company is intent upon seeking longer-term liability for its export business, it must adopt a more proactive approach, which will inevitably involve obtaining a greater understanding of the markets in which its products are sold.

Broker

Another type of agent based in the home country is the export/import broker. The chief function of a broker is to bring a buyer and a seller together. Thus, the broker is a specialist in performing the contractual function, and does not actually handle the products sold or bought. For its services, the broker is paid a commission (about 5 per cent) by the principal. The broker commonly specializes in particular products or classes of product. Being a commodity specialist, there is a tendency for the broker to concentrate on just one or two products. Because the broker deals primarily in basic commodities, for many potential export marketers this type of agent does not represent a practical alternative channel of distribution. The distinguishing characteristic of export brokers is that they may act as the agent for either the seller or the buyer.

Export management company/export house

Export houses (EHs) or export management companies (EMCs) are specialist companies set up to act as the 'export department' for a range of companies. As such, the EMC conducts business in the name of each manufacturer it represents. All correspondence with buyers and contracts are negotiated in the name of the manufacturer, and all quotations and orders are subject to confirmation by the manufacturer.

By carrying a large range, the EMCs can spread their selling and administration costs over more products and companies, as well as reducing transport costs because of the economies involved in making large shipments of goods from a number of companies.

EMCs deal with the necessary documentation, and their knowledge of local purchasing practices and government regulations is particularly useful in markets which might prove difficult to penetrate. The use of EMCs, therefore, allows individual companies to gain far wider exposure of their products in foreign markets at much lower overall costs than they could achieve on their own, but there are a number of disadvantages, too:

- The export house may specialize by geographical area, product or customer type (retail, industrial or institutional), and this may not coincide with the supplier's objectives. So the selection of markets may be made on the basis of what is best for the EMC rather than for the manufacturer.

- As EMCs are paid by commission, they might be tempted to concentrate upon products with immediate sales potential, rather than those which might require greater customer education and sustained marketing effort to achieve success in the longer term.

- EMCs may be tempted to carry too many product ranges and as a result the manufacturer's products may not be given the necessary attention from sales people.

- EMCs may carry competitive products which they may promote to the disadvantage of a particular firm.

Manufacturers should therefore take care in selecting a suitable EMC and be prepared to devote resources to managing the relationship and monitoring its performance.

As sales increase, the manufacturer may feel that it could benefit from increased involvement in international markets, by exporting itself. However, the transition may not be very easy. First, the firm is likely to have become very dependent on the export house, and unless steps have been taken to build contacts with foreign customers and to build up the firm's knowledge of its markets, moving away from using an EMC could prove difficult. Second, the firm could find it difficult to withdraw from its contractual commitments to the export house. Third, the EMC may be able to substitute products from an alternative manufacturer and so use its existing customer contacts as a basis for competing against the original manufacturer.

Trading company

Trading companies are part of the historical legacy from colonial days and, although different in nature now, they are still important trading forces in Africa and the Far East. Although international trading companies have been active throughout the world, it is in Japan that the trading company concept has been applied most effectively. There are thousands of trading companies in Japan that are involved in exporting and importing, and the largest firms (varying in number from 9 to 17 depending upon source of estimate) are referred to as general trading companies or Soge Shosha. This group of companies, which include C. Itoh, Mitsui & Company and Mitsubishi Shoji Kaisha, handle 50 per cent of Japan's exports and 67 per cent of its imports. While the smaller trading companies usually limit their activities to foreign trade, the larger general trading companies are also heavily involved in domestic distribution and other activities.

They play a central role in such diverse areas as shipping, warehousing, finance, technology transfer, planning resource development, construction and regional development (for example, turnkey projects), insurance, consulting, real estate and deal making in general (including facilitating investment and joint ventures). In fact, it is the range of financial services offered which is a major factor distinguishing general trading companies from others. These services include the guaranteeing of loans, the financing of both accounts receivable and payable, the issuing of promissory notes, major foreign exchange transactions, equity investment and even direct loans.

Another aspect of their operations is to manage counter-trade activities, in which sales into one market are paid for by taking other products from that market in exchange. The essential role of the trading company is to find a buyer quickly for the products that have been taken in exchange. Sometimes this can be a very resource-demanding process.

Counter trade is still a very widespread trading form in eastern Europe and developing countries because of their lack of 'hard' currency. One of the motivations for western firms to go into counter trade is the low-cost sources of production and raw materials for use in the firm's own production (Okoroafo, 1994).

Piggyback

In piggybacking the export-inexperienced SME, the 'rider', deals with a larger company (the 'carrier') which already operates in certain foreign markets and is willing to act on behalf of the rider that wishes to export to those markets. This enables the carrier to utilize fully its established export facilities (sales subsidiaries) and foreign distribution. The carrier is either paid by commission and so acts as an agent or, alternatively, buys the product outright and so acts as an independent distributor. Piggyback marketing is typically used for products from unrelated companies that are non-competitive (but related) and complementary (allied).

Sometimes the carrier will insist that the rider's products are somewhat similar to its own, in view of the need to deal with technical queries and after-sales service 'in the field'. Branding and promotional policies are variable in piggybacking. In some instances, the carrier may buy the products, put its own brand on them, and market them as its own products (private labels). More commonly, the carrier retains the brand name of the producer and the two work out promotional arrangements between them. The choice of branding and promotional strategy is a function of the importance of brand to the product and of the degree to which the brand is well established.

Piggybacking has the following advantages/disadvantages for the carrier and the rider.

Carrier

Advantages

A firm that has a gap in its product line or excess capacity in its export operation has two options. One is to develop internally the products necessary to round out its line and fill up its exporting capacity. The other option is to acquire the necessary products outside by piggybacking (or acquisition). Piggybacking may be attractive because the firm can get the product quickly (someone already has it). It is also a low-cost way to get the product because the carrier firm does not have to invest in R & D, production facilities or market testing for the new product. It can just pick up the product from another firm. In this way the firm can broaden its product range without having to develop and manufacture extra products.

Disadvantages

Piggybacking can be extremely attractive for the carrier, but some concerns exist about quality control and warranty. Will the rider maintain the quality of the products sold by another firm? This depends in part on whose brand name is on the product. If the rider's name is on the product, the quality incentive might be stronger. A second concern is continuity of supply. If the carrier develops a substantial market abroad, will the rider firm develop its production capacity, if necessary? Each of these items should be a subject in the agreement between the two parties. If the piggybacking arrangement works out well, there is another potential advantage for the carrier. It might find that the rider is a good acquisition candidate or joint-venture partner for a stronger relationship.

Rider

Advantages

Riders can export conveniently without having to establish their own distribution systems. They can observe carefully how the carrier handles the goods and hence learn from the carrier's experience – perhaps to the point of eventually being able to take over its own export transactions.

Disadvantages

For the smaller company this type of agreement means giving up control over the marketing of its products – something that many firms dislike doing, at least in the long run. Lack of commitment on the part of the carrier and the loss of lucrative sales opportunities in regions not covered by the carrier are further disadvantages.

In summary, piggyback marketing provides an easy, low-risk way for a company to begin export marketing operations. It is especially well suited to manufacturers which either are too small to go directly into exports or do not want to invest heavily in foreign marketing.

9.3 Direct export modes

Direct exporting occurs when a manufacturer or exporter sells directly to an importer or buyer located in a foreign market area. In our discussion of indirect exporting, we examined ways of reaching foreign markets without working very hard. Indeed, in the indirect approaches, foreign sales are handled in the same way as domestic sales: the producer does the global marketing only by proxy (that is, through the firm that carries its products overseas). However, both the global marketing know-how and the sales achieved by these indirect approaches are limited.

As exporters grow more confident, they may decide to undertake their own exporting task. This will involve building up overseas contacts, undertaking marketing research, handling documentation and transportation, and designing marketing mix strategies. Direct exporting modes include export through foreign-based agents and distributors (independent intermediaries).

The terms 'distributor' and 'agent' are often used synonymously. This is unfortunate because there are distinct differences: distributors, unlike agents, take title to the goods, and are paid according to the difference between the buying and selling prices rather than by commission. Distributors are often appointed when after-sales service is required, as they are more likely than agents to possess the necessary resources.

Distributors

Exporting firms may work through distributors, which are the exclusive representatives of the company and are generally the sole importers of the company's product in their markets. As independent merchants, distributors buy on their own accounts and have substantial freedom to choose their own customers and to set the conditions of sale. For each country, exporters deal with one distributor, take one credit risk, and ship to one destination. In many cases, distributors own and operate wholesale and retail establishments, warehouses, and repair and service facilities. Once distributors have negotiated with their exporters on price, service, distribution and the like, their efforts focus on working their own sub-operations and dealers.

The distributor category is broad and includes more variations, but distributors usually seek exclusive rights for a specific sales territory and generally represent the manufacturer in all aspects of sales and servicing in that area. The exclusivity is in return for the substantial capital investment that may be required on the part of the distributor in handling and selling products.

Agents

Agents may be exclusive, where the agent has exclusive rights to specified sales territories; semi-exclusive, where the agent handles the exporter's goods along with other non-competing goods from other companies; or non-exclusive, where the agent handles a variety of goods, including some that may compete with the exporter's products.

An agent represents an exporting company and sells to wholesalers and retailers in the importing country. The exporter ships the merchandise directly to the customers, and all arrangements on financing, credit, promotion, etc. are made between the exporter and the buyers. Exclusive agents are widely used for entering international markets. They cover rare geographic areas and have sub-agents assisting them. Agents and sub-agents share commissions (paid by the exporter) on a pre-agreed basis. Some agents furnish financial and market information, and a few also guarantee the payment of customers' accounts. The commissions that agents receive vary substantially, depending upon services performed, the market's size and importance, and competition among exporters and agents.

The advantages of both agents and distributors are that they are familiar with the local market, customs and conventions, have existing business contacts and employ foreign nationals. They have a direct incentive to sell through either commission or profit margin, but since their remuneration is tied to sales they may be reluctant to devote much time and effort towards developing a market for a new product. Also, the amount of market feedback may be limited as the agent or distributor may see itself as a purchasing agent for its customers rather than as a selling agent for the exporter.

Choice of an intermediary

The selection of a suitable intermediary can be a problematic process. But the following sources may help a firm to find such an intermediary:

- Asking potential customers to suggest a suitable agent.
- Obtaining recommendations from institutions such as trade associations, chambers of commerce and government trade departments.
- Using commercial agencies.
- Poaching a competitor's agent.
- Advertising in suitable trade papers.

In selecting a particular intermediary, the exporter needs to examine each candidate firm's knowledge of the product and local markets, experience and expertise, required margins, credit ratings, customer care facilities and ability to promote the exporter's products in an effective and attractive manner. Specific desirable characteristics of an intermediary are listed in Table 9.1.

When an intermediary is selected by the exporting manufacturer, it is important that a contract is negotiated and developed between the parties. The foreign representative agreement is the fundamental basis of the relationship between the

Table 9.1

Table 9.1   Profile desired of an intermediary

- Trading areas covered.
- Lines handled.
- Size of firm.
- Experience with manufacturer's or similar product line.
- Sales organization and quality of sales force.
- Physical facilities.
- Willingness to carry inventories.
- After-sales servicing capability.
- Knowledge/use of promotion.
- Reputation with suppliers, customers and banks.
- Record of sales performance.
- Cost of operations.
- Financial strength/credit rating.
- Overall experience.
- Relations to local government.
- Knowledge of English or other relevant languages.
- Knowledge of business methods in manufacturer's country.
- Willingness to cooperate with manufacturer.

Source: Root (1994), pp. 86–7.

exporter and the intermediary. Therefore the contract should clearly cover all rele-vant aspects and define the conditions upon which the relationship rests. Rights and obligations should be mutually defined and the spirit of the agreement must be one of mutual interest. The agreement should cover the provisions listed in Table 9.2.

For most exporters, the three most important aspects of their agreement with foreign representatives are sole or exclusive rights, competitive lines and termina-tion of the agreement. The issue of agreeing territories is becoming increasingly important, as in many markets, distributors are becoming fewer in number, larger in size and sometimes more specialized in their activity. The trend to regionaliza-tion is leading distributors increasingly to extend their territories through organic growth, mergers and acquisitions, making it more difficult for firms to appoint different distributors in individual neighbouring markets.

Table 9.2

Table 9.2   Contracts with intermediaries

---

1. **General provisions**
   Identification of parties to the contract.
   Duration of the contract.
   Definition of covered goods.
   Definition of territory or territories.
   * Sole and exclusive rights.
   Arbitration of disputes.

---

2. **Rights and obligations of manufacturer**
   Conditions of termination.
   Protection of sole and exclusive rights.
   Sales and technical support.
   Tax liabilities.
   Conditions of sale.
   Delivery of goods.
   Prices.
   Order refusal.
   Inspection of distributor's books.
   Trademarks/patents.
   Information to be supplied to the distributor.
   Advertising/promotion.
   Responsibility for claims/warranties.
   Inventory requirements.
   * Termination and cancellation.

---

3. **Rights and obligations of distributor**
   Safeguarding manufacturer's interests.
   Payment arrangements.
   Contract assignment.
   * Competitive lines.
   Customs clearance.
   Observance of conditions of sale.
   After-sales service.
   Information to be supplied to the manufacturer.

---

* Most important and contentious issues.
Source: Root (1994), pp. 90–1.

In general, there are some principles that apply to the law of agency in all nations:

- An agent cannot take delivery of the principal's goods at an agreed price and resell them for a higher amount without the principal's knowledge and permission.
- Agents must maintain strict confidentiality regarding their principal's affairs and must pass on all relevant information.
- The principal is liable for damages to third parties for wrongs committed by an agent 'in the course of his or her authority' (e.g. if the agent fraudulently misrepresents the principal's firm).

During the contract period, the support and motivation of intermediaries is important. Usually this means financial rewards for volume sold, but there can also be other means:

- Significant local advertising and brand awareness development by the supplying firm.
- Participation in local exhibitions and trade fairs, perhaps in cooperation with the local intermediary.
- Regular field visits and telephone calls to the agent or distributor.
- Regular meetings of agents and distributors arranged and paid for by the supplying company in the latter's country.
- Competitions with cash prizes, free holidays, etc. for intermediaries with the highest sales.
- Provision of technical training to intermediaries.
- Suggestion schemes to gather feedback from agents and distributors.
- Circulation of briefings about the supplying firm's current activities, changes in personnel, new product developments, marketing plans, etc.

Even if the firm has been very careful in selecting intermediaries, a need can arise to extricate oneself quickly from a relationship that appears to be going nowhere. Cancellation clauses usually involve rights under local legislation, and it is best that a contract is scrutinized by a local lawyer before signature, rather than after a relationship has ended and a compensation case is being fought in the courts.

Termination laws differ from country to country, but the European Union situation has been largely reconciled by a Directive on agency that has been effective in all EU nations since 1994. Under the Directive, an agent whose agreement is terminated is entitled to the following:

- Full payment for any deal resulting from its work (even if concluded after the end of the agency).
- A lump sum of up to one year's past average commission.
- Compensation (where appropriate) for damages to the agent's commercial reputation caused by an unwarranted termination.

Outside western Europe, some countries regard agents as basically employees of client organizations, while others see agents as self-contained and independent businesses. It is essential to ascertain the legal position of agency agreements in each country in which a firm is considering doing business.

9.4 | Cooperative export modes/export marketing groups

Export marketing groups are frequently found among SMEs attempting to enter export markets for the first time. Many such firms do not achieve sufficient scale economies in manufacturing and marketing because of the size of the local market or the inadequacy of the management and marketing resources available. These characteristics are typical of traditional, mature, highly fragmented industries such as furniture and clothing. Frequently the same characteristics are to be found among small, recently established high-technology firms.

Figure 9.1 shows an export marketing group with manufacturers A_1, A_2 and A_3, each having separate upstream functions but cooperating on the downstream functions through a common foreign-based agent.

One of the most important motives for SMEs to join with others is the opportunity of effectively marketing a complementary product programme to larger buyers. The following example is from the furniture industry.

Manufacturers A_1, A_2 and A_3 have their core competences in the upstream functions of the following complementary product lines:

A_1 Living room furniture.

A_2 Dining room furniture.

A_3 Bedroom furniture.

Together they form a broader product concept, which could be more attractive to a buyer in a furniture retail chain, especially if the total product concept targets a certain lifestyle of the end customers.

The cooperation between the manufacturers can be tight or loose. In a loose co-operation the separate firms in a group sell their own brands through the same agent, whereas a tight cooperation often results in the creation of a new export association. Such an association can act as the exporting arm of all member companies, presenting a united front to world markets and gaining significant economies of scale. Its major functions are the following:

● Exporting in the name of the association.

● Consolidating freight, negotiating rates and chartering ships.

● Performing market research.

● Appointing selling agents abroad.

● Obtaining credit information and collecting debts.

● Setting prices for export.

● Allowing uniform contracts and terms of sale.

● Allowing cooperative bids and sales negotiation.

Firms in an association can research foreign markets more effectively together, and obtain better representation in them. By establishing one organization to replace several sellers, they may realize more stable prices, and selling costs can be reduced. Through consolidating shipments and avoiding duplicated effort, firms realize transportation savings, and a group can achieve standardization of product grading and create a stronger brand name, just as the California fruit growers did with Sunkist products.

Considering all the advantages for an SME in joining an export marketing group, it is surprising that so few groups are actually running. One of the reasons for this could be that the firms have conflicting views as to what the group should do. In many SMEs there are strong feelings of independence inspired by the founders and entrepreneurs of the SMEs, which may be contrary, for example, to the common goal setting of export marketing groups.

9.5 Summary

The advantages and disadvantages of the three main types of export mode are summarized in Table 9.3.

Table 9.3   Advantages and disadvantages of the different export modes for the manufacturer

Export mode	Advantages	Disadvantages
Indirect exporting (e.g. export buying agent, broker or export management company)	Limited commitment and investment required. High degree of market diversification is possible as the firm utilizes the internationalization of an experienced exporter. Minimal risk (market and political). No export experience required.	No control over marketing mix elements other than the product. An additional domestic member in the distribution chain may add costs, leaving smaller profit to the producer. Lack of contact with the market (no market knowledge acquired). Limited product experience (based on commercial selling).
Direct exporting (e.g. distributor or agent)	Access to local market experience and contacts to potential customers. Shorter distribution chain (compared to indirect exporting). Market knowledge acquired. More control over marketing mix (especially with agents). Local selling support and services available.	Little control over market price because of tariffs and lack of distribution control (especially with distributors). Some investment in sales organization required (contact from home base with distributors or agents). Cultural differences, providing communication problems and information filtering (transaction costs occur). Possible trade restrictions.
Export marketing groups	Shared costs and risks of internationalization. Provide a complete product line or system sales to the customer.	Risk of unbalanced relationships (different objectives). Participating firms are reluctant to give up their complete independence.

Case study   Pepsi Chart shows

Is it possible to export radio/TV chart shows?

Pepsi-Cola UK is hoping to hit the right note with consumers as it embarks on a global roll-out of its TV chart and radio shows (www.pepsichart.co.uk).

Unlike the BBC, which looks on overseas sales of the Top of the Pops (TOTP) brand as an extra revenue stream, Pepsi is concerned only in using the Pepsi Chart show to drive sales of the drink. Hence the move to provide a localized version of the programme for the Middle East.

Andy Woodford, a director of Pepsi's UK music agency Music Innovations, says: 'The Middle East is a strong market for Pepsi. We are looking to roll out the Pepsi Chart everywhere that Pepsi has business.'

The weekly TV show has been commissioned by Middle Eastern satellite broadcaster MBC and is due to be aired in Saudi Arabia, the Lebanon, Egypt and the United Arab Emirates in April. It will be made in London and Beirut, with up to 90 per cent of content being localized. An Arabic customized Pepsi Chart is also being set up for each of the countries because of the lack of relevant charts.

The plan is that the screening of a Pepsi Chart TV series will coincide with the launch of a Pepsi Chart radio show in the same region. Pepsi will also run promotional activities around the launch in what is one of its key markets for soft drink sales. PepsiCo's fourth quarter results (1998) published on 1 February 1999 reported the drink's 'four per cent international advance reflected strong performance in China, India and the Middle East'.

Localized versions of the Pepsi Chart show have also been commissioned by TV3 in Denmark, TVN in Poland and TV2 in Hungary. In Finland, TV4, which has already bought the UK version of the Pepsi Chart show, plans to commission a localized version by the end of the year. The show's original format is televised in Sweden, Sri Lanka and Ireland. Pepsi will have final approval on all the deals these agencies negotiate.

Overseeing the global rollout of the Pepsi Chart show is Leslie Golding, former TOTP brand manager at BBC Worldwide.

Golding says: 'The first thing we need is a broadcaster which is allowed to, and prepared to, carry advertiser sponsored programmes. Not all countries have one so the BBC may be able to sell its shows to more places than we can.' However, Golding says BBC Worldwide would not have the resources to put together a similar deal for TOTP.

Managing director of music consultancy Music And Media Partnership Rick Blaskey says: 'Pepsi is showing the value of owning a music property as opposed to dipping in and out of music by sponsoring an event.'

Like Pepsi, BBC Worldwide is making inroads in Europe. Recently it announced a deal with Rome production house Einstein Multimedia and the BBC's production team to make a series tailored for the Italian market, which is scheduled to air later this year.

A TOTP set will be created in Rome as a platform for localized content and an Italian presenter will record links for UK. The deal is similar to the one the BBC show has with German broadcaster RTL, which transmits the programme to Germany, Austria and Switzerland. TOTP is also seen in France, New Zealand, Japan and Australia.

Graham Samuels, general manager global marketing of BBC Music, maintains the market is big enough for the Pepsi Chart show and TOTP which first appeared on the network in 1964. But he says: 'What appeals to broadcasters is the longevity of our brand.'

Like Pepsi, BBC Worldwide plans to roll out a radio version of its TV show. It is also looking at the possibility of launching the TOTP magazine, which has an audited circulation of 436,906 per issue, into the German market. But Samuels is cautious and warns against comparing the TOTP brand and its merchandising with the success of the Teletubbies, which earned BBC Worldwide £23m for the year 1997/8.

Laurence Munday, joint managing director of Drum Ltd, says: 'I think the Pepsi brand and chart show have been hugely successful in the UK. Pepsi's show will probably be more successful abroad than TOTP because of the lure of Pepsi as a global brand and the greater marketing support the drinks company has at its disposal.'

But Sanjay Nazerali, managing director of youth consultancy Marketing Depot, asks: 'What is the relevance between Pepsi and the chart? There's an audience synergy, but why is a cola bringing you music? There's a lot more to it than merely shoving a brand on the chart.'

Questions

1. Can the exporting of Pepsi Chart shows give a boost to the global sales of the drink?

2. What parts of the value chain for the Pepsi Chart shows are standardized/localized?

3. Define the differences in the business systems of Pepsi Chart shows and BBC's 'Top of the Pops'.

4. Which of the two chart shows would have the biggest chance of being successful in the international markets?

Source: Adapted from Wilkinson, A. (1999) 'Pepsi plans global hit with chart show', *Marketing Week*, 4 March

Questions for discussion

1. Why is exporting frequently considered the simplest way of entering foreign markets and favoured by SMEs?

2. What procedures should a firm follow in selecting a distributor?

3. Why is it difficult – financially and legally – to terminate a relationship with overseas intermediaries? What should be done to prevent or minimize such difficulties?

4. Identify the ways to reach foreign markets by making a domestic sale.

5. What is the difference between direct and indirect exporting?

6. Discuss the financial and pricing techniques for motivating foreign distributors.

7. Which marketing tasks should be handled by the exporter and which ones by its intermediaries in foreign markets?

8. How can the carrier and the rider both benefit from a piggyback arrangement?

9. When a firm begins direct exporting, what tasks must it perform?

10. Discuss the various ways of communicating with foreign distributors.

11. 'When exporting to a market, you're only as good as your intermediary there.' Discuss.

12. The international marketer and the intermediary will have different expectations concerning the relationship. Why should these expectations be spelled out and clarified in the contract?

Internet exercise

BBC's 'Tweenies'

Please go to:

http://www.bbc.co.uk/education/tweenies/

Children's BBC stars the *Tweenies* are on the road to global stardom after being sold to foreign networks.

The situation in spring 2000 is that the all-singing and dancing capers of the colourful foursome have been bought by broadcasters in France, Australia, Portugal, South Africa and Singapore. The deals have been worth £3m to BBC Wordwide and make the Tweenies the fastest-selling children's product from the corporation's commercial arm – outstripping their famous predecessors the *Teletubbies*.

A further 20 countries are said to be interested in screening the programme and a European deal has been signed with toy makers Hasbro.

The BBC says the Tweenies, made by independent producer Tell-Tale Productions, is primarily for children who have graduated from the Teletubbies.

Questions

1. What are the key success factors (KSFs) in exports of the Tweenies?

2. What export mode would you prefer for the Tweenies?

For further exercises and cases, see this book's website at *www.booksites.net/hollensen*

References

Okoroafo, S.C. (1994) 'Implementing international countertrade: a dyadic approach', *Industrial Marketing Management*, vol. 23, pp. 229–34.

Root, F.R. (1994) *Entry Strategies for International Markets*: Revised and Expanded Edition, The New Lexington Press, Lexington, MA.

Intermediate entry modes

After studying this chapter you should be able to do the following:

● Describe and understand the major intermediate entry modes:
   contract manufacturing;
   licensing;
   franchising; and
   joint venture/strategic alliances.

● Discuss the advantages and disadvantages of the major intermediate entry modes.

● Explain the different stages in joint-venture formation.

● Explore the reasons for the 'divorce' of the two parents in a joint-venture constellation.

● Explore different ways of managing a joint venture/strategic alliance.

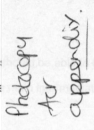

10.1 Introduction

So far we have assumed that the firm entering foreign markets is supplying them from domestic plants. This is implicit in any form of exporting. However, sometimes the firm may find it either impossible or undesirable to supply all foreign markets from domestic production. Intermediate entry modes are distinguished from export modes because they are primarily vehicles for the transfer of knowledge and skills, although they may also create export opportunities. They are distinguished from the hierarchical entry modes in the way that there is no full ownership (by the parent firm) involved, but ownership and control can be shared between the parent firm and a local partner. This is the case with the (equity) joint venture.

Intermediate entry modes include a variety of arrangements, such as licensing, franchising, management contracts, turnkey contracts, joint ventures and technical know-how or co-production arrangements. In Figure 10.1 the most relevant intermediate modes are shown in the usual value chain perspective.

Figure 10.1 Intermediate modes

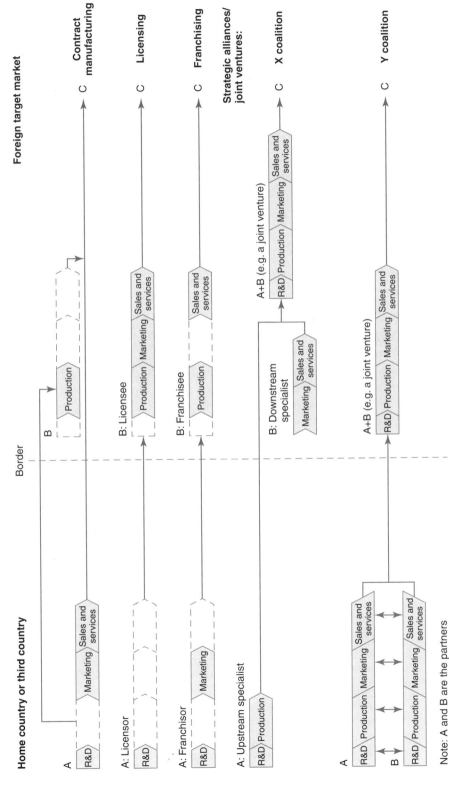

Generally speaking, contractual arrangements take place when firms possessing some sort of competitive advantage are unable to exploit this advantage because of resource constraints, for instance, but are able to transfer the advantage to another party. The arrangements often entail long-term relationships between partner firms and are typically designed to transfer intermediate goods such as knowledge and/or skills between firms in different countries.

10.2 Contract manufacturing

Several factors may encourage the firm to produce in foreign markets:

- Desirability of being close to foreign customers. Local production allows better interaction with local customer needs concerning product design, delivery and service.
- Foreign production costs (e.g. labour) are low.
- Transportation costs may render heavy or bulky products non-competitive.
- Tariffs or quotas can prevent entry of an exporter's products.
- In some countries there is government preference for national suppliers.

Contract manufacturing enables the firm to have foreign sourcing (production) without making a final commitment. Management may lack resources or be unwilling to invest equity to establish and complete manufacturing and selling operations. Yet contract manufacturing keeps the way open for implementing a long-term foreign development policy when the time is right. These considerations are perhaps most important to the company with limited resources. Contract manufacturing enables the firm to develop and control R & D, marketing, distribution, sales and servicing of its products in international markets, while handing over responsibility for production to a local firm (Figure 10.1).

Payment by the contractor to the contracted party is generally on a per unit basis, and quality and specification requirements are extremely important. The product can be sold by the contractor in the country of manufacture, its home country, or some other foreign market.

This form of business organization is quite common in particular industries. For example, Benetton and IKEA rely heavily on a contractual network of small overseas apparel manufacturers.

Contract manufacturing also offers substantial flexibility. Depending on the duration of contract, if the firm is dissatisfied with product quality or reliability of delivery, it can shift to another manufacturer. In addition, if management decides to exit the market, it does not have to sustain possible losses from divesting production facilities. On the other hand, it is necessary to control product quality to meet company standards. The firm may encounter problems with delivery, product warranties or fulfilling additional orders. The manufacturer may also not be as cost efficient as the contracting firm, or may reach production capacity, or may attempt to exploit the agreement.

Thus, while contract manufacturing offers a number of advantages, especially to a firm whose strength lies in marketing and distribution, care needs to be exercised in negotiating the contract. Where the firm loses direct control over the manufacturing function, mechanisms need to be developed to ensure that the contract manufacturer meets the firm's quality and delivery standards.

10.3 Licensing

Licensing is another way in which the firm can establish local production in foreign markets without capital investment. It differs from contract manufacturing in that it is usually for a longer term and involves much greater responsibilities for the national firm, because more value chain functions have been transferred to the licensee by the licensor (see Figure 10.1).

A licensing agreement

A licensing agreement is an arrangement wherein the licensor gives something of value to the licensee in exchange for certain performance and payments from the licensee. The licensor may give the licensee the right to use one or more of the following things:

● A patent covering a product or process.

● Manufacturing know-how not subject to a patent.

● Technical advice and assistance, occasionally including the supply of components, materials or plant essential to the manufacturing process.

● Marketing advice and assistance.

● The use of a trade mark/trade name.

In the case of trade mark licensing the licensor should try not to undermine a product by overlicensing it. For example, Pierre Cardin diluted the value of his name by allowing some 800 products to use the name under licence. Overlicensing can increase income in the short run, but in the long run it may mean killing the goose that laid the golden egg.

In some situations the licensor may continue to sell essential components or services to the licensee as part of the agreement. This may be extended so that the total agreement may also be one of cross-licensing, wherein there is a mutual exchange of knowledge and/or patents. In cross-licensing there might not be a cash payment involved.

Licensing can be considered a two-way street because a licence also allows the original licensor to gain access to the licensee's technology and product. This is important because the licensee may be able to build on the information supplied by the licensor. Some licensors are very interested in grantbacks and will even lower the royalty rate in return for product improvements and potentially profitable new products. Where a product or service is involved, the licensee is responsible for production and marketing in a defined market area. This responsibility is followed by all the profits and risks associated with the venture. In exchange the licensee pays the licensor royalties or fees, which are the licensor's main source of income from its licensing operations and which usually involve some combination of the following elements:

- A lump sum not related to output. This can include a sum paid at the beginning of an agreement for the initial transfer of special machinery, parts, blueprints, knowledge and so on.

- A minimum royalty – a guarantee that at least some annual income will be received by the licensor.

- A running royalty – normally expressed as a percentage of normal selling price or as a fixed sum of money for units of output.

Other methods of payment include conversions of royalties into equity, management and technical fees, and complex systems of counter purchase, typically found in licensing arrangements with eastern European countries.

If the foreign market carries high political risk, then it will be wise for the licensor to seek high initial payments and perhaps compress the timescale of the agreement. Alternatively, if the market is relatively free of risk and the licensee is well placed to develop a strong market share, then payment terms will be somewhat relaxed and probably influenced by other licensors competing for the agreement.

The licensing agreement or contract should always be formalized in a written document. The details of the contract are probably the subject of detailed negotiation and hard bargaining between the parties, and there can be no such thing as a standard contract.

In the following we see licensing from the viewpoint of a *licensor* (licensing out) and a *licensee* (licensing in). This section is written primarily from the licensor's viewpoint, but licensing in may be an important element in smaller firms' growth strategies, and therefore some consideration is given to this issue too.

Licensing out

Generally, there is a wide range of strategic reasons for using licensing. The most important motives for licensing out are as follows:

- The licensor firm will remain technologically superior in its product development. It wants to concentrate on its core competences (product development activities) and then outsource production and downstream activities to other firms.

- The licensor is too small to have financial, managerial or marketing expertise for overseas investment (own subsidiaries).

- The product is at the end of its product life cycle in the advanced countries because of obsolescing technology or model change. A stretching of the total product life cycle is possible through licensing agreements in less developed countries.

- Even if direct royalty income is not high, margins on key components to the licensee (produced by the licensor) can be quite handsome.

● If government regulations restrict foreign direct investment or if political risks are high, licensing may be the only realistic entry mode.

● There may be constraints on imports into the licensee country (tariff or non-tariff barriers).

When setting the price for the agreement, the costs of licensing should not be underestimated. Table 10.1 presents a breakdown of costs of licensing out by Australian firms.

Licensing in

Empirical evidence shows (Young *et al.*, 1989, p. 143) that many licensing agreements actually stem from approaches by licensees. This would suggest that the licensee is at an immediate disadvantage in negotiations and general relations with the licensor. In other cases, licensing in is used as the easy option, with the licence being renewed regularly and the licensee becoming heavily dependent on the technology supplier (the licensor).

As Figure 10.2 shows, licensing in can improve the net cash flow position of the licensee, but mean lower profits in the longer term. Because technology licensing allows the firms to have products on the market sooner than otherwise, the firm benefits from an earlier positive cash flow. In addition, licensing means lower development costs. The immediate benefits of quick access to new technology, lower development costs and a relatively early cash flow are attractive benefits of licensing.

Table 10.1

Table 10.1 Relative costs of licensing overseas (%)

Breakdown of total costs of licensing overseas	
Protection of industrial property	24.4
Establishment of licensing agreement	46.6
Maintenance of licensing agreement	29.0
	100.0
Breakdown of establishment costs	
Search for suitable licensee	22.8
Communication between involved parties	44.7
Adoption and testing of equipment for licensee	9.9
Training personnel for licensee	19.9
Other (additional marketing activity and legal expenses)	2.7
	100.0
Breakdown of maintenance costs	
Audit of licensee	9.7
Ongoing market research in market of licensee	7.2
Back-up services for licensee	65.0
Defence of industrial property rights in licensee's territory	11.0
Other	7.1
	100.0

Sources: Carstairs and Welch (1981); Young *et al.* (1989), p. 132

| Figure 10.2 | Life cycle benefits of licensing |

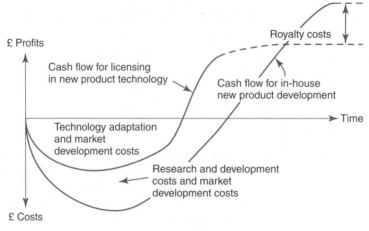

(Sources: Lowe and Crawford, 1984; Bradley, 1995, p. 388)

Table 10.5 (section 10.7) summarizes the advantages and disadvantages of licensing for the licensor.

10.4 Franchising

The term 'franchising' is derived from the French meaning 'to be free from servitude'. Franchise activity was almost unknown in Europe until the beginning of the 1970s. The concept was popularized in the USA, where over one-third of retail sales are derived from franchising, in comparison with about 10 per cent in Europe (Young *et al.*, 1989, p. 110).

A number of factors have contributed to the rapid growth rate of franchising. First, the general world-wide decline of traditional manufacturing industry and its replacement by service-sector activities has encouraged franchising. It is especially well suited to service and people-intensive economic activities, particularly where these require a large number of geographically dispersed outlets serving local markets. Second, the growth in popularity of self-employment is also a contributory factor to the growth of franchising. Government policies in many countries have improved the whole climate for small businesses as a means of stimulating employment.

A good example of the value of franchising is the Swedish furniture manufacturer IKEA, which franchises its ideas throughout the western world, especially in Europe and North America. In terms of retail surface area and the number of visitors to retail stores, this company has experienced very significant growth through franchising in recent years.

Franchising is a marketing-oriented method of selling a business service, often to small independent investors who have working capital but little or no prior business experience. However, it is something of an umbrella term which is used to mean anything from the right to use a name to the total business concept. Thus there are two major types of franchising:

● Product and trade name franchising. This is very similar to trade mark licensing. Typically it is a distribution system in which suppliers make contracts with dealers to buy or sell products or product lines. Dealers use the trade name, trade mark and product line. Examples of this type of franchising are soft drink bottlers like Coca-Cola and Pepsi.

● Business format 'package' franchising.

The latter is the focus of this section.

International business format franchising is a market entry mode that involves a relationship between the entrant (the franchisor) and a host country entity, in which the former transfers, under contract, a business package (or format), which it has developed and owns, to the latter. This host country entity can be either a franchisee or a subfranchisor. The package transferred by the franchisor contains most elements necessary for the local entity to establish a business and run it profitably in the host country in a prescribed manner, regulated and controlled by the franchisor. The package can contain the following items:

● Trade marks/trade names.

● Copyright.

● Designs.

● Patents.

● Trade secrets.

● Business know-how.

● Geographic exclusivity.

The package may also include the right for the local entity, a subfranchisor, to establish and service its own subsystem of subfranchisees within its appointed territory.

In addition to this package, the franchisor also typically provides local entities with managerial assistance in setting up and running local operations. All locally owned franchisees, subfranchisees and subfranchisors can also receive subsupplies from the franchisor and benefit from centrally coordinated advertising. In return for this business package the franchisor receives from the franchisee or subfranchisor an initial fee up-front and/or continuing franchise fees, based typically on a percentage of annual turnover as a mark-up on goods supplied directly by the franchisor.

There is still a lively debate about the differences between licensing and franchising, but if we define franchising in the broader 'business format' (as here), we see the differences presented in Table 10.2.

Types of business format franchise include business and personal services, convenience stores, car repairs and fast food. US fast-food franchises are some of the best-known global franchise businesses, including McDonald's, Burger King and Pizza Hut.

The fast-food business is taken as an example of franchising in the value chain approach of Figure 10.1. The production (e.g. assembly of burgers) and sales and service functions are transferred to the local outlets (e.g. McDonald's restaurants), whereas the central R & D and marketing functions are still controlled by the franchisor (e.g. the McDonald's head office in the United States). The franchisor will develop the general marketing plan (with the general advertising messages) that will be adapted to local conditions and cultures.

As indicated earlier, business format franchising is an ongoing relationship that includes not only a product or a service, but also a business concept. The business concept usually includes a strategic plan for growth and marketing, instruction on the operation of the business, elaboration of standards and quality control, continuing guidance for the franchisee, and some means of control of the franchisee by the franchisor. Franchisors provide a wide variety of assistance for franchisees, but not all franchisors provide the same level of support. Some examples of assistance

Table 10.2 | **How licensing and franchising differ**

Licensing	Franchising
The term 'royalties' is normally used	'Management fees' is regarded as the appropriate term.
Products, or even a single product, are the common element	Covers the total business, including know-how, intellectual rights, goodwill, trade marks and business contacts. (Franchising is all-encompassing, whereas licensing concerns just one part of the business).
Licences are usually taken by well-established businesses.	Tends to be a start-up situation, certainly as regards the franchisee.
Terms of 16–20 years are common, particularly where they related to technical know-how, copyright and trademarks. The terms are similar for patents.	The franchise agreement is normally for 5 years, sometimes extending to 10 years. Franchises are frequently renewable.
Licensees tend to be self-selecting. They are often established businesses and can demonstrate that they are in a strong position to operate the licence in question. A licensee can often pass its licence on to an associate or sometimes unconnected company with little or no reference back to the original licensor.	The franchisee is very definitely selected by the franchisor, and its eventual replacement is controlled by the franchisor.
Usually concerns specific existing products with very little benefit from ongoing research being passed on by the licensor to its licensee.	The franchisor is expected to pass on to its franchisees the benefits of its ongoing research programme as part of the agreement.
There is no goodwill attached to the licence as it is totally retained by the licensor.	Although the franchisor does retain the main goodwill, the franchisee picks up an element of localized goodwill.
Licensees enjoy a substantial measure of free negotiation. As bargaining tools, they can use their trade muscle and their established position in the marketplace.	There is a standard fee structure and any variation within an individual franchise system would cause confusion and mayhem.

Sources: Perkins, (1987), pp. 22, 157; Young *et al.* (1989), p. 148.

and support provided by franchisors are in the areas of finance, site selection, lease negotiation, cooperative advertising, training and assistance with store opening. The extent of ongoing support to franchisees also varies among franchisors. Support areas include central data processing, central purchasing, field training, field operation evaluation, newsletters, regional and national meetings, a hotline for advice and franchisor–franchisee advisory councils. The availability of these services is often a critical factor in the decision to purchase a franchise, and may be crucial to the long-term success of marginal locations or marginally prepared owners.

International expansion of franchising

Franchisors, like other businesses, must consider the relevant success factors in making the decision to expand their franchising system globally. The objective is to search for an environment that promotes cooperation and reduces conflict. Given the long-term nature of a franchise agreement, country stability is an important factor.

Where should the international expansion start? The franchising development often begins as a response to a perceived local opportunity, perhaps as an adaptation of a franchising concept already operating in another foreign market. In this case the market focus is clearly local to begin with. In addition, the local market provides a better environment for testing and developing the franchising format. Feedback from the marketplace and franchisees can be obtained more readily because of the ease of communication. Adjustments can be made more quickly because of the close local contact. A whole variety of minor changes in the format may be necessary as a result of early experience in areas such as training, franchisee choice, site selection, organization of suppliers, promotion and outlet decoration. The early stages of franchise development represent a critical learning process for the franchisor, not just about how to adapt the total package to the market requirements, but also regarding the nature of the franchising method itself. Ultimately, with a proven package and a better understanding of its operation, the franchisor is in a better position to attack foreign markets, and is more confident about doing so with a background of domestic success.

Developing and managing franchisor–franchisee relationships

Franchising provides a unique organizational relationship in which the franchisor and franchisee each bring important qualities to the business. The franchise system combines the advantages of economy of scale offered by the franchisor with the local knowledge and entrepreneurial talents of the franchisee. Their joint contribution may result in a success. The franchisor depends on franchisees for fast growth, an infusion of capital from the franchise purchase fee, and an income stream from the royalty fee paid by franchisees each year. Franchisors also benefit from franchisee goodwill in the community and, increasingly, from franchisee suggestions for innovation. The most important factor, however, is the franchisee's motivation to operate a successful independent business. The franchisee depends on the franchisor for the strength of the trade mark, technical advice, support services, marketing resources and national advertising that provides instant customer recognition.

There are two additional key success factors, which rest on the interdependence of the franchisee and the franchisor:

● Integrity of the whole business system.
● Capacity for renewal of the business system.

Integrity of the business system

The business will be a success in a viable market to the extent that the franchisor provides a well-developed, proven business concept to the franchisee and the franchisee is motivated to follow the system as it is designed, thereby preserving the integrity of the system. Standardization is the cornerstone of franchising: customers expect the same product or service at every location. Deviations from the franchising business concept by individual franchisees adversely affect the franchisor's reputation. The need for the integrity of the system requires that the franchisor exerts control over key operations at the franchise sites.

Capacity for renewal of the business system

Although most franchisors conduct research and development within the parent company, the highest proportion of innovation originates from franchisees in the field. Franchisees are most familiar with customers' preferences. They sense new trends and the opportunity to introduce a new product and service. The issue is getting the franchisee to share new ideas with the parent company. Not all franchisees are willing to share ideas with the franchisor, for a number of reasons. The most common is failure of the franchisor to keep in close contact with the franchisees; the most troubling is a lack of trust in the franchisor. The franchisor needs to promote a climate of trust and cooperation for mutual benefit.

Handling possible conflicts

Conflict is inherent in the franchisor–franchisee relationship, since all aspects that are good for the franchisor may not be good for the franchisee. One of the most basic conflicts is failure of either the franchisor or the franchisee to live up to the terms of the legal agreement.

Disagreement over objectives may be the result of poor communication on the part of the franchisor, or failure on the part of the franchisee to understand the franchisor's objectives. Both franchisor and franchisee agree on the need for profits in the business, not only to provide a living but to stay competitive. However, the two parties may disagree on the means of achieving profits. The number of conflicts between franchisors and franchisees may be reduced by establishing extensive monitoring of the franchisee (e.g. computer-based accounting, purchasing and inventory systems). Another way of reducing the number of conflicts is to view franchisors and franchisees as partners in running a business; both objectives and operating procedures have to be in harmony. This view requires a strong common culture with shared values established by the use of intensive communication between franchisor and franchisees in different countries (e.g. cross-national/regional meetings, cross-national/regional advisory councils).

10.5 Joint ventures/strategic alliances

A joint venture or a strategic alliance is a partnership between two or more parties. In international joint ventures, these parties will be based in different countries, and this obviously complicates the management of such an arrangement.

A number of reasons are given for setting up joint ventures, including the following:

● Complementary technology or management skills provided by the partners can lead to new opportunities in existing sectors (e.g. multimedia, in which information processing, communications and the media are merging).

● Many firms find that partners in the host country can increase the speed of market entry.

● Many less developed countries, such as China and South Korea, try to restrict foreign ownership.

● Global operations in R & D and production are prohibitively expensive, but necessary to achieve competitive advantage.

The formal difference between a joint venture and a strategic alliance is that a strategic alliance is typically a non-equity cooperation, meaning that the partners do not commit equity into or invest in the alliance. The joint venture can be either a contractual non-equity joint venture or an equity joint venture.

In a contractual joint venture, no joint enterprise with a separate personality is formed. Two or more companies form a partnership to share the cost of investment, the risks and the long-term profits. An equity joint venture involves the creation of a new company in which foreign and local investors share ownership and control.

Thus, according to these definitions, strategic alliances and non-equity joint ventures are more or less the same (Figure 10.3).

The question of whether to use an equity or a non-equity joint venture is a matter of how to formalize the cooperation. Much more interesting is to consider the roles that partners are supposed to play in the collaboration.

In Figure 10.4 two different types of coalition are shown in the value chain perspective. These are based on the possible collaboration pattern along the value chain. In Figure 10.4 we see two partners A and B, each having its own value chain.

Figure 10.3   **Joint ventures and strategic alliances**

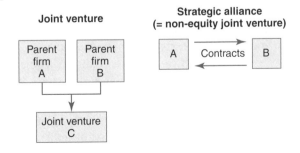

Figure 10.4   **Collaboration possibilities for partners A and B in the value chain**

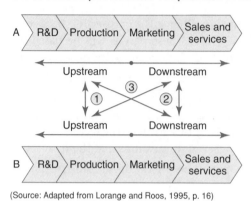

(Source: Adapted from Lorange and Roos, 1995, p. 16)

Three different types of value chain partnership appear:

1. *Upstream-based collaboration.* A and B collaborate on R & D and/or production.

2. *Downstream-based collaboration.* A and B collaborate on marketing, distribution, sales and/or service.

3. *Upstream/downstream-based collaboration.* A and B have different but complementary competences at each end of the value chain.

Types 1 and 2 represent the so-called Y coalition and type 3 represents the so-called X coalition (Porter and Fuller, 1986, p. 336–7):

● *Y coalitions.* Partners share the actual performance of one or more value chain activities: for example, joint production of models or components enables the attainment of scale economies that can provide lower production costs per unit. Another example is a joint marketing agreement where complementary product lines of two firms are sold together through existing or new distribution channels, and thus broaden the market coverage of both firms.

● *X coalitions.* Partners divide the value chain activities between themselves: for example, one partner develops and manufactures a product while letting the other partner market it. Forming X coalitions involves identifying the value chain activities where the firm is well positioned and has its core competences. Take the case where A has its core competences in upstream functions, but is weak in downstream functions. A wants to enter a foreign market but lacks local market knowledge and does not know how to get access to foreign distribution channels for its products. Therefore A seeks and finds a partner B, which has its core competences in the downstream functions, but is weak in the upstream functions. In this way A and B can form a coalition where B can help A with distribution and selling in a foreign market, and A can help B with R & D or production.

In summary, X coalitions imply that the partners have asymmetric competences in the value chain activities: where one is strong, the other is weak and vice versa. In

Y coalitions, on the other hand, partners tend to be more similar in the strengths and weaknesses of their value chain activities.

Stages in joint-venture formation

The various stages in the formation of a joint venture are shown in Table 10.3.

Step 1: Joint-venture objectives

Joint ventures are formed for a variety of reasons, which include entering new markets, reducing manufacturing costs, and developing and diffusing new technologies rapidly. Joint ventures are also used to accelerate product introduction and overcome legal and trade barriers expeditiously. In this period of advanced technology and global markets, implementing strategies quickly is essential. Forming alliances is often the fastest, most effective method of achieving objectives. Companies must be sure that the goal of the alliance is compatible with their existing businesses, so their expertise is transferable to the alliance. Firms often enter

Table 10.3	Stages in joint-venture formation

1. **Joint venture objectives**
   Establish strategic objectives of the joint venture and specify time period for achieving objectives.

2. **Cost/benefit analysis**
   Evaluate advantages and disadvantages of joint venture compared with alternative strategies for achieving objectives (e.g. licensing) in terms of:
   (a) financial commitment;
   (b) synergy;
   (c) management commitment;
   (d) risk reduction;
   (e) control;
   (f) long-run market penetration; and
   (g) other advantages/disadvantages

3. **Selecting partner(s)**
   (a) profile of desired features of candidates;
   (b) identifying joint-venture candidates and drawing up short list;
   (c) screening and evaluating possible joint-venture partners;
   (d) initial contact/discussions; and
   (e) choice of partner.

4. **Develop business plan**
   Achieve broad agreement on different issues.

5. **Negotiation of joint-venture agreement**
   Final agreement on business plan.

6. **Contract writing**
   Incorporation of agreement in legally binding contract, allowing for subsequent modifications to the agreement

7. **Performance evaluation**
   Establish control systems for measuring venture performance.

Source: Adapted from Young *et al.* (1989), p. 233.

into alliances based on opportunity rather than linkage with their overall goals. This risk is greatest when a company has a surplus of cash.

There are three principal objectives in forming a joint venture:

● *Entering new markets.* Many companies recognize that they lack the necessary marketing expertise when they enter new markets. Rather than trying to develop this expertise internally, the company may identify another organization that possesses those desired marketing skills. Then, by capitalizing on the product development skills of one company and the marketing skills of the other, the resulting alliance can serve the market quickly and effectively. Alliances may be particularly helpful when entering a foreign market for the first time because of the extensive cultural differences that may abound. They may also be effective domestically when entering regional or ethnic markets.

● *Reducing manufacturing costs.* Joint ventures may allow companies to pool capital or existing facilities to gain economies of scale or increase the use of facilities, thereby reducing manufacturing costs.

● *Developing and diffusing technology.* Joint ventures may also be used to build jointly on the technical expertise of two or more companies in developing products that are technologically beyond the capability of the companies acting independently.

Step 2: Cost/benefit analysis

A joint venture/strategic alliance may not be the best way of achieving objectives. Therefore this entry mode should be evaluated against other entry modes. Such an analysis could be based on the selection criteria set out in Chapter 9.

Step 3: Selecting partner(s)

If it is accepted that a joint venture is the best entry mode for achieving the firm's objectives, the next stage is the selection of the joint-venture partner. This normally involves five stages.

Establishing a desired partner profile

Companies frequently search for one or more of the following resources in a partner:

● Development know-how.
● Sales and service expertise.
● Low-cost production facilities.
● Strategically critical manufacturing capabilities.
● Reputation and brand equity.
● Market access and knowledge.
● Cash.

Identifying joint-venture candidates

In many cases, this part of the partner selection is not performed thoroughly. The first candidate, generally discovered through contacts established by mail, arranged by a banker or a business colleague already established in the country, is often the one with whom the company undertakes discussions. Little or no screening is done; nor is there an in-depth investigation of the motives and capabilities of the candidate. At other times the personal network that executives maintain with senior managers from other firms shapes the set of prospective joint-venture partners which companies will generally consider. All too often, however, alliances are agreed upon informally by these top managers without careful attention to how appropriate the partner match may be. Instead of taking this reactive approach, the firm should proactively search for joint-venture candidates. Possible candidates can be found among competitors, suppliers, customers, related industries and trade association members.

Screening and evaluating possible joint-venture partners

Relationships get off to a good start if partners know each other. Table 10.4 gives some criteria that may be used to judge a prospective partner's effectiveness.

These suggestions form only an outline sketch of the type of information which can be used to grade partners. They cover areas where there is a reasonable chance of forming a view by the appraisal of published information and by sensible observation and questioning.

Initial contacts/discussions

Since relationships between companies are relationships between people, it is important that the top managers of the firm meet personally with top managers from the remaining two or three possible partners. It is important to highlight the personal side of a business relationship. This includes discussion of personal and social interests to see if there is a good 'chemistry' between the prospective partners.

Choice of partner

The chosen partner should bring the desired complementary strength to the partnership. Ideally, the strengths contributed by the partners are unique, for only these strengths can be sustained and defended over the long term. The goal is to develop synergies between the contributions of the partners, resulting in a win–win situation for both. Moreover, the partners must be compatible and willing to trust one another.

It is important that neither partner has the desire to acquire the other partner's strength, or the necessary mutual trust will be destroyed. Dow Chemical Company, a frequent and successful alliance practitioner, uses the negotiation process to judge other corporate cultures and, consequently, their compatibility and trustworthiness.

Commitment to the joint venture is essential. This commitment must be both financial and psychological. Unless there is senior management endorsement and enthusiasm at the operating level, an alliance will struggle, particularly when tough issues arise.

Step 4: Develop business plan

Issues that have to be negotiated and determined prior to the establishment of the joint venture include the following:

Table 10.4	Analysis of prospective partners: examples of criteria that may be used to judge a prospective partner's effectiveness by assessing existing business ventures and commercial attitudes

1.   Finance
Financial history and overall financial standing (all the usual ratios).
Possible reasons for successful business areas.
Possible reasons for unsuccessful business areas.

2.   Organization
Structure of organization.
Quality and turnover of senior managers.
Workforce conditions/labour relations.
Information and reporting systems; evidence of planning.
Effective owner's working relationship with business.

3.   Market
Reputation in marketplace and with competitors.
Evidence of research/interest in service and quality.
Sales methods; quality of sales force.
Evidence of handling weakening market conditions.
Results of new business started.

4.   Production
Condition of existing premises/works.
Production efficiencies/layouts.
Capital investments and improvements.
Quality control procedures.
Evidence of research (internal/external); introduction of new technology.
Relationship with main suppliers.

5.   Institutional
Government and business contacts (influence).
Successful negotiations with banks, licensing authorities, etc.
Main contacts with non-national organizations and companies.
Geographical influence.

6.   Possible negotiating attitudes
Flexible or hardline.
Reasonably open or closed and secretive.
Short-term or long-term orientation.
Wheeler-dealer or objective negotiator.
Positive, quick decision making or tentative.
Negotiating experience and strength of team support.

Sources: Walmsley (1982); Paliwoda (1993).

- Ownership split (majority, minority, 50–50).
- Management (composition of board of directors, organization, etc.).
- Production (installation of machinery, training, etc.).
- Marketing (the four Ps, organization).

Step 5: Negotiation of joint-venture agreement

As Figure 10.5 shows, the final agreement is determined by the relative bargaining power of both prospective partners.

Figure 10.5 **Partner-to-partner relationships creating a joint venture**

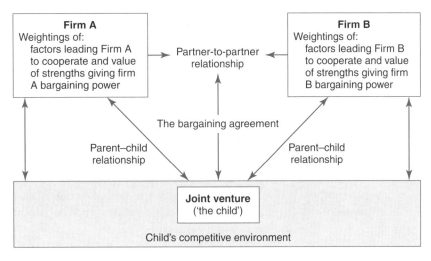

(Source: Harrigan, 1985, p. 50.)

Step 6: Contract writing

Once the joint-venture agreement has been negotiated, it needs to be written into a legally binding contract. Of course, the contract should cover the 'marriage' conditions of the partners, but it should also cover the 'divorce' situation, such as what happens with 'the child' (the joint venture).

Step 7: Performance evaluation

Evaluating joint-venture performance is a difficult issue. Managers often fall into the trap of assessing partnerships as if they were internal corporate divisions with unambiguous goals operating in low-risk, stable environments. Bottom-line profits, cash flow, market share and other traditional financially oriented output measures become standard indicators of performance. These measures may be inappropriate for two reasons. First, they reflect a short-term orientation, and maximization of initial output too soon can jeopardize the prospects for alliances positioned for the long term. Second, the goals of many alliances may not be readily quantifiable. For instance, a partnership's objectives may involve obtaining access to a market or blocking a competitor.

Many alliances need considerable time before they are ready to be judged on conventional output measures. Only after partnerships mature (i.e. when the operations of the alliance are well established and well understood) can managers gradually shift to measure output, such as profits and cash flows.

Thus expecting too much too soon in terms of profits and cash flows from an alliance working under risky conditions can endanger its future success.

Managing the joint venture

In recent years we have seen an increasing number of cross-border joint ventures. But it is dangerous to ignore the fact that the average life span for alliances is only about seven years and nearly 80 per cent of joint ventures ultimately end in a sale by one of the partners.

Harrigan's model (Figure 10.6) can be used as a framework for explaining this high 'divorce rate' (see also Exhibit 10.1 as an example of the problems in a joint-venture marriage).

Changes in bargaining power

According to Bleeke and Ernst (1994), the key to understanding the 'divorce' of the two parents is changes in their respective bargaining power. Let us assume that we have established a joint venture with the task of penetrating markets with a new product. In the initial stages of the relationship, the product and technology

Figure 10.6   Model of joint-venture activity

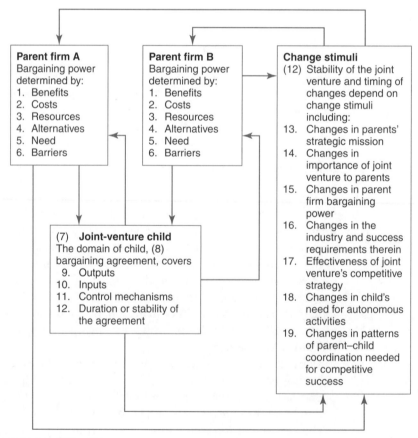

(Source: Harrigan, 1985, p. 52.)

provider generally has the most power. But unless those products and technologies are proprietary and unique, power usually shifts to the party that controls distribution channels and thus customers.

The bargaining power is also strongly affected by the balance of learning and teaching. A company that is good at learning can access and internalize its partner's capabilities more easily, and is likely to become less dependent on its partner as the alliance evolves. Before entering a joint venture, some companies see it as an intermediate stage before acquiring the other partner. By entering a joint venture, the prospective buyer of the partner is in a better position to assess the true value of such intangible assets as brands, distribution networks, people and systems. This experience reduces the risk that the buyer will make an uninformed decision and buy an expensive 'lemon' (Nanda and Williamson, 1995).

Exhibit 10.1 | ### Joint ventures: parents do not always have a happy relationship

In 1992 Samsung formed a joint venture with Slovakia's refrigerator maker, Calex. The South Koreans took a 45 per cent stake in the venture, while state-owned Calex kept the rest. Calex received a much-needed $11 million in investment. Samsung got a cheap production site for its refrigerators, from which to attack the European market. But things went very wrong.

Calex was already on the way down. It had 80 per cent of the Czech and Slovakian market, but was destroyed by the split from the Czech Republic and by the flood of foreign refrigerators into both the Czech and Slovakian markets. By late 1995 Calex had less than 12 per cent of the Slovakian market, only half the share of its own joint venture with Samsung. But while Samsung Calex is expanding its presence throughout the region (85 per cent of production is exported), it is also in deep trouble. In 1995 it made a Sk197 million ($6.4 million) loss, compared to profits of Sk22 million in 1994 and Sk124 million in 1993. Production is well below the plant's 450,000-unit capacity.

Some of its problems are caused by its Slovakian parent. The joint venture is forced to buy parts and supplies from Calex, even though they cost 30 per cent more than the same parts sourced abroad. Worse, as relations between the Koreans and the Slovakians deteriorated, Calex was turning angry. In an electrical bill dispute in 1995, it turned the power off at the Zlaté Moravce plant. Production was halted for several days. The situation was getting out of control. To sort it out, Samsung has been trying to buy a controlling stake in Calex. But it is not that easy. Calex is saddled with $200 million in debts, leading to a financial crisis which forced the company to stop production four times in 1995 and 1996. Not surprisingly, Samsung refuses to take over the debt mountain. Politics are also a problem. Calex is on the list of strategic companies in which the Slovakian government decided to maintain a veto over strategic decisions. Samsung's offer of $70 million was turned down and the government is now considering $100 million for 100 per cent control.

Source: Adapted from Zalatorius (1996).

Other change stimuli and potential conflicts

Diverging goals

As the joint venture progresses, the goals of the two partners may diverge. For example, unacceptable positions can develop in the local market when the self-interest of one partner conflicts with the interest of the joint venture as a whole, as in the pricing of a single-source input or raw material.

Double management

A potential problem is the matter of control. By definition, a joint venture must deal with double management. If a partner has less than 50 per cent ownership, that partner must in effect let the majority partner make decisions. If the board of directors has a 50–50 split, it is difficult for the board to make a decision quickly if at all.

Repatriation of profits

Conflicts can also arise with regard to issues such as repatriation of profits, where the local partner desires to reinvest them in the joint venture while the other partner wishes to repatriate them or invest them in other operations.

Mixing different cultures

An organization's culture is the set of values, beliefs and conventions that influence the behaviour and goals of its employees. This is often quite different from the culture of the host country and the partner organization. Thus, developing a shared culture is central to the success of the alliance.

Partnering is inherently very people oriented. To the extent that the cultures of the partners are different, making the alliance work may prove difficult. Cultural differences often result in an 'us versus them' situation. Cultural norms should be consistent with management's vision of the alliance's ideal culture. This may entail creating norms as well as nurturing those that already exist. The key to developing a culture is to acknowledge its existence and to manage it carefully. Bringing two organizations together and letting nature take its course is a recipe for failure. Language differences are also an obvious hurdle for an international alliance.

Ignoring the local culture will almost certainly destroy the chances of it accepting the alliance's product or service. Careful study of the culture prior to embarking on the venture is vital. Again, extensive use of local managers is usually preferred.

Shared equity

Shared equity may also involve an unequal sharing of the burden. Occasionally, international companies with 50–50 joint ventures believe that they are giving more than 50 per cent of the technology, management skill and other factors that contribute to the success of the operation, but are receiving only half the profits. Of course, the national partner contributes local knowledge and other intangibles that may be underestimated. Nevertheless, some international companies believe that the local partner gets too much of a 'free ride'.

Developing trust in joint ventures

Developing trust takes time. The first two times that companies work together, their chances of succeeding are very slight. But once they find ways to work together, all sorts of opportunities appear. Working together on relatively small projects initially helps develop trust and determine compatibility while minimizing economic risk. Each partner has a chance to gauge the skills and contributions of the other, and further investment can then be considered. Of course, winning together in the marketplace on a project of any scale is a great way to build trust and overcome differences. It usually serves as a precursor to more ambitious joint efforts.

Providing an exit strategy

As indicated earlier, there is a significant probability that a newly formed joint venture will fail, even if the previously mentioned key principles are followed. The anticipated market may not develop, one of the partner's capabilities may have been overestimated, the corporate strategy of one of the partners may have changed, or the partners may simply be incompatible. Whatever the reason for the failure, the parties should prepare for such an outcome by addressing the issue in the partnership contract. The contract should provide for the liquidation or distribution of partnership assets, including any technology developed by the alliance.

10.6 | Other intermediate entry modes

Management contracting emphasizes the growing importance of services and management know-how. The typical case of management contracting is where one firm (contractor) supplies management know-how to another company that provides the capital and takes care of the operating value chain functions in the foreign country. Normally, the contracts undertaken are concerned with management operating/control systems and training local staff to take over when the contracts are completed.

Management contracts typically arise in situations where one company seeks the management know-how of another company with established experience in the field. The lack of management capability is most evident for developing countries. Normally, the financial compensation to the contractor for the management services provided is a management fee, which may be fixed irrespective of the financial performance or may be a percentage of the profit (Luostarinen and Welch, 1990). The advantages and disadvantages of management contracting are listed in Table 10.5.

Other management contracts may be part of a deal to sell a processing plant as a *project* or a *turnkey* operation. This issue will be dealt with more intensively in Chapter 12 (section 12.8).

Table 10.5	Advantages and disadvantages of the different intermediate modes	
Intermediate entry mode	**Advantages**	**Disadvantages**
Contract manufacturing (seen from the contractor's viewpoint)	Permits low-risk market entry. No local investment (cash, time and executive talent) with no risk of nationalization or expropriation. Retention of control over R & D, marketing and sales/after-sales service. Avoids currency risks and financing problems. A locally made image, which may assist in sales, especially to government or official bodies. Entry into markets otherwise protected by tariffs or other barriers. Possible cost advantage if local costs (primarily labour costs) are lower. Avoids intra-corporate transfer-pricing problems that can arise with a subsidiary.	Transfer of production know-how is difficult. Contract manufacture is only possible when a satisfactory and reliable manufacturer can be found – not always an easy task. Extensive technical training will often have to be given to the local manufacturer's staff. As a result, at the end of the contract, the subcontractor could become a formidable competitor. Control over manufacturing quality is difficult to achieve despite the ultimate sanction of refusal to accept substandard goods. Possible supply limitation if the production is taking place in developing countries.
Licensing (seen from the licensor's viewpoint)	Increases the income on products already developed as a result of expensive research. Permits entry into markets that are otherwise closed on account of high rates of duty, import quotas and the like. A viable option where manufacture is near the customer's base. Requires little capital investment and should provide a higher rate of return on capital employed. There may be valuable spin-off if the licensor can sell other products or components to the licensee. If these parts are for products being manufactured locally or machinery, there may also be some tariff concessions on their import. The licensor is not exposed to the danger of nationalization or expropriation of assets.	The licensor is ceding certain sales territories to the licensee for the duration of the contract; should it fail to live up to expectations, renegotiation may be expensive. When the licensing agreement finally expires, the licensor may find he or she has established a competitor in the former licensee. The licensee may prove less competent than expected at marketing or other management activities. Costs may even grow faster than income. The licensee, even if it reaches an agreed minimum turnover, may not fully exploit the market, leaving it open to the entry of competitors, so that the licensor loses control of the marketing operation. Danger of the licensee running short of funds, especially if considerable plant expansion is involved or an injection of capital is required to sustain the project. This danger can be turned to advantage if the licensor has funds available by a general expansion of the business through a partnership.
	Because of the limited capital requirements, new products can be rapidly exploited, on world-wide basis, before competition develops. The licensor can take immediate advantage of the licensee's local marketing and distribution organization and of existing customer contacts.	Licence fees are normally a small percentage of turnover, about 5%, and will often compare unfavourably with what might be obtained from a company's own manufacturing operation. Lack of control over licensee operations. Quality control of the product is difficult – and the product will often be sold under the licensor's brand name.

Table 10.5   (*Continued*)

Intermediate entry mode	Advantages	Disadvantages
	Protects patents, especially in countries which give weak protection for products not produced locally. Local manufacture may also be an advantage in securing government contacts.	Negotiations with the licensee, and sometimes with local government, are costly. Governments often impose conditions on transferral of royalties or on component supply.
Franchising (seen from franchisor's viewpoint)	Greater degree of control compared to licensing. Low-risk, low-cost entry mode (the licensees are the ones investing in the necessary equipment and know-how). Using highly motivated business contacts with money, local market knowledge and experience. Ability to develop new and distant international markets, relatively quickly and on a larger scale than otherwise possible. Generating economies of scale in marketing to international customers. Precursor to possible future direct investment in foreign market.	The search for competent franchisees can be expensive and time consuming. Lack of full control over franchisee's operations, resulting in problems with cooperation, communications, quality control, etc. Costs of creating and marketing a unique package of products and services recognized internationally. Costs of protecting goodwill and brand name. Problems with local legislation, including transfers of money, payments of franchise fees and government-imposed restrictions on franchise agreements. Opening up internal business knowledge may create potential future competitor. Risk to the company's international profile and reputation if some franchisees underperform ('free riding' on valuable brand names).
Joint venture (seen from parents viewpoint)	Access to expertise and contacts in local markets. Each partner agrees to a joint venture to gain access to the other partner's skills and resources. Typically, the international partner contributes financial resources, technology or products. The local partner provides the skills and knowledge required for managing a business in its country. Each partner can concentrate on that part of the value chain where the firm has its core competence. Reduced market and political risk. Shared knowledge and resources: compared to wholly owned subsidiary, less capital and fewer management resources are required. Economies of scale by pooling skills and resources (resulting in e.g. lower marketing costs). Overcomes host government restrictions. May avoid local tariffs and non-tariff barriers. Shared risk of failure.	Objectives of the respective partners may be incompatible, resulting in conflicts. Contributions to joint venture can become disproportionate. Loss of control over foreign operations. Large investments of financial, technical or managerial resources favour greater control than is possible in a joint venture. Completion might overburden a company's staff. Partners may become locked into long-term investments from which it is difficult to withdraw. Transfer pricing problems as goods pass between partners. The importance of the venture to each partner might change over time. Cultural differences may result in possible differences in management culture among participating firms. Loss of flexibility and confidentiality. Problems of management structures and dual parent staffing of joint ventures. Nepotism perhaps the established norm.

(Continued)

Table 10.5 *(Continued)*

Intermediate entry mode	Advantages	Disadvantages
	Less costly that acquisitions. Possibly better relations with national governments in through having a local partner (meets host country pressure for local participation).	
Management contracting (seen from contractor's viewpoint)	If direct investment or export is considered too risky – for commercial or political reasons – this alternative might be relevant. As with other intermediate entry modes, management contracts may be linked together with other forms of operation in foreign markets. Allows a company to maintain market involvement, so puts it in a better position to exploit any opportunity which may arise. Organizational learning: if a company is in its early development stages of internationalization, a management contract may offer an efficient way of learning about foreign markets and international business.	Training future competitors: the management transfer package may in the end create a competitor for the contractor. Places a great demand for key personnel. Such staff are not always available, especially not in SMEs. Considerable effort needs to be put into building lines of communication at local level as well as back to contractor. Potential conflict between the contractor and the local government as regards the policy of the contract venture. Little control, which also limits the ability of a contractor to develop the capacity of the venture.

Exhibit 10.2   McDonald's + Coca-Cola + Disney = a powerful alliance

Figure 10.7   The alliance between McDonald's, Coca-Cola and Disney

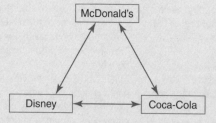

Today, business is being driven by two fashionable ideas: globalization and core competences. The first compels companies to look for ways to sell their product in as many different places as possible, which often requires other people to help them. The second, the fashion for a firm sticking to what it does best, means that they must often let outsiders help them with everything else.

The ties binding Coca-Cola, McDonald's and Disney vary enormously:

McDonald's ↔ Disney

In 1997 McDonald's and Disney began a formal ten-year alliance. The first specific outcome was a Disney film, 'Flubber', whose box-office returns were helped by tie-ins at McDonald's. In July 1998 a promotion started of 'Armageddon', a $100m film starring Bruce Willis, with McDonald's selling tickets and special 'Astromeals' at each of it 23,500 restaurants world-wide. This time the target was not children but young adults – a market in which McDonald's is weaker.

McDonald's ↔ Coca-Cola

This alliance has no formal agreement – no piece of paper to fall back on. Although Coca-Cola sells drinks to other restaurants, its relationship with McDonald's goes far beyond that of a mere supplier. It has helped its partner to set up new operations around the world. Coca-Cola is sold in almost twice as many countries as McDonald's.

Coca-Cola ↔ Disney

Coca-Cola's ties to Disney are probably the weakest of the three – but they are still considerable. Coca-Cola has been the sole provider of soft drinks at Disney parks since 1955, and it has had a marketing alliance in place since 1985. Coca-Cola has also helped Disney overseas.

Questions

1. What is it that makes the Coca-Cola–Disney–McDonald's triumvirate so powerful in the globalization process?
2. Which factors could make the alliance of Coca-Cola–Disney–McDonald's break up?

10.7 Summary

The advantages and disadvantages of the different intermediate entry modes are summarized in Table 10.5.

Case study Ka-Boo-Ki

Licensing-in the LEGO brand

The Danish toy manufacturer LEGO is known world-wide for its LEGO bricks. LEGO is a strong and well-known brand. At the end of 1991 LEGO management received the result of three consumer surveys which confirmed this statement:

● Landour Associates completed a survey at the end of 1991 of the best brands' 'image power' among 10,000 representatively chosen adults aged between 18 and

65 in the USA, Japan and Europe (Belgium, France, the Netherlands, Italy, Spain, the UK and Sweden). 'Image power' is a measure of brands' impact, where consumers' awareness of the world's leading brands is combined with their judgement of the brands' quality. In the USA and Japan LEGO was not placed among the top ten, but the results from Europe were impressive. Here LEGO was placed at no. 5 after four car brands: Mercedes-Benz, Rolls-Royce, Porsche and BMW. LEGO was in front of brands like Nestlé, Rolex, Jaguar and Ferrari.

● An American survey, conducted in Europe, the USA and Japan, showed that LEGO is no. 13 in the list of most appreciated brands.

● A survey by a German market analysis institute showed that LEGO is one of the most well-known brands in toys in the new German Federal Republic, with an awareness share of 67 per cent. Matchbox is no. 2 with 41 per cent.

The LEGO management has decided to exploit this strong brand image. A managing director for the new business area LEGO Licensing A/S has been employed. The company's objective is to generate income from licensing suitable partners, which use the LEGO brand in marketing their own products.

The LEGO management has noticed that Coca-Cola has an income of DKK3 billion from licensing lalone. Coca-Cola's strategy can be characterized as 'brand milking', where a brand is sold to the highest bidder in each product area.

Ideas become viable

In 1993 ideas of licensing the LEGO brand became viable for the Danish textile firm Ka-Boo-Ki, as it was given the rights to use the LEGO brand in connection with production and sale of children's clothes (see Plate 5). For Ka-Boo-Ki's managing director, Torben Klausen, the idea of producing children's clothes is not new. He was earlier employed in LEGO's international marketing department, where he was in charge of coordinating the European marketing of LEGO bricks. From this position in the LEGO company, Torben Klausen was able to follow the development of the licensing concept. Since 1993 things have been developing very fast for LEGO children's clothes. Ka-Boo-Ki, which has invested a considerable amount of money in the R & D of LEGO children's clothes, at the middle of 1997 sells to approximately 900 shops, primarily in Scandinavia and England.

Torben Klausen says:

> We received a strong international brand from the first day. But from the sale of LEGO children's clothes follows an obligation to live up to the LEGO company's unique quality demands. The LEGO company must approve all new models which are sent on the market and that is between 350 and 400 a year.

LEGO children's clothes distinguish themselves from other brands by being functional and having strong colours and an uncompromising quality. This means a relatively high price for the clothes and that the products are not sold in discount shops. The clothes are sold on the basis of a shop-in-shop concept, where merchandising and display facilities are very important.

You have just been employed by LEGO Licensing A/S in connection with development of the licensing data. You are given the following assignments.

Questions

1. What are the most important factors determining future market demand for LEGO children's clothes from Ka-Boo-Ki?

2. Which other products could be considered for licensing-out the LEGO brand?

3. List some criteria for choice of suitable licensees and future products for the LEGO brand (licensing-out).

4. What values/benefits can the LEGO company transfer to the licensee (e.g. Ka-Boo-Ki) apart from the use of the LEGO brand?

5. What values/benefits can the licensee transfer to the licensor?

Questions for discussion

1. Why are joint ventures preferred by host countries as an entry strategy for foreign firms?

2. Why are strategic alliances used in new product development?

3. Under what circumstances should franchising be considered? How do these circumstances vary from those leading to licensing?

4. Do you believe that licensing in represents a feasible long-term product development strategy for a company? Discuss in relation to in-house product development.

5. Why would a firm consider forming partnerships with competitors?

6. Apart from the management fees involved, what benefits might a firm derive from entering into management contracts overseas?

Internet exercise

JV in Asian music netcasting

Please go to:

www.pacific.net.sg

www.com

In May 2000 Pacific Internet announced that it has entered into a Memorandum of Understanding (MOU) with WWW.COM, Inc. (http://www.com), the premier business-to-business music netcasting company. The MOU resulted in a joint venture company based in Singapore, which is set to lead the proliferation of Internet broadcast services in Asia and boost the popularity of the Internet as an alternative broadcasting medium.

The joint venture will provide music netcasting products and services to Asian Internet and e-commerce companies, Web sites, portals, entertainment outlets, shops and malls. It will initially target the markets in the Asia-Pacific, including Australia and New Zealand, if applicable.

About Pacific Internet

Pacific Internet offers services in six countries (Singapore, Hong Kong, the Philippines, Australia, India and Thailand) including Internet access, portal sites and the ultimate Web lifestyle with the '4Cs' (connection, commerce, content and community) under Pacfusion.com.

About WWW.COM

Los Angeles-based WWW.COM is the Internet's leading business-to-business music webcasting company and the largest provider of turnkey solutions for Web sites world-wide. The company broadcasts originally programmed stations, supported by a digitized music collection of 350,000 songs and more than 200 music stations. Launched in July 1999, the companys mission is to be the dominant provider of music and entertainment on the Internet, building a powerful broadcast network on the convergence of radio, television and print with a wide range of compelling programming.

Questions

1. Describe the role of the two partners in the joint venture.
2. What are the benefits of the joint venture for each partner?
3. Are there any disadvantages of this joint venture for any of the partners?
4. Describe a possible course of internationalization.

 For further exercises and cases, see this book's website at *www.booksites.net/hollensen*

References

Bleeke, J. and Ernst, D. (1994) *Collaborating to Compete: Using strategic alliances and acquisitions in the global marketplace*, John Wiley, New York.

Bradley, F. (1995) *International Marketing Strategy* (2nd edn), Prentice Hall, Hemel Hempstead.

Carstairs, R.T. and Welch, L.S. (1981) *A Study of Outward Foreign Licensing of Technology by Australian Companies*, Licensing Executives Society of Australia, Canberra.

Harrigan, K.R. (1985) *Strategies for Joint Ventures*, Lexington Books and D.C. Heath, Lexington, MA.

Lorange, P. and Roos, J. (1995) *Strategiske allianser i globale strategier*, Norges Eksportråd, Oslo.

Lowe, J. and Crawford, N. (1984) *Technology Licensing and the Small Firm*, Gower, Aldershot.

Luostarinen, R. and Welch, L. (1990) *International Business Operations*, Helsinki School of Economics, Helsinki.

Nanda, A. and Williamson, P.J. (1995) 'Use joint ventures to ease the pain of restructuring', *Harvard Business Review*, November–December, pp. 119–28.

Paliwoda, S. (1993) *International Marketing*, Heinemann, Oxford.

Perkins, J.S. (1987) 'How licensing and franchising differ', *Les Nouvelles*, vol. 22, no. 4, pp. 155–8.

Porter, M.E. and Fuller, M.B. (1986) 'Coalition and global strategy', in Porter, M.E. (ed.), *Competition in Global Strategies*, Harvard Business School Press, Boston, MA.

Walmsley, J. (1982) *Handbook of International Joint Ventures*, Graham and Trotman Ltd, London.

Young, S., Hamill, Wheeler S. and Davies, J. R. (1989) *International Market Entry and Development*, Harvester Wheatsheaf/Prentice Hall, Hemel Hempstead.

Zalatorius, G. (1996) 'Samsung's Slovak disaster: cool reception', *Business Central Europe*, July/August, p. 26.

Chapter 11

Hierarchical modes

After studying this chapter you should be able to do the following:

● Describe the main hierarchical modes:
  domestic-based representatives;
  resident sales representatives;
  foreign sales subsidiary;
  sales and production subsidiary; and
  region centres.

● Compare and contrast the two investment alternatives: acquisition versus greenfield.

● Explain the different determinants that influence the decision to withdraw investments from a foreign market.

11.1 Introduction

The final group of entry modes is the hierarchical modes, where the firm completely owns and controls the foreign entry mode. Here it is a question of where the control in the firm lies. The degree of control that head office can exert on the subsidiary will depend on how many and which value chain functions can be transferred to the market. This again depends on the allocation of responsibility and competence between head office and the subsidiary, and how the firm wants to develop this on an international level. An organization which is not 100 per cent owned will here be viewed as an export mode or an intermediate mode. The following example, though, may suggest some of the problems involved in this sharp division: a majority-owned (e.g. 75 per cent) joint venture is according to definition an intermediate mode, but in practice a firm with 75 per cent will generally have nearly full control, similar to a hierarchical mode.

If a producer wants greater influence and control over local marketing than export modes can give, it is natural to consider creating own companies in the foreign markets. However, this shift involves an investment, except in the case of the firm having its own sales force, which is considered an operating cost (Figure 11.1).

As a firm goes through Figure 11.1, it chooses to decentralize more and more of its activities to the main foreign markets. In other words, it transfers the responsibility of performing the value chain functions to the local management in the different countries. While moving through Figure 11.1, the firm also goes from one internationalization stage to another (Perlmutter, 1969):

● *Ethnocentric orientation*, represented by the domestic-based sales representatives. This orientation represents an extension of the marketing methods used in the home country to foreign markets.

● *Polycentric orientation*, represented by country subsidiaries. This orientation is based on the assumption that markets/countries around the world are so

Figure 11.1   Hierarchial modes in a value chain perspective

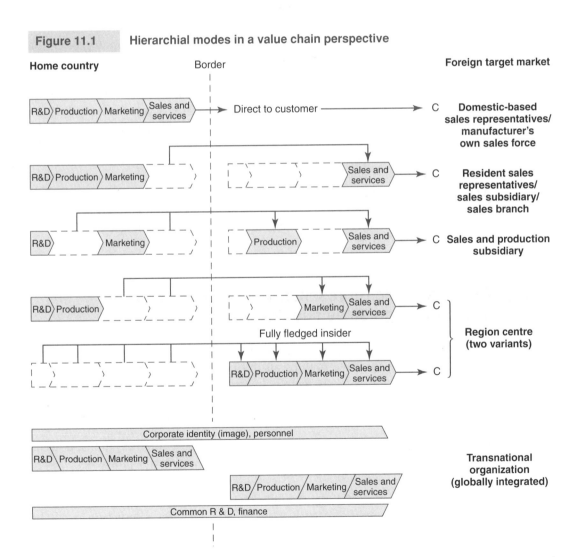

different that the only way to succeed internationally is to manage each country as a separate market with its own subsidiary and adapted marketing mix.

● *Regiocentric orientation*, represented by a region of the world (section 11.5).

● *Geocentric orientation*, represented by the transnational organization. This orientation is based on the assumption that the markets around the world consist of similarities and differences and that it is possible to create a transnational strategy that takes advantage of the similarities between the markets by using synergy effects to leverage learning on a world-wide basis.

The following description and discussion concerning the hierarchical modes takes Figure 11.1 as its starting point.

11.2 Domestic-based sales representatives

A domestic-based sales representative is one who resides in one country, often the home country of the employer, and travels abroad to perform the sales function. As the sales representative is a company employee, better control of sales activities can be achieved than with independent intermediaries. Whereas a company has no control over the attention that an agent or distributor gives to its products or the amount of market feedback provided, it can insist that various activities be performed by its sales representatives.

The use of company employees also shows a commitment to the customer that the use of agents or distributors may lack. Consequently, they are often used in industrial markets, where there are only a few large customers which require close contact with suppliers, and where the size of orders justifies the expense of foreign travel. This method of market entry is also found when selling to government buyers and retail chains, for similar reasons.

11.3 Resident sales representatives/foreign sales branch/foreign sales subsidiary

In all these cases, the actual performance of the sales functions is transferred to the foreign market. These three options all display a greater customer commitment than using domestic-based sales representatives. In making the decision whether to use travelling domestic-based representatives or resident sales representatives in any particular foreign market, a firm should consider the following:

● *Order making or order taking*. If the firm finds that the type of sales job that it needs done in a foreign market tends towards order taking, it will probably choose a travelling domestic-based sales representative; and vice versa.

● *The nature of the product*. If the product is technical and complex in nature and a lot of servicing/supply of parts is required, the travelling salesperson is not an efficient entry method. A more permanent foreign base is then needed.

Sometimes firms find it relevant to establish a formal branch office, to which a resident salesperson is assigned. A foreign branch is an extension and a legal part of the firm. A foreign branch also often employs nationals of the country in which it is located as salespeople. If foreign market sales develop in a positive direction, the firm (at a certain point) may consider establishing a wholly owned sales subsidiary. A foreign subsidiary is a local company owned and operated by a foreign company under the laws of the host country.

The sales subsidiary provides complete control of the sales function. The firm will often keep a central marketing function at its home base, but sometimes a local marketing function can be included in the sales subsidiary. When the sales function is organized as a sales subsidiary (or when sales activities are performed), all foreign orders are channelled through the subsidiary, which then sells to foreign buyers at normal wholesale or retail prices. The foreign sales subsidiary purchases the products to be sold from the parent company at a price. This, of course, creates the problem of intracompany transfer pricing. In Chapter 15 this problem will be discussed in further detail.

One of the major reasons for choosing sales subsidiaries is the possibility of transferring greater autonomy and responsibility to these sub-units, being close to the customer. However, another reason for establishing sales subsidiaries may be the tax advantage. This is particularly important for companies headquartered in high-tax countries. With proper planning companies can establish subsidiaries in countries having low business income taxes and gain an advantage by not paying taxes in their home country on the foreign-generated income until such income is actually repatriated to them. Of course, the precise tax advantages that are possible with such subsidiaries depend upon the tax laws in the home country compared to the host country.

11.4 Sales and production subsidiary

Especially in developing countries, sales subsidiaries may be perceived as taking money out of the country and contributing nothing of value to the host country in which they are based. In those countries a sales subsidiary will generally not be in existence long before there are local demands for a manufacturing or production base.

Generally, if the company believes that its products have long-term market potential in a politically relatively stable country, then only full ownership of sales and production will provide the level of control necessary to meet fully the firm's strategic objectives. However, this entry mode requires great investment in terms of management time, commitment and money. There are considerable risks, too, as subsequent withdrawal from the market can be extremely costly – not simply in terms of financial outlay, but also in terms of reputation in the international and domestic market, particularly with customers and staff.

Japanese companies have used this strategy to build a powerful presence in international markets over a long period of time. Their patience has been rewarded with high market shares and substantial profits, but this has not been achieved overnight. They have sometimes spent more than five years gaining an understanding of markets, customers and competition, as well as selecting locations for manufacturing, before making a significant move.

The main reasons for establishing some kind of local production are as follows:

● To defend existing business. Japanese car imports to Europe were subject to restrictions, and as their sales increased, so they became more vulnerable. With the development of the single European market, Nissan and Toyota have set up operations in the UK.

● To gain new business. Local production demonstrates strong commitment and is the best way to persuade customers to change suppliers, particularly in the industrial markets where service and reliability are often the main factors when making purchasing decisions.

● To save costs. By locating production facilities overseas, costs can be saved in a variety of areas such as labour, raw materials and transport.

● To avoid government restrictions which might be in force to restrict imports of certain goods.

Assembly operations

An assembly operation is a variation of the production subsidiary. Here a foreign production plant might be set up simply to assemble components manufactured in the domestic market or elsewhere. The firm may try to retain key component manufacture in the domestic plant, allowing development, production skills and investment to be concentrated, and maintaining the benefit from economies of scale. Some parts or components may be produced in various countries (multisourcing) in order to gain each country's comparative advantage. Capital-intensive parts may be produced in advanced nations, and labour-intensive assemblies may be produced in a less developed country (LDC), where labour is abundant and labour costs are low. This strategy is common among manufacturers of consumer electronics. When a product becomes mature and faces intense price competition, it may be necessary to shift all of the labour-intensive operations to LDCs. This is the principle behind the international product life cycle (IPLC): see also Chapter 14 (section 14.4).

11.5 Region centres (regional headquarters)

Until now choice of foreign entry mode has mainly been discussed in relation to one particular country. If we suspend this condition, we consider option 3 in Figure 11.2, where 'geographically focused start-up' is an attempt to serve the specialized needs of a particular region of the world. It is very difficult for competitors to imitate a successful coordination of value chain activities in a particular region, as it involves tacit knowledge and is socially complex.

The world is increasingly being regionalized through the formation of such groupings as the European Union, the North American Free Trade Area (NAFTA) and the Association of South-East Asian Nations (ASEAN).

Figure 11.2   **Types of international new venture**

Coordination of value chain activities	Few activities coordinated across countries (primarily logistics)	New international market makers	
		Export/import start-up ①	Multinational trader ②
	Many activities coordinated across countries	③ Geographically focused start-up	④ Global start-up
		Few	Many
		Number of countries involved	

Source: Oviatt and McDougall, 1994, p. 59. Reprinted with permission by *Journal of International Business Studies (JIBS)*: Georgetown University, Washington DC)

In Figure 11.1 two examples of region centres are shown. The first variant shows that the downstream functions have been transferred to the region. In the second variant even greater commitment is shown to the region because here all the value chain activities are moved to the region, whereby the firm has become a fully fledged insider in the region. At this stage the firm has all the necessary functions in the region to compete effectively against local and regional competitors. At the same time, the firm can respond to local customer needs.

Formation of region centres implies creation of a regional headquarters (RHQ) or appointment of a 'lead country', which will usually play the role of coordinator and stimulator with reference to a single homogeneous product group (see Figure 11.3).

The coordination role consists of ensuring three things:

● Country and business strategies are mutually coherent.

● One subsidiary does not harm another.

● Adequate synergies are fully identified and exploited across business and countries.

The stimulator role consists of two functions:

● Facilitating the translation of 'global' products into local country strategies.

● Supporting local subsidiaries in their development (Lasserre, 1996).

Figure 11.3 (an example of a multinational company having its head office in Germany) shows that different countries/subsidiaries can have a leading function for different product groups. In the diagram there is a world market such that for products A and E only one country/subsidiary has the coordination function on a global basis (France and Great Britain, respectively). For product D there are three regions with a lead country in each region.

The choice of a lead country is influenced by several factors:

● The marketing competences of the foreign subsidiaries.

● The quality of human resources in the countries represented.

Figure 11.3   The lead country concept

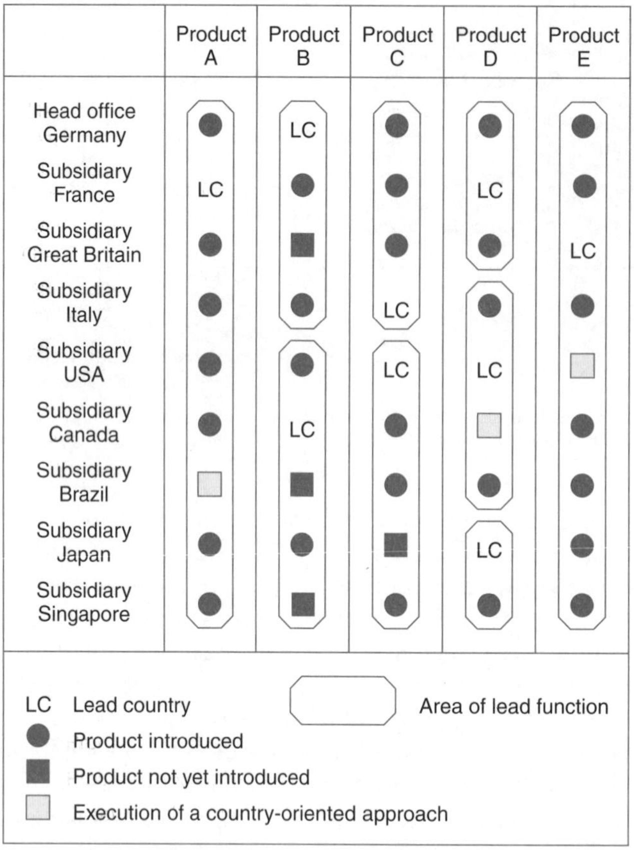

	Product A	Product B	Product C	Product D	Product E
Head office Germany	●	LC	●	●	●
Subsidiary France	LC	●	●	LC	●
Subsidiary Great Britain	●	■	●	●	LC
Subsidiary Italy	●	●	LC	●	●
Subsidiary USA	●	●	LC	LC	□
Subsidiary Canada	●	LC	●	□	●
Subsidiary Brazil	□	■	●	●	●
Subsidiary Japan	●	●	■	LC	●
Subsidiary Singapore	●	■	●	●	●

LC   Lead country   Area of lead function
●   Product introduced
■   Product not yet introduced
□   Execution of a country-oriented approach

(Source: Raffée and Kreutzer, 1989. Reproduced with kind permission from *European Journal of Marketing*, MCB University Press; http://www.mcb.co.uk)

● The strategic importance of the countries represented.

● Location of production.

● Legal restrictions of host countries.

The country with the best 'leading' competences should be chosen for the job as lead country.

Figure 11.4 shows how a firm can develop the region centre concept in the Asia Pacific area. The countries in the Asia Pacific area are so different that you have to proceed in a sequential way. The example is based on a country-by-country approach together with developing a regional view (Lasserre, 1995).

One can distinguish five types of country in Asia, which are represented in Figure 11.4.

● The *platform countries*, such as Singapore or Hong Kong, which can be used in the starting phase as bases for gathering intelligence and initiating first contacts

Figure 11.4   **Developing the region centre concept in Asia Pacific**

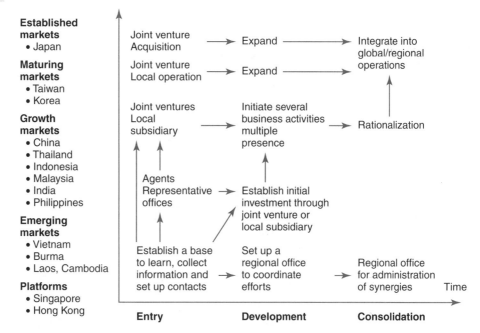

(Source: Lasserre, 1995, p. 21. Reprinted with permission from Elsevier Science Ltd., The Boulevard, Langford Lane, Kidlington, OX5 1GB, UK)

which can later become the centre of regional coordination. For instance, medium-sized companies with no prior experience in the region could establish their presence by setting up a 'listening post' in these countries.

● The *emerging countries*, such as Vietnam today and Myamar (Burma) and Cambodia in the near future. The task in these countries is to establish an initial presence through a local distributor and build the necessary relationships in order to prepare for the establishment of a local operation either directly or through a joint venture.

● The *growth countries*, such as China and the ASEAN countries, where it is becoming urgent to establish a significant presence in order to capitalize on the opportunities generated by rapid economic development.

● The *maturing* and *established countries*, such as Korea and Taiwan, which already have significant economic infrastructures and well-established local and international competitors. In the entry phase the task here is to find a way to acquire, through massive investment, the necessary operational capability to catch competitors up.

The particular entry and pathway to development will depend upon the company's prior experience and capabilities, and on the particular strategic attractiveness of an industrial sector in a country.

Gradually, the firm will start to look at all the countries in one region, because some activities, notably strategic, intelligence, financial, engineering, R & D, training and specialized services, can reap the benefits of economies of scale only by servicing the whole region.

| Exhibit 11.1 | Region centres and the case of Henkel |

The German-based Henkel is a specialist in applied chemistry, selling 11,000 different products world-wide to industrial customers and end consumers. The detergent brand, Persil, is Henkel's largest single product and the market leader in Germany.

On an aggregate level, several surveys had shown that 20–25 per cent of all chemicals in the world were sold in Asia. There was consensus that this percentage would increase considerably over the coming decades, on account of declining sales in Europe and the United States. The problem was that Henkel still had only 4.4 per cent of its business in Asia.

Because of these facts, Henkel had become increasingly aware that it had to boost its exposure in Asia significantly, if it was to continue to grow and prosper. Thus, on 1 November 1991, Henkel announced the establishment of the region centre, Henkel Asia-Pacific Ltd (HAP) with headquarters in Hong Kong. In a press release the holding group's objectives were defined as: the centralization of management; the intensification of advisory services; and the reinforcement of the management of subsidiaries and joint ventures. One of the senior managers became chairman of this holding group, and all the heads of the subsidiaries reported directly to him, including Japan. The region consisted of twelve countries: Australia, China, Hong Kong, Indonesia, Japan, Malaysia, New Zealand, Philippines, Singapore, South Korea, Taiwan and Thailand. Some 1,600 people were employed in fifteen subsidiaries that generated sales of around DM 450 million.

While most subsidiaries were pleased with the establishment of HAP in Hong Kong, the Japanese resisted and stressed that their market had little in common with the region, with the possible exception of Korea and Taiwan. They saw their operation as more in line with medium-sized European subsidiaries, which were not asked to report to a regional office.

Strategically, the region had gained in importance for Henkel, but its total share in world-wide sales and profits was still tiny. Much of Henkel's growth in the region now depends on progress in China and its future development.

Source: Adapted from Schütte, H. (1995) 'Henkel's Strategy for Asia Pacific', *Long Range Planning*, vol. 28, pp. 95–103. Copyright © 1995, with permission from Elsevier Science Ltd, The Boulevard, Longford Lane, Kidlington, OX5 1GB, UK.

| 11.6 | ## Transnational organization |

In this final stage of internationalization, companies attempt to coordinate and integrate operations across national boundaries so as to achieve potential synergies on a global scale. Management views the world as a series of interrelated markets. At this stage, the employees tend to identify more strongly with their company than with the country in which they operate.

Common R & D and frequent geographical exchange of human resources across

Figure 11.5 **Unilever's differentiation organization**

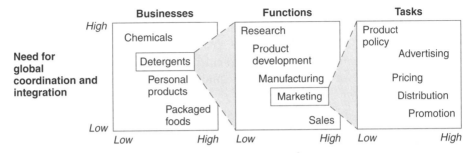

borders are among the characteristics of a transnational company. The overall goal for the transnational company will be to achieve global competitiveness through recognizing cross-border market similarities and differences, and linking the capabilities of the company across national boundaries. One of the relatively few international companies that have reached this stage is Unilever.

Bartlett and Ghoshal (1989) used the global integration/national responsiveness grid (Bartlett, 1984) in an extended form as an illustration of Unilever's attempt to balance conflicting demands for both global efficiency and local responsiveness (see Figure 11.5).

Unilever's 'special chemicals' business is selling ingredients and processing aid to industrial customers. This business is managed globally so as to maximize global efficiency. The packaged foods business, on the other hand, has to adapt to local cultural tastes and country-specific distribution infrastructures. Figure 11.5 also shows that the 'upstream' value chain functions (R & D, manufacturing) allow for a higher degree of global coordination, whereas the 'downstream' value chain functions (marketing, sales, service) most often require adaptation to the local environment.

In summary, managing a transnational company requires the sensitivity to know the following:

● When a global brand makes sense or when local requirements should take precedence.

● When to transfer innovation and expertise from one market to another.

● When a local idea has global potential.

● When to bring international teams together fast to focus on key opportunities.

11.7 Establishing wholly owned subsidiaries – acquisition or greenfield

All the hierarchical modes presented in this chapter (except domestic-based sales representatives) involve investment in foreign-based facilities. In deciding to establish wholly owned operations in a country, a firm can either acquire an existing company or build its own operations from scratch (greenfield investment).

Acquisition

Acquisition enables rapid entry and often provides access to distribution channels, an existing customer base and, in some cases, established brand names or corporate reputations. In some cases, too, existing management remains, providing a bridge to entry into the market and allowing the firm to acquire experience in dealing with the local market environment. This may be particularly advantageous for a firm with limited international management expertise, or little familiarity with the local market.

In saturated markets the industry is highly competitive or there are substantial entry barriers, and therefore there is little room for a new entrant. In these circumstances, market acquisitions may be the only feasible way of establishing a base in the host country.

Acquisitions take many forms. According to Root (1987), acquisition may be horizontal (the product lines and markets of the acquired and acquiring firms are similar), vertical (the acquired firm becomes supplier or customer of the acquiring firm), concentric (the acquired firm has the same market but different technology, or the same technology but different markets) or conglomerate (the acquired firm is in a different industry from that of the acquiring firm). No matter what form the acquisition takes, coordination and styles of management between the foreign investor and the local management team may cause problems.

Greenfield investment

The difficulties encountered with acquisitions may lead firms to prefer to establish operations from the ground up, especially where production logistics is a key industry success factor, and where no appropriate acquisition targets are available or they are too costly.

The ability to integrate operations across countries, and to determine the direction of future international expansion, is often a key motivation to establish wholly owned operations, even though it takes longer to build plants than to acquire them.

Furthermore, if the firm builds a new plant, it can not only incorporate the latest technology and equipment, but also avoid the problems of trying to change the traditional practices of an established concern. A new facility means a fresh start and an opportunity for the international company to shape the local firm into its own image and requirements.

11.8 ▌ Foreign divestment: withdrawing from a foreign market

While a vast theoretical and empirical literature has examined the determinants of entering into foreign direct investments (FDI), considerably less attention has been given to the decision to exit from a foreign market.

Most of the studies undertaken show a considerable 'loss' of foreign subsidiaries over time:

● Between 1967 and 1975 the 180 largest US-based multinationals added some 4,700 subsidiaries to their networks, but more than 2,400 affiliates were divested during the same period (Boddewyn, 1979).

● Out of 225 FDIs undertaken by large Dutch multinationals in the period 1966–88, only just over half of them were still in existence in 1988 (Barkema *et al.*, 1996).

Closing down a foreign subsidiary or selling it off to another firm is a strategic decision, and the consequence may be a change of foreign entry mode (e.g. from a local sales and production subsidiary to an export mode or a joint venture), or a complete withdrawal from a host country.

The most obvious incentive to exit is profits that are too low, which in turn may be due to high costs, permanent decreases in local market demand or the entry into the industry of more efficient competitors. Besides being voluntary, the divestment may also be a result of expropriation or nationalization in the foreign country.

In order to investigate further the question of why foreign divestments take place, it is necessary to look at the specific factors that may influence incentives and barriers to exit, and thereby the probability of exiting from a foreign subsidiary. Benito (1996) classifies the specific factors into four main groups (Figure 11.6).

Environmental stability

This is a question of the predictability of the environment – competitively and politically – in which the foreign subsidiary operates.

Figure 11.6   **Divestment of foreign operation: a framework**

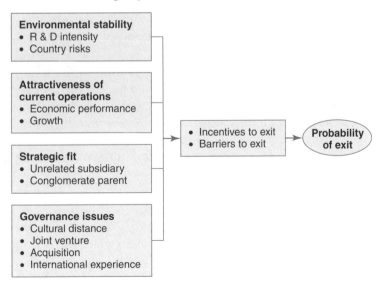

(Source: Benito, 1996, Figure 2)

- *R & D intensity*. Perceived barriers to exit are likely to increase due to large market-specific investments made in R & D and the marketing of the products.
- *Country risks*. These risks are typically outside the firm's scope of control. Political risks may often lead to forced divestment, with the result that expropriation takes place.

Attractiveness of current operations

- *Economic performance*. Unsatisfactory economic performance (i.e. inability to produce a net contribution to overall profits) is the most obvious reason why particular subsidiaries are sold off or shut down. On the other hand, if the subsidiary is a good economic performer, the owners may see an opportunity to obtain a good price for the unit while it is performing well.
- *Growth*. Economic growth in the host country would normally make FDI even more attractive, thereby increasing the barriers to exit from such a country. However, the attractiveness of the location would make such operations more likely targets for takeovers by other investors.

Strategic fit

Unrelated expansion (i.e. diversification) increases the governance cost of the business, and economies of scale and scope are also rarely achieved by unrelated subsidiaries. Hence these factors increase the incentives to exit.

The same arguments apply to a conglomerate parent.

Governance issues

- *Cultural distance*. Closeness between home country and host countries results in easier monitoring and coordination of production and marketing activities in the various locations. Thus, culturally close countries increase the barriers to exit and vice versa.
- *Joint venture and acquisition*. A joint venture with a local partner can certainly reduce barriers to the penetration of a foreign market by giving rapid access to knowledge about the local market. On the other hand, whenever a joint venture is set up with a foreign partner, both different national and corporate cultures may have an impact on its success. Joint ventures and acquisitions are put in a difficult situation in the often critical initial phases of the integration process. Thus, a lack of commitment in the parent company or companies may increase the incentive to exit.
- *Experience*. Firms learn from experience how to operate in the foreign environment, and how to search for solutions to problems that emerge. As experience is accumulated, it becomes easier to avoid many of the problems involved in running foreign subsidiaries and to find workable solutions if problems should arise. This also includes the unpleasant decision to close down a subsidiary.

11.9   Summary

The advantages and disadvantages of the different hierarchical entry modes are summarized in Table 11.1.

Furthermore, this chapter discussed under what circumstances foreign divestment is likely to take place. The most obvious reason to exit from a market seems to be low profits earned in the market.

Table 11.1   Advantages and disadvantages of different hierarchical entry modes

Hierarchical entry mode	Advantages	Disadvantages
Domestic-based sales representatives	Better control of sales activities compared to independent intermediaries. Close contact to large customers in foreign markets close to home country.	High travel expenses. Too expensive in foreign markets, far away from home country.
Foreign sales branch/sales and production subsidiary	Full control of operation. Eliminates the possibility that a national partner gets a 'free ride'. Market access (sales subsidiary). Acquire market knowledge directly (sales subsidiary). Reduce transport costs (production subsidiary). Elimination of duties (production subsidiary). Access to raw materials and labour (production subsidiary).	High initial capital investment required (subsidiary). Loss of flexibility. High risk (market, political and economic). Taxation problems.
Region centres/transnational organization	Achieves potential synergies on a regional/global scale. Regional/global scale efficiency. Leverage learning on a cross-national basis. Resources and people are flexible and can be put into operating units around the world.	Possible threats: Increasing bureaucracy. Limited national-level responsiveness and flexibility. A national manager can feel he or she has no influence. Missing communication between head office and region centres.
Acquistion	Rapid entry to new markets. Gaining quick access to: distribution channels; a qualified labour force; existing management experience; local knowledge; contacts with local market and government; established brand names/reputation.	Usually an expensive option. High risk (taking over companies which are regarded as part of a country's heritage can raise considerable national resentment if it seems that they are being taken over by foreign interests). Possible threats: Lack of integration with existing operation. Communication and coordination problems between acquired firm and acquirer.
Greenfield investment	Possible to build in an 'optimum' format, i.e. In a way that fits the interests of the firm (e.g. integrating production with home base production). Possible to integrate state-of-the-art technology (resulting in increased operational efficiency).	High investment cost. Slow entry of new markets (time-consuming process).

Case study   Durex condoms in Japan

SSL will sell Durex condoms in the Japanese market through their own organization

Durex condoms will go on sale in Japan for the first time after SSL International, the manufacturer and distributor of healthcare products, announced it is to expand its operation in the country.

SSL International was formed in June 1999 by the merger of Seton Scholl Health Care with LIG (London International Group). Durex is the most-sold condom-brand around the world with a world-wide market share of approximately 20 per cent. Generally the SSL managers run a brand-oriented strategy: 'We want Durex to be the Coca-Cola of the condom world'.

The move in Japan was made possible by the 1999 merger. Seton Scholl has its own presence in Japan, with marketing and distribution networks set up, whereas LIG did not. Through Seton Scholl Japan, it already distributes Scholl products such as shoes and footwear products throughout the country as well as surgical and dental gloves which are manufactured by the old LIG company.

SSL has terminated a long-term contract with Okamoto, the largest supplier of condoms in Japan, freeing it to vie for a share of the country's 200m condom market. Iain Carter, chief executive, says 'It now makes sense for us to take control of our own destiny in Japan'. SSL aims to have won 5 per cent of the market within five years, generating £10m of new revenue. SSL has bought out its partner in Seton Scholl Japan, giving it full control. Iain Carter, chief executive, said: 'We saw more prospect of generating value for shareholders by going it alone in Japan.' He said Durex products would be channelled through the established distribution network of *Seton Scholl Japan*, selling footwear, footcare and surgical gloves. He added that Durex was already well known as an international brand in the country.

The Japanese market for condoms is said to be the world's largest with annual turnover worth about £200 million. It is dominated by Okamoto (42 per cent market share) and other locally produced products. The Japanese market is so large because until June 1999 the contraceptive pill was banned and most people had to reply on condoms for birth control. Experts say that it will still take one or two generations before the pill is widely used in Japan.

One reason why it took 40 years for the contraceptive pill to be legalized in Japan was lobbying by condom-makers against its introduction. Japanese health officials said that they were concerned that use of the pill, instead of condoms, would spread sexually transmitted disease. It was even claimed, by other opponents, that the urine of women on the pill would pollute rivers and deform fish.

Questions

1. What have been the main motives for SSL to establish their own distribution channels for condoms in Japan?

2. What are the major barriers for SSL to reach higher market share for condoms in Japan?

Source: Adapted from:
Financial Times, (2000) 'SSL goes it alone in Japan with Durex', 3 February.
New Media Age (1997) 'Condom brand goes global on web', 1 May.

Questions for discussion

1. By what criteria would you judge a particular foreign direct investment activity to have succeeded or failed?

2. What are the firm's major motives in the decision to establish manufacturing facilities in a foreign country?

3. Is the establishment of wholly owned subsidiaries abroad an appropriate international market development mode for SMEs?

4. What is the idea behind appointing a 'lead country' in a region?

5. Why is acquisition often the preferred way to establish wholly owned operations abroad? What are the limitations of acquisition as an entry method?

6. What are the key problems associated with profit repatriation from subsidiaries?

Internet exercise

Rover

Please go to

http://www.rovercars.com/

http://newsvote.bbc.co.uk/hi/english/talking_point/newsid_741000/741920.stm

In May 2000 Phoenix signed a contract with BMW to buy Rover Cars for a nominal sum of £10.

The deal followed almost two months of frenetic negotiations involving Phoenix, BMW, the original bidders Alchemy Partners and the UK government. Rover's previous owner, German car giant BMW, had threatened to close its subsidiary's Longbridge plant by the end of the month if it could not find a buyer.

The Phoenix consortium includes two Rover dealers and racing car group Lola.

Questions

1. What are the advantages for the Phoenix consortium of this acquisition model compared with other relevant entry modes?

2. Do you believe it will be possible to penetrate the global car market with the Rover brand?

For further exercises and cases, see this book's website at *www.booksites.net/hollensen*

References

Barkema, H.G., Bell, J. and Pennings, J.M. (1996) 'Foreign entry, cultural barriers and learning', *Strategic Management Journal*, vol. 17, pp. 151–66.

Bartlett, C.A. (1984) *Organization and Control of Global Enterprises: Influences, characteristics and guidelines*, Harvard Business School Press, Boston, MA.

Bartlett, C.A. and Ghoshal, S. (1989) *Managing Across Borders: The transnational solution*, Harvard Business School Press, Boston, MA.

Benito, G. (1996) 'Why are subsidiaries divested? A conceptual framework', Working Paper No. 3–93, Institute of International Economics and Management, Copenhagen Business School.

Boddewyn, J.J. (1979) 'Foreign divestment: magnitude and factors', *Journal of International Business Studies*, vol. 10, pp. 21–7.

Lasserre, P. (1995) 'Corporate strategies for the Asia Pacific region', *Long Range Planning*, vol. 28, no. 1, pp. 13–30.

Lasserre, P. (1996) 'Regional headquarters – the spearhead for Asian Pacific markets', *Long Range Planning*, vol. 29, no. 1, pp. 30–7.

Oviatt, B.M. and McDougall, P.P. (1994) 'Toward a theory of international new ventures', *Journal of International Business Studies*, vol. 25, no. 1, pp. 45–64.

Perlmutter, H. (1969) 'The torturous evolution of multinational corporations', Columbia Journal of World Business, January–February, pp. 9–18.

Raffée, H. and Kreutzer, R. (1989) 'Organisational dimensions of global marketing', *European Journal of Marketing*, vol. 23, no. 5, pp. 43–57.

Root, F.R. (1987) *Entry Strategies for International Markets*, Lexington Books, Lexington, MA.

Schütte, H. (1995) 'Henkel's strategy for Asia Pacific', *Long Range Planning*, vol. 28, no. 1, pp. 95–103.

Chapter 12

International sourcing decisions and the role of the subsupplier

After studying this chapter you should be able to do the following:

● Describe the role of subcontractor in the vertical chain.

● Explore the reasons for international outsourcing.

● Explain the development of a buyer–seller relationship.

● Discuss alternative routes of subcontractor internationalization.

● Explain how turnkey contracts differ from conventional subcontracting.

12.1 Introduction

Recent studies of subcontracting and competitiveness have emphasized the importance of outsourcing: moving functions or activities out of an organization. Outsourcing is often more efficient, except in the case of the firm's core competences, which are considered central to its success. Thus, the issue is whether an organization should perform certain functions itself ('make') or source ('buy') these activities from outside. If LSEs outsource an increasing number of value chain functions, it provides business opportunities for the SMEs as subcontractors to LSEs (main contractors).

A subcontractor can be defined as a person or a firm that agrees to provide semi-finished products or services needed by another party (main contractor) to perform another contract to which the subcontractor is not a party. According to this definition, the characteristics of subcontractors that distinguish them from other SMEs are as follows:

● Subcontractors' products are usually part of the end product, not the complete end product itself.

● Subcontractors do not have direct contact with the end customers, because the main contractor is usually responsible to the customer.

The position of subcontractors in the vertical production chain is shown in Figure 12.1.

In the OEM contract (where OEM stands for original equipment manufacturer), the contractor is called the OEM or 'sourcer', whereas the parts suppliers are

Figure 12.1 **Subcontractor's position in the vertical chain**

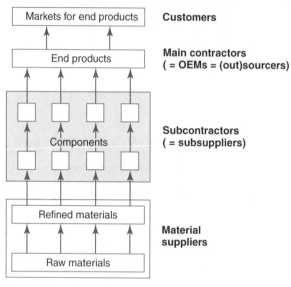

(Source: Adapted from Lehtinen, 1991, p. 22)

Figure 12.2 **Structure of Chapter 12**

regarded as 'manufacturers' of OEM products (= subcontractors = subsuppliers). Typically the OEM contracts are different from other buyer–seller relationships in the way that the OEMs (contractors) often have much stronger bargaining power than the subcontractors. However, in a partner-based buyer–seller relationship, the power balance will be more equal. There are cases where a subcontractor improved its bargaining position and went on to become a major force in the market (Cho and Chu, 1994).

The structure of the remainder of this chapter is shown in Figure 12.2.

12.2 Reasons for international sourcing

More and more international firms are buying their parts, semi-finished components and other supplies from international subcontractors. Creating competitiveness through the subcontractor is based on the understanding that the supplier can be essential to the buyer (contractor) for a number of reasons.

Concentration on in-house core competences

A contractor wishes to concentrate management time and effort on those core business activities that make the best use of in-house skills and resources. There may also be special difficulties in obtaining suitably skilled labour in-house.

Lower product/production costs

In this respect there are two underlying reasons for outsourcing:

- *Economies of scale*. In many cases the subcontractor produces similar components for other customers, and by use of the experience curve the subcontractor can obtain lower production costs per unit.

- *Lower wage costs*. The labour costs involved in the domestic country can make the in-house operation uneconomic and motivate international sourcing. For example, 80 per cent of the labour cost of clothing manufacture is in the sewing stage. Short production runs of different sizes of clothes permit only a low degree of mechanization. Moreover, adjusting the tooling for each run is relatively labour intensive (Hibbert, 1993). Therefore a large part of labour-intensive clothing production is moved to low-wage countries in eastern Europe and the Far East.

General cost efficiency

If a firm plans to be more cost efficient than its competitors, the firm has to minimize the total costs towards the end (ultimate) customer. Figure 12.3 shows a model of the different cost elements from basic price of materials to the ultimate customer cost.

Each element of the supply chain is a potential candidate for outsourcing. Quality costs, inventory costs (not explicitly mentioned in Figure 12.3) and buyer/supplier transaction costs are examples of costs that should be included in every calculation.

Figure 12.3   The total cost/value hierarchy model

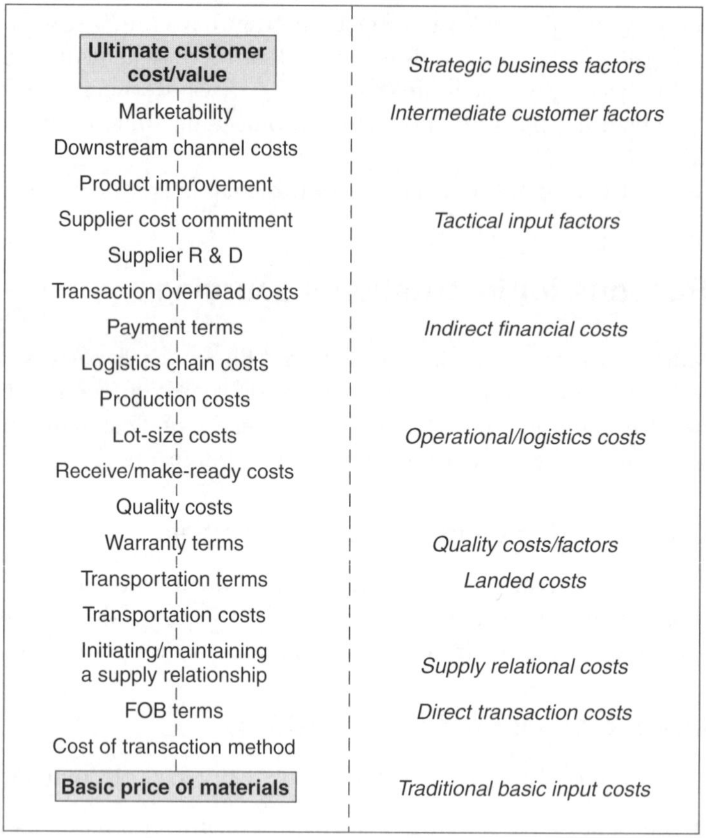

Ultimate customer cost/value	Strategic business factors
Marketability	Intermediate customer factors
Downstream channel costs	
Product improvement	
Supplier cost commitment	Tactical input factors
Supplier R & D	
Transaction overhead costs	
Payment terms	Indirect financial costs
Logistics chain costs	
Production costs	
Lot-size costs	Operational/logistics costs
Receive/make-ready costs	
Quality costs	
Warranty terms	Quality costs/factors
Transportation terms	Landed costs
Transportation costs	
Initiating/maintaining a supply relationship	Supply relational costs
FOB terms	Direct transaction costs
Cost of transaction method	
Basic price of materials	Traditional basic input costs

(Source: Cavinato, 1992)

However, some of these costs are difficult to estimate and are consequently easily overlooked when evaluating a subcontractor.

For example, the quality of a subcontractor's product or service is essential to the buyer's quality. However, it is not only a question of the quality of the product or service. The quality of the delivery processes also has a major impact on the buyer's performance. Uncertainties, as far as lead times are concerned, have an impact on the buyer's inventory investments and cost efficiency, and they may cause delays in the buyer's own delivery processes. Thus the buyer's own delivery times towards the end customers are determined by the subcontractors and their delivery. Another important fact is that the cost of components and parts is to a large extent already determined at the design stage. Thus, close cooperation between buyer and seller at this stage can give rise to considerable cost advantages in production and distribution.

Increased potential for innovation

Ideas for innovation can be generated by the subcontractor due to its more in-depth understanding of the component. New ideas can also be transferred from other customers of the subcontractor.

Fluctuating demand

If the main contractor is confronted with fluctuating demand levels, external uncertainty and short product life cycles, it may transfer some risk and stock management to the subcontractor, leading to better cost and budget control.

Finally, it should be mentioned that, when buying from international sources, fluctuations in exchange rates become particularly important, especially when there is a lag from the time the contract is signed to when payment is made. When the currency in the country of the main contractor is very strong against a particular country, this can be an incentive for the main contractor to buy from this country.

In summary, price is a very important reason for (international) outsourcing, but the main contractors increasingly regard cooperation with critical subcontractors as advantageous to the buying firm's competitiveness and profitability.

12.3 A typology of subcontracting

Traditionally, a subcontractor has been defined as a firm carrying out day-to-day production based on the specifications of another firm (the main contractor). The variety of subcontracting relationships that are appearing indicates a need for a more differentiated typology.

Figure 12.4 displays a typology of subcontractors based on differences in the contractor–subcontractor relationship. The typology displays the interplay between the degree of coordination needed and the complexity of the tasks to be solved.

- *Standard subcontracting.* Economies of scale often operate in the global market with standardized products, in which case no adaptation to specific customers is needed.
- *Simple subcontracting.* Information exchange is simple since the contractor specifies criteria for contribution. The contractor's in-house capacity is often a major competitor.
- *Expanded subcontracting.* There is some mutual specialization between the two parties and exit costs are higher for both parties. Therefore single sourcing (one supplier for a product/component) may replace multisourcing (more suppliers for a product/component).
- *Strategic development subcontracting.* This is very important to the contractor. Subcontractors possess a critical competence of value to the contractor. They are involved in the contractor's long-term planning, and activities are coordinated by dialogue.
- *Partnership-based subcontracting.* This is a relationship based on a strong mutual strategic value and dependency. The subcontractor is highly involved in R & D activities of the contractor.

Figure 12.4   **Typology of subcontracting**

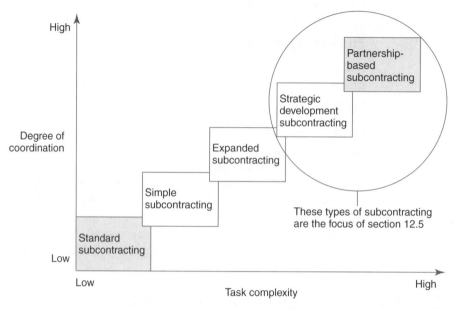

(Source: Adapted from Blenker and Christensen, 1994)

There is a certain overlap between the different types of subcontractor and in a specific relationship it can be very difficult to place a subcontractor in a certain typology. Depending primarily on the task complexity, a main contractor may have both standard subcontractors and partnership-based subcontractors. Also a subcontractor may play more than one role in Figure 12.4, but only one at a time.

12.4   Buyer–seller interaction

Traditionally, subcontracting has been defined as the production activities that one firm carries out on the day-to-day specification of another firm. Outsourced activities increasingly include R & D, design and other functions in the value chain. Thus what starts with simple transactions (so-called episodes) may, if repeated over time, evolve into a relationship between buyer and seller.

Interaction theory was developed by the Swedes but spread into France, Britain, Italy and Germany when a group of like-minded researchers formed what became known as the IMP Group, basing their research on the interaction model (Figure 12.5).

The interaction model has four basic elements:

● The interaction process, which expresses the exchanges between the two organizations along with their progress and evolution throughout time.

● The participants in the interaction process, meaning the characteristics of the supplier and the customer involved in the interaction process.

Figure 12.5   **The buyer–seller interaction**

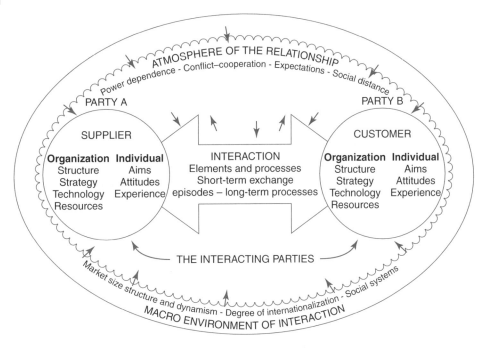

(Source: Turnbull and Valla, 1986. Reproduced with permission from The Braybrooke Press Ltd.)

● The atmosphere affecting and being affected by the interaction.

● The environment within which interaction takes place.

Interaction process

The interaction process can be analyzed in both a short-term and a long-term perspective. Over time, the relationship is developed by a sequence of episodes and events that tends to institutionalize or destabilize it, depending on the evaluations made by the two firms in the interaction. These episodes may vary in terms of types of exchange: commercial transactions, periods of crisis caused by delivery, price disputes, new product development stages, etc.

Through social exchange with the supplier, the customer attempts to reduce decision-making uncertainty. Over time and with mutual adaptation, a relationship-specific mode of operation emerges and may act as a 'shock absorber' in case of crisis. This mode of operation can take the form of special procedures, mutual developments, communication style between individuals, and more or less implicit rules. These rules are modified through past exchanges and form the framework for future exchanges.

Interacting parties

The participants' characteristics strongly influence the way they interact. Three analytical perspectives of buyer and seller, at different levels, may be taken into account.

The social system perspective

Dimensions such as culture – languages, values and practices – and the operating modes of the firm influence the distance between actors that will limit or encourage collaboration.

The organizational perspective

The relationship between buyer and seller is influenced by three organizational dimensions:

● The characteristics of each firm's technology (i.e. products and production technology) strongly influence the nature of the interaction between the two organizations.

● The complexity of products sold, for example, conditions the very nature and the density of the interaction between supplier and customer.

● Relationship characteristics: a supplier can choose to develop a stable relationship with a customer, or the supplier can regard the relationship as a pure transaction-based exchange where the supplier typically makes 'one-shot' business with a customer purely to increase sales volume and with no further involvement.

The individual perspective

The individuals' characteristics, their objectives and their experience will influence the way social exchanges and social contacts take place, and subsequently the development of supplier–customer interaction.

Atmosphere of the relationship

The atmosphere is the 'climate' that has developed between the two firms. This atmosphere can be described in terms of power–dependence, cooperation–conflict and trust–opportunism, and in terms of understanding and social distance. The atmosphere concept is central to the understanding of the supplier–customer relationship. In the case of key account management (discussed further in section 16.7), atmosphere plays a particularly important role. As buyer and seller approach each other the marketing exchanges are changing from single transactions to a relationship. The further characteristics of these two situations are described in Table 12.1 and Figure 12.6.

Interaction environment

Supplier–customer relationships evolve in a general macro environment that can influence their very nature. The following analytical dimensions are traditionally considered: political and economic context, cultural and social context, market structure, market internationalization and market dynamism (growth, innovation rate).

Table 12.1

Table 12.1 Marketing exchange understanding

	Transaction	Relationship
Objective	To make a sale (sale is end result and measure of success) Customer needs satisfaction (customer buys values)	To create a customer (sale is beginning of relationship) Customer integration (interactive value generation)
Customer understanding	Anonymous customer Independent buyer and seller	Well-known customer interdependent buyer and seller
Marketers' task and performance criteria	Assessment on the basis of products and prices Focus on gaining new customers	Assessment on the basis of problem-solving competence Focus on value enhancing of existing customers
Core aspects of exchange	Focus on products Sale as a conquest Discrete event Monologue to aggregated broad customer segments	Focus on service Sale as an agreement Continuing process Individualized dialogue

Source: Jüttner and Wehrli (1994). Reproduced with permission from MCB University Press; http://www.mcb.co.uk

Figure 12.6

Market exchange understanding

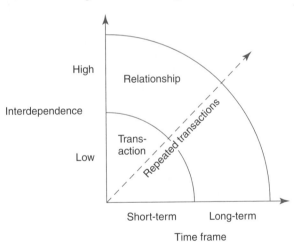

(Source: Jüttner and Wehrli, 1994. Reproduced with permission from MCB University Press; http://www.mcb.co.uk)

12.5

Development of a relationship

A relationship between two firms begins, grows and develops – or fails – in ways similar to relationships between people. The development of a relationship has been mapped out in a five-phase model: awareness, exploration, expansion, commitment and dissolution. The first four phases are shown in Figure 12.7.

Figure 12.7 The relationship development process

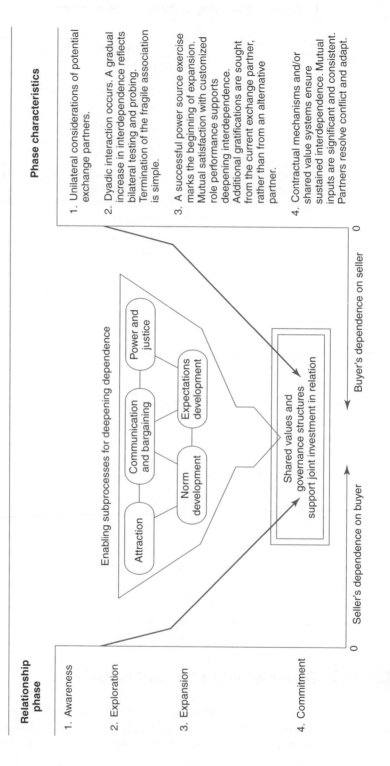

(Source: Dwyer *et al.*, 1987p. 15.)

Within such a framework, one might easily characterize a marketing relationship as a marriage between a seller and a buyer (the dissolution phase being a 'divorce'). The use of the marriage metaphor emphasizes the complexity as well as some affective determinants of the quality of the relationship. Dwyer *et al.* (1987) call the first phase in a relationship *awareness*, which means that the partners recognize each other as potential partners. In other words, in their model the decisions made about cooperating and choosing the partner are combined. In our opinion, both types of decision making can exist at the beginning of cooperation, but it is difficult to state any definite chronological order between them.

In SMEs it is likely that the decision making is reactive, in the way that the SME probably first realizes the existence of a potential partner (maybe 'love at first sight') and then decides to cooperate. The selection process may go better if companies look for three key criteria (Kanter, 1994):

● *Self-analysis*. Relationships get off to a good start when partners know themselves and their industry, when they have assessed changing industry conditions and decided to seek an alliance. It also helps if executives have experience in evaluating potential partners. They will not be easily attracted by the first good-looking prospect that comes along.

● *Chemistry*. To highlight the personal side of business relationships is not to deny the importance of sound financial and strategic analysis. But successful relations often depend on the creation and maintenance of a comfortable personal relationship between senior executives. This will include personal and social interests. Signs of managers' interests, commitment and respect are especially important in high-context countries. In China, as well as in Chinese-dominated businesses throughout Asia, the top manager of the western company should show honour and respect to the potential partner's decision by investing his or her personal time.

● *Compatibility*. The courtship period tests compatibility on broad historical, philosophical and strategic grounds: common experiences, values and principles, and hopes for the future. While analysts examine financial viability, managers can assess the less tangible aspects of compatibility. What starts out as personal rapport, philosophical and strategic compatibility, and shared vision between two companies' top executives must eventually be institutionalized and made public ('getting engaged'). Other stakeholders get involved, and the relationship begins to become depersonalized. But success in the engagement phase of a new alliance still depends on maintaining a careful balance between the personal and the institutional.

In Figure 12.7's *exploration phase*, trial purchases may take place and the exchange outcomes provide a test of the other's ability and willingness to deliver satisfaction. In addition, electronic data interchange (EDI) can be used to reduce the costly paperwork associated with purchase orders, production schedule releases, invoices and so on.

At the end of the exploration phase it is time to 'meet the family'. The relations between a handful of leaders from the two firms must be supplemented with approval, formal or informal, by other people in the firms and by stake holders.

Each partner has other outside relationships that may need to approve the new relationship.

When a party (as is the case in the *expansion phase*) fulfils perceived exchange obligations in an exemplary fashion, the party's attractiveness to the other increases. Hence motivation to maintain the relationship increases, especially because high-level outcomes reduce the number of alternatives that an exchange partner might use as a replacement.

The romance of courtship quickly gives way to day-to-day reality as the partners begin to live together ('setting up house'). In the *commitment phase* the two partners can achieve a level of satisfaction from the exchange process that actually precludes other primary exchange partners (suppliers) which could provide similar benefits. The buyer has not ceased attending other alternative suppliers, but maintains awareness of alternatives without constant and frequent testing.

During the description of the relationship development, the possibility of a withdrawal has been implicit. The *dissolution phase* may be caused by the following problems:

● Operational and cultural differences emerge after collaboration is under way. They often come as a surprise to those who created the alliance. Differences in authority, reporting and decision-making styles become noticeable at this stage.

● People in other positions may not experience the same attraction as the chief executives. The executives spend a lot of time together both informally and formally. Other employees have not been in touch with one another, however, and in some cases have to be pushed to work with their overseas counterparts.

● Employees at other levels in the organization may be less visionary and cosmopolitan than top managers and less experienced in working with people from different cultures. They may lack knowledge of the strategic context in which the relationship makes sense and see only the operational ways in which it does not.

● People just one or two tiers from the top might oppose the relationship and fight to undermine it. This is especially true in organizations that have strong independent business units.

● Termination of personal relationships, because managers leave their positions in the companies, is a potential danger to the partnership.

Firms have to be aware of these potential problems before they go into a relationship, because only in that way can they take actions to prevent the dissolution phase.

12.6 Reverse marketing: from seller to buyer initiative

Reverse marketing describes how purchasing actively identifies potential subcontractors and offers suitable partners a proposal for long-term cooperation. Similar terms are proactive procurement and buyer initiative (Ottesen, 1995). In recent years, the buyer–seller relationship has changed considerably. The traditional relationship, in which a seller takes the initiative by offering a product, is increasingly

Figure 12.8   **Supplier development strategies**

	Current activities	New activities
Existing suppliers	Intensify current activities	Develop and add new activities
New potential suppliers	Replace existing suppliers Add suppliers: secure deliveries	Develop new activities not covered by existing suppliers

being replaced by one in which the buyer actively searches for a supplier that is able to fulfil its needs.

Today, many changes are taking place in the utilization of the purchasing function:

● Reduction in the number of subcontractors.

● Shorter product life cycles, which increase the pressure to reduce the time to market (just-in-time).

● Upgraded demands on subcontractors (zero deficits). In addition, firms are demanding that their suppliers become certified. Those that do not comply may be removed from the approved supplier list.

● Purchasing which no longer just serves the purpose of getting lower prices. The traditional arm's-length relationships are increasingly being replaced by long-term partnerships with mutual trust, interdependence and mutual benefits.

Implementing a reverse marketing strategy starts with fundamental market research and with an evaluation of reverse marketing options (i.e. possible suppliers). Before choosing suppliers the firm may include both present and potential suppliers in the analysis as well as current and desired activities (Figure 12.8).

Based on this analysis the firm may select a number of suitable partners as suppliers and rank them in order of preference.

12.7 Internationalization of subcontractors

In Chapter 3 the internationalization process was described as a learning process (the Uppsala school). Generally speaking, it is something that can be described as a gradual internationalization. According to this view, the international development of the firm is accompanied by an accumulation of knowledge in the hands of management and by growing capabilities and propensities to manage international affairs. The main consequence of this way of thinking is that firms tend to increase their commitment towards foreign markets as their experience grows. The number of adherents to this theory has grown, but there has also been much criticism of it.

The main problem with the model is that it seems to suggest the presence of a deterministic and mechanistic path that firms implementing their internationalization strategy must follow. Sometimes it happens that firms leapfrog one or more stages in the establishment chain; at other times firms stop their internationalization altogether (Welch and Luostarinen, 1988).

Concerning internationalization among contractors and subcontractors, there is a central difference. The internationalization of subcontractors is closely related to their customers. The concept of subcontractor indicates that the strategies of such a firm, including its internationalization strategy, cannot be seen in isolation from the strategies of its partner, the contractor. Therefore the internationalization of subcontractors may show irregular paths, such as leapfrogging.

Andersen *et al.* (1995) introduce four basic routes of internationalization (please note that sometimes there may be some overlap between the different routes, e.g. between routes 2 and 3).

Route 1: Following domestic customers

If a contractor is internationalizing and establishing a production unit in a foreign market, some subcontractors (standard or simple in Figure 12.4) may be replaced with local suppliers, because they might be able to offer the standard components at cheaper prices. However, subcontractors in the upper part of Figure 12.4 and with a strategic value to the contractor will be maintained if they commit themselves to foreign direct investment: claims for direct delivery to the foreign production unit or claims for after-sales service on delivered components may result in the establishment of a local sales and/or production subsidiary by the subcontractor. In most cases, such a direct foreign investment related directly to a specific contractor is based on a guarantee of procurement over some years (until the pay-back period has passed).

When the furniture chain IKEA established itself in the North American market, it took along some strategically important Scandinavian subcontractors, some of which also established subsidiaries in North America. Other examples are the Japanese car manufacturers which established production units in the United States and pulled along a lot of Japanese subcontractors to establish subsidiaries there. This route is similar to the 'late starters' in the model of Johanson and Mattson (1988) in Figure 3.9.

Route 2: Internationalization through the supply chain of an MNC

Deliveries to one division of a multinational corporation may lead to deliveries to other divisions, or parts of its network. One case is when mergers and acquisitions take place between firms, and create new business opportunities for dynamic subcontractors.

The strategic alliance between the French car manufacturer Renault and the Swedish Volvo is one example, where Swedish subcontractors have become involved in the subcontracting system of Renault, and French subcontractors have opportunities to get into the subcontracting system of Volvo (Christensen and Lindmark, 1993).

Route 3: Internationalization in cooperation with domestic or foreign system suppliers

In collaboration with other specialized subcontractors, system suppliers may be involved in international system supplies by taking over the management of whole supplies of subsystems (Figure 12.9).

Systems supplies result in the development of a new layer of subcontractors (second-tier subcontractors). Through the interaction between a system supplier and a domestic main contractor, the system supplier can get access to the network of a global contractor (the dotted line in Figure 12.9) because of the network/contract between the contractor and the global contractor. For example, a Japanese car seat supplier supplies the Japanese Toyota factory (domestic main contractor). This can eventually give the supplier access to other Toyota factories around the world (global contractors) and their global networks.

In many cases the collaboration between the subcontractors will be characterized by exchange of tacit, not easily transferable knowledge. The reason for this is that the complete subsystem is frequently based on several fields of competence, which have to be coordinated by use of tacit knowledge and communication. In the case of the Japanese car seat supplier, the system supplier should have a tight relationship with the subcontractors (suppliers of leather head rests, etc.) in order to adapt the car seat to the individual car models. (See also Exhibit 12.1.)

Route 4: Independent internationalization

The need to gain economies of scale in production forces the standard contractor, in particular, to use the route of independent internationalization. In other cases it cannot be recommended that small subcontractors follow the independent route. The barriers of independent internationalization are too high for small firms with limited resources. For these firms, route 3 (collaboration with other subcontractors) seems to be a more realistic way to internationalize.

Figure 12.9   **Possible internationalization of system suppliers**

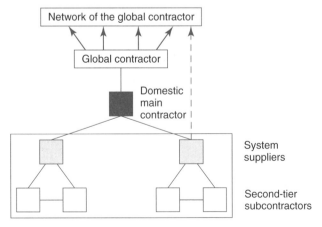

Exhibit 12.1	An example of Japanese network sourcing: the Mazda seat-sourcing case

Mazda adopts a policy of splitting its seat purchases between two suppliers, Delta Kogyo and the Toyo Seat Company. The present division is approximately 60 per cent to Delta and 40 per cent to Toyo. Each of these companies is responsible for different models of seats. The reader should note that each individual item, such as a seat for the Mazda 626, is single sourced for the product life cycle of typically three to five years, but seat production in general is, in effect, dual sourced.

Both Delta Kogyo and the Toyo Seat Company are informally assured of a certain percentage of the Mazda seat business at any one time. This percentage is approximately one-third of the total Mazda seat purchases. Thus, each firm has an assured long-term share of Mazda's seat business. Indeed, when asked about the length of relationship that Mazda has with its suppliers, Mr Nakamichi of Mazda's marketing division noted that relationships with all suppliers, whether they are affiliates, subcontractors or common part suppliers, were established for an 'indefinite' period of time. In addition, the last third of the seat business was available to whichever of the suppliers had performed the best over the life cycle of previous car models.

The two seat makers rely on Mazda for a very high percentage of their business. In the case of Delta Kogyo, Mazda business represents around two-thirds of its total sales. In addition, both suppliers are members of Mazda's Keiretsu (network) and hence come into direct contact with each other on a regular basis. Additionally, since they are direct competitors for only a third of Mazda's seat business, there is a significant degree of openness between the two firms. This openness in some instances takes the form of cooperation in solving mutual or individual problems, because the other seat supplier is often in a better position to give advice than Mazda itself.

However, competition for the remaining third of the Mazda seat business is very intense, since both firms know that they have only one chance to gain the orders for a new car model every three to five years. The most interesting aspect of this competition is that it is based primarily on past performance since the last contract was awarded. The areas of competition include design abilities, management strength, cost reduction progress, quality record and, perhaps surprisingly, the amount of assistance that the supplier has given to its direct competitor either within the auspices of the Keiretsu or on separate occasions. Thus, either firm can obtain new business as long as the other does not fall below 33 per cent of Mazda's total seat purchases. A situation has been created in which there is a creative tension between cooperation and competition.

Indeed, when one of the suppliers approaches the lower limit of its 33 per cent supply, Mazda typically uses its own engineers, and possibly those of the supply competitor, to help the weaker supplier in terms of a joint value analysis/value engineering programme. Because neither supplier wants to be forced into this situation, both will work diligently to avoid this fate – and at the same time to enhance their own competitiveness.

Mazda is careful to ensure that neither supplier is forced into a situation of unprofitability, since this would obviously mean that Mazda would suffer in the long term. This is not to say that either supplier is allowed to make excessive profits. Indeed, profit as a percentage of sales is roughly equalized throughout the supply network, including the Mazda organization itself. During recessionary periods, Mazda and its network of suppliers would make no more than about 2 per cent profit on sales. Thus, members of the supply network stand or fall together, increasing the shared bonds and the willingness to help any member of the network.

Source: Hines (1995), pp. 22–3. Reproduced with permission from the publisher, the National Association of Purchasing Management.

12.8 Project export (turnkey contracts)

This chapter has dealt mainly with sourcing (subcontracting) in the industrial market. Although marketing of subsupplies to international projects has a number of similarities with subsupplies in the industrial market in general, it also has the characteristics of the special marketing situation in the project market: for example, the long and often very bureaucratic selection of subsuppliers for *ad hoc* supplies.

The subsupplier market in project export, however, is also very internationalized, and the main part of marketing should be conducted in those centres or countries where the main contractor is domiciled. For example, London is the domicile of a number of building contracting businesses, which work in those countries that used to be in the British Empire.

Project export is a very complex international activity involving many market players. The preconditions for project export are a technology gap between the exporting and importing countries and that the exporter possesses the specific product and technology know-how which is being demanded in the importing country.

Project export involves supplies or deliveries that contain a combination of hardware and software. When the delivery is concluded it will constitute an integrated system which is able to produce the products and/or the services which the buyer requires. An example of this type of project is the construction of a dairy in a developing country.

Hardware is the blanket term for the tangible, material or physical contribution of the project supply. Hardware is buildings, machines, inventory, transport equipment, etc. and is specified in the quotation and contract between buyer and seller in the form of drawings, unit lists, descriptions and so on.

Software is the blanket term for the intangible contributions in a project supply. Software includes know-how and service. There are three types of know-how:

● *Technology know-how*, comprising product, process and hardware know-how.

● *Project know-how*, comprising project management, assembly and environmental know-how.

● *Management know-how*, which in general terms involves tactical and operational management, and specifically includes marketing and administrative systems.

Service includes advisory services and assistance in connection with various applications and approvals (environmental approval, financing of the project, planning permission, etc.).

The marketing of projects is different from the marketing of products in the following respects:

● Decision of purchase, apart from local business interests, often involves decision processes in national and international development organizations. This implies the participation of a large number of people and a heavily bureaucratic system.

● The product is designed and created during the negotiation process where the requirements are put forward.

● It often takes years from the disclosure of needs to the purchase decision being taken. Therefore total marketing costs are very large.

● When the project is taken over by the project buyer, the buyer–seller relations cease. However, by cultivating these relations before, during and after the project, a 'sleeping' relationship can be woken again in connection with a new project (Hadjikhani, 1996).

Financing a project is a key problem for seller as well as buyer. The project's size and the time used for planning and implementation result in financial demands which make it necessary to use external sources of finance. In this connection the following main segments can be distinguished. The segments arise from differences in the source of financing for the projects.

● Projects where *multilateral organizations*, such as the World Bank or regional development banks, are a primary source of finance.

● Projects where *bilateral organizations* are a primary or essential source of finance.

● Projects where a *government institution* acts as buyer. This was normal in the command economies, where government companies acted as buyers. However, it can also be found in liberal economies: for example, in connection with the development of social infrastructure or the building of a bridge.

● Projects where a *private person or firm* acts as buyer, as when Unilever builds a factory in Vietnam for the production of ice-cream.

Organizing export projects involves establishing an interaction between different firms from the West on the one side, and firms and authorities typically from developing countries on the other. Creating or adapting an organization which is able to function under these conditions is a precondition of project marketing.

12.9 Summary

This chapter has analyzed the buyer–seller relationship from different angles in the internationalized environment. The advantages and disadvantages for the contractor and subcontractor of going into a relationship are summarized in Table 12.2.

The project export situation differs from the 'normal' buyer–seller relationship in the following ways:

● The buying decision process often involves national and international development organizations. This often results in very bureaucratic selection of subcontractors.

Table 12.2   **Advantages and disadvantages of buyer–seller relationships for contractor and subcontractor**

	Advantages	Disadvantages
Contractor (buyer)	The contractor is flexible by not investing in manufacturing facilities. The subcontractor can source the products more cheaply (because of e.g. cheaper labour costs) than by own production. The contractor can concentrate on in-house core competences. Complementation of the contractor's product range. New ideas for product innovation can be carried over from the subcontractor.	The availability of suitable manufactureres (subcontractors) cannot be assumed. Outsourcing tends to be relatively less stable than in-house operations. The contractor has less control over the activities of the subcontractor. Subcontractors can develop into competitors. Quality problems of outsourced products can harm the business of the contractor. Assistance to the subcontractor may increase the costs of the whole operation.
Subcontractor (seller)	Access to new export markets because of the internationalization of the contractor (especially relevant for the so-called late starters). Exploits scale economies (lower cost per unit) through better capacity utilization. Learns product technology of the contractor. Learns marketing practices of the contractor.	Risk of becoming dependent on the contractor because of expanding production capacity and concurrent overseas expansion of sale and marketing activities in order to meet the demands of the contractor.

● Financing of the project is a key problem.

Case study   # LM Glasfiber in the international wind turbine industry

Following their customers' international expansion

LM Glasfiber A/S is the world's leading supplier of rotor blades for wind turbines. Its headquarters is located in Lunderskov, Denmark. It has 14 manufacturing bases in 10 Danish towns, with more than 1,700 employees in modem production areas covering some 100,000 sq. m.

The company is internationally represented with manufacturing facilities and sales offices in Germany, the Netherlands, Spain, the USA, India and China. Its customers are thus guaranteed prompt and punctual delivery with a high level of service world-wide.

The establishment in India can be explained and illustrated as shown in Figure 12.10. Typically, rotor blades represent approximately 20 per cent of a wind turbine's value (excluding mounting, installation etc.).

Figure 12.10 shows the phases that LM Glasfiber (as subsupplier) has had to go through in order to globalize via the buyers'/wind turbine manufacturers' network, especially Micon's network.

The ① in the figure indicates that LM Glasfiber has very large deliveries of rotor blades to the Danish network of wind turbine manufacturers, the largest being NEG Micon (1999), Vestas (wind systems), Bonus (energy), and Nordex. Even though the total Danish network covers more than 50 per cent of the world market for wind turbines, it should not be forgotten that the competition between the companies in the international markets is very keen. To support the Danish wind turbine manufacturers' interests the Danish Wind Turbine Manufacturers' Association was established. Having exceeding close relations with and deliveries to this network ('domestic contractors', LM Glasfiber also cooperates very closely with the research environment within wind turbine technology by way of relations with the 'Risø National Laboratory'.

This example is based on LM Glasfiber's relations with Micon – the biggest or second-biggest wind turbine manufacturer in the world (Micon is fighting with Vestas for the first place). As regards subsuppliers Micon's strategy has been to outsource the biggest part of the rotor blade production. However, Micon has always aimed at having an adequate share of internal subsuppliers of rotor blades, in order

Figure 12.10   **LM Glasfiber's globalization through the network of the customer**

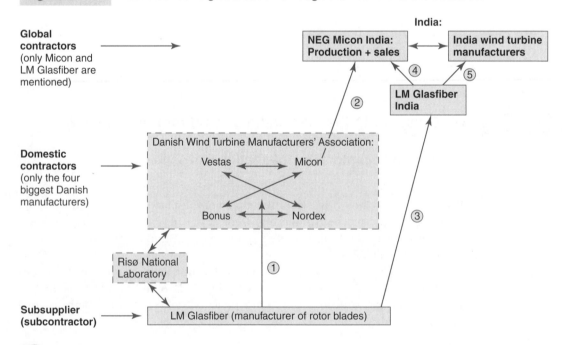

for the company to have the necessary technological preparedness compared to competitors and external subsuppliers (LM Glasfiber being by far the biggest). This flexible sourcing concept is an essential precondition for Micon's continued globalization process.

② shows Micon's establishment of a sales and manufacturing company in India at the beginning of the 1990s. India is an attractive market for wind turbines, as India's power supply is poor, especially in the country. Therefore, the Indian government has supported the mounting of wind turbines that can contribute to stabilizing the power supply (often in cooperation with foreign development aid organizations).

In continuation of establishing this production LM Glasfiber realizes that it has to start manufacturing rotor blades in India. ③ shows the 1994 establishment of LM Glasfiber India Ltd. – a joint venture between LM Glasfiber AIS, the Industrialization Fund for Developing Countries (IFU), and the Indian wind turbine manufacturer NEPC. ④ therefore shows the local deliveries of rotor blades and the back-up service that LM Glasfiber India can provide by being a local company. As a consequence of the partnership with the local Indian wind turbine manufacturer (NEPC), LM Glasfiber has now (via the local joint venture) gained access to NEPC's network, which includes several markets in Asia. ⑤ thus shows that LM Glasfiber has been able to take advantage of the relationship with NEPC as a 'springboard' to other markets in Asia.

Questions

1. Are there any threats to LM Glasfiber's strategy in following the key customer abroad?

2. How does this case relate to the network model in Chapter 3?

Questions for discussion

1. What are the reasons for the increasing level of outsourcing to international subcontractors?

2. Describe the typology of subcontractors based on the differences in the contractor/subcontractor relationship.

3. Explain the shift from seller to buyer initiative in subcontracting.

4. Explain the main differences between the American and the Japanese subsupplier systems.

5. How are project exports/turnkey projects different from general subcontracting on the industrial market?

6. Project export is often characterized by a complex and time-consuming decision-making process. What are the marketing implications of this for the potential subcontractor?

Internet exercise

Lear Corp.

Please go to:

www.lear.com

Lear Corporation is one of the ten largest independent automotive suppliers in the world. The company is also the leading supplier of automotive interior systems in the global automotive interior market and the third largest supplier in the global automotive electrical distribution systems market. The company has established in-house capabilities in all five principal segments of the automotive interior market: seat systems; flooring and acoustic systems; door panels; headliners; and instrument panels. The company is the largest supplier in the global seat systems market. In North America, it is one of the two largest suppliers in each of the other principal automotive interior markets, with the exception of the instrument panels market in which it is the fourth largest supplier. The company is also one of the leading global suppliers of automotive electrical distribution systems.

Questions

1. How can Lear Corp. be characterized as a subsupplier?
2. Describe the relationships that Lear Corp. has to its customers.
3. How would you consider the international competitiveness of Lear Corp. compared to its Japanese customers?

For further exercises and cases, see this book's website at *www.booksites.net/hollensen*

References

Andersen, P.H., Blenker, P. and Christensen, P.R. (1995) *Internationalization of Subcontractors: In search of a theoretical framework*, The Southern Denmark Business School, Kolding.

Blenker, P. and Christensen, P.R. (1994) 'Interactive strategies in supply chains – a double-edged portfolio approach to SME', *Subcontractors Positioning Paper* presented at the 8th Nordic Conference on Small Business Research.

Cavinato, J.L. (1992) 'A total cost/value model for supply chain competitiveness', *Journal of Business Logistics*, vol. 13, no. 2, pp. 285–301.

Cho, Dong-Sung and Chu, Wujin (1994) 'Determinants of bargaining power in OEM negotiations', *Industrial Marketing Management*, vol. 23, pp. 342–55.

Christensen, P.R. and Lindmark, L. (1993) 'Location and internationalization of small firms', in Lindquist, L. and Persson, L.O. (eds.), *Visions and Strategies in European Integration*, Springer Verlag, Berlin/Heidelberg.

Dwyer, R.F., Schurr, P.H. and Oh, S. (1987) 'Developing buyer–seller relationships', *Journal of Marketing*, vol. 51, April, pp. 11–27.

Hadjikhani, A. (1996) 'Project marketing and the management of discontinuity', *International Business Review*, vol. 5, no. 3, pp. 319–36.

Hibbert, E.P. (1993) 'Global make or buy decisions', *Industrial Marketing Management*, vol. 22, pp. 67–77.

Hines, P. (1995) 'Network sourcing: a hybrid approach', *International Journal of Purchasing and Materials Management*, Spring, pp. 18–24.

Johanson, J. and Mattson, L.G. (1988) 'Internationalization in industrial systems', in Hood, N. and Vahlne, J.E. (eds.), *Strategies in Global Competition*, Croom Helm, Beckenham (UK).

Jüttner, U. and Wehrli, H.P. (1994) 'Relationship marketing from a value system perspective', *International Journal of Service Industry Management*, no. 5, pp. 54–73.

Kanter, R.M. (1994) 'Collaborative advantage', *Harvard Business Review*, July–August, pp. 96–107.

Lehtinen, U. (1991) 'Alihankintajärjestelmä 1990-luvulla (Subcontracting system in the 1990s)', *Publications of SITRA*, no. 114, Helsinki.

Ottesen, O. (1995) 'Buyer initiative: ignored, but imperative for marketing theory', Working Paper, Department of Business Administration, Stavanger College, Norway.

Overgaard, B.B. (1987) 'Project export' (in Danish), Working Paper, Aarhus Business School.

Turnbull, P.W. and Valla, J.P. (1986) *Strategies for International Industrial Marketing*, Croom Helm, London.

Welch, L.S. and Luostarinen, R. (1988) 'Internationalization: evolution of a concept', *Journal of General Management*, vol. 14, no. 2, pp. 36–64.

Global e-commerce

After studying this chapter you should be able to do the following:

● Describe the development of Internet and e-commerce in the main regions of the world.

● Explain the reasons for the rapid development of e-commerce.

● Explore how e-commerce functions in the two main market types: B-t-B, B-t-C, C-t-B, C-t-C.

● Discuss the reality behind 'disintermediation' (bypassing resellers).

● Discuss alternative routes of global e-commerce strategies.

13.1 Introduction

In the past few years there has been an explosion of on-line commercial activity enabled by the Internet or World Wide Web (WWW). This is generally referred to as electronic commerce (e-commerce), with a major component of e-commerce being electronic transactions taking place on Internet-based markets (electronic markets or e-markets).

The development of the Internet as a 'new' distribution channel will result in a shift of power from the manufacturers and the traditional retail channels to the consumers. This increasing consumer power can be explained in the following way:

1. *The search for convenience.* The Internet gives people a new tool to gather information and purchase more easily than through traditional channels.

2. *The incorporation of the Net into the purchase process.* Pre-purchase and post-sale use of the Net is exploding, regardless of where the product is bought.

3. *A shift in loyalties.* Consumers reward on-line merchants with higher repeat-purchase behaviour.

4. *Future buying plans.* Survey results indicate an increasing consumer disposition to buy on-line (IDC, 2000a; Boston Consulting Group, 2000).

Today's technology only scratches the surface of efficient comparison-shopping and product search. The development of automated buying profiles, networked buying clubs, and on-line auctions will bring greater price competition to the Internet. Merchants must be prepared to live up to 'We will match any price' marketing guarantees (see also Chapter 15, Pricing decisions).

Competing on the Internet is different from the traditional industrial world. Competition no longer takes place in the physical *marketplace*, but in the *market space* (Rayport and Sviokla, 1996). This computer-mediated environment has profound implications for how business is transacted between buyer and seller. The nature of transaction is different in that it is based on information about the product or services rather than on its physical appearance or attributes. The context of the transaction is different; instead of taking place in a physical world, it occurs in a computer-mediated environment with the buyer conducting the transaction from a personal computer screen. Consequently, to be a player in many industries does not require a physical infrastructure like buildings and machinery; a computer and communications platform is sufficient.

Like so many 'buzz words' in use today, e-commerce tends to mean different things to different people. For the purpose of introducing the subject, e-commerce is defined in this way: *The enablement of a business vision supported by advanced information technology to increase the effectiveness of the business relationships between trading partners*.

Examples of e-commerce transactions are:

● An individual purchases a book on the Internet.

● A government employee reserves a hotel room over the Internet.

● A business calls a toll-free number and orders a computer using the seller's interactive telephone system.

● A retailer orders merchandise using an EDI network or a supplier's extranet.

● A manufacturing plant orders electronic components from another plant within the company using the company's intranet.

● An individual withdraws funds from an automatic teller machine (ATM).

13.2 | Types of products

The products sold in e-commerce markets can roughly be grouped into two categories: physical products and purely digital goods and services.

Physical products

Marketing physical products over the Web has led to some of the biggest success stories in e-commerce. The key to success is marketing that takes advantage of the interface and the networked environment. Transferring a conventional mail-order business to the Web adds little value.

The potential advantages of the Internet include the scope for real-time interaction within a vast networked community, the possibility of using sophisticated market mechanisms, and the illusion of almost infinite inventory (when an intermediary acts for many suppliers). Businesses that exploit these opportunities, such as Amazon.com and E-Bay, have been very successful.

Digital goods and services

This category includes information goods and services, such as financial information, news services, reference and learning material, entertainment and multimedia products, software distribution services, distributed database services and remote computation services. In addition, the Internet has spawned innovative digital products such as on-line gaming, chat rooms, search engines, on-line advertising, yellow pages and certification services. These products are characterized by being difficult to value and easy to copy.

Companies use different strategies to price and market these goods. They include customization and bundling, bundling valuable content with advertising to provide 'free' goods, introducing different versions of the same product to suit different users, charging subscriptions and, most important, using market mechanisms to help set price.

The individualization of goods

The digital world, in which information can be acquired and processed with ease, lets sellers tailor their products to individual customers. Further, the electronic environment allows companies to respond quickly to consumer feedback.

The ease of customization, and the ability to adapt to variations in consumer preferences, lead to the possibility of individualizing goods in the electronic markets. As each consumer will prefer (and be offered) a different version of the basic product, the total perceived value of the same (basic) product may be higher than with only one version of the product.

Comparison between the industrial economy (the physical marketplace) and the digital economy (the market space)

Electronic commerce is more than home shopping. It encompasses a range of electronic interactions between organizations and their up- and downstream trading partners. Many of their transactions have been occurring for quite some time, long before the Internet opened to commercial traffic. Platforms for electronic commerce that precede the Internet include the use of the Teletel in France for inter-organizational commercial transactions, as well as the use of EDI over private networks.

The Internet has become a powerful business tool. This new approach to the communication and distribution of information and services has transformed the fundamental dynamics behind many social and business interactions. The barriers and obstacles which often accompanied traditional commerce are giving way to new

Figure 13.1	The new business dynamics

Industrial economy
(Marketplace = physical products)

- Manufacturing dominates
- Barrier: physical distribution
- Barrier: lack of capital
- First-mover advantage was years
- Innovative ideas contained internally
- Relationships constrained by human capital

Digital economy
(Market space = e-commerce)

- Knowledge and relationships dominate
- E-distribution is the new barrier
- Capital is a commodity
- First-mover advantage is months
- Innovation is in the public domain
- Relationships can be established electronically

business approaches. Consumers, producers and distributors now all have flexible, fast and inexpensive ways of participating in the market for products and services round the world. Individual and corporate customers can approach the marketplace differently as the variety and depth of information on products and services speed up decision-making processes. Moreover, this new virtual marketplace is providing a significant boost to economic activity.

The Internet's unprecedented impact on the way the world does business stems from the way it has altered basic business dynamics. The dynamics that have shaped markets and market leaders since the 19th century – dynamics rooted in an industrial economy – have been replaced with a new set of fundamental principles based on a digital economy (Figure 13.1).

In the industrial economy, manufacturing dominates. The physical production of goods is the principal driver of economic activity. In the digital economy, knowledge and relationships dominate. It is a world where information and ideas are becoming more important than physical objects.

In the industrial economy, the most serious market barriers were lack of a physical distribution infrastructure and lack of capital. These significant barriers-to-entry in the physical world meant first-mover advantage could typically be measured in years. The Internet, however, has turned traditional distribution models upside down. With distribution models changing and capital roadblocks removed, markets are wide open and first-mover advantage is now measured in months. The new distribution roadblock is 'e-distribution', or the first-mover advantage earned by companies which are able to lock up exclusive business relationships with the new e-business drivers, such as the leading Web portals. Becoming an exclusive retail partner of a portal such as America Online, for example, would enable a retailer to leapfrog ahead of its competition.

13.3 The global rise and structure of e-commerce

The following sections describe the rise and structure of e-commerce on three geographic levels:

- Global level
- USA level
- European level

The rise and structure of e-commerce on a global level

Internet activity is growing both in popularity and in profitability. In less than four years, the Internet has evolved from a basic communication tool into a vast communications and interactive market of products, services and ideas. According to Nua, an Internet strategy firm, as of May 1999, 171 million people across the globe had access to the Internet, over half of them in the United States and Canada (Figure 13.2). According to Global Report (1999) the number of world-wide Internet users is expected to double during the next three years.

Not only do the United States and Canada occupy the largest absolute share (56.6 per cent) of all the Internet users, they also have a high level of Internet participation on a per capita basis. More disaggregate data derived from a variety of sources show the percentage of the population with access to the Internet, either at home or at work, by country or country group (Figure 13.3).

Relative to population, the United States, Canada, the Nordic countries, and Australia have at least twice the level of Internet access so far achieved by the United Kingdom, Germany, Japan, and France.

The rise and structure of e-commerce in North America

As the world's biggest e-commerce market, the potential 'US Internet Universe' can be broken down as shown in Table 13.1.

| Figure 13.2 | **Number of people with Internet access, by region (May 1999), total 171.4 million** |

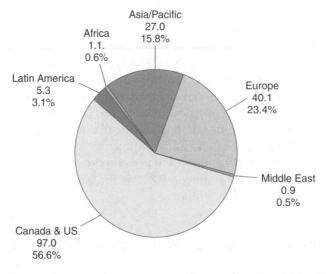

(Source: Department of Commerce (1999), p. 2; (*http://www.ecommerce.gov/ede/chapter1.html* and NUA: http://www.nua.ie/surveys, 1999))

Figure 13.3   Percentage of the population with Internet access at home or at work

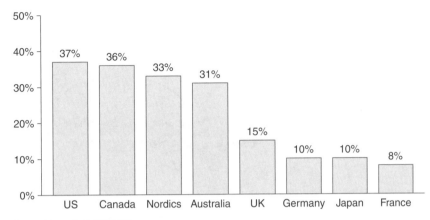

(Source: Elmer, S. *IDC* (2000b))

Table 13.1   The US Internet universe

	Millions	%
Total US adults (+14 years)	198	100
Total US adults with Internet access	98	49
Total US adults with Internet in the past 30 days	78	39
Where did the 78 million use the Internet?		
● From their home and work	16	8
● From their work only	21	11
● From their home only	41	20
Total	78	39

Source: Lake (1999) and Mediamark Research (1999), (http://www.thestandard.com)

It is one thing is to estimate the number of Web users; it is another thing to look at the number of people who actually buy on the Internet (Table 13.2).

Nearly half of Web users are now women. However, according to a recent survey (Cyber Dialogue, 2000), only 28 per cent of them buy on-line. Cyber Dialogue further points out that among the 24 million women who have not bought on-line, 40 per cent cite concerns about security of information on Web sites.

Nearly 70 per cent of women who seek product information on-line still end up going off-line to make purchases. (Source: Cyber Dialogue, 2000.)

Table 13.2   On-line buyers (buying minimum one time per year) on the Internet as a percentage of total US population

	1997	1998	1999	2000	2001	2002
On-line buyers (% of the total US population)	3.2	7.9	17.8	21.4	26.6	30.0

Source: Mediamark Research (1999).

Figure 13.4 | **Computer vs. Internet usage in Europe**

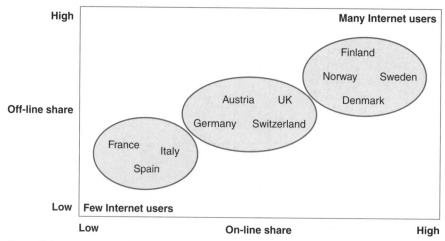

(Source: IDC (2000b) *A preview of IDC's Consumer Survey.*)

The rise and structure of e-commerce in Europe

Several countries in Europe had been doing on-line shopping long before the Web became popular. Their various teletext systems have had varying degrees of success in e-commerce, with the French Minitel leading the pack (20 per cent of the French adult population have made purchases by Minitel). There are 18 million people using the Minitel in France, the English and Dutch have teletext systems, and 2 million people use T-Online in Germany. It will take some time to migrate their habits onto the Web, as well as invest in on-line stores on the Web (which mirror what they already have on Minitel and T-Online). Once the French and Germans migrate to the Web, their on-line spending habits should naturally follow and e-commerce will explode.

By the end of 1999, 25 per cent of Europeans had access to the Internet and 5 per cent had made on-line purchases. There are still extremes in Internet usage across the region. For example, Sweden's penetration rate is 60 per cent, but France's is 16 per cent. Furthermore, more than 25 per cent of UK users have purchased something on-line, but only 1–2 per cent of Spain's users have.

It appears from Figure 13.4 that there is a close connection between the percentage of PCs in the population (off-line share) and the percentage of computer users who are on the Internet (on-line share). Again it shows that Internet information technology is much more developed in the northern part of Europe than in the southern part.

A major factor inhibiting growth of consumer e-commerce in Europe is lack of confidence in on-line security. Europeans remain reluctant to use credit cards over the Net (IDC, 2000b).

The European e-retailing business[1]

In the European business-to-consumer (e-retailing) there seems to be two main

---

[1] This section is mainly based on information given in Boston Consulting Group (2000) *The Race for Online Riches – E-Retailing in Europe.*

types of players – European start ups and US on-line retailers – fighting to capture market share.

A report from Boston Consulting Group (2000) says that unless European retailers become more aggressive in creating innovative e-commerce businesses, they will continue to lose a share of their home market to more experienced US competitors.

US players (for example Amazon.com) have already been able to capture up to 20 per cent of the European market by coming in with large-scale pan-European businesses. This approach contrasts with that of typical European incumbents who have focused on their national markets only. US on-line retailers, however, will also find it difficult to deal with the European on-line market since it is a conglomeration of regional markets, each at a different level of development.

Total on-line revenue in 1999 was Euro 3.5 billion and will reach about Euro 9 billion by the end of year 2000. On-line retailing will continue to grow at exceptional rates over the next few years. Total European on-line retail revenue is expected to reach approximately Euro 45 billion in 2002, a thirteen-fold increase from 1999.

Multichannel retailers, those with other existing sales channels, are taking advantage of their strong existing brands and established customer service functions and, as a result, account for two thirds of the on-line market.

'*Pure-plays*', retailers who sell only on-line, account for 'only' one third of the market but they are outperforming multichannel retailers, experiencing growth rates that are on average 25 percentage points higher.

Four categories – travel, computer hardware/software, books and financial brokerage – account for three-quarters of the market.

As a whole, European on-line retailers have preferred to take a narrow focus, generating 93 per cent of their sales in their home markets. Total exports beyond national borders account for only 7 per cent of European on-line retailers' revenue; exports out of Europe generate just 2 per cent. This is partly due to the tremendous differences amongst on-line markets within Europe, which pose a significant challenge for retailers trying to span the entire continent. Even established on-line retailers from the US are finding it difficult to adapt their one-size-fits-all approach to the diverse European market. Some of these differences include:

- Sweden has developed a relatively advanced on-line market. With an on-line retail penetration of 0.7 per cent, second only to the US, it clearly stands out from the rest of Europe. Its absolute market size, however, is relatively small.

- Despite lower levels of penetration, Germany and the UK are the most important markets by virtue of the size of their economies. Already, they account for 60 per cent of the on-line market and the majority of market growth in absolute terms by expanding more than three-fold over the space of a year.

- In Spain/Portugal and Italy the development of on-line retailing lags behind the rest of Europe, as shown by their lower on-line retail penetration rates. They do, however, have the potential to become important markets as their penetration rates rise and they migrate more of their sizeable retail markets on-line.

- France's population has been buying direct through Minitel for almost two decades. These high Minitel penetration rates have yet to be translated to the Internet-based on-line retail market.

Table 13.3	Internet usage according to language			
	1999	**2001**	**2003**	**2005**
English-speaking (%)	54	51	46	43
Non-English speaking (%)	46	49	54	57
Total %	100	100	100	100
Total number of Internet users (million)	171	213	268	346

Source: *Computer Economics*, 6 July 1999.

● Belgium, the Netherlands, Switzerland, Austria, Norway, Finland and Denmark claim smaller positions in the European on-line retail market as a result of moderate on-line retail penetration rates and small market sizes.

European retailers need to step up to meet above mentioned challenges and determine what part of their business can be scaled on a pan-European basis and what part needs to be tailored to appeal to local preferences within the European market.

Languages used on the Web

In 1999 54 per cent of all Internet users were English speaking (Table 13.3), but by 2003, Internet users will be predominately non-English speaking, according to research by *Computer Economics* (1999). By 2005, nearly 60 per cent of Internet users will speak a language other than English. The language groups that most significantly 'attack' the dominance of English on the Internet are those in Asia Pacific (primarily Japanese and Chinese) and Latin America (*Computer Economics*, 1999). Of course this has also to do with the increasing penetration of Internet in these areas of the world.

The growth of the non-English-speaking market will mean that it will become imperative that companies offer multiple-language Web sites.

The introduction of the Euro as a single currency

The next two years are set to bring dramatic changes in Europe: not only are most European countries going on-line at an unprecedented rate, but 11 countries of the European Union are phasing out their own currency and accepting a common currency (the Euro) during 2000. The combination of these two factors is widely thought to give strong stimulation to e-commerce. See also Chapter 15 for a further discussion of this Euro issue.

13.4 Types of e-commerce – defining new business models

The impact of e-commerce on the economy extends far beyond the dollar value of e-commerce activity. Businesses use e-commerce to develop competitive advantages by providing more useful information, expanding choice, developing new services, streamlining purchasing processes, and lowering costs. The Internet also imposes price discipline as customers have access to price and product information from many sources.

The different e-commerce markets may be divided into four categories:

Table 13.4

Four different e-commerce markets

	Business	Consumer
Business	**B-t-B** ● EDI relation ● GM, Ford and DaimlerChrysler join forces in sourcing of autoparts in e-markets	**B-t-C** ● Dell ● Furniture.com (see Exhibit 13.1) ● eToys ● CDnow
Consumer	**C-t-B** (reverse auctions) ● Priceline ● HobShop (earlier name: Accompany) ● LetsBuyIt	**C-t-C** (traditional auctions) ● eBay ● QXL

In the following, the four markets shown in Table 13.4 will be further discussed.

Today *the market volume on the B-t-B is much bigger than on the B-t-C market* – five times more, according to Forrester (http:www.forrester.com/).

Business-to-business (B-to-B) e-commerce

Electronic-based commerce is not a new phenomenon on the B-to-B market. Instead of Internet-based solutions, many industries have been using electronic data interchange (EDI) for years to streamline business processes and reduce the cost of doing business. Suppliers, manufacturers, wholesalers, distributors and retailers share inventory information and send orders, invoices and shipping data electronically. EDI enhances the flow of information and goods through the supply chain and eliminates a manual re-entry of data, thereby eliminating errors and costly delays.

EDI is used for the exchange of structured data between the computer systems of trading partners. It is frequently used as an electronic replacement for traditional 'paper' documents such as the order form or invoice but EDI is developed also in the world of finance, administration etc. In essence EDI is used for the exchange of structured data between originators and recipients of such information. EDI can be defined as *the transfer of structured data, by agreed message standards, from one computer system to another by electric means.*

A brief definition of the terms used in this definition will help readers understand the concept, which is also known as 'paperless trading':

● The use of *structured data* refers to a precise, recognized method of assembling data. Such data items as item code, customer reference, delivery point and limit price all come together to form a purchase order invoice, packing list, acknowledgement of order etc.

● The phrase *by agreed message standards* implies that such discrepancies between documents (an invoice is one such message) will be minimized by providing a fixed and agreed method of specifying and presenting the data. Much effort has been expended by respected national and international bodies (ISO bodies) in producing standards for presenting the data, via syntax rules and message guidelines.

● The definition also uses the phrase *from one computer system to another*, and implies that the two systems belong to distinct organizations. However, EDI can be used for both intra-company and inter-company communications.

● The phrase *by electronic means* implies no human intervention. In Table 13.5 a comparison between the traditional EDI and the Internet is made.

Traditional EDI, however, is expensive and time consuming to implement. Many smaller companies simply cannot justify the price of entry. According to *Business Week*, adding a single trading partner to an EDI network can cost up to $50,000. In contrast, some Internet-based EDI links cost less than $1,000, making them affordable for a much broader audience.

EDI on the Web supports much richer information exchange. Traditional EDI supports only highly structured documents such as purchase orders and invoices. The Internet supports the exchange of multimedia information, including engineering drawings, full-colour photographs, audio and even video clips. As a result, Internet-based EDI fosters much tighter relationships among participants, providing a sense of teamwork and shared goals, and enabling all components and systems of a value chain to communicate with each other. Today, EDI has further developed and hybrid solutions are now available, most of them based on Web technology.

Many of the same advantages that arise from retail e-commerce hold for business-to-business e-commerce. For example, e-commerce can permit businesses to increase services they can offer their business customers. By opening an immediate and convenient channel for communicating, exchanging and selecting information, e-commerce is allowing firms to reconsider which functions they should perform 'in-house' and which are best provided by others. The new technology has helped to create new relationships and to streamline and augment supply chain processes. As these changes are occurring, the roles of logistic and financial intermediaries (e.g. FedEx, UPS, American Express) are expanding.

These changes will result in aggressive growth rates during the next few years: in January 2000, Gartner Group forecasted the worldwide B-t-B market to grow from $145 billion in 1999 to $7.29 trillion in 2004. (Source: Gartner Group, press release, January 2000.)

The catalyst for B-t-B e-commerce is e-market maker activity. E-market makers are projected to facilitate $2.71 trillion e-commerce sales transactions in 2004, representing 37 per cent of the overall B-t-B market. (See also Figure 13.5 for the illustration of the principle behind e-markets.)

Table 13.5	A comparison between EDI and the Internet
Traditional EDI	**Internet**
Proprietary, dedicated network	Open network
Highly structured, machine-readable data	E-mail, video, voice, image
High cost	Low cost
More secure	Less secure

Boston Consulting Group's (BCG's) research shows that the size of the business-to-business e-commerce is far greater than is commonly reported, in part because it recognizes the establishment of electronic data interchange (EDI) over private networks and its extensions to the Internet. While EDI over private networks represented the biggest share of 1998 volume (86 per cent), nearly all of the additional volume until 2003 (90 per cent, or $2.0 trillion) will be Internet-based transactions. BCG predicts that business-to-business e-commerce will account for *24 per cent* of total business-to-business commerce by 2003.

Figure 13.5 illustrates the shift from EDI to Internet-based B-t-B e-commerce.

While business-to-business e-commerce is a global phenomenon, the North American market currently dominates. The $700 billion North American market is twice the size of business-to-business e-commerce in the rest of the world combined ($330 billion). North America will likely retain its significant lead over the next few years, but the global dynamics of business-to-business e-commerce will shift. In Western Europe, which lags 18 months behind North America in e-commerce adoption, several countries have accelerated their e-commerce investments and will significantly close this gap. Asia and Latin America remain further behind, but this may change rapidly as global supply chains go on-line. For local suppliers in local markets, business-to-business e-commerce presents significant growth opportunities, as they expand their networks and customer bases by accessing new export markets.

Growth is expected to be strong in every market until 2003:

● In North America e-commerce penetration will triple from 7 per cent to 24 per cent.

● In Western Europe it will grow from 3 per cent to 11 per cent.

Figure 13.5   **The development of B-t-B e-commerce**

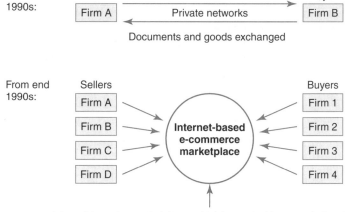

Internet-based e-marketplace, which is created by *e-market makers*, (e.g. Chemdex, Vertical Net etc., who develop e-marketplaces of buyers and sellers with a particular industry or geographic region).

- In Asia Pacific it will flow from 2 per cent to 9 per cent.
- Latin America will move from 2 per cent to 7 per cent.

By 2003, North America will reach $3.0 trillion in business-to-business e-commerce. The rest of the world will reach $1.8 trillion.

By 2003, more than 65 per cent of all business-to-business e-commerce purchases will be in the sectors of retail, motor vehicles, shipping, industrial equipment, high tech, and cost savings rather than strategic opportunities will drive most of the initial growth. Companies which have moved aggressively into business-to-business e-commerce will have cost savings on materials of up to 15 per cent as purchasing and record keeping processes are simplified (Boston Consulting Group, 2000).

Business-to-consumer (B-t-C) e-commerce

Many of the advantages of e-commerce were first exploited (in the mid 1990s) by retail 'e-businesses' such as Amazon.com, eTrade, and Auto-by-tel that were created as Internet versions of traditional bookstores, brokerage firms, and auto dealerships. Freed from the geographic confines and costs of running actual stores, such firms could deliver almost unlimited content on request and could react and make changes in close to real time. Compared to traditional retail or catalogue operations, this new way of conducting business is changing cost structures. The emergence of these e-businesses has made their competitors consider their own e-commerce strategies, and many now operate their own on-line stores (e.g. Barnes and Noble, Merill Lynch).

Exhibit 13.1	**Furniture.com (B-t-C)**

Unlike many on-line retailers, Furniture.com, is not technically an Internet start-up. It began 50 years ago as the 'bricks-and-mortar' and family-owned Empire Furniture Showroom in Worcester, Mass, USA. In early 1999, after simplifying the name to Furniture.com and moving to its suburban offices, the company closed the bricks-and-mortar business and converted the old showroom to a photo studio for creating furniture groupings shown on the site. Today the company (with almost no stock) sell its wares on the Web, working with manufacturers who ship purchases (at all price levels) directly to consumers. As the CEO/President says: '*It is matchmaking, really. We're creating a marriage between the customer and a perfect piece of furniture*'.

E-businesses do more than simply provide alternative shipping sites to real-world stores; they can also expand existing markets and even create new ones. Not included in the cost savings listed above are the additional value that Internet-based businesses can provide in terms of increased information and choice and time savings. These advantages make it possible for buyers and sellers to come together in significantly more efficient ways than would otherwise be possible. For example, musicfile.com serves as a clearing house where music collectors and retailers can post their out-of-print vinyl records and CDs, and buyers can post their 'wants'.

The move towards providing goods and services through a digital medium does not need to be 'all or nothing'. In the retail business the Web store and the physical store can support each other in many different ways, capitalizing on natural complementarities. These include cross-promotions, joint-service provisions, and value-added services. Cross-promotions are perhaps the most straightforward example of a natural complementarity. Web stores may provide the bargains that people may expect when shopping on the Internet, but also offer coupons for in-store purchases. Marketers are accustomed to the use of 'loss-leaders' as an approach to increasing store traffic, and realize that once in the store, other purchases for non-discounted merchandise are more likely. A physical store can use its Web site to highlight local events, such as a reading or performance at the store, helping to bring in traffic. The Web store may also provide information about additional services, available at the store, that add value to products purchased on-line. A company might use electronic mail for direct marketing not only to advertise the Web site, but also to provide information about in-store products and services. Some services might be provided jointly, leveraging the investment in physical and Web presence. A good example would be when a computer store offers a product on-line, but provides installation and repair services at their premises for customers purchasing from their Web site. Finally, the Web store may function as a source of value-added service for customers who have purchased or plan to purchase goods at the physical store.

With the emergence of Web-based grocery sites customers gain convenience by shopping on-line. A local grocery store then delivers the chosen items. Finally, a number of stores have initiated in-store Web kiosks as a means of lowering costs and improving service. In-store shoppers gain the ability to search for products not on display, gather in-depth information without taking up the salesperson's time, and even purchase or pay for products for immediate or subsequent delivery. These various complementary approaches represent a sampling of strategies a retailer might use to leverage its investment in physical and Web distribution channels.

Consumer-to-business (C-t-B) e-commerce

This type of e-commerce is a kind of 'reverse auction' where the buyer (consumer) rather than the seller initiates the transaction.

LetsBuyIt and MobShop (earlier it had the name Accompany) are direct competitors in this C-t-B market. The word 'mob' is defined as: 'to crowd with excessive enthusiasm'. The business principle of both companies is that consumers join together to drive down the price of products through the benefits of bulk buying. Both companies launched their first co-buying site in April 1999, but the geographical markets of the two companies are different: MobShop is mainly based in North America, whereas LetsBuyIt mainly targets the European market.

A more comprehensive description of LetsBuyIt is included as the Case Study to Chapter 3.

| Exhibit 13.2 | Priceline.com (B-t-C) |

Priceline.com has got a type of e-commerce known as a 'demand collection system' that enables consumers to use the Internet to save money on a wide range of products and services while enabling sellers to generate incremental revenue. Using a simple and compelling consumer proposition – 'name your price', Priceline.com collects consumer demand (in the form of individual customer offers guaranteed by a credit card) for a particular product or service at a price set by the customer and communicates that demand directly to participating sellers or to their private databases. Consumers agree to hold their offers open for a specified period of time to enable Priceline.com to fulfil their offers from inventory provided by participating sellers. Once fulfilled, offers generally cannot be cancelled. By requiring consumers to be flexible with respect to brands, sellers and/or product features, they enable sellers to generate incremental revenue without disrupting their existing distribution channels or retail pricing structures

Let's say that a customer wants a hotel room in San Francisco on a certain date, but he only wants to pay $100 per night. Priceline will take this offer to their participating, name-brand hotels in San Francisco to see if any will agree to the price. If they are successful, the customer has got the room he wants at the price he wants to pay! Since airlines fly with many empty seats every day, and thousands of hotel rooms go unsold every night, it is easy to understand why companies would be willing to consider the offer from a potential customer.

Consumer-to-Consumer (C-t-C) e-commerce

This e-commerce type covers the new fashion for consumer-to-consumer auctions. They are not so much a new marketplace as a new form of entertainment. Auctions did not develop by chance; for many products they suit both buyers and sellers. Fixed prices did not develop by chance; for many (standardized) products they suit both buyers and sellers. However, despite these reservations, the new auction-pricing portals will not disappear, because it is great fun for many people. The bidding and close interaction between buyers and sellers promotes a sense of community – a near addiction that keeps them coming back.

The US-based *eBay Inc.* is the world's largest and most popular person-to-person trading community on the Internet. eBay pioneered on-line person-to-person trading by developing a Web-based community in which buyers and sellers are brought together in an efficient and entertaining auction format to buy and sell personal items such as antiques, coins, collectibles, computers, memorabilia and toys. The eBay service permits sellers to list items for sale, buyers to bid on items of interest and all eBay users to browse through listed items in a fully automated, topically arranged, intuitive and easy-to-use on-line service that is available 24 hours a day, seven days a week

The eBAY-user spends 130 minutes a month at the site – 10 times more than the typical Amazon-user. Of all consumer e-commerce spending in 1998, some 15 per cent came through auctions (*Business Week*, 1999b).

Amazon's response to this development came on 12 April 1999 when Amazon announced its plans to acquire the Internet-based auction company, LiveBid.com Inc., after eBAY also approached the company about a possible buyout. In *Business Week* (1999b) Bezos was asked if he thought that the dynamic pricing of auctions would come to other products of Amazon.com. Bezos answered (*Business Week,* 1999b):

> No, no, no. Auction pricing is most useful when it's hard to assess a fair value. So that means either that the thing you are selling is unique, or maybe it's not unique, but its value fluctuates rapidly. Stock prices are sort of like that. For most things, fixed prices are more efficient. The reason is that you don't have to negotiate. You don't want to negotiate the price of simple things you buy every day.

This answer is in line with the principles of the transactions cost analysis model which implies that transaction costs increase when the transactions are characterized by a high degree of complexibility (see the TCA approach in Chapter 3).

The proportion of eBay's customers outside North America is still under 5 per cent, but the company is trying to boost these numbers with its purchase of a big German on-line auctioneer, Alando.de.

QXL.com is eBay's direct European competitor. It is a pan-European auction community, conducting consumer-to-consumer and business-to-consumer auctions across seven countries in Western Europe.

13.5 Exploring buying behaviour in the e-commerce market

This section deals with buying behaviour on the two main markets: the business-to-consumer (B-t-C) market and the business-to-business (B-t-B) market.

Segmenting and exploring consumer behaviour in the B-t-C market

Hofacker (1999) divides Internet users into two main segments:

1. *Hedonic surfers.* Hedonic surfers use a Web site by experiencing it in the same way they do movies and sports events. Often there is a strong non-verbal aspect to the hedonic experience – the images are quite important. Surfers are relatively unfocused and their browsing is spontaneous. The goal is escapist, to achieve immersion in the site, or at least a high degree of personal enjoyment either through arousal or pleasure or both. The idea is to gather interesting and exciting experiences from the Web.

   A unique site works best for these surfers, one which is novel and interesting. They can be drawn into a Web site via links everywhere and ad banners on other sites.

2. *Utilitarian searchers.* In contrast to hedonic surfers, utilitarian searchers are on a mission and they have a work mentality. The utilitarian searcher uses the Web in a way that is instrumental and rational. Such a visitor is looking for some kind of specific information. A well-organized and searchable site works best for these seekers.

Figure 13.6   Consumer purchasing decision process: the marketplace vs. market space

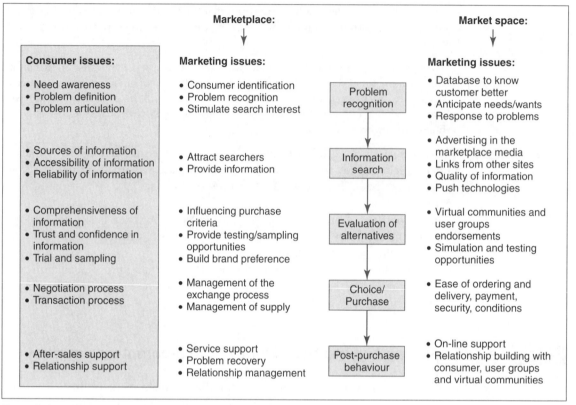

(Source: Butler and Peppard (1998), p. 603).

Utilitarian searchers often use search engines and they can often find a Web address that is easy to guess.

In the following we will further discuss consumer buying behaviour in the B-to-C market. Despite the fundamental difference between the 'physical marketplace' and the 'virtual market space', one principle still holds true in both worlds: the marketer must understand how the consumer makes decisions as to purchase choice before he/she can effectively respond to these demands.

Figure 13.6 provides an overview of the main differences between 'marketplace' and 'market space' in the consumer decision process. Of course, iteration exists between the different stages.

Each of these stages is now examined in turn and compared in the context of the marketplace and the market space.

Problem recognition

The first stage, consumer decision, triggers all subsequent activity. The consumer is compelled to fill the gap between the actual and the desired state. When problem awareness is reached, problem recognition may be triggered by a number of external and internal factors.

In traditional markets, conventional marketing communications stimulate demand via conventional media, e.g. an advertisement on television. However, on the Internet the medium is new, and so new kinds of communications are required. In the traditional mass marketing approaches much of the audience will not be interested, and there is considerable wastage. But new information technologies fundamentally change that. Computer-mediated environments enable identification of individual consumer needs and wants, and subsequent design and delivery of individual and customized communications.

Information search

The information gathered, be it from internal sources (e.g. memory) or external sources (e.g. discussions, brochures, sales promotions) provides the basis for this stage. The physical marketplace imposes limitations on information. Economic and access barriers constrain what can efficiently be known, and consequently what can realistically be evaluated. On the Internet, however, intelligent shopping agents can scan the entire Web to find the data necessary for comparison. The relevant criteria can be presented and explained and can be ordered to suit individual needs.

The management of information is the primary role of the agent or broker in the marketplace. The intermediary function is here largely based on information provision and exchange. This is the effective function of travel agents, for instance. But, in the market space, when an airline sets up its own Web site with interactive flight information and booking facilities, for example, then the traditional intermediary is bypassed in a classic case of disintermediation. As channel disintermediation and re-intermediation become important, a match between information content and consumer requirements also becomes important. As individuals come to utilize the Internet for consumer purchases, a situation of perfect information is almost attainable. However, it must be noted that consumers' sense of uncertainty can actually increase as they gain more information. Information 'overload' occurs when we learn more about the alternatives available to us, and the search becomes 'psychologically costly'.

Evaluation of alternatives

In the marketplace the word-of-mouth communication, the reference of family, colleagues and friends, are a central influence at this stage. In the market space, new reference groups appear. The virtual community, consisting of discussion groups of interested parties, can have the power of the traditional reference groups, but with even greater quality and quantity of evaluative information. A simple version of a virtual community is Amazon.com's open book reviews, whereby a potential buyer can read book reviews by other Web site visitors.

Purchase decision

This stage involves decisions on *where* and *how* to buy. *Where* to buy is a decision regarding the choice of seller. Competition on the Web is driven by sellers attempting to build more exciting and interesting sites than their competitors, attracting the right customers to those sites, and providing superior shopping experiences to induce purchase. *How* to buy concerns the nature of the transaction and contract. Many of the products and services currently available to individual consumers on the Internet are digital, e.g. software and upgrades, or easily physically transported, e.g. music CDs and books. The future broadening of the base will require particular analysis of physical delivery issues. The actual delivery routines for such a service are probably more complex than the ordering, packing and payment routines. Whereas the order can be met within the one organization and under one roof, the logistics of physical delivery of relatively bulky but relatively low-value grocery orders is an entirely different proposition.

Post-purchase behaviour

In this stage the actual sale should be perceived as a starting point rather than an end. How the customer takes delivery of the product, how the product is used, the degree and satisfaction, quality of the service dimensions, customer complaints and suggestions are all critical to understanding consumer behaviour. This, of course, applies both in the *marketplace* and in the *market space*.

The main difference between relationship development in the two types of markets is that the *market space* emphasizes 'high tech', and is more characterized by the power of information and communication technologies to satisfy customer needs and thereby continue business relationships. For the seller in the market space the big issue is to update the Web site continuously. Post-purchase activity involves consumers returning to the seller's site with queries, for *new* information, and to repurchase.

Finally, how do features from marketplace retail stores relate to market space retail stores? Table 13.6 illustrates analogies between physical stores (also called 'bricks-and-mortar') and on-line retail stores. Obviously, some features like atmosphere are difficult to measure and characterize in on-line retail stores. Other features like store promotions are less difficult to measure in on-line retail stores.

Exploring business behaviour in B-t-B market

Web information systems hold great potential to streamline and improve business-to-business transactions. Instead of regarding the Internet as a mere sales channel, companies also utilize emerging technologies to cut costs out of the supply chain by streamlining procurement processes and improving collaboration. In times of intense competition and increasingly open markets, the ability to achieve efficiency improvements can become key to commercial success.

In the following we will look at how businesses make buying decisions and how they can be supported by an e-commerce information system. A conceptual framework is introduced in Figure 13.7. The interorganizational transactions are analyzed from a process-oriented perspective. We distinguish between four phases: information, negotiation, settlement, and after-sales and transaction analysis.

Participants

Transactions usually involve three categories of participants: buyers, sellers, and

Table 13.6

Differences between physical and on-line stores

Physical store: marketplace	On-line retail store: market space
Salesclerk service	Product descriptions, information pages, gift services, search function, clerk on the phone/email
Store promotion	Special offers, on-line games and lotteries, links to other sites of interest, appetizer information
Store window displays	Home page
Store atmosphere	Interface consistency, store organization, interface and graphics
Aisle products	Featured product on hierarchical levels of the store
Store layout	Screen depth, browse and search functions, indices, image maps
Number of floors in the store	Hierarchical levels of the store
Number of store entrances and store outlets/branches	Number of links to a particular on-line retail store
Checkout cashier	On-line shopping basket and/or order form
Look and touch of the merchandise	Limited to image quality and description, potential for sound and visual applications
Number of people entering the store	Number of unique visits to the on-line retail store
Sales per period	Sales per period

Source: Lohse and Spiller, 1999, p. 4

intermediaries. Buyers and sellers are the active groups in terms of exchanging goods and services (sellers) for some form of compensation (buyer). Regarding the third group, intermediaries, we will expand the role from a traditional distributor of goods as described in Chapters 9 and 10. The intermediaries are supposed to offer a variety of services to support and facilitate transactions. This includes financial institutions such as banks, credit-card companies and insurance brokers; providers of shipping, logistics and warehousing services; and consultants, industry associations and market researchers offering advice, product data or market information. Providers of information technology to automate transactions or to help set up electronic marketplaces can be characterized as intermediaries as well.

In the case of business-to-business transactions, both buyers and sellers are business organizations, whereas business-to-consumer and consumer-to-consumer transactions involve end-consumers or private households as buyers or sellers, respectively.

In the following we refer to the four phases of the buyer/seller transaction process model (Figure 13.7). In particular the role of the e-commerce information system will be described.

Figure 13.7   **The buyer/seller transaction process model**

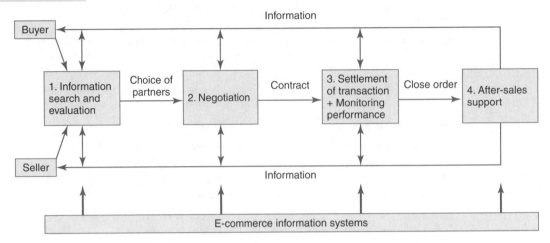

Phase 1: Information search and evaluation

In the information phase of a transaction, both buyers and sellers reach out to the world in search of information. In the physical world (marketplace), buyers locate information sources such as product catalogues, use them to scan product listings, obtain offerings from prospective suppliers, and gather additional information about products, vendor or transaction-specific requirements. Before a purchasing transaction can be performed, internal approval frequently has to be obtained from upper-level management.

The information phase comprises both searching for a particular electronic catalogue or source of information and locating required information and commodities within the information repository. In this phase, buyers and sellers are not yet focused on specific transaction partners. Information gathering and knowledge creation are at the centre of attention, and information is the primary object of exchange between prospective transaction partners.

A variety of Web-based information systems and other applications are available to provide support for the information phase of a transaction. Electronic catalogues, for example, feature comprehensive product descriptions and search tools, configuration support for complex purchases, workflow routing for approval processes, and access to additional information such as market research data and product review. Catalogues can be provided by suppliers, set up by the buyer, or developed by a third party. They can be hosted on the supplier's Web server, or be integrated into internal systems. Links to back-end systems provide access to human resources data, as they are required to manage purchasing authorization.

Phase 2: Negotiation

Of all transaction phases, the negotiation phase shows the broadest range of variations ranging from simple processes where price is the most important factor ('always-a-share'), to very complex arrangements where the buyer–seller relationship is regarded as a long-term strategic partnership ('lost-for-good'), according to Jackson (1985). Negotiations are often perceived as processes where a small number of prospective customers and sellers (often only one participant on each side) bargain on product prices and other terms of a deal. The parties jointly identify possible solutions with the goal of reaching a consensus, usually in the form of a contract. Bargaining processes alter with decisions whether to accept or reject the offering, and with the outlining of counter-suggestions until a mutually satisfactory agreement is reached. As prospective buyers and seller start communicating directly with each other, interaction is at the centre of attention. In this phase, influence is the primary object of exchange between the transaction partners. Not every transaction process features such complex negotiations. In fact, the negotiation phase is very often quite simple or even non-existent, such as in the case of retail buys and pre-negotiated contracts.

Negotiations can range from a single transaction to multiple-year contracts. The longer the time span that is covered, the more complex the structure of the bargaining process tends to be. In the following, we focus on complex forms of negotiations (be it for one transaction or a large number), but acknowledge the simpler forms as well.

Information systems support negotiations in a number of ways. They can provide transaction information and decision support by assessing the value of specific offerings, by identifying new bargaining options, and by increasing the negotiation's productivity. Participants may improve their bargaining positions through additional on-line information, such as the volume of previous business, supplier performance, or spending patterns.

Phase 3: Settlement of transaction + monitoring performance

Upon execution of the contract the objects of the transaction are exchanged according to the conditions previously stipulated. In addition, the settlement phase regularly includes some form of mutual performance monitoring. After the rather unstructured negotiation phase, the process of executing a transaction can be relatively straightforward. It is formally initiated as soon as a purchase order is confirmed by the supplier. The supplier ships the goods (often in collaboration with a third party, for example a local provider of logistic services), announces the shipment, and sends out a corresponding invoice. At the buyer side, orders are tracked, items are received, and payment is initiated after matching the invoice with the delivery. Naturally, there are many variations of this standard scenario. Consider, for example, the differences between the shipment of physical goods and the on-line delivery of information goods.

In the settlement phase of a transaction, activities and procedures are comparatively well defined, as they are part of the contract. Thus, attention centres on execution and efficiency. At this point, the main objects of exchange are goods and services. Information technologies to support transaction settlement may include EDI systems on the Web and various tools to process orders internally and between transaction partners, facilitate order tracking, and support payment processes.

Phase 4: After-sales analysis

After a transaction has taken place, both sellers and buyers store the transaction data to provide after-sales support (seller), or to assess supplier performance and analyze internal buying patterns (buyer). At the buyer side, the information flow is often split. While the purchase data is stored with central procurement, the end-user keeps the product-related documentation. In case of unexpected irregularities, it is often the end-user who contacts the supplier (e.g. to request a repair). Without proper access to the transaction file, communication problems and delays can occur. Capturing, storing, and managing data are vital at this point. Similar to the first phase (information), it is mainly information that is being exchanged between buyer and seller.

The electronic support of after-sales activities ranges from simple electronic mail services to automated help desks and sophisticated electronic maintenance manuals. Ideally, systems to support after-sales and transaction analysis provide central access to the transaction information. Data warehousing applications support the storing, accessing and processing of large amounts of data. They allow the firm to assess supplier performance, analyze internal buying patterns, provide the basis for consolidation corporate buys, and improve future bargaining positions with suppliers. At the supplier side, data about past transactions – including information of system configurations, preferred payment options, and so forth – support the maintenance process and subsequently improve the quality of the information phase of future transactions.

13.6 Disintermediation in e-commerce – myth or reality?

According to transaction cost analysis or TCA (see Chapter 3), firms will choose the entry and distribution mode that economizes on transaction cost, e.g. in particular the coordination cost between producer and intermediaries.

Today, as information technology continues its rapid cost performance, information infrastructures are extending to reach individual consumers. The potential for transformations in the value chain of many firms is thus far greater now than it has been in the past, as technology begins to enable producers to interact directly with consumers. It has been noted that intermediaries add significant costs to the value chain, which are reflected in a higher prices of products or services to the end customers. One fundamental question, therefore, is to what extent producers would take advantage of direct electronic links with consumers, and whether, in the process, intermediaries will be eliminated from the value system.

The essential argument is that the use of IT allows manufacturers to internalize activities that have been traditionally performed by intermediaries. Producers will 'capture value' and in the resultant redistribution of profits along the value system, traditional intermediaries will disappear. Benjamin and Wigand (1995) argue that if transactions take place directly between manufacturers and consumers, both manufacturers and consumers will benefit: the manufacturers will try to retain a higher portion of surplus value or profits that are generated along the value system, while the consumers will benefit from both a larger choice and lower prices. In other words, the network's ability to support direct exchanges efficiently will increase both producer and consumer welfare. Thus, it is predicted that manufacturers will sell directly to consumers, and consumers will prefer to buy directly from manufacturers.

Thus the myth has been that the Internet will eliminate the need for intermediaries. Early predictions called for *disintermediation* (e.g. Wunderman, 1998), that is, the disappearance of physical distribution chains as people moved from buying through distributors and resellers to buying directly from manufacturers. The reality is that the Internet may eliminate the traditional 'physical' distributors, but in the transformation process of the value chain new types of intermediaries may appear. So the disintermediation process has come to be balanced by a re-intermediation force – the evolution of new intermediaries tailor-made for the on-line world (Figure 13.8).

The traditional distribution model is linear. The manufacturer builds products. Wholesalers and distributors aggregate products from multiple manufacturers and bring them through several levels of distribution in small lots to resellers who deal directly with consumers. The value-added of the distribution chain lies in shipping, warehousing and delivering products.

With the Internet, value chains are being deconstructed and reconstructed in different ways – into value webs. *This process has given rise to a new class of intermediaries.* Companies such as Yahoo! aggregate information and make it easier to access information and see new possibilities of doing business. *The value-add is no longer in logistic aggregation but rather an information aggregation* – or eyeball aggregation. Consumers come to these sites looking for information and opportunities to purchase.

Companies such as Amazon.com and E*Trade are dramatically changing traditional models of selling goods and services by acting as a new type of intermediary. These new types of intermediaries offer new opportunities for existing companies as

| Figure 13.8 | Disintermediation and re-intermediation |

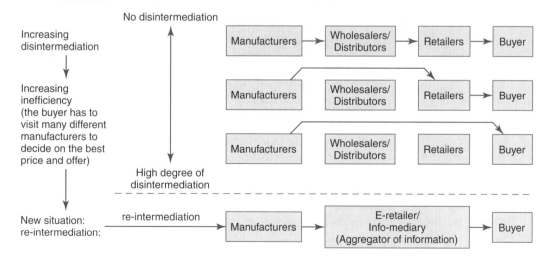

well as start-ups. Companies need to examine their current value chain and determine how the Internet might change it. Then they can adapt their business processes to take advantage of the new model – protecting their major sources of revenue and also developing new ones.

As an example, consider the airline industry. In the physical economy, who are the distributors of travel tickets? Thousands of travel agents, spread around the world. In the on-line economy, who are the distributors? Travel-related Web sites such as Microsoft's Expendia, among others. Consider another data point: in some big cities of the United States various reports indicate that almost 20 per cent of automobile sales take place on Internet sites. The distribution channels haven't gone away; they've simply shifted to new intermediaries.

| Exhibit 13.3 | **Disintermediation in the Japanese distribution system** |

If Japan is anything it is a nation of middlemen. It seems that the Internet and particularly the B-to-B e-commerce will eliminate inefficient distributors, disrupting long-established supply chains and lowering distribution costs. This could create tremendous opportunities for new entrants and could raise consumers' spending power.

'There are six and sometimes seven layers of distribution between us, the manufacturers of agrochemicals, and the end users – the farmers', says Peter Loescher, president and chief executive of Hoechst Japan, a bioscience company. 'We must fundamentally change both marketing and distribution. Marketing, because the farmers will be able to access information about the products directly from us via the Internet, and distribution, because many of the intermediaries will become redundant.'

B-to-B e-commerce could hit Japan's wholesalers hard. Ken Okamura, strategist at Dresdner Kleinwort Benson, notes that the Internet's transparent pricing mechanism could have a difficult time competing with the competitors who use Internet solutions to streamline operations. The overall implications for Japan's economy are tremendous; wholesalers account for about 4m jobs, according to Mr Okamura, so an overhaul of the industry could further inflate Japan's unemployment level which is already at a record high.

A number of factors could slow the growth of Japan's B-to-B e-commerce market. These include:

● High telecom charges. Miti says telecom charges are the largest constraint to the development of Japan's e-commerce market. Prices for a dedicated line used to access the Internet can be more that $1,000 (¥610) a month between Tokyo and Osaka, more than twice the cost of their US equivalent, according to Goldman Sachs.

● Low penetration of personal computers among smaller Japanese businesses. Less than 40 per cent of small companies in Japan own PCs, and less than 20 per cent have Internet access, compared with the US where 80 per cent of small businesses use computers and 60 per cent are on-line.

● Japan's stuttering economy. Many companies have frozen or even slashed information technology budgets, according to Kathy Matsui, strategist at Goldman Sachs. As a result, Japanese groups may not be investing sufficiently in new software technologies to create the necessary e-commerce platforms.

However, Mr Hirose of Fujitsu, a dominants force in Japan's Internet industry, disagrees. He says that managers may be reluctant to increase spending across the board but are increasingly willing to invest in new information technology initiatives that could change their businesses.

The distribution system in Japan is very much influenced by the special Japanese phenomenon, Keiretsu, which is a system of business groupings, combined with the cross-shareholdings among companies. The Keiretsu structure has traditionally limited competition among suppliers, a key dynamic of the price-driven e-commerce market. But companies are loosening Keiretsu ties and unwinding cross-shareholdings. This is expected to fuel competitive dynamics in the e-commerce market.

'In e-commerce, the Keiretsu does not matter. The concern is not how to stay in the Keiretsu but how to win in the international marketplace,' says Mr Hirose. 'Companies concerned with the Keiretsu will be wiped out.'

All in all, the changes in the Japanese distribution system may very well be gradual because of the existence of traditions, but it is a development that cannot be stopped.

Source: Nusbaum, A. (2000).

13.7 Developing dynamic global e-commerce

Many commercial Web sites have moved from providing basic company and product information to becoming an integral part of product and service launch strategies. Yet many firms are realizing that even this more coordinated approach is not taking full advantage of the Internet environment.

Figure 13.9 explores the development of a firm's Web strategy from a low-level strategy with the same one-way communication to a fully integrated e-commerce strategy, where the customer feels that he/she is treated on a one-to-one interactive basis. The following discusses the three commitment levels in detail.

Level 1: One-to-many broadcast ('use Internet representation as a company and product brochure')

Companies use the Internet for something that could be considered little else than a formal presence. These companies feel that they have to be present on the Web, but do not follow any concrete marketing objectives with the establishment of their Web site.

The motivation of the management in establishing such a page is most probably mainly reactive: as competitors move onto the Web, it is felt that a presence has become necessary. Often, however, the management will doubt that few if any customers or prospects will ever care to go near the page. The only tangible benefit from the Web is seen in the ability to use the Web site on traditional marketing channels in order to project a 'high-tech' image, an image of a company that keeps abreast with the latest developments. Although such an Internet 'strategy' will certainly not double the company's turnover, it can nonetheless be an economically plausible move because investments are low.

Figure 13.9   **Increasing commitment to e-commerce**

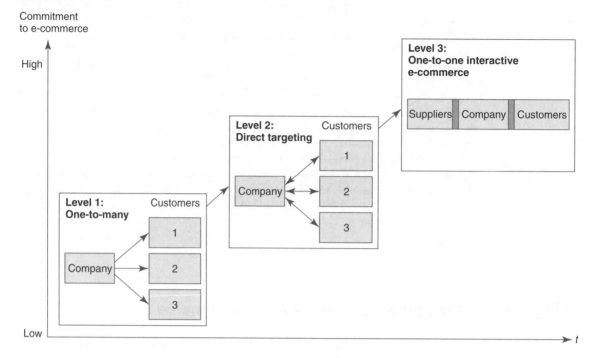

The Web representation is regarded as an additional tool to channel information on a firm's products or services to potential and existing customers. Companies following this strategy do consider that the World Wide Web is a useful tool, but perceive it more or less as no different from the traditional one-to-many marketing channels. The focus of such a Web presence will therefore lie on the firm providing as much information as possible through the Web rather than establishing a dialogue with the customer. Consequently, these companies will spend considerable time designing their Web site and ensuring the information is complete, accurate and kept up to date. The site will be easy to access, quick to load, and easily found using search engines. Products or services may be displayed in great detail in this virtual showroom to enhance their visibility and exposure in the marketplace and thus increase purchase probability.

However, these sites will not be designed as a communication device. The site will not explicitly encourage customer feedback such as service requests or complaints beyond product enquiries. Moreover, if a customer wants to purchase a product they will often have to use the traditional channels to do so. In summary, these informational sites represent company and product brochures. Economically speaking this is a valid strategy for companies that rely heavily on mass communication. The Web presence will allow these firms to keep their customers and prospects constantly up to date. It will also decrease the amount of printed information and the likelihood of having boxes full of outdated brochures awaiting disposal.

Level 2: Direct targeting

For the firms on this level, the key difference between traditional marketing media and the new cyber marketing is the degree of interactivity. Communication is no longer based on businesses feeding information to customers. Rather, the customers play an active role not only in looking for information relevant to the specific product and service needs in their buying process, but also in communicating these needs to the company. Hence, some degree of segmentation is possible. In some cases, the customers can also buy standard products on the Web site. The interaction (feedback) is still not on the highest level, as the basic exchange of information takes place through e-mails.

The most fundamental capability of a Web site is the presentation of information about products, services, people, events or ideas. Web sites with a strategic orientation emphasize both the gathering (feedback) and diffusion of information. It is possible to evaluate the extent to which an organization fulfils the informing function by examining the efforts to exchange information with key stakeholders. These stakeholders are customers, investors, suppliers, affiliates, employees, managers, and community members. In addition to providing information on the company's vision, history, products and services, many Web sites include information on organizational structure, financials, recruiting, executive teams and customer surveys.

After establishing a presence on the Internet, one of the primary objectives of a new Web site is to attract a variety of interested parties to visit the company's on-line presence. This is done in a variety of ways. It may simply be a matter of mentioning the address of the firm's home page in all possible connections. On the other hand, the company may have found differences among the customers and have differentiated the home page to its different customer groups around the world.

Many companies try to duplicate their US e-commerce strategy in European countries, but it is not as easy as it might seem. Companies cannot create a single Web site and expect to reach customers and distributors around the world.

Global e-commerce with one world-wide standardized Web site will probably not be successful in the long run, but for the small company ('Born Global') it may be the only way to get started in global e-commerce, without using too many resources. The moment a company has to deliver physical goods, it is up against every piece of legislation that exists in the real world (e.g. tariff barriers, VAT). Not to mention every cultural, legal and ethical and language barrier.

Let us further explore the language barrier. Today, there are only seven countries where English is the primary language spoken, some half a billion people, and where the combined economies represent 30 per cent of the world's economy. The combined population of these countries represent 8 per cent of the world's population. Companies that continue to target this small fraction of the world market will miss out on capturing a large potential market.

| Exhibit 13.5 | Laura Ashley is going into e-commerce |

Laura Ashley, the struggling clothes retailer, has gone into e-commerce in the second quarter of 2000, with a Web site (*www.laura-ashley.com*) selling clothes and home furnishings across Europe. The site focuses on personalization. It tailors offers and incentives to individual consumers, contacting them with product recommendations in real time while they visit the site.

Laura Ashley will also contact regular visitors by e-mail, although visitors will not be forced to register on the site.

On-line buying will be restricted initially to European consumers, but Laura Ashley hopes to roll it out globally.

Laura Ashley will promote the site with an on-line ad campaign, while press ads will feature the Web site address from next year.

Source: Jardine, A. (1999).

According to the latest statistics (*http://www.euromktg.com/glostats*), 91 million people access the Internet from English-speaking countries, whereas 80 million people access the Internet in other languages. Recent figures from Forrester Research state that 80 per cent of European-based corporate sites are multilingual. (See http//www.glreach.com/eng/ed/art/reasonsforglobal.html)

An example of the use of multilingual Web sites is Eastman Kodak Co. which has region-specific versions of its Kodak.com Web sites in 16 countries. Also, search engines like Yahoo! and Alta Vista have country-specific Web sites, at least on their major markets.

Level 3: One-to-one interactive e-commerce strategy

This is the final level where we see a high degree of interaction between buyer and seller. Here, the company is moving from providing company and product information to becoming an integral part of the whole vertical value chain from supplier to end-consumer. This virtual integration works faster than Level 2 (Direct Targeting) by blurring traditional boundaries between suppliers, manufacturers and customers in the value chain. Dell Computers gained the position as a market leader in the personal computer industry by using this model (Magretta, 1998).

A Web site that supports e-commerce can provide an important strategic asset for a business. A successful site has many benefits:

- It tightens relationships with existing customers and business partners.
- It offers new revenue-generating opportunities – through new channels as well as new business models.
- It offers opportunities to reduce costs by streamlining processes.
- It provides a competitive advantage.

Building a site can represent a significant investment in time and resources. A haphazard approach often results in wasted money and lost opportunity. To be successful, companies must integrate e-commerce into their overall business strategies and processes. They must understand the role of e-commerce in the context of other revenue-generating channels as well as re-engineering and cost-reduction initiatives.

Exhibit 13.6	**Amazon.com and its integrative role as 'information broker'**

Amazon.com is a firm that is solely dependent upon the WWW for its revenues and survival. The firm competes as 'information broker' for books and not just retailer of books as do physical bookstores. It has found a way to use the emerging medium to offer services that a physical bookstore cannot match. To keep customers interested in Amazon, the firm offers e-mail-based services to its registered customers. These include e-mail updates on the latest books which the customers have been reading. These 'virtual' services are automated and available 'free-of-charge' to all registered users.

The CEO of Amazon.com, Mr Bezos, has now expanded its role as 'information broker' to other product areas like auctions, music, DVDs etc.

Source: Hollensen, S. (1999).

Companies must also recognize that e-commerce may have a dramatic impact on existing business models and distribution channels. It may be necessary to redefine the current business model and perhaps modify relationships with the current channel or supply chain – or develop entirely new relationships or supply chains. Some industries will be more affected than others by the supply chain transformation that the Internet is causing. In some industries, a complete redefinition of the business model may be the only way to maintain a competitive edge. As a result, a careful examination of the existing business model and how e-commerce may affect it is essential for success in the on-line arena.

The following phases are involved in developing and implementing a successful e-commerce strategy:

1. *Identification of the process, product or business area that is most applicable for an e-commerce initiative.*

2. *The company's e-commerce goods.* Questions that need to be answered include:

   (a) What portion of the business will e-commerce represent in 12 months, two years and five years?

   (b) What volume of business does the company expect over the next five years?

   (c) What level of return on investment does the company expect?

   (d) How will return on investment be measured?

   (e) What cost savings can the company realize through e-commerce?

   (f) Will on-line sales reduce the sales volumes in existing channels? If so, what will be the impact on each channel?

3. *Definition of 'internal' and 'external' actors.* Defining the audience or customer is one of the primary tasks because it determines how and when internal and external actors should be involved. This includes identifying internal audiences, such as marketing, sales, channel sales, finance, IT and other internal groups, as well as external customers, suppliers, vendors, resellers and other business partners. This element of the overall plan affects many other aspects of the e-commerce system, from site design to on-line marketing techniques.

4. *Evaluation of competitor strategies.* The company's traditional competitors may already have an e-commerce initiative. It is essential to identify what these competitors are doing. Are they aggressively pursuing an e-commerce strategy or are they taking a wait-and-see approach? Are they extending their existing offerings to the new channel or are they creating an entirely new business? Although current competitors are a threat, non-traditional competitors often represent the biggest competitive risk. These are the companies that find new ways to reconstruct traditional value chains into value webs – gaining a significant head-start over companies that simply move existing business processes to the Internet.

5. *Integration of e-commerce with existing distribution channels and partners.* E-commerce is one component of an overall business value chain. It integrates with existing business processes and systems, and should complement existing channels rather than compete with them.

6. *Putting the right internal competences/skills in place.* Moving into the electronic commerce area requires new skills, knowledge and expertise in the three areas of strategy, technology and creativity:

   (a) *Strategy*: Strategic planning must be approached in a totally different way because of the dynamic nature of the Internet. Therefore the time perspective of strategic plans in the 'physical' firms (e.g. five years) should normally be shortened to maybe one year in 'virtual' firms.

   (b) *Technology*: Internet technologies are rapidly evolving, and keeping pace with the new breakthroughs is difficult. Technological expertise involves in-depth understanding of current hardware and software solutions, new technologies, site development, systems integration and security issues.

   (c) *Creativity*: Creative skills involve more than just basic Web site design. This discipline encompasses the entire user experience – what users see, how they navigate, how they obtain information and how they conduct transactions.

It also encompasses the audience development activities that drive traffic to the site. Marketing and promotional techniques that are effective in traditional media do not always translate well into the on-line marketplace.

After considering these phases, the company may go to the phase with design and implementation of the desired e-commerce system.

13.8 The legal environment of e-commerce

Companies that conduct e-commerce must are subject to the same laws, regulations and taxes that govern operations of all businesses. Companies operating on the Web face at least one complicating factor as they try to follow the laws. A company that uses the Web immediately becomes an international business, and as such the company can become subject to many more laws, more quickly than it would if it had been a traditional bricks-and-mortar company tied to one specific physical location. Furthermore any country's legal issues are difficult to interpret and follow because of the newness of electronic commerce and the unsettled nature of the laws. Some of the legal issues (in different countries) on which companies might need to seek specific legal advice are: ownership of company's domains (URLs), advertising/marketing standards, taxation on e-commerce.

If the Internet is used to promote and sell product overseas, the company has to be aware of various marketing legislation in the different countries. For example, Germany has specific laws that prohibit explicit comparisons between products.

One interesting issue is the *data protection and privacy laws*. The European Union's comprehensive privacy legislation, the Directive on Data Protection (the Directive), became effective on 25 October 1998. It requires that transfers of personal data take place only to non-EU countries that provide an 'adequate' level of privacy protection.

The United States and the EU have been trying to set common rules on data privacy. The US is concerned that strict EU laws would stop companies from sending some data to the United States from the EU. The United States also says the EU rules are likely to give US consumers a false sense of security because such rules are impossible to enforce. In November 1999, the Commerce Department released a plan to issue 'safe harbor' regulations that would protect US companies operating in Europe from sanctions under a new EU law as long as they meet certain guidelines. The EU, meanwhile, is concerned the United States won't enforce privacy guidelines strictly enough. It also wants the United States to set clear rules that allow consumers access to their own personal information that has been collected by businesses. At the time of writing (May 2000), the outcome of these negotiations between USA and EU is not yet clear.

13.9 Summary

During the last few years there has been an explosion of on-line commercial activity enabled by the Internet or World Wide Web (WWW). This is generally referred to as electronic commerce (e-commerce), with a major component of e-commerce being electronic transactions taking place on Internet-based markets (electronic markets, or e-markets).

The development of the Internet as a 'new' direct distribution channel has resulted in a shift of power from the manufacturers and the traditional retail channels to the consumers.

Generally, the development of e-commerce in Europe has been behind the development in USA. A major factor inhibiting growth of consumer e-commerce in Europe is lack of confidence in on-line security. However, for those selling via the Internet, the new European currency, the Euro, will make it easier to do business, and give encouragement to companies selling to European customers. Since Europeans will now be able to shop and compare prices at a click of a mouse, they will be more favourably inclined towards e-commerce.

The market volume of e-commerce on the B-t-B is much bigger than on the B-t-C market – five times more, according to some research results. The reason for this difference is that e-commerce is not a new phenomenon on the B-to-B market. Instead of Internet-based solutions, many industries have been using electronic data interchange (EDI) for years to streamline business processes and reduce the cost of doing business.

The main difference between buying behaviour in the 'physical marketplace' and the 'virtual market space' is that the *market space* emphasizes 'high tech', and is more characterized by the power of information and communication technologies to satisfy customer needs and thereby continue business relationships.

The myth has been that the Internet will eliminate the need for intermediaries. Early predictions called for *disintermediation*, that is, the disappearance of physical intermediaries as people moved from buying through distributors and resellers to buying directly from manufacturers. The reality is that the Internet may eliminate the traditional 'physical' distributors, but the transformation process of the value chain *has given rise to a new class of intermediaries*. Companies such as Yahoo aggregate information and make it easier to access new information and see new business possibilities. *The value-added is no longer in logistic aggregation but rather in information aggregation.*

Three alternative strategy levels of e-commerce commitment has been presented:

● *Level 1*. One-to-many strategy: use Internet presence as a company- and product-brochure.
● *Level 2*. Direct targeting: here the company starts selling on the Internet.
● *Level 3*. One-to-one interactive e-commerce.

On level 3 the company is moving from providing company and product information to becoming an integral part of the whole vertical value chain from supplier to end-consumer. This virtual integration works faster than Level 2 (direct targeting) by blurring traditional boundaries between suppliers, manufacturers and customers in the value chain.

Companies that conduct e-commerce must be subject to the same laws, regulations and taxes that govern operations of all businesses. But a company that uses the Web immediately becomes an international business, and as such the company can become subject to many more laws, more quickly than if it were a traditional bricks-and-mortar company tied to one specific physical location. Furthermore many countries' legal issues are difficult to interpret and follow because of the newness of electronic commerce.

What are the drivers and barriers of e-commerce?

Drivers

● For the supplier:
- reduced working capital (less inventory, reduced administration);
- global reach;
- more efficient distribution (disintermediation means fewer distribution channels);
- ability to develop relationships with customers.

● For the customer:
- more choices (greater product depth and global reach);
- ease of purchase and monitoring delivery;
- more individual products (via 'mass customization' of products);
- cost savings;
- faster product cycle time (ordering, shipping, billing);
- on the B-t-B market the customer has better possibilities of swapping between suppliers than with EDI.

Barriers (for both supplier and customer)

● When entering the global market there may be different barriers to different countries: language barriers, cultural barriers, limited Internet access, different legislation, logistical barriers, etc.

● Web-technology is not user friendly.

● Security fears.

● E-commerce is not suitable for certain types of product, for example 'high touch' products (fashion clothes) or very complex products or projects, where face-to-face communication is necessary.

● Conflicting interests (e.g. distributors, who may be bypassed, have another interest to the manufacturer).

● WWW = World Wide Wait (poor performance leading to slow download).

Case study Levi Strauss

First on-line, then off-line

Levi's on-line

Blue-jeans maker Levi Strauss's foray into on-line selling just in time for the Christmas 1998 holiday shopping season illustrated one of the biggest challenges traditional retailers face in the Web age: competing against suppliers.

The new Levi Strauss Web sites included:

- A virtual dressing room, where consumers can download images of clothes in their 'shopping bag' in eight seconds or less, without installing special graphics software. The images can be arranged on-screen so customers can see how they look together.
- A service allowing customers to order custom-tailored blue jeans.
- Virtual salespeople offering tips on matching pants and shirts.

Levi offered two-thirds of its men's and women's jeans line, or 32 styles, on the Internet (www.levi.com), and only eight styles were carried in stores. It sold 85 per cent of its khakis styles on-line (www.dockers.com).

Levi Strauss claimed that their move to sell directly to consumers via the Internet enabled them to broaden brand awareness, which would also benefit retail partners. The Web sites were backed by an estimated $5 million in on-line, newspaper and radio advertising, primarily in top college markets.

The physical retail stores (bricks-and-mortar stores) were worried: having fewer people browsing and buying on impulse in bricks-and-mortar stores is a problem for retailers because it could erode sales. Retailers also feared that suppliers could undercut their prices or introduce products on-line before rolling them out in stores.

Levi's off-line

Then in January 1999 the message came that Levi Strauss & Co. had called a halt to selling merchandise on its own Web sites, and has moved instead to allow two of its customers, JCPenney Co. and Macy's, to sell its products via their Web sites. The decision came after a year in which Levi had prohibited its larger retailers from selling its goods on the Web.

Speaking with Bobbin, Jeff Beckman, senior manager of communications for Levi, said the move came on the heels of a new strategic direction for the company, which involves a renewed focus on working hand-in-hand with retailers to meet consumer needs. Calling its own flagship e-commerce initiative 'unprofitable', Levi is looking to shift the responsibility for on-line sales to its retail customers.

'One of the things we learned this past year was what it takes to truly have a world-class e-commerce site, both in terms of money and time,' Beckman emphasized. 'Although the [Levi] sites have been successful and produced strong sales, the costs remain high. It's simply not affordable for us right now. We say this realizing that some of the retailers run really terrific, top-notch e-commerce sites. And these sites have the full capacity to fully meet the needs of our consumers while representing the product well.'

Questions

1. What are the advantages and disadvantages for a clothing manufacturer like Levi Strauss to sell on-line on the WWW?

2. Would you recommend that Levi Strauss sell products on-line or not, and if yes, in what form?

3. Why did Levi Strauss mainly approach top college markets in their advertising campaign for their Web sites?

4. Do you agree with Levi's decision to withdraw from the direct Web sales and instead let the two big retailers JCPenney and Macy's take over the Web selling at Levi?

Adapted from different sources:
Grant, L. (1998) 'On-line shopping soars Net sales nag retailers', *USA Today*, 15 December.
Rosenbush, S. (1998) 'Personalizing service on Web', *USA Today*, 16 November.
Jastrow, D. (1999) 'Saying no to Web sales', *Computer Reseller News*, 29 November.

Questions for discussion

1. Explain the term virtual value chain.

2. Explain what is meant by electronic commerce.

3. What are transaction costs and why are they important to consider in e-commerce?

4. 'The WWW represents a pull medium for marketing rather than a push-medium'. Discuss.

5. What types of channel conflict are caused by the Internet?

6. How does the demographic profile of Internet users differ from the general population of a country?

7. Explain the main benefits that a company selling fast-moving consumer products could derive by creating a Web site

8. Describe sticky features that Web sites use to attract and keep visitors. Why is stickiness important to companies operating Web sites?

9. How do companies that create global Web strategies need to accommodate cultural differences and can they turn them to their advantage?

10. For the following stages in the buying process, explain how the Internet can be used to help achieve the communication objectives: supplier search, evaluation and selection, purchase, post-purchase.

11. Why is the Internet a suitable medium for one-to-one marketing?

12. 'Companies should spend a higher proportion of their Web site budgets on promotion than on designing and developing the site'. Discuss.

13. 'It is inevitable that the transparency of information on products and price on the WWW will drive down product prices'. Discuss.

Internet exercise

Auctions on the Internet

Please go to:

http://www.ft.com/ftsurveys/q69e6.htm

http://www.ft.com/ftsurveys/q6a06.htm

http://www.cio.com/archive/webbusiness/060199_auct.html

Questions

1. Explain how the different auctions types work.
2. Which auction type works on the B-t-C and B-t-B market?

For further exercises and cases, see this book's website at *www.booksites.net/hollensen*

References

Benjamin, R. and Wigand, R. (1995) 'Electronic markets and virtual chains on the information highway', *Sloan Management Review*, Winter, pp. 62–72.

Boston Consulting Group (2000) *The Race for Online Riches – E-Retailing in Europe* (http://www.bcg.com/new_ideas/new_ideas_subpage3.asp).

Butler, P. and Peppard, J. (1998) 'Consumer purchasing on the Internet: process and prospects', *European Management Journal*, vol. 16, no 5, October, pp. 600–610.

Business Week (1999a) 'A hard sell online? Guess again – Clothes, furniture, even food are starting to move', *Business Week*, 12 July, pp. 78–80.

Business Week (1999b) 'In the ring: eBAY vs. Amazon.com', *Business Week*, 31 May, pp. 49–55.

Computer Economics (1999) 'Internet usage according to language', 6 July 1999 (read more on http://www.glreach.com/globstats/).

Cyber Dialogue (2000) *American Internet Survey*, 2000. (http://cyberatlas.internet.com/big_picture/demographics/article/0,1323,5911_246241,00.html)

Department of Commerce (1999) *The Emerging Digital Economy II*. Chapter 1: Electronic Commerce in the Digital Economy (http://www.ecommerce.gov/ede/chapter1.html).

Financial Times (1999) 'Gucci doubles its net profit for third quarter', *Financial Times*, Companies & Finance Section, 11 December.

Gartner Group (2000), 'GartnerGroup forecasts worldwide business-to-business e-commerce to reach $7.29 trillion in 2004', GartnerGroup Corporate Headquarters, Connecticut, January.

Global Report (1999) 'The world's online populations' (http://cyberatlas.internet.com/big_picture/demographics/article/0,1323,5911_246241,00.html)

Hofacker, Charles F. (1999) *Internet Marketing* (2nd edn), Digital Springs, Inc.

Hollensen, S. (1999): 'Globalization of Internet-based services: The case of Amazon.com'. AIMS Conference 1999 (http://www.indiainfoline.com/bisc/amaz.html)

IDC (2000a) 'Europe sees big gains in Internet usage, 2000' (http://cyberatlas. internet.com/big_picture/demographics/article/0,1323,5911_281021,00.html)

IDC (2000b) 'A preview of IDC's Consumer Survey: European Internet and eCommerce', IDC European Internet Center (PowerPoint-presentation download at http://www.idc.com)

Jackson, B. (1985) 'Build customer relationships that last', *Harvard Business Review*, November–December, pp. 120–28.

Jardine, A. (1999) 'Laura Ashley site to offer net sales', *Marketing*, London, 9 December.

Kotha, S. (1998) 'Competing on the internet: The case of Amazon.com', *European Management Journal*, vol. 16, pp. 212–22.

Lake, D. (1999) 'Spotlight: How big is the US net population', *The Standard: Intelligence for the Internet Economy*, 29 November.

Lohse, G.L. and Spiller, P. (1999) 'Internet retail store design: How the user interface influences traffic and sales', *Journal of Computer Mediated Communication*, vol. J, no. 2, December, pp. 1–20.

Magretta, J. (1998) 'The power of virtual integration: An interview with Dell's Computer's Michael Dell', *Harvard Business Review*, March–April, pp. 73–84.

Mediamark Research (1999) 'Spotlight: How big is the US Net population?' (http://www.the standard.com/metrics/display/0,2149,1071,00.html)

Nusbaum, A. (2000) 'Web cuts out entire order of middlemen: 'Information Technology Internet in Japan: B-t-B e-commerce is threatening the livelihoods of thousands of intermediaries', *Financial Times*, 11 January.

Rayport, J.F. and Sviokla, J.J. (1996) 'Exploiting the virtual value chain', *McKinsey Quarterly*, no. 1, pp. 21–36.

Thompson, M.J. (1999) 'Customer feeding frenzy: E-retailers vie for $185 billion', *http://www.thestandard.com*, 15 November.

Wunderman, W. (1998) 'The future of selling via the Internet. The online progress of disintermediation', *Web Commerce Today*, Issue 10, 15 May.

Case III.1   Hong Guan Technologies

Seeking new business opportunities in the east Asian market

Introduction

Established in Singapore, Hong Guan Technologies is a medium-sized engineering service and manufacturing firm. Although the firm has been designing and building factory automation systems, it has also integrated vertically into specialized manufacturing activities. Between 1990 and 1995, Hong Guan's annual sales volume averaged US$20 million and this is projected to reach US$30 million in 1997. The firm currently employs about 200 people, of whom 85 per cent are involved in fabricating automation systems and manufacturing machine/electronic component parts, and the remaining 15 per cent are in managerial and R & D activities.

Since the firm's inception in 1986, its sales have been progressing steadily, in tandem with the buoyant economic growth of the country. While sales growth in the past five years may be considered to be very good, the company perceives that, unless it develops new business and explores overseas markets, its revenue growth could plateau. Thus, Hong Guan Technologies is currently evaluating strategic options to achieve growth in the next five years.

Background to the company

Hong Guan Technologies started under the ownership of Mr James Teo, an entrepreneur who hailed from an accounting background. In its early days, the firm concentrated on the assembly of component parts in building machinery for factories. Sensing the need to augment the technical expertise of the firm, Mr Teo sought collaboration with Sanwa Koki Co. Ltd of Japan. The collaboration entailed the transfer of technology in machinery design and building an automated production system. To a large extent this collaboration worked well and, with an enhanced level of technological competence, the firm was able to expand its scope and volume of business. The elevation of its technical expertise also secured an important advantage

for the firm. In 1989 Hong Guan was awarded a five-year pioneer status by the government of Singapore, in recognition of the specialized and high-tech nature of its business and its potential contribution to the economy of the country. The pioneer status enabled the company to enjoy certain concessionary tax benefits for a five-year period, which encouraged the firm to intensify its investment in the acquisition of technical expertise through licensing and collaborations with other firms. This period of pioneer status was reviewed and extended for another five years to end in the year 1999.

Today, Hong Guan's main business activities have broadened to include total systems design on turnkey projects, systems integration, precision engineering and high-speed, computer-aided design assembly. Its customer base has also expanded considerably and now includes major multinational firms such as Hitachi Electronic Devices, Sony, Molex, EG & G Heimann Optoelectronics, Thai CRT and Samsung Electronic Devices.

Organizational structure

Hong Guan is organized on the traditional basis of strategic business units (SBUs) and structured in the form of a product–customer matrix. Owing to its simplicity and ease of implementation, this concept appeals to a growing medium-sized company such as Hong Guan. Broadly, the company is structured under two main lines of business: engineering (with four SBUs) and manufacturing (with three SBUs).

The SBUs involved in engineering are as follows:

● Engineering 1 provides turnkey services to key customers. Its main customers are Hitachi, Hibex, Heimann, Samsung and Thai CRT.

● Engineering 2 specializes in connector assembly and equipment for Molex (S) Pte Ltd.

● Engineering 3 focuses on original equipment manufacturing (OEM) sales.

● Engineering 4 specializes in machining facilities and supports other SBUs as well as outside customers.

The SBUs involved in manufacturing are as follows:

● Manufacturing 1 specializes in the integrated manufacturing of component parts of compact disc players for Sony, and in auto vision inspection and injection moulding.

● Manufacturing 2 is based in Johore (a state in neighbouring Malaysia). Its activities are mainly labour-intensive inspection of output and certain manual manufacturing operations (where full automation is not economically feasible). It supports Manufacturing 1 in some of the manufacturing processes.

● Manufacturing 3 is involved in the integrated manufacturing of components for colour picture tube assembly. Its main customer is Hitachi.

In addition to engineering and manufacturing groups, there are staff units comprising of personnel and administration; procurement; finance; and quality assurance.

While the engineering group has remained the mainstay of the company business, the manufacturing group is gradually gaining in importance. Over recent years, Hong Guan has begun contract manufacturing of component parts for some of its clients. This line of business, essentially 'transplanting' certain production activities from the clients to Hong Guan, conveys reciprocal benefits on both parties. From the perspective of the clients, they can avoid many of the problems arising from the breakdown of production systems, reduce maintenance costs and focus on the design and quality of their products. Some clients too are facing undercapacity, but are unable to expand in the face of spatial limitations. For Hong Guan, the 'coupling' of the production systems of firms provides a stronger business alliance with its clients. It offers Hong Guan an opportunity to capitalize on its expertise and increase the value added of its output. Furthermore, it benchmarks the firm's technological proficiency in building cost-effective production infrastructures and provides feedback for continuous improvement.

The contract manufacturing arrangement is usually formulated on a cost-plus basis: customers are charged the cost of production plus a percentage to cover Hong Guan's overhead cost and profit. Following industrial norms, the unit price of the output decreases with the accumulated volume of the order, and is based on a formula agreed between Hong Guan and its clients. This decrease in price is due to the 'learning curve' effect of efficiency resulting from repetitive production. The contract manufacturing arrangement includes a provision for reimbursement to Hong Guan for any modification to the production system resulting from a change in client specifications.

Financial status

Sales revenue has been progressing steadily over the past five years, as shown in Table 1. After 1996/7, it is perceived that any increase in sales revenue must necessarily come from an expansion of the scope of business.

Nature of technology-based business

A prevailing framework for viewing the operations of a technology-based company such as Hong Guan is to examine the continuum of activities ranging from research to applied science to development to engineering to production. At the core level of the business is fundamental research, the primary focus of which is to seek the principles and relationships underlying knowledge of a particular phenomenon. Firms that are heavily involved in research are usually those with deep pockets to finance experiments whose commercial gains could have indefinite time periods. Pure research usually brings about patent and proprietary knowledge that may be locked up in patents with low returns.

Table 1	Hong Guan sales revenue, 1989–1996/7
Year	Sales[a] (US$m)
1989	6.9
1993/4	11.0
1994/5	16.6
1995/6	27.6
1996/7	35.5 (estimated)

[a] Based on a conversion rate of US$1 to S$1.45 as at January 1997.

In order for business to reap the economic benefits of proprietary knowledge, the next level of the continuum concerns applied science, which further crystallizes the true nature of the knowledge and demonstrates its potential utility. This is followed by development, which reduces the knowledge to practice in workable prototype forms. Next comes engineering, which refines the knowledge for commercial exploitation or other practical uses. Finally, production and sales put the technology into use.

In terms of research and applied science, Hong Guan currently has a joint research programme with the Nanyang Technological University in Singapore; this collaboration in the field of power electronics is in its infancy stage. Hong Guan's strength lies in the development and engineering areas. The strategy provides for swift commercialization of technology, and avoids placing the company in research that has an uncertain success outcome. The firm keeps abreast of technology by sourcing specialized technical expertise through licensing or management contracts with specialist firms. Another source of organizational learning is contract manufacturing, whereby clients disclose information on their products and their production process.

New business development

In addition to supporting Singapore-based foreign firms such as Sony and Hitachi, Hong Guan is pursuing regional markets aggressively. Importantly, the firm is considering how it could utilize its technological competence in factory automation and integrated manufacturing as a springboard to entering new business.

Against the backdrop of the economic development taking place in the Pacific Rim region, the top management of Hong Guan has identified the production of automobile parts as a strong possibility. For many countries in the region, the continuing brisk pace of economic growth coupled with a higher standard of living has fuelled a strong demand for cars in both the private and commercial sectors of the economy. The recognition of a growing market plus the imposition of import restrictions following governmental concerns about the loss of foreign exchange through car imports have encouraged many car manufacturers to set up plants in the region. For example, General

Motors has assembly plants in Thailand and China. Last year, Kia Motors of South Korea entered into a joint-venture partnership with a local firm to produce the Timor in Indonesia. This is in addition to the several Japanese car makers that have already established a foothold in the market. In Malaysia, a national car, Proton, has emerged as the best-selling car in the country, its success being partly attributed to government protection against foreign competition. The car plant, set up with technical support from Mitsubishi of Japan, has progressed over the last decade to become self-reliant in design and production. Recently in Singapore, the state Economic Development Board (EDB) has given an innovation grant to Daimler-Benz to undertake vehicle customization for the Asia-Pacific market. The focus of the grant is on the design and development of commercial vehicle concepts with the potential to be marketed under the Mercedes-Benz name.

With the increasing level of activity in the car industry, Hong Guan senses that the supply of automotive components could be a promising avenue of business. There are, of course, several barriers that the company must overcome. One of the problems is that many of the automotive parts have protected designs which require approval from and royalty payment to copyright holders. Hong Guan figures that to overcome the complications of copyright, the company could link up with major car plants through contract manufacturing, an arrangement that the company is familiar with. However, this strategy is possible only if Hong Guan is able to achieve a lower cost base than those of the parent automotive plants.

As Hong Guan's production predominantly embodies electronic components, a feasible progression would be a specific segment of the car industry: electronic components. To venture into the new business domain, an important starting point is building up technological competence. One possible ally is Bodine, a US firm specializing in consumer electronics and automotive parts assembly, which has linkages with the 'big three' car makers in the USA. Hong Guan has collaborated with this ally since 1991 on other projects, and this could be augmented to include components for automobiles.

Apart from acquisition of expertise from this US firm, there are other considerations that must be evaluated. One concerns whether to locate in the country of the manufacturer, or to supply the components from Singapore. The production of the components from Singapore could eliminate many of the difficulties of moving overseas, such as training labour, setting up production facilities, and governmental bureaucracy. However, such advantages are outweighed by other elements essential to operating successfully in the car industry. For one, there is a requirement for just-in-time production and timely delivery of parts. This is possible only if Hong Guan has a factory in the proximity of its manufacturer. Moreover, the costs of labour and land in Singapore compare unfavourably with those in the neighbouring countries, especially in countries where the car plants have been located. This would, in any event, foil Hong Guan's plan to achieve a lower cost base than the parent plants.

Another factor is the choice of entry mode. While setting up a wholly owned subsidiary would keep proprietary knowledge within the firm, this mode requires a large investment outlay. The risk is accentuated by the fact that Hong Guan is in the process of building up its experience of operating overseas, and may be inadequate to manage effectively in the country of investment. Moreover, its current technological expertise may not be fully utilized in the automotive industry and other parties may be required to fill the gap in technology. An alternative to operating a wholly owned subsidiary is for Hong Guan to enter into a joint venture. Here, Hong Guan has to seek out reliable partners which could provide complementary expertise in managing the joint venture successfully. In addition to sorting out home and host country cross-cultural issues, Hong Guan has to weigh up its share equity position and the level of control it has against the operation of the joint venture.

Decision

The company is working on its own and with the Singapore Economic Development Board (EDB) to seek out business opportunities and prospective partners in Thailand, Malaysia, Vietnam and others. The EDB has an extensive network of offices world-wide and is a good source of important contacts. It also has intimate knowledge of the economic and political environment in the region. It may take several months before Hong Guan finally decides on an appropriate course of action.

Questions

1. How do you think Hong Guan Technologies (as a sub-supplier) will establish links with big companies like Samsung and General Motors? Is Hong Guan only a supplier of components or will it also be involved in product development at its customers?

2. Would it be better for Hong Guan to supply component parts by (a) setting up production facilities in host countries or (b) manufacturing and exporting them from Singapore?

3. If Hong Guan chooses to manufacture component parts in the host countries, what form of entry mode would you recommend – wholly owned subsidiaries or joint-venture partnerships? Explain your choice.

4. List the criteria that Hong Guan ought to consider when choosing alliance partners.

Prepared by Dr Benjamin Tan Lin Boon, Nanyang Technological University, Singapore. The author is indebted to Mr Mike Choo, assistant general manager of Hong Guan Technologies, for information and advice. Any errors, however, are the author's own.

Case III.2   Bertelsmann Music Group (BMG)

Part A: Global marketing strategy for the music business

On a spring day in 1997 the managing director of the Entertainment Group in BMG, Marcus Schmidt,[1] gets on a plane in Frankfurt. The plane is bound for New York, where Marcus, among other things, is going to participate in the launch of Toni Braxton's new CD. Toni Braxton was one of BMG's best-selling artists in 1996, and Marcus is looking forward to meeting the megastar personally. (Plate 6 shows photographs of Toni Braxton and another big recording star of BMG, David Bowie.)

As Marcus is new in his job as managing director, he uses the plane trip over the Atlantic to study the global music industry more thoroughly. Marcus has noticed that BMG is very proud of being one of the top five record companies in the world. But BMG is 'only' no. 5 in this group, with a worldwide market share of 14 per cent.

Fortunately, Marcus has brought his portable PC which he turns on to read a report that one of his marketing associates has written. But first a little general information about BMG:

● It is the third largest media corporation in the world.

● The group's holding company is Bertelsmann AG, which is based in Gütersloh, Germany.

● The group employs 58,000 people in more than 570 companies and profit centres spread across 40 countries.

● Revenues in 1995/6 topped $15 billion and the net income was $595 million, an increase of 8 per cent on 1994/5.

Bertelsmann is divided into four product lines:

● Books.

● Entertainment.

● Press.

● Industry.

It publishes and distributes books, magazines and newspapers. It runs record and film companies, TV

and radio networks, and is active in all related businesses. The entertainment business (of which recorded music is an important part) amounts to one-third of its total revenues.

The global market for music on CDs, LPs and cassettes

According to the International Federation of the Phonographic Industry (IFPI), the retail value of global music in 1995 was nearly $40 billion. From 1991 to 1995 the global sales volume of CDs, LPs and cassettes rose from 2.8 billion to 3.8 billion units.

About 34 per cent of all compact discs, tapes and records are sold in Europe. The European market share has risen from 28 to 34 per cent in the past ten years, while the American share has fallen from 36 to 33 per cent (Table 1). Behind Europe's huge market share is an increase in sales of 12 per cent in the last five years and 40 per cent in the last ten years. At the same time, the sale of music stagnated in the large American market in 1995 after a long period with strong growth.

About 80 per cent of the world's retail sales come from pop/rock/dance/soul/reggae/country/folk while classic/jazz accounts for the remaining 20 per cent.

The largest market in Europe is Germany ($3 billion) followed by the UK ($2.5 billion).

Table 1	World retail music sales by region, 1995
Region	**Market share (%)**
Europe	34
North America	33
Japan	19
Far East (excluding Japan)	5
Latin America	5
Pacific	2
Middle East	1
Africa	1

Source: IFPI.

[1] All similarities to past or present BMG managing directors are coincidental.

Table 2   The 'big five' of the global recorded music industry (pop/rock category, 1994)

	Polygram	EMI/Virgin	Warner Music Group	BMG	Sony
Ownership	The holding company is 75% owned by Philips (Netherlands)	Owned by Thorn EMI plc (England)	Owned by Time Warner Group (USA)	Owned by Bertelsman AG (Germany)	Owned by Sony Corporation (Japan)
World-wide market share	19%	15%	18%	14%	17%
Sales/pre-tax net income	$4.7 billion/ $685 million	$3.4 billion/ $450 million	$4 billion/ $366 million	$3.8 billion/ n/a	$4.9 billion/ n/a
Major international record labels	Polydor, Phonogram, Island, A&M, Motown, Decca, Philips	EMI, Virgin records, Parlophone, Chrysali Records	WEA, EastWest	RCA, Ariold, Arista	Columbia (CBS), Epic, S2
Top international artists	Bon Jovi, Stevie Wonder, Dire Straits, Elton John, U2, Ace of Base, Boyz II Men	Frank Sinatra, Janet Jackson, Meat Loaf, Cliff Richard, Paul McCartney, Queen	Madonna, REM, Simply Red, Enya, Chris Rea, Hootie and the Blowfish	Toni Braxton, ZZ Top, Whitney Houston, Annie Lennox, Take That, David Bowie, Eros Ramazotti	Michael Jackson, Bruce Springsteen, Mariah Carey, Billy Joel George Michael, Sade
Top regional artists	Jacky Cheung (Hong Kong), MC Solaar (France)	Yumi Matsutoya (Japan), Jon Secada (Cuba), Eric Moo (Taiwan), Mamonas Assassinas (Brazil)	Laura Pausini (Italy), Aaron Kwok (Hong Kong), Dadawa (China), Luis Miguel (Mexico)	Masaharu Fukuyama (Japan), So Pro Contrariar (Brazil), Diego Torres (Argentina), Peter Maffay (Germany)	TUBE (Japan), Harlem Yu (Taiwan), Patricia Kaas (France), Roberto Carlos (Brazil)
Strengths/weaknesses	No. 1 world-wide. Early focus on building local repertoire in international markets now paying off, but top management is distracted by demands of new film unit.	Boosted world-wide market share from 10% in 1991 after buying Virgin records in 1991 and Japanese affiliate in 1994, but is weak in the USA.	Dominates the USA with 22% market share, but is playing catch-up in the global market, building local repertoire fast.	Publishing hard to develop local talent in central Europe. Weak in the USA.	No. 2 spot in USA, dominates Latin America, but in other markets is overly dependent on American talent.

The global music industry

The IFPI estimates that 60 per cent of all the music that Europeans buy is recorded by European artists. This is the exact opposite of the film market, which is totally dominated by the USA.

Today the global music industry is dominated by five 'majors', which control more than 80 per cent of the market. They are Polygram (the Netherlands), BMG (Germany), Sony (Japan), Warner (USA) and EMI (UK). Table 2 gives a description of these companies. Right behind the 'big five' comes a 'little' no. 6, the record company MCA, which the American Seagram bought in 1994 from the Japanese Matsushita concern. The rest of the industry is divided among 1,100 minor record companies.

All companies operate under several labels and are part of large multimedia conglomerates which also deal with film, TV, books, magazines and other entertainment. The only exception is EMI, which at the moment is being separated from Thorn EMI which is to be divided in two. EMI has expanded into the retail business with the international music chain HMV, but has until now refused to expand into other media activities.

Table 3 shows the market shares of the 'big five' and the independents in a number of countries in 1995. The largest market growth (till year 2005) is expected to take place in Latin America, eastern Europe and Asia, which stand to grow by 13 per cent a year compared to a global growth in the same period of 7.5 per cent a year.

Growth of the local/regional music scene

The 'big five' are also battling new regional independents, such as Taiwan's Rock Records, Brazil's Sigla and Japan's Pony Canyon. Often run by street-wise local entrepreneurs, the independents can spot new talents more easily. In the past sixteen years, Rock Records has built itself into eastern Asia's largest independent record company, with 50 Chinese-language artists, including the region's most popular stars. Sales were estimated at $85 million for 1995.

In Asia, tastes are changing even more rapidly. In the early 1990s, as political winds shifted in markets such as Taiwan, newly liberated music fans went for western pop idols such as Whitney Houston. Later a Cantopop genre developed, mostly bubblegum music lip-synched by film and soap opera stars. Now, local music is becoming more sophisticated. Fans seem to want songs that rediscover a common heritage and are sung in their own language.

Take China, where 32-year-old singer Wei Wei soared to fame with ballads and love songs. She cut four albums that sold 106 million copies, making her more popular than Madonna. But in 1994, when she began singing in English to broaden her appeal, her popularity plummeted at home.

In Malaysia, America's 'gangsta rap' is not popular, but Malaysian teenagers love their home-grown rap group, Kru. An EMI scout heard the three brothers who make up Kru singing a jazzy song for the local Selangor soccer team on the radio. He signed them to a contract in 1993, and in two years they have sold 300,000 albums. After a slow start, the 'big five' music companies are catching on to the demand for local talent.

Threats to the global music industry

The exploding pirate copy market has put a damper

Table 3	International market shares of the 'big five' and the independents, 1995 (%)						
	UK	USA	Germany	France	Denmark	Netherlands	Japan
Polygram	23.3	11.5	22.0	32.0	24.1	24.1	12.3
EMI/Virgin	19.2	10.7	20.7	19.0	30.1	12.4	13.6
Warner	11.7	22.5	17.6	10.0	11.4	12.6	8.0
Sony	10.5	17.5	11.7	15.0	13.3	15.5	25.9
BMG	8.1	11.0	17.6	11.0	11.8	17.7	5.0
'Big five'	72.8	73.2	89.6	87.0	90.7	82.3	64.8
Independents	27.2	26.8	10.4	13.0	9.3	17.7	35.2
Total	100	100	100	100	100	100	100

on the expected growth in Asia and eastern and central Europe. It is estimated that between 5 and 10 per cent of the world's total sales volume does not go through registered record companies.

China produces 40 per cent of all pirate CDs sold in the world. After a long tug-of-war with the EU and USA, China has promised to take action against the illegal copying, and at the same time make it easier for foreign music companies to establish themselves in China. But according to the IFPI it is a very slow process and the organization has just filed a complaint to the EU on this matter. In Europe the music industry is becoming still more concerned about Bulgaria, which is known as 'a China on Europe's doorstep'. That country alone is responsible for a huge part of the illegal sales in Europe, with an export of 20 million pirate CDs a year. The exports go mainly to eastern Europe and Russia, but the Bulgarian copies have also been found in the UK, Germany and the Netherlands.

Another threat towards the established record companies is on-line music delivery via the telephone line and the Internet directly to the world consumer's home. According to the IFPI much of the conventional sale of music on CDs and cassettes will soon be replaced.

Large retail concerns estimate that as much as 15 per cent of the global sales in music shops will be replaced by on-line delivery in the next five years. In Europe this is equivalent to a market of nearly $2 billion. The on-line market is a golden opportunity for music companies, but only if they are protected by copyright. The American music organization RIAA has also warned that competition from the Internet and computer games will increase, and the market for electronic entertainment is expected to overtake the music market in the USA within a few years.

BMG's basis for challenging the market leaders in the music market

BMG has traditionally been strong in markets that were geographically close to Germany, but in buying the American record company RCA in 1986, many possibilities were suddenly opened up in the USA. The new markets in eastern Europe and the Far East have also been discussed, but top management of BMG has not yet decided which marketing strategy to use in these markets.

When the plane arrives at JFK airport in New York, Marcus Schmidt feels that BMG still needs to consider some very important strategic questions. When Marcus enters the arrival hall of the airport, he hurries to a fax machine to send some questions home to head office in Gütersloh in Germany.

As you have just been employed by Marcus Schmidt as marketing coordinator, you are presented with the following questions:

Questions

1. Which geographic market areas should be chosen for closer analysis?
2. Which marketing strategy and entry mode should be used in these markets?

Case III.3 Autoliv Air Bags

Transforming Autoliv into a global company

Chief executive officer of Autoliv AB, Gunnar Bark, is in the middle of a board of directors' meeting in Stockholm in March 1996, discussing how it is possible to transform Autoliv from a European company to a global company. He takes out a situation report for the business area of air bags. As there are a couple of new members on the board of directors, Gunnar takes the opportunity to give a broader introduction to the business area than he usually does. The following is Gunnar Bark's status report concerning the business area of air bags.

Situation report for the business area of air bags

Business concept

Autoliv shall develop, manufacture and market systems and components for *personal safety* in automobiles. In this aspect, Autoliv wants to be the systems supplier and the development partner to the car producers that satisfy all the needs in the area of personal safety.

To fulfil the business concept, Autoliv has strong product lines: seat belts and air bags. The following will primarily concern the business area of air bags.

The product: air bag

Even the best belt designs cannot prevent all head and chest injuries in serious frontal crashes. This is where air bags help, by creating an energy-absorbing cushion between an occupant's upper body and the steering wheel, instrument panel or windshield. Independent research has shown that driver deaths in frontal crashes are about 20 per cent lower in cars with air bags than in similar cars with belts only. In all kinds of crash, deaths are down about 15 per cent over and above lives already being saved by belts.

Although air bags may seem complicated, they are relatively simple. In moderate and severe frontal crashes, sensors signal inflators to fill the bags with harmless gas. The bags fill in a fraction of a second and begin deflating instantly as they cushion people. Peak inflation is in less than 1/20th of a second, faster than the blink of an eye. The speed and force of air bag inflation may occasionally cause injuries, mostly minor abrasions or bruises, but in the United States some small children have died of a broken neck caused by an air bag that inflated with great force. Those at the greatest risk of injury caused by an air bag are anyone who drives or rides unbelted, small children, short or obese adults, and certain disabled people.

Injury risk from the bag itself can be reduced by choosing a seating position that does not put your face or chest close to the steering wheel or instrument panel. The combination of seat belt and air bag provides maximum protection in all kinds of crash.

Together with Volvo, Autoliv has also developed the first side air bags to protect drivers and right-front passengers in side-impact crashes. These bags are typically smaller than frontal air bags and they inflate more quickly. Volvo was first to offer side air bags in its 850 model for 1995. Volvo's bag is mounted on the outboard side of driver and right-front passenger seat backs. For 1996, side bags are standard in all Volvo models.

The history of air bags goes back to the early 1950s. The product idea was patented in 1951 by Walter Linderer from Munich. It was in the USA, however, that the concept really struggled into existence, driven by the North Americans' reluctance to use a seat belt and hindered by the car manufacturers, which initially ridiculed the idea. In 1981 only 2,636 air bag systems were produced.

However, in late 1989 automatic restraint systems became compulsory in all passenger cars in the USA and, while this included automatically fastening seat belts, it seemed that the air bag had at last arrived. By 1992 10 million air-bag-equipped cars had been delivered in the USA. With model year 1994 came the requirement that all new cars produced in the USA had to be fitted with air bags. The next stage will be the compulsory fitting of air bags to both the driver and front passenger sides.

Autoliv introduced its first air bag system in 1990. The first system was designed to meet US requirements where not all states have laws on wearing seat belts. The air bag therefore had to be relatively large. Some of Autoliv's competitors still sell only such systems, including outside the United States. Autoliv has developed a special system (the Eurobag system) for markets where wearing a seat belt is compulsory. In this system the air bags have less volume (but they are still effective) and therefore the price can be kept at a lower level than some of the competitors. In the Eurobag system the air bags are 30–45 litres on the driver's side and 60–100 litres on the passenger's side. Furthermore, the Eurobag system is lighter and less bulky.

An air bag system consists of an electronic control unit and an air bag module. The electronic control unit contains (among other things) a sensor, while the module essentially consists of a gas generator, a nylon bag and a cover for the steering wheel centre or the instrument panel, depending on where the air bag module is placed. Autoliv typically supplies entire systems adapted to individual car models.

The world market for air bags

In 1995, 35 million frontal air bags were sold (see Table 1) compared to just 25 million in 1994. The total world market for air bags and seat belts was US$8 billion. The world market for frontal air bags is expected to be in excess of 75 million by the year 2000. Thus, this part of the market should almost double, but the prices are falling.

The potential market for side air bags is difficult to assess. This is because side-impact air bags will be optional accessories in many cars and not standard equipment – at least initially, until the car producers have had time to evaluate the reaction of the market.

Table 1		The world market for air bags, 1995			
	Production of light vehicles (millions)	% of vehicles equipped with air bags (dual air bags, both driver and passenger)	Total market for frontal air bags (driver + passenger) (millions)	Autoliv's sales (millions)	Autoliv's market share (%)
Europe East West	 2 12	50% with driver's air bag 30% with dual air bags	11	4.4	40
USA	9	95% with driver's air bag 80% with dual air bags	14	0 (only seat belts)	0
Asia Japan Asia (exc. Japan)	 13 5	35% with driver's air bag 25% with dual air bags	8	0.2	2
Others	7	15% with driver's air bag 10% with dual air bags	2	—	—
Total	48		35	4.6	13

Sources: W.J. Trein, *Wirtschaftsordnung, Unternehmensorganisation und internationale Wettbewerbsfähigkeit – Ein intergrativer Ansatz – Dargestellt am Beispeil der Automobilindustrie* (Peter Lang, 1994); EIU, 'The European market passenger car air bags', *Europe's Automotive Components Business*, 3rd quarter, 1995, pp. 52–63.

Table 2	Five years of economic development at Autoliv AB				
	1991	**1992**	**1993**	**1994**	**1995**
Sales (SEKm)	2,691	3,534	5,333	8,947	10,201
Pre-tax profit (SEKm)	93	167	240	680	1,009
Capital employed (SEKm)	838	1,259	1,370	1,234	1,773
Number of employees at 31 December	3,566	4,531	4,392	5,740	6,670

Competitors

Autoliv's major competitors are the American companies TRW and Allied Signal and the Japanese Takata, all of which offer both seat belts and air bags. The American company Morton and the German Petri and MST are also significant competitors in air bags, but they do not offer seat belts. TRW is the biggest supplier of air bags with about 25 per cent of the world market, while Autoliv, Morton and Takata each have about 10–20 per cent of the world market.

Customers

Several of the world's largest car producers are among Autoliv's customers. Autoliv typically accounts for between 25 and 75 per cent of customers' purchases of seat belts and air bags. The contract with the customer usually applies to the entire production run of a particular model.

In development of a new car model, a process that takes several years, Autoliv functions in many cases as a development partner. This means that Autoliv takes the initiative in creating new safety-enhancing products and assumes responsibility for adaptation and evaluation of the systems.

During the last couple of years, Autoliv has shown a strong development in profits and sales (Table 2).

With this positive development Gunnar Bark finishes his presentation of Autoliv's situation in the market for air bags. He would like a discussion of the following, to which you are asked to contribute:

Questions

1. Describe the causes of Autoliv's success by using, among other things, the Porter diamond model.

2. Characterize Autoliv's role as a subsupplier for large car producers.

3. Which strategic alternatives (entry modes) does Autoliv have to strengthen its competitive position outside Europe? Give a conclusion.

Case III.4 Imax Corporation

Globalization of the film business

One morning in 1997 CEO of Imax, Richard L. Gelfond, sees himself quoted in the newspaper in connection with receiving the 1997 Special Academy Award (Oscar) for scientific and technical achievement. He reads: 'Technology is the star of the show. People don't go for a story.' Richard L. Gelfond leans back smiling in his chair, thinking: Imax's advanced technology may carry the company for a while, but for how long? He has often heard criticism of IMAX® films' missing story, but as he says: 'It is too expensive and risky for us to put all our eggs in one basket and hire a major movie star.'

Imax Corporation

The Imax Corporation is involved in a wide variety of out-of-home entertainment business activities. It designs and manufactures projection and sound systems for giant-screen theatres based on a patented technology. The Imax Corporation is the world's largest producer and distributor of films for giant-screen theatres. Another part of the corporation is the IMAX® simulation ride system, which combines giant-screen technology with aspects of an amusement park ride.

History

The Imax system has its roots in EXPO '67 in Montreal, Canada, where multiscreen films were the hit at the fair. A small group of Canadian film-makers/entrepreneurs (Graeme Ferguson, Roman Kroitor and Robert Kerr), who had made some of those popular films, decided to design a new system using a single powerful projector rather than the cumbersome multiple projectors used at that time. The result was the Imax motion picture projection system, which would revolutionize giant-screen cinema. As the Imax screen is about ten times the size of a conventional movie screen – up to eight storeys high – picture quality has to be very good. Thus the IMAX® projection system uses 70 mm/15 perforation film, the largest film frame in motion picture history. The camera is also much

bigger than a conventional movie camera, but for anyone with film experience it is not hard to learn to use the camera.

There are more than 125 films in Imax's film library. Educational and entertaining, these films take viewers where they are unable to go: to explore the hidden secrets of natural wonders like the Grand Canyon, the inside of an atom or the magic of space. The first IMAX 15/70 space film, *The IMAX 15/70 Space Trilogy* (*The Dream is Alive*, *Blue Planet* and *Destiny in Space*), has earned more than $200 million and has been seen by more than 63 million people world-wide. The much acclaimed *Fires of Kuwait* was nominated for an Academy Award in the Feature Documentary category in 1993. Since the première in 1970 more than 550 million people have enjoyed the IMAX® Experience™.

Imax subsidiaries include Ridefilm Corporation, manufacturers and producers of motion simulation theatres or movie rides; Sonics Associates, Inc., world leaders in sound design; and David Keighley Productions/70MM, Inc., award-winning specialists in image quality control and laboratory production and post-production.

Imax Ridefilm (Ridefilm Corporation) was originally founded in 1989 by visionary film-maker and entrepreneur Douglas Trumbull as a privately owned company specializing in the development and production of simulation rides. As early as 1974, Trumbull combined 35 mm film with a flight simulator, creating the world's first movie ride. To simulate the experience of physical movement within a theatre environment, Trumbull synchronized the audio and visual elements of film with a hydraulic motion system which convinced the audience that they were actually flying, diving and accelerating. One of Ridefilm Corporation's new state-of-the-art projects became reality in 1993. *Back to the Future – The Ride*, directed by Douglas Trumbull, premièred in June at Universal Studios, Hollywood. This high-tech attraction is considered by entertainment industry experts to be the paradigm for the film experience of the future.

Currently in development and production are six movie rides to be included in the library of films for the IMAX® *Ridefilm*™ system. In cooperation with Imax, the company provides complete site design and installation supervision services for its film-based simulator attractions, as well as the assembly, integration, service and maintenance of all film, hardware and software components.

IMAX *Ridefilm* simulator systems and films are marketed world-wide to such venues as theme parks, shopping malls, multiplex theatres, festival retail centres, urban entertainment centres, speciality retail chains and other high-traffic locations.

In March 1994, Ridefilm Corporation and the former Trumbull Company, Inc. were purchased by an investment group as part of a transaction involving the acquisition of Imax Corporation, the Toronto-based pioneer and leader in giant-screen, large-format film technology. Ridefilm is now a US-based wholly owned subsidiary of Imax. In June 1994, Imax Corporation became a publicly traded company listed on the Nasdaq Exchange. Douglas Trumbull served as vice-chairman of Imax Corporation and president CEO of Ridefilm Corporation until 1 March 1997, when he left Imax. However, Douglas Trumbull is still involved in projects with Imax.

Business of the company

Generally speaking, the company does not own the IMAX theatres, but rather leases its projection and sound systems and licenses the use of its trade marks. Imax derives revenue principally from theatre system lease agreements, maintenance agreements, film production agreements and distribution of films. Regarding film production, Imax has struck an agreement with ABC, Inc., a Walt Disney Co. subsidiary, to develop IMAX films. Such movies would have greater entertainment value than IMAX's education-oriented productions.

During 1996 Imax signed contracts for 29 IMAX theatre systems valued at a record of nearly $90 million. At the end of 1996 there were 149 Imax theatres in operation in 22 countries with a backlog of 45 theatre systems. Table 1 summarizes revenue, cost and profit figures for Imax Corporation between 1994 and 1996. Table 2 gives an overview of the location of existing IMAX theatres plus a market and product overview.

Table 1	Imax Corporation (US$m)		
	1994	**1995**	**1996**
Revenue			
Systems	37.5	52.0	86.0
Films	30.9	28.8	28.4
Other	6.6	7.7	15.5
Total revenue	75.0	88.5	129.9
Cost and expenses	56.1	44.3	58.3
Gross margin	18.9	44.2	71.6
Other expenses	35.3	35.1	41.0
Earnings before income tax	−16.4	9.1	30.6

Table 2	Overview of existing 149 IMAX theatres				
Geographic location (%) (*n* = 149)		**Market (%) (*n* = 149)**		**Product (%) (*n* = 149)**	
United States	46	Science and natural history	57	2-dimensional	89
Europe	15	Commercial	20	(trend going down)	
Japan	15	Theme parks	15	3-dimensional	11
Canada	9	Destination sites	4	(trend going up)	
Asia (excluding Japan)	7	Zoos and aquaria	3		
Mexico	5	Temporary	1		
Australia	2				
South Africa	1				
	100		100		100

Source: IMAX Annual Report, 1995, 1996.

In 1995 Imax introduced the three-dimensional theatre in which the viewers wear goggles that make it appear that they are inside the film.

At the end of 1996 the total number of IMAX *Ridefilm* theatres in operation was eleven. During 1996 the company signed contracts for 24 IMAX *Ridefilm* systems. As indicated earlier, nearly all of the theatres are owned by someone else, but Imax has started a push to take ownership positions in some of the new theatres and especially in some of the IMAX *Ridefilm* systems.

Building on its business relationship with ITT Corporation, Imax and ITT will joint venture on two IMAX *Ridefilm* systems scheduled to open in December 1996 at ITT's Delta Station at the Tren de la Costa entertainment centre in Buenos Aires, Argentina. Imax and ITT have previously announced a joint venture to operate the world's first large-scale, 3D motion simulator attraction, which is scheduled to open in December 1997 at the Forum Shops at Caesar's Palace in Las Vegas.

Imax has forged an alliance with Japan's Sega Enterprises Ltd to install two IMAX *Ridefilm* systems in Japan, at Sega's high-tech amusement parks in Niigata and Daiba. The IMAX *Ridefilm* system can also be experienced at the Magical World of Fantasy Island, in Lincolnshire, north-east of London. 'The advantages are that it has great economics,' Gelfond says. 'We can charge $5 for a four-minute ride, people seem to love it and it doesn't take up a lot of space.' The drawbacks are that it needs highly populated locations, such as theme parks and casinos.

Questions

1. Suggest a product/market expansion strategy for the Imax Corporation. Give reasons for your suggestion.

2. Discuss the statement: 'Technology is the star of the show. People don't go for a story.'

3. Discuss alternative cooperation strategies with film companies.

4. Can Imax's core competences be transferred to the marketing of high-volume commercial products? Which types of product could these be?

Case III.5 Timex watches

Timed out in India by Titan

Timex USA, the leading low-priced lifestyle watch-maker in the USA, decided in the 1990s to enter India. It chose a joint venture with Titan Industries Ltd., the leading brand of Indian wristwatches and jewelry. The joint venture started with great optimism as a win–win initiative, prospered but soon encountered problems and was finally terminated by early 1998. Timex (India) is now left on its own. Timex is now in a fix. It is a new challenge for Timex in India – one of the biggest emerging markets in Asia.

Timex USA

Timex, a $600 million turnover company in the year 1999, is one of the oldest watchmaking companies in the world and certainly in the USA. In existence now for 150 years, Timex was originally known as Waterbury's clocks. It is located in Connecticut – once known as the 'Switzerland of America' for its multiple watchmaking units and Timex.

Timex has a long tradition of bringing innovations in clock- and watchmaking. Its dalliance with domestic markets began with its introducing Waterbury's clocks. The company aimed to make *timekeeping affordable for all working-class Americans*. The Waterbury shelf and mantel clocks were simple, low-cost and were more like the mass-produced stamped brass movements. They also imitated expensive models. In the next two decades of its existence, Timex introduced the first mechanical pocket watch in 1880. Like its clocks, Waterbury watches were inexpensive. They received enthusiastic acceptance throughout North America and Europe. By the turn of the twentieth century, Timex introduced the 'Yankee' pocket watch, the first watch to cost just one US dollar. With the sale of nearly forty million units, 'Yankee' became the world's largest selling pocket watch attracting all segments and persons ranging from Mark Twain to miners, from farmers to factory workers and from office clerks to sales clerks. Yankee's wristwatch version came into the market when, during the

First World War, the US Army required Waterbury to re-tool the Yankee pocket watch into a convenient new *wristwatch* for soldiers. After the war, returning veterans continued to wear the handy timepiece, and civilians took them up in huge numbers during the 1920s.

During the Second World War, the Waterbury clock assumed a new identity – the U.S. Time Company. The company's wartime expertise in research and development and advanced mass production techniques led to the creation of the world's first low-price mechanical watch movement. The new wristwatch was named Timex. Launched in 1950, print advertisements featured the new watch strapped to Mickey Mantle's bat, frozen in an ice cube tray, spun for seven days in a vacuum-cleaner, taped to a giant lobster's claw, or wrapped around a turtle in a tank to show its quality. By the end of the 1950s, one out of every three watches bought in the US was a Timex. The Timex brand became a household word during the 1960s.

By the 1970s, the US Time Company itself was re-christened as Timex. Having completely conquered the low-priced market, Timex then upgraded and diversified its product line. It introduced 'Cavatina' – its first women's brand in 1959. With this, Timex also introduced a new merchandising concept in watch selling – as an impulse item. Technological advances allowed Timex to offer a wide range of products, including the first low-priced electric watches for men and women, as well as several other, inexpensive jewelled models. In the decade, every other watch bought in the US was a Timex. It retailed in 250,000 different outlets. The decade was also a testing period for all American watch manufacturers. The industry was shaken out by the arrival of a new digital watch technology and by fierce price competition from the Far East. Naturally Timex too was affected. It feverishly searched for a winning brand of its own in digital watches. However, it had to wait until 1986 when finally Timex launched 'Ironman-Triathlon'.

Within a year, the brand became America's best-selling watch and later diversified into a full line for men and women. It became the world's largest selling sports watch.

Leveraging on its ability in negotiating the new digital technology, Timex introduced the industry's first electro-luminescent watch face in 1992, when the blue-green 'Indiglo' night-light feature appeared on some of its digital and analogue watches. Today, more than 75 per cent of all Timex watches are equipped with 'Indiglo'. As the era of information technology dawned, Timex was not found wanting this time. It launched a variety of wristwatches with sophisticated IT. For instance, it launched a brand 'Data Link' which was a sophisticated wrist instrument featuring scheduling, phone numbers, and other personal information. It collaborated with Microsoft to create the necessary software. Its IT-based products include 'Turn and Pull' – an analogue alarm watch, and Beepwear, a new wrist pager developed with Motorola.

Timex is now an established global brand. Annual markets and brands surveys consistently rank Timex as number one out of 50 fashion brands in jewelry and accessories and the third most popular of all women's accessory brands in the world. It employs globally 7,500 employees in all continents. Timex is selling in more than 80 countries and has its own offices in 50 countries. Naturally, as Indian markets were freed in 1991 onwards, Timex wanted to be there.

The India initiative

Timex entered India in 1991 through a company called Timex Watches Ltd. It was a joint venture between Timex USA and Titan Industries Ltd., the leading watchmaker in India. Titan was a part of Tatas, the leading business group of companies in India. The US$10 billion Tata group is highly diversified with business interests in automobiles, steel, power, engineering services and goods, chemicals, telecommunications, information technology, plantations, agro-industries, hotels and consumer goods. The Tatas are internationally known and respected for their ethical business practices – a reputation that has helped the group to enter several international business partnerships. The Titan plant is one of the most sophisticated watchmaking

plants in India, costing over US$100 million in 1986. In 1999, Titan employed over 2,500 employees. Titan manufactures quartz watches with a world-class standard of quality inspection and is currently one of the largest integrated watch and jewelry manufacturers in the world. It also produces over 1,50,000 pieces of jewelry annually in the brand name of Tanishq. Though Titan began with the objective of catering to the Indian markets, it has now grown international. Titan is deemed to be a model corporate citizen in India. It stayed for six years, from 1992–99, as India's most admired company in consumer durables. The zenith of the Titan was in year 2000 when it was voted as the most respected brand in India, ahead of such international names as Coca-Cola, P&G and Pepsi etc. The most liked attributes of Titan are its quality and brand image. Taking all these dimensions into account, Timex aligned itself with Titan.

India provides a curious mix of both good and bad as far as global business is concerned. India is now ranked as the seventh largest country in the world. It has a continuous and documented history from about 2000 BC. Today it is a sovereign, socialist, secular, democratic republic housing one billion inhabitants, second in population only to China. Internationally, India has of late been growing in importance. It is not only a profitable destination for consumer items from the West, it is also considered a good manufacturing base by multinationals. They found India an interesting market to enter after 1991 when the then Narasimha Rao Government pursued a programme of market reforms and economic liberalization. Currently, the annual growth rate of India ranges from 5 to 6 per cent. There has been a steady increase in foreign investment, joint ventures, partnerships, and direct ownership by American, Japanese, and European businesses in India since then. The Clinton administration also recognized these changes and designated India as one of the world's 10 big emerging markets.

The Indian watch market

Indian has traditionally been a basic and functional watch market. As a developing country where 40 per cent of the population still lived below a prosperity cutoff, owning a wristwatch was a luxury for most Indians. The wristwatches were bought as timekeeping, functional devices, not as fashion accessories; the buying attributes for wristwatches were quality and functionality. For most Indians, wristwatches were considerable a durable item good for another 5–8 years or until they broke. Price was a major segment variable in India. For instance, in 1999, watches costing less than Rs 450[1] constituted half of the watch market. Those between Rs 450 and Rs 1,000 constituted another 30 per cent, leaving only a fifth of the market for watches above Rs 1,000. Titan is credited with changing the Indian watch market. Offering premium quartz watches in a variety of styles, Titan succeeded in turning Indian wristwatch buyers into a style-conscious segment.

Timex eyed India for the segment branded as Indian Made Foreign Quartz (IMFQ). Mostly operated as an unorganized sector, demand for IMFQ watches was estimated at 18 million pieces a year. The IMFQ watches were stylish, fashionable, cheap and disposable. The IMFQ category was driven solely by price, with most of the watches falling in the Rs 200–400 price band. Mostly they were bought by children, youngsters and by low-income consumers. As per another estimate, the IMFQ segment accounted for as high as 75 per cent of the informal and fun watch product category in India in 1999. Thus, assuming the total market size to be at 40 million units, the IMFQ watch segment accounted for 20–30 million pieces. The IMFQ players imported watch movements and dials at very cheap prices. With a low-cost, low overhead operation, they were able to sell for as low as Rs 350. As mentioned earlier, the segment was a global forte of Timex.

The joint venture

Timex entered a joint venture with Titan in 1991. A new company was set up as Timex Watches Ltd. Both Timex and Titan held 28.5 per cent in equity. The rest of the equity was in the market and foreign financial institutions (FFIs). The joint venture was billed as a win–win solution to both. For instance, through the joint operation, Timex added to the product line of Titan. Titan was also looking at the

huge potential in the India Made Foreign Quartz (IMFQ) segment. The IMFQ players offered flashy watches and more variety at a much lower price to Indian consumers. Titan, due to its own movements manufacturing, was no match in the IMFQ segment. Timex filled this gap. Titan offered the retailing infrastructure to Timex. Timex also eyed the thriving grey market, then estimated at about 6 million pieces a year.

When the Timex–Titan joint venture came about in 1990, the two partners envisaged distinct roles for themselves. It was decided that Timex, an all-plastic watch, would chiefly operate in the sub-Rs 1,000 segment, and directly compete with the grey market. Since Titan, on the other hand, was positioned as a more premium watch selling upwards of Rs 1,000, it was calculated that it would appeal more to the formal office workers. While the Titan was a watch for special occasions, Timex was a tough, sporty watch for the adventurous. Thus, a lot of planning and care went into building distinct identities for the two brands. It was important to avoid confusion at the retail outlets, which were common for the two brands.

Timex gained on the vast distribution network of Titan shops. The retailing and distribution of Titan included, as Titan claimed, the world's largest chain of exclusive showrooms for watches and jewelry. In 1999, the numbers of Titan retailing outlets exceeded 5,500 and were located in more than 1,500 cities in 33 countries. The exclusive retail network of Titan too was pretty strong. It had two shops – the World of Titan and Time Zones. Up to the end of 1999, the World of Titan was at 107 locations across 68 towns in India. In 1999 Time Zones could be found in 52 Indian cities. All Titan showrooms were artistically designed and offered customer service in a spacious and stylish retail ambience. Since Titan also sold branded jewelry (Tanishq), it set up exclusive Tanishq outlets. These were more exclusive up-market premium show-rooms and provided a rich ethnic Indian buying experience. The network of Tanishq showrooms touched almost every capital town in India and other major towns.

Besides Titan's own retailing network, Timex could use the bigger but traditional and independent stores, thanks to Titan. The Indian partner was

---

[1] Exchange rate in March 2000, 1US$ = Indian Rupees 43.80.

fairly successful in cultivating these independent retailers in India. In fact, Titan is credited with exploding several traditions in Indian watch retailing. Before Titan's arrival, wristwatches in India were never sold in the high streets; the interested buyers had to seek out specialized watch shops. These shops were poorly styled and had virtually no retailing infrastructure and ambience to interest the customers: they wanted to get out of the shop the moment they were done. Titan changed all that: it introduced lifestyle buying. Titan also made its brands available in all those shops where the right segment of customer traffic was assumed to be higher and more frequent (like the general provision stores, cloth shops, electronic shops etc.). These shops were fresh, younger looking and were visited by younger customer and female buyers. Titan also made its brands available in gift stores and departmental stores to position them as gift items and to encourage impulse purchases. To provide its customers easy access to enhanced after-sales service, Titan expanded its network of watch care centres to number over 350 in India and around the world. The influence of Titan on the independent stores was so unmistakable that in 1997, Titan even contemplated levying a 2 per cent royalty on sales at these independent shops. Naturally, Timex hoped that the distribution network would help its watch sales grow all over India. Titan helped Timex in another way too: Titan's retail channel played a crucial role in establishing Timex as a credible brand by keeping it side by side the Titan brand. It was beneficial for Timex in its initial years since an all-plastic watch, which Timex watches were, had a low acceptability in India.

The eventual break-up

The joint venture produced results instantly. Timex sales grew from 0.4 million watches in the first year to 2 million in 1996. It notched a 15 per cent share of the organized market, which translated into a comfortable 25 per cent share of the urban market. However, offtake of Timex was poor in 1997. As Timex retailers started complaining of mounting stocks (stocks worth Rs 400 million or US$ 10 million were lying at the factory at one point in 1996) Timex slashed production drastically, and its prices. It failed to perk up Indian consumers.

There was no doubt that the Indian watch market was flattening out. Titan too was affected during this period. However, the joint venture ran into problems that could have been expected. Their apparent difference was about the size of the market and growth rate pattern of the IMQW market. Market experts, however, attributed the strains to the fundamental mismatch of the cultures of the two. Timex was a price warrior that leveraged on the low-price, high-volume segment world-wide. Titan, on the other hand, produced a formal brand of wristwatches. The Titan showrooms were hardly visited by the Indian masses. Timex argued that Titan's retail channel was not geared to tap the lower end of the market effectively enough to give it large volumes. Whenever Timex looked at the grey market of watches in India (roughly 6–7 million pieces were sold in the India grey markets) it felt that its own brand should have replaced the sales. But Titan showrooms could not penetrate as deep into India as grey marketers did. Timex privately complained that Titan's marketing group, which also handled Timex's marketing, was responsible for flooding the market with Timex watches in 1996. Predictably, the trade receivables grew more unmanageable.

Another problem was the price difference between the two brands. While Timex sold primarily below the Rs 1,000 price level, most of the Titan sales came from the Rs 1,500–3,000 bracket. When the joint venture was forged, it was understood that Titan would gradually move up the price ladder while Timex catered to the lower price segments. However, Titan found it more difficult to win the required volumes for its higher priced watches. Most of its sales still came from the models in the Rs 1,500–3,000 price band. Strains were further added when Titan launched 'PSI2000' – deemed to be a Timex lookalike.

The product positioning of the two was conflicting. Titan watches appealed more as formal wear for office workers and for special occasions. Timex, on the other hand, was positioned as a tough, sporty watch for the adventurous. The alliance also suffered from poor coordination in sales and support. A marketing group within Dealers complained that the engineers from Titan were not trained on Timex movements and were unable to repair Timex watches. Consumers began to perceive Timex as a watch which could not be repaired. The joint venture broke up in early 1998.

Timed out

The break-up had very severe consequences for Timex. In the first full financial year after the break-up, its profits crashed by nearly 80 per cent from the previous US$17 million.

Questions

1. Analyze the working of an international joint venture. What factors determine its success?

2. Review the Timex and Titan break-up. Can it be explained within a conceptual framework?

3. What options does Timex have now?

Prepared by Dr Mohan Lal Agrawal, Professor, Marketing, XLRI Jamshedpur (India) and Associate Professor Svend Hollensen. Inputs for the case were sourced from a variety of public media.

Designing the global marketing programme

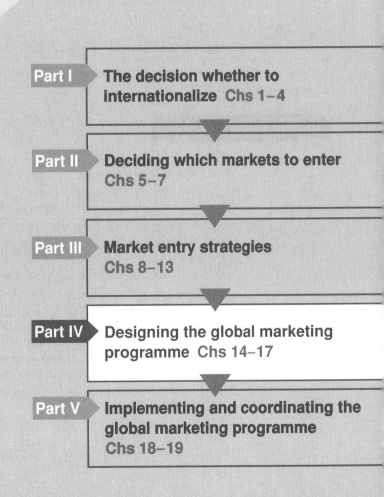

Part I The decision whether to internationalize Chs 1–4

Part II Deciding which markets to enter Chs 5–7

Part III Market entry strategies Chs 8–13

Part IV Designing the global marketing programme Chs 14–17

Part V Implementing and coordinating the global marketing programme Chs 18–19

Part IV Cases

Introduction

Once the firm has decided how it will enter the international market(s) (Part III), the next issue is how to design the global marketing mix.

Since the beginning of the 1980s, the term 'globalization' has increasingly become a matter of debate. Levitt's contribution on 'The globalization of markets' (Levitt, 1983) provoked much controversy concerning the most appropriate way for companies to become international. Levitt's support of the globalization strategy received both support and criticism. Essentially, the two sides of this debate represented local marketing versus global marketing and focused on the central question of whether a standardized, global marketing approach or a country-specific differentiated marketing approach has the most merits. In Part IV we learn that there are different forces in the international environment that may favour either 'increasing globalization' or 'increasing adaptation' of a firm. The starting point is illustrated by the existing balance-point on the scale illustrated in Figure 1. Which force will win not only depends on the environmental forces but also on the specific international marketing strategy that the firm might favour. Figure 2 shows the extremes of these two strategies.

Hence, a fundamental decision that managers have to make regarding their global marketing strategy is the degree to which they should standardize or adapt their global marketing mix. The following three factors provide vast opportunities

Figure 1

Environmental factors influencing the balance between standardization and adaptation

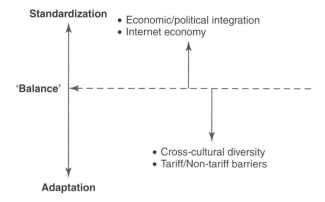

Figure 2

Standardization and adaptation of the international marketing mix

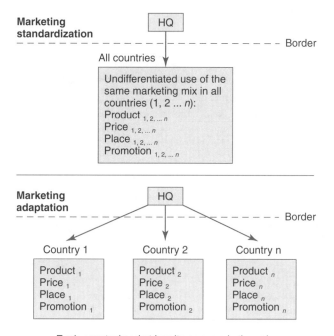

for marketing standardization (Meffert and Bolz, 1993):

● *Globalization of markets*. Customers are increasingly operating on a world-wide basis and are characterized by an intensively coordinated and centralized purchasing process. As a countermeasure, manufacturers establish a global key account management in order to avoid individual country subsidiaries being played off against each other in separate negotiations with, for example, global retailers.

391

- *Globalization of industries.* Many firms can no longer depend on home markets for sufficient scale economies and experience curve effects. Many industries, such as computers, pharmaceuticals and automobiles, are characterized by high R & D costs which can be recouped only via world-wide high-volume sales.

- *Globalization of competition.* As a consequence of the world-wide homogenization of demand, the different markets are interrelated. Therefore the firms can plan their activities on a world-wide scale and attempt to establish a superior profile *vis-à-vis* other global competitors. Hence, country subsidiaries no longer operate as profit centres, but are viewed as parts of a global portfolio.

The standardized marketing concept can be characterized by two features:

- Standardization of marketing processes is mainly concerned with a standardized decision-making process for cross-country marketing planning. By standardization of the launching of new products, controlling activities, etc., rationalization of the general marketing process is sought.

- Standardization of marketing programmes and the marketing mix is concerned with the extent to which individual elements of the 4 Ps can be unified into a common approach for different national markets.

| Figure 3 | Analysis of a company's standardization potential |

- Standardization profile of a special disposable nappy (e.g. Pampers)
- Standardization profile of a special hard drink (e.g. Johnny Walker)

(Source: Adapted from Kreutzer, 1988. Reproduced with kind permission from MCB University Press; http//www.mcb.co.uk)

Table 1   **Main factors favouring standardization versus adaptation**

Factors favouring standardization	Factors favouring adaptation
Economies of scale in R & D, production and marketing (experience curve effects)	Local environment-induced adaptation: government and regulatory influences (no experience curve effects)
Global competition	Local competition
Convergence of tastes and consumer needs (consumer preferences are homogeneous)	Variation in consumer needs (consumer needs are heterogeneous)
Centralized management of international operations	Fragmented and decentralized management with independent country subsidiaries
A standardized concept is used by competitors	An adapted concept is used by competitors

These two characteristics of standardization are often interrelated: for many strategic business units, process-oriented standardization is the precondition for the implementation of standardized marketing programmes.

Many writers discuss standardization and adaptation as two distinct options. The commercial reality, however, is that few marketing mixes are totally standardized or adapted. Instead it is more relevant to discuss degrees of standardization. Therefore Figure 3 shows a standardization-potential profile for two different products by the same company (Procter & Gamble).

The results indicate that there are different ways of realizing a standardized concept within the marketing mix. In the case of both products it is possible to standardize the package at least on an average level. Difficulties arise as far as the price policy is concerned. Here it is possible to reach a standardized price positioning only for disposable nappies. So Procter & Gamble selects only those markets that possess the necessary purchasing power to pay a price within the target price range. In the case of hard drinks, it is nearly impossible to gain a standardized price positioning due to legal constraints. In Denmark, for example, consumers have to pay twice as much for the same Johnny Walker whisky as in Germany because of tax regulations. In many cases it is possible to use one brand name on a world-wide basis. There are negative effects connected with particular names in only a few cases; you have to change brand names to avoid these unintentional images.

We end this introduction to Part IV by listing in Table 1 the main factors favouring standardization versus adaptation of the global marketing programme.

References

Kreutzer, R. (1988) 'Standardisation: an integrated approach in global marketing', *European Journal of Marketing*, vol. 22, no. 10, pp. 19–30.

Levitt, T. (1983) 'The globalization of markets', *Harvard Business Review*, May–June, pp. 92–102.

Meffert, H. and Bolz, J. (1993) 'Standardization of marketing in Europe', in Halliburton, C. and Hünerberg, R. (eds) *European Marketing: Readings and cases*, Addison Wesley, Wokingham, England.

Chapter 14

Product decisions

After studying this chapter you should be able to do the following:

● Discuss the influences that lead a firm to standardize or adapt its products.

● Explore how international service strategies are developed.

● Distinguish the product life cycle (PLC) and international product life cycle (IPLC).

● Discuss the challenge of developing new products for foreign markets.

● Explain and illustrate the alternatives in the product communication mix.

● Define and explain the different branding alternatives.

● Explain what is meant by a green product.

● Discuss alternative environmental management strategies.

● Define and explain the different standards of ISO 9000.

14.1 Introduction

The product decision is among the first decisions that a marketing manager makes in order to develop a global marketing mix. This chapter examines product-related issues and suggests conceptual approaches for handling them. Also discussed are international brand (labelling) strategies and service policies.

14.2 The dimensions of the international product offer

In creating an acceptable product offer for international markets, it is necessary to examine first what contributes to the 'total' product offer. Kotler (1997) suggests five levels of the product offer, which should be considered by marketers in order to make the product attractive to the international markets. In the product dimensions of Figure 14.1 we include not just the core physical properties, but also

Figure 14.1   **The three levels of a product**

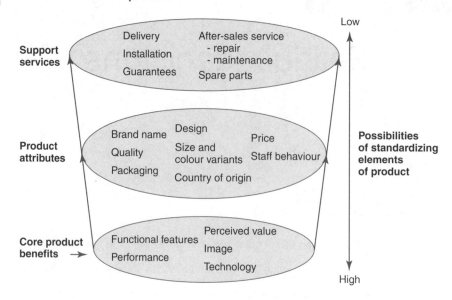

additional elements such as packaging, branding and after-sales service that make up the total package for the purchaser.

We can also see from Figure 14.1 that it is much easier to standardize the core product benefits (functional features, performance, etc.) than it is to standardize the support services, which often have to be tailored to the business culture and sometimes to individual customers.

Exhibit 14.1   **Exporting Belarus tractors to North America: adding value to the product**

When exporting eastern European products to North America, product modifications are often required. Take the tractor-maker Belarus Machinery, which has annual US sales of $50 million. Once a tractor is shipped to North America, its journey has only just begun. Painting is redone, electrical systems are upgraded and American-made hydraulics are added. 'Our job is to bring the product up to American standards,' says Eldrid Muehlhausen, manager of operations. 'All in all, we add about 30 per cent of the value to the tractor right here in Milwaukee.'

Source: Tomesco (1995), p. 34. Reproduced with permission from Business Central Europe.

14.3   **Developing international service strategies**

We have seen from the definition of a product that services often accompany products, but products are also an increasingly important part of our international economy in their own right. As Figure 14.2 shows, the mix of product and service elements may vary substantially.

Figure 14.2   Scale of elemental dominance

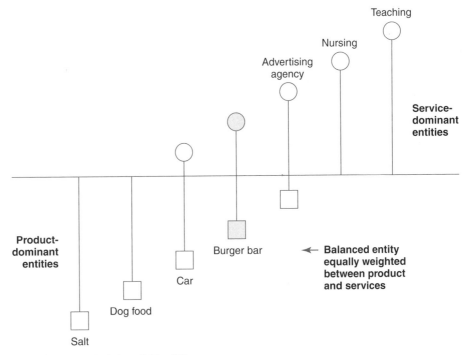

(Source: Czinkota and Ronkainen, 1995, p. 526)

Characteristics of services

Before considering possible international service strategies, it is important to consider the special nature of global service marketing. Services are characterized by the following features:

● *Intangibility*. As services like air transportation or education cannot be touched or tested, the buyers of services cannot claim ownership or anything tangible in the traditional sense. Payment is for use or performance. Tangible elements of the service, such as food or drink on airlines, are used as part of the service in order to confirm the benefit provided and to enhance its perceived value.

● *Perishability*. Services cannot be stored for future usage – for example, unfilled airline seats are lost once the aircraft takes off. This characteristic causes considerable problems in planning and promotion in order to match supply and demand. To maintain service capacity constantly at levels necessary to satisfy peak demand will be very expensive. The marketer must therefore attempt to estimate demand levels in order to optimize the use of capacity.

● *Heterogeneity*. Services are rarely the same because they involve interactions between people. Furthermore, there is high customer involvement in the production of services. This can cause problems of maintaining quality, particularly in international markets where there are quite different attitudes towards customer service.

- *Inseparability*. The time of production is very close to or even simultaneous with the time of consumption. The service is provided at the point of sale. This means that economies of scale and experience curve benefits are difficult to achieve, and supplying the service to scattered markets can be expensive, particularly in the initial setting-up phase.

Global marketing of services

There are some specific problems in marketing services internationally. There are particular difficulties in achieving uniformity of the different marketing parameters in remote locations where exerting control can be especially problematic. Pricing, too, can be extremely difficult, because fixed costs can be a very significant part of the total service costs. Consumers' ability to buy and their perceptions of the service they receive may vary considerably between markets, resulting in significantly different prices being set and profits generated. Moreover, preserving customer loyalty in order to obtain repeat business may prove difficult because of the need to provide personalized services.

Categories of service

All products, both goods and services, consist of a core element that is surrounded by a variety of optional supplementary elements. If we look first at the core service products, we can assign them to one of three broad categories depending on their tangibility and the extent to which customers need to be physically present during service production. These categories are presented in Table 14.1.

Categories of supplementary service

The core service provider, whether a bed for the night or a bank account, is typically accompanied by a variety of supplementary elements, which can be grouped into eight categories (Lovelock and Yip, 1996):

- *Information*. To obtain full value from any good or service, customers need relevant information about it, ranging from schedules to operating instructions, and from user warnings to prices. Globalization affects the nature of that information (including the languages and format in which it is provided). New customers and prospects are especially information hungry and may need training in how to use an unfamiliar service.

- *Consultation and advice*. Consultation and advice involve a dialogue to probe customer requirements and then develop a tailored solution. Customers' need for advice may vary widely around the world, reflecting such factors as level of economic development, nature of the local infrastructure, topography and climate, technical standards and educational levels.

- *Order taking*. Once customers are ready to buy, suppliers need to make it easy for them to place orders or reservations in the language of their choice, through telecommunications and other channels, at times and in locations that are convenient to them.

Table 14.1   Three categories of service

Categories of service	Characteristics	Examples (service provider)	Possibilities of world-wide standardization (hence utilizing economies of scale, experience effects, lower costs)
People processing	Customers become part of the production process. The service firm needs to maintain local geographic presence.	Education (schools universities). Passenger transportation (airlines, car rent). Health care (hospitals). Food service (fast food, restaurants). Lodging service (hotel).	No good possibilities: because of 'customer involvement in production', many local sites will be needed, making this type of service very difficult to operate globally.
Possesion processing	Involve tangible actions to physical objects so to improve their value to customers. The object needs to be involved in the production process, but the owner of the object (the customer) does not. A local geographic presence is required.	Car repair (garages). Freight transport (forwarding agent). Equipment installation (e.g. electrician). Laundry service (laundrette).	Better possibilities: compared to people-processing services, this involves a lower degree of contact between the customer and the service personnel. This type of service is not so culture-sensitive.
Information-based services	Collecting, manipulating, interpreting and transmitting data to create value. Minimal tangibility. Minimal customer involvement in the production process.	Telecommunication services (telephone companies). Banking. News. Market analysis. Internet services (producers of homepages on www, database providers).	Very good possibilities: of world-wide standardization from one central location (single sourcing) because of the 'virtual' nature of these services.

- *Hospitality: taking care of the customer.* Well-managed businesses try, at least in small ways, to treat customers as guests when they have to visit the supplier's facilities (especially when, as is true for many people-processing operations, the period extends over several hours or more). Cultural definitions of appropriate hospitality may differ widely from one country to another, such as the tolerable length of waiting time (much longer in Brazil than in Germany) and the degree of personal service expected (not much in Scandinavia, but lavish in Indonesia).

- *Safekeeping: looking after the customer's possessions.* When visiting a service site, customers often want assistance with their personal possessions, ranging from car parking to packaging and delivery of new purchases. Expectations may vary by country, reflecting culture and levels of affluence.

- *Exceptions.* Exceptions fall outside the routine of normal service delivery. They include special requests, problem solving, handling of complaints/suggestions/compliments, and restitution (compensating customers for performance failures). Special requests are particularly common in people-processing services, such as in the travel and lodging industries, and may be complicated by differing cultural norms. International airlines, for example, find it necessary to respond to an array of medical and dietary needs, sometimes reflecting religious and cultural values. Problem solving is often more difficult for people who are travelling overseas than it would be in the familiar environment of their native country.

● *Billing*. Customers need clear, timely bills that explain how charges are computed. With abolition of currency exchange restrictions in many countries, bills can be converted to the customer's home currency. Hence, currencies and conversion rates need to be clarified on billing statements. In some instances, prices may be displayed in several currencies, even though this policy may require frequent adjustments in the light of currency fluctuations.

● *Payment*. Ease and convenience of payment (including credit) are increasingly expected by customers when purchasing a broad array of services. Major credit cards and travellers' checks solve the problem of paying in foreign funds for many retail purchases, but corporate purchasers may prefer to use electronic fund transfers in the currency of their choice.

Copyright © 1996, by the Regents of the University of California. Reprinted from *California Management Review*, vol. 38, no. 2. By permission of the Regents.

Not every core service is surrounded by all eight supplementary elements. In practice, the nature of the product, customer requirements and competitive pressures help to determine which supplementary service must be offered. In many cases the provider of the supplementary services can be located in one part of the world and the services delivered electronically to another.

For example, order taking/reservations and payment can be handled through telecommunication channels, ranging from voice telephone to the world-wide web (www). As long as appropriate languages are available, many such service elements could be delivered from almost anywhere.

In summary, the information-based services offer the best opportunities of global standardization. The two other types of service (people processing and possession processing) both suffer from their inability to transfer competitive advantages across borders. For example, when Euro Disneyland in Paris opened, Disney suffered from not being able to transfer the highly motivated staff of its US parks to Europe.

The accelerating development within information technology (Internet/www) has resulted in the appearance of new types of information service (e.g. information on international flight schedules), which offer great opportunities for standardization.

Service in the business-to-business market

Business-to-business markets differ from customer markets in many ways:

● Fewer and larger buyers, often geographically concentrated.
● A derived, fluctuating and relatively inelastic demand.
● Many participants in the buying process.
● Professional buyers.

- A closer relationship.
- Absence of intermediaries.
- Technological links.

For services in consumer markets, an alternative for dissatisfied consumers is always to exit from the supplier–consumer relationship, as the number of firms offering the same kind of products is usually high. Therefore it is easy to switch between products and firms.

In the business-to-business market, however, bonds between the buyer and seller make the firms more unwilling to break the relationship. Of course, the exit opportunity also exists to some extent in the business-to-business market, but the loss of investment in bonds and commitment tends to create exit barriers, because the costs of changing supplier are high. Furthermore, it can be difficult to find a new supplier.

Professional service firms, like consulting engineering firms, have similarities with typical business-to-business service firms, but they involve a high degree of customization and have a strong component of face-to-face interaction. The service frequently takes the form of a hundred-million-dollar project and is characterized by the development of long-term relationships between firms, but also the management of day-to-day relations during the project. When a professional service firm (whether it be an accountant, architect, engineer or management consultant) sells to its clients, it is less the services of the firm than the services of specific individuals that it is selling. As a consequence, professional service firms require highly skilled individuals.

Filiatrault and Lapierre (1997) made a study of the cultural differences in consulting engineering projects between Europe (France) and North America (Canada). In North America the consulting engineering firms are generally smaller and they work in an economic environment closer (than in Europe) to pure competition. The contracts in Europe are very large and often awarded by government. The French consultants recognize that there is more flexibility in managing in North America than in Europe. Subcontracting also appears to be more popular in North America.

14.4 ❚ The product life cycle

The concept of the product life cycle (PLC) provides useful inputs into making product decisions and formulating product strategies.

Products, like individuals, pass through a series of stages. Each stage is identified by its sales performance and characterized by different levels of profitability, various degrees of competition and distinctive marketing programmes. The four stages of the product life cycle are introduction, growth, maturity and decline. The basic model of the PLC is shown in Figure 14.3.

The PLC emphasizes the need to review marketing objectives and strategies as products pass through various stages. It is helpful to think of marketing decisions during the lifetime of a product, but managers need to be aware of the limitations of the PLC so they are not misled by its prescriptions.

Figure 14.3 **Product life cycle**

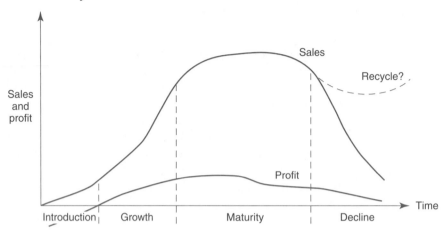

Limitations of the product life cycle

Misleading strategy prescriptions

The PLC is a dependent variable which is determined by the marketing mix; it is not an independent variable to which firms should adapt their marketing programmes (Dhalla and Yuspeh, 1976). If a product's sale is declining, management should not conclude that the brand is in the decline stage. If management withdraws marketing resources from the brand, it will create a self-fulfilling prophecy and the brand's sales will continue to decline. Instead, management might increase marketing support in order to create a recycle (see Figure 14.3). This could be realized by use of one or more of the following measures:

● Product improvements (e.g. new product packaging).
● Reposition perception of the product.
● Reach new users of the product (via new distribution outlets).
● Promote more frequent use of the product (fulfilling same need).
● Promote new uses of the product (fulfilling new needs).

Fads

Not all products follow the classic PLC curve. Fads are fashions that are adopted very quickly by the public, peak early and decline very fast. It is difficult to predict whether something will be only a fad, or how long it will last. The amount of mass-media attention together with other factors will influence the fad's duration.

Unpredictability

The duration of the PLC stages is unpredictable. Critics charge that markets can seldom tell what stage the product is in. A product may appear to be mature when actually it has only reached a temporary plateau prior to another upsurge.

Levels of product life cycle

The PLC concept can be examined at various levels, from the life cycle of a whole industry or product form (the technological life cycle or TLC) (Popper and Buskirk, 1992) to the life cycle of a single model of a specific product. It is probably most useful to think in terms of the life cycle of a product form such as photocopiers or video cassette recorders (see Exhibit 14.2). Life cycles for product forms include definable groups of direct and close competitors and a core technology. These characteristics make life cycles for product forms easier to identify and analyze, and would seem to have more stable and general implications. In Figure 14.4 an example of different PLC levels is shown.

| Exhibit 14.2 | **The global VHS/Betamax contest in the VCR business** |

Figure 14.4 shows that the Betamax-format introduced by Sony lost ground when the VHS standard (introduced by JVC) was adopted world-wide as the VCR diffused into global markets. The VHS/Betamax contest was a fight to the death by two virtually equal but incompatible formats. Market forces decided that there was room for only one successful format. Product performance was apparently not the crucial factor in the outcome, as an independent test found little difference between Betamax and VHS, in, for example, picture and sound quality. However, JVC was quicker than Sony to add features that consumers could immediately see the value of, such as longer recording and extended delay times. In promoting Betamax, Sony evidently created an awareness of VCRs from which VHS subsequently benefited. The fierce competition between the formats (resulting in lower prices) accelerated total VCR sales. Today the VHS system is in the late maturity stage and a new digital VCR system has been introduced.

| Figure 14.4 | **Comparisons of PLCs for product forms (technological life cycles, TLCs) and a single product model: example with different VCR systems** |

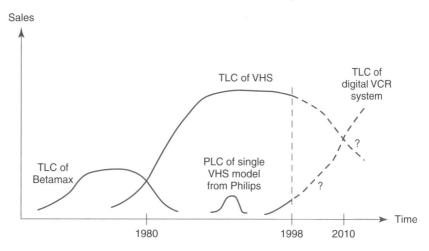

Another example of a TLC shift happened when the compact disc (CD) format was introduced as a result of a joint development between Philips and Sony. A key factor in the success of the CD format displacing the old LP record format was the ownership by Sony of CBS in the USA, and by Philips of Polygram in Europe, two of the biggest music software companies in the world. This contributed to the new CD format establishing itself as the industry standard. However, there were also a number of barriers to the adoption of the new format. The potential users had already invested in LP record collections and the prices of discs and players were relatively high at the beginning of the TLC.

Product life cycles for different products of the firm

So far in this chapter we have treated products as separate, distinct entities. However, many firms are multiproduct, serving multimarkets. Some of these products are 'young' and some are 'older'. Young products will require investment to finance their growth, others will generate more cash than they need. Somehow firms have to decide how to spread their limited resources among the competing needs of products so as to achieve the best performance of the firm as a whole. Figure 14.5 shows an example of a company (British Leyland) which did not succeed in achieving a balanced product portfolio (note that the PLC curves are represented by profit and not sales).

Product life cycles for different countries

When expanding the concept of the PLC to international markets two different approaches appear:

● International product life cycle (IPLC): a macroeconomic approach.
● PLCs across countries: a microeconomic approach.

The international product life cycle

The IPLC theory (originally Vernon, 1966) describes the diffusion process of an innovation across national boundaries (Figure 14.6). For each curve, net export results when the curve is above the horizontal line; if the curve is below the horizontal line, net import results for a particular country.

Typically, demand first grows in the innovating country (here the USA). In the beginning, excess production in the innovating country (greater than domestic demand) will be exported to other advanced countries, where demand also grows. Only later does demand begin in less developed countries (LDCs). Production, consequently, takes place first in the innovating country. As the product matures and technology is diffused, production occurs in other industrialized countries and then in less developed countries. Efficiency/comparative advantages shift from developed countries to developing countries. Finally, advanced countries, no longer cost-effective, import products from their former customers.

Figure 14.5 **Situation of British Leyland in the late 1970s**

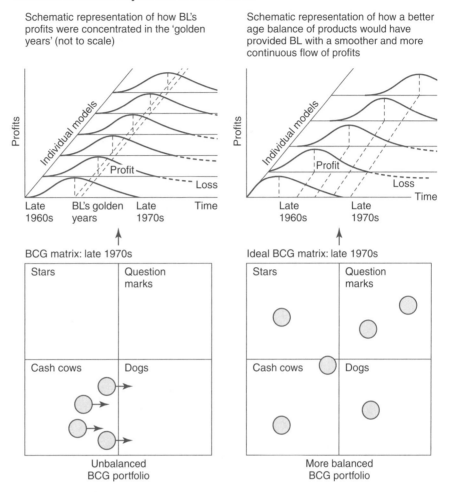

Schematic representation of how BL's profits were concentrated in the 'golden years' (not to scale)

Schematic representation of how a better age balance of products would have provided BL with a smoother and more continuous flow of profits

(Partly reprinted from McNamee (1984), with permission from Elsevier Science Ltd, The Boulevard, Langford Lane, Kidlington OX5 1G, UK)

Examples of typical IPLCs can be found in the textile industry and the computer/software industry. For example, many software programs today are made in Bangalore, India.

Product life cycles across countries: a microeconomic approach

In foreign markets, the time span for a product to pass through a stage may vary from market to market. In addition, due to different economic levels in different countries, a specific product can be in different PLC stages in different countries. Figure 14.7 shows that the product (at a certain time, t_1) is in the decline stage in the home market, while it is in the maturity stage for country A and in the introduction stage for country B.

Figure 14.6 **IPLC curves**

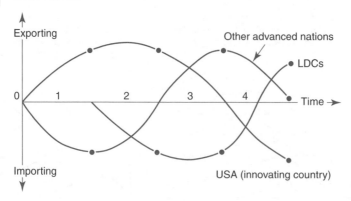

(Source: Onkvisit and Shaw, 1993, p. 483. Reprinted by permission of Prentice-Hall, Inc.)

Figure 14.7 **PLCs of different countries for a specific product**

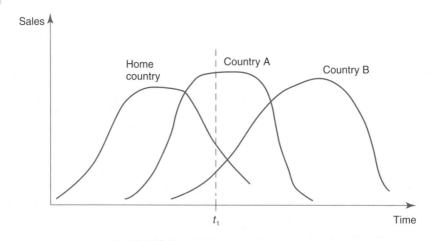

14.5 New products for the international market

Customer needs are the starting point for product development, whether for domestic or global markets. In addition to customer needs, conditions of use and ability to buy the product form a framework for decisions on new product development for international markets.

Developing new products/cutting the time to market

As a consequence of increasing international competition, time is becoming a key success factor for an increasing number of companies which manufacture technologically sophisticated products. This time competition and the level of technological development mean that product life cycles are getting shorter and shorter (see Figure 14.8).

In parallel to shorter PLCs, the product development times for new products are being greatly reduced. As can be seen from Table 14.2, this applies not only to technical products in the field of office communication equipment, but also to cars and consumer electronics. In some cases there have been reductions in development times of more than half.

Similarly, the time for marketing/selling, and hence also for R & D cost to pay off, has gone down from about four years to only two years. This new situation is illustrated in Figure 14.9.

For all types of technological product it holds true that the manufactured product must be as good as required by the customer (i.e. as good as necessary), but not as good as technically feasible. Too frequently, technological products are over-optimized and therefore too expensive from the customer's point of view.

| Figure 14.8 | Gillette's product life cycles are getting shorter |

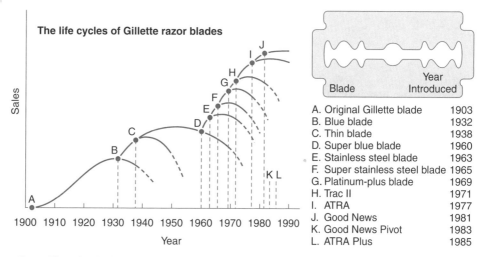

(Source: Zikmund and D'Amico, 1989, p. 247. Reprinted by permission of John Wiley & Sons, Inc.)

| Table 14.2 | Development times of new products |

Company	Product	Development time in years	
		1980	1990
Rank Xerox	Copiers	5	3
Brother	Printers	4	2
Hewlett Packard	Printers	4.5	2
Apple	Computers	3.5	1
Volvo	Trucks	7	5.5
Honda	Cars	8	3
AT&T	Telephone systems	2	1
Sony	Television Sets	2	0.75

Source: Töpfer (1995), p. 68. Reprinted from Elsevier Science Ltd, The Boulevard, Longford Lane, Kedlington, OX5 1GB, UK

Figure 14.9 **Compression of R & D cycles and product life cycles**

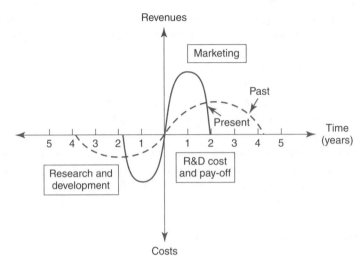

(Source: Töpfer, 1995, p. 64. Reprinted with permission from Elsevier Science Ltd, The Boulevard, Langford Lane, Kidlington, OX5 1GD, UK)

As we have indicated in earlier chapters, Japanese and European suppliers to the car industry have different approaches to the product development process. Figure 14.10 shows an example with suppliers of dashboard instruments for cars. The two Japanese manufacturers start the engineering design phase two years later than the European manufacturer. This enables the Japanese fully to develop a product in a shorter time using the newest technology and to launch it almost simultaneously with their competitors.

Figure 14.10 **Development and test periods for suppliers to the car industry**

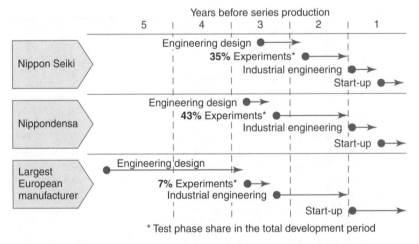

(Source: Töpfer, 1995, p. 72. Reprinted with permission from Elsevier Science Ltd, The Boulevard, Langford Lane, Kidlington, OX5 1GB, UK)

The reason for the better time competition of the Japanese manufacturers is the intensive use of the following measures:

● Early integration of customers and suppliers.

● Multiskilled project teams.

● Interlinking of R & D, production and marketing activities.

● Total quality management.

● Parallel planning of new products and the required production facilities (simultaneous engineering).

● High degree of outsourcing (reduction of internal manufacturing content).

Today product quality is not enough to reach and to satisfy the customer. Quality of design and appearance play an increasingly important role. A highly qualified product support and customer service is also required.

Degrees of product newness

A new product can have several degrees of newness. A product may be an entirely new invention (new to the world) or it may be a slight modification of an existing product. In Figure 14.11 newness has two dimensions: newness to the market (consumers, channels and public policy) and newness to the company. The risk of

Figure 14.11   **Different degrees of product newness**

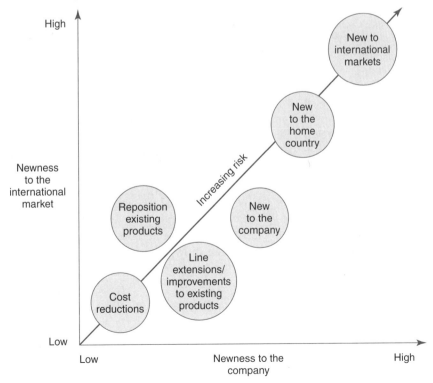

market failure also increases with the newness of the product. Hence, the greater the newness of the product, the greater the need for a thorough internal company and external environment analysis, in order to reduce the risk involved. Exhibit 14.3 describes an example of brand extension.

Exhibit 14.3 | **Mars: brand extensions**

One company that has been successful with the extension of its brand name is Mars. It developed a strong brand name and image with Mars chocolate confectionery and then stretched the name into a Mars drink and Mars ice-cream. The Mars bar ice-cream was introduced on to the UK market in 1988, and rolled out in fifteen countries in Europe and in the USA the following year. The company had been experimenting with ice-cream products for a number of years, finally choosing the UK as a test market for the new product. The product was priced at a premium level above then existing hand-held ice-cream products. The ice-cream concept was later applied to other Mars confectionery products, which were subsequently introduced around Europe. At the turn of the decade, retail sales of Mars ice-cream in Europe were estimated at £200 million. The combined sales of the Mars bar chocolate bar and the Mars bar ice-cream had increased by about one-third.

Source: MacNamee and McDonnell (1995), pp. 113–14.

The product communication mix

Having decided upon the optimum standardization/adaptation route and the newness of the product, the next most important (and culturally sensitive) factor to be considered is that of international promotion.

Product and promotion go hand in hand in foreign markets and together are able to create or destroy markets in very short order. We have considered above the factors which may drive an organization to standardize or adapt its product range for foreign markets. Equally important are the promotion or the performance promises which the organization makes for its product or service in the target market. As with product decisions, promotion can be either standardized or adapted for foreign markets.

Keegan (1995) has highlighted the key aspects of marketing strategy as a combination of standardization or adaptation of the product and promotion of elements of the mix, and offers five alternative and more specific approaches to product policy. These approaches are shown in Figure 14.12.

Straight extension

This involves introducing a standardized product with the same promotion strategy throughout the world market (one product, one message world-wide). By applying this strategy successfully, major savings can be made on market research and product development. Since the 1920s, Coca-Cola has adopted a global approach, which has allowed the company to make enormous cost savings and benefits from

Figure 14.12 **Product/communication mode**

		Product		
		Standard	*Adapt*	*New*
Promotion	*Standard*	Straight extension	Product adaptation	Product invention
	Adapt	Promotion adaptation	Dual adaptation	

(Source: Adapted from Keegan, 1995. With permission of Prentice-Hall, Inc.)

continual reinforcement of the same message. While a number of writers have argued that this will be the strategy adopted for many products in the future, in practice only a handful of products might claim to have achieved this already. A number of firms have tried and failed. Campbell's soups, for example, found that consumers' taste in soup was by no means international.

An example of successful extension is Unilever's world-wide introduction of Organics Shampoo, which was first launched in Thailand in late 1993 after joint development work by Unilever's Hair Innovation Centres in Bangkok and Paris. By 1995 the brand was sold in over 40 countries, generating sales of £170 million. Plate 7 shows a two-page advertisement from a magazine, used during the product's introduction into Argentina. The basic advertising concept all over the world (including Argentina) has been 'Organics – the first ever root-nourishing shampoo'.

Promotion adaptation

Use of this strategy involves leaving a product unchanged but fine-tuning promotional activity to take into account cultural differences between markets. It is a relatively cost-effective strategy as changing promotion messages is not as expensive as adapting products. An example of this strategy is given in Plate 8, which shows Motorola's cellular phone advertisement for the Korean market. An advertising campaign for the south-east Asian market was developed in Singapore. However, the advertising proposal from Singapore was redeveloped in Korea. A juggler was switched to a well-known Korean drummer as it was thought to be more familiar and appealing to Korean consumers. The English translation of the original Korean script is as follows:

Only those who challenge the limits can open the new world of possibilities

Percussionist Kim Dae Hwan challenges the boundaries of performance technique and creates a new world of sound that no one previously has imagined. We sometimes meet situations in our lives which seem too difficult to overcome, but with our constant challenging spirit, we can certainly overcome them. Motorola Cellular constantly challenges the boundaries of technology. We create the new world of cellular technology which no one could have thought possible by creating smaller and lighter cellular phones. The new world of cellular phones, a result of our challenging spirit, helps many of us in the world to accomplish more in our lives. Rest assured, only those who challenge the limits can open the new world of possibilities.

Motorola. A world you never thought possible.

Product adaptation

By modifying only the product, a manufacturer intends to maintain the core product function in the different markets. For example, electrical appliances have to be modified to cope with different electrical voltages in different countries. A product can also be adapted to function under different physical environmental conditions. Exxon changed the chemical composition of petrol to cope with the extremes of climate, but still used the 'Put a tiger in your tank' campaign unchanged around the world.

Dual adaptation

By adapting both products and promotion for each market, the firm is adopting a totally differentiated approach. This strategy is often adopted by firms when one of the previous three strategies has failed, but particularly if the firm is not in a leadership position and is therefore reacting to the market or following competitors. It applies to the majority of products in the world market. The modification of both product and promotion is an expensive but often necessary strategy.

An example of dual adaptation is shown in Plate 9, with the launching of Kellogg's Basmati Flakes in the nascent breakfast cereal market in India. This product was specially created to suit Indian tastes, India being a large rice-eating country. The advertising campaign was a locally adapted concept based on international positioning. Please note that the product is available only in the Bombay area.

Product invention

Product invention is adopted by firms usually from advanced nations which are supplying products to less developed countries. Products are specifically developed to meet the needs of the individual markets. Existing products may be too technologically sophisticated to operate in less developed countries, where power supplies may be intermittent and local skills limited. Keegan (1995) uses a hand-powered washing machine as a product example.

14.6　Product positioning

Product positioning is a key element in the successful marketing of any organization in any market. The product or company which does not have a clear position in the customer's mind consequently stands for nothing and is rarely able to command more than a simple commodity or utility price. Premium pricing and competitive advantage are largely dependent upon the customer's perception that the product or service on offer is markedly different in some way from competitive offers. How can we achieve a credible market position in international markets?

Since it is the buyer/user perception of benefit-generating attributes that is important, product positioning is the activity by which a desirable 'position' in the mind of the customer is created for the product. Positioning a product for international markets begins with describing specific products as different attributes which are capable of generating a flow of benefits to buyers and users.

The global marketing planner puts together these attributes into bundles so that the benefits generated match the special requirements of specific market segments. This product design problem involves not only the basic product components (physical, package, service and country of origin) but also brand name, styling and similar features.

Viewed in a multidimensional space (commonly denoted as 'perceptual mapping'), a product can be graphically represented as a point specified by its attributes. The location of a product's point in perceptual space is its 'position'. Competitors' products are similarly located (see also Johansson and Thorelli, 1985). If points representing other products are close to the point of the prototype, then these other products are close competitors to the prototype. If the prototype is positioned away from its closest competitors in some international markets and its positioning implies important features for customers, then it is likely to have a significant competitive advantage.

Country-of-origin effects

The country of origin of a product, typically communicated by the phrase 'made in [country]', has a considerable influence on the quality perception of that product. Some countries have a good reputation and others have a bad reputation for certain products. For example, Japan and Germany have good reputations for producing cars. The country-of-origin effects are especially critical among eastern European consumers. A study (Ettensén, 1993) examined the brand decision for televisions among Russian, Polish and Hungarian consumers. These consumers evaluated domestically produced television products much lower than western-made products, regardless of brand name. There was a general preference for televisions manufactured in Japan, Germany and the USA.

The country of origin is more important than the brand name and can be viewed as good news for western firms that are attempting to penetrate the eastern European region with imports whose brand name is not yet familiar. Another study (Johansson et al., 1994) showed that some products from eastern Europe have done well in the West, despite negative country-of-origin perceptions. For example, Belarus tractors have sold well in Europe and the United States not only because of their reasonable price, but also because of their ruggedness. Only the lack of an effective distribution network has hindered the firm's ability to penetrate western markets to a greater degree.

When considering the implications of product positioning it is important to realize that positioning can vary from market to market, because the target customers for the product differ from country to country. In confirming the positioning of a product or service in a specific market or region, it is therefore necessary to establish in the consumer's perception exactly what the product stands for and how it differs from existing and potential competition. In developing a market-specific product positioning, the firm can focus upon one or more elements of the total product offer, so the differentiation might be based upon price and quality, one or more attributes, a specific application, a target consumer or direct comparison with one competitor.

14.7 Brand equity

A study by Cittibank and Interbrand in 1997 found that companies basing their business on brands had outperformed the stock market for 15 years. The same study does, however, note the risky tendency of some brand owners to have reduced investments in brands in the mid-1990s with negative impacts on their performance (Hooley *et al.*, 1998, p. 120).

The following two examples show that brands add value for the customers:

● The classic example is that in blind test 51 per cent of consumers prefer Pepsi to Coca-Cola, but in open tests 65 per cent prefer Coca-Cola to Pepsi: soft drink preferences are based on brand image, not taste (Hooley *et al.*, 1998, p. 119).

● Skoda cars have been best known in Britain as the butt of bad jokes, reflecting a widespread belief that the cars are of very low quality. In 1995, Skoda was preparing to launch a new model in the UK, and did 'blind and seen' tests of the consumers' judgement of the vehicle. The vehicle was rated as better designed and worth more by those who did not know the make. With the Skoda name revealed, perceptions of the design were less favourable and estimated value was substantially lower. This leads us from the reputation of the company to branding (Hooley *et al.*, 1998, p. 117).

Definitions of 'brand equity'

Although the definition of brand equity is often debated, the term deals with the brand value, beyond the physical assets associated with is manufacture.

Dr David Aaker of the University of California at Berkeley, one of the leading authorities on brand equity, has defined the term as 'a set of *brand assets and liabilities* linked to the brand, its name and symbol, that add to or subtract from the value provided by a product or service to a firm or to the firm's customers (Aaker, 1991, p. 15).

Professor Aaker has clustered those assets and liabilities into five categories:

1. *Brand loyalty*. Encourages customers to buy a particular brand time after time and remain insensitive to competitors' offerings.

2. *Brand awareness*. Brand names attract attention and convey images of familarity. May be translated to: how big a percentage of the customers know the brand name.

3. *Perceived quality*. 'Perceived' means that the customers decide upon the level of quality, not the company.

4. *Brand associations*. The values and the personality linked to the brand.

5. *Other proprietary brand assets*. Include trademarks, patents, and marketing channel relationships.

Brand equity can be thought of as the additional cash flow achieved by associating a brand with the underlying values of the product or service. In this connection it is useful (although incomplete) to think of a brand's equity as *the premium a customer/consumer would pay for the branded product or service compared to an identical unbranded version of the same product/service.*

Hence, brand equity refers to the strength, depth, and character of the consumer-brand relationship. A strong equity implies a positive force that keeps the consumer and the brand together, in the face of resistance and tension. The strength, depth, and character of the customer–brand relationship is referred to as the *brand relationship quality (BRQ)* (Marketing Science Institute, 1995).

14.8 Branding decisions

Closely linked to product positioning is the question of branding. The basic purposes of branding are the same everywhere in the world. In general, the functions of branding are as follows:

● To distinguish a company's offering and differentiate one particular product from its competitors.

● To create identification and brand awareness.

● To guarantee a certain level of quality and satisfaction.

● To help with promotion of the product.

Figure 14.13   **Branding decisions**

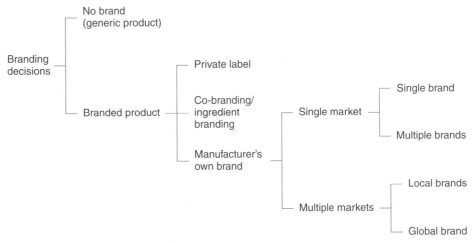

(Source: Adapted from Onkvisit and Shaw, 1993, p. 534. With permission of Prentice-Hall, Inc.)

| Table 14.3 | Advantages and disadvantages of branding alternatives |

	Advantages	Disadvantages
No brand	Lower production cost. Lower marketing cost. Lower legal cost. Flexible quality control.	Severe price competition. Lack of market identity.
Branding	Better identification and awareness. Better chance for production differentiation Possible brand loyalty. Possible premium pricing.	Higher production cost. Higher marketing cost. Higher legal cost.
Private Label	Possibility of larger market share. No promotional problems.	Severe price competition. Lack of market identity.
Co-branding/ingredient branding	Adds more value to the brand. Sharing of production and promotion costs Increases manufacturer's power in gaining access to retailers' shelves. Can develop into long-lasting relationships based on mutual commitment.	Consumers may become confused. Ingredient supplier is very dependent on the success of the final product. Promotion cost for ingredient supplier.
Manufacturer's own brand	Better price due to higher price inelasticity. Retention of brand loyalty. Better bargaining power. Better control of distribution.	Difficult for small manufacturer with unknown brand. Requires band promotion.
Single market, single brand	Marketing efficiency. Permits more focused marketing. Eliminates brand confusion. Good for product with good reputation (halo effect).	Assumes market homogeneity. Existing brand's image harmed when trading up/down. Limited shelf space.
Single market, multiple brands	Market segmented for varying needs. Creates competitive spirit. Avoids negative connotation of existing brand. Gains more retail shelf space. Does not harm existing brand's image.	Higher marketing cost. Higher inventory cost. Loss of economies of scale.
Multiple markets, local brand	Meaningful names. Local identification. Avoidance of taxation on international brand. Allows variations of quantity and quality across markets.	Higher marketing cost. Higher inventory cost. Loss of economies of scale. Diffused image.
Multiple markets, global brand	Maximum markerting efficiency. Reduction of advertising costs. Elimination of brand confusion. Good for culture-free product. Good for prestigious product. Easy identification/recognition for international travellers. Uniform world-wide image.	Assumes market homogeneity. Problems with black and grey markets. Possibility of negative connotation. Requires quality and quantity consistency. LDCs' opposition and resentment. Legal complications.

Source: Adapted from Onkvisit and Shaw (1989). With kind permission from *International Marketing Review*, MCB University Press.

All of these purposes have the same ultimate goals: to create new sales (market shares taken from competitors) or induce repeat sales (keep customers loyal).

As seen from Figure 14.13 there are four levels of branding decisions. Each alternative at the four levels has a number of advantages and disadvantages, which are presented in Table 14.3. We will discuss these options in more detail below.

Brand versus no brand

Branding is associated with added costs in the form of marking, labelling, packaging and promotion. Commodities are 'unbranded' or undifferentiated products. Examples of products with no brand are cement, metals, salt, beef and other agricultural products.

Private label versus co-branding versus manufacturer's own brand

These three options can be graded as shown in Figure 14.14.

The question of consumers having brand loyalty or shop loyalty is a crucial one. The competitive struggle between the manufacturer and the retailer actualizes the need for a better understanding of shopping behaviour. Both actors need to be aware of determinants of shop choice, shopping frequency and in-store behaviour. Where manufacturers pay little attention to the shopping behaviour of their consumers, this information helps to anticipate the increasing power of certain retail chains.

Private label

Private labelling is most developed in the UK, where Marks & Spencer, for instance, only sell own-label products. At Sainsbury own labels account for 60 per cent of the sales. Contrary to the high share of private labelling in North Europe, the share in South Europe (e.g. Spain and Portugal) is not higher than 10 per cent.

| Figure 14.14 | The three brand options |

| Exhibit 14.4 | Coca-Cola: Adaption to the local drinking habits |

Though Coca-Cola is mostly known for its standardized world marketing strategy, consumers in different countries drink Coca-Cola for different reasons. In China, it is a luxury item, served on silver trays at government functions. In Spain, it is used as a mixer with wine, for example. In California, it is kept in coolers to be used as a refreshment; in Tromsö, Norway, it is kept in warmers, rather than coolers. Even the generic description of Coca-Cola varies from country to country, as does the listing of ingredients.

Format also varies. In Zimbabwe, Coca-Cola is almost exclusively limited to 200 ml and 300 ml glass bottles. In nearby Botswana, 340 ml cans are common while Coca-Cola bottles are unheard of. In Australia and in the USA, Coca-Cola is available in both bottles and cans. In the USA, a standard can size is 12 US ounces, which is 335 ml. In the UK, the 150 ml can is popular.

Product line is also adapted from place to place. In some markets, such as Argentina, Australia, Canada, Israel, Norway, South Africa and the US, a sugarless cola was made available, targeted to up-scale, style-consious, weight-concerned urbanites. In Canada and the USA, the name 'Diet Coke' is used; in Israel, the name 'Diet Coca-Cola has been selected. In countries where the word 'diet' implies weight-reducing (as opposed to minimal weight-gaining), the product is known as Coca-Cola Light. Because of governmental regulation the combination of ingredients in Coca-Cola vary according to the market. Government regulation may also necessitate a product having an expiry date. For example in France, Coca-Cola shows an expiry date; in Holland, the product shows the date packed and an expiry date (18 months later).

Source: Pana, L.-P. and Oldfield, B.M. (1999) 'Dublin Coca-Cola Bottles Ltd', *International Marketing Review*, vol. 45, no. 4/5, pp. 291–298

The retailer's perspective

For the retailer there are two main advantages connected with own-label business:

● *Own labels provide better profit margins.* The cost of goods typically makes up 70–85 per cent of a retailer's total cost (*The Economist*, 4 March 1995, p. 10). So if the retailer can buy a quality product from the manufacturer at a lower price, this will provide a better profit margin for the retailer. In fact, private labels have helped UK food retailers to achieve profit margins averaging 8 per cent of sales, which is high by international standards. The typical figure in France and the USA is 1–2 per cent.

● *Own labels strengthen the retailer's image with its customers.* Many retail chains try to establish loyalty to their particular chain of shops by offering their own quality products. In fact, premium private-label products (e.g. Marks & Spencer's St Michael) that compete in quality with manufacturers' top brands have seen a growth in market share, whereas the share of cheap generics is tiny and declining.

The manufacturer's perspective

Although private brands are normally regarded as threats for manufacturers, there may be situations where private branding is a preferable option:

● Since there are no promotional expenses associated with private branding for the producer, the strategy is especially suitable for SMEs with limited financial resources and limited competences in the downstream functions.

● The private brand manufacturer gains access to the shelves of the retail chains. With increasing internationalization of the big retail chains, this may also result in export business for the SME which has never been in international markets.

Exhibit 14.5

Molten: A producer of sports balls moving from private branding to manufacturer's branding

When Fumiya Tamiaki graduated from the University of Tokyo in 1966, he joined the car maker Mazda. And that is where he planned on staying until his father-in-law, Molten's president, fell ill and designated him successor. It was the summer of 1976 and the choice between Mazda and Molten was not easy, but Tamiaki decided to take over at Molten.

From the beginning Tamiaki had turned his sights overseas. Molten was already an exporter of sports balls, but they were all private brands, handled by trading houses and sold under the purchaser's brand. A major breakthrough came when Molten began to negotiate direct with major international customers.

In May 1979, Tamiaki took off for the Adidas office in France. Adidas is a large German manufacturer of sporting goods, but its ball division was located outside Strasbourg. Adidas made the balls for World Cup soccer and was very good at it. Tamiaki knew there was no way he could beat the company at its own game, so he tried to join it instead, asking Adidas for a licence to produce its soccer balls. The negotiations with the president of Adidas were more like an interrogation, Tamiaki recalls. For almost an hour he was fed rapid-fire questions about the current state of the sporting industry. Only when he had passed that grilling could he begin business discussions with lower-level officers. Two days later he had a contract.

According to Tamiaki, 'Before we ever began negotiating, Adidas had checked the quality of every ball manufacturer in Japan and judged ours best'. The Adidas contract boosted Molten's international reputation overnight. Today, it still produces more than 50 per cent of Adidas soccer balls.

Molten's next big break came in the summer of 1980. Tamiaki flew to Los Angeles, where Peter Ueberroth, chairman of the Los Angeles Olympic Organizing Committee, met him to discuss Molten's producing basketballs for the games. It took a year, but Molten finally won the contract for the official balls. Needless to say, the contract carried with it the obligation to contribute lots of financial support for the games, but it also gave Molten another boost in recognition.

Today Molten claims over half the Japanese market for sports balls and about 13 per cent of the world market. It has large plants in Thailand and Mexico, with sales offices in Germany and the USA. This network of factories and sales offices gives it world-wide coverage.

Molten has a goal of being more profitable. To reach this goal Tamiaki is sure that Molten has to sell more of its own brands. Tamiaki says: 'No one in this industry had ever been successful as a manufacturer of private-brand products alone. You had to sell your own brand.'

Source: Adapted from Katayama (1995). With kind permission from O. Katayama/*Look Japan*

There are also a number of reasons why private branding is bad for the manufacturer:

● By not having its own identity, the manufacturer must compete mainly on price, because the retail chain can always switch supplier.

● The manufacturer loses control over how its products should be promoted. This may become critical if the retailer does not do a good job in pushing the product to the consumer.

● If the manufacturer is producing both its own brands and private brands, there is a danger that the private brands will cannibalize the manufacturer's brand name products.

Exhibit 14.5 shows an example of a Japanese sports ball firm moving from a private brand strategy to a manufacturer's brand strategy. Exhibit 14.6 shows an example with Kellogg, who has moved the other way, from a brand strategy to a private brand strategy.

Exhibit 14.6 **Kellogg is under pressure to produce under Aldi's own-label**

In February 2000 Kellogg (the cereal giant) made an own-label deal with German supermarket chain Aldi. It is the first time that Kellogg has supplied own-label.

A slogan on Kellogg's cereal packets claims: 'If you don't see Kellogg's on the box … it isn't Kellogg's in the box. But now Kellogg has negotiated a deal with Aldi to supply products in Germany bearing a different brand name. Reports in Germany say that the deal was made after Aldi announced it would no longer pay brand suppliers' prices and threatened to cut top brands from its shelves.

Source: The information for this case was adapted from various public media.

Quelch and Harding (1996) argue that many manufacturers have over-reacted to the threat of private brands. Increasing numbers of manufacturers are beginning to make private-label products to take up excess production capacity. According to Quelch and Harding (1996), more than 50 per cent of US manufacturers of branded consumer packaged goods already make private-label goods as well.

Managers typically examine private-label production opportunities on an incremental marginal cost basis. The fixed overhead costs associated with the excess capacity used to make the private-label products would be incurred anyway. But if private-label manufacturing were evaluated on a full-cost basis rather than on an incremental basis, it would, in many cases, appear much less profitable. The more private-label production grows as a percentage of total production, the more an analysis based on full costs becomes relevant (Quelch and Harding, 1996).

Manufacturer's own brand

From the Second World War until the 1960s the brand manufacturers managed to build a bridge over the heads of the retailers to the consumers. They created consumer loyalty for their particular brand by using sophisticated advertising (culminating in TV advertising) and other promotional techniques.

Since the 1960s various sociological changes (notably the car) have encouraged the rise of large efficient retailers. Nowadays the distribution system is being turned upside down. The traditional supply chain, powered by manufacturer 'push', is becoming a demand chain, driven by consumer 'pull'. Retailers have won control over distribution not just because they decide the price at which goods are sold, but also because both individual shops and retail companies have become much bigger and more efficient. They are able to buy in bulk and to reap economies of scale, mainly due to advances in transport and, more recently, in information technology. Most retail chains have not only set up computer links between each store and the distribution warehouses, they are also hooked up with the computers of the firm's main suppliers, through an EDI (Electronic Data Interchange) system.

After some decades of absence, private labels reappeared in the 1970s as generic products pioneered by Carrefour in France but were soon adopted by UK and American retailers. Ten years ago, there was a distinct gap in the level of quality between private-label and brand name products. Today the gap has narrowed: private-label quality levels are much higher than ever before, and they are more consistent, especially in categories historically characterized by little product innovation.

Co-branding/ingredient branding

Despite the similarities between co-branding and ingredient branding, there is also an important difference, as we shall see below.

Co-branding

Co-branding is a form of cooperation between two or more brands with significant customer recognition, in which all the participants' brand names are retained. It is of medium to long-term duration and its net value creation potential is too small to justify setting up a new brand and/or legal joint venture. The motive for co-branding is the expectation of synergies which create value for both participants, above the value they would expect to generate on their own.

Figure 14.15   **Illustration of co-branding and ingredient branding**

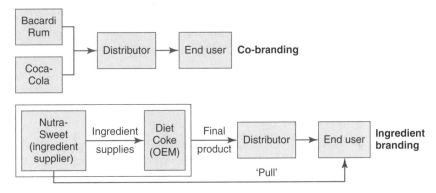

In the case of co-branding, the products are often complementary, in the way that one product can be used or consumed independently of the other (e.g. Bacardi Rum and Coca-Cola). Hence, co-branding may be an efficient alternative to traditional brand extension strategies (Figure 14.15).

| Exhibit 14.7 | Shell's co-branding with Ferrari and Lego |

In 1999–2000 Shell is running a £50m co-branding campaign, together with Ferrari and Lego. Some people would think that it is an attempt to persuade people, mainly in the West, that Shell's controversial attempt to dump the Brent Spar oil platform in the North Sea was not a true reflection of the company.

However, it may be more accurate to say that Shell is seeking a 'brand image transfer'. In the petrol retailer market traditionally driven by price and more price promotions, Shell wants both Ferrari's sexy, sporty image and the family values of Lego. Furthermore Shell is no longer only in the petroleum and oils business, where price promotions is the main focus of marketing activity. They are also involved in food retailing where also loyalty programmes are important.

What are the benefits for Ferrari and Lego?

Ferrari gains sponsorship and royalty income from model car sales, while Lego gets improved global distribution. The co-branding strategy involves the use of ten exclusive small box toys and a big Ferrari Lego car carrying a Shell logo. Shell wants to sell between 20 and 40 million units of Lego globally. It will make Shell one of the world's largest toy distributors.

Source: The information for this case was adapted from various public media

Ingredient branding

Normally the marketer of the final product (OEM) creates all of the value in the consumer's eyes. But in the case of Intel and NutraSweet (see Exhibit 14.8) the ingredient supplier is seeking to build value in its products by branding and promoting the key component of an end product. When promotion (pull strategy: see Figure 14.15) of the key component brand is initiated by the ingredient supplier, the goal is to build awareness and preference among consumers for that ingredient brand. Simultaneously, it may be the manufacturer (OEM) that seeks to benefit from a recognized ingredient brand. Some computer manufacturers are benefiting from the quality image of using an Intel chip.

However, ingredient branding is not suitable for every supplier of components. An ingredient supplier should fulfil the following requirements:

● The ingredient supplier should be offering a product that has a substantial advantage over existing products. DuPont's Teflon, NutraSweet, Intel chips and the Dolby noise reduction system are all examples of major technological innovations, the result of large investments in R & D.

● The ingredient should be critical to the success of the final product. NutraSweet is not only a low-calorie sweetener, but has a taste that is nearly identical to that of sugar.

Exhibit 14.8	Examples of ingredient branding

NutraSweet

An example of a successful ingredient labelling strategy is Monsantos' NutraSweet – an artificial sweetener – which in 1993 was used in about 5,000 food and drink brands, including Pepsi-Cola's and Coca-Cola's products. By using traditional marketing tools in an untraditional way, Monsantos created a market for its product NutraSweet by catching the attention of household customers and in this way creating a pull effect in the chain of distribution.

NutraSweet is an example of how successful ingredient labelling can be done. NutraSweet contained a much lower amount of calories than sugar, but still tasted like it. Monsantos' idea was that the customer should use its sweetener as a substitute for sugar. In the beginning it was difficult to convince soft-drink producers, Coca-Cola and Pepsi-Cola, of NutraSweet's uniqueness, but when Monsantos finally succeeded, problems arose with delivery as all customers suddenly wanted NutraSweet as an ingredient in their soft drink. Today Monsantos works closely with soft-drink and food producers to minimize production costs on both sides.

Intel's Pentium

Intel had used the strategy of a corporate brand for a number of years ('Intel inside'), when it launched 286, 386 and 486 chips, but in 1993 it branded its component 'Pentium Chip'. Intel is the latest example of how a supplier can successfully create equity in its product and the end product by branding.

Intel has two-thirds of the world market and is thus the global leader in microprocessors, the 'brain' in personal computers. Capturing such a large market share has been expensive, but Intel has, through network television advertising and advertising in different computer magazines, been able to build up awareness of Intel's name among buyers of PCs, and has in spite of intensive competition in the computer industry had success with differentiation.

The technology in microchips develops with explosive speed, where every new chip generation makes its predecessor's capabilities look old fashioned. Intel has benefited from NutraSweet's ingredient labelling strategy, but Intel has also been able to create a brand strategy for a product which is not so 'close' to the customer as NutraSweet.

Danfoss Cool Quality

Danfoss is a well-reputed Danish manufacturer of critical components (controls) for cooling equipment, such as beverage coolers. The cooperation between Danfoss and the (OEM) manufacturer of the end product involves, among other things, a joint brochure and joint appearances at trade fairs. At the same time, Danfoss obtains a label profile towards the end user when the OEM puts the Danfoss label on its product (Figure 14.16).

Figure 14.16   **The Danfoss label**

Single brand versus multiple brands (single market)

A single brand or family brand (for a number of products) may be helpful in convincing consumers that each product is of the same quality or meets certain standards. In other words, when a single brand on a single market is marketed by the manufacturer, the brand is assured of receiving full attention for maximum impact.

The company may also choose to market several (multiple) brands on a single market. This is based on the assumption that the market is heterogeneous and consists of several segments.

Local brands versus a global brand (multiple markets)

A company has the option of using the same brand in most or all of its foreign markets, or using individual, local brands. A single, global brand is also known as an international or universal brand. A Eurobrand is a slight modification of this approach, as it is a single product for a single market of twelve or more European countries, with an emphasis on the search for intermarket similarities rather than differences.

A global brand is an appropriate approach when a product has a good reputation or is known for quality. In such a case, a company would be wise to extend the brand name to other products in the product line. Examples of global brands are Coca-Cola, Shell and the Visa credit card. Although it is possible to find examples of global brands, local brands are probably more common among big multinational companies than people realize. Boze and Patton (1995) have studied the branding practices in 67 countries all over the world of six multinational companies:

● Colgate-Palmolive – headquartered in the USA.

● Kraft General Foods (now part of Philip Morris) – headquartered in the USA.

● Nestlé – headquartered in Switzerland.

● Procter & Gamble – headquartered in the USA.

Table 14.4   **Brands of six MNCs in 67 countries**

Company	Total no. of brands	Brands found in 50% or more countries		Brands in only one country	
		Number	% of total	Number	% of total
Colgate	163	6	4	59	36
Kraft GF	238	6	3	104	44
Nestlé	560	19	4	250	45
P & G	217	18	8	80	37
Quaker	143	2	1	55	38
Unilever	471	17	4	236	50
Total	1792	68	4	784	44

Source: Boze and Patton (1995, p. 22). Reproduced with kind permission from the *Journal of Consumer Marketing*, MCB University Press.

- Quaker Oats – headquartered in the USA.
- Unilever – headquartered in the UK and the Netherlands.

The findings of the research are summarized in Table 14.4. Of the 1,792 brands found in the 67 countries, 44 per cent were only marketed in one country. Only 68 brands (4 per cent) could be found in more than half of the countries. Of these 68 brands, only the following six brands were found in all 67 countries: Colgate, Lipton, Lux, Maggi, Nescafé and Palmolive. Hence these were the only true world brands.

Surprisingly, each of the six MNCs seems to follow the practice of multiple brands in a single market. No official explanation was offered for this strategy, but a Nestlé manager explained 'that he believed it is a very important marketing advantage to provide a brand name not found in any other country, especially those adjacent to the nation or bigger than it' (Boze and Patton, 1995, p. 24).

The use of umbrella brands varies a lot among the MNCs examined. Of the six MNCs, Colgate is the most intensive user of its two company names:

- *Colgate.* Mostly dental products, toothpaste, tooth powder, toothbrushes, dental floss, mouthwash and shaving cream.
- *Palmolive.* Hair products, shaving products, hand lotions, talc, deodorant, sun screen, toilet soap, bath products, liquid detergent (dishes and fine fabrics), and automatic dishwasher detergent.

It should be emphasized that the big MNCs prefer to acquire some local brands instead of using a global brand.

14.9   Implications of Internet/e-commerce for product decisions

Types of product

The products sold over electronic markets were roughly grouped in Chapter 13 into two categories: *physical products* and purely *digital goods and services*.

Customization and closer relationships

The new business platform recognizes the increased importance of customization of products and services. Increased commoditization of standard features can only be countered through customization, which is most powerful when backed up by sophisticated analysis of customer data.

Mass-marketing experts such as Nike and Levi Strauss are experimenting with ways of using digital technology to enable customization. Web sites that can display three-dimensional images, for example, will certainly boost the attractiveness of custom tailoring. Levi Strauss has provided a truly personal service that dates back to 1994, when Levi's initiated its 'Personal Pair' programme. Women who were prepared to pay up to $15 more than the standard price and wait for delivery could go to Levi's Stores and have their measurements taken and a pair of custom jeans made. Later this service migrated to the Web and was branded as Original Spin (read more about Levi's on-line/off-line strategy in the Case Study in Chapter 13).

The challenge is clear: to use IT to get closer to customers. There are already many examples of this. Dell is getting a closer relationship with their end-customer by letting them design their own PC on the Internet. Customers who have ordered their computers from Dell can then follow their computers along the various stages of the production process in real time on their personalized Web site. Such experimentation is advisable because the success of 'build-to-order' models such as Dell's represents a challenge to current 'build-to-stock' business platforms, which Compaq generally uses. In Exhibit 14.9 there is a comparison of the business models of Dell and Compaq. Dell's basic business principle is the close relationship between the PC manufacturer and the end-customer without further intermediaries in the distribution channel. This allows Dell to individualize the computers to the specific needs of the customers.

Computers can also be remotely diagnosed and fixed over the network today; this may soon be true of many other appliances. Airlines now communicate special fares to preferred customers through e-mails and special Web sites. Cars will soon have Internet protocol addresses, which will make possible a range of personal in-vehicle information services.

Customers can also be involved in the early stages of product development so that their inputs can shape product features and functionality. Pharmaceutical companies are experimenting with the possibility of analyzing patients' genes to determine precisely what drugs should be administered in what dosages.

The transformation in the business platform can be seen in college textbook publishing. This industry – which has seen little innovation since the advent of the printing press – is now in the midst of major changes. Publishers are creating supplementary Web site links to provide additional ways for students and professors to be connected during courses (e.g. www.pearson.com and www.wiley.com). The publisher's role, which traditionally was selling textbooks at the beginning of term, is becoming that of an educational consultant or value-adding partner throughout the term.

Exhibit 14.9	**Business models of Dell and Compaq**

In the personal computer industry, Dell and Compaq are world-wide market leaders. However, the business model of the two companies differs a lot, as the following table demonstrates:

	Dell	**Compaq**
Target customer	Knowledgeable customer buying multiple units	Multiple customer segments with varied needs
Value proposition	Customized PC at competitive price	'Brand' with quality image
Value capture	Through pushing latest components upgrades and low-cost distribution system	Through premium for the 'brand' and reseller push
Business system		
R&D	Limited	Considerable
Manufacturing	Flexible assembly, cost advantage	High speed, low-variety, low-cost manufacturing system
Supply chain	Made-to-order; inventory: one-week, mainly component	Made-to-stock; delivery; inventory: one-month finished-product
Marketing	Moderate advertising	Expensive brand advertising
Sales and distribution	Primarily through sales force, telemarketing and Internet	Primarily through third-party resellers

Compaq has business systems of the type traditionally associated with branded products. It has high R&D expenditures, low cost, low-variety, large-run manufacturing systems, one month finished-products inventory.

Dell primarily targets corporate accounts but with built-to-order, customized PCs at reasonable prices. Dell has minimal R&D expenditures, made-to-order, flexible manufacturing system (which give Dell a slight disadvantage compared to Compaq), one-week parts inventory and an efficient distribution system. Dell has been a pioneer in PC sales through the Internet.

Source: Adapted from Kumar (1999).

Dynamic customization of product and services

The second stage of the customer interaction vector focuses on the opportunities and challenges in dynamically customizing products and services. Competitive markets are rapidly eroding margins due to price-based competition, and companies are seeking to enhance margins through customized offering. Dynamic customization is based on three principles: modularity, intelligence, and organization.

● *Modularity:* An approach for organizing complex products and processes efficiently. Product or service modularity requires the partitioning of a task into independent modules that function as a whole within overall architecture.

● *Intelligence:* Continuous information exchange with consumers allows companies to create products and processes using the best possible modules. Web site operators can match buyer and seller profiles and make recommendations based on their shared interests. The result is intelligent sites that learn their visitors' (potential buyers') tastes and deliver dynamic personalized information about products and services.

● *Organization:* Dynamic customization of products and services requires a customer-oriented and flexible approach that is fundamentally committed to operation in this new way.

How can the Internet be integrated in the future product innovation?

Figure 14.17 shows some of the implications of the Internet on the future product innovation. The internet is seen as the medium through which each 'box' communicates with the R & D function in the company.

● *Design.* Data is gathered directly from the product and is part of designing and developing the product. New product features (such as new versions of software programs) may be built into the product directly from the Internet.

● *Service and support.* The service department can perform troubleshooting and correction directly through the Internet set-up. For example a Mercedes car driving

Figure 14.17   **Product innovation through the Internet**

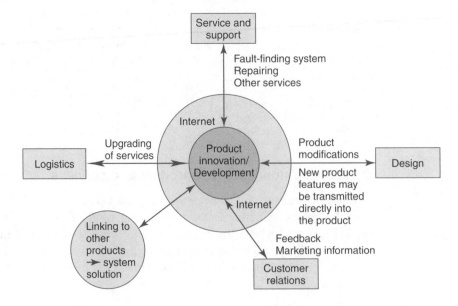

on the highway may be directly connected to the Mercedes service department. They will monitor the main functions of the car and if necessary make on-line repairs of e.g. the software of the car.

● *Customer relations.* Data gathered from the product may form part of statistics, comparisons between customers etc. In this way the customer can compare the performance of his product (e.g. a car) with other customers' product (a kind of benchmarking). This may also strengthen an existing customer relationship.

● *Logistics.* Concurrently with increasing demands to Just-In-Time deliveries, the Internet will automatically find the distribution and transport that will take the goods from the subsupplier to the producer and then to the customers in the cheapest and most efficient way (on time).

A fundamental shift in thinking is to replace the term 'supply chain' with 'demand-chain'. The critical difference is that demand-chain thinking starts with the customers and works backwards. This breaks out of parochial approaches that focus solely on reducing transport costs. It supports a 'mass customization' viewpoint, in which bundles of goods and services are offered in ways that support customers' individual objectives.

This does not necessarily imply product differentiation. In fact, the service aspects often require differentiation. For example, a company such as Unilever will provide the same margarine to both Tesco and Sainsbury. However, the ways in which the product is delivered, transactions are processed and other parts of the relationship are managed, can and should be different, since these two competing supermarket chains each have their own ways of evaluating performance. The information systems required to coordinate companies along the demand chain require a new and different approach to that required within individual companies. Some managers believe that if they and their suppliers choose the same standard software package, such as SAP, they will be able to integrate their information systems.

● *Link to other products.* Sometimes a product is used as a sub-component in other products. Through links in the Internet such sub-components may be essential inputs for more complex product solutions. The car industry is an example of an industry that already makes a targeted effort in this direction. New 'stylish' cars are linked together by the Internet. In the wake of this development a new industry is created, the purpose of which is to provide integrated transport. In this new, integrated transport industry, developing and producing cars is only one of several important services. Instead, systems are to be developed that can diagnose cars (and correct the error) while the car is running, systems for regulation of traffic, interactive systems that enable drivers to have the desired transport at their disposal when and where they want it without tiresome rental agreements etc.

The music industry is also undergoing a change. Today, you can buy portable 'players' that can download music from the Internet using the MP3 format, and subsequently play the music that is stored in the 'player'. The CD is skipped – and so is the whole distribution facility. The music industry will become completely changed through the different economic conditions. The costs paid by the listeners when downloading a piece of music will probably bear the earnings – not the player. The struggle will therefore be about creating the best portal to the Internet, where the consumer can find the best information on music and the largest selection of music. The problems regarding rights are, however, still being discussed, and the lawyers and politicians have to find a final solution, before the market can increase significantly.

Thus, innovative product development of the future demands that a company possesses the following characteristics:

● Innovative product development and strategic thinking. Product development will contain much technology and demand interdisciplinary, strategic overview and knowledge in order to find out what new services are worth aiming at.

● Management of alliances. Few companies have all the necessary qualifications themselves – the innovative product development and the resulting services demand that the companies enter into alliances very dynamically and yet in a structured way.

● New customer relations. The above-mentioned car industry example clearly shows that the customers are not car buyers any longer but *buyers of transport services*, and that is quite another matter. This means that the companies have to focus on understanding the customers' needs in a quite different way.

Developing brands on the Internet

Clearly, consumer product companies like Procter & Gamble, Colgate, Kraft Foods, and consumer durables and business-to-business companies like General Motors, General Electric, Allied Signal and Caterpillar have crafted their business strategies by leveraging physical assets and developing powerful global brands supported by mass advertising and mass distribution. But remote links with customers apply equally well to these companies. Remote and continuous links with customers become critical as the concepts of brand identity and brand equity are redefined by the Internet.

Kraft Interactive Kitchen (*www.kraftfoods.com*) is an example of a consumer products company keeping in touch with its consumers by providing information-based services like meal planners, recipes, tips, and cooking techniques. Kraft's intent is to have remote connections and interactions with consumers in new ways.

However, some companies find it difficult to translate a strong off-line brand (like Nike and Levi's) to the Internet, because many of the well-known brands are based on an extensive physical' retail distribution system, and many of the retailers are reluctant to support on-line brands because of the fear for disintermediation (see section 13.6 for more discussion of this issue).

In fact, many sites that are run by top brands register minimal on-line traffic, according to a report by Forrester Research. Forrester studied brand awareness and Web surfing behaviour among 16 to 22-year-olds, whom advertisers consider to be strongly brand-conscious.

Companies are taking a broad approach to branding, integrating it with an overall advertising and marketing strategy. On the Net, branding is more than logos and colour schemes; it is about creating experiences and understanding customers. Consequently, Web brand-building is not cheap. Building a brand requires a persistent on-line presence. For some brands, that entails a mass-appeal site; for others, brand-building requires a combination of initiatives, from banner ads to sponsorships.

14.10 Green marketing strategies

Environmentalists were once considered the only people concerned about the depletion of natural resources, waste accumulation and pollution. Environmentalists around the world are now becoming global in their scope and scale of operations. Their aim is to increase people's awareness of the importance of environmental preservation on a global scale and how the lack of it will have a harmful effect on our planet. Global awareness about the environment is also being aroused by media reports on ecological disasters such as Chernobyl, the Exxon Valdez oil spill, acid rain and global warming.

The scientific community asserts that atmospheric pollution is having a damaging effect on the ozone layer. Two major factors influencing the depletion of the ozone layer are the use of aerosol sprays and the manufacture of certain types of plastic and foam insulation.

Because ecological grassroot campaigns gain widespread recognition and support, and global media networks such as CNN continue to report on environmental issues and disasters, today's consumer is becoming environmentally conscious. Various polls and surveys reveal that many consumers are taking environmental issues into consideration as they buy, consume and dispose of products. Consequently, there is a direct connection between a company's ability to attract and keep consumers and its ability to develop and execute environmentally sound strategies.

As consumer preferences and government policies increasingly favour a balanced business approach to the environment, managers are paying more attention to the strategic importance of their environmental decisions. Irresponsible behaviour by some firms has led to consumer boycotts, lengthy lawsuits and large fines. Such actions may have harmed firms in less direct ways such as negative public relations, diversion of management attention and difficulty in hiring top employees.

In Europe particularly, the green consumer movement is large and growing, and certain countries can be considered leaders and standard-setters in green awareness. Eighty per cent of German consumers, for instance, are willing to pay premiums for household goods that are recycled, recyclable and non-damaging to the environment; in France 50 per cent of consumers will pay more at the supermarket for products they perceive as environmentally friendly. This trend is growing elsewhere too: according to a European study, consumers throughout the OECD area are willing to pay more for green goods (Vandermerwe and Oliff, 1991).

Several retailers have also committed themselves to marketing green products. The example of The Body Shop is described in Exhibit 14.11.

Clearly, failing to consider the environmental impact of strategic decisions may affect the financial stability of the firm and the ability of that firm to compete with others in the industry.

Strategic options

Figure 14.18 presents four strategic options that are available for the firm with environmental concerns. The choice of strategic environmental posture will depend on how an organization wants to create value for its green customers and how change oriented its approach is.

As can be seen from the diagram, if a firm is more oriented to cost reduction than to benefit enhancement for customers, pollution prevention strategies (options 3 and 4) would probably be chosen in preference to the development of 'green' products: for example, by using natural or recycled materials. If a firm is more proactive than accommodative, it tends to be more innovative than otherwise (options 1 and 3).

Although going beyond compliance (i.e. doing more than required according to environmental legislation) is generally perceived as highly desirable, SMEs may not have the resources to act proactively, and hence need to focus on compliance and minor product modification (options 2 and 4).

Environmental management in the value chain perspective

Management cannot afford to be myopic in looking at the finished product without considering the manufacturing and R & D phases as they relate to consumers' perceptions of what constitutes a green product. Nor can a company use traditional marketing principles to gain product acceptance. Put differently, both the input and output activities associated with the design, manufacture and delivery of products must be considered, and each step within the value-creating process must be assessed in the light of its overall environmental impact and consequences.

Figure 14.18   **Types of environmental strategic posture**

| | | Value creation approach | |
		Benefit enhancement for customers	Cost reduction
Change orientation	Proactive	Green product Innovation (major modification) ①	Pollution prevention Beyond compliance ③
	Accommodative	Green product ② Differentiation (minor modification)	④ Pollution prevention Compliance

(Source: Adapted from Starik et al., 1996, p. 17)

Figure 14.19   **Value-adding logistics and the environment interface**

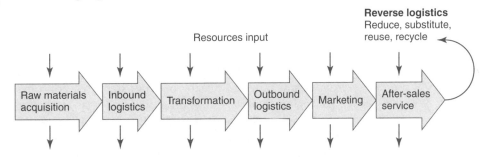

(Source: Adapted from Wu and Dunn, 1995, p. 23 with permission from *International Journal of Physical Distribution and Logistics Management*, MCB University Press; http://www.mcb.c.uk)

Figure 14.19 illustrates the resource conversion and pollutant generation relationships. As resources are used to create desired utilities, pollutants are implicitly produced as byproducts during each step of the integrated supply chain process. For example, packaging is used to protect the products from damage and is an undesired item once they are consumed. Proper management and awareness of the environmental implications of logistical activities can significantly reduce their negative impact.

Exhibit 14.10   ## Levi Strauss's recycling programme

Levi Strauss is a privately owned, global corporation, headquartered in San Francisco, California, with 1993 sales figures of nearly US$6 billion. It markets jeans, jeans-related products and casual apparel in over 60 countries. The company employs over 36,000 people world-wide and operates over 76 production facilities, including cutting, pressing, finishing and other manufacturing centres.

One programme introduces recycled jeans as an important and growing segment of some retail channels of distribution. Another programme involves the recycling of denim scraps. Levi Strauss has created a process to make paper from 100 per cent recycled denim. Denim-Paper, a unique product made from scraps of denim, reduces shipping and disposal of denim scrap to landfills. Levi's blue-hued stationery and business cards are all made from recycled denim. It is estimated that 8,000 trees are saved annually as a result of this recycling programme. Efforts to recycle Levi's materials represent a way of dealing with environmental concerns and contribute to reputational effects in the post-production segment of the value chain. Numerous other environmentally sensitive initiatives are also part of the company's activities, including recycled paper tags, copper rivets and buttons from natural copper (avoiding chemical processing in copper plating), waste water treatment in denim-treatment plants, as well as fostering the production of naturally coloured cotton which generates what has been described as eco-friendly clothing.

Source: Preece *et al.* (1995). Adapted with permission from Elsevier Science Ltd, The Boulevard, Langford Lane, Kidlington, OX5 1GB, UK.

Integrative environmental management means that every element in the corporate value chain is involved in minimization of the firm's total environmental impact from start to finish of the supply chain, and also from beginning to end of the product life cycle.

Reverse logistics in Figure 14.19 results in the shipment of packaging waste, recyclable packages and consumer returns in the logistics system.

Germany and other European countries state that consumers have the right to leave packaging materials at retail stores and that stores must dispose of them properly. Denmark has for many years also required beer bottles to be reusable. The shipment of these packaging materials back to original sites creates demand for logistical capacity and adds no direct value to the goods.

Management has to consider how to reduce the reverse flows. In relation to Figure 14.19, reverse logistics emphasizes source reduction and substitution over reuse and recycling. Source reduction refers to doing the same things with less resources. The practice reduces total waste in the system. Substitution means using more environmentally friendly materials instead of regular ones that end up as pollutants. Reuse is employing the same item many times in its original form so that little is discarded. Recycling gives discarded materials a new life after some chemical or physical processes.

Eco-labelling schemes

Over the years, eco-labelling schemes have been implemented in a number of EU countries in an attempt to promote the use of products and production methods which are less harmful to the environment. The first scheme was introduced in West Germany in 1978. Today the organizers of the scheme claim that 80 per cent of German households are aware of the scheme and it receives widespread support from manufacturers.

The label should affect all businesses along the supply chain because the suppliers have to provide detailed information about their own components and their manufacturing process. The criteria for the award of an eco-label for a product are based on a cradle-to-grave analysis or life cycle assessment (Table 14.5). National bodies that award the eco-labels for products act as a kind of jury, assessing the environmental performance of a product by reference to agreed specific environmental criteria for each product group.

Green alliances between business and environmental organizations

Strategic alliances with environmental groups (e.g. Greenpeace) can provide five benefits to marketers of consumer goods (Mendleson and Polonsky, 1995):

● *They increase consumer confidence in green products and their claims*. It can be assumed that, if an environmental group supports a firm, product or service, consumers are more likely to believe the product's environmental claims.

● *They provide firms with access to environmental information*. It is in their role as an information clearing house that environmental groups may be of immense benefit to organizations with which they form strategic alliances. Manufacturers

Table 14.5 Eco-labelling scheme indicative assessment

Environmental fields	Product life cycle				
	Pre-production	Production	Distribution	Utilization	Disposal
Waste relevance	× ×	× ×	× ×	× ×	× ×
Soil pollution and degradation	× ×	× ×	× ×	× ×	× ×
Water contamination	× ×	× ×	× ×	× ×	× ×
Air contamination	× ×	× ×	× ×	× ×	× ×
Noise	× ×	× ×	× ×	× ×	× ×
Consumption of energy	× ×	× ×	× ×	× ×	× ×
Consumption of natural resources	× ×	× ×	× ×	× ×	× ×
Total effects on eco-systems	× ×	× ×	× ×	× ×	× × >

Source: Welford, R. and Prescott, K. (1996), *European Business: An issue-based approach*, Pearson Education Limited.

facing environmental problems may turn to their strategic partners for advice and information. In some cases, environmental partners may actually have technical staff who can be used to assist in solving organizational problems or implementing existing solutions.

● *They give the marketer access to new markets.* Most environmental groups have an extensive support base, which in many cases receives newsletters or other group mailings. Their members receive catalogues marketing a variety of licensed products, all of which are less environmentally harmful than other commercial alternatives. Environmental group members represent a potential market that can be utilized by producers, even if these groups do not produce specialized catalogues. An environmental group's newsletter may discuss how a firm has formed a strategic alliance with the group, as well as the firm's less environmentally harmful products. Inclusion of this information in a newsletter is a useful form of publicity.

● *They provide positive publicity and reduce public criticism.* Forming strategic alliances with environmental groups may also stimulate increased publicity. When the Sydney Olympic Bid Committee announced that Greenpeace was the successful designer for the year 2000 Olympic Village, the story appeared in all major newspapers and on the national news. It is highly unlikely that this publicity would have been generated if a more conventional architect had been named as the designer of the village. Once again the publicity associated with the alliance was positive and credible.

● *They educate consumers about key environmental issues for the firm and its product(s).* Environmental groups are valuable sources of educational information and materials. They educate consumers and the general public about environmental problems and also inform them about potential solutions. In many cases the public views these groups as credible sources of information, without a vested interest. Marketers can also play an important role as providers of environmental information through their marketing activities. In doing so they create environmental awareness of specific issues, their products and their organizations. For example, Kellogg's in Norway educated consumers and promoted its environmental concern by placing environmental information on the packaging of its cereals relating to various regional environmental problems (World Wide Fund for Nature, 1993).

Choosing the correct alliance partner is not a simple task, as environmental groups have different objectives and images. Some groups may be willing to form exclusive alliances, where they partner only one product in a given product category. Other groups may be willing to form alliances with all products that comply with their specific criteria.

The marketer must determine what capabilities and characteristics an alliance partner can bring to the alliance. As with any symbiotic relationship, each partner must contribute to the success of the activity. Poor definition of these characteristics may result in the firm searching out the wrong partner.

Exhibit 14.11 **The Body Shop: a business with green ideals**

It is twenty years since Anita Roddick opened her first The Body Shop in Brighton. She did it to be able to support her two daughters.

The business concept is to produce products from a combination of traditional knowledge, ancient herbal recipes and modern scientific research. The Body Shop offers minimally packaged, natural-ingredient products that have not been tested on animals. It stands for environmental consciousness and Anita Roddick has become famous for her engagement in different environmental issues. She participates in a number of different projects, from increasing living standards for Indians in the Amazonas to improving orphanages in Romania.

When Anita Roddick decided to use the franchising principle on The Body Shop, following the same concept as McDonald's and Burger King, the story became an adventure. The first Body Shop outside England opened in Belgium in 1978, and has since expanded. The Body Shop became listed on the Stock Exchange in 1984 and today there are more than 1,400 shops in 50 different countries. On average, a new shop opens every third day.

The main idea behind Anita Roddick's business – protection of the environment, human rights and threatened animals – has never been compromised. And she is even more engaged today than earlier. For six months every year she travels around the world visiting primitive tribes in Africa, Asia and South America, finding old recipes of health mixtures and beauty treatments which she produces and sells in The Body Shop.

In the past couple of years the price of The Body Shop shares has dropped. One of the problems is the American market, where Roddick neglected to follow her own system for success. The Body Shop owns 113 of its 272 stores in the USA, and this is one of the key reasons for the company's stumble there, analysts say. Rather than perfecting sales in its existing shops, the company charged into the top malls, in the hope of gaining a foothold against the fast-expanding Bath & Body Works. But it did not work. The US operation lost money in 1996.

Bath & Body Works, by contrast, which has opened 412 stores in the past five years, is making a profit. Its chairman, Leslie H. Wexner, says his rival's background as a manufacturer (and foreigner) worked against her in the USA. 'They're not retailers,' he says. 'We have an advantage – we know the territory.' 'It was just awesome to watch how fast they got into the market,' Roddick admits.

Having been burned in retailing, Roddick now seems to have learned her lesson. As The Body Shop expands, it is sticking to its more profitable franchising strategy, the approach that made it successful in the first place. Today all but 12 of its 841 shops outside the USA and the UK are franchises.

Source: Adapted from Wallace (1996) and Brown (1996).

14.11 ▌ Total quality management and ISO 9000 certification

With product quality becoming the cornerstone of global competition, companies are increasingly requiring assurances of standard performance from suppliers. In this sense, total quality management (TQM) is a broad organizational approach. TQM may be defined as follows:

- *Total.* All persons in the firm are involved (and where possible also the customers and suppliers of the firm).
- *Quality.* Customer requirements are met precisely.
- *Management.* Senior executives are fully committed.

As part of TQM, ISO 9000 does not relate to specific products, but is the registration and certification of a manufacturer's quality system. The ISO 9000 standards ensure that products are produced using certified methods of manufacture, thereby eliminating product quality variation. However, the ISO 9000 certification does not guarantee that a manufacturer produces a 'quality' product. The end product is only as good as the design and process specifications require.

Headquartered in Geneva, Switzerland, the International Standards Organization (ISO) promotes the development of standardization and standards with a view to facilitating the international exchange of goods and services. Currently made up of the national standard bodies of 91 countries, ISO initiated the ISO 9000 standards in 1987. The standards are revised periodically to ensure that they do not become outdated.

The five standards of ISO 9000

The five standards that collectively make up the ISO 9000 are as follows:

- *ISO 9000.* This is the road map for the series. It is the overall term covering the other four standards in the series: 9001, 9002, 9003 and 9004.
- *ISO 9001.* This is the most comprehensive of the standards. It is a quality assurance that requires the demonstration of a supplier's capability to fulfil the

requirements during all phases of operation: design, development, production, installation and servicing.

- *ISO 9002*. This standard is a subset of ISO 9001 with the areas of design and development of the product removed. The standard is sometimes used as an interim standard before expanding to the more comprehensive ISO 9001. It is also the most commonly used standard for service companies. The quality guidelines are used to ensure that the service is provided using a consistent process that is described in the quality documents.

- *ISO 9003*. This model provides a standard of quality assurance for firms only involved in final inspection and testing of products. Firms using this standard are basically performing the inspection function of the product that would normally be done by the customer when the product is received.

- *ISO 9004*. This standard provides a set of guidelines by which the management of a company can implement and develop an effective quality management system. There is heavy emphasis on meeting company and customer needs.

Implementing ISO 9000

Considerable work is needed before obtaining a certification to a chosen ISO 9000 standard. The costs can also be large, especially for small companies when external consultants are needed to perform much of the work.

When the firm is ready, it requests a certifying body (a third party authorized to provide an ISO 9000 audit) to conduct a registration assessment: that is, an audit of the key business processes in the company. In some countries, there is more than one registration body. For example, in the UK companies can register under BSI, Lloyd's, Yardsley and others approved by the National Council for Certification Award Bodies (Ho, 1995). When accreditation is granted, the company receives certification. A complete assessment for recertification will be done every four years with intermediate evaluations during the four-year period.

The strong level of interest in ISO is being driven by market requirements, and ISO 9000 is becoming an important competitive marketing tool in international markets, especially in the European Union. Industrial buyers often use the list of ISO-registered suppliers as a screening device to identify potential suppliers (Ferguson, 1996).

Exhibit 14.12	Dell Computers

Patents – a hidden weapon for Dell

Dell is getting a closer relationship to its end-customers by letting them design their own PC on the Internet. Customers who have ordered their computers from Dell can then follow their computers along the various stages of the production process in real time on their personalized Web site. Such experimentation is advisable because the success of 'build-to-order' models such as Dell's represents a challenge to current 'build-to-stock' business platforms, which Compaq generally uses. Dell's basic business principle is the close relationship between PC manufacturer and the end-customer without further intermediatries in the distribution channel. This allows Dell to individualize the computers to the specific needs of the customers.

For Dell, the build-to-order system has resulted in the highest margins and the lowest manufacturing and inventory costs in the industry, a cash-conversion cycle of an incredible eight days, and the fervent loyalty of millions of satisfied customers. It has also earned Dell the unabashed envy of its competitors, several of whom are now attempting to mimic its direct sales approach. Imitation, of course, is the sincerest form of flattery.

Unknown to most of its rivals, Dell has already secured four patents on its build-to-order direct sales model. And by the time you read this, an additional 38 patents still pending on this system may also have been granted. These patents cover not only the on-line customer-configurable ordering system, but also the way it is integrated into the company's manufacturing, inventory, distribution, and customer service operations. In short, Dell has patented its pioneering method of doing business.

It is Dell's innovation: how they run their factory, how their ordering system allows customers to configure their PCs with whatever hardware and software they choose, and how they advise customers of shipment. And Dell intends to protect that innovation.

This is a rather unorthodox intellectual property strategy, to be sure, especially for a firm competing in a commodity business like computers. Most companies, to the extent that they even have patent strategies, focus those strategies on protecting their products or technologies. Dell, however, uses its patents to protect and leverage the most valuable component of its business and the true source of its competitive advantage: its build-to-order business model.

Information for this case is sourced from a variety of public media.

14.12 Summary

In deciding the product policy abroad, it is an important issue to decide what parts (product levels) should be standardized and what parts should be adapted to the local environment. This chapter has discussed the variety of factors that are relevant to this decision.

A very important issue is the question of branding. Different branding alternatives have been discussed. For example, because large (often transnational) retail chains have won control over distribution, they try to develop their own labels. For the retailer, private labels provide better profit margins and strengthen the retailer's image with its customers. Because of the power shift to the retailers, the percentage of retail grocery sales derived from private brands has increased in recent years.

This chapter has also discussed two issues, which are experiencing increasing interest: total quality management (TQM)/ISO 9000 and green marketing strategies, including the need for product adaptation in a 'green' direction.

Case study | Danish Klassic

Launch of a cream cheese in Saudi Arabia

In the spring of 1987, the product manager of Danish Cheese Overseas, KA, was pleased to note that after some decline, e.g. in Iran, feta sales were improving in the Middle East. However, the company was a little concerned that the feta, according to several expert opinions, could lose ground to the cream cheese which was apparently becoming more and more popular among Arabs in both big cities and in provincial areas.

Saudi Arabia in general

Because of its immense income from oil, Saudi Arabia has developed fantastically during the past 30 years. With the Islamic tradition as its basis, the country has become more modern.

In 1987, the population was 11.5 million, more than 50 per cent of whom were under 15 years of age, which makes Saudi Arabia a 'young' nation.

According to the Saudi Arabic Ministry of Agriculture, the population was forecast to rise to 19 million in 2000. The expected development in population in the three biggest cities is shown in Table 1.

Table 1 — **Development in population in the three biggest cities in Saudi Arabia**

	Population (m.) 1974	Population (m.) 2000
Riyadh	0.7	2.4
Jeddah	0.6	2.1
Dammam	0.2	0.8

Source: *Demographic Yearbook 1985*, p. 270, and prognosis from the Saudi Arabic Ministry of Agriculture.

Table 2 — **Total import of cheese (tons) in 1986**

	Total import
Processed cheese (including cream cheese)	29,500
Feta	18,400
Other types of cheese	2,400
Total	50,300

Source: Saudi Arabic import statistic.

The cheese market in Saudi Arabia

Traditionally, Danish Cheese Overseas has had a strong position in Saudi Arabia, having been the market leader for several years, especially as regards feta and other types of cheese. However, Danish Cheese Overseas has had some difficulties in the cream cheese market. The market has risen, but to date two globally large exporters of cheese have dominated the market, that is France and Australia.

The total import of cheese into Saudi Arabia (there is very little local production) is shown in Table 2. So far the share of cheese from Denmark has been about 25 per cent (£10 million).

On the basis of this, Danish Cheese decided to develop a new cream cheese in order to compete with the big exporters of cheese within the cream/processing segment. The product was also to be targeted at the Middle East, where Saudi Arabia is the main market, but was also to form the basis for an international brand: *Danish Klassic* (see Plate 10).

In order to plan the specific details of the product parameter Danish Cheese contacted an international market research bureau that specialised in the Middle East. The objective was to analyze the cream cheese consumption among typical Middle East families living in the cities. The final result showed that between 85 and 100 per cent of all family members eat cream cheese on a regular basis (mostly in the middle of the day), and the consumption is especially high among children. Thus, the company could set forth the product development of the new cheese. Different product concepts were tested among typical families, with the final result being a 200 gram cream cheese in brick cartons. The brick carton is a new type of packaging, because until then cream cheese had mostly been sold in glass packaging.

Marketing plan for Danish Klassic

The following describes the launch actually made by Danish Cheese Overseas in 1987.

An introduction was held in October 1987, in the form of three trade seminars in the three big cities, Riyadh, Jeddah and Dammam. Here, the product concept and the advertising campaign were presented to a large number of distributors and wholesalers – see Plate 10, a–e.

TV commercials

In Saudi Arabia television is considered to be the most effective medium for mass communication. It therefore became the foundation of the company's marketing. In total, 128 commercial spots were planned during the first year (see Plate 10b).

Print advertisements

- *Consumer oriented.* The most popular newspapers and family magazines in the big cities, especially directed at women as the decisive buyer unit (Plate 10c).
- *Distributor oriented.* Trade magazines.
- *In-store promotion.* Displays, taste sample demonstrations etc. (Plate 10d).

The campaign material was introduced in both Arabic and English, and Plate 10, a–e are a mixture of both English and Arabic.

The campaign was influenced by a high degree of pull strategy (consumer influence). In this way, distributors were induced to build up stocks in order to meet the expected end-user demand. The risk the distributors would face when buying large quantities was limited because the cheese could be kept for a year without being refrigerated.

Plate 10a can be translated as follows:

Product information:

● *Danish Klassic* – cream cheese spread for the whole family.

● Created from fresh cow's milk from the vigorous fields of Denmark.

● Product facts
  – It takes 1.5 litres of fresh cow's milk to produce a single box of 200 g.
  – *Danish Klassic* is packed in a practical, unbreakable box.
  – This cream cheese spread will remain healthy and delicious for a whole year after production – even if it's not kept under refrigeration.
  – *Danish Klassic*, a combination of high nutrition value and a delicious taste.

This enclosure was also used as an advertisement for many consumer oriented newspapers and magazines.

Plate 10d can be translated as follows:

Shop demonstrations:

● To let your customers know *Danish Klassic* is in town, we plan shop demonstrations in a number of supermarkets all over the country.

● The selected shops will be decorated with some giant *Danish Klassic* boxes.
  – Your customers are bound to notice this cream cheese.
  – Tastes will be distributed.
  – Taste it. It's delicious. It's healthy, and full of energy.

What happened to Danish Klassic?

About half a year after the introduction in Saudi Arabia, 24 October 1988, the following was part of an article in *Jyllandsposten*, a Danish newspaper:

> So far MD Foods has shipped 700–800 tons of the new, long-life cheese from the harbour of Esbjerg, but the sales are expected to rise to 5000 tons per year during the next few years ... According to the plan, 'Danish Klassic' is to be marketed in Denmark and in other parts of the world such as South America, where it has scored top marks in recent taste tests.
>
> The new, long-life cheese that comes in completely sealed 200 g packages is marketed massively through TV spots, the company's own sales representatives, shop promotions, and print advertisements. About half of the total investment of DKK30–35 million is allocated to marketing. Thus, MD Foods challenges the multinational food concern, Kraft Food, which, through its various types of cheese in glass packaging, controls the majority of the markets in the Middle East.

However, at the beginning of 1993, MD Foods realized that Danish Klassic could not meet the international sales budget, and therefore, in 1989/90, MD Foods withdrew the product from the market.

Today, MD Foods sells cheese to the Middle East through its sales company, Chesco Cheese Ltd. The cream cheese and other types of cheese are now sold under the brand 'Puck' (Plate 10f) in glass packaging. Its market share of cream cheese is increasing again and today the total sales are very close to those of the market leader, Kraft Food.

Questions

1. What could be the reasons for Danish Klassic not being able to meet the expectations? In relation to this, please comment on the following:
   – the change of packaging – from glass to plastic brick carton;
   – the consumer oriented advertisement (Plate 10a) – is it targeted at the Saudi Arabic market?
2. What do you think of the brand name Danish Klassic?

Questions for discussion

1. How would you distinguish between services and products? What are the main implications of this difference for the global marketing of services?

2. What implications does the product life cycle theory have for international product development strategy?

3. To what degree should international markets be offered standardized service and warranty policies that do not differ significantly from market to market?

4. Why is the international product policy likely to be given higher priority in most firms than other elements of the global marketing mix?

5. Describe briefly the IPLC theory and its marketing implications.

6. What are the requirements that must be met so that a commodity can effectively be transformed into a branded product?

7. Discuss the factors that need to be taken into account when making packaging decisions for international product lines.

8. When is it appropriate to use multiple brands in (a) a single market and (b) several markets/countries?

9. What is the importance of 'country of origin' in international product marketing?

10. What are the distinguishing characteristics of services? Explain why these characteristics make it difficult to sell services in foreign markets.

11. Identify the major barriers to developing international brands.

12. Discuss the decision to add or drop products to or from the product line in international markets.

13. Why should customer-service levels differ internationally? Is it, for example, ethical to offer a lower customer-service level in developing countries than in industrialized countries?

14. What are the characteristics of a good international brand name?

Internet exercise

Global branding and KFC

Please go to:

http://www.cio.com/archive/enterprise/031598_marketing.html

http://www.kfc.com/

http://www.triconglobal.com/triconroot/default.htm

Questions

1. How can companies build brand awareness on a global basis?

2. How is the KFC Corporation building their brand image on a global basis?

For further exercises and cases, see this book's website at *www.booksites.net/hollensen*

References

Aaker, D. (1991) *Managing the Brand Equity: Capitalizing on the Value of the Brand Name*. The Free Press, New York.

Boze, B.V. and Patton, C.R (1995) 'The future of consumer branding as seen from the picture today', *Journal of Consumer Marketing*, vol. 12, no. 4, pp. 20–41.

Brown, P. (1996) *Anita Roddick and The Body Shop*, Great Business Stories, Exley Publications, Watford, UK.

Czinkota, M. R. and Ronkainen, I.A. (1995) *International Marketing* (4th edn), Dryden Press, Fort Worth, TX.

Dhalla, N.K. and Yuspeh, S. (1976) 'Forget the product life concept', *Harvard Business Review*, January–February, pp. 102–12.

Ettensén, R. (1993) 'Brand name and country of origin: effects in the emerging market economies of Russia, Poland and Hungary', *International Marketing Review*, no. 5, pp. 14–36.

Ferguson, W. (1996) 'Impact of ISO 9000 series standards on industrial marketing', *Industrial Marketing Management*, vol. 25, pp. 305–10.

Filiatrault, P. and Lapierre, J. (1997) 'Managing business-to-business marketing relationships in consulting engineering firms', *Industrial Marketing Management*, vol. 26, pp. 213–22.

Ho, S.K.M. (1995) 'Is the ISO 9000 series for total quality management?', *International Journal of Physical Distribution and Logistics Management*, vol. 25, no. 1, pp. 51–66.

Hooley, Saunders and Piercy (1998) *Marketing Strategy and Competitive Positioning* (2nd edn), Prentice Hall Europe.

Johansson, J.K. and Thorelli, H.B. (1985) 'International product positioning', *Journal of International Business Studies*, vol. 16, Fall, pp. 57–75.

Johansson, J.K., Ronkainen, I.A. and Czinkota, M.R. (1994) 'Negative country-of-origin effects: the case of the new Russia', *Journal of International Business Studies*, vol. 25, 1st quarter, pp. 1–21.

Katayama, O. (1995) 'Life is a ball', *Look Japan*, December, pp. 18–19.

Keegan, W.J. (1995) *Global Marketing Management* (5th edn), Prentice Hall, Englewood Cliffs, NJ.

Kotler, P. (1997) *Marketing Management: Analysis, planning, implementation and control* (9th edn), Prentice Hall, Englewood Cliffs, NJ.

Kumar, N. (1999) 'Internet distribution strategies: Dilemmas for the incumbent', Mastering Information Management Part 7, Electronic Commerce, *Financial Times*, 15 March.

Lovelock, C.H. and Yip, G.S. (1996) 'Developing global strategies for service business', *California Management Review*, vol. 38, no. 2, pp. 64–86.

MacNamee, B. and McDonnell, R. (1995) *The Marketing Casebook*, Routledge, London.

Marketing Science Institute (1995) *Brand Equity and Marketing Mix: Creating customer value.* Conference Summary, Report no. 95–111, September, p. 14.

McNamee, P. (1984) 'Competitive analysis using matrix displays', *Long Range Planning*, vol. 17, no. 3, pp. 98–114.

Mendleson, N. and Polonsky, M.J. (1995) 'Using strategic alliances to develop credible green marketing', *Journal of Consumer Marketing*, vol. 12, no. 2, pp. 4–18.

Onkvisit, S. and Shaw, J.J. (1989) 'The international dimension of branding: strategic considerations and decisions', *International Marketing Review*, vol. 6, no. 3, pp. 22–34.

Onkvisit, S. and Shaw, J.J. (1993) *International Marketing: Analysis and strategy* (2nd edn), Macmillan, London.

Popper, E.T. and Buskirk, B.D. (1992) 'Technology life cycles in industrial markets', *Industrial Marketing Management*, vol. 21, pp. 23–31.

Preece, S., Fleisher, C. and Toccacelli, J. (1995) 'Building a reputation along the value chain at Levi Strauss', *Long Range Planning*, vol. 28, no. 6, pp. 88–98.

Quelch, J.A. and Harding, D. (1996) 'Brands versus private labels: fighting to win', *Harvard Business Review*, January–February, pp. 99–109.

Starik, M., Throop, G.M., Doody, J.M. and Joyce, M.E. (1996) 'Growing on environmental strategy', *Business Strategy and the Environment*, vol. 5, pp. 12–21.

Tomesco, F. (1995) 'Central Europeans in North America: pioneering spirit', *Business Central Europe*, September, p. 34.

Töpfer, A. (1995) 'New products – cutting the time to market', *Long Range Planning*, vol. 28, no. 2, pp. 61–78.

Vandermerwe, J. and Oliff, M.D. (1991) 'Corporate challenges for an age of reconsumption', *Columbia Journal of World Business*, vol. 26, no. 3, pp. 6–25.

Vernon, R. (1966) 'International investment and international trade in the product life cycle', *Quarterly Journal of Economics*, May, pp. 190–207.

Wallace, C.P. (1996) 'Can the Body shape up?' *Fortune*, 15 April, pp. 62–4.

Welford, R. and Prescott, K. (1996) *European Business: An issue-based approach* (3rd edn), Pitman, London.

World Wide Fund for Nature (1993) *Corporate Relationships*, Sydney.

Wu, H.J. and Dunn, S.C. (1995) 'Environmentally responsible logistics systems', *International Journal of Physical Distribution and Logistics Management*, vol. 25, no. 2, pp. 20–38.

Zikmund, W. and D'Amico, M. (1989) *Marketing* (3rd edn), John Wiley, New York.

Chapter 15

Pricing decisions and terms of doing business

After studying this chapter you should be able to do the following:

- Explain how internal and external variables influence international pricing decisions.

- Explain why and how prices escalate in export selling.

- Discuss the strategic options in determining the price level for a new product.

- Explain the necessary sales volume increase as a consequence of a price decrease.

- Explain what is meant by experience curve pricing.

- Explore the special roles and problems of transfer pricing in global marketing.

- Discuss how varying currency conditions challenge the international marketer.

- Identify and explain the different terms of sale (price quotations).

- Discuss the conditions that affect terms of payment.

- Discuss the role of export credit and financing for successful export marketing.

15.1 Introduction

Pricing is part of the marketing mix. Pricing decisions must therefore be integrated with the other three Ps of the marketing mix. Price is the only area of the global marketing mix where policy can be changed rapidly without large direct cost implications. This characteristic, plus the fact that overseas consumers are often sensitive to price changes, results in the danger that pricing action may be resorted to as a quick fix instead of changes being made in other areas of the firm's marketing programme. It is thus important that management realizes that constant fine tuning of prices in overseas markets should be avoided and that many problems are not best addressed by pricing action.

Generally, pricing policy is one of the most important yet often least recognized of all the elements of the marketing mix. The other elements of the marketing mix all lead to costs. The only source of profit to the firm comes from revenue, which in turn is dictated by pricing policy. In this chapter, we focus on a number of pricing issues of special interest to international marketers.

15.2 International pricing strategies compared with domestic pricing strategies

For many SMEs operating in domestic markets, pricing decisions are based on the relatively straightforward process of allocating the total estimated cost of producing, managing and marketing a product or service and adding an appropriate profit margin. Problems for these firms arise when costs increase and sales do not materialize or when competitors undercut them. In international markets, however, pricing decisions are much more complex, because they are affected by a number of additional external factors, such as fluctuations in exchange rates, accelerating inflation in certain countries and the use of alternative payment methods such as leasing, barter and counter-trade.

Of special concern to the global marketing manager are pricing decisions on products made or marketed locally, but with some centralized influence from outside the country in which the products are made or marketed. Broadly speaking, pricing decisions include setting the initial price as well as changing the established price of products from time to time.

15.3 Factors influencing international pricing decisions

An SME exporting for the first time, with little knowledge of the market environment that it is entering, is likely to set a price that will ensure that the sales revenue generated at least covers the cost incurred. It is important that firms recognize that the cost structures of products are very significant, but they should not be regarded as sole determinants when setting prices.

Pricing policy is an important strategic and tactical competitive weapon that, in contrast to the other elements of the global marketing mix, is highly controllable and inexpensive to change and implement. Therefore, pricing strategies and action should be integrated with the other elements of the global marketing mix.

Figure 15.1 presents a general framework for international pricing decisions. According to this model, factors affecting international pricing can be broken down into two main groups (internal and external factors) and four subgroups, which we will now consider in more detail.

Firm-level factors

International pricing is influenced by past and current corporate philosophy, organization and managerial policies. The short-term tactical use of pricing in the form of discounts, product offers and reductions is often emphasized by managers at the

Figure 15.1 International pricing framework

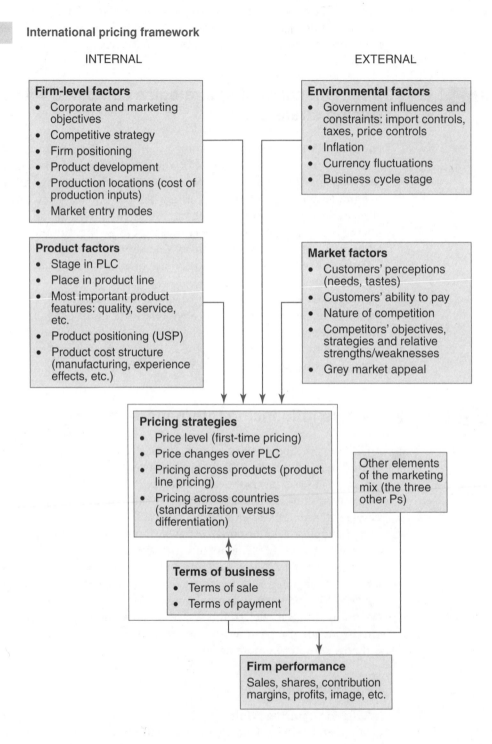

Plate 13 Habits of cognac drinking in western Europe and Asia (Chapter 17)

Plate 14 Advertisements for Prince cigarettes in the UK and Germany (Chapter 17)

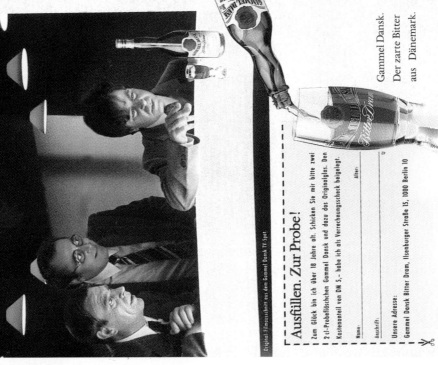

Plate 15 Advertisements for Gammel Dansk in Denmark and Germany (Chapter 17)

For Angels With Dirty Faces.

LUX

(a)

Plate 16 Lux in UK (a) and Indian (b) advertisements (Chapter 17)

Plate 16 (continued)

BUILD YOUR CHILD'S MIND.

LEGO SYSTEM FreeStyle is much more than a toy. It encourages children of 3 years and above to develop vital skills for their future. It helps to build their practical skills, their imagination and their minds. More importantly, there are no rights and no wrongs because LEGO SYSTEM FreeStyle is about building and exploring your own imagination. Give your child a headstart with LEGO SYSTEM FreeStyle today.

LEGO SYSTEM FreeStyle

BUILDS YOUR CHILD'S MIND

Plate 17 Advertisements for LEGO FreeStyle in Europe and the Far East (Chapter 17)

Plate 18 American rap group Bad Boys in Helly Hansen clothes (Case Study Chapter 17)

Plate 19 Absolut Vodka (Case IV.1)

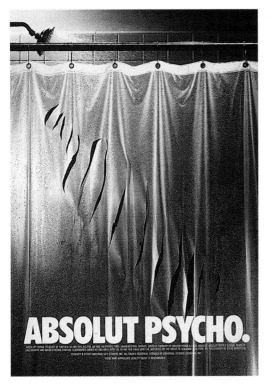

ABSOLUT PSYCHO.

ABSOLUT MILAN.

ABSOLUT BERLIN.

ABSOLUT MARINÉ.

Plate 19 (continued)

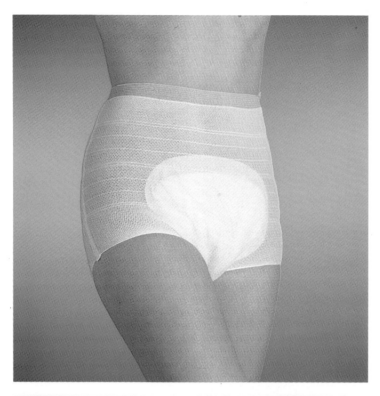

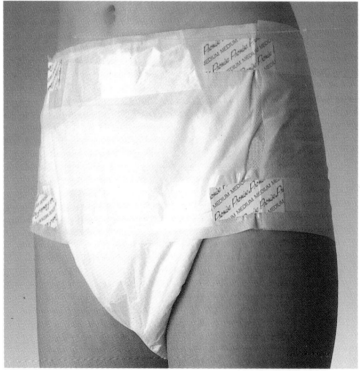

Plate 20 Tytex's two-piece systems (top), and one-piece system (bottom) (Case IV.4)

Plate 21 Martini (Case V.1)

Plate 21 (continued)

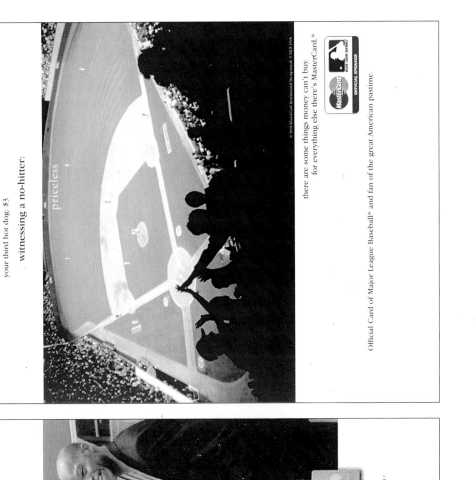

four more desks: $625

second laser printer: $999

larger conference table: $755

becoming a bigger fish in the pond:

priceless

the new Executive BusinessCard has a higher credit limit and
a range of payment options designed to help manage your cash flow.
to learn how to apply call 1-800-727-8825 or visit us at www.mastercard.com

there are some things money can't buy

for everything else there's MasterCard.®

bleacher seat: $7

binoculars: $30

your third hot dog: $3

witnessing a no-hitter:

priceless

© 1998 MasterCard International Incorporated. © MLB 1998.

there are some things money can't buy.
for everything else there's MasterCard.®

Official Card of Major League Baseball® and fan of the great American pastime.

Plate 22 Eurocard (Case V.1)

climbing harnesses and helmets: $325

raft for rapids: $400

venom antidote: $2

last-minute changes to will: $150

surviving: priceless

there are some things money can't buy.

for everything else there's MasterCard.*

The Official Card of the Discovery Channel Eco-Challenge and Supporter of the Great Outdoors.

two front-row tickets: $62

John Harkes key chain: $10

souvenir poster: $16

seeing your heroes life-size: priceless

there are some things money can't buy.

for everything else there's MasterCard.*

Official Card of Major League Soccer, World Cup '98, and friend of soccer fanatics everywhere.

Plate 22 (continued)

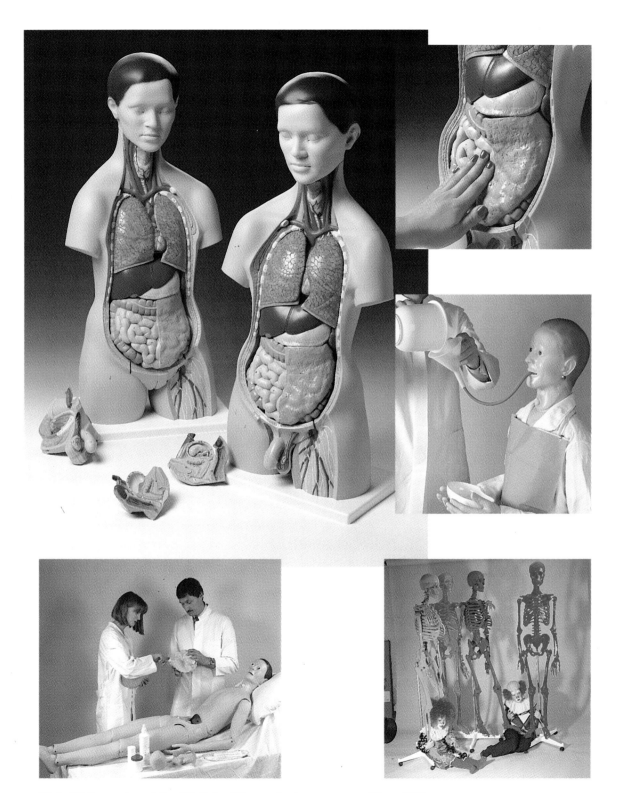

Plate 23 Examples of the 3B Scientific product programme (Case V.2)

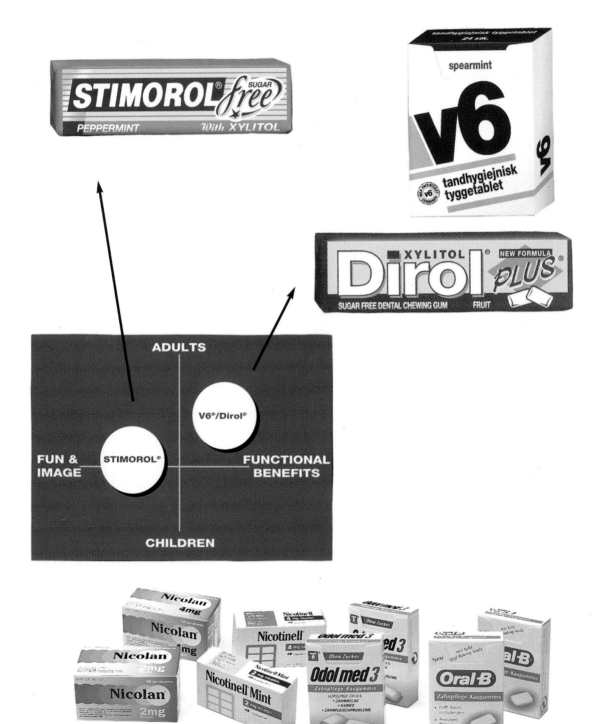

Plate 24 Dandy's brands and their positioning (top) and Dandy's private-label programme (bottom) (Case V.3)

expense of its strategic role, and yet pricing over recent years has played a very significant part in the restructuring of many industries, resulting in the growth of some businesses and the decline of others. In particular, Japanese firms have approached new markets with the intention of building market shares over a period of years by reducing price levels, establishing the brand name, and setting up effective distribution and servicing networks. The market share objectives of the Japanese firms have usually been accomplished at the expense of short-term profits, as international Japanese firms have consistently taken a long-term perspective on profit. They are usually prepared to wait much longer for returns on investments than some of their western counterparts.

The choice of foreign market entry mode also affects the pricing policy. A manufacturer with a subsidiary in a foreign country has a high level of control over the pricing policy in that country.

Product factors

Key product factors include the unique and innovative features of the product and the availability of substitutes. These factors will have a major impact on the stage of the product life cycle, which will also depend on the market environment in target markets. Whether the product is a service or a manufactured or commodity good sold into consumer or industrial markets is also significant.

The extent to which the organization has had to adapt or modify the product or service, and the level to which the market requires service around the core product, will also affect cost and thereby have some influence on pricing.

Costs are also helpful in estimating how rivals will react to the setting of a specific price, assuming that knowledge of one's own costs helps in the assessment of competitors' reactions. Added to the above is the intermediary cost, which depends on channel length, intermediary factors and logistical costs. All these factors add up and lead to price escalation.

The example in Table 15.1 shows that, due to additional shipping, insurance and distribution charges, the exported product costs some 21 per cent more in the export market than at home. Through the use of an additional distribution link (an importer), the product costs 39 per cent more abroad than at home.

Many exporters are not aware of rapid price escalation; they are preoccupied with the price they charge to the importer. However, the final consumer price should be of vital concern because it is on this level that the consumer can compare prices of different competitive products and it is this price that plays a major role in determining the foreign demand.

Price escalation is not a problem for exporters alone. It affects all firms involved in cross-border transactions. Companies that undertake substantial intracompany shipment of goods and materials across national borders are exposed to many of the additional charges that cause price escalation.

The following management options are available to counter price escalation:

● Rationalizing the distribution process. One option is to reduce the number of links in the distribution process, either by doing more in-house or by circumventing some channel members.

Table 15.1	Price escalation (examples)

	Domestic channel (a)	Foreign marketing channel (b)	(c)
	Firm → Wholesaler → Retailer → Consumer	Firm → [Border] → Wholesaler → Retailer → Consumer	Firm → [Border] → Importer → Wholesaler → Retailer → Consumer
	£	£	£
Firm's net price	100	100	100
Insurance and shipping costs	—	10	10
Landed cost	—	110	110
Tariff (10% of landed cost)	—	11	11
Importer pays (cost)	—	—	121
Importer's margin/mark-up (15% of cost)	—	—	18
Wholesaler pays (cost)	100	121	139
Wholesaler'/mark-up (20% of cost)	20	24	28
Retailer pays (cost)	120	145	167
Retail margin/mark-up (40% of cost)	48	58	67
Consumer pays (price) (exclusive VAT)	168	203	234
% price escalation over domestic channel	—	21	39

- Lowering the export price from the factory (firm's net price), thus reducing the multiplier effect of all the mark-ups.
- Establishing a local production of the product within the export market to eliminate some of the cost.
- Pressurizing channel members to accept lower profit margins. This may be appropriate if these intermediaries are dependent on the manufacturer for much of their turnover.

It may be dangerous to overlook traditional channel members. In Japan, for example, the complex nature of the distribution system, which often involves many different channel members, makes it tempting to consider radical change. However, existing intermediaries do not like to be overlooked, and their possible network with other channel members and the government may make it dangerous for a foreign firm to attempt to cut them out.

Environmental factors

The environmental factors are external to the firm and thus uncontrollable variables in the foreign market. The national government control of exports and imports is usually based on political and strategic considerations.

Generally speaking, import controls are designed to limit imports in order to protect domestic producers or reduce the outflow of foreign exchange. Direct restrictions commonly take the form of tariffs, quotas and various non-tariff barriers. Tariffs directly increase the price of imports unless the exporter or importer is willing to absorb the tax and accept lower profit margins. Quotas have an indirect impact on prices. They restrict supply, thus causing the price of the import to increase.

Since tariff levels vary from country to country, there is an incentive for exporters to vary the price somewhat from country to country. In some countries with high customs duties and high price elasticity, the base price may have to be lower than in other countries if the product is to achieve satisfactory volume in these markets. If demand is quite inelastic, the price may be set at a high level, with little loss of volume, unless competitors are selling at lower prices.

Government regulation on pricing can also affect the firm's pricing strategy. Many governments tend to have price controls on specific products related to health, education, food and other essential items. Another major environmental factor is fluctuation in the exchange rate. An increase (revaluation) or decrease (devaluation) in the relative value of a currency can affect the firm's pricing structure and profitability.

Market factors

One of the critical factors in the foreign market is the purchasing power of the customers (customers' ability to pay). The pressure of competitors may also affect international pricing. The firm has to offer a more competitive price if there are other sellers in the market. Thus, the nature of competition (e.g. oligopoly or monopoly) can influence the firm's pricing strategy.

Under conditions approximating pure competition, price is set in the marketplace. Price tends to be just enough above costs to keep marginal producers in business. Thus, from the point of view of the price setter, the most important factor is costs. The closer the substitutability of products, the more nearly identical the prices must be, and the greater the influence of costs in determining prices (assuming a large enough number of buyers and sellers).

Under conditions of monopolistic or imperfect competition, the seller has some discretion to vary the product quality, promotional efforts and channel policies in order to adapt the price of the total product to serve preselected market segments. Nevertheless, the freedom to set prices is still limited by what competitors charge, and any price differentials from competitors must be justified in the minds of customers on the basis of differential utility: that is, perceived value.

When considering how customers will respond to a given price strategy, Nagle (1987) has suggested nine factors which influence the sensitivity of customers to prices. Price sensitivity is reduced in the following cases:

● More distinctive product.

● Greater perceived quality of products.

● Consumers less aware of substitutes in the market.

● Difficulty in making comparisons (e.g. in the quality of services such as consultancy or accountancy).

● The price of a product represents a small proportion of total expenditure of the customer.

● The perceived benefit for the customer increases.

● The product is used in association with a product bought previously, so that, for example, components and replacements are usually extremely highly priced.

● Costs are shared with other parties.

● The product or service cannot be stored.

In the following sections we discuss the different available pricing strategies.

15.4 International pricing strategies

In determining the price level for a new product, the general alternatives are as shown in Figure 15.2.

Skimming

In this strategy, a high price is charged to 'skim the cream' from the top end of the market, with the objective of achieving the highest possible contribution in a short time. For a marketer to use this approach, the product has to be unique, and some segments of the market must be willing to pay the high price. As more segments are targeted and more of the product is made available, the price is gradually lowered. The success of skimming depends on the ability and speed of competitive reaction.

Products should be designed to appeal to affluent and demanding consumers, offering extra features, greater comfort, variability or ease of operation. With skimming, the firm trades off a low market share against a high margin.

Figure 15.2   **Strategies for pricing a new product**

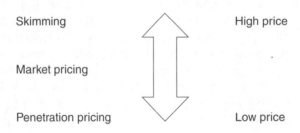

Problems with skimming are as follows:

● Having a small market share makes the firm vulnerable to aggressive local competition.

● Maintenance of a high-quality product requires a lot of resources (promotion, after-sales service) and a visible local presence, which may be difficult in distant markets.

● If the product is sold more cheaply at home or in another country, grey marketing (parallel importing) is likely.

Market pricing

If similar products already exist in the target market, market pricing may be used. The final customer price is based on competitive prices. This approach requires the exporter to have a thorough knowledge of product costs, as well as confidence that the product life cycle is long enough to warrant entry into the market. It is a reactive approach and may lead to problems if sales volumes never rise to sufficient levels to produce a satisfactory return. Although firms typically use pricing as a differentiation tool, the global marketing manager may have no choice but to accept the prevailing world market price.

From the price that customers are willing to pay, it is possible to make a so-called retrograde calculation where the firm uses a 'reversed' price escalation to calculate backwards (from market price) to the necessary (ex factory) net price. If this net price can create a satisfactory contribution margin, then the firm can go ahead.

Penetration pricing

A penetration pricing policy is used to stimulate market growth and capture market shares by deliberately offering products at low prices. This approach requires mass markets, price-sensitive customers and reduction in unit costs through economies of scale (experience curve effects). The basic assumption that lower prices will increase sales will fail if the main competitors reduce their prices to a correspondingly low level. Another danger is that prices might be set so low that they are not credible to consumers. There exist 'confidence levels' for prices below which consumers lose faith in the product's quality.

Motives for pricing at low levels in certain foreign markets might include the following:

● Intensive local competition from rival companies.

● Lower income levels of local consumers.

● Some firms argue that, since their R & D and other overhead costs are covered by home sales, exporting represents a marginal activity intended merely to bring in as much additional revenue as possible by offering a low selling price.

Japanese companies have used penetration pricing intensively to gain market share leadership in a number of markets, such as cars, home entertainment products and electronic components.

Price changes

Price changes on existing products are called for when a new product has been launched or when changes occur in overall market conditions (such as fluctuating foreign exchange rates).

Table 15.2 shows the percentage sales volume increase or decrease required to maintain the level of profit. An example (the marked figure in Table 15.2) shows how the table functions. A firm has a product with a contribution margin of 20 per cent. The firm would like to know how much the sales volume should be increased as a consequence of a price reduction of 5 per cent, if it wishes to keep the same total profit contribution. The calculation is as follows:

Before price reduction

Per product	sales price	£100
	variable cost per unit	£80
	contribution margin	£20

Total contribution margin: 100 units @£20 = £2,000

After price reduction (5%)

Per product	sales price	£95
	variable cost per unit	£80
	contribution margin	£15

Total contribution margin: 133 units @£15 = £2,000

Table 15.2   Sales volume increase or decrease (%) required to maintain total profit contribution

Price reduction (%)	Profit contribution margin (price – variable cost per unit as % of the price)								
	5	10	15	20	25	30	35	40	50
	Sales volume increase (%) required to maintain total profit contribution								
2.0	67	25	15	11	9	7	7	5	4
3.0	150	43	25	18	14	11	9	8	6
4.0	400	67	36	25	19	15	13	11	9
5.0		100	50	33	25	20	17	14	11
7.5		300	100	60	43	33	27	23	18
10.0			200	100	67	50	40	33	25
15.0				300	150	100	75	60	43

Price reduction (%)	Profit contribution margin (price – variable cost per unit as % of the price)								
	5	10	15	20	25	30	35	40	50
	Sales volume reduction (%) required to maintain total profit contribution								
2.0	29	17	12	9	7	6	5	5	4
3.0	37	23	17	13	11	9	8	7	6
4.0	44	29	21	17	14	12	10	9	7
5.0	50	33	25	20	17	14	12	11	9
7.5	60	43	33	27	23	20	18	16	13
10.0	67	50	40	33	29	25	22	20	17
15.0	75	60	50	43	37	33	30	27	23

As a consequence of a price reduction of 5 per cent, a 33 per cent increase in sales is required.

If a decision is made to change prices, related changes must also be considered. For example, if an increase in price is required, it may be accompanied, at least initially, by increased promotional efforts.

When changing prices, the degree of flexibility enjoyed by decision makers will tend to be less for existing products than for new products. This follows from the high probability that the existing product is now less unique, faces stronger competition and is aimed at a broader segment of the market. In this situation, the decision maker will be forced to pay more attention to competitive and cost factors in the pricing process.

The timing of price changes can be nearly as important as the changes themselves. For example, a simple tactic of time lagging competitors in announcing price increases can produce the perception among customers that you are the most customer-responsive supplier. The extent of the time lag can also be important.

In one company, an independent survey of customers (Garda, 1995) showed that the perception of being the most customer-responsive supplier was generated just as effectively by a six-week lag in following a competitor's price increase as by a six-month lag. A considerable amount of money would have been lost during the unnecessary four-and-a-half-month delay in announcing a price increase.

Experience curve pricing

Price changes usually follow changes in the product's stage in the life cycle. As the product matures, more pressure will be put on the price to keep the product competitive despite increased competition and less possibility of differentiation.

Let us also integrate the cost aspect into the discussion. The experience curve has

Figure 15.3   **Experience curves of value chain activities**

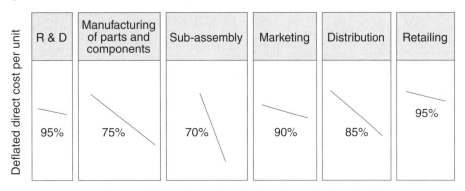

(Source: Czepiel, 1992, p. 154)

its roots in a commonly observed phenomenon called the learning curve, which states that as people repeat a task they learn to do it better and faster. The learning curve applies to the labour portion of manufacturing cost. The Boston Consulting Group extended the learning effect to cover all the value-added costs related to a product – manufacturing plus marketing, sales, administration and the like.

The resulting experience curves, covering all value chain activities (see Figure 15.3), indicate that the total unit costs of a product in real terms can be reduced by a certain percentage with each doubling of cumulative production. The typical decline in cost is 30 per cent (termed a 70 per cent curve), although greater and lesser declines are observed (Czepiel, 1992, p. 149).

If we combine the experience curve (average unit cost) with the typical market price development within an industry, we will have a relationship similar to that shown in Figure 15.4.

Figure 15.4 shows that after the introduction stage (during part of which the price is below the total unit cost), profits begin to flow. Because supply is less than demand, prices do not fall as quickly as costs. Consequently, the gap between costs and prices widens, in effect creating a price umbrella, attracting new competitors. However, the competitive situation is not a stable one. At some point the umbrella will be folded by one or more competitors reducing the prices in an attempt to gain market shares. The result is that a shake-out phase will begin: inefficient producers will be shaken out by rapidly falling market prices, and only those with a competitive price/cost relationship will remain.

Figure 15.4   **Product life cycle stages and the industry price experience curve**

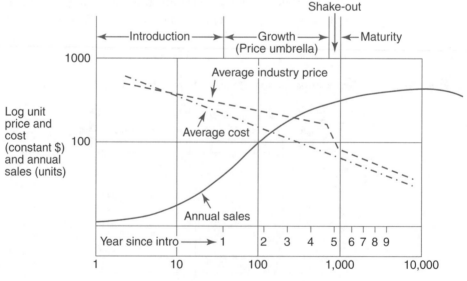

(Source: Czepiel, 1992, p. 167)

Exhibit 15.1	**Sony's pricing strategy for compact disc players**

As a result of a joint development between Sony and Philips, the first CD player was introduced in 1982, but in the beginning it was only an alternative product to the analogue LP player connected to a full-size hi-fi audio system. This player could not significantly increase the market demand. The prices of the CD players were also higher than the standard analogue LP players at that time. Consequently, the market size of CD players was smaller than the industry had expected.

Then in 1984 Sony made the strategic decision to promote the CD heavily. It introduced the Discman D-50 to the market, at a price of ¥49,800, half the price of other stationary CD models.

Figure 15.5 shows only two price curves on the Japanese market, not the corresponding cost curves. However, the least expensive curve, showing a V-shape around 1984, has been able to pull down the average price curve by expanding the market for CD players. The competitor to Sony's Discman D-50, Matsushita's SL-XP7 CD player, appeared on the market in July 1985, nine months after the introduction of the Discman. The new portable CD player attracted new customers, not just the hi-fi enthusiasts, but also the general audio users, just as had happened with the introduction of the Walkman.

In 1985 Sony was the first company to introduce the CD radio cassette, which was a combination unit of a radio, a stereo cassette recorder and a built-in CD player. The small CD player unit was also introduced into the car stereo field. Besides being a CD player manufacturer, Sony is also an OEM supplier of the key components in a CD player (optical pick-up, laser diodes, etc.) and it has taken a 10 per cent market share of the OEM business in Japan, including Sony's in-house use. Thus, the strategic concept of Sony's CD player business is: 'Pushing out the competitors, while at the same time pulling them into the market'. Sony is selling to them anyway, as an OEM supplier. Furthermore, Sony has made integrative moves into the CD software business (music) by acquiring CBC Records in the USA in 1987. Sony now holds 10 per cent of the CD software world-wide.

Source: Shibata (1993). Reprinted with permission from Elsevier Science Ltd, The Boulevard, Langford Lane, Kidlington, OX5 1GB, UK.

Pricing across products (product line pricing)

With across-product pricing, the various items in the line may be differentiated by pricing them appropriately to indicate, for example, an economy version, a standard version and the top-of-the-line version. One of the products in the line may be priced to protect against competitors or to gain market share from existing competitors.

Products with less competition may be priced higher to subsidize other parts of the product line, so as to make up for the lost contribution of such 'fighting brands'. Another strategy is price bundling (total 'package' price), where a certain price is set for customers who simultaneously buy several items within the product line (one price for a personal computer package with software and printer). In all such cases, a key consideration is how much consumers in different countries want to save

Figure 15.5   **Pushing down the experience curve**

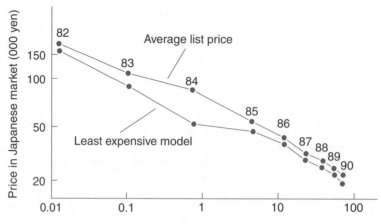

Cumulative production quantity of CD players (millions world-wide)

money, to spend time searching for the 'best buy' and so forth. Furthermore, some items in the product line may be priced very low to serve as loss leaders and induce customers to try the product. A special variant of this is the so-called buy in–follow on strategy (Weigand, 1991). A classic example of this strategy is the razor blade link where Gillette, for example, uses a penetration price on its razor (buy in) but a skimming pricing (relatively high price) on its razor blades (follow on). Thus, the linked product or service – the follow on – is sold at a significant contribution margin. This inevitably attracts hitchhikers who try to sell follow-on products without incurring the cost of the buy in.

The buy in–follow on strategy is different from a low introductory price, which is based on the hope that the customer (of habit) will return again and again at higher prices. With the buy in–follow on strategy, sales of two products or services are powerfully linked by factors such as legal contracts, patents, trade secrets, experience curve advantages and technological links.

Other examples of the strategy are as follows:

● The price of a Polaroid instant camera is very low, but Polaroid hopes that this will generate sales of far more profitable films for many years.

● The telephone companies sell mobile (cellular) telephones at a near giveaway price, hoping that the customer will be a 'heavy' user of the profitable mobile telephone network.

Pricing across countries (standardization versus differentiation)

A major problem for companies is how to coordinate prices between countries. There are two essential opposing forces: first, to achieve similar positioning in different markets by adopting largely standardized pricing; and second, to maximize profitability by adapting pricing to different market conditions. In determining to what extent prices should be standardized across borders, two basic approaches appear:

- *Price standardization*. This is based on setting a price for the product as it leaves the factory. At its simplest, it involves setting a fixed world price at the headquarters of the firm. This fixed world price is then applied in all markets after taking account of factors such as foreign exchange rates and variance in the regulatory context. For the firm this is a low-risk strategy, but no attempt is made to respond to local conditions and so no effort is made to maximize profits.

- *Price differentiation*. This allows each local subsidiary or partner (agent, distributor, etc.) to set a price which is considered to be the most appropriate for local conditions, and no attempt is made to coordinate prices from country to country. The weakness with this policy is the lack of control that the headquarters has over the prices set by the subsidiary operations or external partner. Significantly different prices may be set in adjacent markets, and this can reflect badly on the image of multinational firms. It also encourages the creation of parallel importing/grey markets (which are dealt with in greater detail later in this chapter), whereby products can be purchased in one market and sold in another, undercutting the established market prices in the process.

The underlying forces favouring standardization or differentiation are shown in Figure 15.6.

| Figure 15.6 | **Structural factors of standardized versus differentiated pricing in European consumer goods markets** |

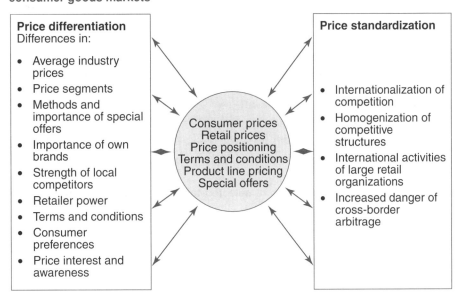

(Source: Diller and Bukhari, 1994, p. 168. Reprinted with permission from Elsevier Science Ltd, the Boulevard, Langford Lane, Kidlington OX5 1GB, UK)

European pricing strategy

In 1991 price differentials for identical consumer goods across Europe were around 20 per cent on average, but much greater differences were apparent in certain products (Simon and Kucher, 1993). Another study (Diller and Bukhari, 1994) shows a case of considerable price differences for identical take-home ice-cream products (see Table 15.3).

The causes of price differentials are differences in regulations, competition, distribution structures and consumer behaviour, such as willingness to pay. Currency fluctuations can also influence short-term price differences. The pressures of regionalization are accelerating the move to uniform pricing, but Simon and Kucher (1993) warn that this is a potential time bomb, as the pressure is for uniform pricing to be at the lowest pricing levels.

Europe was a price differentiation paradise as long as markets were separated. But it is becoming increasingly difficult to retain the old price differentials. There are primarily two developments which may force companies to standardize prices across European countries:

● International buying power of cross-European retail groups.

● Parallel imports/grey markets. Because of differentiated prices across countries, buyers in one country are able to purchase at a lower price than in another country. As a result there will be an incentive for customers in lower-price markets to sell goods to higher-price markets in order to make a profit. Grey marketing will be examined further in section 16.8.

Simon and Kucher (1993) suggest a price 'corridor' (Figure 15.7 and Exhibit 15.2). The prices in the individual countries may only vary within that range. Figure 15.7 is also interesting in the light of the Euro, which is going to be fully implemented by January 2002, when new Euro notes and coins will circulate. But this does not mean that a uniform price across Europe is required. Price differences which can be justified by transportation costs, short-term exchange rate fluctuations, etc. may still be maintained.

They recommend that business in smaller countries should be sacrificed, if necessary, in order to retain acceptable pricing levels in the big markets like France, Germany, the UK and Italy. For example, for a pharmaceutical manufacturer it is more profitable not to sell in the Portuguese pharmaceutical market than to accept a price reduction of 10 per cent in the German market due to parallel imports from Portugal.

Table 15.3   **Consumer prices of selected take-home ice-cream brands: deviation from German price (%)**

	France	Italy	Spain	Netherlands	Belgium
Industry average	+37	+86	+99	−12	−3
Mars	+7	+24	+41	+4	+32
Cart D'Or	−7	+48	+54	−16	+24
Vienetta	+37	+98	+56	+1	+31

Source: Diller and Bukhari (1994), p. 166. Reprinted with permission from Elsevier Science Ltd, The Boulevard, Longford Land, Kidlington, OX5 1GB, UK.

Figure 15.7	Development of prices in Europe

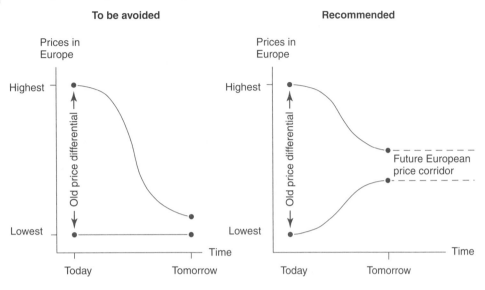

(Source: Simon and Kucher, 1993, p. 26)

Exhibit 15.2 | **Fujitsu's European price corridor**

One of the world's largest manufacturers of computer equipment, Fujitsu, makes disks, scanners and printers as its main products.

'We decided to create a uniform price for our products because our pan-European customers order centrally from the territory where they can buy the cheapest. Also, we saw that European Commission policy is to encourage a reduction in differentials,' a Fujitsu manager explains.

Fujitsu's pricing policy in Europe was dictated by three factors: the company's commitment to uniform prices; customer demand for a single price throughout Europe; and a desire to stop the flow of parallel imports from the USA. Fujitsu priced each item in dollars, then made a currency conversion for the local market.

The company has six regional marketing divisions, which fix prices in the local currency. The regions are Italy, Spain, France, Germany, UK/Benelux and Scandinavia. Small variations still occur from time to time in dollar prices because the price in local currency is fixed at regular intervals, between which dates actual exchange rates fluctuate. The company's aim is to keep these differentials between ±3 per cent. In practice, the differentials can be as high as 8 per cent.

One of the main issues arising from the decision to apply common pricing has been the profitability of specific products for individual operating subsidiaries. Overheads are higher in some markets than in others, which means that some operating companies need to achieve higher performance targets than others. 'We need to move more goods in the UK than, for example, Benelux or Germany because overheads are higher in the UK.'

This is solely due to the impact of overheads on profits within such margins. In the UK, while variable costs such as staffing have fallen significantly, fixed costs such as property rentals and taxes have risen a lot.

Italy is cheaper because premises are older and wage rates lower. Another factor in Italy used to be varying rates of value added tax by region. In some of the poor areas in the south, VAT on computer hardware was charged at 2 per cent, whereas in Rome it was fixed at 12 per cent. This made a profound difference to the marketability of the product. It meant that where products were sold within Italy was crucial to the price. However, VAT on computer hardware has since been harmonized.

Looking at Europe as a whole, profit margins vary by operating area, product group and the nature of the product: either off-the-shelf or integrated. Fujitsu makes a wide range of goods for the European market. These include scanners, printers and disks. Where the products are off-the-shelf, price variation is very small. In the case of products which need to be integrated with other discrete units of technology, the opportunity for price variation grows.

Source: Adapted from EIU (1995).

Transfer pricing

Transfer prices are those charged for intracompany movement of goods and services. Many purely domestic firms need to make transfer-pricing decisions when goods are *transferred* from one domestic unit to another. While these transfer prices are internal to the company, they are important externally because goods being transferred from country to country must have a value for cross-border taxation purposes.

The objective of the corporation in this situation is to ensure that the transfer price paid optimizes corporate rather than divisional objectives. This can prove difficult when a company internationally is organized into profit centres. For profit centres to work effectively, a price must be set for everything that is transferred, be it working materials, components, finished goods or services. A high transfer price – for example, from the manufacturing division to a foreign subsidiary – is reflected in an apparently poor performance by the foreign subsidiary (see the high mark-up policy in Table 15.4), whereas a low price would not be acceptable to the domestic division providing the goods (see the low mark-up policy in Table 15.4). This issue alone can be the cause of much mistrust between subsidiaries.

The 'best' of Table 15.4's two mark-up policies seen from the consolidated point of view is to use a high mark-up policy, since it generates a net income of $550, as against $475 from using a low mark-up policy. The 'best' solution depends on the tax rates in the countries of the manufacturing and distribution affiliates (subsidiaries).

There are three basic approaches to transfer pricing:

● *Transfer at cost.* The transfer price is set at the level of the production cost, and the international division is credited with the entire profit that the firm makes. This means that the production centre is evaluated on efficiency parameters rather

Table 15.4   **Tax effect of low versus high transfer price on net income ($)**

	Manufacturing affiliate (division)	Distribution/selling affiliate (subsidiary)	Consolidated company Total
Low mark-up policy			
Sales	1,400	2,000	2,000
Less cost of goods sold	1,000	1,400	1,000
Gross profit	**400**	**600**	**1,000**
Less operating expenses	100	100	200
Taxable income	**300**	**500**	**800**
Less income taxes (25%/55%)	75	250	325
Net income	**225**	**250**	**475**
High mark-up policy			
Sales	1,700	2,000	2,000
Less cost of goods sold	1,000	1,700	1,000
Gross profit	**700**	**300**	**1,000**
Less operating expenses	100	100	200
Taxable income	**600**	**200**	**800**
Less income taxes (25%/50%)	150	100	250
Net income	**450**	**100**	**550**

Note: Manufacturing affiliate pays income taxes at 25%. Distribution affiliate pays income taxes at 50%.
Source: Adapted from Eitmann and Stonehill (1986).

than profitability. The production division normally dislikes selling at production cost because it believes it is subsidizing the selling subsidiary. When the production division is unhappy, the selling subsidiary may get sluggish service, because the production division is serving more attractive opportunities first.

● *Transfer at arm's length.* Here the international division is charged the same as any buyer outside the firm. Problems occur if the overseas division is allowed to buy elsewhere when the price is uncompetitive or the product quality is inferior, and further problems arise if there are no external buyers, making it difficult to establish a relevant price. Nevertheless the arm's-length principle has now been accepted world-wide as the preferred (not required) standard by which transfer prices should be set (Fraedrich and Bateman, 1996).

● *Transfer at cost plus.* This is the usual compromise, where profits are split between the production and international divisions. The actual formula used for assessing the transfer price can vary, but usually it is this method which has the greatest chance of minimizing executive time spent on transfer-price disagreements, optimizing corporate profits and motivating the home and international divisions. A senior executive is often appointed to rule on disputes.

A good transfer-pricing method should consider total corporate profile and encourage divisional cooperation. It should also minimize executive time spent on transfer-price disagreements and keep the accounting burden at a minimum.

Currency issues

A difficult aspect of export pricing is the decision about what currency the price should be quoted in. The exporter has the following options:

● The foreign currency of the buyer's country (local currency).
● The currency of the exporter's country (domestic currency).
● The currency of a third country (usually dollars or Deutschmarks).
● A currency unit such as the Euro.

If the exporter quotes in the domestic currency, then not only is it administratively much easier, but also the risks associated with changes in the exchange rate are borne by the customer, whereas by quoting prices in the foreign currency the exporter bears the exchange rate risk. However, there are benefits to the exporter in quoting in foreign currency:

● Quoting in foreign currency could be a condition of the contract.
● It could provide access to finance abroad at lower interest rates.
● Good currency management may be a means of gaining additional profits.

Table 15.5 **Exporter strategies under varying currency conditions**

When domestic currency is weak	When domestic currency is strong
Stress price benefits.	Engage in non-price competition by improving quality, delivery and after-sales service.
Expand product line and add more costly features.	Improve productivity and engage in vigorous cost reduction.
Shift sourcing and manufacturing to domestic market.	Shift sourcing and manufacturing overseas.
Exploit export opportunities in all markets.	Give priority to exports to countries with relatively strong currencies.
Conduct conventional cash-for-goods trade.	Deal in counter-trade with countries that have weak currencies.
Use full-costing approach, but use marginal cost pricing to penetrate new/competitive markets.	Trim profit margins and use marginal cost pricing.
Speed repatriation of foreign-earned income and collections.	Keep the foreign-earned income in host country, slow collections.
Minimize expenditures in local, host country currency.	Maximize expenditures in local, host country currency.
Buy needed services (advertising, insurance, transportation etc.) in domestic market.	Buy needed services abroad and pay for them in local currencies.
Minimize local borrowing.	Borrow money needed for expansion in local market.
Bill foreign customers in domestic currency.	Bill foreign customers in their own currency.

Source: Cavusgil (1988), p. 57.

● Customers normally prefer to be quoted in their own currency in order to be able to make competitive comparisons and know exactly what the eventual price will be.

Another difficult problem that exporters face is caused by fluctuating exchange rates. A company in a country with a devalued currency can (all other things being equal) strengthen its international competitive position. It can choose to reduce prices in foreign currencies or it can leave prices unchanged and instead increase profit margins.

When the Italian lira dropped by 15–20 per cent in value against the German mark, it gave the Italian car producer Fiat a competitive advantage in pricing. The German car exporters, such as Volkswagen, were adversely affected and had to raise the list prices. In this respect the geographic pattern of a firm's manufacturing and sales subsidiaries compared with those of its main competitors becomes very important, since a local subsidiary can absorb most of the negative effects of a devaluation. Table 15.5 gives some general advice to an international marketer in the case that the domestic currency is either strong or weak.

15.5 Implications of Internet/e-commerce for pricing across borders

Europe's single currency, the Euro (http://europa.eu.int/euro/) has finally become a reality after more than a decade of planning and preparations. In one stroke, the single currency has created the largest single economy in the world with a larger share of global trade and a greater number of consumers than in the US.

The implication is that Europe suddenly becomes a single market by the end of 2000, and people can purchase from another country as easily as they can from a store across the street. The same currency will be used; only the language issue remains. Opinion in Europe is that, as more of the population goes on-line, and as Europe starts using its new single currency, on-line shopping will experience a tremendous growth.

Most of this growth has been fuelled by aggressive price-cutting from Internet service providers. A number of UK companies, for example, are now offering free Internet access or pay-as-you-go models, which have encouraged new sections of the population to try the Internet for the first time.

A European single currency has been a long-held ambition for members of the European Union (EU). The idea was first considered in the 1970s, but knocked off-course by the oil price rises. It re-emerged in the early 1980s, and was finally agreed to in the 1992 Maastricht Treaty. There were many accounting criteria to be met by each country, such as the control of the rate of inflation and the debt/GDP ratio. Most countries have met these criteria and were permitted to join the European Monetary Union.

This goal has now been achieved by 11 countries. EU currencies like the German mark, the French franc, and the Italian lira are now replaced by the Euro. The Euro zone includes all European Union countries except the UK, Sweden, Denmark and Greece. The UK being outside the Euro region will be quite inconvenient for many

US companies who trade heavily with UK companies or have subsidiaries there. The exact timetable has been as follows:

- *1 January 1999* the Euro became an official currency.

- *1999–2002*: existing national currencies and the Euro operate side by side at fixed rates. The Euro is not imposed as currency, but inter-bank transfer can be made in Euros.

- *By January 2002* new Euro notes and coins will circulate.

- *By July 2002*, at the latest, local currencies are completely phased out and no longer allowed. Only Euro transactions (cash or transfer) are possible.

The current value of the Euro is now (May 2000) below the value of one US$ as it has fallen 25–30 per cent from its introduction on 1 January 1999.

The main detailed implications of the Euro will be that it will:

- lower prices for consumers by making the prices transparent across Europe;

- create a real single market by reducing 'friction' to trade caused by high transaction costs and fluctuation currencies;

- enhance competition by forcing companies to concentrate on price, quality and production instead of hiding behind weak currencies;

- benefit SMEs and consumers by making it easier for the former to enter 'foreign' markets, and allowing the latter, increasingly via the Internet, to shop in the lowest priced markets;

- establish inflation and interest rate stability via the new European Central Bank; and

- lower the costs of doing business through lower prices, lower interest rates, no transaction costs or loss through exchanging currencies, and the absence of exchange rate fluctuations.

In short, the single currency will significantly increase competition, lower transaction costs, and bring about greater certainty. These new forces will bring about structural reforms in Europe. Almost every aspect of Europe's business and political environment will be affected.

Perhaps most importantly, marketing and pricing strategies need rethinking. Because the Euro will allow easy price comparison across Europe (especially via the Internet), it will reveal the differences between higher and lower priced markets.

For those selling via the Internet, the Euro will make it easier to do business, and give encouragement to companies selling to European customers. Since Europeans will now be able to shop and compare prices at a click of a mouse, they will also be more favourably inclined towards e-commerce.

In any single European country, there is usually not much competition for a given product, since purchasing habits have always been local (in one's own country). Now that Europeans will be able to shop internationally at the click of a mouse, they will become aware of other choices and prices for the same product that were not previously known. Competition will heat up for the buyer's Euro, and this should put a downward pressure on prices.

15.6 ❱ Terms of sale/delivery terms

The price quotation describes a specific product, states the price for the product as well as a specified delivery location, sets the time of shipment and specifies payment terms. The responsibilities of the buyer and the seller should be spelled out as they relate to what is and what is not included in the price quotation and when ownership of goods passes from seller to buyer. Incoterms are the internationally accepted standard definitions for terms of sale set by the International Chamber of Commerce (ICC). They have been fully revised for the new millennium in line with developments in commercial practice. Published in September 1999, *Incoterms 2000* may be used to define the responsibilities of buyer and seller in contracts effective from 1 January 2000.

The 13 terms contained in *Incoterms 2000* are the following:

EXW: *Ex works* (… named place)
FCA: *Free carrier* (… named place)
FAS: *Free alongside ship* (… named port of shipment)
FOB: *Free on board* (… named port of shipment)
CFR: *Cost and freight* (… named port of destination)
CIF: *Cost, insurance and freight* (… named port of destination)
CPT: *Carriage paid to* (… named place of destination)
CIP: *Carriage and insurance paid to* (… named place of destination)
DAF: *Delivered at frontier* (… named place)
DES: *Delivered ex ship* (… named port of destination)
DEQ: *Delivered ex quay* (… named port of destination)
DDU: *Delivered duty unpaid* (… named place of destination)
DDP: *Delivered duty paid* (… named place of destination)

Table 15.6 describes the point of delivery and risk shift for some terms of sale. The following is a description of some of the most popular terms of sale:

● *Ex works (EXW)*. The term 'Ex' means that the price quoted by the seller applies at a specified point of origin, usually the factory, warehouse, mine or plantation,

Table 15.6 **Point of delivery and where risk shifts from seller to buyer**

	EXW	FAS	FOB	CFR	CIF	DEQ	DDP
Supplier's factory/warehouse	×						
Dock at port of shipment (export dock)		×					
Port of shipment (on board vessel)			×	×	×		
Port of destination (import dock)					×*	×	
Buyer's warehouse (destination)							×
Main transit risk on	buyer	buyer	buyer	buyer	seller	seller	seller

* The seller transfers the risk to its insurance company.
Source: Adapted from Onkvisit and Shaw (1993), p. 799. Reprinted by permission of Prentice-Hall, Inc.

and the buyer is responsible for all charges from this point. This term represents the minimum obligation for the exporter.

● *Free alongside ship (FAS)*. Under this term the seller must provide for delivery of the goods free alongside, but not on board, the transportation carrier (usually an ocean vessel) at the point of shipment and export. This term differs from that of FOB, since the time and cost of loading are not included in the FAS term. The buyer has to pay for loading the good on to the ship.

● *Free on board (FOB)*. The exporter's price quote includes coverage of all charges up to the point when goods have been loaded on to the designated transport vehicle. The designated loading point may be a named inland shipping point, but is usually the port of export. The buyer assumes responsibility for the goods the moment they pass over the ship's rail.

● *Cost and freight (CFR)*. The seller's liability ends when the goods are loaded on board a carrier or are in the custody of the carrier at the export dock. The seller pays all the transport charges (excluding insurance, which is the customer's obligation) required to deliver goods by sea to a named destination.

● *Cost, insurance, freight (CIF)*. This trade term is identical with CFR except that the seller must also provide the necessary insurance. The seller's obligations still end at the same stage (i.e. when goods are loaded or aboard), but the seller's insurance company assumes responsibility once the goods are loaded.

● *Delivered Ex Quay (DEQ)*. Ex Quay means from the import dock. The term goes one step beyond CIF and requires the seller to be responsible for the cost of the goods and all other costs necessary to place the goods on the dock at the named overseas port, with the appropriate import duty paid.

● *Delivered duty paid (DDP)*. The export price quote includes the costs of delivery to the importer's premises. The exporter is thus responsible for paying any import duties and costs of unloading and inland transport in the importing country, as well as all costs involved in insuring and shipping the goods to that country. These terms imply maximum exporter obligations. The seller also assumes all the risks involved in delivering to the buyer. DDP used to be known as 'Franco domicile' pricing.

Export price quotations are important because they spell out the legal and cost responsibilities of the buyer and seller. Sellers favour a quote that gives them the least liability and responsibility, such as ex works, which means the exporter's liability finishes when the goods are loaded on to the buyer's carrier at the seller's factory. Buyers, on the other hand, would prefer either DDP, where responsibility is borne by the supplier all the way to the customer's warehouse, or CIF port of discharge, which means that the buyer's responsibility begins only when the goods are in its own country.

Generally, the more market-oriented pricing policies are based on CIF, which indicates a strong commitment to the market. By pricing ex works, an exporter is not taking any steps to build relations with the market and so may be indicating only short-term commitment.

15.7 Terms of payment

The exporter will consider the following factors in negotiating terms of payment for goods to be shipped:

● Practices in the industry.

● Terms offered by competitors.

● Relative strength of the buyer and the seller.

If the exporter is well established in the market with a unique product and accompanying service, price and terms of trade can be set to fit the exporter's desires. If, on the other hand, the exporter is breaking into a new market or if competitive pressures call for action, pricing and selling terms should be used as major competitive tools.

The basic methods of payment for exports vary in terms of their attractiveness to the buyer and the seller, from cash in advance to open account or consignment selling. Neither of the extremes will be feasible for longer-term relationships, but they do have their uses in certain situations. The most common payment methods are presented in Figure 15.8.

The most favourable term to the exporter is cash in advance because it relieves the exporter of all risk and allows for immediate use of the money. On the other hand, the most advantageous option seen from the buyer's perspective would be consignment or open account.

The most common arrangements, in decreasing order of attractiveness to the exporter, will now be described.

Figure 15.8   **Different terms of payment**

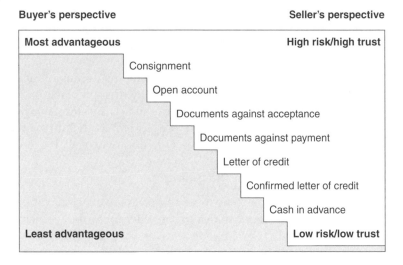

(Source: Chase Manhattan Bank, 1984, p. 5)

Cash in advance

The exporter receives payment before shipment of the goods. This minimizes the exporter's risk and financial costs, since there is no collection risk and no interest cost on receivables. However, importers will rarely agree to these terms, since it ties up their capital and the goods may not be received. Consequently, such terms are not widely used. They are most likely either when the exporter lacks confidence in the importer's ability to pay, often the case in initial export transactions, or where economic and political instability in the importing country may result in foreign exchange not being made available for importers.

Letter of credit

World-wide letters of credit are very important and very common. A letter of credit is an instrument whereby a bank agrees to pay a specified amount of money on presentation of documents stipulated in the letter of credit, usually the bill of lading, an invoice and a description of the goods. In general, letters of credit have the following characteristics:

● They are an arrangement by banks for settling international commercial transactions.

● They provide a form of security for the parties involved.

● They ensure payment, provided that the terms and conditions of the credit have been fulfilled.

● Payment by such means is based on documents only and not on the merchandise or services involved.

The process for handling letters of credit is illustrated in Figure 15.9.

In the process, the customer agrees to payment by a confirmed letter of credit. The customer begins the process by sending an enquiry for the goods (1). The price and terms are confirmed by a pro-forma invoice (2) by the supplier, so that the customer knows for what amount (3) to instruct its bank (the issuing bank) to open a letter of credit (L/C)(4). The L/C is confirmed by a bank (5) in the supplier's country.

When the goods are shipped (6), the shipping documents are returned to the supplier (7), so that shipment is confirmed by their presentation (8) together with the L/C and all other stipulated documents and certificates for payment (9). The money is automatically transmitted from the customer's account via the issuing bank. The customer may collect the goods (10) only when all the documents have been returned (Phillips *et al.*, 1994, p. 453).

The letter of credit has three forms:

● *Revocable L/C.* Now a rare form, this gives the buyer maximum flexibility as it can be cancelled without notice to the seller up to the moment of payment by the bank.

● *Irrevocable but unconfirmed L/C.* This is as good as the credit status of the establishing bank and the willingness of the buyer's country to allow the required use

Figure 15.9   **The process for handling letters of credit**

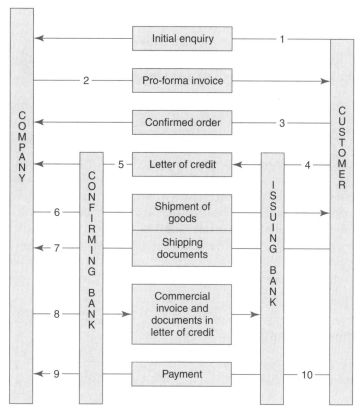

(Source: Phillips *et al.*, 1994, p. 454, with permission from ITBP Ltd.)

of foreign exchange. An unconfirmed L/C should not necessarily be viewed with suspicion. The reason for the lack of confirmation may be that the customer has been unwilling to pay the additional fee for confirmation.

● *Confirmed irrevocable L/C.* This means that a bank in the seller's country has added its own undertaking to that of the issuing bank, confirming that the necessary sum of money is available for payment, awaiting only the presentation of shipping documents. While it guarantees the seller its money, it is much more costly to the buyer. Generally, the buyer pays a fixed fee plus percentage of the value, but where the letter of credit is confirmed, the confirming bank will also charge a fee. On the other hand, the confirmation of an irrevocable letter of credit by a bank gives the shipper the most satisfactory assurance that payment will be made for the shipment. It also means that the exporter does not have to seek payment under any conditions from the issuing bank – invariably located in some foreign country – but has a direct claim on the confirming bank in the exporter's home country. Thus, the exporter need not be concerned about the ability or willingness of the foreign bank to pay.

Documents against payment and acceptance

In the following two 'documents against' situations, the seller ships the goods and the shipping documents, and the draft (bill of exchange) demanding payment is presented to the importer through banks acting as the seller's agent. There are two principal types of bill of exchange: sight draft (documents against payment) and time draft (documents against acceptance).

● *Documents against payment.* Here the buyer must make payment for the face value of the draft before receiving the documents conveying title to the merchandise. This occurs when the buyer first sees the draft (*sight draft*).

● *Documents against acceptance (D/A).* When a draft is drawn 'documents against acceptance', credit is extended to the buyer on the basis of the buyer's acceptance of the draft calling for payment within a specified time and usually at a specified place. Acceptance means that the buyer formally agrees to pay the amount specified by the draft on the due date. The specified time may be expressed as certain number of days after sight (*time draft*). A time draft offers less security for the seller than a sight draft, since the sight draft demands payment prior to the release of shipping documents. The time draft, on the other hand, allows the buyer a delay of 30, 60 or 90 days in payment.

Open account

The exporter ships the goods without documents calling for payment, other than the invoice. The buyer can pick up the goods without having to make payment first. The advantage of the open account is its simplicity and the assistance it gives to the buyer, which does not have to pay credit charges to banks. The seller in return expects that the invoice will be paid at the agreed time. A major weakness of the method is that there are no safeguards for payment. Exporters should sell on open account only to importers which they know very well or which have excellent credit ratings, and to markets with no foreign exchange problems. Open account sales are less complex and expensive than drafts, since there are no documentation requirements or bank charges.

Consignment

Here the exporter retains title of the goods until the importer sells them. Exporters own the goods longer in this method than any other, and so the financial burden and risks are at their greatest. The method should be offered only to very trustworthy importers with an excellent credit rating in countries where political and economic risk is very low. Consignments tend to be mainly used by companies trading with their own subsidiaries.

The credit terms given are also important in determining the final price to the buyer. When the products of international competitors are perceived to be similar, the purchaser may choose the supplier that offers the best credit terms, in order to achieve a greater discount. In effect, the supplier is offering a source of finance to the buyer.

15.8

Export financing

Exporters need financing support in order to obtain working capital and because importers will often demand terms that allow them to defer payment. Principal sources of export finance include commercial banks, government export financing programmes, export credit insurance, factoring houses and counter-trade.

Commercial banks

The simplest way of financing export sales is through an overdraft facility with the exporter's own bank. This is a convenient way to finance all the elements of the contract, such as purchasing, manufacturing, shipping and credit. The bank is generally more favourably disposed towards granting an overdraft if the exporter has obtained an export credit insurance policy.

Export credit insurance

Export credit insurance is available to most exporters through governmental export credit agencies or through private insurers. Such insurances usually cover the following:

● *Political risks* and non-convertibility of currency.
● *Commercial risks* associated with non-payment by buyers.

Exporters may be able to use credit insurance to enable them to grant more liberal credit terms or to encourage their banks to grant them financing against their export receivables. The costs of such insurance are often quite low in many markets, ranging from 1 to 2 per cent of the value of the transaction. Specialized insurance brokers handle such insurance.

Factoring

Factoring means selling export debts for immediate cash. In this way, the exporter shifts the problems of collecting payment for completed orders over to organizations or factors that specialize in export credit management and finance.

Ideally, the exporter should go to the factor before any contract is signed or shipment made, and secure its willingness to buy the receivable. The factor will check out the credit rating and so forth of the prospective buyer(s) typically by having a correspondent in the importer's country do the necessary checking. Thus, the factor acts as a credit approval agency as well as facilitator and guarantor of payment.

The factor does not usually purchase export debts on terms exceeding 120 days. The factor normally charges a service fee of between 0.75 and 2.5 per cent of the sales value, depending on the workload and the risk carried by the factor.

Forfeiting

This is a finance method developed in Switzerland in the 1950s. It is an arrangement whereby exporters of capital goods can obtain medium-term finance (between one and seven years). The system can briefly be explained as follows.

An exporter of capital goods has a buyer that wishes to have medium-term credit to finance the purchase. The buyer pays some of the cost at once and pays the balance in regular instalments for, say, the next five years. The principal benefit is that there is immediate cash for the exporter, and along with the first cash payment by the buyer, forfeiting can finance up to 100 per cent of the contract value.

Bonding

In some countries (e.g. in the Middle East), contracts are cash or short term. Whereas this is an ideal situation for suppliers, it means that the buyer loses some of its leverage over the supplier as it cannot withhold payment. In this situation, a bond or guarantee is a written instrument issued to an overseas buyer by an acceptable third party, either a bank or an insurance company. It guarantees compliance of its obligations by an exporter or contractor, or the overseas buyer will be indemnified for a stated amount against the failure of the exporter/contractor to fulfil its obligations under the contract.

Leasing

Exporters of capital equipment may use leasing in one of two ways:

- To arrange cross-border leases directly from a bank or leasing company to the foreign buyer.
- To obtain local leasing facilities either through overseas branches or subdivisions of international banks or through international leasing associations.

With leasing, the exporter receives prompt payment for goods directly from the leasing company. A leasing facility is best set up at the earliest opportunity, preferably when the exporter receives the order.

Counter-trade

Counter-trade is a generic term used to describe a variety of trade agreements in which a seller provides a buyer with products (commodities, goods, services, technology) and agrees to a reciprocal purchasing obligation with the buyer in terms of an agreed percentage (full or partial) of the original sales value.

Barter

This is a straightforward exchange of goods for goods without any money transfer. Bilateral barter, where only two parties are involved, is relatively uncommon. The bartering process can, however, be facilitated when a third (trilateral barter) or even more countries (multilateral barter) become involved in a trading chain.

Compensation deal

This involves the export of goods in one direction. The 'payment' of the goods is split into two parts:

● Part payment in cash by the importer.

● For the rest of the 'payment', the original exporter makes an obligation to purchase some of the buyer's goods. These products can be used in the exporter's internal production or they may be sold on in the wider market.

Buy-back agreement

The sale of machinery, equipment or a turnkey plant to the buyer's production is financed at least in part by the exporter's purchase of some of the resultant output. Whereas barter and compensation deals are short-term arrangements, buy-back agreements are long-term agreements. The contract may last for a considerable period of time, such as 5–10 years. The two-way transactions are clearly linked, but are kept financially separate.

Counter-trade has arisen because of shortages of both foreign exchange and international lines of credit. Some have estimated the size of counter-trade as high as 10–15 per cent of world trade.

15.9 ▌ Summary

The major issues covered in this chapter include the determinants of price, pricing strategy, how foreign prices are related to domestic prices, price escalation, the elements of price quotation, and transfer pricing.

Several factors must be taken into consideration in setting price, including cost, competitors' prices, product image, market share/volume, stage in product life cycle and number of products involved. The optimum mix of these ingredients varies by product, market and corporate objectives. Price setting in the international context is further complicated by such factors as foreign exchange rates, different competitive situations in each export market, different labour costs and different inflation rates in various countries. Also local and regional regulations and laws in setting prices have to be considered.

The international marketer must quote a meaningful price by using proper international trade terms. When there is doubt about how to prepare a quotation, freight forwarders may be consulted. These specialists can provide valuable information with regard to documentation (e.g. invoice, bill of lading) and the costs relevant to the movement of goods. Financial documents, such as letters of credit, require a bank's assistance. International banks have international departments that can facilitate payment and advise clients regarding pitfalls in preparing and accepting documents.

Case study | Coca-Cola

Automatically price-changing in vending machines

The Coca-Cola Co. is studying wireless technology that could allow bottlers automatically to raise or lower soda prices in its vending machines, but a company spokesman said Coke is not planning to launch a machine that would raise soft drink prices in hot weather.

'Contrary to what has been reported, we are not introducing vending machines that are going to raise the price of soft drinks in hot weather,' said Ben Deutsch, spokesman for Coca-Cola. *The New York Times* had reported that the company was testing such a machine, quoting chairman and chief executive M. Douglas Ivester's comments on the subject to a Brazilian news magazine, *Veja*.

In the article, Ivester had said that since the desire for a cold drink increases during the summer heat, 'It is fair that it should be more expensive. The machine will simply make this process automatic.'

No time frame for launch

Deutsch said the example of raising soft drink prices in hot weather was used only as a 'hypothetical' situation, and he noted that the two-way technology would serve other purposes, such as lowering prices during promotions or informing the company that a machine was out of stock.

'Sure, you could adjust the prices, but that's one application,' Deutsch said. 'The example that has been framed for hot weather was a hypothetical application.'

Deutsch said that the technology, which has been developing for a few years, is still in the exploratory phase and the company has no time frame for when these machines would be introduced to the public.

Industry watchers said they doubted that Coca-Cola would launch such a controversial technology in its vending machines without first doing extensive research into public opinion. 'Though the Coke system may be testing these machines, it would surprise me if they would appear on any broad scale unless Coke determined whether or not this would be a consumer-friendly device,' said John Sicher, editor and publisher of *Beverage Digest*.

Questions

1. What are the advantages and disadvantages for Coca-Cola of automatically changing prices in vending machines, even across borders?

2. What do you think of the idea of automatically raising Coca-Cola prices in hot weather?

3. Would there be other events that could automatically result in price changes of Coca-Cola in vending machines?

4. How should Coca-Cola conduct research to find out whether automatic price change is a good idea?

Source: Adapted from: Valenti, C. (1999) 'Coke denies pricing plan', ABCNEWS.com from TheStreet.com, 28 October.

Questions for discussion

1. What are the major causes of international price escalation? Suggest possible courses of action to deal with this problem.

2. Explain how exchange rate and inflation affect the way you price your product.

3. In order to protect themselves, how should marketers price their product in a country with high inflation?

4. International buyers and sellers of technology frequently disagree on the appropriate price for knowledge. Why?

5. What methods can be used to compute a transfer price (for transactions between affiliated companies)?

6. What relevance has the international product life cycle (IPLC) theory for pricing strategy in international firms?

7. Why is it often difficult to compute fair arm's-length transfer prices?

8. Explain these terms of sale: EXW, FAS, FOB, CFR, CIF, DEQ and DDP. Which factors will determine the terms of sale?

9. Explain these types of letter of credit: revocable/irrevocable, confirmed/unconfirmed. Under what sets of circumstances would exporters use the following methods of payment:

    (a)   revocable letter of credit;

    (b)   confirmed letter of credit;

    (c)   confirmed irrevocable letter of credit;

    (d)   time draft (i.e. bill of exchange)?

10. Name some of the financing sources for exporters.

11. How does inflation affect a country's currency value? Is it a good idea to borrow or obtain finance in a country with high inflation?

12. How and why are export credit financing terms and conditions relevant to international pricing?

13. What is counter-trade? Why should firms be willing to consider counter-trade arrangements in their global marketing efforts?

Internet exercise

Gillette Co.

Please go to:

www.gillette.com

The latest Gillette shaving innovation, the MACH3 triple-blade shaving system, is now available in North America, western Europe, the Former Soviet Union and selected markets in Asia-Pacific, eastern Europe and Latin America. Plans call for distribution of the MACH3 system to be extended to nearly all major markets world-wide in 1999.

This new product has further strengthened the world-wide leadership position Gillette holds in blades and razors, its principal line of business.

Questions

1. Discuss if it is possible for Gillette to standardize pricing across borders for their MACH3 triple-blade. Which factors would favour price standardization and which factors would favour price differentiation?

For further exercises and cases, see this book's website at *www.booksites.net/hollensen*

References

Cavusgil, S.T. (1988) 'Unravelling the mystique of export pricing', *Business Horizons*, vol. 31, no. 3, pp. 54–63.

Chase Manhattan Bank (1984) *Dynamics of Trade Finance*, New York.

Czepiel, J.A. (1992) *Competitive Marketing Strategy*, Prentice Hall, Englewood Cliffs, NJ.

Diller, H. and Bukhari, I. (1994) 'Pricing conditions in the European Common Market', *European Management Journal*, vol. 12, no. 2, pp. 163–70.

Eitemann, D.K. and Stonehill, A.I. (1986) *Multinational Business Finance* (4th edn), Addison Wesley, Reading, MA.

EIU (1995) 'The EU50 – corporate case studies in single market success' Research Report, pp. 93–5.

Fraedrich, J.P. and Bateman, C.R. (1996) 'Transfer pricing by multinational marketers: risky business', *Business Horizons*, vol. 39, no. 1, pp. 17–22.

Garda, R.A. (1995) 'Tactical pricing', in Paliwoda, S.J. and Ryans, J.K. (eds.), *International Marketing Reader*, Routledge, London.

Nagle, T.T. (1987) *The Strategies and Tactics of Pricing*, Prentice Hall, Englewood Cliffs, NJ.

Onkvisit, S. and Shaw, J.J. (1993) *International Marketing Analysis and Strategy* (2nd edn), Macmillan, London.

Phillips, C., Doole, I. and Lowe, R. (1994) *International Marketing Strategy: Analysis, development and implementation*, Routledge, London.

Shibata, T. (1993) 'Sony's successful strategy for compact discs', *Long Range Planning*, vol. 26, no. 4, pp. 16–21.

Simon, H. and Kucher, E. (1993) 'The European pricing bomb – and how to cope with it', *Marketing and Research Today*, February, pp. 25–36.

Weigand, R.E. (1991) 'Buy in – follow on strategies for profit', *Sloan Management Review*, Spring, pp. 29–38.

Distribution decisions

After studying this chapter you should be able to do the following:

- Explore the determinants of channel decisions.

- Discuss the key points in putting together and managing global marketing channels.

- Discuss the factors influencing channel width (intensive, selective or exclusive coverage).

- Explain what is meant by integration of the marketing channel.

- Describe the most common export documents.

- Define and explain the main modes of transportation.

- Explain how the internationalization of retailing affects the manufacturer.

- Define grey markets and explain how to deal with them.

16.1 Introduction

Access to international markets is a key decision area facing firms at the end of the 1990s and beyond the year 2000. In Part III we considered the firm's decision of an appropriate market entry mode that can assure the entry of a firm's products and services into a foreign market.

After the firm has chosen a strategy to get its products into foreign markets, the next challenge (and the topic of this chapter: see Figure 16.1) is the distribution of the products within foreign markets. The first part of this chapter concerns the structure and management of foreign distribution. The second part of the chapter is concerned with the management of international logistics.

According to Table 16.1, distribution channels typically account for 15–40 per cent of the retail price of goods and services in an industry.

Over the next few years, the challenges and opportunities for channel management will multiply, as technological developments accelerate channel evolution.

Table 16.1

Value added in the vertical chain (% of retail price, estimated)

Actor in the vertical chain	Cars	Software	Petrol	Laser printers	Packaged goods
Supplier of raw materials/ components	45	10	53	40	26
Manufacturer of finished goods	40	65	19	30	33
Distribution channel	15	25	28	30	41
Total	100	100	100	100	100

Source: Bucklin *et al.* (1996), p. 106. The figures in the table are based on research made by, among others, the Economist Intelligence Unity and McKinsey.

Data networks are increasingly enabling end users to bypass traditional channels and deal directly with manufacturers and service providers.

Electronic data interchange (EDI) is now used for the exchange of orders and invoices between suppliers and their customers. By on-line monitoring of stocks, customers are also able to order directly from suppliers on a just-in-time (JIT) basis, and thereby to avoid holding stock altogether or to minimize the time it is held.

At the same time, new channels are continuing to emerge in one industry after another, opening up opportunities for companies to cut costs or improve their effectiveness in reaching specific market segments. Catalogue retailing, telephone

Figure 16.1

Channel decisions

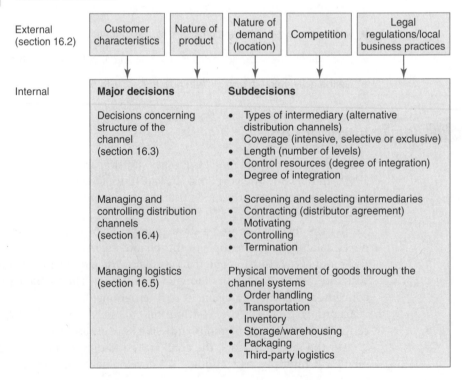

480

Figure 16.2   **Alternative distribution channels for foreign markets**

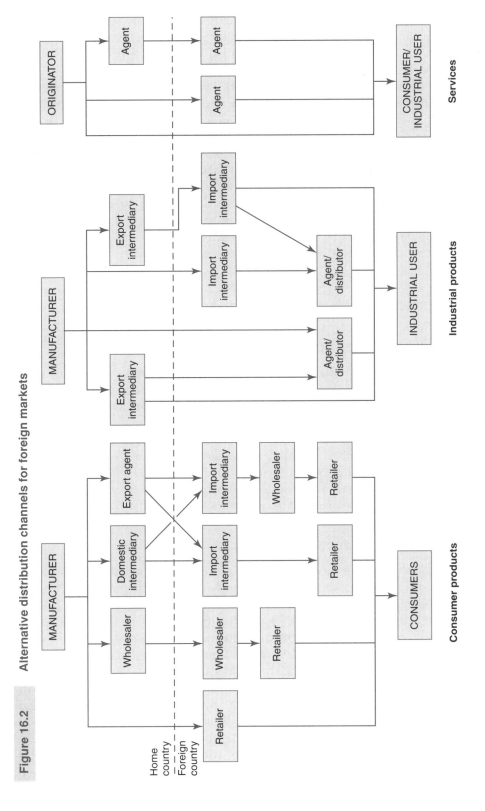

Home
country
– – –
Foreign
country

Consumer products

Industrial products

Services

(Source: Chee, H. and Harris, R. (1994) *Marketing: A global perspective*, Pearson Education Limited.)

ordering, cable TV shopping and Internet ordering are all becoming increasingly important to consumer goods manufacturers. Despite the scale and importance of these opportunities, however, few companies manage to take full advantage of them.

The following presents a systematic approach to the major decisions in international distribution. The main channel decisions and their determinants are illustrated in Figure 16.1.

Distribution channels are the link between producers and final customers. As Figure 16.2 shows, there are numerous ways of creating this link.

In general terms, an international marketer distributes either directly or indirectly. As we saw in Chapter 9, direct distribution amounts to dealing with a foreign firm, while the indirect method means dealing with another home country firm that serves as an intermediary. Figure 16.1 shows that the choice of a particular channel link will be strongly influenced by various market characteristics of the host markets. We will now consider these in more detail.

16.2 External determinants of channel decisions

Customer characteristics

The customer, or final consumer, is the keystone in any channel design. Thus, the size, geographic distribution, shopping habits, outlet preferences and usage patterns of customer groups must be taken into account when making distribution decisions.

Consumer product channels tend to be longer than industrial product channels because the number of customers is greater, the customers are more geographically dispersed, and they buy in smaller quantities. Shopping habits, outlet preferences and usage patterns vary considerably from country to country and are strongly influenced by sociocultural factors.

Nature of product

Product characteristics play a key role in determining distribution strategy. For low-priced, high-turnover convenience products, the requirement is an intensive distribution network. On the other hand, it is not necessary or even desirable for a prestigious product to have wide distribution. In this situation a manufacturer can shorten and narrow its distribution channel. Consumers are likely to do some comparison shopping and will actively seek information about all brands under consideration. In such cases, limited product exposure is not an impediment to market success.

Transportation and warehousing cost of the product are also critical issues in the distribution and sale of industrial goods such as bulk chemicals, metals and cement. Direct selling, servicing and repair, and spare parts warehousing dominate the distribution of such industrial products as computers, machinery and aircraft. The product's durability, ease of adulteration, amount and type of customer service required, unit costs and special handling requirements (such as cold storage) are also significant factors.

Nature of demand/location

The perceptions that the target customers hold about particular products can force modification of distribution channels. Product perceptions are influenced by the customer's income and product experience, the product's end use, its life cycle position and the country's stage of economic development.

The geography of a country and the development of its transportation infrastructure can also affect the channel decision.

Competition

The channels used by competing products and close substitutes are important because channel arrangements that seek to serve the same market often compete with one another. Consumers generally expect to find particular products in particular outlets (e.g. speciality stores), or they have become accustomed to buying particular products from particular sources. In addition, local and global competitors may have agreements with the major wholesalers in a foreign country that effectively create barriers and exclude the company from key channels.

Sometimes the alternative is to use a distribution approach totally different from that of the competition and hope to develop a competitive advantage.

Legal regulations/local business practices

A country may have specific laws that rule out the use of particular channels or intermediaries. For example, until recently, all alcoholic beverages in Sweden and Finland had to be distributed through state monopoly-owned outlets. Other countries prohibit the use of door-to-door selling. Channel coverage can also be affected by law. In general, exclusive representation may be viewed as a restraint of trade, especially if the product has a dominant market position. EU antitrust authorities have increased their scrutiny of exclusive sales agreements. The Treaty of Rome prohibits distribution agreements (e.g. grants of exclusivity) that affect trade or restrict competition.

Furthermore, local business practices can interfere with efficiency and productivity and may force a manufacturer to employ a channel of distribution that is longer and wider than desired. Because of Japan's multitiered distribution system, which relies on numerous layers of intermediaries, foreign companies have long considered the complex Japanese distribution system as the most effective non-tariff barrier to the Japanese market.

Exhibit 16.1 shows how the Japanese distribution system differs from its counterparts in the United States and Europe.

Figure 16.3 **Comparison of distribution channels in car parts between Japan and the USA**

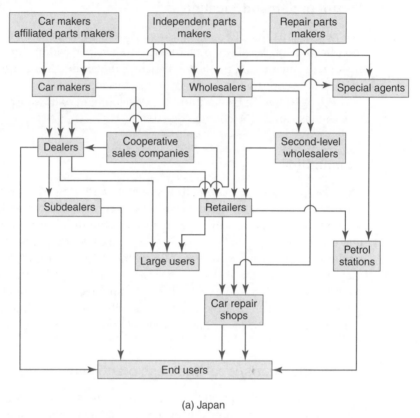

(a) Japan

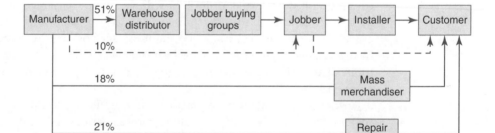

―――― Primary channel

― ― ― ― Secondary channel

(b) USA

(Source: Cateora, 1993, p. 432. Reproduced with kind permission of the McGraw-Hill Companies)

Exhibit 16.1

The distribution system in Japan

The distribution network in Japan has more wholesalers and retailers per capita than any other industrial nation (Onkvisit and Shaw, 1993, p. 598). Figure 16.3 illustrates the difference between shorter US channels and the long and complex Japanese channels.

A consequence of the more complex Japanese distribution system is the considerable price escalation from producer to consumer, as shown in Figure 16.4. (The principle behind price escalation is shown in Table 15.1.)

The first transaction in Figure 16.4, from producer to wholesaler, is a *vertical* exchange, whereas the next transaction (from one wholesaler to another) is a *horizontal* exchange. Small Japanese distributors often lack adequate inventory to serve another distributor at the same vertical level (i.e. horizontal exchange). According to economic criteria, the Japanese distribution system would seem to be inefficient, resulting in higher consumer prices.

However, the complex Japanese distribution system exists to serve social as well as economic purposes. Channel members are like family members and their relations to each other are tightly interlocked by tradition and emotion. Because of these social considerations, inefficient channel members are sometimes retained and tolerated in order to maintain employment and income flows. For example, one of the primary concerns of Japanese channel managers is to help other channel members preserve their dignity. Going out of business is viewed as disgraceful, so stronger channel members (typically producers) must often support weak distributors. The Japanese system is often seen as a trade barrier by western firms, but it is likely that these foreign firms have merely failed to understand the system.

Sources: Cateora (1993); Onkvisit and Shaw (1993); Pirog and Lancioni (1997).

Figure 16.4   **A hypothetical channel sequence in the Japanese consumer market**

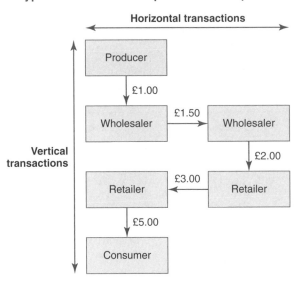

(Source: Pirog and Lancioni, 1997, p. 57. Adapted with kind permission from *International Journal of Physical Distribution and Logistics Management*, MCB University Press; http://www.mcb.co.uk)

Let us now return to the major decisions concerning the structure of the distribution channel (Figure 16.1).

The structure of the channel

Market coverage

The amount of market coverage that a channel member provides is important. Coverage is a flexible term. It can refer to geographical areas of a country (such as cities and major towns) or the number of retail outlets (as a percentage of all retail outlets). Regardless of the market coverage measure(s) used, the company has to create a distribution network (dealers, distributors and retailers) to meet its coverage goals.

As shown in Figure 16.5, three different approaches are available:

● *Intensive coverage*. This calls for distributing the product through the largest number of different types of intermediary and the largest number of individual intermediaries of each type.

Figure 16.5 **Three strategies for market coverage**

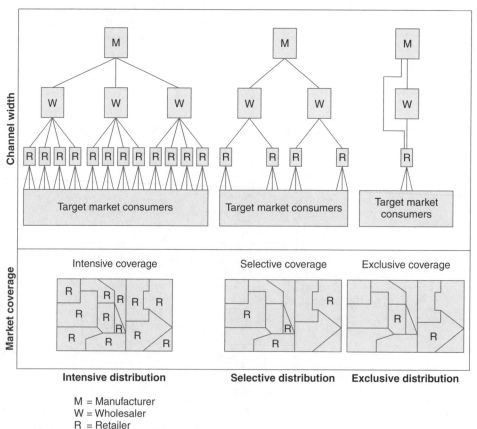

M = Manufacturer
W = Wholesaler
R = Retailer

(Source: Lewison, 1996, p. 271)

● *Selective coverage*. This entails choosing a number of intermediaries for each area to be penetrated.

● *Exclusive coverage*. This involves choosing only one intermediary in a market.

Channel coverage (width) can be identified along a continuum ranging from wide channels (intensive distribution) to narrow channels (exclusive distribution). Figure 16.6 illustrates some factors favouring intensive, selective and exclusive distribution.

Channel length

This is determined by the number of levels or different types of intermediaries. Longer channels, those with several intermediaries, tend to be associated with convenience goods and mass distribution. As seen in Exhibit 16.1, Japan has longer channels for convenience goods because of the historical development of its system. One implication is that prices increase considerably for the final consumer (price escalation: see section 15.3).

Control/cost

The control of one member in the vertical distribution channel is its ability to influence the decisions and actions of other channel members. Channel control is of critical concern to international marketers wanting to establish international brands and a consistent image of quality and service world-wide.

| Figure 16.6 | **Factors influencing channel width** |

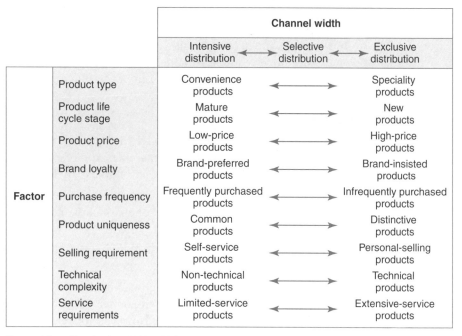

(Source: Adapted from Lewison, 1996, p. 279)

The company must decide how much control it wants to have over how each of its products is marketed. The answer is partly determined by the strategic role assigned to each market. It is also a function of the types of channel member available, the regulations and rules governing distribution activity in each foreign market, and to some extent the roles traditionally assigned to channel members.

Normally, a high degree of control is provided by the use of the firm's own sales force in international markets. The use of intermediaries will automatically lead to loss of some control over the marketing of the firm's products.

An intermediary typically performs certain functions:

● Carrying of inventory.

● Demand generation, or selling.

● Physical distribution.

● After-sales service.

● Extending credit to customers.

In getting its products to end-user markets, a manufacturer must either assume all of these functions or shift some or all of them to intermediaries. As the old saying goes, 'You can eliminate the intermediary, but not the functions of the intermediary.'

In most marketing situations, there is a trade-off between a producer's ability to control important channel functions and the financial resources required to exercise that control. The more intermediaries involved in getting a supplier's product to user customers, the less control the supplier can generally exercise over the flow of its product through the channel and the way it is presented to customers. On the other hand, reducing the length and breadth of the distribution channel usually requires that the supplier perform more functions itself. In turn, this requires the supplier to allocate more financial resources to activities such as warehousing, shipping, credit, field selling or field service.

In summary, the decision to use an intermediary or to distribute via a company-owned sales force requires a major trade-off between the desire to control global marketing efforts and the desire to minimize resource commitment costs.

Degree of integration

Control can also be exercised through integration. Channel integration is the process of incorporating all channel members into one channel system and uniting them under one leadership and one set of goals. There are two different types of integration:

● *Vertical integration*: seeking control of channel members at different levels of the channel.

● *Horizontal integration*: seeking control of channel members at the same level of the channel (i.e. competitors).

Integration is achieved either through acquisitions (ownership) or through tight cooperative relationships. Getting channel members to work together for their own mutual benefit can be a difficult task. However, today cooperative relationships are essential for efficient and effective channel operation.

Figure 16.7   Vertical integration

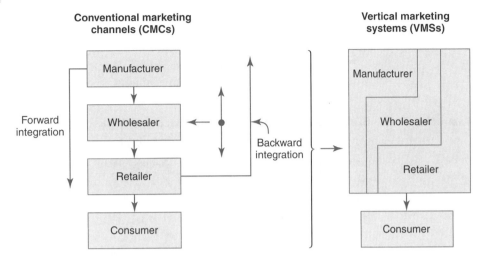

Figure 16.7 shows an example of vertical integration. The starting point in Figure 16.7 is the conventional marketing channels (CMCs), where the channel composition consists of isolated and autonomous participating channel members. Channel coordination is here achieved through arm's-length bargaining. At this point, the vertical integration can take two forms: forward and backward.

● The manufacturer can make forward integration, when it seeks control of businesses of the wholesale and retail levels of the channel.

● The retailer can make backward integration, seeking control of businesses at wholesale and manufacturer levels of the channel.

● The wholesaler has two possibilities: both forward and backward integration.

The result of these manoeuvres is the vertical marketing system (Figure 16.7). Here the channel composition consists of integrated participating members, where channel stability is high due to assured member loyalty and long-term commitments.

16.4 Managing and controlling distribution channels

Once the basic design of the channel has been determined, the international marketer must begin to fill it with the best available candidates, and must secure their cooperation.

Screening and selecting intermediaries

At this stage, the international marketer knows the type of distributor that is needed. The potential candidates must now be compared and contrasted against determining criteria.

The example in Table 16.2 uses thirteen criteria for screening potential channel members. The criteria to be used depend on the nature of a firm's business and its distribution objectives in given markets. The list of criteria should correspond closely to the marketer's own determinants of success – all the things that are important to beating the competition.

The hypothetical consumer packaged goods company used in Table 16.2 considered the distributor's marketing management expertise and financial soundness to

Table 16.2 **Examples of distributor (dealer) selection criteria**

Criteria (no ranking implied)	Weight	Distributor 1 Rating	Distributor 1 Score	Distributor 2 Rating	Distributor 2 Score	Distributor 3 Rating	Distributor 3 Score
Financial soundness and depth of channel member	4	5	20	4	16	3	12
Marketing management expertise and sophistication	5	4	20	3	15	2	10
Satisfactory trade, customer relations and contacts	3	4	12	3	9	3	9
Capability to provide adequate sales coverage	4	3	12	3	12	3	12
Overall positive reputation and image as a company	3	5	15	4	12	4	12
Product compatibility (synergy or conflict?)	3	3	9	4	12	4	12
Pertinent technical know-how at staff level	–	–	–	–	–	–	–
Adequate technical facilities and service support	–	–	–	–	–	–	–
Adequate infrastructure in staff and facilities	1	5	5	3	3	3	3
Proven performance record with client companies	2	4	8	3	6	3	6
Positive attitude towards the company's products	1	3	3	3	3	3	3
Mature outlook regarding the company's inevitable progression in market management	1	3	3	3	3	3	3
Excellent government relations	1	4	4	3	3	3	3
Score			**111**		**94**		**84**

Scales:

Rating		Weighting	
5	Outstanding	5	Critical success factor
4	Above average	4	Prerequisite success factor
3	Average	3	Important success factor
2	Below average	2	Of some importance
1	Unsatisfactory	1	Standard

Source: Toyne and Walters (1993), p. 520.

be of greatest importance. These indicators will show whether the distributor is making money and is able to perform some of the necessary marketing functions such as extension of credit to customers and risk absorption. Financial reports are not always complete or reliable, or may lend themselves to differences of interpretation, pointing to the need for a third-party opinion. In the example, Distributor 1 would be selected by the company.

Alternatively, an industrial goods company may consider the distributor's product compatibility, technical know-how, and technical facilities and service support of high importance, and the distributor's infrastructure, client performance and attitude toward its products of low importance. Quite often, global marketers find that the most desirable distributors in a given market are already handling competitive products and are therefore unavailable.

A high-tech consumer goods company, on the other hand, may favour financial soundness, marketing management expertise, reputation, technical know-how, technical facilities, service support and government relations. In some countries, religious or ethnic differences might make an agent suitable for one part of the market coverage but unsuitable for another. This can result in more channel members being required to give an adequate market coverage.

Contracting (distributor agreements)

When the international marketer has found a suitable intermediary, a foreign sales agreement is drawn up. Before final contractual arrangements are made, it is wise to make personal visits to the prospective channel member. The agreement itself can be relatively simple, but given the numerous differences in the market environments, certain elements are essential. These are listed in Table 16.3.

The long-term commitments involved in distribution channels can become particularly difficult if the contract between the company and the channel member is not carefully drafted. It is normal to prescribe a time limit and a minimum sales level to be achieved, in addition to the particular responsibilities of each party. If this is not carried out satisfactorily, the company may be stuck with a weak

Table 16.3	Items to include in an agreement with a foreign intermediary (distributor)

Names and addresses of both parties.
Date when the agreement goes into effect.
Duration of the agreement.
Provisions for extending or terminating the agreement.
Description of sales territory.
Establishment of discount and/or commission schedules and determination of when and how paid.
Provisions for revising the commission or discount schedules.
Establishment of a policy governing resale prices.
Maintenance of appropriate service facilities.
Restrictions to prohibit the manufacture and sale of similar and competitive products.
Designation of responsibility for patent and trade mark negotiations and/or pricing.
The assignability or non-assignability of the agreement and any limiting factors.
Designation of the country and state (if applicable) of contract jurisdiction in the case of dispute.

Source: Jain (1996), p. 523.

performer that either cannot be removed or is very costly to buy out from the contract.

Contract duration is important, especially when an agreement is signed with a new distributor. In general, distribution agreements should be for a specified, relatively short period (one or two years). The initial contract with a new distributor should stipulate a trial period of either three or six months, possibly with minimum purchase requirements. Duration is also dependent on the local laws and their stipulations on distributor agreements.

Geographic boundaries for the distributor should be determined with care, especially by smaller firms. Future expansion of the product market might be complicated if a distributor claims rights to certain territories. The marketer should retain the right to distribute products independently, reserving the right to certain customers.

The *payment section* of the contract should stipulate the methods of payment as well as how the distributor or agent is to draw compensation. Distributors derive compensation from various discounts, such as the functional discount, whereas agents earn a specific commission percentage of net sales (typically 10–20 per cent). Given the volatility of currency markets, the agreement should also state the currency to be used.

Product and conditions of sale need to be agreed on. The products or product lines included should be stipulated, as well as the functions and responsibilities of the intermediary in terms of carrying the goods in inventory, providing service in conjunction with them, and promoting them. Conditions of sale determine which party is to be responsible for some of the expenses (e.g. marketing expenses) involved, which will in turn have an effect on the price to the distributor. These conditions include credit and shipment terms.

Means of communication between the parties must be stipulated in the agreement if a marketer–distributor relationship is to succeed. The marketer should have access to all information concerning the marketing of its products in the distributor's territory, including past records, present situation assessments and marketing research.

Motivating

Geographic and cultural distance make the process of motivating channel members difficult. Motivating is also difficult because intermediaries are not owned by the company. Since intermediaries are independent firms, they will seek to achieve their own objectives, which will not always match the objective of the manufacturer. The international marketer may offer both monetary and psychological rewards. Intermediaries will be strongly influenced by the earnings potential of the product. If the trade margin is poor and sales are difficult to achieve, intermediaries will lose interest in the product. They will concentrate upon products with a more rewarding response to selling efforts, since they make their sales and profits from their own assortment of products and services from different companies.

It is important to keep in regular contact with agents and distributors. A consistent flow of all relevant types of communication will stimulate interest and sales performance. The international marketer may place one person in charge of distributor-related communications and put into effect an exchange of personnel so that both organizations gain further insight into the workings of the other.

Controlling

Control problems are reduced substantially if intermediaries are selected carefully. However, control should be sought through the common development of written performance objectives. These performance objectives might include some of the following: sales turnover per year, market share growth rate, introduction of new products, price charged and marketing communications support. Control should be exercised through periodic personal meetings.

Evaluation of performance has to be done against the changing environment. In some situations, economic recession or fierce competition activity prevents the possibility of objectives being met. However, if poor performance is established, the contract between the company and the channel member will have to be reconsidered and perhaps terminated.

Termination

Typical reasons for the termination of a channel relationship are as follows:

● The international marketer has established a sales subsidiary in the country.

● The international marketer is unsatisfied with the performance of the intermediary.

Open communication is always needed to make the transition smooth. For example, the intermediary can be compensated for investments made, and major customers can be visited jointly to assure them that service will be uninterrupted.

Termination conditions are among the most important considerations in the distribution agreement. The causes of termination vary and the penalties for the international marketer may be substantial. It is especially important to find out what local laws say about termination and to check what type of experience other firms have had in the particular country.

In some countries terminating an ineffective intermediary can be time consuming and expensive. In the EU one year's average commissions are typical for termination without justification. A notice of termination has to be given three to six months in advance. If the cause for termination is the manufacturer's establishment of a local sales subsidiary, then the international marketer may consider engaging good employees from the intermediary as, for example, managers in the new sales subsidiary. This can prevent a loss of product know-how that has been created at the intermediary's firm. The international marketer could also consider an acquisition of this firm if the intermediary is willing to sell.

16.5 | Managing logistics

Logistics is used as a term to describe the movement of goods and services between supplier(s) and end users.

Two major phases in the movement of materials are of logistical importance. The first phase is *materials management*, or the timely movement of raw materials, parts and supplies into and through the firm. The second phase is *physical distribution*, or the movement of the firm's finished product to its customers. The basic goal of logistics management is the effective coordination of both phases and their various components to result in maximum cost-effectiveness while maintaining service goals and requirements.

The primary area of concern in this section is the second phase: that is, order handling, transportation, inventory and storage/warehousing.

Order handling

The general procedure for order handling, shipment and payment is shown in Figure 16.8:

1. The sale
   Importer makes enquiry of potential supplier.
   Exporter sends catalogues and price list.
   Importer requests pro forma invoice (price quote).
   Exporter sends pro forma invoice.
   Importer sends purchase order.
   Exporter receives purchase order.
2. Importer arranges financing through its bank.
3. Importer's bank sends letter of credit (most frequently used form of payment).
4. Exporter's bank notifies exporter that letter of credit is received.
5. Exporter produces or acquires goods.
6. Exporter arranges transportation and documentation (obtained by exporter or through freight forwarding company).
   Space reserved on ship or aircraft.
   Documents acquired or produced, as required:

   (a) exporter's licence;

Figure 16.8 **The export procedure**

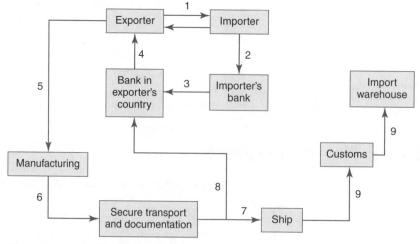

(Source: Albaum *et al.*, 1994, p. 419.)

(b) shipper's export declaration;

(c) commercial invoice;

(d) bills of lading;

(e) marine insurance certificate;

(f) consular invoice;

(g) certificate of origin;

(h) inspection certificates;

(i) dock receipts.

7. Exporter ships goods to importer.

8. Exporter presents documents to bank for payment.

9. Importer has goods cleared through customs and delivered to its warehouse. (Source: Albaum *et al.*, 1994, p. 419).

Most common export documents

This section is drawn from Albaum *et al.* (1994), p. 440.

Transportation documents

- *Bill of lading*. This is a receipt for the cargo and a contract for transportation between a shipper and a transport carrier. It may also be used as an instrument of ownership.

- *Dock receipt*. This is the document acknowledging receipt of the cargo by an ocean carrier.

- *Insurance certificate*. This is evidence that insurance is provided to cover loss or damage to the cargo while in transit.

Banking documents

- *Letter of credit*. This is a financial document issued by a bank at the request of the importer, guaranteeing payment to the exporter if certain terms and conditions surrounding a transaction are met.

Commercial documents

- *Commercial invoice*. This is a bill for the products from the exporter to the buyer.

Government documents

- *Export declaration*. This includes complete information about the shipment.

- *Consular invoice*. This is a document signed by a consul of the importing country that is used to control and identify goods shipped there.

- *Certificate of origin*. This is a document certifying the origin of products being exported, so that the buying country knows in which country the products were produced.

The enquiry or order for products and/or services may be unsolicited or the result of a firm's efforts (the manufacturer or the agent). When the actual order is received, the international marketer will normally send a confirmation of receipt, followed by a commitment to fulfil the order if all of the terms and payment arrangements are acceptable for the international marketer.

A pro forma invoice may be prepared by the exporter to indicate the terms that have been agreed upon (or are proposed). The pro forma invoice normally shows the type and amount of merchandise, unit costs and extensions, expected weights and measures, and often other terms (including payment terms). If accepted by the prospective buyer, it may serve as a contract.

Order cycles are shortened by rapid processing of orders, and the role of communications technology (such as electronic data interchange, EDI) is critical in reducing the time factor. Few countries have efficient and reliable communication systems; however, possessing an efficient international order-processing system would give a firm a competitive advantage.

Transportation

This deals primarily with the mode of transportation, which usually constitutes 10–15 per cent of the retail costs of imported goods. There are four main modes of transport: road, water, air and rail.

Road

Roads are very efficient for short hauls of high-value goods, being very flexible in route and time. Goods can be delivered direct to customers' premises. However, restrictions at border controls can be time consuming, and long distances and the need for sea crossings reduce the attractiveness of freight transport by road. In some parts of the world, particularly in LDCs, road surfaces are poor.

Water

Water transportation is a key mode for international freight movements because it provides a very low-cost way to transport bulky products such as coal and oil. However, water transport is slow and is subject to difficulties caused by the weather – for example, some ports are iced over for part of the winter. Water transport usually needs to be combined with other modes of transport to achieve door-to-door delivery.

Increasingly, nations have begun to recognize the importance of appropriate port structures and are developing such facilities in spite of the heavy investments necessary. If such investments are accompanied by concurrent changes in the overall infrastructure, transportation efficiency should, in the long run, more than recoup the original investment.

Air

Air freight is available to and from most countries. There has been a tremendous growth in international air freight over past decades. Air freight is considerably more expensive per tonne/kilometre than the other modes of transport. It accounts for less than 1 per cent of the total volume of international transport, but represents more than 20 per cent of the value shipped by industrialized countries (Sletmo and

Picard, 1984). High-value items are more likely to be shipped by air, particularly if they have a high weight-to-volume ratio.

Rail

Rail services provide a very good method of transporting bulky goods over long land distances. The increasing use of containers provides a flexible means to use rail and road modes, with minimal load transfer times and costs. High-speed trains are also emerging in Europe and the United States as attractive alternatives. For example, in Europe trains travelling at 190 miles per hour have cut the travel time between major European cities.

The decision about what transportation mode to use is affected by a number of factors, including the following:

● Cost of different transportation alternatives.

● Distance to the location.

● Nature of the product.

● Frequency of the shipment.

● Value of the shipment.

● Availability of transportation.

The level of economic development is a major determinant of the availability of transportation – in some markets, air freight is highly developed compared to rail transportation.

Freight forwarders

Freight forwarders provide an important service to exporters. The full-service foreign freight forwarder can relieve the producer of most of the burdens of distribution across national borders. This is particularly so for small and medium-sized companies and those that are inexperienced in exporting. Freight forwarders provide a wide range of services, but the general activities and services provided are as follows:

● Coordination of transport services.

● Preparation and processing of international transport documents.

● Provision of warehousing.

● Expert advice.

The traditional view of the freight forwarder is that of a provider of services, a company that does not own transport facilities but which buys from the most appropriate transport provider, and a company that acts as the agent of the exporter. Various changes have taken place which have impacted upon freight forwarders. There has been a tendency for transport companies to extend their activities to include an in-house forwarding function. In addition, larger and more experienced exporters have developed their own in-house transport and documentation expertise. Both these trends have threatened the freight forwarder.

Inventory (at the factory base)

The purpose of establishing inventory – to maintain product movement in the delivery pipeline, in order to satisfy demand – is the same for domestic and international inventory systems.

There are many different cost elements involved in managing an inventory: storage, interest on capital tied up, taxes, lost sales, etc. Since these costs may sometimes be sizeable, management must be concerned about inventory control. This involves determining the proper level of inventory to hold, so that a balance is maintained between customer service and inventory cost.

In deciding the level of inventory to be maintained, the international marketer must consider two factors:

● *Order cycle time*: the total time that passes between the placement of an order by a customer and the receipt of the goods. Depending on the choice of transportation mode, delivery times may vary considerably. As a result, the marketer has to keep larger safety stock in order to be able to satisfy demand in any circumstance. However, the marketer could attempt to reduce order cycle time, thereby reducing costs, by altering transportation method, changing inventory locations, or shifting order placement to direct computer-order entry (EDI).

● *Customer service levels*: the ability to fulfil customer orders within a certain time. For example, if within three days 80 per cent of the orders can be fulfilled, the customer service level is 80 per cent. The choice of customer service level for the firm has a major impact on the inventories needed. Because high customer service levels are costly (inventory constitutes tied-up capital), the goal should not be the highest level possible but rather an acceptable level, based on customer expectations. For some products, customers may not demand or expect quick delivery. In addition, if higher customer service levels result in higher prices, this may reduce the competitiveness of a firm's product.

Besides these two factors, international inventories can also be used as a strategic tool in dealing with currency valuation changes or hedging against inflation.

Storage/warehousing (in foreign markets)

Sometimes goods and materials need to be stored in the export markets. However, this activity involves more than just storage. In addition to storing products in anticipation of consumer demand, warehousing encompasses a broad range of other activities, such as assembling, breaking bulk shipments into smaller sizes to meet customer needs, and preparing products for reshipment.

Warehousing decisions focus on three main issues:

● Where the firm's customers are geographically located.

● The pattern of existing and future demands.

● The customer service level required (i.e. how quickly a customer's order should be fulfilled).

The following general observations can be made about warehousing facilities:

● If products need to be delivered quickly, storage facilities will be required near the customer.

● For high-value products (e.g. computer software), the location of the warehouse will be of minimal importance as these lightweight products can be air freighted.

Exhibit 16.2

How Bosch-Siemens (BS) improved customer service and reduced costs by reducing its warehouses

Bosch-Siemens (BS) is a leading European manufacturer of consumer white goods, with handsome market shares in Germany, Scandinavia, Spain and Greece. Recently the company decided to reduce the number of its European warehouses from thirty-six to ten. BS aimed to cut costs and reduce the amount of stock it held. The company also wanted to improve its distribution, enhance customer service and reform its logistics structure to boost its share of other markets, particularly the UK and France.

The process of continent-wide rationalization took three years to plan. BS fixed on ten sites as its current optimum, based on effective delivery criteria. It wanted to be able to reach customers within 24–48 hours. On the other hand, the optimum size of a warehouse in terms of cost is 20,000–30,000 square metres. Hence BS arrived at ten as the optimum number of warehouses in Europe. These are shown in Figure 16.9.

BS seeks to serve several territories from each warehouse. Thus, for example, it has a warehouse in Sweden that also covers Norway and Finland; and its south German warehouse supplies Luxembourg, Austria and parts of France.

By cutting warehouses it has reduced total distribution and warehousing costs, has brought down staff numbers, holds fewer items of stock, provides greater access to regional markets, makes better use of transport networks and has improved service to customers.

The financial benefit is a saving of DM30 million a year, or a reduction of 21 per cent in total logistics costs. BS has also achieved greater flexibility in the use of transport systems such as rail and waterways. It has brought stock numbers down from 1 million items to 700,000.

Source: EIU (1995).

Packaging

A good balance needs to be achieved between the high costs of the substantial export packing required to eliminate all damage, and the price and profit implications that this has for the customer and the exporter.

Export packing has been modified over the years from wooden crates. Different countries have different regulations about what materials are acceptable. One example of this is the recycling of containers for reuse. This requires a system for deposits and returns into the distribution channels. In addition, export packing influences customer satisfaction through its appearance and its appropriateness to minimize handling costs for the customer.

Figure 16.9   **Bosch Siemens' European distribution centres**

During recent years, packaging has been simplified by palletization. Computer software is now available from packaging suppliers, which can now design individual product packaging to maximize the number of units per pallet, and thus per container load. Palletization with shrink-wrap protection, together with containerization, has served both to protect goods against damage and to diminish losses through theft.

Third-party logistics (contract logistics)

A growing preference among international firms is to employ outside logistical expertise. The main thrust behind the idea is that individual firms are experts in their industry and should therefore concentrate only on their operations. Third-party logistics providers, on the other hand, are experts solely at logistics, with the knowledge and means to perform efficient and innovative services for those companies in need. The goal is improved service at equal or lower cost.

One of the greatest benefits of contracting out the logistics function in a foreign market is the ability to take advantage of an in-place network complete with resources and experience. The local expertise and image are crucial when a business is just starting up.

One of the main arguments levelled against contract logistics is the loss of the firm's control in the supply chain. Yet contract logistics does not and should not require the handing over of control. Rather, it offers concentration on one's core competence, a division of labour. The control and responsibility towards the customer remain with the firm, even though operations may move to a highly trained outside organization.

16.6] # Implications of Internet/e-commerce for distribution decisions

The Internet has the power to change drastically the balance of power among consumers, retailers, distributors, manufacturers and service providers. Some participants in the distribution chain may experience an increase in their power and profitability. Others will experience the reverse; some may even find that they have been bypassed and have lost their market share.

Physical distributors and dealers of goods and services that are more conveniently ordered and/or delivered on-line are indeed subject to increasing pressure from e-commerce. This *disintermediation* process, with increasing direct sales through the Internet, leads manufacturers to compete with their resellers, which results in *channel conflict*. The extent to which these effects are salient depends upon which of the following *four Internet distribution strategies* are adopted by the manufacturer:

1. Present only product information on the Internet

As less than 5 per cent of retail sales (in both Europe and USA) presently occur over the Internet, only a few manufacturers would be willing to endanger their relationships with their distributors for that volume. The risk of distribution conflicts with the existing distributors would be too great. So, manufacturers may decide not to sell their products through the Internet and prohibit their resellers also from using the Internet for sales. Only product information is provided on the Internet, with any customer queries being passed on to the appropriate channel member. In industries, such as aircraft manufacturing, where sales are large, complex and customized, this may be an appropriate strategy.

2. Leave Internet business for distributors

Some companies prefer distributors to leave the Internet business for resellers and not to sell directly through the Internet. How effective this strategy is depends on the existing distribution structure. It can be effective when manufacturers assign exclusive territories to resellers, since resellers can be restricted to either delivering only to customers within their assigned territory or they can be compensated through profit pass-over agreements if they are adversely affected. Any leads generated by the manufacturer's Web site are passed on to the appropriate regional reseller.

By contrast, for intensively distributed products where resellers have no assigned territories, resellers simply compete with each other as they would do in the normal, physical marketplace. The global nature of the Internet creates price transparency, which may conflict with differential prices charged by the manufacturer in various markets. Another limitation of this approach is that most consumers search for manufacturers' Web sites rather than resellers' Web sites. Inability to purchase from the manufacturer's Web site can be frustrating for the consumer and can result in lost sales for the manufacturer.

3. Leave Internet business only to the manufacturer

A third strategy for the manufacturer is to restrict Internet sales exclusively to itself. This strategy is only profitable if the manufacturer has a business model that is aligned with sales through the Internet. The business system of most manufacturers (such as consumer packaged goods companies) is not set up for sales to end-users who place numerous small orders. Alternatively, by selling through the Internet a manufacturer may aim not to generate profits, but rather to learn about this new channel of distribution, collect information on consumers, or build its brand. But regardless of a manufacturer's objectives, resellers dislike having to yield the market space to manufacturers. Exhibit 16.3 illustrates how Sony has used this strategy in Japan.

If the manufacturer uses this strategy he also risks channel conflicts, i.e. creating competition with his own customers (distributors). The PC-manufacturer Compaq also realized this when they struggled to exploit the Internet, because to do so properly would mean bypassing its distributors. For Compaq it was difficult to remit sales through the Internet without upsetting their distributors and jeopardizing their historically strong relationships with them. In order to limit the direct competition with their customers, Compaq introduced a differentiated product-line of PCs, Prosignia, for sales through the Internet (Kumar, 1999).

Exhibit 16.3 | **Sony Corp. is starting to sell direct to consumers in Japan**

On 1 February 2000 Sony Corp. (through a newly formed company, Sony Style) launched a Web site that will sell mass-customized personal computers and peripherals directly to consumers in Japan.

Sony Style will be Japan's first consumer electronics manufacturer to sell directly to consumers on the Internet. Consumers will be able to buy personal computers and specify the memory, software and peripherals that will make up the package.

In the US, Dell Computer Corp. has led mass customization of computers for consumers.

Though Sony Style will launch with the sales of customized personal computers for consumers, Sony plans to add a range of consumer electronics later in the year. Additional products slated to go up on Sony Style this spring include digital cameras, portable music players, digital video cameras and other audio/visual equipment. The site will gradually add set-top boxes as well as digital televisions.

As an incentive to create direct relationships with on-line consumers, Sony Style will offer frequent customers free Internet access through Sony's So-net Internet provider. The programme will be based on a point system derived from the total amount consumers spend at the site.

Sony aims to sell 20 per cent of its consumer and enterprise products on-line over the next three to five years. The site will initially sell only consumer-designed packages that are not available through retailers.

Sony's move to direct sales comes as a shock to Japanese retailers that sell Sony products. Japan has a tradition of strong ties with its dealer networks, which has kept Japanese e-commerce subdued. Companies such as Matsushita Electric Industrial

▶

Company and Toyota Motor Corporation have been careful to maintain their dealer relationships in the face of e-commerce opportunities. Much like the US auto industry, Japan's manufacturers are cautious to protect their dealer network while making moves towards selling directly to consumers.

Some analysts believe that Sony's actions are likely to have a substantial impact on the willingness of other electronics manufacturers to sell directly on-line, although such decisions are fraught with problems. Most significantly, analysts point to pricing as a key issue. What price will manufacturers sell at on-line? If they sell at their suggested retail price, they will not compete effectively with most e-tailers that sell at discounted prices. In effect, pricing at suggested retail does their customers a disservice. If they decide to discount, however, where do they set their prices? Furthermore, what does that say for the integrity of their suggested retail pricing?

In short, while Sony has taken a bold step into direct sales on-line, analysts see many tough decisions down the road as manufacturers try to satisfy customer demand, while at the same time maintaining good relationships with their existing distributors.

Source: Spegel (2000) www.EcommerceTimes.com.

4. Open Internet business to everybody

The fourth strategy is to let the market decide the winners and open the Internet to everybody – for direct sales and resellers. Manufacturers who have ventured on-line, either through the third or the fourth strategy, usually sell at retail prices and/or provide only a limited line because of their desire not to compete with their resellers. However, this limits the attractiveness of the Internet's value proposition.

Conclusion

The fear of cannibalizing existing distribution channels and potential channel conflict requires manufacturers to trade off existing sales through the traditional distribution network and potential future sales through the Internet. Unfortunately, history suggests that most companies tend to stay at declining distribution networks for too long.

16.7 Special issue 1: International retailing

In the continuing integration of the world economy, internationalization not only concerns advertising, banking and manufacturing industries, it also affects the retailing business. The trend in all industrialized countries is towards larger units and more self-service. The number of retail outlets is dwindling, but the average size is increasing.

However, retailing still shows great differences between countries, reflecting their different histories, geography, culture and economic development. The cultural importance attached to food in Italy provides an opportunity for small specialist food retailers to survive and prosper. In other developed countries, such as the USA, the trend is towards very large superstores which incorporate a wide range of speciality foods. The Italian approach relies on small-scale production by the retail proprietor. The US approach encourages mass production, branding and sophisticated distribution systems to handle inventory and freshness issues.

A consequence of the greater economies of scale and efficiency in American retailing is that the USA tends to have larger retail outlets and a smaller number per capita than other developed countries. Some industrialized countries do not have an extensive modern retail sector. Among them are Japan, France and Italy. Japan has more retail outlets than the United States with only half the population (Jain, 1996, p. 536).

Legislation

A major reason for the lack of growth of large-scale retailing in these countries is legislation. Compared to the USA, retailing in Europe and to some extent Japan is subject to rather stringent legislation. In order to protect the independent retailer in town centres, legislation primarily targets competition, new shops, and days and hours of opening.

Legislative conditions differ across Europe. In the UK legislation is liberal, which explains the rapid development of large supermarkets in the 1980s and large specialized stores in the 1990s. In Italy, where legislation is much stricter, the opening of department stores and hypermarkets has been limited.

Legislation can hamper the development of some forms of retailing. Though France was one of the creators of the hypermarket (a giant market), France passed a law regulating the establishment or expansion of retail stores in 1973. The effect of this law and similar laws in Italy is to allow existing retailers to protest against the establishment of any new large-scale retailers in their area.

Internationalization of retailing

Both US retailers and European retailers are internationalizing their business. Among large international US retailers are: 7-eleven, McDonald's, Pizza Hut, Blockbuster Video and Toys 'R' Us. Among the large international European retailers are IKEA, Benetton, Body Shop, Laura Ashley and Carrefour.

The Japanese are relative newcomers to this internationalization of retailing, but they are getting deeply involved. One of the Japanese food retailers, Jusco, has supermarkets in Hong Kong, Thailand and Malaysia. South-east Asia seems to be the natural zone of influence for Japanese retailers, and they have spread throughout the region.

Despite the trend towards internationalization in retailing, a prospective international retailer also faces some serious challenges and problems. The problems begin with the consumers. Retailers' performance in local markets is highly sensitive to variations in consumer behaviour. These are differences in consumer tastes, buying habits and spending patterns from country to country. Such differences have implications for a more differentiated merchandise offering along dimensions such as colour, fabric and site for clothing, and flavour for confectionery and snack foods.

Other problems that retailers will encounter when operating internationally include shortages of key resources such as land and labour, unfavourable tax and tariff structures, restrictions on trading hours and foreign ownership, and impenetrable established supplier relationships.

A case study of one US speciality retailer (made by McKinsey) has pinpointed the problems of establishing a retail business in Europe (Table 16.4). The reasons for the relatively large 'drop' in the European figures from top line to bottom line can be sought in the following factors:

● Higher expenses for acquiring real estate in Europe.

● More expensive labour in Europe.

● The complex legislation for establishing large retail stores in Europe.

Stages of internationalization

The 'stages' concept (the Uppsala school: see section 3.2) has been applied to depict the typical movement by retailers towards internationalization. Given the considerable risks and costs involved in expansion outside home markets, most have viewed the prospect with a degree of reluctance. The retail companies will typically move from reluctance to cautious expansion abroad, starting with the closest markets.

The internationalization of retailing has produced different styles of international operation, ranging from multinational to global (Figure 16.10). Global retailers such as Toys 'R' Us vary their format very little across national boundaries, achieving the greatest economies of scale but showing the least local responsiveness. Multinational retailers, on the other hand, operate as autonomous entities within each country. A middle course is termed 'transnational' retailing, whereby the company seeks to achieve global efficiency while responding to national opportunities and constraints.

Trade marketing

For too long manufacturers have viewed vertical marketing channels as closed systems, operating as separate, static entities. The most important factors creating

Table 16.4	**Profitability of retailing in United States versus Europe (example: US speciality retailer)**		
		USA	Europe
Top line			
Sales per square foot		$459	$580
Cross margin		35.6%	55.2%
Bottom line			
Operating profit per store		$0.4m	$0.2m
Operating margin		14%	5%

Source: Barth *et al.* (1996), p. 118.

Figure 16.10 International development positions

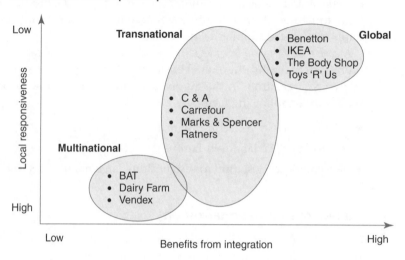

(Source: McGoldrick, P.J. and Davies, G. (1995) *International Retailing: Trends and Strategies*, Pearson Education Limited.)

long-term, integrated strategic plans and fostering productive channel relationships were largely ignored. Fortunately, a new philosophy about channel management has emerged, but to understand its potential we must first understand how power has developed at the retailer level.

Power in channel relationships can be defined as the ability of a channel member to control marketing decision variables of any other member in a channel at a different level of distribution. A classic example of this is the amount of power wielded by retailers against the food and grocery manufacturers. As the balance of power has shifted, more merchandise is controlled by fewer and fewer retailers (Table 16.5).

There is a world-wide tendency towards concentration in retailing. As Table 16.5 shows, the concentration in the European food sector is most evident in the northern part of Europe.

A consequence of this development is that there has been a world-wide shift from manufacturer to retailer dominance. Power has become concentrated in the hands of fewer and fewer retailers, and the manufacturers have been left with little choice

Table 16.5 Concentration in food retailing: food market share of the top five retailers

	Belgium	Germany	France	Italy	Netherlands	UK
Top five retailers	GIB	Aldi	Leclerc	Crai	Ahold	Sainsbury
	Delhaize	Rewe	Intermarche	Conad	Super-Unie	Tesco
	Aldi	Edeka	Carrefour	Coop	Vendex	Argyll
	Colruyt	Markant	Promodes	Vege	Aldi	Asda
	Edeku	Asko	Auchan	Rinascente	Hermans	Co-op
Food market share of top five retailers	43%	41%	40%	20%	44%	48%

Source: Adapted from McGoldrick, P.J. and Davies, G. (1995), *International Retailing: Trends and Strategies*, Pearson Education Limited.

but to accede to their demands. This often results in manufacturing of the retailers' own brands (private labels). This phenomenon was discussed in section 14.8.

Therefore, we can see that traditional channel management, with its characteristics of power struggles, conflict and loose relationships, is no longer beneficial. New ideas are emerging to help channel relationships become more cooperative. This is what is known as 'trade marketing'. Trade marketing is when the manufacturer (supplier) markets directly to the trade (retailers) to create a better fit between product and outlet. The objective is to create joint marketing and strategic plans for mutual profitability.

For the manufacturer (supplier), it means creating twin marketing strategies: one to the consumer and another to the trade (retailers). However, as Figure 16.11 shows, potential channel conflicts exist because of differences in the objectives of the channel members.

Despite potential channel conflicts, what both parties share, but often forget, is their common goal of consumer satisfaction. If the desired end result is to create joint marketing plans, a prerequisite must be an improved understanding of the other's perspective and objectives.

Figure 16.11 **Channel relationships and the concept of trade marketing**

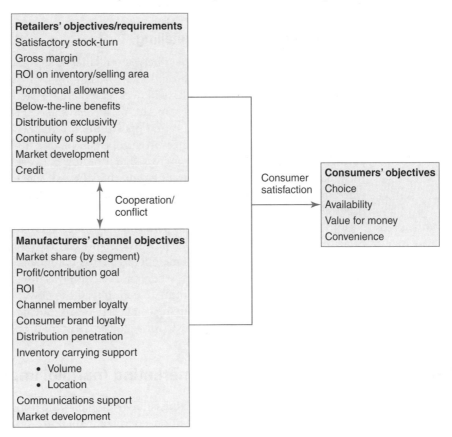

Retailers are looking for potential sales, profitability, exclusivity in promotions and volume. They are currently in the enviable position of being able to choose brands which fulfil those aims.

A private label manufacturer has to create different packages for different retailers. By carefully designing individual packages, the manufacturer gains a better chance of striking up a relationship with the best-matched retailer.

Manufacturers can offer retailers a total 'support package' by stressing their own strengths. These include marketing knowledge and experience, market position, proven new product success, media support and exposure, and a high return on investment in shelf space.

If a joint strategy is going to be successful, manufacturers and retailers must work together at every level, perhaps by matching counterparts in each organization. As a consequence of the increasing importance of the individual customer, the concept of the key account (key customer) was introduced. Key accounts are often large retail chains with a large turnover (in total as well as of the supplier's products), which are able to decide quantity and price on behalf of different outlets.

Segmentation of customers is therefore no longer based only on size and geographic position, but also on customers' (retailers') structure of decision making. This results in a gradual restructuring of sales from a geographic division to a customer division. This reorganization is made visible by creating key account managers (managers responsible for customers).

Cross-border alliances in retailing

The focus of this section is alliances between retailers that are both horizontal (i.e. retailer to retailer) and also international, in that they cross the boundaries of nation states. Cross-border retailer alliances are emerging predominantly between western European retailers and can, in many cases, be interpreted as explicit responses to the perceived threats and opportunities of the EU internal market.

None of the cross-border alliances in Europe can be described as 'equity participating alliances', which include a cross-shareholding between members. None of the alliances involves the sharing of equity, but they all have a central secretariat with the function of coordinating operational activities – buying, branding, expertise exchange and product marketing.

Until now, the range of activities performed by the secretariats of the alliances has been limited and excludes actual processing and central payments. The present advantage for an individual retail member in a cross-border alliance lies primarily in central purchasing from suppliers, where price advantages flow to all members, suggesting that the alliance is attempting to countervail the power of the manufacturer (supplier). Cross-border central buying can be a relevant starting point for both manufacturers and retailers attempting to move towards a pan-European supply network.

16.8 ▌ Special issue 2: Grey marketing (parallel importing)

Grey marketing or parallel importing can be defined as the importing and selling of products through market distribution channels which are not authorized by the manufacturer. It occurs when manufacturers use significantly different market prices for the same product in different countries. This allows an unauthorized dealer (in Figure 16.12, a wholesaler) to buy branded goods intended for one market at a low price and then sell them in another higher-priced market, at a higher profit than could have been achieved in the 'low-price' market.

Grey marketing often occurs because of the fluctuating value of currencies between different countries, which makes it attractive for the 'grey' marketer to buy products in markets with weak currencies and sell them in markets with strong currencies.

Grey markets can also be the result of a distributor in one country having an unexpected oversupply of a product. This distributor may be willing to sell its excess supply for less than the normal margin to recover its investment. Other reasons for lower prices in some countries (which can result in grey marketing) might be lower transport costs, fiercer competition and higher product taxes (high product taxes put pressure on the ex-works price to keep the end-consumer price at an acceptable level).

The particular problem with grey marketing for the manufacturer is that it results in authorized intermediaries losing motivation. The grey marketer usually competes only on price and pays little attention to providing marketing support and after-sales service.

Possible strategies to reduce grey marketing

Sometimes companies hope that it is a short-term problem and that it will disappear. Indeed, it might be if the price difference is the result of the fluctuating

Figure 16.12   **Grey marketing (parallel importing)**

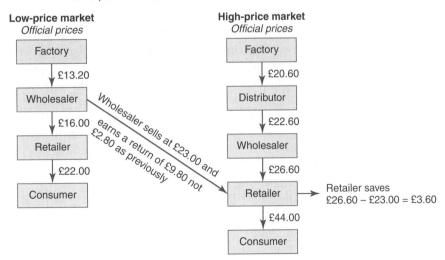

Two markets kept separate by the manufacturer.
Same product sold in the two markets.

(Source: Paliwoda, 1993, p. 300. Reprinted with permission from Butterworth-Heinemann Publishers; http://www.heinemann.co.uk)

value of currencies. At other times a more proactive approach to the problem is needed:

● Seek legal redress. Although the legal option can be time consuming and expensive, some companies (e.g. Seiko) have chosen to prosecute grey marketers.

● Change the marketing mix.

The latter involves three elements:

● *Product strategy*. This strategy is about moving away from the standardization concept (same product for all markets), and introducing a differentiated concept with a different product for each main market.

● *Pricing strategy*. The manufacturer can change the ex-works prices to the channel members to minimize price differentials between markets. The manufacturer can also narrow the discount schedules it offers for large orders. This will reduce the incentive for intermediaries to over-order to get lower prices and later sell unsold stock on the grey market, still at a profit.

● *Warranty strategy*. The manufacturer may reduce or cancel the warranty-period for grey market products. This will require that the products can be identified through the channel system.

16.9 Summary

In this chapter we have examined the management of international distribution channels and logistics. The main structure of this chapter was given in Figure 16.1, and from the discussion it is evident that the international marketer has a broad range of alternatives for selecting and developing an economical, efficient and high-volume international distribution channel.

In many instances, the channel structure is affected by external factors and it may vary from nation to nation. Physical distribution (external logistics) concerns the flow of goods from the manufacturer to the customer. This is one area where cost savings through efficiency are feasible, provided the decision is systematically made. The changing nature of international retailing influences distribution planning. During the last decade, the balance of power (between manufacturers and retailers) has shifted in favour of the retailers. The manufacturer often has no other choice than to cooperate with large and increasingly concentrated retailers in terms of the 'trade marketing' concept.

A phenomenon of growing importance in international markets is the grey market, which consists of unauthorized traders buying and selling a company's product in different countries. Companies confronted with a grey market situation can react in many ways. They may decide to ignore the problem, take legal action or modify elements of their marketing mix. The option chosen is strongly influenced by the nature of the situation and its expected duration.

Case study   Vivid Video

International distribution strategy for erotic videos/DVDs

Welcome to the international sex industry, turnover $20 billion a year.

Let us start with some categories. There are what may be called services: prostitution, striptease and telephone sex. And there are products: pornography and sex aids. In both parts of the industry, a handful of well-run and imaginative businesses are making money as never before – through upmarket escort agencies, for instance, or over the Internet, or by intelligently exploiting market niches. Traditional businesses, especially the small and amateurish ones, are threatened with extinction.

At the bottom of the market, few language or other skills are required. Increasingly, western providers of sexual services are finding it difficult to compete with foreigners. As in other industries, these new competitors work longer hours, for less money, and with less concern for safety and comfort than their western counterparts.

What is going on? The biggest change, as in so many industries, is globalization. On the product side of the business, sex aids these days are produced almost exclusively in China. Most West European producers of sex videos use East European actors wherever possible. 'They cost less and do more', an executive at Germany's Silwa production company explains bluntly. In only eight years, Budapest has become probably the biggest centre for pornography production in Europe, eclipsing rivals such as Amsterdam and Copenhagen. Stars' fees have dropped sharply. Even excruciating or humiliating acts usually cost the producer only two or three hundred dollars, roughly a third of the fees paid ten years ago.

The same applies to pornography; the bottom of the market is hopelessly oversupplied. Staying awake could be a big problem: most porn films are barely distinguishable from each other, with feeble plots and dialogue. Demand for basic porn is all but saturated.

As in any business threatened with commoditization, what really makes money is building a brand or finding a niche. European consumers will pay a premium for a familiar face – such as Teresa Orlowski, the Hanover-based porn star who now runs one of Germany's biggest sex-video businesses. Offering customers something new or different works too. Videos on subjects which would have been considered odd, or even kinky, a few years ago, such as tickling or foot fetishes, can now be found occupying a shelf or two in the 'adult' section of any well-stocked video store.

The US industry gained the opportunities to open up to a larger audience partly because young adults grew up with VCRs, cable TV and the Internet and thus have been exposed to more adult material. The AIDS epidemic has prompted a turn to voyeurism as a prudent alternative to sex. But an equally big factor, say the porn manufacturers, is the Bill Clinton–Lewinsky case.

Vivid Video

American porn barons such as Steven Hirsch of Vivid Video have made a fortune by producing (slightly) more upmarket fare, featuring such innovations as connected dialogue and intimations of a plot.

Vivid is the most powerful studio in America's porn-film industry. Nationally, adult videos totally bring in $2 billion a year, according to *Adult Video News*, and account for more than a quarter of all sales and rentals at the typical video store. Most of the industry resides in the San Fernando Valley, on the north side of LA's Santa Monica mountains.

In 1999 Vivid Video generated more than $30 million in revenue, mainly by selling videos in the US market. Vivid has focused on producing couples-friendly, plot-heavy 35-mm films costing up to $200,000 and selling them to the Playboy Channel, the Spice Channel and Spectravision systems in hotel rooms, as well as overseas television. With Playboy, Vivid co-owns AdulTVision, an adult-movie channel available on many US cable systems. Vivid is also negotiating with Playboy to buy Hot Spice, a new hard-core cable channel.

Vivid Video has revived the Hollywood studio system, signing actors on exclusive contracts and promoting its actresses as 'Vivid girls', a cut above the regular porno crowd. The studio system provides Vivid with brand identity. Now that anyone with a hand-held video camera can make a film, the market is being saturated. Vivid employs an in-house director to give its films a 'Vivid feel'; it even makes sure that the boxes that the film comes in have a 'Vivid look'. Significantly, Vivid's biggest competitors, notably VCA, are adopting a similar strategy to deal with the glut in the market.

Vivid Video has won Adult Video News Awards several times (in 1997, Vivid won no fewer than 15 of these adult Oscars, an all-time high).

At retail, the selling of porn has become less lurid. Vivid is happy to peddle video-tapes in a more Main Street manner through the Adam & Eve catalogue, which is mailed to 2.5 million people a month, and Tower and Virgin record stores, where the 'Vivid girls' have done signings.

But Vivid is looking to the future as well as the past. Technologically, it is ahead of the rest of the industry. Fifteen years ago the pornography business was one of the first to turn the videocassette recorder into a cash machine. Today it is doing the same for DVD and the Internet. The Internet is the most important of all the changes, technological or otherwise, affecting the global sex industry. Vivid is not only cranking out DVD faster than any other studio, it is also using the medium's capabilities to their limit to enhance the viewer's experience – by, for instance, allowing viewers to watch a single scene from several angles. And by supplying video to other sites, rather than by running its own, Vivid is even making money out of its website (www.vividvideo.com).

Video companies in general have started to market their products more aggres-sively. For big releases, there are screenings and premiere parties. VCA, one of the four big adult-film companies, has put promotional billboards along Sunset Boulevard in Los Angeles, and Vivid has placed ads at the Burbank airport as well as along Sunset. Vivid's actresses also appear in commercials for clothing and sunglasses.

Questions

1. What are the main differences between the business systems of Vivid Videos and Playboy (see Playboy Internet exercise, Chapter 1)?

2. Steven Hirsch has decided to enter the main European and Asian markets with his videos. What advice would you give Mr Hirsch regarding selection of the right distribution channels on these markets?

3. Should there be a difference in the distribution strategy for Europe and Asia?

Source: adapted from 'Branded flesh', *Economist*, 14 August 1999.

Stein, Joel, 'Porn goes mainstream', *Time*, 7 September 1998.

Questions for discussion

1. Discuss current distribution trends in world markets.

2. What are the factors that affect the length, width and number of marketing channels?

3. In attempting to optimize global marketing channel performance, which of the following should an international marketer emphasize: training, motivation or compensation? Why?

4. When would it be feasible and advisable for a global company to centralize the coordination of its foreign market distribution systems? When would decentralization be more appropriate?

5. Do grey marketers serve useful marketing functions – for consumers and manufacturers?

6. Why is physical distribution important to the success of global marketing?

7. Discuss the reasons why many exporters make extensive use of the services of freight forwarders.

8. Discuss the implications for the international marketer of the trend towards cross-border retailing.

9. Many markets have relatively large numbers of small retailers. How does this constrain the international marketer?

10. What are the ways in which retailing know-how is transferred internationally?

11. What services would the manufacturer like to receive from the retailer?

Internet exercise

Travelstore.com

Please go to:

www.travelstore.com

Question

Discuss the problems and possibilities of disintermediation for Travelstore.com.

For further exercises and cases, see this book's website at *www.booksites.net/hollensen*

References

Albaum, G., Strandskov, J., Duerr, E. and Laurence Dowd (1994) *International Marketing and Export Management*, Addison Wesley, Reading, MA.

Barth, K., Karch, N.J., Mclaughlin, K. and Shi, C.S. (1996) 'Global retailing – tempting trouble', *The McKinsey Quarterly*, no. 1, pp. 117–25.

Bucklin, C.B., Defalco, S.P., DeVincentis, J.R. and Levis III, J.P. (1996) 'Are you tough enough to manage your channels?', *The McKinsey Quarterly*, no. 1, pp. 105–14.

Cateora, P.R. (1993) *International Marketing* (8th edn), Irwin, Homewood, IL.

Chee, H. and Harris, R. (1994) *Marketing: A global perspective*, Pitman, London.

EIU (1995) 'The EU50 – corporate case studies in single market success', Research Report, pp. 77–8.

Jain, S. (1996) *International Marketing Management* (5th edn), South-Western College Publishing, Cincinnati, OH.

Kumar, N. (1999) 'Internet distribution strategies: Dilemmas for the incumbent', Mastering Information Management, Part 7, Electronic Commerce, *Financial Times*, 15 March.

Lewison, D.M. (1996) *Marketing Management: An overview*, The Dryden Press/Harcourt Brace College Publishers, Fort Worth, TX.

McGoldrick, P.J. and Davies, G. (1995) *International Retailing: Trends and strategies*, Pitman, London.

Onkvisit, S. and Shaw, J.J. (1993) *International Marketing: Analysis and strategy* (2nd edn), Macmillan, London.

Paliwoda, S. (1993) *International Marketing*, Heinemann, Oxford.

Pirog III, S.F. and Lancioni, R. (1997) 'US–Japan distribution channel cost structures: is there a significant difference?', *International Journal of Physical Distribution and Logistics Management*, vol. 27, no. 1, pp. 53–66.

Sletmo, G.K. and Picard, J. (1984) 'International distribution policies and the role of air freight', *Journal of Business Logistics*, vol. 6, pp. 35–52.

Spegel, R. (2000) 'Sony shocks Japanese dealers with direct sales web site', *E-Commerce Times*, 1 February.

Toyne, B. and Walters, P.G.P. (1993) *Global Marketing Management: A strategic perspective* (2nd edn), Allyn and Bacon, Needham Heights, MA.

Chapter 17

Communication decisions (promotion strategies)

After studying this chapter you should be able to do the following:

- Define and classify the different types of communication tool.
- Describe and explain the major steps in advertising decisions.
- Describe the techniques available and appropriate for setting the advertising budget in foreign markets.
- Discuss the possibilities of marketing via the Internet.
- Discuss which points should be considered when creating a World Wide Web site on the Internet.
- Explain how important personal selling and sales force management are in the international marketplace.
- Discuss how standardized international advertising has both benefits and drawbacks.

17.1 Introduction

Communication is the fourth and final decision about the global marketing programme. The role of communication in global marketing is similar to that in domestic operations: to communicate with customers so as to provide information that buyers need to make purchasing decisions. Although the communication mix carries information of interest to the customer, in the end it is designed to persuade the customer to buy a product – at the present time or in the future.

To communicate with and influence customers, several tools are available. Advertising is usually the most visible component of the promotion mix, but personal selling, exhibitions, sales promotions, publicity (PR) and direct marketing (including the Internet) are also part of a viable international promotion mix.

One important strategic consideration is whether to standardize world-wide or to adapt the promotion mix to the environment of each country. Another consideration is the availability of media, which varies around the world.

The communication process

In considering the communication process we normally think about a manufacturer (sender) transmitting a message through any form of media to an identifiable target segment audience. Here the seller is the initiator of the communication process. However, if the seller and the buyer have already established a relationship, it is likely that the initiative to the communication process will come from the buyer. If the buyer has positive post-purchase experience with a given offering in one period of time, this may dispose the buyer to rebuy on later occasions: that is, take initiatives in the form of making enquiries or placing orders (so-called reversed marketing).

The likely development of the split between total sales volume attributable to buyer and seller initiatives is shown in Figure 17.1. The relative share of sales volume attributable to buyer initiative will tend to increase over time. Present and future buyer initiatives are a function of all aspects of a firm's past market performance: that is, the extent, nature and timing of seller initiative, the competitiveness of offerings, post-purchase experience, the relationships developed with buyers as well as the way in which buyer initiative has been dealt with (Ottesen, 1995).

Key attributes of effective communication

The rest of the chapter will be devoted to the communicative process and communicative tools based on seller initiatives. All effective marketing communication has four elements: a sender, a message, a communication channel and a receiver (audience). The communication process in Figure 17.2 highlights the key attributes of effective communication.

Figure 17.1 **The shift from seller initiative to buyer initiative in buyer/seller relationships**

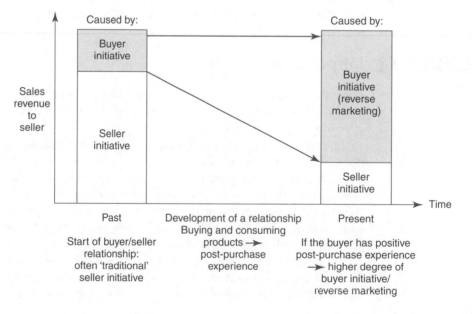

Figure 17.2   **Elements of the international communication process**

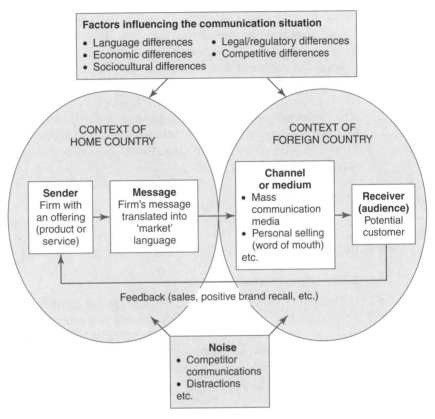

To communicate in an effective way, the sender needs to have a clear understanding of the purpose of the message, the audience to be reached and how this audience will interpret and respond to the message. However, sometimes the audience cannot hear clearly what the sender is trying to tell about its product because of the 'noise' of rival manufacturers making similar and often contradictory claims about their products.

Another important point to consider in the model of Figure 17.2 is the degree of 'fit' between medium and message. For example, a complex and wordy message would be better for the press than for a visual medium such as television or cinema.

Other factors affecting the communication situation

Language differences

A slogan or advertising copy that is effective in one language may mean something different in another language. Thus, the trade names, sales presentation materials and advertisements used by firms in their domestic markets may have to be adapted and translated when used in other markets.

There are many examples of unfortunate translations of brand names and slogans. General Motors has a brand name for one of its models called the Vauxhall Nova – this does not work well in Spanish-speaking markets because there it means 'no go'. In Latin America, 'Avoid embarrassment – Use Parker Pens' was translated as 'Avoid pregnancy – Use Parker Pens'.

A Danish company made the following slogan for its cat litter on the British market: 'Sand for Cat Piss'. Unsurprisingly, sales of the firm's cat litter did not increase! Another Danish company translated 'Teats for baby's bottles' as 'Loose tits'. In Copenhagen Airport the following poster could be seen until recently: 'We take your baggage and send it in all directions'. A slogan thus used to express a wish of giving good service might give rise to some concern as to where the baggage might end up (Joensen, 1997).

Economic differences

In contrast to industrialized countries, the developing countries may have radios but not television sets. In countries with low levels of literacy, written communication may not be as effective as visual or oral communication.

Sociocultural differences

Dimensions of culture (religion, attitudes, social conditions and education) affect how individuals perceive their environment and interpret signals and symbols. For example, the use of colour in advertising must be sensitive to cultural norms. In many Asian countries, white is associated with grief; hence an advertisement for a detergent where whiteness is emphasized would have to be altered for promotional activities in, say, India.

Exhibit 17.1   ## In Moslem markets only God is great

One of the major car manufacturers was using Muhammed Ali in one of its Arab advertising campaigns. Muhammed Ali is very popular in the Middle East, but the theme was him saying 'I am the greatest', which offended people because the Moslems only regard God as the greatest.

Source: Harper (1986)

Legal and regulatory conditions

Local advertising regulations and industry codes directly influence the selection of media and content of promotion materials. Many governments maintain tight regulations on content, language and sexism in advertising. The type of product that can be advertised is also regulated. Tobacco products and alcoholic beverages are the most heavily regulated products in terms of promotion. However, the manufacturers of these products have not abandoned their promotional efforts. Philip Morris engages in corporate-image advertising using its Marlborough man. Regulations are found more in industrialized economies than in developing economies, where the advertising industry is not yet as highly developed.

Competitive differences

As competitors vary from country to country in terms of number, size, type and promotional strategies used, a firm may have to adapt its promotional strategy and the timing of its efforts to the local environment.

17.3 ▌ Communication tools

Earlier in this chapter we mentioned the major forms of promotion. In this section the different communication tools, listed in Table 17.1, will be further examined.

Advertising

Advertising is one of the most visible forms of communication. Because of its wide use and its limitations as a one-way method of communication, advertising in international markets is subject to a number of difficulties. Advertising is often the most important part of the communications mix for consumer goods, where there are a large number of small-volume customers who can be reached through mass media. For most business-to-business markets, advertising is less important than the personal selling function.

The major decisions in advertising are shown in Figure 17.3. We will now discuss these different phases.

Objectives setting

Although advertising methods may vary from country to country, the major advertising objectives remain the same. Major advertising objectives (and means) might include some of the following:

● *Increasing sales from existing customers* by encouraging existing customers to increase the frequency of their purchases; maintaining brand loyalty via a strategy that reminds customers of the key advantages of the product; and stimulating impulse purchases.

| Table 17.1 | **Typical communication tools (media)** |

One-way communication ◄──────────────────────► Two-way communication

Advertising	Public relations	Sales promotion	Direct marketing	Personal selling
Newspapers	Annual reports	Rebates and	Direct	Sales
Magazines	Corporate image	price discounts	mail/database	presentations
Journals	House magazines	Catalogues and	marketing	Sales force
Directories	Press relations	brochures	Internet marketing	management
Radio	Public relations	Samples,	(WWW)	Trade fairs and
Television	Events	coupons and gifts	Telemarketing	exhibitions
Cinema	Lobbying	Competitions		
Outdoor	Sponsorship			

Figure 17.3   The major international advertising decisions

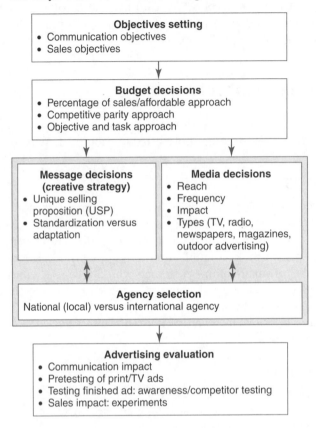

● *Obtaining new customers* by increasing consumer awareness of the firm's products and improving the firm's corporate image among a new target customer group.

Budget decisions

Controversial aspects of advertising include determining a proper method for deciding the size of the promotional budget, and its allocation across markets and over time.

In theory, the firm (in each of its markets) should continue to put more money into advertising, as an amount of money spent on advertising returns more than an amount of money spent on anything else. In practice, it is not possible to set an optimum advertising budget. Therefore firms have developed more practical guidelines. The manager must also remember that the advertising budget cannot be regarded in isolation, but has to be seen as one element of the overall marketing mix.

Affordable approach/percentage of sales

These budgeting techniques link advertising expenditures directly to some measure of profits or, more commonly, to sales. The most popular of these methods is the 'percentage of sales method', whereby the firm automatically allocates a fixed percentage of sales to the advertising budget.

Advantages of this method are as follows:

- For firms selling in many countries, this simple method appears to guarantee equality among the markets. Each market seems to get the advertising it deserves.
- It is easy to justify in budget meetings.
- It guarantees that the firm only spends on advertising as much as it can afford. The method prevents 'good money being thrown after bad'.

Disadvantages of this method are as follows:

- It uses historical performance rather than future performance.
- It ignores the possibility that extra spending on advertising may be necessary when sales are declining, in order to reverse the sales trend by establishing a 'recycle' on the product life cycle curve (see section 14.4).
- It does not take into account variations in the firm's marketing goals across countries.
- The 'percentage of sales' method encourages local management to maximize sales by using the easiest and most flexible marketing tool: price (that is, lowering the price).
- The method's convenience and simplicity encourage management not to bother investigating the relationships between advertising and sales or analyzing critically the overall effectiveness of its advertising campaigns.
- The method cannot be used to launch new products or enter new markets (zero sales = zero advertising).

Competitive parity approach

This involves estimating and duplicating the amounts spent on advertising by major rivals. Unfortunately, determining the marketing expenditures of foreign-based competitors is far more difficult than monitoring home country businesses, whose financial accounts (if they are limited companies) are open to public inspection and whose promotional activities are obvious the moment they occur. Another danger in following the practice of competitors is that they are not necessarily right.

Furthermore, the method does not recognize that the firm is in different situations in different markets. If the firm is new to a market, its relationships with customers are different from those of existing domestic companies. This should also be reflected in its promotion budget.

Objective and task approach

The weaknesses of the above approaches have led some firms to follow this approach, which begins by determining the advertising objectives and then ascertaining the tasks needed to attain these objectives. This approach also includes a cost/benefit analysis, relating objectives to the costs of achieving them. To use this method, the firm must have good knowledge of the local market.

A research study (Hung and West, 1991) showed that only 20 per cent of companies in the USA, Canada and the UK used the objective and task approach. Although it is the 'theoretically correct' way of determining the promotion budget, it is sometimes more important to be operational and to use a 'percentage of sales' approach. This is not necessarily a bad method if company experience shows it to be reasonably successful. If the percentage is flexible, it allows different percentages in different markets.

Message decisions (creative strategy)

This concerns decisions about what unique selling proposition (USP) needs to be communicated, and what the communication is intended to achieve in terms of consumer behaviour in the country concerned. These decisions have important implications for the choice of advertising medium, since certain media can better accommodate specific creative requirements (use of colour, written description, high definition, demonstration of the product, etc.) than others.

An important decision area for international marketers is whether an advertising campaign developed in the domestic market can be transferred to foreign markets with only minor modifications, such as translation into the appropriate languages. Complete standardization of all aspects of a campaign over several foreign markets is rarely attainable. Standardization implies a common message, creative idea, media and strategy, but it also requires that the firm's product has a USP that is clearly understood by customers in a cross-cultural environment.

Standardizing international advertising can lead to a number of advantages for the firm. For example, advertising costs will be reduced by centralizing the advertising campaign in the head office and transferring the same campaign from market to market, as opposed to running campaigns from different local offices.

However, executing an advertising campaign in multiple markets requires a balance between conveying the message and allowing for local nuances. The adaptation of global ideas can be achieved by various tactics, such as adopting a modular approach, adapting international symbols and using international advertising agencies.

Exhibit 17.2   Developing the 'Me and my Magnum' campaign: the power of persuasion

In 1989 Unilever launched the ice-cream brand Magnum (see also Exhibit 19.2) in a number of European countries. A special and unique relationship arose between Magnum and the customer due to the backbone of the advertising campaign 'Me and my Magnum', which was developed in 1991–2 by Barry Day, creative consultant at Lintas, together with Langnese-Iglo's marketing director, Klaus Rabbel, and Michael Bronsten, Ice Cream Group advertising member.

The ironic thing about the advertising – and the key to its success, says Barry Day – was that 'The Magnum campaign was not dreamt up by some ad man: the consumer "wrote" it. The advertising is based on what consumers were saying about the brand.

▶

The advertisement (see Plate 11) contains three elements, two visual and one audio. The first visual element surrounds one particular aspect of Magnum: its size. Consumers have related that Magnum's size makes it awkward and unwieldy. Thus, they say, it cannot be eaten quickly: time is needed to consume a Magnum and this special moment should not be interrupted. They have also confessed that eating it can be quite an erotic experience. These two elements come together in the second visual image: the body language of the Magnum consumer, who eats it slowly and with great care, gently toying with the crisp, cracking chocolate before teasing out the ice-cream underneath.

Binding these two visual elements together is a soundtrack which gives the consumer 'licence to indulge', says Barry Day. It consists of genuine testimonies from consumers reflecting on what Magnum means to them. The advertisement works, Barry Day believes, because the words it uses to describe the experience of eating a Magnum really do accord with those of the consumer. This recognition is translated into a close affinity between one Magnum consumer and another. 'It gives the viewer the feeling that he or she is part of some sort of élite or club – the Magnum Club,' he explains. It is, however, a singles club. Magnum is purely personal indulgence: people eating one are not going to share it with anyone else.

Where does the Magnum advertising go from here? Barry Day feels that future campaigns can go deeper into the psychology of the brand, but should never take away from the values which have made Magnum the success it is today.

Source: Shelly (1995).

Media decisions

The selection of the media to be used for advertising campaigns needs to be done simultaneously with the development of the message theme. A key question in media selection is whether to use a mass or target approach. The mass media (television, radio and newsprint) are effective when a significant percentage of the general public are potential customers. This percentage varies considerably by country for most products, depending on, for example, the distribution of incomes in different countries.

The selection of the media to be used in a particular campaign typically starts with some idea of the target market's demographic and psychological characteristics, regional strengths of the product, seasonality of sales, and so on. The media selected should be the result of a careful fit of local advertising objectives, media attributes and target market characteristics. Furthermore, media selection can be based on the following criteria:

- *Reach*. This is the total number of people in a target market exposed to at least one advertisement in a given time period ('opportunity to see', or OTS).

- *Frequency*. This is the average number of times within a given time period that each potential customer is exposed to the same advertisement.

- *Impact*. This depends on compatibility between the medium used and the message. *Penthouse* magazine continues to attract advertisers for high-value-added consumer durables, such as cars, hi-fi equipment and clothes, which are geared primarily to a high-income male segment.

High reach is necessary when the firm enters a new market or introduces a new product so that information about, for example, a new product's availability is spread to the widest possible audience. A high level of frequency is appropriate when brand awareness already exists and the message is about informing the consumer that a campaign is under way. Sometimes a campaign should have both a high frequency and extensive reach, but limits on the advertising budget often create the need to trade off frequency against reach.

A media's gross rating points (GRPs) are the result of multiplying its reach by the frequency with which an advertisement appears within the media over a certain period. Hence it contains duplicated exposure, but indicates the 'critical mass' of a media effort. GRPs may be estimated for individual vehicles, for entire classes of media or for a total campaign.

The cost of running a media campaign also has to be taken into consideration. Traditionally, media planning is based on a single measure, such as 'cost per thousand GRPs'. When dealing with two or more national markets, the selection of media also has to take the following into account:

● Differences in the firm's market objectives across countries.

● Differences in media effectiveness across countries.

Since media availability and relative importance will not be the same in all countries, plans may require adjustment in cross-border campaigns.

As a way of distributing advertising messages through new communication channels, co-promotion has got a strong foothold (see Exhibit 17.3).

Let us now take a closer look at the main media types.

Exhibit 17.3 **Co-promotion in practice: McDonald's and LEGO**

In 1994 LEGO carried out its then largest European co-promotion with McDonald's as collaborator. The family restaurant's children's menu Happy Meal contained a LEGO product for four weeks, one every week. The activity was marketed on television and in print media.

The campaign included sixteen countries in Europe plus Turkey and Israel. LEGO's motives for an increasing interest in co-promotion, says brand manager Carsten Sørensen, are twofold:

● There is increasing competition in media which are becoming more and more crowded. Co-promotion offers the opportunity of getting more value for money from the marketing budget.

● In some markets, LEGO needs an increased market share. The more it is in contact with consumers, the better they know the company. Co-promotion can thus be a relevant tool if a company is introducing a new product in an existing market or existing products in new markets.

Source: Nørmark (1994).

Television

Television is an expensive but commonly used medium in attempting to reach broad national markets. In most developed countries, coverage is no problem. However, television is one of the most regulated communications media. Many countries have prohibited the advertising of cigarettes and alcohol other than beer. In other countries (e.g. in Scandinavia) there are limits on the number of minutes that TV advertising is permitted to be sent. These countries also prohibit commercial breaks in TV programmes.

Exhibit 17.4

Mercedes uses Janis Joplin's hit to market its cars in the USA

'Oh, Lord, won't you buy me a Mercedes Benz. My friends all drive Porsches, I must make amends. Worked hard all my lifetime. No help from my friends. So, Lord, won't you buy me a Mercedes Benz.'

Twenty-four years ago rock singer Janis Joplin begged the Lord for a Mercedes Benz. The vocal version of a poor woman's evening prayer was a hit then and is still played frequently on radio stations all over the world.

Buying power of the generation of 1968

The generation of 1968 have now reached an age with purchasing power, and the German car company has decided to let the prayer be heard as part of a huge advertising campaign. Mercedes Benz has bought the rights to use the song in its advertisements in coming years. The campaign has already been launched on American TV, where Joplin's whisky voice accompanies the delicate pictures of two of Mercedes' newest luxury models. Many classic rock hits from the 1950s and 1960s have been used commercially in advertisements during recent years. But Joplin's hit is different in two ways. First, it mentions the product directly. Second the song was originally a satire of the poor's dream that happiness was found in one of yesterday's most materialistic status symbols.

'It was never meant to be taken seriously,' songwriter Bob Neuwirth recollects, who back in 1970 helped Joplin fabricate the song in a break between two concerts. He has nothing to do with the song today and has not been asked for advice. 'But I am surprised that it took them so long to think of the idea,' he says, and maintains that Joplin had no desperate personal need for an expensive status symbol.

Drove Porsche

In those days, Joplin owned a Porsche. Mercedes Benz has chosen Joplin as part of an attempt to reach a younger audience through advertisements which, according to the director for Mercedes' North American department Andrew Goldberg, create an instant emotional and physical connection to the product.

The reactions of a test audience have documented that the song produced warm, nostalgic feelings and created a more positive attitude towards Mercedes. 'What she meant by the song 25 years ago can be freely interpreted by anyone. But when a cus-

▶

tomer sees the advertisement, it is solely about emotions and not sociology,' says Andrew Goldberg.

Janis Joplin became a world name with the group Big Brother and the Holding Co. at the end of the 1960s, but died alcoholized from an overdose of heroin on 4 October 1970. Six months later her solo LP *Pearl* was released. It contained among others the Mercedes song, which a chuckling Joplin finishes with the words 'That's it', after the famous refrain: 'So Lord won't you buy me a Mercedes Benz'. Exactly as she is doing now a quarter of a century later in the advertisement.

Source: Translated from an article by Jan Lund in the Danish newspaper *Jyllandsposten*, 24 March 1995.

Radio

Radio is a lower-cost broadcasting activity than television. Commercial radio started several decades before commercial television in many countries. Radio is often transmitted on a local basis and therefore national campaigns have to be built up on an area-by-area basis.

Newspaper (print)

In virtually all urban areas of the world, the population has access to daily newspapers. In fact, the problem for the advertiser is not having too few newspapers, but rather having too many of them. Most countries have one or more newspapers that can be said to have a truly national circulation. However, in many countries newspapers tend to be predominantly local or regional and, as such, serve as the primary medium for local advertisers. Attempting to use a series of local papers to reach a national market is considerably more complex and costly.

Many countries have English-language newspapers in addition to local-language newspapers. For example, the aim of the *Asian Wall Street Journal* is to supply economic information in English to influential Asian business-persons, politicians, top government officials and intellectuals.

Magazines (print)

In general, magazines have a narrower readership than newspapers. In most countries, magazines serve to reach specific segments of the population. For technical and industrial products, magazines can be quite effective. Technical business publications tend to be international in their coverage. These publications range from individual businesses (e.g. beverages, construction, textiles) to world-wide industrial magazines covering many industries.

Marketers of international products have the option of using international magazines that have regional editions (e.g. *Newsweek*, *Time* and *Business Week*). In the case of *Reader's Digest*, local-language editions are distributed.

Cinema

In countries where it is common to subsidize the cost of showing movies by running advertising commercials prior to the feature film, cinema advertising has become an important medium. India, for example, has a relatively high level of cinema attendance per capita (few have television at home). Therefore cinema advertisements play a much greater role in India than in, for example, the United States.

Cinema advertising has other advantages, one of the most important being that it has a truly captive audience (no channel hopping!). The problem, of course, is that people know that commercials will be shown before the film. So they will not turn up until the main feature begins.

Outdoor advertising

Outdoor advertising includes posters/billboards, shop signs and transit advertising. This medium shows the creative way in which space can be sold to customers. In the case of transit advertising, for example, a bus can be sold as an advertising medium. In Romania transit advertising is very effective. According to a survey by Mueller (1996), in Bucharest 91 per cent of all consumers surveyed said they remembered the content of transit advertisements, compared with 82 per cent who remembered the content of print adverts. The use of transit media is expanding rapidly in China as well. Outdoor posters/billboards can be used to develop the visual impact of advertising. France is a country associated with the effective use of poster/billboard advertising. In some countries, legal restrictions limit the poster space available.

Agency selection

Confronted with the many complex problems that international advertising involves, many businesses instinctively turn to an advertising agency for advice and practical assistance. Agencies employ or have instant access to expert copywriters, translators, photographers, film makers, package designers and media planners who are skilled and experienced in the international field. Only the largest of big businesses can afford to carry such people in-house.

If the international marketer decides to outsource the international advertising functions, he or she has a variety of options including the following:

- Use different national (local) agencies in the international markets where the firm is present.
- Use the services of a big international agency with domestic overseas offices.

In Table 17.2 the different factors favouring a national or an international agency are listed. The single European (pan-European) market is used as an example of an international agency.

The criteria relevant to the choice of a national or an international agency include the following:

- *Policy of the company*. Has the company got any realistic plans for a more standardized advertising approach?
- *Nature of the advertising to be undertaken*. Corporate image advertising might be best undertaken by a single large multinational agency which operates throughout the

Table 17.2	European agency selection: national (local) or pan-European (international)	
	National (local)	**Pan-European (international)**
	Supports national subsidiary.	Reflects new European reality and trends.
	Investment in existing brand best handled nationally.	Economies of scale in new product development and branding.
	Closer to marketplace.	Uniformity of treatment across Europe.
	Smaller size more conducive to personalized service and greater creativity.	Resources and skills of major European or global agency.
	Diversity of ideas.	Easier to manage one agency group.

Source: Adapted from Lynch (1994), Table 11-4.

world via its own subsidiaries. For niche marketing in specialist country sectors, a local agency might be preferred.

● *Type of product.* The campaign for an item that is to be presented in a standardized format, using the same advertising layouts and messages in all countries, might be handled more conveniently by a single multinational agency.

Advertising evaluation

Advertising evaluation and testing is the final stage in the advertising decision process shown in Figure 17.3. Testing advertising effectiveness is normally more difficult in international markets than in domestic markets. An important reason for this is the distance and communication gap between domestic markets and foreign markets. Thus, it can be very difficult to transfer testing methods used in domestic markets to foreign markets. For example, the conditions for interviewing people can vary from country to country. Consequently, many firms try to use sales results as a measure of advertising effectiveness. First we discuss some testing procedures (the following is primarily based on Griffin (1993)).

Pretesting print advertisements/direct mail

When an advertising manager doubts which of two print advertisements he should use for a campaign, he can use a 'split-run' test to determine the reader response from the two versions. This technique can be used to test alternative headlines, illustrations and slogans. This is possible only where a newspaper or magazine to be used in the advertiser's media schedule can provide an 'A–B' split. Advertisements using, for example, two different headlines are produced. In all other respects, the advertisements are identical. The printing presses are then set to produce version A in every second paper or magazine coming off the press; the alternative paper or magazine carries version B. All advertisements carry the same offer to induce reader response, but they are coded differently so that it can be determined how many responses each version produced. In this way, the relative strengths of the two headlines, illustrations or slogans can be measured. This technique can be used equally well in testing alternative elements in a direct-mail campaign.

Pretesting TV advertisements

The purpose of pretesting TV adverts is similar. It is not the final version that will be tested, but a story board that is presented to potential customers. Simulation of the commercial in this manner will cost only a fraction of the finished product. This preliminary advertisement can be shown to individuals or a group in a central location. Afterwards, the viewers can be asked a number of questions:

● What went on?

● What was said?

● What was the main point of the commercial?

● What, if anything, was hard to understand?

● What was liked and disliked?

● What was the name of the product being advertised?

Results of this type of testing will either strengthen the advertiser's conviction that the commercial has the communication values sought, or lead to changes and improvements. Some drawbacks have been cited for preliminary message testing. Advertisements that have not been produced in final form may not include important details and may thereby reduce communication effectiveness. Subjects being interviewed may not represent the real target market. Because of the artificial environment, the results may be inaccurate.

Testing finished advertisements

More techniques exist for testing advertisements once they have been produced.

Awareness testing is designed to measure the effectiveness of an advertising campaign after it has begun and is in progress. Brand awareness is of crucial importance during the early stages of a new product launch.

Telephone surveys (if telephones are available) are common during test market programmes and new product launches because of the need to obtain feedback as quickly as possible in order to find out if the advertising is producing the intended levels of awareness. Personal interviews are used when not only awareness but other types of information are sought. In conducting these surveys, it is necessary to qualify the respondent at the outset to make sure that he or she is in the target market. For awareness, the early questions may be of an unaided nature, as in the following example which lists questions concerning awareness of detergent brands.

Unaided awareness:

1. What is the first brand that comes to mind when you think of detergent?

2. Please tell me all the other brands of detergent you have heard of.

3. Within the past six months, have you seen or heard any advertising for detergent?

Aided awareness:

4. Here is a list of different brands of detergent. Please read this list and tell

me which brands you have heard of, including those you may have already mentioned.

5. Do you recall seeing or hearing any advertising for each brand not mentioned in question 3?

6. Where did you see or hear the advertising for each brand mentioned?

7. For each brand you saw or heard advertising for (ask separately), please tell me everything that you remember. What else do you remember seeing or hearing?

It is not only important to evaluate the advertisements of the particular firm. Sometimes it is relevant to compare the firm's advertisements against those of competitors.

Testing the impact of advertising on sales is very difficult because it is difficult to isolate the advertising effect. One way to solve this problem is to use a kind of *experiment*, where the markets of the firm are grouped according to similar characteristics. In each group of countries, one or two countries are used as test markets. Independent variables to be tested against the sales (dependent variable) might include the amount of advertising, the media mix, the unique selling proposition (USP) and the frequency of placement.

This kind of experiment is also relevant for testing other types of communication tool mentioned in Table 17.1.

Exhibit 17.5 | **Bailey's Irish Cream liqueur: sales expansion with market and product development**

In 1993 R&A Bailey and Co. decided to increase sales of its brand in Europe by expanding usage of the drink. A cross-border television advertising campaign, 'Bailey's with ice', was developed to reinforce the contemporary all-year-round image of the drink and to distinguish it from the 'stuffy' image of traditional liqueurs with their mainly after-dinner role. The appeal was to younger consumers to drink Bailey's on a greater number of occasions. Special promotional packs were also developed, consisting of a one-litre bottle together with two free liqueur glasses.

In early 1993 Bailey's was also launched on the Japanese market after a period of test marketing. The regular brand was offered in addition to a specially developed brand for the Japanese called Bailey's Gold, which was developed with ten-year-old malt whiskey to appeal to the Japanese taste for premium-quality spirits. This Bailey's Gold was also priced at double the price of the regular brand.

Source: MacNamee and McDonnell (1995).

Public relations

Word-of-mouth advertising is not only cheap, it is very effective. Public relations (PR) seeks to enhance corporate image building and influence favourable media treatment. PR (or publicity) is the marketing communications function that carries out programmes designed to earn public understanding and acceptance. It should be viewed as an integral part of the global marketing effort.

PR activities involve both internal and external communication. Internal communication is important to create an appropriate corporate culture. The target groups for public relations are shown in Table 17.3.

The range of target groups is far wider in public relations than it is for the other communications tools. Target groups are likely to include the main stakeholder groups of employees, customers, distribution channel members and shareholders. For companies operating in international markets, this gives a very wide range of communication tasks. Internal communications in different country subsidiaries, employing people from a number of different countries, with different cultural values, will be particularly challenging.

In a more market-oriented sense, the PR activity is directed towards an influential, though relatively small, target audience of editors and journalists who work for newspapers/magazines, or towards broadcasting aimed at the firm's customers and stakeholders.

Since the target audience is small, it is relatively inexpensive to reach. Several methods can be used to gain PR. Such methods include the following:

● Contribution of prizes at different events.
● Sponsorship of events (sporting, cultural, etc.). According to Meenaghan (1996), the world-wide sponsorship market grew from $2 billion in 1984 to $13.02 billion in 1994. In 1994 Europe and the United States together accounted for 32.6 per cent of world-wide sponsorship expenditures.
● Press releases of news about the firm's products, plant and personnel.
● Announcements of the firm's promotional campaign.
● Lobbying (government).

Table 17.3	Target groups for public relations	
	Publics or target groups: domestic markets	**Extra international dimensions: international markets**
	Directly connected with the organization	
	Employees	Wider range of cultural issues
	Shareholders	The degree of remoteness of the corporate headquarters
	Suppliers of raw materials and components	
	Providers of financial services	Is this to be handled on a country-by-country
	Providers of marketing services (e.g. marketing research, advertising, media)	basis, or is some overall standardization desirable?
	Customers of the organization	
	Existing customers	May have less knowledge of the company
	Past customers	The country-of-origin effect will influence
	Those capable of becoming customers	communications
	Environment	
	The general public	Wide range of general publics
	Government: local, regional, national	Host governments
	Financial markets generally	Regional grouping (e.g. EU), world groupings

Source: Phillips *et al.* (1994), p. 362. Reproduced with permission from International Thomson Publishing Services Ltd.

The degree of control of the PR messages is quite different. Journalists can use PR material to craft an article of so many words, or an interview of so many seconds. How material is used will depend on the journalist and the desired story line. On occasions a thoroughly negative story can result from a press release that was designed to enhance the company image.

Hence, PR activity includes anticipating criticism. Criticisms may range from general ones against all multinational corporations to more specific ones. They may also be based on a market: for example, doing business with prison factories in China.

Sales promotion

Sales promotion is defined as those selling activities that do not fall directly into the advertising or personal selling category. Sales promotion also relates to so-called below-the-line activities such as point-of-sale displays and demonstrations, leaflets, free trials, contests and premiums such as 'two for the price of one'. Unlike media advertising which is 'above the line' and earns a commission, below-the-line sales promotion does not. To an advertising agency, 'above the line' means traditional media for which they are recognized by the media owners, entitling them to commission.

Sales promotion is a short-term effort directed primarily to the consumer and/or retailer, in order to achieve specific objectives:

● Consumer product trial and/or immediate purchase.

● Consumer introduction to the shop.

● Encouraging retailers to use point-of-purchase displays for the product.

● Encouraging shops to stock the product.

In the United States, the sales promotion budgets for fast-moving consumer goods (FMCG) manufacturers are larger than the advertising budgets. In Europe, the European Commission estimates that the rate of growth of spending on sales promotions was double that for conventional advertising throughout the period 1991–4 (Bennett, 1995, p. 321). Factors contributing to the expansion of sales promotion activities include the following:

● Greater competition among retailers, combined with increasingly sophisticated retailing methods.

● Higher levels of brand awareness among consumers, leading to the need for manufacturers to defend brand shares.

● Improved retail technology (e.g. electronic scanning devices that enable coupon redemptions etc. to be monitored instantly).

● Greater integration of sales promotion, public relations and conventional media campaigns.

In markets where the consumer is hard to reach because of media limitations, the percentage of the total communication budget allocated to sales promotions is also relatively high. Here are some of the different types of sales promotion:

- *Price discounts.* These are very widely used. A variety of different price reduction techniques is available, such as cash-back deals.

- *Catalogues/brochures.* The buyer in a foreign market may be located at quite a distance from the closest sales office. In this situation, a foreign catalogue can be very effective. It must be able to close the gap between buyer and seller in the way that the potential buyer is supplied with all the necessary information from prices, sizes, colours and quantities to packing, shipping time and acceptable form of payment. In addition to catalogues, brochures of various types are useful for salespersons, distributors and agents. Translations should be done in cooperation with overseas agents and/or distributors.

- *Coupons.* Coupons are a classic tool for FMCG brands, especially in the United States. A variety of coupon distribution methods exists: door-to-door, on pack, in newspapers. Coupons are not allowed in all European countries.

- *Samples.* A sample gives the potential foreign buyer an idea of firm and quality that cannot be attained by even the best graphic picture. Samples may prevent misunderstandings over style, sizes, models and so on.

- *Gifts.* Most European countries have a limit on the value of the premium or gift given. Furthermore, in some countries it is illegal to offer premiums that are conditional on the purchase of another product. The United States does not allow alcoholic beer to be offered as a free sample.

- *Competitions.* This type of sales promotion needs to be communicated to the potential customers. This can be done on the pack, in stores via leaflets or through media advertising.

The success of sales promotion depends on local adaptation. Major constraints are imposed by local laws which may not permit premiums or free gifts to be given. Some countries' laws control the amount of discount given at retail level; others require permits for all sales promotions. Since it is impossible to know the specific laws of each and every country, international marketers should consult local lawyers and authorities before launching a promotional campaign.

Direct marketing

According to Onkvisit and Shaw (1993, p. 717), direct marketing is the total of activities by which products and services are offered to market segments in one or more media for informational purposes or to solicit a direct response from a present or prospective customer or contributor by mail, telephone or personal visit.

Direct marketing covers direct mail (marketing database), telephone selling and marketing via the Internet. A number of factors have encouraged the rapid expansion of the international direct marketing industry (Bennett, 1995, p. 318):

- Developments in mailing technology which have reduced the costs of distributing direct-mail literature.

- Escalating costs of other forms of advertising and sales promotion.

- The increasing availability of good-quality lists of prospective customers.

- Developments in information technology (especially database technology and desktop publishing) which enable smaller companies to produce high-quality direct marketing materials in-house.

- The increasing availability throughout the developed world of interactive television facilities, whereby consumers may order goods through a teletext system.

Direct mail

Direct mail is a viable medium in many countries. It is especially important when other media are not available. Direct mail offers a flexible, selective and potentially highly cost-effective means of reaching foreign consumers. Messages can be addressed exclusively to the target market, advertising budgets may be concentrated on the most promising market segments, and it will be some time before competitors realize that the firm has launched a campaign. In addition, the size, content, timing and geographical coverage of mailshots can be varied at will: the firm can spend as much or as little as necessary to achieve its objectives. There are no media space or airtime restrictions, and no copy or insertion deadlines to be met. All aspects of the direct-mail process are subject to the firm's immediate control, and it can experiment by varying the approach used in different countries. Direct mail can take many forms – letters, catalogues, technical literature – and it can serve as a vehicle for the distribution of samples. A major problem in the effective use of direct mail is the preparation of a suitable mailing list (marketing database).

European marketers are still far behind the United States in exploiting the medium and also with regard to the response to direct mail in the form of mail orders. Per capita mail-order sales in the USA are more than double those of any European country (Desmet and Xardel, 1996, p. 58).

The use of direct mail in Japan is also below that in the USA. One reason for this discrepancy is that the Japanese feel printed material is too impersonal and insufficiently sincere.

Direct mail is not only relevant for the consumer market. However, effective use of direct mail for business-to-business purposes requires the preparation of an accurate customer profile (marketing database), including industry classification, size of target company (measured, for example, by turnover, number of employees or market share), the people to approach in each business (purchasing officer, project development engineer, product manager, etc.), industry purchasing procedures and (where known) supplier selection criteria and the buying motives of prospective customers.

Telemarketing is today used for both consumer and business-to-business campaigns throughout the industrialized world. The telephone can be used both to obtain orders and to conduct fast, low-cost market research. Telemarketing covers cold calling (unsolicited calls) by salespeople, market surveys conducted by telephone, calls designed to compile databases of possible sales prospects, and follow-ups to customer requests for further information, resulting from print and broadcast advertisements. Currently, the majority of cross-border telemarketing campaigns focus on business-to-business contacts, essentially because of the combined telephone/fax/database facilities that an increasing number of companies possess and, in consequence, the greater reliability of business-to-business communications.

The administration of international telemarketing normally requires the use of a commercial telemarketing agency. Language skills are required, plus considerable skills and experience in identifying decision-makers in target firms.

In some European countries, cold calling of consumers is receiving close scrutiny in the name of consumer protection and respect for privacy. For example, Germany has prohibited calls on the grounds of privacy invasion, and this ban even applies to an insurance salesperson's announcement of a visit.

In the light of the development within Internet technologies it is very relevant to consider the World Wide Web as a direct marketing tool. This issue is further discussed in Chapter 13.

Personal selling

The differences between advertising and personal selling were indicated in Table 17.1. Advertising is a one-way communication process that has relatively more 'noise', whereas personal selling is a two-way communication process with immediate feedback and relatively less 'noise'. Personal selling is an effective way to sell products, but it is expensive. It is used mainly to sell to distribution channel members and in business-to-business markets. However, personal selling is also used in some consumer markets – for example, for cars and for consumer durable

Figure 17.4   **Combination of direct mail (database marketing) and personal selling**

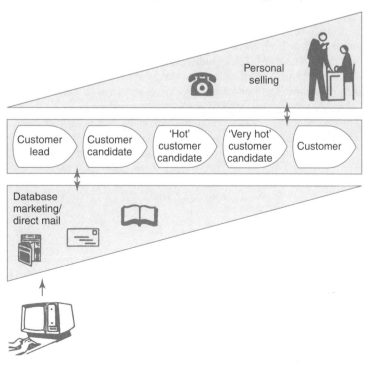

products. In some countries, labour costs are very low. In these instances, personal selling will be used to a greater extent than in high-cost countries.

If personal selling costs on business-to-business markets are relatively high, it is relevant to economize with personal selling resources, and use personal selling only at the end of the potential customer's buying process (Figure 17.4). Computerized database marketing (direct mail, etc.) is used in a customer screening process, to point out possible customers, who will then be 'taken over' by salespersons. Their job is to turn 'hot' and 'very hot' customer candidates into real customers.

Exhibit 17.6	Sales-force automation (SFA) programs are hard to sell in Latin America

The idea behind SFA is using technology to put customer information in the hands of all a company's employees via a database, not just in the files of the field salesperson in charge of the account. When a customer makes a purchase or a prospect indicates interest, a salesperson, using a laptop or Palm Pilot-type device, takes and executes the order, and pertinent information such as demographics or size of capital-spending budget are compiled and made available within hours to, say, the peripheral-equipment department salesperson. In addition, the salespeople can check for real-time information regarding inventory and delivery times when making a pitch.

Sales-force automation is often considered part of a company's customer relationship management (CRM) programme and may be linked with call-centre technologies, customer-service departments and the company's Web site.

Some 10 to 12 per cent of all US companies have automated some aspect of CRM; by comparison, the percentage of Latin American companies is probably closer to between 5 and 8 per cent, depending on the country.

Much of the drag on progress in this area is the resistance from Latin America's traditional salesforces. Culturally, sales practices in the region are geared toward personal relationships, not technological wizardry. Sales professionals typically view their customer accounts as proprietary; they are reluctant to embrace automation for fear of sharing information and losing a competitive edge. They may not understand the benefits to the company – and themselves – of sharing client information.

Language presents another problem; usually the software's language is English, and while company top brass often speak English, middle-management – and salespeople – frequently do not speak it well.

However, the situation may change soon: German-based software maker SAP AG, for example, holds more than 33 per cent of the CRM/SFA market-share in Latin America and is preparing to offer software in Spanish, Portugese and French in the near future.

Source: Adapted from Schmidt (2000).

Assessing sales force effectiveness

There are five essential questions to ask in assessing sales force effectiveness:

1. *Is the selling effort structured for effective market coverage?*
   Organization.
   Size of sales force.
   Territory deployment.

2. *Is the sales force staffed with the right people?*
   Type of international sales force: expatriates/host country/third country.
   Age/tenure/education profile.
   Interpersonal skills.
   Technical capabilities.
   Selling technique.

3. *Is strong guidance provided?*
   Written guidelines.
   Key tasks/mission definition.
   Call frequency.
   Time allocation.
   People to be seen.
   Market/account focus.
   Territory planning and control tools.
   On-the-job coaching.

4. *Is adequate sales support in place?*
   Training.
   Technical back-up.
   Inside sales staff.
   Product and applications literature.

5. *Does the sales compensation plan provide the proper motivation?*
   Total compensation.
   Split of straight salary/straight commission.
   Incentive design/fit with management objectives.
   Non-cash incentives.

In the following we will go into further details with questions 1 and 2.

International sales force organization

In international markets, firms often organize their sales forces similarly to their domestic structures, regardless of differences from one country to another. This means that the sales force is organized by geography, product, customer or some combination of these (Table 17.4).

A number of firms organize their international sales force along simple geographical territories within a given country or region. Firms that have broad product lines and large sales volume, and/or operate in large, developed markets may prefer more specialized organizations, such as product or customer assignment. The firm may also organize the sales force based upon other factors such as culture or languages spoken in the targeted foreign markets. For example, firms often divide Switzerland into different regions reflecting French, Italian and German language usage.

Type of international sales force

Management should consider three options when determining the most appropriate international sales force. The salespeople hired for sales positions could be expa-

Table 17.4   Sales force organizational structure

Structure	Factors favouring choice of organizational structure	Advantages	Disadvantages
Geographic	Distinct languages/cultures Single product line Underdeveloped markets	Clear, simple Incentive to cultivate local business and personal ties Travel expenses	Breadth of customers Breadth of products
Product	Established market Broad product lines	Product knowledge	Travel expenses Overlapping territories/customers Local business and personal ties
Customer*	Broad product lines	Market/customer knowledge	Overlapping territories/products Local business and personal ties Travel expenses
Combination	Large sales volume Large/developed markets Distinct language/cultures	Maximum flexibility Travel expenses	Complexity Sales management Product/market/geography overlap

* By type of industry, size of account, channel of distribution, individual company.

triates, host country nationals or third country nationals. For example, a German working for a German company in the United States is an expatriate. The same German working for a US company in Germany is a host country national. He or she is a third country national if assigned to France.

● *Expatriate salespersons.* These are viewed favourably because they are already familiar with the firm's products, technology, history and policies. Thus the 'only' kind of preparation they would need is a knowledge of the foreign market. Yet this may be a great problem for the expatriate salesperson. Whereas some may enjoy the challenge and adjustment, other expatriate personnel find it difficult to come to terms with a new and unfamiliar business environment. The failure to understand a foreign culture and its customers will hinder the effectiveness of an expatriate sales force. The family of the expatriate may also face adaptation problems. However, very expensive items often require selling directly from the head office, which usually involves expatriates.

● *Host country nationals.* These are personnel who are based in their home country. As native personnel, they bring extensive market and cultural knowledge, language skills and familiarity with local business traditions. Since the government and local community undoubtedly prefer that their own nationals be hired instead of outsiders, the firm can avoid charges of exploitation while gaining goodwill at the same time. Using local sales representatives also permits the firm to become active more quickly in a new market because the adjustment period is minimized.

● *Third country nationals.* These are employees transferred from one country to another. They tend to be born in one country, employed by a firm based in another country and working in a third country: for example, a German engineer who works for a French company in Spain.

The advantages and disadvantages of the three types of international sales force are summarized in Table 17.5.

Expatriates and third country nationals are seldom used in sales capacities for long periods of time. They are used for three main reasons: to upgrade a subsidiary's selling performance; to fill management positions; and to transfer sales policies, procedures and techniques. However, most companies use local nationals as their sales personnel. They are familiar with local business practices and can be managed accordingly.

Trade fairs and exhibitions

A trade fair or exhibition is a concentrated event at which manufacturers, distributors and other vendors display their products and/or describe their services to current and prospective customers, suppliers, other business associates and the press. It appears from Figure 17.5 that trade fairs (TFs) are multi-purpose events involving many interactions between the TF exhibitor and numerous parties.

TFs can enable a company to reach in a few days a concentrated group of interested prospects which might otherwise take several months to contact. Potential buyers can examine and compare the outputs of competing firms in a short period at the same place. They can see the latest developments and establish immediate contact with supplying businesses.

Traditionally, TFs have been regarded as a personal selling tool, but Sharland and Balogh (1996) conclude that TFs are an excellent environment for non-selling activities such as information exchange, relationship building and channel partner assessment. TFs offer international firms the opportunity to gather vital

Table 17.5 **Advantages and disadvantages of sales force types**

Category	Advantages	Disadvantages
Expatriates	Product knowledge High service levels Train for promotion Greater home control	Highest costs High turnover High training cost
Host country	Economical High market knowledge Language skills Best cultural knowledge Implement actions sooner	Needs product training May be held in low esteem Importance of language skills declining Difficult to ensure loyalty
Third country	Cultural sensitivity Language skills Economical Allows regional sales coverage May allow sales to country in conflict with the home country	Face identity problems Blocked promotions Income gaps Needs product/company training Loyalty assurance

Source: Honeycutt and Ford (1995), p. 138. Reprinted with permission from Elsevier Science Ltd.

Figure 17.5   Three conceptions of trade fairs: major interactions for a local exhibitor

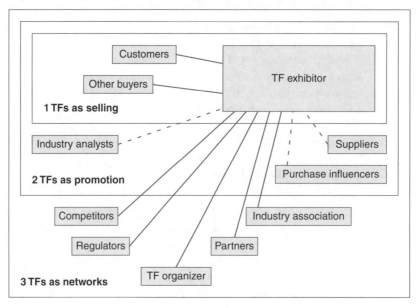

(Source: Adapted from Rossen and Seringhaus, 1996, p. 1181, with kind permission of P. Rossen, Dalhousie University)

information quickly, easily and cheaply. For example, within a short period, a firm can learn a considerable amount about its competitive environment, which would take much longer and cost much more to get through other sources (e.g. secondary information).

We conclude this section by listing the arguments for and against participation in TFs.

Arguments for participation in TFs

- Marketers are able to reach a sizeable number of potential customers in a brief time period at a reasonable cost per contact. Orders may be obtained on the spot.

- Some products, by their very nature, are difficult to market without providing the potential customer with a chance to examine them or see them in action. TFs provide an excellent opportunity to introduce, promote and demonstrate new products.

- SMEs without extensive sales forces have the opportunity to present their outputs to large buying companies on the same face-to-face basis as large local rivals.

- Finding an intermediary may be one of the best reasons to attend a TF. A show is a cost-effective way to solicit and screen candidates to represent the firm, especially in a new market.

- Although many technical specialists and company executives refuse to see or take telephone calls from outsiders who try to sell them things at their places of work, these same managers often do attend trade exhibitions. The customer goes to the exhibition in order to see the seller. This is also an important aspect in the concept of reverse marketing or buyer initiative (see, for example, Figure 17.1).

● An appearance also produces goodwill and allows for cultivation of the corporate image. Beyond the impact of displaying specific products, many firms place strong emphasis on 'waving the company flag' against competition. This facet also includes supporting the morale of the firm's sales personnel and intermediaries.

● TFs provide an excellent chance for market research and collecting competitive intelligence. The marketer is able to view most rivals at the same time and to test comparative buyer reactions.

● Visitors' names and addresses may be used for subsequent mailshots.

Arguments against participation in TFs

● There is a high cost in terms of time and administrative effort needed to prepare an exhibition stand in a foreign country. However, a marketer can lower costs by sharing expenses with distributors or representatives. Furthermore, the costs of closing a sale through trade shows are estimated to be much lower than those for a sale closed through personal representation.

● It is difficult to choose the appropriate trade fairs for participation. This is a critical decision. Because of scarce resources, many firms rely on suggestions from their foreign distributors on which TFs to attend and what specifically to exhibit.

● Coordination problems may arise. In LSEs with multiple divisions, more divisions may be required to participate in the same TF under the company banner. In SMEs coordination is required with distributors and agents if joint participation is desired, and this necessitates joint planning.

● Furthermore, the firm faces a lot of practical problems. For example, most people visit exhibitions to browse rather than to buy. How does the exhibiting firm obtain the names and addresses of the callers who influence major buying decisions within their companies? Second, gimmicks may be highly effective in attracting visitors to a stand, but they can attract the wrong people. An audience may be greatly impressed by the music, dancing, demonstration or whatever is provided, yet not be remotely interested in the product. Third, how can the employees who staff a stand be prevented from treating the exercise as a holiday, paying more attention to the social aspects of their involvement with the exhibition than to finding customers? What specific targets can the staff be given and how can the attainment of targets be measured?

Whether a marketer should participate in a trade fair depends largely on the type of business relationship it wants to develop with a particular country. A company looking only for one-off or short-term sales might find the TF expense prohibitive, but a firm looking for long-term involvement may find the investment worthwhile.

| Exhibit 17.7 | No tobacco advertising in China but there are alternatives |

The big international tobacco companies have pinned high hopes on China's booming cigarette market in the face of flagging sales in western nations, particularly in the United States. China is the world's largest producer and consumer of tobacco products. With an estimated 300 million smokers among the country's 1.2 billion people, China is viewed as a huge market for international cigarette makers.

While smokers often feel like outcasts in the West, the habit is still socially acceptable in China. Regulations prohibiting smoking in public places are widely flouted and Chinese officials are often seen on television puffing away during Communist Party meetings. The government's attitude towards the industry has been ambivalent: despite government-led anti-smoking campaigns, tobacco is the country's largest source of tax revenue. As a result, the foreign tobacco companies R.J. Reynolds and Philip Morris of the USA and Rothmans International of the UK have set up joint-venture cigarette-producing operations in China.

At the beginning of 1995 the Chinese government passed a law that bans tobacco advertising in the broadcast and print media as well as in public places such as theatres and sports stadiums. But China's advertising law is nothing new for international tobacco companies, analysts say. Cigarette makers have faced similar bans on advertising in other countries and have still managed to get their message out. For example, the law does not ban sponsorship by tobacco companies, which has become an increasingly popular strategy on the mainland. Another strategy is being pursued by Marlboro, which is promoting a line of fashion clothes bearing its popular name.

Source: Billing (1994).

17.4 International advertising strategies in practice

In the introduction to Part IV, the question of standardization or adaptation of the whole marketing mix was discussed. Standardization allows the realization of economies of scale in the production of advertising materials, reducing advertising costs and increasing profitability. On the other hand, since advertising is based largely on language and images, it is mostly influenced by the sociocultural behaviour of consumers in different countries.

In reality, it is not a question of either/or. For the internationally oriented firm it is more a question of the degree of standardization/localization. A study by Hite and Frazer (1988) showed that a majority (54 per cent) of internationally oriented firms were using a combination strategy (localizing advertising for some markets and standardizing advertising for other markets). Only 9 per cent of the firms were using totally standardized advertising for all foreign markets, much lower than in previous studies (Sorenson and Weichman, 1975; Boddewyn et al., 1986). This could indicate a trend towards less standardization. A total of 37 per cent of the firms reported that they were using only localized advertising. Many of the global companies using standardized advertising are well known (e.g. Coca-Cola, Intel, Philip Morris/Marlboro).

Plate 12 shows an example of an air freight service firm, which uses a standard-ized strategy in the south-east Asian area. The only element of adaptation in Plate 12 is the translation of the English text into Japanese.

Examples of adaptation (localization) strategies

Courvoisier Cognac: Hong Kong/China versus Europe

The Chinese love affair with western alcohol goes back a long way. The first imported brandy arrived in Shanghai in 1859 when Hennessy unloaded its first cargo. Then in 1949 the favourite drink of 'the Paris of the East' suddenly became a symbol of western capitalist decadence; alcohol shipments came to an abrupt halt and did not resume for the next 30 years. However, when foreign liquor once again became available in the late 1970s, cognac quickly resumed its place as guest at the Chinese banquet table.

Today cognac and brandy still account for about 80 per cent of all imported spirits in China. Most of the imported brandy goes through Hong Kong via grey markets (see also section 16.8). Chinese awareness of brand and category of cognac is particularly high in the south, where the drinking habits of visiting Hong Kong businessmen set a strong example. This impact is reinforced by alcohol advertising on Hong Kong television, available to millions of viewers in Guangdong province.

The key to Chinese consumption patterns lies in the importance of 'face'. Whatever the occasion, be it the father of the bride toasting his son-in-law's family in Beijing or a Shenzhen entrepreneur's night out on the town, brandy is of para-mount importance. Unlike their western counterparts, who like to curl up on the couch with a snifter of brandy, the Chinese consider cognac drinking an extremely social – and conspicuous – pastime.

Plate 13 shows two different advertisements for Courvoisier Cognac. The one for the western European market shows couples drinking cognac with their coffee. The Asian advertisement shows people drinking cognac from beer glasses during the meal.

Folklore as much as marketing has propelled the growth of cognac sales. Cognac has long had the inestimable commercial benefit of being widely regarded by the Chinese as enhancing a man's sexual prowess. And much to the delight of the liquor companies, the Chinese believe that the older (and pricier) the cognac, the more potent its effect.

(Source: Adapted from Business Week, 1984; Balfour, 1993)

Prince cigarettes: UK versus Germany

The Danish cigarette company House of Prince has high market shares (50–90 per cent) in Scandinavian countries, but outside this area the market shares are very low, typically 1–2 per cent.

Advertisements for House of Prince cigarettes in the UK and Germany are shown in Plate 14. The UK version is based on an invitation to try the product ('I go for Prince'). The target group is also above average in education and income. The German advertisement is somewhat different from the English. Prince is promoted as an 'original import from Denmark'. Apparently there is no 'buy German' mentality preventing the use of this slogan. In the German consumer's mind, Danish cigarettes are strongly positioned compared to the light German cigarettes. Therefore, the product's position is emphasized as 'men's business', with Viking associations and ideas of freedom. Incidentally, the two products Prince and Prince Denmark are not identical. The German Prince Denmark has a less strong taste than Prince.

Gammel Dansk (Danish Distillers/Danisco): Denmark versus Germany

The Danish bitter Gammel Dansk has a 75 per cent share of the bitter market in Denmark. Thus, the product has a high degree of recognition there (nearly all Danish adults knows the label). The objective of the Danish advertisement (Plate 15) has therefore primarily been to maintain Gammel Dansk's high degree of recognition.

Although the market share in Denmark is very high, Gammel Dansk does not have any position worth mentioning outside Denmark. In Germany the situation is totally different. Here the knowledge (and trial share) is at a minimum. The Germans have their own Jägermeister and competition is tough. The strategy behind the German campaign has therefore been to make people try Gammel Dansk by letting them fill out a coupon. By sending it in they receive a little bottle of Gammel Dansk and two original Gammel Dansk glasses.

LUX soap (Unilever): UK versus India

The UK version of the LUX advertisement (Plate 16a) is based on the classic transborder advertising campaign, 'the beauty soap of film stars', which has been standardized to a high degree. In India the LUX campaign has been given a special local touch.

The Indian version is one of three advertisements that trace LUX's association with film stars from the past era to the current stars of today and the potential film stars of tomorrow. Plate 16b shows the first advertisement, focusing on three past legendary beauties of Indian cinema, who have endorsed the brand. The creative statement is in a cinema poster style, keeping the brand image in mind, and in a sepia colour tone to give it a nostalgic feel.

LEGO FreeStyle: Europe versus the Far East

European and Far Eastern versions of an advertisement for LEGO FreeStyle are shown in Plate 17. The Asian version, 'Build your child's mind', appeals to Asian parents' desire for their children to do well in school. The Asian educational system is very competitive and only those with the highest grades are admitted to university. In many places in Asia it is a defeat for parents if their child does not do well in school. The Asian version has been run in Hong Kong, Taiwan and Korea (preferably in the local languages because the majority of consumers do not understand English. In Hong Kong the advertisements are run in English or Chinese dependent on the language of the magazine).

The European version implies creativity when playing with the different FreeStyle bricks: 'What will your child make of it?'

17.5 Implications of Internet/e-commerce for communication decisions

In the physical marketplace different communication tools are used in the buying process of customers (see Figure 17.6). Traditional mass communication tools (print advertising, TV and radio) can create awareness and this can result in consumers' identification of new needs. From then on other elements of the communication mix take over such as direct marketing (direct marketing, personal selling) and in-store promotion. Unlike marketing in the physical marketplace the Internet/e-commerce encompasses the entire 'buying' process.

Market communication strategies change dramatically in the on-line world. On the Internet, it is easier than ever to actually *communicate* a message to large numbers of people. However, in many cases, it is much harder for your message to be heard above the noise by your target audience. Various strategies for conducting on-line marketing have been developed in the past several years – from the most common (Web site linking) to the most expensive (banner advertising) to the most offensive (e-mail spamming), and everything in between. It is almost certain that a continual stream of new market communication strategies will emerge as the Internet medium evolves.

Although some companies do business exclusively on the Web, for most the Internet offers exciting opportunities to develop an additional sales channel. This new channel can extend a company's reach significantly, enabling it to do business with a new customer base that was previously unreachable. Customer preferences are driving e-commerce because many consumers simply prefer on-line shopping because of the convenience, reach and availability of products and services. Companies that do not develop an Internet presence risk losing these customers to more aggressive competitors.

Developing a successful on-line marketing programme boils down to the same objectives as in the physical world: how to create an audience. 'Audience development' is the preferred phrase for on-line marketing, because it more precisely communicates the point of the activity.

Figure 17.6   The role of Internet communication in the buying process of customers

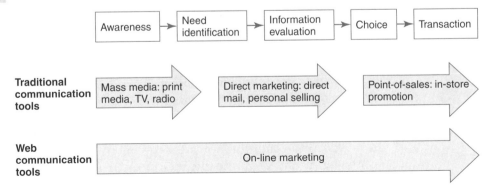

How, then, can a Web audience be created? The Web audience development process consists of the following six phases (USWeb/CKS, 1999):

1. Integration.
2. Design requirements that are unique.
3. Techniques for audience creation.
4. Methods of advertising the site.
5. Effective promotions that attract attention.
6. Measurement and analysis to ensure ongoing success.

Re 1: Integration of Internet strategy into an overall business strategy

Before a company builds a site, it should determine how the site will fit into the company's overall business strategy. A holistic approach does not look at the site in isolation, but in the context of overall marketing and sales efforts. Marketers must understand the role of each medium within the company's marketing mix and utilize the strengths of each. Creating the right on-line corporate identity is the first step for audience development, the step from which all other components of a successful Web marketing programme flow. Synergy and consistency are essential. Although individual messages may vary to apply the unique strengths of each medium, the overall flavour should be consistent across media.

All marketing and sales activities should work together, and each marketing objective should be supported across multiple media where possible. A company should cross-promote among media, for example, promoting its Web site in brochures and print advertising.

Re 2: Design requirements that are unique

Given the free flow of information in the *marketspace* and the potential for overload, the marketer with the best-designed information package will generate the competitive advantage.

While audience creation, advertising and promotions drive traffic to a site, it is the design that either encourages visitors to explore or drives them away in frustration. A good design is, of course, aesthetically pleasing. More importantly, though, it engages visitors, makes it easy for them to navigate the site and compels them to explore the site further, purchase products and return another day. Attractive graphics that support the company's message are important, but large graphics that take a long time to load frustrate users. Many visitors will not wait long enough for the graphic to finish loading. Additionally, visitors are less likely to return to a site that has confusing navigational cues.

The design should use clear, consistent navigational cues that make it easy for visitors to determine where they are within the site structure. With more than a million sites competing for users' attention, first impressions are critical. A confusing, poorly organized site structure can negate even the highest quality content.

Web design differs significantly from design for other media. The most important difference is that the Web is interactive, incorporating hyperlinks and devices for immediate visitor feedback. Some sophisticated designs include dynamically generated pages that are custom-tailored to each visitor's interests, preferences and buying habits.

Re 3: Techniques for audience creation

Developing traffic on a site requires expert knowledge of the numerous on-line search devices. The audience creation methods described in this section are highly cost-effective for generating a large number of repeat site visitors:

● *Search engine optimization.* Search engines and directories play a critical role in Internet marketing, because the majority of Web surfers rely on these navigation guides to conduct their research. Because users typically explore only the first 10 or 20 sites on the list, an understanding of how search ranking works can make a huge difference in traffic volume. Effective optimization of search engine results requires carefully designed meta tags and other HTML code and pointer pages specialized for individual search engines.

● *Editorial placement in new media.* In addition to using the Internet as a communication tool to contact traditional journalists, companies can reach out to the new and rapidly increasing breed of 'on-line-only' news media. Most on-line stories contain hyperlinks to the sites of featured marketers. Because on-line stories are typically archived in news databases and indexed by search engines, they provide a source of new visitors for an indefinite period.

● *Strategic linking.* A major differentiator between the Web and other media is the use of hyperlinks, in which a user clicks on a link and is instantly transported to another site. The more inbound links a company establishes on other sites, the more qualified visitors the site will attract. Unlike banner ads, links frequently stay in place for months and bear the credibility of editorial selection. Best of all, they are usually free. Some of the best investments of time marketers can make is to contact Webmasters of affinity sites in an attempt to place inbound links on their sites. Webmasters of many popular sites actively seek out quality sites to which they can link.

● *Interactive public relations.* Interactive public relations facilitates world-wide new delivery as well as direct interactivity with individuals. Newsgroups, mailing lists, forums, bulletin boards and other virtual communities are important sources of visitors for a site.

One method for tapping into virtual communities is to employ interactive public relations with materials such as electronic press releases or other stories that may be of interest to specific groups.

Re 4: Methods of advertising the site

To take full advantage of the power of Internet marketing, companies must understand the differences between on-line advertising and other more traditional media.

● *Banner advertising*. On-line banner ads use eye-catching multimedia effects such as animation, interactivity, sound, video and 3D to attract attention and draw visitors to a site. Even in-the-banner commerce transactions are becoming common.

With on-line advertising, companies can target ads with far greater precision than with any other medium. Today's ad server technology offers highly sophisticated, automatic targeting that uses factors such as demographic data and visitor behaviour while at the site. In addition, technology is emerging that allows on-line ads to be tailored automatically to each individual visitor.

Marketers can take advantage of this targeting capability to place banner ads on sites that attract visitors who match the demographic profile for companies' products. As a result, they can increase brand awareness among a carefully targeted audience and drive highly qualified traffic to their site.

● *Sponsorships*. Exclusive sponsorship of site content is a growing trend. Sponsoring strategic editorial content is an effective way to establish long-term brand identification among target audiences.

Sponsorship of content or pages on certain sites – for example, a site maintained by an influential industry group or a leader in a particular industry – associate a company with that group or industry leader. This association lends credibility and helps increase customer interest and brand awareness.

● *Barter advertising*. In addition to paid advertising, many sites are performing banner exchanges and ad barter arrangements. Even among top content sites, bartering is a common, cost-effective way to boost traffic. Companies can take advantage of this low-cost advertising method by establishing personal relationships and negotiating barter deals with other sites.

Re 5: Effective promotions that attract attention

Promotions offer an excellent opportunity for public relations exposure and on-line community awareness. These promotions can take a variety of forms:

● *Contests*. Quizzes, sweepstakes and other contests are sometimes effective components of on-line marketing. Companies can use contests for a variety of purposes, including sales generation, brand recognition establishment, customer loyalty building and market research.

● *Loyalty programmes*. It is well known that the cost of retaining a current customer is about one-tenth that of acquiring a new one. As a result, customer loyalty programmes can have a dramatic impact on the bottom line. Loyalty programmes and similar on-line campaigns can help retain customers and motivate them to recruit new customers by recommending a company's site or products to friends and associates.

● *On-line events*. Live events (for example live sporting events) in which users from around the world participate have proven tremendously popular with the on-line public. Promoters have seized on this trend to capture audiences for a variety of on-line events, including celebrity chats, live concert broadcasts, virtual conferences and auctions. Such events can be effective for gaining mindshare among new users and positioning a company or site at the cutting edge of its market.

Re 6: Measurement and analysis to ensure ongoing success

The Internet is one of the most measurable of all communication media. The ability to monitor the effectiveness and continually fine-tune sites and campaigns is one of the medium's greatest benefits.

Paul (1996) argues that the Web has the ability to compile statistics about the *reach* (how many people have viewed each advertisement) and *exposure time* (how long have the viewers looked at the advertisement). This helps companies to measure the effectiveness of their advertisements.

Server logs and other performance data are valuable indicators that can be used to develop insights that are far beyond what any print circulation figures or TV ratings data can provide. It is important, however, to combine these quantitative measures with qualitative measures to achieve a meaningful evaluation of effectiveness. Tracking which external sources refer the most visitors to the home page is useful when evaluating the success of ad banners, affinity links and other promotional campaigns.

Audience qualification

Counting Web page hits alone is not sufficient to determine effectiveness of audience development strategies. It's more important to determine *who* the visitors are. Are they prospective customers or simply confused and curious surfers who will never return? How many pages past the first home page does the average visitor explore from a particular banner ad? What percentage of visitors return again, and which ones become paying customers?

Customer feedback

Perhaps the most valuable form of analysis comes not from technology, but directly from site visitors. Sites that post their e-mail addresses or telephone numbers to encourage contact from visitors are sending a strong message that invites relationship building with prospects and customers. An interactive process that incorporates visitor feedback enables the company to raise the site to its full potential and keep it there.

Marketers can get information on visitors' perception of the site through on-line visitor surveys. Because they are convenient and even fun to respond to, response rates are typically high. For additional opinions, marketers can monitor discussions about the brand and general product category on discussion boards in newsgroups as well as other independent forums. Such feedback is a natural by-product of many on-line marketing activities and can be effectively incorporated into the other components of audience development.

Exhibit 17.8	Johnnie Walker: Has the image of Scotland and Scotch whisky become clichéd and stereotyped?

The world's biggest spirits company, Diageo, is dropping images of misty mountains and kilted pipers as part of its global advertising strategy for Johnnie Walker whisky.

Diageo, whose brand names include Burger King, Smirnoff vodka, Guinness beer,

►

Johnny Walker Whisky and Pillsbury bakery goods, was formed by the merger of Guinness and GrandMet in December 1997. Now Diageo is launching a £100m campaign to boost sluggish sales by appealing to a younger generation who still regard whisky as a 'dad's' drink in a fireside armchair.

The campaign focuses on the brand's Striding Man logo as a symbol of everyone's personal journey in life and features such diverse characters as actor Harvey Keitel, Abraham Lincoln and a pair of father-and-son French tightrope walkers. Out go images of Bravehearts, castles and old men waxing lyrical about past times over a nip or two.

Ivan Menezes, head of global marketing at Diageo's drinks unit United Distillers and Vinters (UDV), said: 'We've tended to put Scotch up on a pedestal. It's been skewed towards older, knowing consumers.

'The imagery of Scotland has become clichéd and stereotyped and not that relevant to today's young adults.'

Sales hit by slump

In the 1980s, sales began to slow in 'mature' markets like the United States and the UK, where drinkers were turning increasingly to lighter, mixable white spirits like vodka.

Sales continued to grow in developing markets like Latin America and Asia until both regions were hit by economic crises. In 1998, volume sales of Johnnie Walker Red Label fell 6 per cent and Black Label tumbled 13 per cent, although sales of both appear to have rebounded slightly last year along with most Asian economies.

Overall the global market for Scotch whisky has grown slowly, carried almost entirely by the growth of premium and single malt whiskies, the one type that seems to appeal to younger drinkers in the US and UK.

Diageo relies on Scotch to generate a quarter of the volume and half the profits of its spirits division, and Scotch is one of the UK's top five export earners, contributing £2bn a year.

Industry 'complacent'

'The industry needs to be more dynamic and recruit younger drinkers in the "mature" markets like the United States,' said Alan Gray, an analyst at Sutherlands brokerage in Edinburgh and a leading expert on the industry. 'Overall, it has been a bit complacent in the past 20 years, and missed a generation of drinkers.'

Last September, Diageo said business overall was bouncing back, following disappointing first-half results. The group reported a 4.5 per cent drop in annual profits. But it said sales growth returned in the second half of the year, boosted by strong growth in Europe and the US and a recovery in the Far East. Operating profits rose 15 per cent in the second half.

Diageo said it was seeing the benefits of the merger of Guinness and GrandMet in December 1997, now that the integration was complete. Annual pre-tax profits fell to £1.767bn ($2.83bn) for the year to 30 June, while the year dividend was raised 8 per cent to 19.5 pence a share.

Source: BBC *Business News*, 6 January 2000;
http://news.bbc.co.uk/hi/english/uk/scotland/newsid_593000/593014.stm

17.6 ▌ Summary

Five ingredients of international communication have been presented in this chapter:

- Advertising.
- Public relations.
- Sales promotion.
- Direct marketing.
- Personal selling.

As international marketers manage the various elements of the promotions mix in differing environmental conditions, decisions must be made about what channels are to be used in the communication, the message, who is to execute or help execute the programme, and how the results of the communication plan are to be measured. The trend is towards greater harmonization of strategy, at the same time allowing for flexibility at the local level and early incorporation of local needs into the communication plans.

Hence, an important decision for international marketers is whether the different elements of the communication should be standardized world-wide or localized. The main reasons for seeking standardization are as follows:

- Customers do not conform to national boundaries.
- The company is seeking to build an international brand image.
- Economies of scale can be achieved.
- The few high-quality creative ideas can be exploited as widely as possible.
- Special expertise can be developed and exploited.

However, some communication tools, especially personal selling, have to be localized to fit conditions of individual markets. Another reason for localization of the personal selling tool is that distribution channel members are normally located firmly within a country. Consequently, decisions concerning recruitment, training, motivation and evaluation of salespersons have to be made at the local level.

The process of selecting agencies has also been considered. The requisite blend of local knowledge, cultural understanding and management expertise across international markets is elusive. Too much centralization and standardization results in inappropriate marketing communications.

A very important communication tool for the future is the Internet. Any company eager to take advantage of the Internet on a global scale must select a business model for its Internet ventures and estimate how information and transactions delivered through this new direct marketing medium will influence its existing distribution and communication system.

| Case study | Helly Hansen (HH) |

Sponsoring fashion clothes in the American market

On a warm autumn day in 1997 Johnny Austad, president of the Norwegian clothing manufacturer Helly Hansen Co., arrives at Helly Hansen's American subsidiary. Johnny can still not quite understand the incredible development that Helly Hansen Co. has been through in the American market. During the last couple of years, Helly Hansen USA has had an increase in turnover of 10 per cent per year, but in 1996 turnover doubled in the American market, thus amounting to one-third of HH's world-wide sales.

How it all started

Helly Hansen Co. was founded in 1877 by the Norwegian captain Helly Juell Hansen. During the era of the sailing ship he felt the forces of nature when he had to stand at the helm in all kinds of weather. Many hours were spent oiling clothes so they would become waterproof before rough weather set in. However, the clothes became stiff and sticky, so when Helly Juell Hansen finally went ashore, he decided to develop better rain clothes for Norwegian sailors. Today HH sells its products in more than twenty countries. Production takes place in the company's own factories in Norway and Portugal, as well as in the Far East, and via contract manufacturing. Design of the new collections takes place in the concern's headquarters in Norway.

From a producer of functionalistic clothes to a supplier of fashion clothes to the American underground

The honourable, nearly 100-year-old Norwegian producer of functionalistic clothes for sailors has by chance become the supplier of fashion clothes to black hip-hoppers in New York's underground. The label, which for generations has been connected with wind and waterproof leisure wear, and work clothes for the quality-conscious consumer who likes to be dressed 'sensibly', has now become a signal of the avant-garde and the different (see Plate 18). The young think that the clothes are smart and don't care if they have taped seams and that it might be difficult to breathe through four layers of waterproof coating.

In earlier days, the first and last thing that HH thought of when making jackets was functionalism. The result was very large collection of jackets with small specialized differences which only real enthusiasts could appreciate. HH's prices, on the other hand, became unreasonably high. By gathering several of the functions in the same jacket, HH is able to make allowances for its choosy customers, as well as producing at a price which a larger part of the market is able to pay. Where HH used to directs its collections toward alpine skiers, fishermen, sea sportspeople and snow boarders, it is now beginning to look more at the current fashion trends. HH is trying to link its look to street fashion and hopes that in this way its core customers will feel smarter, while new customers are encouraged to buy because of the smartness of the clothes.

Before Johnny Austad gets on the plane back to Norway, the American subsidiary receives an enquiry of sponsorship from one of the most well-known rap groups in the USA. The manager of the rap group in question demands $200,000 of HH for Bad Boys to perform in HH clothes at all their concerts in the next six months as well as in their coming music video.

As a newly employed marketing assistant in the American HH subsidiary, you are asked to take care of this enquiry. You are specifically asked the following questions.

Questions

1. Would you recommend HH to sponsor the American rap group? Give reasons for your answer.
2. How can an eventual sponsorship be integrated into the total marketing plan for HH clothes in the American market?

Questions for discussion

1. Identify and discuss problems associated with assessing advertising effectiveness in foreign markets.

2. Compare domestic communication with international communication. Explain why 'noise' is more likely to occur in the case of international communication processes.

3. Why do more companies not standardize advertising messages world-wide? Identify the environmental constraints that act as barriers to the development and implementation of standardized global advertising campaigns.

4. Explain how personal selling may differ overseas from how it is used in the home market.

5. What is meant by saying that advertising regulations vary around the world?

6. Evaluate the 'percentage of sales' approach to setting advertising budgets in foreign markets.

7. Explain how the multinational firm may have an advantage over local firms in training the sales force and evaluating its performance.

8. Identify and discuss problems associated with allocating the company's promotion budget across several foreign markets.

Internet exercise

Easyfair.com

Please go to:

www.easyfair.com

Easyfair.com is a new European Internet company which has specialized in creating virtual fairs for exhibitors and exhibition organizers.

Virtual fairs can take place as separate exhibitions or as a parallel to physical (on-the-ground) trade fairs.

Questions

1. What are the advantages and disadvantages of virtual fairs for:
   (a) exhibition organizers
   (b) exhibitors

2. Easyfair.com has the goal of being the leading virtual fair supplier in Europe. Which communication strategy (communication mix) would you recommend easyfair.com to follow in order to reach their goal?

For further exercises and cases, see this book's website at *www.booksites.net/hollensen*

References

Balfour, F. (1993) 'Alcohol industry: companies in high spirits', *China Trade Report*, June, pp. 4–5.

Bennet, R. (1995) *International Marketing: Strategy, planning, market entry and implementation*, Kogan Page, London.

Billing, C. (1994) 'No to Joe Camel', *China Trade Report*, December, p. 9.

Boddewyn, J.J., Soehl, R. and Picard, J. (1986) 'Standardization in international marketing: is Ted Levitt in fact right?', *Business Horizons*, pp. 69–75.

Business Week (1984) 'Advertising Europe's new Common Market', July, pp. 62–5.

Desmet, P. and Xardel, D. (1996) 'Challenges and pitfalls for direct mail across borders: the European example', *Journal of Direct Marketing*, vol. 10, no. 3, pp. 48–60.

Griffin, T. (1993) *International Marketing Communications*, Butterworth Heinemann, Oxford.

Harper, T. (1986) 'Polaroid clicks instantly in Moslem markets', *Advertising Age* (special report on 'Marketing to the Arab world'), 30 January, p. 12.

Hite, R.E. and Frazer, C. (1988) 'International advertising strategies of multinational corporations', *Journal of Advertising Research*, vol. 28, August–September, pp. 9–17.

Honeycutt, E.D. and Ford, J.B. (1995) 'Guidelines for managing an international sales force', *Industrial Marketing Management*, vol. 24, pp. 135–44.

Hung, C.L. and West, D.C. (1991) 'Advertising budgeting methods in Canada, the UK and the USA', *International Journal of Advertising*, vol. 10, pp. 239–50.

Joensen, S. (1997) 'What hedder it now on engelsk?', *Politikken* (Danish newspaper), 24 April 1997.

Lynch, R. (1994) *European Marketing*, Irwin, Homewood, IL.

MacNamee, B. and McDonnell, R. (1995) *The Marketing Casebook*, Routledge, London.

Meenaghan, T. (1996) 'Ambush marketing – a threat to corporate sponsorship', *Sloan Management Review*, Fall, pp. 103–13.

Mueller, B. (1996) *International Advertising: Communicating across cultures*, Wadsworth, Belmont, CA.

Nørmark, P. (1994) 'Co-promotion in growth', *Markedsføring* (Danish marketing magazine), no. 14, p. 14.

Onkvisit, S. and Shaw, J.J. (1993) *International Marketing: Analysis and strategy* (2nd edn), Macmillan, London.

Ottesen, O. (1995) 'Buyer initiative: ignored, but imperative for marketing management – towards a new view of market communication', *Tidsvise Skrifter*, no. 15, avdeling for Økonomi, Kultur og Samfunnsfag ved Høgskolen i Stavanger.

Paul, P. (1996) 'Marketing on the Internet', *Journal of Consumer Marketing*, vol. 13, no. 4, pp. 27–39.

Phillips, C., Poole, I. and Lowe, R. (1994) *International Marketing Strategy: Analysis, development and implementation*, Routledge, London/New York.

Rossen, J.R. and Seringhaus, F.H.R. (1996) 'Trade fairs as international marketing venues: a case study', paper presented at the 12th IMP Conference, University of Karlsruhe.

Schmidt, K.V. (2000) 'Why SFA is a tough sell in Latin America', *Marketing News*, Vol. 34, no. 1, pp. 4–5.

Sharland, A. and Balogh, D. (1996) 'The value of non selling activities at international trade shows', *Industrial Marketing Management*, vol. 25, pp. 59–66.

Shelly, B. (1995) 'Cool customer', *Unilever Magazine*, no. 2, pp. 13–17.

Sorenson, R.Z. and Weichman, V.E. (1975) 'How multinationals view marketing standardization', *Harvard Business Review*, May–June, pp. 38–56.

USWeb/CKS (1999) *Audience Development: A comprehensive process for building a profitable customer base on the Internet*. White Paper, Washington.

Case IV.1 Absolut Vodka

Defending and attacking for a better position in the global vodka market

On a lovely spring day in May 1996, Claes G. Fick (marketing director of the Absolut Company, the international wing of the Swedish state-owned Vin & Sprit AB) packs his suitcase for the third time this month for a business trip to the USA. While packing he thinks of how hard the Absolut Company must fight to keep and increase its market share for Absolut Vodka in the USA and other markets. Until 1994 Absolut Vodka was distributed by Carillon Importers with the charismatic Michael Roux in charge.

In 1994 the Absolut Company entered into an agreement with the somewhat larger Seagram Co. to distribute Absolut Vodka in the USA and a number of other countries. Seagram is the world's fourth largest distributor of spirits with world-wide sales of nearly $6 billion. Seagram distributes (in the USA) such well-known labels as Chivas Regal, Coyote Tequila and Martell Cognac. But it needed a well-known vodka label in its assortment. Seagram is an international distributor with local distributors in 150 countries.

The shift from Carillon Importers to Seagram Co. has not been without problems and drama. Michael Roux was very upset when he heard he had been fired as importer for the American market. As a countermove, he has taken the Russian competitor Stolichnaya into his assortment, thus intensifying the 'vodka war'.

In 1995 the Latin American and south-east Asian markets were transferred to Seagram. In January 1996 Canada was also transferred to Seagram.

When Claes G. Fick gets on the plane in Stockholm's airport bound for Seagram's headquarters in New York, there are three things that worry him:

● Isn't it dangerous to transfer most of the Absolut Company's world-wide distribution and marketing to only one company, Seagram, which is much larger than Absolut?

● Has the Absolut Company reached the top of its market share in the USA or is it time for a frontal attack on the no. 1 brand, Smirnoff?

● Until now the market share for Absolut Vodka in Europe (especially in eastern Europe) has been a lot smaller. This can be a problem when 80 per cent of the world's vodka is consumed in Russia and the other countries of eastern Europe.

On his way over the Atlantic, Claes sits back and thinks back on the story and adventure of Absolut Vodka.

The history of Absolut Vodka

The Swedish state-owned Vin & Sprit AB can justly call the launching of its Absolut Vodka an absolute success. Absolut Vodka is probably the biggest success story in the world of spirits. It has become an icon.

The shape of the bottle

The shape of the bottle dates back to the mid-nineteenth century. Far earlier, in the sixteenth century, Swedish pharmacies sold a clear distilled liquid as a cure for ailments like colic or even the plague. The custom was to ingest it by spoon, not with a shot glass.

Rediscovered at an antique store in Stockholm by Gunnar Broman, of the now defunct advertising agency Carlsson & Broman, the clear medicine bottle has since been fine-tuned by Absolut's team of shrewd marketers. The neck was lengthened, curves were adjusted and labels were replaced by printed typeface.

To top it off, a medallion bearing the portrait of Lars Olsson Smith, known as 'The King of Vodka', was stamped on each bottle. In 1879 Smith successfully broke Stockholm's spirit monopoly by distilling and marketing Absolut Rent Bränvin, or Absolute Pure Vodka. His tipple was the beginning of a dynasty.

Introduction to the US market

Independent market research in the USA concluded in 1979 that no one would buy Swedish vodka. Nevertheless the first shipment of Absolut Vodka was sent off to the USA in April 1979. The destination for the first shipment of vodka was Boston. Some 90,000 litres were sold world-wide in 1979 and in 1995 world-wide sales were 41.5 million litres. About 70 per cent of this amount was exported to the USA. Apart from the USA the most important markets are Sweden, Canada and certain markets in Europe.

The marketing of the bottle

For more than fifteen years, advertisements for Absolut Vodka have been based on the same fundamental concept, with focus placed on the product. The very first advertisement, 'Absolut Perfection' (see Plate 19), was created in 1981 and today stands as one of the most often used.

Since Andy Warhol, patron saint of pop art, created his first Absolut painting in 1985 (see Plate 19 'Absolut Warhol'), artists around the world have been asked to render their interpretation of the bottle.

In the advertisement 'Absolut Essence' magazine readers were able to fold back the cover and smell the scent of Absolut Kurant.

Distinctive advertising campaigns like 'Absolut London' (see Plate 19), in which the door of 10 Downing Street resembles an Absolut bottle, have made the vodka brand nearly as famous as Coca-Cola or Nike. Most countries maintain strict rules concerning alcohol advertisements to consumers. But Absolut's PR machine has milked the free publicity that its advertising generates.

Claes G. Fick's thoughts have become dream-like on the plane to New York, but he wakes with a start when the stewardesses ask passengers to buckle their seat belts. To use his time sensibly before landing, Claes takes a report out of his suitcase describing conditions in the US and world markets. The following is the essence of the report.

The world market for vodka

Table 1 shows that eastern European countries amount to 80 per cent of the world's total vodka sales.

The average consumption per capita per year is also very large in eastern Europe. In Poland the average vodka consumption per capita per year is about 10 litres, while the average in the CIS is

5 litres. As a comparison, the average consumption in the USA is 1.3 litres and in the UK 0.6 litres. It should be noted that all these figures are based on registered sales. In addition to this is home distillery, which takes place in quite a large part of eastern Europe as well as in Sweden and Finland.

The markets of eastern Europe are distinguished not only by their high vodka consumption, but also by how much consumers know about alcoholic beverages and their feeling for quality. However, political uncertainty and lack of a well-functioning infrastructure in several eastern European countries make short-term developments difficult to predict.

For several years Absolut Vodka has been sold to most eastern European countries, and in 1995 the brand was introduced in Poland as well. Thus, Absolut Vodka is now represented in all the major vodka markets of the world.

The US market for vodka

In the last fifteen years the consumption of alcohol in the USA has decreased by 20 per cent. There are several reasons for this decrease. One of the main reasons is the 'health trend' in the USA, which has caused a greater consciousness of the harmful effects of alcohol. At the same time there has been a tendency towards greater consciousness of drinking 'less but better'. Thus many people now drink cleaner and more pure alcohol. This has meant that the sale of 'super-premium' (high-quality) brands has not fallen and has been stable in the last five years.

Nearly all imported brands are in the super-premium segment and are the main reason that

Table 1	Distribution of world vodka sales
Region	**% of distribution**
CIS (the former USSR)	60
East Europe	20
USA	12
Others	8
Total	100
World's total vodka sales	2,250 million litres

Source: Impact International.

vodka imports have not fallen. Although the vodka importers' share of the total market is only 12–15 per cent, the gross margin on imported vodka represents about 40 per cent of the total gross margin of all vodka sales in the USA.

Historically, vodka has not been a differentiated product, but more and more flavoured brands have gradually been introduced to the market, including Absolut Lemon, Absolut Pepper and Absolut Kurant.

Today it is not without risk introducing new brands to the US market, as American consumers' tastes are so volatile. A producer can risk introducing a flavour one year, which is unpopular the next.

Product segments

The different product segments are as follows:

● *Platinum.* The most expensive category with prices around $20 per bottle. Labels in this category include Stolichnaya Cristall. This segment has under 1 per cent of total US vodka consumption.

● *Super-premium.* Nearly all labels here are imported. The leading labels are Swedish Absolut, Russian Stolichnaya and Finnish Finlandia. The price level is $15–16 per bottle. This category's share of the total vodka consumption in the USA is about 10 per cent.

● *Premium.* Here we find the world's most popular vodka, the American Smirnoff, sold for $9–10 a bottle. This group's share is 22 per cent of the USA's total vodka consumption.

● *Standard priced.* Here the two English labels Gilbey's and Gordon's are sold for $7 a bottle. The category's share is 14 per cent of US vodka consumption.

● *Popular priced.* This is the largest group. Its share of the total US vodka consumption is about 54 per cent, and the group consists of a number of local labels at about $6 a bottle.

Table 2 lists the market shares of the largest producers in the US market. The three largest imported brands are Absolut (no. 3), Stolichnaya (no. 11) and Finlandia (no. 17). Absolut's two

main competitors can be characterized as follows:

● *Stolichnaya.* The pioneer among imported vodka brands, this was the first vodka to be introduced in the USA, in 1972. Stolichnaya was at this time a good alternative to the USA-produced vodka brands as it tasted milder due to a more refined distilling process. But Stolichnaya's popularity has been dependent on the political climate between the USA and the former USSR. Today Stolichnaya is distributed by Absolut Vodka's former importer, Carillon Importers.

● *Finlandia.* This brand was introduced to the USA in 1976. Despite many marketing campaigns, Finlandia has never been able to get hold of the vodka market. In the trade, it is estimated that Finlandia has the most exposed position as all new importers go for the esteemed third place, which seems to be a realistic goal for a new importing vodka brand.

The distribution system for vodka in the USA

Generally the sale of spirits goes through the distribution system shown in Figure 1. For American producers, producer/supplier and importer/agent coincide. The retail ('off-premise') sale of wine, spirits and beer takes place through two different distribution systems. In the 'open states' (licence

Figure 1 The general distribution system for spirits in the USA

| Producer/supplier |
| Importer/agent |
| Distributor |

'On-premise' institutional market	'Off-premise' retail market
● Bars ● Restaurants ● Cafés ● Discos	● Supermarkets ● Discount markets ● Liquor stores ● Drug stores ● Convenience stores

Table 2	Vodka brand shares in the US market, 1990 and 1995		
Brand	**Company**	**% in volume (1990)**	**% in volume (1995)**
1. Smirnoff	Heublein	16.8	17.9
2. Popov	Heublein	9.8	11.1
3. Absolut	Seagram	6.9	9.7
4. Gordon's	Schenley Ind	5.6	7.0
5. Barton	Canadaigua	2.2	3.9
6. Kamchatka	Jim Beam Brands	5.6	3.8
7. Gilbey's	Jim Beam Brands	3.3	3.7
8. Wolfschmidt	Jim Beam Brands	2.6	3.7
9. Skol	UD Glenmore	2.2	2.7
10. McCormick	McCormick Distilling	2.0	3.5
11. Stolichnaya	Carillon	3.0	2.8
12. Fleischmann's	UD Glenmore	2.2	2.7
13. Aristocrat	Heaven Hill	1.3	2.2
14. Nikolai	Sazerac	1.4	2.0
15. Taaka	Sazerac	1.5	1.7
16. Relska	Heublein	1.6	1.4
17. Finlandia	Heublein	0.7	1.4
18. Crystal Palace	Canadaigua	1.0	1.3
19. Crown Russe	Sazerac/Southland	1.0	1.2
20. Majorska	Star Liquor Imports	1.0	0.9
Total top twenty		71.7	84.6
Others		28.3	15.4
Total		100	100

Total sales volume (1995): 280 million litres.

Source: Jobson's Handbook Advance/Euromonitor/Impact Databank

states) the market is free, and sale takes place in liquor stores, supermarkets or other grocery stores where the owner has a licence to sell spirits. In 'control states', spirits can only be sold in liquor stores owned by the state, similar to the Nordic monopoly system.

The importer/agent usually has only a minor sales force, which concentrates on selling to and servicing a distributor. An importer/agent usually cooperates with one distributor in every state (although one distributor can handle several states), and in large states a distributor can have up to 500 salespeople (geographically divided). Generally, these salespeople pay for their own car and receive a low basic wage and commission.

The salesperson in the area concerned visits both the institutional market and the retail market, often once a week, taking orders and in exceptional cases delivering goods and collecting payment.

Having read the above report, Claes G. Fick acknowledges that it is necessary to get some external input on some essential strategic questions. When Claes lands in New York he has written down the following questions which he asks you to answer.

Questions

1. State the advantages and disadvantages of having Seagram distribute and market not only in the USA, but also in a number of other markets. Give a conclusion.

2. Which alternative marketing strategies does the Absolut Company/Seagram have to increase its market share for:
   (a) Absolut Vodka in the USA;
   (b) Absolut Vodka in Europe (including eastern Europe)?

3. Where would you recommend the Absolut Company to allocate its resources: the USA or Europe (including eastern Europe)?

Case IV.2   Dandy

Part A: Chewing gum in Russia

If you want to get a more general introduction to Dandy and its business areas, read Case V.3.

In a very few years the Russian market had developed by 1996 into the biggest market for the Danish chewing gum producer Dandy's brands, DIROL and STIMOROL. In 1996 the turnover in Russia amounted to about DKK0.5 billion, out of total sales in the Dandy group of about DKK1.8 billion.

A brief review

Before 1991 Dandy chewing gum was sold primarily via state trading companies and resold to subsidiaries. In 1991 state trading broke down and new channels of distribution arose. TV commercials became common and in the beginning were very cheap: US$500 for a 30-second spot at the peak broadcasting time on the national TV channel.

At that time, Dandy's sales in Russia were handled by the Danish exporter Jahn International A/S. In 1991 Dandy's main competitor, Wrigley, also introduced its first products on the market. At an exhibition in Moscow in 1992, Dandy and Jahn International received the first reactions to the STIMOROL commercials: people loved them because they saw STIMOROL as an American product and eastern European consumers associate America with quality. Dandy continues to advertise on Russian national television, with a budget of $100,000.

In 1993 demand increased even more and the distribution contract with Jahn International was terminated. The media budget had now reached $1.5 million. 1993 was also the year when Wrigley launched Orbit sticks and Dandy launched DIROL.

In 1994 Dandy established its own sales company in Moscow and the distribution strategy was changed from central to regional distribution, which led to an increased number of distributors, numbering about 25–30. At the same time, a new business unit (SBU) was established in the Dandy group: Russian Brands Division.

In April 1996 demand began to stabilize and Dandy started a packing plant in Novgorod near St Petersburg. The chewing gum tablets are now sent in boxes from Denmark to Novgorod, where the boxes are emptied before the tablets are packed into the familiar packages and sent to the Russian shops.

From being a chaotic mess, the system of distribution has now become more organized with a network of regional distributors and merchandisers.

The Russian chewing gum market

The major part of chewing gum sales takes place in the 33 cities with more than 500,000 citizens. These cities are spread over the eleven time zones in Russia. The distribution of incomes among the Russian consumers is very uneven and it is assumed that only people with high wages can afford to buy chewing gum. Table 1 shows that the distribution of consumption between the two main types of chewing gum has changed considerably in a couple of years.

Dandy has benefited from this development and now has a market share of 60 per cent as opposed to Wrigley's 40 per cent. The distribution of chewing gum in Russia is very different from what is known in the West. Some 68 per cent of chewing gum sales take place from commercial kiosks, of which 8,000 are located in Moscow alone. Kiosks in the Metro have 11 per cent of the total chewing gum sales. Supermarkets have only 2 per cent of sales.

Market communication for chewing gum

The consumer behaviour towards chewing gum is characterized by impulse buying. Consumers do

Table 1	Distribution of the Russian chewing gum market between main types (%)	
	1994	1996
Sticks ('the long ones')	40	20
Dragee ('the tablet ones')	60	80
Total	100	100

Figure 1   Advertisements for DIROL in Russian and English

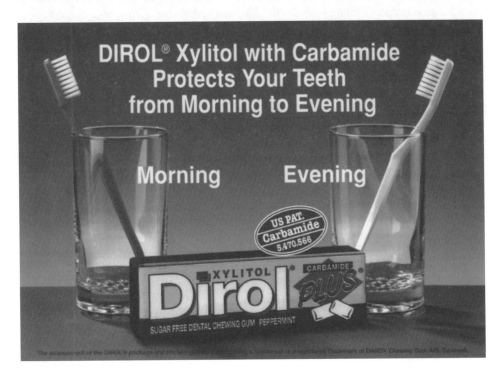

not decide to buy until they discover the product on the shelf. Therefore consumers must constantly be reminded of the reasons to buy a certain brand of chewing gum.

The Russians are bombarded with reminders from Dandy. The national television station broadcasts STIMOROL commercials five or six times a day. Since March 1995 Dandy has been the main sponsor of the Russian football league, called the STIMOROL League. The STIMOROL name is printed on the score board, the players' clothes, tickets and programmes. Russian television broadcasts four hours from the STIMOROL League each week, with an obligation to interrupt the transmission five times to make room for commercials.

The weather forecasts on Russian national television are sponsored by DIROL and are finished with the remark that DIROL keeps your mouth clean and fresh from morning till night (see the advertisements for DIROL in Figure 1). Dandy also sponsored the Russian ice hockey team during the 1996 World Championship. As time goes by, STIMOROL posters, streamers and billboards are increasingly to be found all over Russian cities. House ends and buses are painted in STIMOROL colours and STIMOROL arranges rock concerts and disco nights at the University of Moscow.

Production in Russia

Dandy's management has got hold of the news that Wrigley is contemplating building a plant for chewing gum production in Russia. This has hurried up Dandy's plans for building a chewing gum plant in Novgorod at a price of $100 million. This big investment is co-financed by the Danish Investment Fund for Eastern Countries and the European Bank for Reconstruction and Development (EBRD) in London.

However, the Dandy management is still very cautious about realizing its plans because the Russian government raised the duties on raw and sugar-free chewing gum shortly after the packing department began operations in Novgorod.

Sudden rises in duties on raw chewing gum are such a big threat to the profitability of the potential production plant in Novgorod that the Dandy management has requested the Danish Minister of Foreign Affairs to discuss the matter with the Russian Minister of Foreign Affairs Jevgenij Primakov, who is visiting Copenhagen at the beginning of February 1997.

In addition to these political risks, there are also problems with inconsistent laws and practices in Russia. For this reason, some local dealers manage to avoid paying all or part of the duty. This makes pricing difficult and encourages re-exportation within the CIS. If price differences occur among the countries of the CIS, the dealers in the different countries will quickly know (via cellular telephones) where to buy the cheapest chewing gum.

All these problems sometimes make Dandy's managing director, Lars Funder, ask himself: 'Isn't life too short to deal with this unstable market? Why don't we just produce some chewing gum in Vejle Denmark and leave the responsibility of selling and transportation of the chewing gum to an external partner?'

Questions

1. What would be your answer to Lars Funder's questions if he asked you?

2. If Dandy still chooses to handle things in Russia itself (i.e. internalizes), would you start building the planned production plant, or would you wait and risk Wrigley completing its plant first?

3. Which marketing parameters would you recommend Dandy to use in order to maintain its leading position in Russia?

Part B: Distribution and promotion of BMG records in the UK

Please see Case III.2 for a description of the world-wide music industry and the 'big five' record companies.

On a sunny autumn day in 1997, Colin Bailey[1] (managing director of the UK BMG Entertainment group) is sitting in his office in London in a meeting with one of his employees. During the meeting, Colin's secretary Shirley puts a fax on Colin's desk from Marcus Schmidt of BMG headquarters in Gütersloh (see Case III.2). After the meeting Colin reads:

Dear Colin,

Our board of directors' meeting in BMG Entertainment is scheduled in two days. We will be discussing the sales situation and marketing strategies in the different markets. According to the latest figures BMG has a UK market share of 8.5% in the sale of CDs, records and cassettes.

Although our market share has been rising slightly for the last couple of years, I still expect that I will be bombarded with questions as to how we are going to increase our market share to the average of other European markets (about 14%).

I would appreciate it if you could send me some background material on the English market and a suggestion for a marketing strategy that could bring the market share in the UK up to the same level as other markets in Europe.

Regards,

Marcus Schmidt, managing director of BMG Entertainment, Gütersloh, Germany

Straight away Colin gets hold of one of his market reports from 1995 regarding the UK market. This report gives some background information on the UK market, and contains the following material.

Structure of the industry

The most important participants in the industry are the record companies, composers, artists, publishing companies, music retailers and all those indi-

viduals and companies involved in the creation of sound recordings. The functions of some of these participants are briefly summarized below.

The record companies

The five largest record companies are usually referred to as 'the majors' or the 'big five'. They own and operate national distribution systems, distributing their own and third-party sound recordings to retailers, wholesalers and smaller distributors. Several of the majors also own and operate their own manufacturing plants, where cassettes, CDs and vinyl records are manufactured. The five majors are BMG, EMI, Polygram, Sony and Warner.

Besides the principal activities of the record companies there are: finding and developing new artists, recording music (which will involve hiring studios, sound engineers, technicians, producers and equipment), releasing recordings, marketing and promoting them in the UK and in the international marketplace, obtaining licences for the repertoire of overseas companies and selling it in the UK, and making royalty payments to artists, music publishers and others out of the proceeds of record sales.

There are some 600 independent record companies in the UK. They carry out a more limited range of activities than the majors, and are centred around the production of a recording. In terms of size they vary from significant operations such as MCA and Mute Records Ltd to very small businesses issuing only a handful of recordings a year. Independent record companies make an important contribution to the discovery and development of new talent, particularly (although by no means exclusively) in niche areas of musical taste such as dance, jazz, modern classical music and early music. They may also specialize, for example, in the licensing in of music originated by other record companies to create compilations or in the budget end of the classical sector. Some independent record companies have become very successful: for example, Virgin before its sale to EMI.

[1] All similarities to past or present BMG directors are coincidental.

Distributors

The major record companies each operate centralized distribution systems in the UK, serving both their own record labels and third parties. The recorded music market also supports independent distributors which are closely tied both to the independent record companies and to the smaller, independent retailers. Wholesalers (such as Entertainment UK Ltd (EUK) and TBD) also play an important role in this market.

Promoters

Promoters of live performances organize venues, concerts and support services. Live performances play an important part in marketing by the record companies of individual groups and artists.

Retailers

Music retailing can be divided into a number of categories in the UK market: specialist music chains, such as HMV, Our Price and Virgin; non-specialist chains such as W. H. Smith and Woolworths; and independent specialists, either small chains or single outlets. 'Non-traditional' outlets such as supermarkets, petrol stations and convenience stores also sell a limited selection of records.

The largest record retailers in terms of overall sales of records are: W. H. Smith and its subsidiary, Our Price; HMV, which is owned by Thorn EMI plc; and Woolworths, which is part of the Kingfisher group. W. H. Smith also has a 50 per cent shareholding in Virgin Retail, which is a joint venture with the Virgin Retail Group Ltd.

The direct-mail selling of sound recordings has increased in importance in recent years. Record clubs, of which the Britannia Music Company Ltd (Britannia) and BCA are the largest, supply their members from a select list of titles. Mail-order companies are much smaller in terms of volume and range of orders. Some, such as Reader's Digest, market their own compilations.

Ancillary activities

There are a number of other organizations and activities which are important to the functioning of the music industry. These include the following:

● Radio stations, clubs, pubs and discos, which play records and generate revenues for composers, performers and record companies in the form of royalties.

● Trade organizations. There are a large number of these in the music industry, including the British Phonographic Industry (BPI), which represents record companies and manufacturers, and the British Association of Record Dealers (BARD), which represents retailers.

● The music press.

● A large miscellaneous service and support sector including lawyers, accountants, managers, graphic designers, public relations companies and advertising agencies.

The UK music scene

A further characteristic of the UK music scene is its diversity. Although there is no universally accepted categorization, the BPI analyzes music sales into the following categories: classical, country/folk, jazz, pop, rock, dance/soul/reggae, middle-of-the-road (MOR) and other. However, the music scene is even more diverse than this analysis would suggest, including punk, rap, heavy metal, acid-house, techno-rave, grunge and swing-beat; and new genres are constantly emerging. Accordingly, musical styles are not readily categorized.

Of the generally accepted categories mentioned above, pop and rock taken together account for nearly 60 per cent of album sales. Classical music accounts for a little more than 9 per cent. There is an accelerating trend towards fragmentation of musical genres and taste, and an increased rate at which styles of music and individual releases become popular with consumers and then decline.

Distribution system

In the record industry, the term 'distribution' refers to the ways in which records are delivered from the record companies to the retailers (or mail-order companies/record clubs). The BPI estimates that some 60 per cent of recorded music in the UK is distributed to retailers directly by the record companies' distributors, 28 per cent goes via a wholesaler and the remaining 12 per cent is supplied to mail-order and record club operators. Figure 1

Figure 1   Distribution of records in the UK

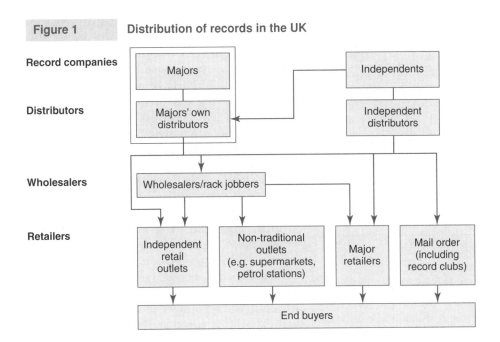

summarizes the main channels of distribution. Distributors and wholesalers are considered below.

Distributors

A distributor normally acts on an exclusive basis for a record company. This means that all the finished products of a record company are bulk-shipped from the manufacturer or a central warehouse to the exclusive distributor, where they are broken, picked and packed for onward distribution. Any dealer (i.e. wholesaler or retailer) wishing to obtain the record company's products must contact the distributor. The supply by the distributor to a retail outlet is deemed to be a sale by the record company. The record companies therefore bear the cost of delivery to retail outlets.

Distributors need to carry full catalogue ranges, and to hold sufficient stocks to satisfy anticipated demand. Because of frequent fluctuations in demand for individual titles and the unpredictability of sales, the distribution system has to ensure that records are delivered as quickly as possible, usually within 24 hours of receipt of an order from the retailer. Most of the major retail chains do not have central warehouses and require delivery direct to each of their stores.

Each of the five major record companies has its own centralized distribution operation (e.g. EMI at Leamington Spa, Sony at Aylesbury). A major might also act as a distributor for an independent record company: for example, Warner distributes for Beggars Banquet. There are also a number of independent distributors. Pinnacle Records, a division of Lambourne Productions Ltd, is the main independent distributor and acts in an exclusive capacity for many independent record companies. Independents therefore have a choice of distributors and there is evidence that switching takes place. For example, MCA switched from Polygram to BMG in 1990.

Table 1 shows the shares of distribution held by the nine leading distributors. The shares of the majors generally reflect their parent company's sales. The exception is BMG, which has a larger share of the distribution market since it acts as distributor for a number of independents.

Wholesalers

Wholesalers purchase catalogues from distributors and offer a range of products, sometimes on a sale-or-return basis. They do not stock every line item offered by the distributors, but typically restrict

Table 1	Market shares of distributors (by value of album sales), 1992
Distributor	**Market share (%)**
Polygram	23.9
EMI	23.1
BMG	15.8
Warner	13.1
Sony	11.0
Pinnacle	7.9
Pickwick	1.0
TBD	0.4
Conifer	0.4
Others	3.4
Total	100

Source: Based on information supplied by Gallup

their stock to the 'mainstream' artists. They also provide 'top-up' stocks for next-day delivery for many of the multiples and independent retailers which otherwise deal directly with the main distributors. This role has diminished recently as the main distributors have reduced order-response times. A wholesaler may also act as exclusive distributor for a small record company.

Recent developments in distribution

Over the last five years there has been increased concentration at both retail and wholesale levels. This has resulted in a higher percentage of business going through fewer accounts and an increase in the bargaining power of some retail chains. However, increased retail and wholesale concentration has not had any great impact on the number of delivery points that the record companies have to service because most retailers do not carry out their own wholesaling.

Marketing and promotion

Record companies use marketing and promotion to help ensure that an individual artist is established in the consumer's mind and that there is maximum exposure of each record release. The ultimate aim is to ensure the sales of albums. The returns from marketing and promotion may take time to accrue. For example, a campaign to raise the profile of an artist may boost sales of not only the current album but all future albums.

The sales success of a new release depends on consumers being able to hear the recording. The record companies estimate that fewer than 10 per cent of the albums are bought by consumers who have not heard the music before. However, in order to achieve playing time in the first place and in order to exploit any playing time that is achieved, it is also necessary to promote the recording. It must be promoted to retailers, to persuade them to stock it, to the media, to draw the recording to the public's attention, and directly to consumers. The process is complex and mixes various elements in different degrees depending on the characteristics of each artist and recording. These elements include: media exposure in the form of airplay and comment on radio, television and in the press; live performances and touring; personal appearances in dance clubs; advertising in the press, on radio and television, and on posters; in-store promotion; and retail cooperative advertising and direct mail.

Media exposure

Radio airplay is a very important medium for record promotion. BBC Radio One, Capital, Virgin 1215 and some 50 independent local radio stations are usually supplied with free samples of records prior to release. Deregulation of radio in the UK has led to an increasing number of new radio stations (both regional and national), some of which target a particular musical taste.

The record company devotes considerable effort to securing mention of a recording in the general press and specialist music press, and on radio and television, and to ensuring that the record is played on the radio and in clubs and discos. Television exposure is also a significant factor. This may involve the artist's live performance or the showing of video clips on BBC's *Top of the Pops*, ITV's *The Chart Show* or MTV.

Press coverage divides into two areas: specialist and general. The UK has a tradition of specialist music papers such as *New Musical Express* and *Melody Maker*. New magazines such as *Q* and *Vox* also feature music. This area of the press reviews new releases of singles and albums, and carries news, features and interviews on artists and on the music scene generally. The releases of the independent record companies in particular are featured in the specialist music press. The general press is also important for music coverage.

Advertising

All forms of advertising media are used, ranging from radio and television to outdoor posters. Advertising is normally funded by the record company, although cooperative activity with retailers and concert promoters is common.

Retailers ('push' activities)

Retailers are notified in advance of new releases, and in the period leading up to the release date the record company will seek advance orders from the retailer to ensure that the records are in stock on that date. Some form of cooperative marketing may be agreed between the record company and the retailer to accompany the release.

Campaigns in conjunction with retailers can take various forms. Television and press advertising, posters and other material advertising the retailer may feature particular recordings. The costs of such cooperative advertising are normally borne by the record company. The record companies also pay for in-store advertising material in the form of posters, carrier bags, etc., bearing the image of the artist or reproducing the cover of the record, and for space in the window display of the store. Retailers and record companies may cooperate to mount back-catalogue campaigns, whereby the retailer offers a reduced price to the consumer and receives a discounted price from the record company for stocks to be included in those campaigns.

The role of singles and charts

Release of singles is the most common and most effective means of promoting a pop album. It is success in the singles chart which is particularly important because the Top 40 is the basis for play lists on radio and for pop programmes on television, and generates demand from consumers and retailers.

Singles are usually not in themselves a profitable format for the record companies: they usually have a catalogue life of less than six months from release to deletion and most do not generate enough sales to cover all the costs of the promotional activity

and manufacturing. However, they play an important role in establishing an artist and improving or maintaining his or her popularity. For a new artist the release of the first single generally precedes the release of the album. The main function of the single is to attract media attention to the artist by focusing on a specific song. If the single is successful and enters the charts, this will generate more media interest which in turn increases the amount of exposure the record receives.

Free records

The singles charts in the UK are based on sales of records through a range of retail outlets. In general, only the specialist multiples and the independent retailers are willing to stock a wide range of singles. The generalist chains and multiples are generally willing to stock only singles which are already in the Top 40 or 60 of the singles charts. However, given the volatility of singles sales and competition for display and storage space, the specialist multiples and the independents require some incentive to stock a particular singles title. The supply of free singles constitutes such an incentive.

Expenditures on marketing and promotion

According to the BPI, total marketing expenditure by record companies is 15–20 per cent of net sales. More than 80 per cent of marketing and promotion expenditure is on new releases.

Future developments

The main developments likely to affect the industry in the next ten years are related to technological developments in the supply of home entertainment. In the shorter term, it is likely that the record industry in the UK will follow the developments that have already been taking place in countries such as Japan and the USA. The CD is becoming the principal carrier not only for music, but also for video, games and information. The introduction of two new audio-only digital carriers, Philips' DCC and Sony's MiniDisc system, represents attempts by these companies to provide alternative digital carriers for consumers. One of these may succeed as there appears to be a requirement for a portable digital format to replace the analogue cassette.

The traditional core business of the record companies, the production and sale of copies of recordings, may begin to be replaced by other means of distributing music. The consumer will begin to order and buy CDs on the Internet. Digital broadcasting by satellite or cable is also currently under development. The ability to compress multiple signals to be carried by fiber optic cables will mean that households will be able to receive a wide range of specialist radio and television stations, catering for a variety of musical tastes.

New technologies are likely to allow delivery of music as part of multimedia (i.e. film, video, music, information, communication) in a physical format such as the CD or via broadcast media.

The ownership structure of the major record companies means that links are growing between the music, entertainment, media, communications, information technology and consumer electronics industries. Apart from EMI, all the large companies in the music industry are parts of international corporations with extensive interests in one or more of these sectors.

It is unlikely that in the next ten years the physical distribution of products will disappear completely, given the perceived consumer benefits associated with the packaging and tactile qualities of the object (portability, durability and convenience). Nevertheless it seems likely that the balance between physical and non-physical distribution will change and that direct access via satellite, cable systems or the Internet will assume much greater importance.

After reading the report briefly, Colin Bailey leaves the job to you, a newly employed marketing assistant in the UK BMG company. You are asked to prepare the presentation which is to be sent to the German headquarters.

Questions

You are asked to prepare the following:

1. Which marketing mix would you suggest to increase BMG's market share in the UK market?

2. Discuss acquisition as a possible growth strategy.

Source: Monopolies and Mergers Commission, *The Supply of Recorded Music: A report on the supply in the UK of prerecorded compact discs, vinyl discs and tapes containing music*, HMSO, London, 1994.

Marketing of an incontinence product to the retail market in the USA

Introduction

Tytex is part of the Thygesen group, a holding company for limited companies Søren Thygesen Trikotagefabrik, Fascia Trikotagegaarden and Tytex.

The holding company was founded on 1 July 1991 after a merger between the three companies. The first year after the merger, the group's turnover rose by DKK66 million or 22 per cent, from DKK299 million to DKK365 million in 1991/2. Profits after tax rose from DKK21.2 million to DKK29.5 million in 1991/2. The total number of employees is about 500. Approximately 80 per cent of the turnover comes from export activities. (The comparison figures are from 1.5.90 to 30.4.91 and from 1.5.91 to 30.4.92.)

To maintain the smaller companies' creativity and efficiency, the three companies are run as independent units with their own management and board of directors.

Søren Thygesen Trikotagefabrik produces highly refined/value-added materials, synthetic as well as cotton. Fascia Trikotagegaarden produces clothes for babies and children as well as ladies' leisure wear.

Tytex was founded in 1971. The entrepreneurs were the brothers Eskild and Niels Laurits Thygesen and their cousin Niels Bruun Thygesen. The company's mission was to produce and sell underwear produced under a new method, where the product was knitted in one run.

In 1981 a company in the USA was established, Tytex Inc., with a view to entering the American market. The company is situated in Providence in the state of Rhode Island. Changes in the American dollar's exchange rate caused the company to stop its own production in the USA, which started up again in 1988. However, since 1981 Tytex has been represented in the American market in one way or another.

Ninety per cent of the production in the USA aims at American hospitals, nursing homes and the health sector. Production is 100 per cent automatic and results in 200,000 units a day. The rest of Tytex's production includes fashion stockings which are marketed to the whole world.

Incontinence

Incontinence means that a person, for one reason or another, is not able to control urination or faeces. It is regarded as one of the most widespread but least-known handicaps today. It is important to point out that incontinence is not a disease but a symptom that one or more of the body's normal functions is not functioning optimally.

The risk of developing incontinence is twice as large for women as for men and the risk increases with age. The Alliance for Aging Research estimates that 40 per cent of women and 20 per cent of men over 60 years in the USA suffer from incontinence. The disorder is increasingly the reason that Americans apply to nursing homes, where nearly two-thirds of the 1.5 million residents suffer from incontinence. It is estimated that two-thirds of all geriatric patients are incontinent. Between 15 and 30 per cent of American senior citizens not living in a nursing home or in a hospital suffer from incontinence. The total number of incontinent people in the USA is difficult to determine, as the problem is still taboo for many people, but a qualified guess is between 10 and 15 million.

Incontinence is a practical, but also a highly psychological and social problem. It is considered by many as something embarrassing that you do not talk or consult a doctor about. Only one out of twelve suffering from incontinence seeks active help in spite of the fact that 80 per cent of incontinent people can be cured by the different treatments available today. People who do not seek active help use baby napkins, sanitary towels, paper or several layers of underwear, or stay indoors and avoid contact with others. The problem is especially serious for many incontinent people who are socially active and have jobs.

A variety of good treatments are available:

medicine, training of the muscles in the floor of the pelvis, operation, bladder training, electro stimulation and regulation of medicine, drinking, eating and toilet habits. Drinking and eating habits can be characterized as being an independent treatment.

In the cases where incontinence cannot be cured and involuntary urination becomes a problem in everyday life, the use of aids to relieve inconvenience can be the answer. One of the most commonly used aids is the sanitary towel. One result of the social stigma attached to incontinence is that the name 'sanitary towel' is often used in preference to 'napkin', which is still the official aid classification in most countries. Many incontinent adults associate the word 'napkin' with babies. How much a sanitary towel can absorb is dependent not only on size but also on material and fit. The sanitary towel must sit tight to the body to exploit its absorbency best and thus be safe. Elastic, tight fitting underwear (briefs) can do this.

Tytex produces 'net briefs' which can be used with a sanitary towel. This combination is called a *two-piece system* (Plate 20). Tytex expects the net brief to be replaced after every ten sanitary towels.

In those cases where the sanitary towel and brief are one, the product is called a *one-piece system* (also shown in Plate 20). Apart from this division, there is also talk about disposable systems and reusable (washable) systems, of which disposable systems until now have had the largest share of the market.

The market in 1991 can be characterized by the figures shown in Table 1.

Product grouping/division

Although the one-piece system has by far the largest share of the US market, the two-piece (net) system gives its user the following advantages:

● The net brief is especially suitable for people who want freedom of movement. This group will become larger when the baby boomers grow older.

● The net brief system is more economical in the long run as the brief only has to be replaced after every ten sanitary towels.

Market division

In recent years the retail market has been growing

Table 1	US market for sanitary towels and briefs for incontinence, 1991	
		Distribution (%)
Product grouping/division		
One-piece (approx.)		90
Two-piece (approx.)		10
Market division		
Institutional market (hospitals, nursing homes)		60
Retail market		35
Mail-order		5
Market share (US$)		
Kimberly-Clarke (label: Depend)		29
Procter & Gamble (label: Attends)		26
Johnson & Johnson (label: Serenity)		15
Others (mainly private-label manufacturers)		30
Total market for incontinence products (sanitary towels and, if fastened, briefs)		Approx. US$745 million

fast due to great pressure on nursing homes, and thus people with incontinence have been referred to 'home care'. As a result, the share of the total market taken by institutions has fallen from 75 per cent in 1985 to 60 per cent in 1991. The retail market for incontinence products is currently increasing by 25 per cent a year. The institutional market is increasing by 12 per cent a year.

There are many mobile persons in the retail market for whom movement, quick replacement, comfort and discretion will be determining demand factors, and these are characteristics of Tytex's brief.

Market shares

The market can be characterized as oligopolistic with three large actors and many small. As a result of the continuously increasing market for incontinence products, the three dominant companies, Kimberly-Clark, Procter & Gamble and Johnson & Johnson, are constantly exposed to new products from smaller competing companies. The Marketing Intelligence Service of Naples and New York estimates that in 1987 eight new products were introduced into the market, while in 1991 over twenty new products were introduced.

The category 'private-label manufacturers' covers mainly smaller producers that market their products under the name/label of a retail chain or another producer. The share of retail turnover taken by private labels is rising rapidly.

Two large producers direct themselves only to the retail market: Kimberly-Clark and Johnson & Johnson. Procter & Gamble directs itself mainly to the institutional market.

Tytex's initial position

Tytex Inc. can be characterized as a 'private-label' manufacturer, which means that the company does not use its own label, but goes under the buying company's label.

Scott Health Care (SHC) is the dominant customer with a 40 per cent share of Tytex Inc.'s sales. This share is expected to rise in years to come. SHC is a division of Scott Paper Co., which is a nationwide company with a turnover of approximately $6 billion.

SHC only markets disposable sanitary towels in the incontinence market and buys know-how from Mölnlycke A.B., Tytex's cooperator in Europe. The main product line is Promise, which is marketed with Tytex Inc.'s net brief as the two-piece 'Promise system'. At the moment SHC has no sales to the retail market worth mentioning, although the Promise system is sold to the final customer through mail-order businesses. However, SHC's main market is the institutional market. Tytex Inc. estimates that at present its two-piece system has a 50 per cent share of the market outside the retail sector.

The company's only large competitor in briefs for sanitary towels is the German-owned company MB Products Ltd (MBP). This company has no own production in the USA at the moment, but cuts and packs its own products in the USA. MBP's brief is a licensed production of Tytex Inc.'s patented Tenafix brief and the company pays a royalty per brief sold. The managing director of MBP, John Bouda, is a former president of the Incontinence Association in the USA.

MBP's main customers are Baxter International and Procter & Gamble, and there is a small sale to Kimberly-Clark. Together with Johnson & Johnson these three companies are known as the 'big four' in the market for incontinence products.

It is estimated that Tytex Inc.'s comparative advantage over MBP lies mainly in better product quality. MBP has had problems where the company's quality control has failed in the cutting.

You have been contacted by Tytex, which would like you to work out a penetration strategy for the Tytex brief in the US retail market.

Postscript

In 1997 Tytex acquired the German-owned competitor Müller Elastics and its subsidiary MB Products (MBP), situated in the American state of North Carolina. The German company had a turnover of $8 million in 1996. The German and American companies have 60 employees altogether. Apart from new customer groups in the USA, the acquisition also gives access to the Middle East market, where Müller Elastics has traditionally had a strong position.

Questions

1. Explain differences in buying behaviour between the retail market and the institutional market.

2. Assess the advantages and disadvantages of alternative penetration strategies for Tytex in the retail market. On this basis, choose a strategy and give reasons for your answer.

3. Propose how you plan to implement the strategy you have chosen.

Part V

Implementing and coordinating the global marketing programme

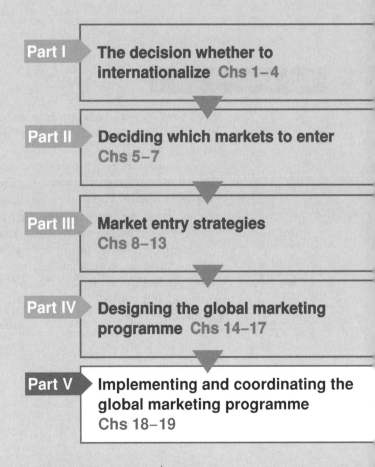

Introduction

While the first four parts of this book have considered the set-up necessary to carry out global marketing activities, *Part V* will discuss the implementation and coordination phase.

An essential criterion for success in selling and negotiating internationally is to be able to adapt to each business partner, company and situation. Therefore, *Chapter 18* discusses how the international negotiator should cope with the different cultural background of his or her counterparts. A special issue in this chapter will be how western negotiators can adapt to the Chinese culture.

As companies evolve from purely domestic firms to multinationals, their organizational structure, coordination and control systems must change to reflect new global marketing strategies. *Chapter 19* is concerned with how organizational structures and control systems have to be adjusted as the firm itself and market conditions change.

International sales negotiations

After studying this chapter you should be able to do the following:

- Discuss why intercultural selling through negotiation is one of the greatest challenges in global marketing.

- Discuss the implications of Hofstede's research for the firm's cross-cultural negotiation.

- Explain some important aspects of the intercultural preparation for expatriates.

- Explain the complexity and dangers of transnational bribery.

- Define and discuss the critical issues when negotiating in China.

18.1 Introduction

All successful international marketers have personal representation abroad. Face-to-face negotiations with the customer are the heart of the sales job. Negotiations are necessary to reach an agreement on the total exchange transaction, comprising such issues as the product to be delivered, the price to be paid, the payment schedule and the service agreement.

International sales negotiations have many characteristics that distinguish them from negotiations in the domestic setting. First and foremost, the cultural background of the negotiating parties is different. Successful negotiations therefore require some understanding of each party's culture and may also require the adoption of a negotiating strategy that is consistent with the other party's cultural system. It is interesting to note that Japanese negotiators, among other things, routinely request background information on American companies and key negotiators. Therefore, Japanese negotiators often know in advance the likely negotiating strategies and tactics of the other side.

At the end of this chapter, China will be used as an example of the issues treated in this and earlier chapters.

Cross-cultural negotiations

Implications of Hofstede's work

From Hofstede's work we see that there are differences (gaps) between national cultures. Each of four dimensions is reflected in the corporate culture patterns exhibited across countries (Hofstede, 1983). For example, Hofstede uses the combination of power distance and uncertainty avoidance to explain prevalent models of corporate culture in the UK, Germany, France and India.

The British model of organization seems to be that of a village market with no decisive hierarchy, flexible rules and a resolution of problems by negotiating. The German model is more like a well-oiled machine. The exercise of personal command is largely unnecessary because the rules settle everything. The French model is more of a pyramidal hierarchy held together by a united command issuing strong rules. If we look at international buyer–seller relations, the national culture is only one level in the cultural hierarchy that will influence the behaviour of the individual buyer or seller.

In negotiation situations, the most fundamental gap influencing the interaction between buyer and seller is the difference between their respective cultural backgrounds (gap 1 in Figure 18.1). This cultural distance can be expressed in terms of differences in communication and negotiation behaviours, the concepts of time, space or work patterns, and the nature of social rituals and norms (Madsen, 1994).

Figure 18.1   **Gap analysis in a cross-cultural negotiation**

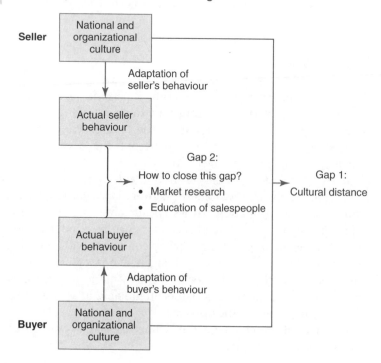

The cultural distance between two partners tends to increase the transaction costs, which may be quite high in crosscultural negotiations.

Both the buyer and especially the seller will adapt their own behaviour in such a way that they think it is acceptable to the other party. In this way, the initial gap 1 is reduced to gap 2, through adaptation of behaviour. But neither the seller nor the buyer obtains full understanding of the other party's culture, so the final result will often still be a difference between the cultural behaviour of the seller and the buyer (gap 2). This gap can create friction in the negotiation and exchange process and hence give rise to transaction costs.

Gap 2 can be reduced through market research and the education of salespeople (see section 18.3). However, salespeople bring different 'baggage' with them in the form of attitudes and skills that result in different stages of intercultural awareness. Each stage of intercultural awareness requires a different training method (Bush and Ingram, 1996). For example, if a trainer chooses to give a basic cultural awareness exercise to salespeople who are already at the acceptance stage and willing to learn about behaviour strategies, then the latter are likely to be bored and not to see the value of some types of diversity training.

Furthermore, face-to-face communication skills remain an important topic in international sales training. This is especially true in consultative selling, where questioning and listening skills are essential in the global marketing context.

| Exhibit 18.1 | Euro Disney becomes Disneyland Paris – The 'American way' did not work in Europe |

In preparing the opening of Euro Disney (near Paris) in 1992, Euro Disney's first chairman proudly announced that his company would 'help change Europe's chemistry'. The French ridiculed the park as a 'cultural Chernobyl'.

Several cross-cultural blunders occurred. Among these were:

● Prior to opening the park, Disney insisted employees comply with a detailed written code regarding clothing, jewelry, and other aspects of personal appearance. Women were expected to wear 'appropriate undergarments' and keep their fingernails short. Disney defended its move, noting that similar codes were used in its other parks. The goal was to ensure that guests receive the kind of experience associated with the Disney name. Despite such statements, the French considered the code to be an insult to French culture, individualism, and privacy.

● The extension of Disney's standard 'no alcohol' policy from USA meant that wine was not available at Euro Disney. This, too, was deemed inappropriate in a country renowned for production and consumption of wine.

It took a series of adaptions such as renaming the park 'Disneyland Paris' and the addition of some special attractions to make the park profitable as of 1996 and the most frequented tourist attraction of France in 1997.

In the fiscal year 1998–99, which ended 30 September, Disneyland Paris drew over 12.5 million visitors, more than any other attraction in France. Only about 41 per cent were from France, with 17 per cent from Belgium, Luxembourg and the Netherlands, 15 per cent from Britain and 10 per cent from Germany.

▶

For the year 1998–99 Disneyland Paris reported a $24 million net profit. Though that was 46 per cent less than the year before, the drop was attributed mainly to a resumption of Euro Disney's payment of management fees to the Walt Disney Company and to stagnant attendance, which was hurt by the World Cup soccer tournament in France in the summer of 1998. Furthermore, Disneyland Paris has announced plans for a new $615 million, 62-acre park that will focus on film studios, animation and television. The official opening is planned for April 2002, 10 years from the inauguration of the first park.

However, Disneyland is not the only company which offers additional theme parks. In a few months, Warner Bros. will break ground on a $300 million theme park, Movie World, Madrid, that will supplement its existing park in Bottrop, Germany. After rejecting sites in England, Warner took advantage of Madrid's desire to 'have something that would compete with Port Aventura', says Nick Winslow, president of the company's international recreation enterprises.

Sources: Tagliabue, J. (2000) 'Lights, action in France for second Disney Park' *New York Times*, 13 February. Della Cava, M.R. (1999) 'Magic kingdoms, new colonies: Theme parks are staking bigger claims in Europe' *USA Today*, 17 February.

Negotiating strategies

Basic to negotiating is, of course, knowing your own strengths and weaknesses, but also knowing as much as possible about the other side, understanding the other's way of thinking and recognizing his or her perspective. Even starting from a position of weakness, there are strategies that a salesperson can pursue to turn the negotiation to his or her advantage.

18.3 | Intercultural preparation

The following discussion can be applied not only to expatriate salespeople, but also to other jobs in the firm based in a foreign country (e.g. an administrative position in a foreign subsidiary). Expatriate salespeople negotiating in foreign cultures often experience a culture shock when confronted with a buyer. Culture shock is more intensely experienced by expatriates whose cultures are most different from the ones in which they are now working. What can the management of the international firm do to minimize the risk of culture shock? The following areas should be considered (Guy and Patton, 1996).

The decision to employ an expatriate salesperson

The first major decision to make is whether the use of home country expatriates is the best choice for entering and serving foreign markets. The firm should first examine its own past experience with culture shock and sales rep adjustment in other cultures. Inexperienced firms would probably be best advised to evaluate possible agents and distributors rather than using home country expatriates. Other options for firms with their own sales force are host country or third country nationals (see also section 17.3).

The firm should try to identify the elements in the expatriate sales job that suggest potential problems with culture shock. If the job is highly technical, is located in an area with other home country nationals, and involves similar tastes and lifestyles as in the home country, then the expatriate sales force may be appropriate.

If, however, the job places the expatriate salesperson in an unfamiliar job with conflicting expectations, the firm should consider other options. The chances of greater culture shock and adjustment problems increase with greater cultural distance. The greater the high context/low context contrast, the greater is the chance of difficulty. When entering a different culture, many familiar symbols and cues are missing. The removal of these everyday reassurances can lead to feelings of frustration, stress and anxiety.

Selection of expatriates

Since being an expatriate salesperson is a critical task, the selection process should be given considerable thought and should not be decided too quickly. The selection should not be based primarily on the technical competence of the salesperson. Substantial emphasis must also be placed on the following attributes:

● Foreign-language skills.

● General relational abilities.

● Emotional stability.

● Educational background.

● Past experience with the designated culture.

● Ability to deal with stress.

Previous research (Guy and Patton, 1996) suggests that the following characteristics of the expatriate are associated with a lower level of cultural shock:

● Open-mindedness.

● Empathy.

● Cultural sensitivity.

● Resilience.

● Low ego identity.

An assessment of the potential expatriate alone is not sufficient if the person has a family which will be making the move as well. Family issues that must be considered include marital stability, the overall emotional stability of family members, and family cohesiveness. In-depth interviews with at least the rep's spouse and preferably other family members as well can be very useful in determining the status of these variables.

| Exhibit 18.2 | **Choice of Rockwell International's managing director for the new subsidiary Rockwell Automation – China** |

Rockwell International is an American multinational corporation with its headquarters at Seal Beach, California and subsidiaries world-wide.

The concern is engaged in development, sales and support of technology to nearly all areas of industrial production, and is divided into four business areas: Automation, Aviation, Automotive and Communication. Rockwell International has a total of 80,000 employees, of which about 16,000 are employed in companies outside the USA. The concern has a turnover of $14 billion a year, of which 40 per cent comes from sales outside the USA. Automation, with an annual turnover of $4.5 billion, is Rockwell's largest independent business area.

In autumn 1996, the managing director of Rockwell Automation's subsidiary in Denmark, Kim Rasmussen, is contacted by Rockwell headquarters, which asks Kim if he would be interested in the job as managing director of Rockwell's new subsidiary in China. Kim Rasmussen has shown entrepreneurial skills (annual growth rate of 60 per cent) in the Danish Rockwell company since he was given responsibility for the Danish company in 1991.

Kim is interested in the job, but Rockwell HQ wants to test his potential as managing director of the Chinese subsidiary. Shortly before Christmas 1996, Kim is asked to come to Rockwell's International HQ at Seal Beach, California, for a two-day job interview with the concern's top management. Top management want a clearer picture of his personality and attitude to business. After the job interview, management turn their attention towards Kim's family; he and his wife are subject to a day-long psychological test, the main objective of which is to assess their ability to function independently and as a couple in (from a western point of view) difficult and foreign conditions. Eighty per cent of unsuccessful US expatriations are due to family problems.

Shortly after Kim and his wife have returned from California, he is offered the job in China if he is ready. In May 1997 the whole family (Kim, his wife and their two boys, 10 and 7 years old) go to Beijing to start a new life.

Source: Volander (1997).

Training

Selecting the most appropriate training programme for each expatriate requires methods for classifying people into various levels of intercultural skills. Each level needs a different training programme. The initial requirement is to train the expatriate, and any accompanying family member, to know the main sociocultural, economic, political, legal and technological factors in the assigned country.

The training activities may include the following:

● Area/country description.

● Cultural assimilation training.

● Role playing.

● Handling critical incidents.

- Case studies.
- Stress reduction training.
- Field experience.
- Extensive language training.

Obviously, many firms will not be able to provide all the training needed in-house or through a single source, but they may need to coordinate a variety of methods and external programmes for their expatriates to take place before and during the foreign assignment.

Support

It is very important to provide a solid support network from the head office so that the expatriate is not simply left alone to 'sink or swim'. Support during expatriate assignment may include a number of elements:

- Adequate monetary compensation or other benefits.
- Constant communication from the home base regarding ongoing operations at head office and in the assigned country/area.
- Providing opportunities for periodic travel to the home country to maintain contacts and relationships within the firm. The home base could also send copies of forthcoming job postings in which the expatriate may be interested.

The expatriate should identify and contact individuals in the host country who can become a part of the expatriate's social network. It is also important that the expatriate's spouse and family are included in a social support network.

Repatriation

Companies employing expatriates should develop an integrated career plan, identifying likely subsequent job positions and career progression. If the expatriates, during their careers, are exposed to a series of international assignments, each assignment should be selected to develop their awareness of different cultures. For example, for a UK company the first non-UK assignment would be a culturally similar or proximate country, say Germany or the USA, the next assignment might be South Africa or Australia, the next Hong Kong, then Japan and so on. In this way cultural shock is minimized, since the process encourages the ability to manage situations in more and more distant cultures.

The return of the expatriate to the home country is sometimes difficult. Lack of job guarantees is one of the most critical challenges faced by expatriates. Some months prior to return, an internal position search should be started with a home visit arranged for the expatriate to meet with appropriate managers. An internal sponsor in the head office should be appointed to maintain ongoing contact and to help the expatriate to secure a desirable position upon return.

Sometimes expatriated families also experience a culture shock upon the return to the home country. Therefore some support is needed during repatriation. This includes spouse job-finding assistance and time to readjust before going back to work.

| Exhibit 18.3 | The political consumer/boycotts |

Historical events

1999	British shoppers shun French produce during the Beef War
1999	Fidel Casto calls for drinkers to buy only Cuban rum in a dispute with Bacardi
1995	Drivers avoid Shell petrol during Brent Spar row
1977	Nestlé targeted for its marketing of baby milk formula
1971	Students boycott Barclays Bank over its South African dealings

Brent Spar

The most dramatic environmental boycott of recent years has to be Greenpeace's 1995 campaign against the dumping of the Brent Spar oil platform (owned by Shell). Sales of Shell petrol were down by 70 per cent in some German outlets and the company gave in after only a few days.

Source: Information was sourced from a variety of public media.

18.4 Transnational bribery in cross-cultural negotiations

On first consideration, bribery is both unethical and illegal. But a closer look reveals that bribery is not really a straightforward issue. The ethical and legal problems associated with bribery can be quite complex. Thus, the definition of bribery can range from the relatively innocuous payment of a few pounds to a minor official or business manager in order to expedite the processing of papers or the loading of a truck, to the extreme of paying millions of pounds to a head of state to guarantee a company preferential treatment.

The difference between lubrication and bribery must be established. Lubrication payments accompany requests for a person to do a job more rapidly or more efficiently. They involve a relatively small cash sum, gift or service made to a low-ranking official in a country where such offerings are not prohibited by law, the purpose being to facilitate or expedite the normal, lawful performance of a duty by that official. This practice is common in many countries of the world. Bribery, on the other hand, generally involves large sums of money, which are frequently not properly accounted for, and is designed to entice an official to commit an illegal act on behalf of the one paying the bribe.

Another type of payment that can appear to be a bribe, but may not be, is an agent's fee. When a businessperson is uncertain of a country's rules and regulations, an agent may be hired to represent the company in that country. This person will do a more efficient and thorough job than someone unfamiliar with country-specific procedures.

There are many intermediaries (attorneys, agents, distributors and so forth) who function simply as channels for illegal payments. The process is further complicated by legal codes that vary from country to country: what is illegal in one country is winked at in another and legal in a third. In some countries, illegal payments can become a major business expense. Hong Kong companies report that bribes account for about 5 per cent of the cost of doing business in China. In Russia the cost is 15–20 per cent, and in Indonesia as high as 30 per cent (Gesteland, 1996, p. 93).

The answer to the question of bribery is not an unqualified one. It is easy to generalize about the ethics of political pay-offs and other types of payment; it is much more difficult to make the decision to withhold payment of money when not making the payment may affect the company's ability to do business profitably or at all. With the variety of ethical standards and levels of morality which exist in different cultures, the dilemma of ethics and pragmatism that faces international business cannot be resolved until more countries decide to deal effectively with the issue.

18.5 An example of sales negotiations in an emergent market: China

The People's Republic of China (PRC) is now becoming a major economic power. Its population makes up approximately one-fifth of the world's consumers and its total GNP is expected to overtake that of the United States within a decade or so (Davies *et al.*, 1995). By the year 2000, some 260 million Chinese people will be able to afford packaged consumer products, making China the world's largest market in many categories such as beer and biscuits (Ayala and Lai, 1996).

Although the Chinese economy is still dominated by state-owned enterprises, a great change in the economic structure took place in 1992 when, for the first time, the output from non-state sectors accounted for more than half (52 per cent) of GNP (Fan, 1996, p. 166). During the economic transition, Chinese enterprises appear to be slowly transforming themselves from production oriented to production and sales oriented, and becoming more responsive to markets. However, the majority of Chinese managers still lack marketing knowledge and have no experience of operating in a real competitive and international marketplace.

Despite the lack of marketing knowledge, a shift of power is taking place from suppliers and manufacturers to Chinese buyers and more discerning consumers. Therefore, it is inevitable that marketers will have to do more customized marketing for the Chinese. That means applying, more than ever, cultural adaptation and cultural sensitivity in dealing and negotiating with Chinese buyers and consumers, as they become more discerning and demanding.

The meaning of 'guanxi'

Anyone who has had experience in dealing with the Chinese would hardly have failed to observe that Chinese people attach great importance to cultivating, maintaining and developing guanxi (best translated as 'personal connections/ relationships'). Guanxi has its roots in Confucianism,[1] where the central goal is to

---

1 Kong Fu Ze, whom the Jeusit missionaries renamed Confucius, was a high civil servant in China around 500 BC. Known for his wisdom, he was always surrounded by a host of disciples who recorded what we know of his teachings. Confucius' teaching are lessons in practical ethics with any religious content.

achieve social harmony and this depends not only on the maintenance of relationships among individuals, but also on the protection of an individual's 'face', or dignity. If a Chinese person loses face, he or she might as well feel, according to Confucius, as if they had lost eyes, nose or mouth.

The Chinese family business

Guanxi plays an extremely important role in the Chinese business world. As most Chinese family businesses (CFBs) are small and managed by core family members, they are heavily dependent on business opportunities and credit lines provided by their guanxi network. The CFBs are not only small, but also simple and informal in structure. Most of them can only concentrate on production, sales or service. The majority of CFBs do not have ancillary departments for R & D, public relations or market research. All employees are expected to be involved in the primary activities of the value chain, where direct profits are made.

The leadership style in CFBs is authoritarian. In order to maintain a large power distance, the top manager controls the spread of information to subordinates, so that they become dependent and unable to outperform him.

Decision making is centralized in the top manager and the owner of the CFB, whose decisions are largely based on intuition and/or experience. As most bosses of the CFBs have started from scratch and know every aspect of the business, they have accumulated a wealth of experience and are capable of powerful intuition.

Due to lack of structure and rules, it may be difficult for Chinese managers at different levels to make objective assessments of employee performance. Consequently, the top manager pays special attention to highly loyal employees, who may receive substantial personal rewards in the form of year-end bonuses. In their external relationships, CFBs remain very flexible and informal. According to Redding (1990), in 34 per cent of subcontracting relationships (in Hong Kong) only a verbal contract existed between buyer and seller. In 53 per cent of these cases, price was determined through discourse between buyer and seller rather than as a result of unilateral decision.

Purchasing decisions in China

A significant number of actors may be involved in decisions where Chinese (end) customers buy from western companies (Björkman and Kock, 1995). The end buyers in China may be any of the following:

● Government organizations (large projects).

● State-owned companies.

● Foreign trade corporations (FTCs).

● Single firms or a collection of firms at the local level.

As only a limited (though growing) number of companies are permitted to trade internationally (the FTCs: see Exhibit 5.1 in Chapter 5), most organizations have to involve an FTC in the transaction. The FTC is usually associated with some level of government, either one of the central ministries or more often part of the provincial or municipal government. FTCs will typically obtain 1–3 per cent commission on the transactions they are involved in.

Local governments may strongly influence investment decisions made by organizations within their geographical area. Design institutes in China play the role of approving technical solutions. Financing of business deals is very important and may involve bank guarantees by a Chinese bank or a foreign financial institution such as the World Bank or the Asian Development Bank.

Social relations with key Chinese actors in the buying decision process are essential in order to obtain important information and to influence Chinese decision makers. It is common to arrange public tenders for very large projects. If the western companies in this situation are able to influence the specifications of the tender, often by influencing foreign experts, their position is strengthened.

Practical implications for the western negotiator in China

Although the Chinese and the Japanese are culturally quite different, they share many negotiating methods. Both have a well-deserved reputation for being tough negotiators. At the same time, Confucianism has left a strong mark on much of east Asian business life. The success of doing business in this part of the world depends heavily on the quality and sometimes the quantity of personal relationships.

The basic rules for negotiating successfully with the Chinese are as follows (partly based on Gesteland, 1996, with kind permission from Handelshøjskolens Forlag/Copenhagen Business School Press):

● *Language of business*. More and more Chinese negotiators speak foreign languages, especially English. However, you may find it advisable to employ an interpreter.

● *The initial contact*. Use the guanxi of the Chinese. You can be introduced by an intermediary, who knows both you and the Chinese party. If you do not have mutual friends to introduce you, a good way to make contact is at a trade show or with an official trade mission.

● *Building relationships*. Developing relationships is a critical and time- consuming part of the overall negotiating process. Prepare ahead of time by knowing as much about the other party as possible, including who are the key decision makers and who are the 'old friends' that are capable of influencing decisions. Be prepared with appropriate gifts for your counterparts. Wining and dining is an essential part of building close relationships.

● *Hierarchy and status in China*. Young marketers must show respect to older, more senior Chinese buyers. Chinese are very rank conscious. If the negotiator sent is of fairly low rank, the Chinese counterpart may assume that there is a lack of sincerity or, worse, may feel insulted.

● *Time-consuming negotiations*. Expect that negotiations will take time and be patient. Generally, the Chinese will not be rushed and the foreign position will be weakened by attempting to hurry them.

● *Maintaining surface harmony*. Avoid anger or displays of temper, as this is seen as infantile and offensive behaviour. The Chinese quickly lose respect for people who cannot retain a calm exterior under stress.

● *Concern with face.* You can cause your counterparts to lose face by embarrassing them or criticizing them in public. You can give face by using polite forms of address and observing local customs and traditions. It is also possible to save the other party's face by allowing him or her a graceful exit from a difficult negotiating position.

● *Verbal communication.* There is less reliance on written communication in China, and more emphasis on meeting face to face. Many Chinese consider it offensive to reply to a request with a 'no'. Thus, the negotiator might answer: 'That will require further study.'

● *Non-verbal communication.* China is a low-contact culture, with little touching. Body language is restrained, with small gestures. When meeting and greeting, a gentle handshake and moderate eye contact is normal.

● *The bargaining range.* Chinese negotiators often bargain. Be prepared for pressure tactics. Leave room for manoeuvre (a relatively high opening offer) and expect compromise to be the rule rather than the exception. The Chinese usually look for long-term relationships rather than a one-off outcome.

● *Role of the contract.* For the Chinese a contract is more an expression of intent and the final written agreement may be regarded as less important than the strength of the relationship with you and your company. The Chinese may expect to renegotiate the contract if circumstances change, and foreign negotiators often complain about Chinese attempts to revisit problems that have supposedly been settled.

● *Facilitation payments/inspection tours overseas.* In the 1990s western business people report demands for expensive gifts, special favours or under-the-table payments in China. Never assume that you will have to give a bribe. Instead an expenses-paid trip to your factory is a much better idea. Chinese businesspeople enjoy going overseas, but it may sometimes be difficult for them to obtain a visa.

● *Conflict management.* If a confrontational situation does arise, western businesspeople tend to look to a legal solution. But avoid the use of litigation to settle disputes. Rather than this appearing tough and in charge, there is a risk of jeopardizing both firm reputation and future business in China.

To companies considering dispatching expatriates to China, the following advice can be given (Johnson, 1996, p. 43):

● Send only those managers with a high stress threshold, the ability to listen and a pioneer spirit. 'In Europe, I spent about 25 per cent of my time listening; here it's more like 60 per cent.'

● Recognize that expatriates need frequent rest and recreation outside China – Bali, Hong Kong, Singapore – and put it in your budget.

● Expect that accommodation will be expensive and hard to find. A 100 square metre apartment in Shanghai costs about US$4,000 a month, and a family house costs about $10,000 a month (1996 prices).

● The expatriates should be able to speak Chinese or English – otherwise, it is impossible to do anything.

18.6 ▶ **Summary**

When marketing internationally, negotiation skills are needed. Negotiation skills and personal selling skills are related to each other. Personal selling typically occurs at the field sales force level and during formal negotiation processes. Cultural factors are critical to understanding the negotiation style of foreigners.

Prior to the negotiation process between two partners, there is a cultural distance between them. This cultural distance causes some transaction costs, which may be quite high. To reduce the cultural distance, training of the negotiators is required.

The culture shock felt by expatriates indicates that sending negotiators and sales-people to foreign markets is often difficult and complex to implement successfully. Five important areas of implementation include (1) making the initial decision to employ an expatriate sales force, (2) identifying and selecting qualified candidates, (3) providing adequate training, (4) maintaining ongoing support and (5) achieving satisfactory repatriation.

The ethical question of what is right or appropriate poses many dilemmas for international marketers. Bribery is an issue that is defined very differently from country to country. What is acceptable in one country may be completely unacceptable in another.

To be successful in Chinese negotiations you have to realize that guanxi (personal relationships) will continue to play an active role in the political, economic, social and cultural life of Chinese societies. Therefore, in dealing with the Chinese, a foreign businessperson requires a basic understanding of guanxi dynamics, even though he or she does not necessarily have to play by Chinese rules.

Case study ▌ **Ericsson, MCA and Hitachi**

Cross-cultural negotiations and communication

The themes in this chapter can be illustrated by three small cases:

Ericsson

The company Ericsson is a world-leading supplier of wired and mobile telecommunications. It has 100,000 employees in 140 countries.

Johan Ljungqvist, director of internal communications, explains: 'Our headquarters are in Stockholm. When we look at the diversity of cultures and languages within our company, we recognize that we can't fully understand the local cultures in Brazil or Chile, for example. So though English is our company language we rely on local communicators to convey a consistent message in the local culture and language.'

MCA

The English market analysis company, MCA, also agree that local language and face-to-face communication work best when trying to build understanding. Here are some of the comments of the client directors:

'I've run focus groups where people are having a discussion in English but it's not their native language. There are so many subtleties – phrases, jokes, repartee – that are lost. As a result, you don't build the same level of understanding or rapport.'

'Companies often use e-mail to make important announcements because of the speed. The visual cues that help people interpret a message are eliminated in e-mail, which is particularly important when the e-mail is not in the recipient's first language.'

'We are working hard to find ways of bringing people from different business unit teams and different geographic areas in Barlow together because it really builds a sense of being a part of one organization.'.

HSE

Hitachi Software Europe (HSE) is producing and selling application and business software for systems ranging from PCs to supercomputers.

Prior to a direct marketing campaign for an interactive white board in Japan the marketing director, Snowball, ran an initial test campaign for Japanese businesses in UK. The results were mixed. The initial response was overwhelming. Most businesses they targeted wrote back saying they were interested. However, when the HSE sales people contacted the Japanese businesses directly and met the Japanese managers face-to-face it turned out that they were interested but did not really want to buy the product. HSE realized that Japanese people are too polite to turn down a request.

Question

What are the managerial implications of the three cases?

Source: Adapted from Hecker, L. (2000) 'International marketers need to appreciate cultural differences', *Brand Strategy*, Features, 21 January.
Dixon, L. (1999) 'Aiming for a Snowball effect in Japan sales', *Precision Marketing*, 30 August.

Questions for discussion

1. Explain why the negotiation process abroad may differ from country to country.

2. You are a European preparing to negotiate with a Japanese firm for the first time. How would you prepare for the assignment if it is taking place (a) in the Japanese headquarters; (b) in one of its European subsidiaries?

3. Should expatriate personnel be used? What are some of the difficulties that they may encounter overseas? What can be done to minimize these problems?

4. Compare and contrast negotiating styles of Europeans and Asians. What are the similarities? What are the differences?

5. What are your views on lobbying efforts by foreign firms?

6. Why is it so difficult for an international marketer to deal with bribery?

Internet exercise

Warner Lambert – chewing gum

http://www.warner-lambert.com/

http://consumer.warner-lambert.com/

http://www.gum-mints.com/

Warner Lambert's chewing gum division is considering building a new chewing gum factory in China together with a Chinese partner.

Question

Which cross-cultural pitfalls are important for the Warner Lambert management to consider before the negotiations with the Chinese partner?

For further exercises and cases, see this book website at *www.booksites.net/hollensen*

References

Ayala, J. and Lai, R. (1996) 'China's consumer market: a huge opportunity to fail?', *The McKinsey Quarterly*, no. 3, pp. 56–71.

Björkman, I. and Kock, S. (1995) 'Social relationships and business networks: the case of western companies in China', *International Business Review*, vol. 4, no. 4, pp. 519–35.

Bush, V.B. and Ingram, T. (1996) 'Adapting to diverse customers: a training matrix for international marketers', *Industrial Marketing Management*, vol. 25, pp. 373–83.

Davies, H., Leung, T.K.P., Luk, S.T.K. and Wong, Y. (1995) 'The benefits of "guanxi" – the value of relationships in developing the Chinese market', *Industrial Marketing Management*, vol. 24, pp. 207–14.

Fan, Y. (1996) 'Cultural factors influencing the transfer of marketing know-how to China', paper presented at the conference on 'The Cultural Dimensions of Marketing', CDIM2, 27–31 May, Department of Marketing, Odense University, Denmark.

Gesteland, R.R. (1996) *Cross-cultural Business Behaviour*, Copenhagen Business School Press, Copenhagen.

Guy, B.S. and Patton, P.W.E. (1996) 'Managing the effects of culture shock and sojourner adjustment on the expatriate industrial sales force', *Industrial Marketing Management*, vol. 25, pp. 385–93.

Hofstede, G. (1983) 'The cultural relativity of organizational practices and theories', *Journal of International Business Studies*, Fall, pp. 75–89.

Johnson, M. (1996) 'China: the last true business frontier', *Management Review*, March, pp. 39–43.

Madsen, T.K. (1994) 'A contingency approach to export performance research', *Advances in International Marketing*, vol. 6, pp. 25–42. FAI Press Inc., Connecticut.

Redding, S.G. (1990) *The Spirit of Chinese Capitalism*, De Gruyter, Berlin.

Volander, M.M. (1997) 'Dansker i spidsen for Amerikansk Kina-eventyr', *Børsen* (Danish newspaper), 4 April.

19

Organization and control of the global marketing programme

After studying this chapter you should be able to do the following:

● Examine how firms build their organizational structure internationally and what roles headquarters can play.

● Identify the variables that affect the reorganization design.

● Describe and evaluate functional, geographic, product and matrix organizations as the key international structural alternatives.

● Describe the key elements of the marketing control system.

● List the most important measures for marketing performance.

● Explain how a global marketing budget is established.

19.1 Introduction

The overall objective of this chapter is to study intra-organizational relationships as part of the firm's attempt to optimize its competitive response in areas most critical to its business. As market conditions change, and companies evolve from purely domestic entities to multinationals, their organizational structure, coordination and control systems must also change.

First, this chapter will focus on the advantages and disadvantages of the main organizational structures available as well as their appropriateness at various stages of internationalization. Then the chapter will outline the need for a control system to oversee the international operations of the company.

19.2 | Organization of global marketing activities

The way in which a global marketing organization is structured is an important determinant of its ability to exploit effectively and efficiently the opportunities available to it. It also determines the capacity for responding to problems and challenges. Companies operating internationally must decide whether the organization should be structured along functions, products, geographical areas or combinations of the three (matrix). The evolutionary nature of organizational changes is shown in Figure 19.1. The following pages discuss the different organizational structures.

Functional structure

Of all the approaches, the functional structure (Figure 19.2) is the simplest. Here management is primarily concerned with the functional efficiency of the company.

Many companies begin their international business activities as a result of having received enquiries from abroad. The company, being new to international business, has no international specialist and typically has few products and few markets. In this early stage of international involvement, the domestic marketing department may have the responsibility for global marketing activities. But as the international involvement intensifies, an export department or international department may become part of the organizational structure. The export department may be a subdepartment of the sales and marketing department (as in Figure 19.2) or may

Figure 19.1   **Structural evolution of international operations**

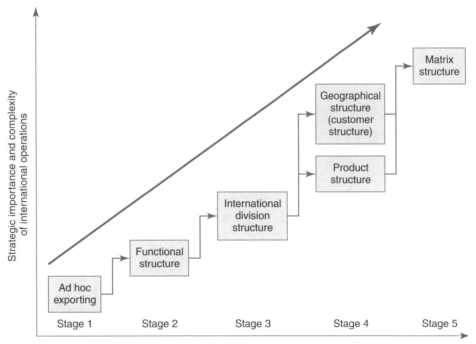

Figure 19.2 **Example of the functional structure**

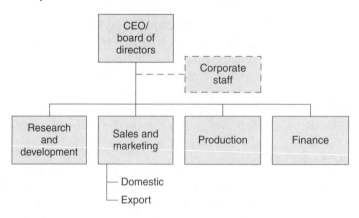

have equal ranking with the other functional departments. This choice will depend on the importance assigned to the export activities of the firm. Because the export department is the first real step in internationalizing the organizational structure, it should be a fully fledged marketing organization and not merely a sales organization. The functional export department design is particularly suitable for small and medium-sized firms, as well as larger companies, which are manufacturing standardized products and are in the early stages of developing international business, having low product and area diversities.

International divisional structure

As international sales grow, at some point an international division may emerge. This division becomes directly responsible for the development and implementation of the overall international strategy. The international division concentrates international expertise, information flows about foreign market opportunities, and authority over international activities. However, manufacturing and other related functions remain with the domestic divisions in order to take advantage of economies of scale.

International divisions best serve firms with new products that do not vary significantly in terms of their environmental sensitivity, and whose international sales and profits are still quite insignificant compared with those of the domestic divisions. Exhibit 19.1 shows how Bandai (Japan's leading toy manufacturer) got rid of the walls between its domestic and overseas divisions.

Exhibit 19.1 | **Bandai is breaking down the walls between domestic and overseas divisions**

Makoto Yamashina, president of Bandai (Japan's leading toy manufacturer), is preparing his company for the multimedia age and the single world toy market. 'The future is certain to see a single world market for toys,' Yamashina explains, 'and when that happens, we are going to have to do a complete 180 degree shift in values in order to survive. That is why – and I know this is going to sound odd – we scrapped our international division. We wanted to get rid of the walls between our domestic and overseas divisions, so we linked the two together. A separate international division places a filter between overseas markets and your employees, making it easier for your employees to think that, because they aren't in the international division, international operations are none of their concern.'

Bandai's international approach has already borne fruit. In September 1993, *Mighty Morphin Power Rangers*, an animated feature produced by Bandai, was aired by 140 television stations in the USA and received surprisingly good ratings. 1.6 million character dolls based on the movie were snatched up by US consumers as soon as they hit the market. As Yamashina says, a single world toy market is indeed emerging.

Bandai currently operates seven marketing companies throughout Europe and North America, and five manufacturing subsidiaries in Asia.

Source: Adapted from Katayama (1994). With kind permission from O. Katayama/*Look Japan*.

Product structure

A typical product division structure is presented in Figure 19.3.

In general, the product structure is more suitable for companies with more experience in international business and marketing, and with diversified product lines and extensive R & D activities. The product division structure is most appropriate under conditions where the products have potential for world-wide standardization. One of the major benefits of the approach is improved cost efficiency through centralization of manufacturing facilities for each product line. This is crucial in industries in which competitive position is determined by world market share,

Figure 19.3 **Example of the product structure**

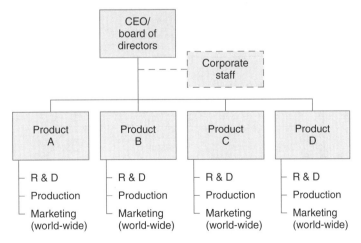

which in turn is often determined by the degree to which manufacturing is rationalized (utilization of economies of scale). The main disadvantages of this type of structure are as follows:

● It duplicates functional resources: you will find R & D, production, marketing, sales force management, etc. in each product division.

● It underutilizes sales and distribution facilities (subsidiaries) abroad.

● The product divisions tend to develop a total independence of each other in world markets. For example, a global product division structure may end up with several subsidiaries in the same foreign country reporting to different product divisions, with no one at headquarters responsible for the overall corporate presence in that country.

Geographical structure

If market conditions with respect to product acceptance and operating conditions vary considerably across world markets, then the geographical structure is the one to choose. This structure is especially useful for companies that have a homogeneous range of products (similar technologies and common end-use markets), but at the same time need fast and efficient world-wide distribution. Typically, the world is divided into regions (divisions), as shown in Figure 19.4.

Many food, beverage, car and pharmaceutical companies use this type of structure. Its main advantage is its ability to respond easily and quickly to the environmental and market demands of a regional or national area through minor modifications in product design, pricing, market communication and packaging. Therefore, the structure encourages adaptive global marketing programmes.

Figure 19.4   **Example of the geographical structure**

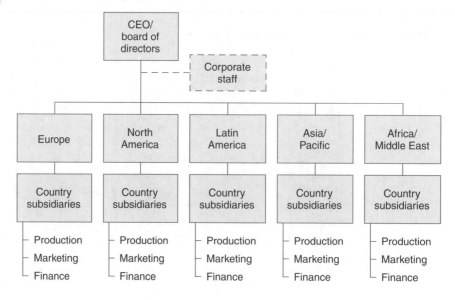

Moreover, economies of scale can be achieved within regions. Another reason for the popularity of this structure is its tendency to create area autonomy. However, this may also complicate the tasks of coordinating product variations and transferring new product ideas and marketing techniques from one country to another.

Hence, the geographical structure ensures the best use of the firm's regional expertise, but it means a less than optimal allocation of product and functional expertise. If each region needs its own staff of product and functional specialists, duplication and also inefficiency may be the result. As indicated in Figure 19.4, the geographical structure may include both regional management centres (Europe, North America, etc.) and country-based subsidiaries.

Regional management centres

There are two main reasons for the existence of regional management centres (RMCs):

● When sales volume in a particular region becomes substantial, there need to be some specialized staff to focus on that region, to realize more fully the potential of an already growing market.

● Homogeneity within regions and heterogeneity between them necessitate treating each important region separately. Therefore a regional management centre becomes an appropriate organizational feature.

Country-based subsidiaries

Instead of or parallel to a regional centre, each country has its own organizational unit. Country-based subsidiaries are characterized by a high degree of adaptation to local conditions. Since each subsidiary develops its own unique activities and its own autonomy, it is sometimes relevant to combine local subsidiaries with an RMC: for example, to utilize opportunities across European countries.

Firms may also organize their operations using a customer structure, especially if the customer groups they serve are very different: for example, businesses and governments. Catering to these diverse groups may require the concentration of specialists in particular divisions. The product may be the same, but the buying processes of the various customer groups may differ. Governmental buying is characterized by bidding, in which price plays a larger role than when businesses are the buyers. Much of what has been said about the geographical structure also applies to the customer structure.

Matrix structure

The product structure tends to offer better opportunities to rationalize production across countries, thus gaining production cost-efficiencies. On the other hand, the geographical structure is more responsive to local market trends and needs, and allows for more coordination in a whole region.

Some global companies need both capabilities, so they have adopted a more complex structure: the matrix structure. The international matrix structure consists of two organizational structures intersecting with each other. As a consequence, there are dual reporting relationships. These two structures can be a combination of the general forms already discussed. For example, the matrix structure might consist of product divisions intersecting with functional departments, or geographical areas intersecting with global divisions. The two intersecting structures will largely be a function of what the organization sees as the two dominant aspects of its environment.

The typical international matrix structure is the two-dimensional structure that emphasizes product and geography (Figure 19.5). Generally, each product division has world-wide responsibilities for its own business, and each geographical or area division is responsible for the foreign operations in its region. If national organizations (subsidiaries) are involved, they are responsible for operations at the country level.

Because the two dimensions of product and geography overlap at the affiliate level, both enter into local decision-making and planning processes. It is assumed that area and product managers will defend different positions. This will lead to tensions and 'creative' conflict. Area managers will tend to favour responsiveness to local environmental factors, and product managers will defend positions favouring cost-efficiencies and global competitiveness. The matrix structure deliberately creates a dual focus to ensure that conflicts between product and geographical area concerns are identified and then analyzed objectively.

The structure is useful for companies that are both product diversified and geographically spread. By combining a product management approach with a market-oriented approach, one can meet the needs both of markets and of products.

Figure 19.5   **Example of a matrix structure**

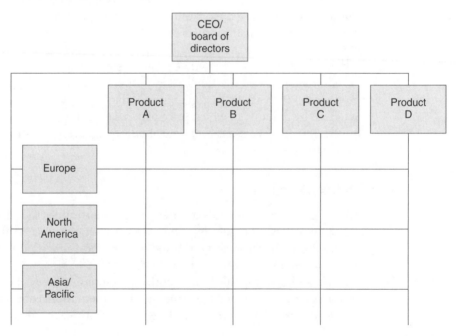

| Exhibit 19.2 | **Unilever and its global marketing of Magnum** |

Unilever describes itself as a 'multi-local multinational' company, not a 'global' company. It tries to think globally and act locally, because it does not attempt to enter all markets with the same product. Half of Unilever's business is in food, where it is essential to take a local view. Only a few products, like ice-cream, can be marketed successfully across borders. Similarly, the formulation of detergents varies from region to region because washing habits, machines, clothes and water quality are all different. Thus, the Unilever portfolio includes a balanced mix of local, regional and international brands, which take account of the differences as well as the similarities in consumer needs.

At Unilever the major product groups are responsible for profits. As the profits are generated in cooperation with the different regions and the national subsidiaries, the international organizational structure can be described as a form of matrix structure. The following describes the organization of the global marketing strategy for one of Unilever's global products: Magnum.

The rise of a global brand: the role of the international product manager

Magnum was an immediate success when it was launched in Germany, the Netherlands, Belgium, Denmark, Sweden and Switzerland in 1989. The 'Me and my Magnum' campaign was created in 1991–2.

In 1993 the position of international brand manager for Magnum was created. 'As ice-cream is basically an emotion-led category, it is clear that the basic approach and motivation are similar across many borders,' says Chris Pomfre, senior marketing member of the Ice Cream Group. 'Taking an international approach thus offered a means of implementing best practice and enjoying economies of scale. So we agreed to appoint four international brand managers for the four core ice-cream brands, Cornetto, Carte d'Or, Viennetta and, of course, Magnum. In each case, the specific role was to aid the development of what was now a global brand.'

Under the auspices of the Ice Cream Group, Jean Callanan (international product manager of Magnum) is responsible for driving the strategic development of Magnum and managing the whole of its advertising and product development. She is very much the Magnum expert. Though she is actually based at Langnese-Iglo, her clear responsibility is Magnum globally, not Magnum in Germany. Since taking up her position, her priority has been to reinforce the brand's global position. She has taken the following steps:

● Establishing a global newsletter to ensure fast spread of best practice around the world and to encourage local creativity.

● Convening a global brand managers' conference in Hamburg – the first ever such event for a Unilever food brand.

● Appointing an international public relations agency for Magnum (Shandwick) – the first time ever for an international ice-cream brand in Unilever.

'We want to use PR not on an ad hoc basis but as an important management tool. Magnum has got enormous potential and exploiting this depends on increasing its

▶

penetration of the adult population. PR is a tool to help us achieve this,' says Jean Callanan. She also works to maintain or improve the degree of harmonization of the brand around the world, a major factor underpinning its success to date. The Magnum name travels remarkably well. Out of the 38 countries in which it has been marketed so far, in only two of them, Greece and Chile, can it not be used (for trade mark reasons).

Sources: Shelly (1995); Unilever (1996).

The future role of the international manager

At the end of the 1980s many internationally oriented companies adopted the transnational model (Bartlett and Ghoshal, 1989). It held that companies should leverage their capabilities across borders and transfer best practices to achieve global economies and respond to the local market. In this way, companies avoided duplicating their functions (product development, manufacturing and marketing). However, it required that senior managers could think, operate and communicate along three dimensions: function, product and geography. Surely there are few such 'super-managers' around!

In a study by Quelch (1992), one manager says of changing managerial roles: 'I am at the fulcrum of the tension between local adaptation and global standardization. My boss tells me to think global and act local. That's easier said than done' (p. 158).

There is no universal solution to the ideal profile for an international manager, but Quelch and Bloom (1996) have predicted the 'fall of the transnational manager and the return of the country manager'. They studied behaviour of country managers in different countries and concluded that the opportunities in expanding emerging markets (e.g. eastern Europe) have to be grasped by entrepreneurial country managers. The transnational manager is better suited to stable and saturated markets, such as western Europe, with its progress towards a single market.

19.3 | Controlling the global marketing programme

The final, but often neglected, stage of international market planning is the control process. Not only is control important to evaluate how we have performed, but it completes the circle of planning by providing the feedback necessary for the start of the next planning cycle. Unfortunately, however, 'control' is often viewed by the people of an organization as being negative. If individuals fear that the control process will be used not only to judge their performance, but as a basis for punishing them, then it will be feared and reviled.

The evaluation and control of global marketing probably represents one of the weakest areas of marketing practice in many companies. Even the organizations that are otherwise strong in their strategic marketing planning have poor control and evaluation procedures for their global marketing. There are a number of possible reasons for this. First of all, there is no such thing as a 'standard' system of control for marketing.

The function of the organizational structure is to provide a framework in which objectives can be met. However, a set of instruments and processes is needed to influence the behaviour and performance of organization members to meet the goals. The critical issue is the same as with organizational structures: what is the ideal amount of control? On the one hand, headquarters needs information to ensure that international activities contribute maximum benefit to the overall organization. On the other hand, controls should not be construed as a code of law.

The key question is to determine how to establish a control mechanism capable of early interception of emerging problems. Considered here are various criteria appropriate for the evaluation process, control styles, feedback and corrective action. These concepts are important for all businesses, but in the international arena they are vital.

Design of a control system

In designing a control system, management must consider the costs of establishing and maintaining it and trade them off against the benefits to be gained. Any control system will require investment in a management structure and in systems designs.

The design of the control system can be divided into two groups dependent on the object of control:

● Output control (typically based on financial measures).
● Behavioural controls (typically based on non-financial measures).

Output control may consist of expenditure control, which involves regular monitoring of expenditure figures, comparison of these with budget targets, and taking decisions to cut or increase expenditure where any variance is believed to be harmful. Measures of output are accumulated at regular intervals and typically forwarded from the foreign subsidiary to headquarters, where they are evaluated and criticized based on comparison to the plan or budget.

Behavioural controls require the exercise of influence over behaviour. This influence can be achieved, for example, by providing sales manuals to subsidiary personnel or by fitting new employees into the corporate culture. Behavioural controls often require an extensive socialization process, and informal, personal interaction is central to the process. Substantial resources must be spent to train the individual to share the corporate culture: that is, 'the way things are done at the company'.

To build common vision and values, managers at the Japanese company Matsushita spend a substantial amount of their first months in what the company calls 'cultural and spiritual training'. They study the company credo, the 'Seven Spirits of Matsushita', and the philosophy of the founder, Kanosuke Matsushita.

However, there remains a strong tradition of using output (financial) criteria. A fixation with output criteria leads companies to ignore the less tangible behavioural (non-financial) measures, although these are the real drivers of corporate success. However, there is a weakness in the behavioural performance measures. To date there has been little success in developing explicit links from behaviour to output criteria. Furthermore, companies and managers are still judged on financial criteria (profit contribution). Until a clear link is established, it is likely that behavioural criteria will continue to be treated with a degree of scepticism.

We will now develop a global marketing control system based primarily on output controls. Marketing control is an essential element of the marketing planning process because it provides a review of how well marketing objectives have been achieved. A framework for controlling marketing activities is given in Figure 19.6.

The marketing control system begins with the company setting some marketing activities in motion (plans for implementation). This may be the result of certain objectives and strategies, each of which must be achieved within a given budget. Hence budgetary control is essential.

The next step in the control process is to establish specific performance standards which will need to be achieved for each area of activity if overall and sub-objectives are to be achieved. For example, in order to achieve a specified sales objective, a specific target of performance for each sales area may be required. In turn, this may require a specific standard of performance from each of the salespeople in the region with respect to, for example, number of calls, conversion rates and, of course, order value. Table 19.1 provides a representative sample of the types of data required. Marketing performance measures and standards will vary by company and product according to the goals and objectives delineated in the marketing plan.

Figure 19.6 **The marketing control system**

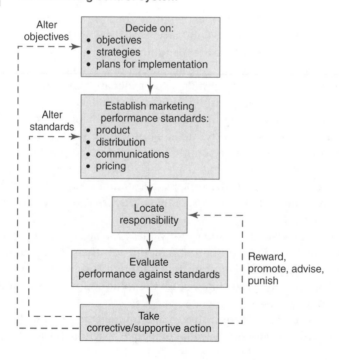

Table 19.1   **Measures of marketing performance**

Product
Sales by market segments
New product introductions each year
Sales relative to potential
Sales growth rates
Market share
Contribution margin
Product defects
Warranty expense
Percentage of total profits
Return on investment

Pricing
Response time to price changes of competitors
Price relative to competitor
Price changes relative to sales volume
Discount structure relative to sales volume
Bid strategy relative to new contacts
Margin structure relative to marketing expenses
Margins relative to channel member performance

Distribution
Sales, expenses and contribution margin by channel type
Percentage of stores carrying the product
Sales relative to market potential by channel, intermediary type and specific intermediaries
Percentage of on-time delivery
Expense-to-sales ratio by channel, etc.
Order cycle performance by channel, etc.
Logistics cost by logistics activity by channel

Communication
Advertising effectiveness by type of media (e.g. awareness levels)
Actual audience/target audience ratio
Cost per contact
Number of calls, enquiries and information requests by type of media
Sales per sales call
Sales per territory relative to potential
Selling expenses to sales ratio
New accounts per time period
Lost accounts per time period

Source: Adapted from Jobber (1995).

The next step is to locate responsibility. In some cases responsibility ultimately falls on one person (e.g. the brand manager); in others it is shared (e.g. the sales manager and sales force). It is important to consider this issue, since corrective or supportive action may need to focus on those responsible for the success of marketing activity.

In order to be successful, the people involved and affected by the control process should be consulted in both the design and implementation stages of marketing control. Above all, they will need to be convinced that the purpose of control is to improve their own levels of success and that of the company. Subordinates need to be involved in setting and agreeing their own standards of performance, preferably through a system of management by objectives.

Performance is then evaluated against these standards, which relies on an efficient information system. A judgement has to be made about the degree of success and failure achieved and what corrective or supportive action is to be taken. This can take various forms:

- Failure which is attributed to the poor performance of individuals may result in the giving of advice regarding future attitudes and actions, training and/or punishment (e.g. criticism, lower pay, demotion, termination of employment). Success, on the other hand, should be rewarded with praise, promotion and/or higher pay.

- Failure which is attributed to unrealistic marketing objectives and performance may cause management to lower objectives or lower marketing standards (Figure 19.6). Success which is thought to reflect unambitious objectives and standards may cause them to be raised in the next period.

Many firms assume that corrective action needs to be taken only when results are less than those required or when budgets and costs are being exceeded. In fact, both 'negative' (underachievement) and 'positive' (overachievement) deviations may require corrective action. For example, failure to spend the amount budgeted for, say, sales force expenses may indicate that the initial sum allocated was excessive and needs to be reassessed, and/or that the sales force is not as 'active' as it might be.

It is also necessary to determine such things as the frequency of measurement (e.g. daily, weekly, monthly or annually). More frequent and more detailed measurement usually means more cost. We need to be careful to ensure that the costs of measurement and the control process itself do not exceed the value of such measurements and do not overly interfere with the activities of those being measured.

The impact of the environment must also be taken into account when designing a control system:

- The control system should measure only dimensions over which the organization has control. Rewards or sanctions make little sense if they are based on dimensions that may be relevant for overall corporate performance, but over which no influence can be exerted (e.g. price controls). Neglecting the factor of individual performance capability would send the wrong signals and severely impair the motivation of personnel.

- Control systems should harmonize with local regulations and customs. In some cases, however, corporate behavioural controls have to be exercised against local customs even though overall operations may be affected negatively. This type of situation occurs, for example, when a subsidiary operates in markets where unauthorized facilitating payments are a common business practice.

Feedforward control

Much of the information provided by the firm's marketing control system is feedback on what has been accomplished in both financial (profits) and non-financial

Figure 19.7 **Adjustment of global marketing strategy**

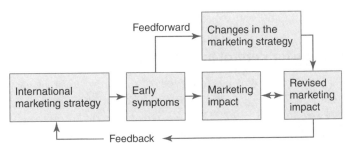

(Source: Samli *et al.*, 1993, p. 425)

(customer satisfaction, market share) terms. As such, the control process is remedial in its outlook. It can be argued that control systems should be forward looking and preventative, and that the control process should start at the same time as the planning process. Such a form of control is feedforward control (Figure 19.7).

Feedforward control would continuously evaluate plans, monitoring the environment to detect changes that would call for revising objectives and strategies. Feedforward control monitors variables other than performance; variables that may change before performance itself changes. The result is that deviations can be controlled before their full impact has been felt. Such a system is proactive in that it anticipates environmental change, whereas after-the-fact and steering control systems are more reactive in that they deal with changes after they occur. Examples of early symptoms (early performance indicators) are presented in Table 19.2.

Feedforward control focuses on information that is prognostic: it tries to discover problems waiting to occur. Formal processes of feedforward control can be

Table 19.2 **Some key early performance indicators**

Early performance indicators	Market implication
Sudden drop in quantities demanded	Problem in marketing strategy or its implementation
Sharp decrease or increase in sales volume	Product gaining acceptance or being rejected quickly
Customer complaints	Product not debugged properly
A notable decrease in competitors' business	Product gaining acceptance quickly or market conditions deteriorating
Large volumes of returned merchandise	Problems in basic product design
Excessive requests for parts or reported repairs	Problems in basic product design, low standards
Sudden changes in fashions or styles	Product (or competitors' product) causing a deep impact on the consumers' lifestyles

Source: Samli *et al.* (1993), p. 421.

incorporated into the business marketer's total control programme to enhance its effectiveness considerably. Utilization of a feedforward approach would help ensure that planning and control are treated as concurrent activities.

Key areas for control in marketing

Kotler (1997) distinguishes four types of marketing control, each involving different approaches, different purposes and a different allocation of responsibilities. These are shown in Table 19.3. Here we will focus on annual plan control and profit control, since they are the most obvious areas of concern to firms with limited resources (e.g. SMEs).

Annual plan control

The purpose of annual plan control is to determine the extent to which marketing efforts over the year have been successful. This control will centre on measuring and evaluating sales in relation to sales goals, market share analysis and expense analysis.

Sales performance is a key element in the annual plan control. Sales control consists of a hierarchy of standards on different organizational control levels. These are interlinked, as shown in Figure 19.8.

We can see from the diagram that any variances in achieving sales targets at the corporate level are the result of variances in the performance of individual salespeople at the operational level. At every level of sales control, variances must be studied with a view to determining their causes. In general, variances may be due to a combination of variances in volume and/or price.

| Table 19.3 | Types of marketing control | | | |

Type of control	Prime responsibility	Purpose of control	Examples of techniques/approaches
Strategic control	Top management Middle management	To examine if planned results are being achieved	Marketing effectiveness ratings Marketing audit
Efficiency control	Line and staff management Marketing controller	To examine ways of improving the efficiency of marketing	Sales force efficiency Advertising efficiency Distribution efficiency
Annual plan control	Top management Middle management	To examine if planned results are being achieved	Sales analysis Market share analysis Marketing expenses to sales ratio Customer tracking
Profit control (budget control)	Marketing controller	To examine where the company is making and losing money	Profitability by e.g. product, customer group or trade channel

Source: Adapted from Kotler (1997).

Figure 19.8   **The hierarchy of sales and control**

Organizational level		
	Strategic (corporate)	Divisional/SBU/geographical area sales targets
		Product-line sales targets
	Tactical	Geographical area/country sales targets
		Individual product/brand sales targets
	Operational	Sales targets by country, e.g. • customer group/individual customer • distribution channel • sales territory/sales manager • individual salesperson

Table 19.4   **An example of an international marketing budget for a manufacturer exporting consumer goods**

International marketing budget	Europe						America		Asia/Pacific				Other markets		Total world Σ	
	UK		Germany		France		USA		Japan		Korea					
Year = ____	B	A	B	A	B	A	B	A	B	A	B	A	B	A	B	A
Net sales (gross sales less trade discounts, allowances, etc.)																
÷ **Variable costs**																
= **Contribution 1**																
÷ **Marketing costs:**																
Sales costs (salaries, commissions for agents, incentives, travelling, training, conferences)																
Consumer marketing costs (TV commercials, radio, print, sales promotion)																
Trade marketing costs (fairs, exhibitions, in-store promotions, contributions for retailer campaigns)																
= **Σ Total contribution 2** (marketing contribution)																

B = budget figures; A = actual.
Note: On a short-term (one-year) basis, the export managers or country managers are responsible for maximizing the actual figures for each country and minimizing their deviation from budget figures. The international marketing manager/director is responsible for maximizing the actual figure for the total world and minimizing its deviation from the budget figure. Cooperation is required between the country managers and the international marketing manager/director to coordinate and allocate the total marketing resources in an optimum way. Sometimes certain inventory costs and product development costs may also be included in the total marketing budget (see main text)

Profit control

In addition to the previously discussed control elements, all international marketers must be concerned to control their profit. The budgetary period is normally one year because budgets are tied to the accounting systems of the company.

Table 19.4 presents an example of a global marketing budget for a manufacturer of consumer goods. Included in the budget are those marketing variables which can be controlled and changed by the sales and marketing functions (departments) in the home country and in the export market. In Table 19.4 the only variable that cannot be controlled by the international sales and marketing departments is variable costs.

The global marketing budget system (as presented in Table 19.4) is used for the following (main) purposes:

● Allocation of marketing resources among countries/markets to maximize profits. In Table 19.4 it is the responsibility of the global marketing director to maximize the total contribution 2 for the whole world.

● Evaluation of country/market performance. In Table 19.4 it is the responsibility of export managers or country managers to maximize contribution 2 for each of their countries.

Please note that besides the marketing variables presented in Table 19.4, the global marketing budget normally contains inventory costs for finished goods. As the production sizes of these goods are normally based on input from the sales and marketing department, the inventory of unsold goods will also be the responsibility of the international marketing manager or director.

Furthermore, the global marketing budget may also contain customer-specific or country-specific product development costs, if certain new products are preconditions for selling in certain markets.

In contrast to budgets, long-range plans extend over periods from two years up to ten years, and their content is more qualitative and judgemental in nature than that of budgets. For SMEs shorter periods (such as two years) are the norm because of the perceived uncertainty of diverse foreign environments.

19.4 Summary

Implementation of a global marketing programme requires an appropriate organizational structure. As the scope of a firm's global marketing strategy changes, its organizational structure must be adequately modified in accordance with its tasks and technology and the external environment. Five ways of structuring an international organization have been presented: functional structure, international divisional structure, product structure, geographical structure (customer structure) and matrix structure. The choice of organizational structure is affected by such factors as the degree of internationalization of the firm, the strategic importance of the firm's international operations, the complexity of its international business and the availability of qualified managers.

Control is the process of ensuring that global marketing activities are carried out as intended. It involves monitoring aspects of performance and taking corrective action where necessary. The global marketing control system consists of deciding marketing objectives, setting performance standards, locating responsibility, evaluating performance against standards, and taking corrective or supportive action.

In an after-the-fact control system, managers wait until the end of the planning period to take corrective action. In a feedforward control system, corrective action is taken during the planning period by tracking early performance indicators and steering the organization back to desired objectives if it goes out of control.

The most obvious areas of control relate to the control of the annual marketing plan and the control of profitability. The purpose of the global marketing budget is mainly to allocate marketing resources across countries to maximize world-wide total marketing contribution.

Case study   Mars Inc.

Merger of the European food, petcare and confectionery divisions

Mars Inc. is a diversified multifunctional company whose primary products include foods, petcare, confectionery, electronics, and drinks. Owned and controlled by the Mars family, this US giant is one of the world's biggest private companies, but also one of the most secretive.

Mars' decision in January 2000 to merge its food, petcare and confectionery divisions across Europe – and eventually with headquarters in the UK – has split the marketing industry.

The most well-known brands within the three divisions are:

● Foods: Uncle Ben's Rice, Uncle Ben's sauces

● Petcare: Whiskas, Pedigree

● Confectionery: M&Ms, Snickers, Milky Way, Mars Bar

Mars UK says the decision to pool the businesses was taken to strike at the company's international competitors in food and confectionery, such as Nestlé and Unilever. The move also coincides with plans to create a single European market and highlights the company's belief that its consumers' needs are the same across the Continent.

But the combination of food and confectionery with petcare is not clear to all industry observers. One industry analyst made the comment: 'Generally speaking, Mars is doing the right thing by merging divisions to squeeze profits out of them. Before the advent of the Euro it was acceptable to run separate companies in different European countries but not any more.'

Another analyst had this opinion: 'I can't imagine it marketing all three sides of the business together. They're too different.'

'The only visible benefit appears to be an improvement in distribution. Tastes across European markets are very different, whether you're selling products for animals or people.'

'It's all very well Mars saying it will tackle competitors such as Nestlé and Unilever, but they are only rivals in food and confectionery.'

'If Mars starts laying down too many controls by merging all its businesses – and therefore also its marketing and management strategies – it may streamline communications, but could lose the creativity available in different regions.'

Questions

1. Discuss the two views of organizing Mars' European activities.
2. Did Mars Inc. do the right thing in your opinion?

Source: McCawley, I. (2000) 'Can Mars bridge gaps in merger?', *Marketing Week*, News Analysis, 13 January.

Questions for discussion

1. This chapter suggests that the development of a firm's international organization can be divided into different stages. Identify these stages and discuss their relationship to the international competitiveness of the firm.

2. Identify appropriate organizational structures for managing international product development. Discuss key features of the structure(s) suggested.

3. What key internal/external factors influence the organizational structure? Can you think of additional factors? Explain.

4. Discuss the pros and cons of standardizing the marketing management process. Is a standardized process of more benefit to the company pursuing a national market strategy or a global market strategy?

5. Discuss to what degree the choice of organizational structure is essentially a choice between headquarters centralization and local autonomy.

6. Discuss how the international organization of a firm may affect its planning process.

7. Discuss why firms need global marketing controls.

8. What is meant by performance indicators? What are they? Why does a firm need them?

9. Performance reviews of subsidiary managers and personnel are required rarely, if at all, by headquarters. Why?

10. Identify the major weaknesses inherent in the international division structure.

11. Discuss the benefits gained by adopting a matrix organizational structure.

Internet exercise

Novartis: Knowledge management and global marketing

Please go to:

http://www.cio.com/archive/enterprise/031599_nova.html

www.novartis.com

Novartis is the result of the merger in 1996 of two venerable Basel-based companies, Sandoz and Ciba-Geigy.

Questions

1. How can Novartis use the concept of knowledge management in its global company?

2. How are 'knowledge management' and 'global marketing' connected?

For further exercises and cases, see this book's website at *www.booksites.net/hollensen*

References

Bartlett, C. and Ghoshal, S. (1989) *Managing Across Borders: The transnational solution*, Harvard University Press, Boston, MA.

Jobber, D. (1995) *Principles and Practice of Marketing*, McGraw-Hill, New York.

Katayama, O. (1994) 'Not toying around', *Look Japan*, November, pp. 22–3.

Kotler, P. (1997) *Marketing Management: Analysis, planning, implementation and control* (9th edn), Prentice Hall, Englewood Cliffs, NJ.

Quelch, J.A. (1992) 'The new country managers', *The McKinsey Quarterly*, no. 4, pp. 155–65.

Quelch, J.A. and Bloom, H. (1996) 'The return of the country manager', *The McKinsey Quarterly*, no. 2, pp. 30–43.

Samli, A.C., Still, R. and Hill, J.S. (1993) *International Marketing: Planning and practice*, Macmillan, London.

Shelly, B. (1995) 'Cool customer', *Unilever Magazine*, no. 2, pp. 12–17.

Unilever (1996) *Introducing Unilever*.

Case V.1 Implementation of international advertising strategies – Martini versus Eurocard

Part A: The 'Martini Man' campaign[1]

Until the launch of the 'Martini Man' campaign, the brand was in terminal decline. It was consumed less frequently, its franchise was ageing and it was failing to attract new drinkers.

Martini Man – the sexy, stylish personification of the brand – changed all that.

Creative strategy

The long-running campaign captures the spirit of the Riviera in the 1960s, but brings it bang up to date. It's a world inhabited by the rich and the beautiful – Jean Paul Belmondo, Bardot and Grace Kelly. A time when men were men and women were blonde and everyone sipped Martinis, it is the Vita Martini – the Martini Life – personified by the 'Martini Man'.

He is the ambassador of the brand; he is cool and slightly dangerous. He is a catalyst for drama and intrigue – a babe magnet. He is the sort of man other men want to be and women fall in love with.

From the outset, the black and white cinema and TV campaign was episodic, touring the glamorous locations of the Mediterranean (see Plate 21). Where one spot ended another began. We follow the 'Martini Man' from adventure to adventure, from one beautiful woman to another. It has the feel of Sean Connery's 'James Bond' or the cult TV classic, 'The Saint'.

'Martini Man' steals a beautiful woman from an ageing tycoon; in another a gorgeous female assassin hired by the tycoon pursues him. Of course, 'Martini Man' foils his plans and the momentum is sustained by all seven ads in the series. The advertising message is consciously provocative – a married woman swallows her wedding ring to be with 'Martini Man', another chooses to lose her dress and bare all.

[1]The advertising agency for this case is Universal McCann Worldwide (henceforth called McCann). The campaign achieved the M&M Award in 1999 for 'Best integrated campaign'. I would like to thank Universal McCann Worldwide, London for the advertising material they have provided.

Media strategy

Since the start of the campaign the world of Martini was brought to life via television and cinema, and has been as creative in the use of media as in the ads themselves. So the launch of a new 'Martini Man' ad is like the launch of a blockbuster movie. When a new version is to be shown for the first time, first of all the audience is teased with short intriguing spots so that it knows a new Martini ad is on the way. Then the advertising agency 'road blocks' entire time slots across all TV stations to ensure maximum reach and to build the fame of the campaign. McCann also advertised the launch of new ads in TV listing magazines and ran a 15-minute 'making of' programme in Greece that covered the shoot and interviews with the stars.

Cinema

Cinema was invented for the 'Martini Man' campaign!

The Martini 'mini films' are placed amid trailers of relevant films (i.e. James Bond). Posters are placed in the cinema foyer to announce the forthcoming 'Martini Man' film and Martini cocktails are served to the audience at movie premieres after the movie showing.

Press

Press is used to create a buzz around the new 'Martini Man' films and to expand the audience's knowledge of the context, the dramas and the 'stars'.

Selected lifestyle magazines and leading newspapers are given exclusive interviews with the 'Martini Man' in the form of advertorials.

Outdoors

Martini was originally advertised on posters in the 1960s, so posters have been placed in areas with a high concentration of hotels, restaurants, cafes and clubs.

The advertising people also used 'Martini Man' himself in silhouette on bus shelters and painted buses, and laser-projected on to prominent buildings. Finally, last year McCann took him up, up and away – painted on to a full-sized Spanish Air Europa jet.

Local activities

To meet the needs of local markets and to make Martini appear vibrant at all levels, a number of different promotional and PR solutions have run.

- Spain: To increase the number of young men drinking Martini, a radio campaign runs on Thursday and Saturday evenings when they are getting ready to go out. It highlights 'Martini Man's' attractiveness to women.

- Denmark: The product was not being served cold so ads on magazines are 'cool sensitive' – the logo is only revealed when it is cold enough.

- Italy: To stop over-45-year-olds switching to supermarket own-label Vermouth, promotional packs have been introduced offering free videos of Fellini's film 'La dolce vita'.

- Across all markets: postcards and posters are given away, and 'Martini Man' sunglasses, watches and T-shirts have been used promotionally. In clubs the advertising agency runs cocktail competitions and asks consumers to dress as characters from the ads. 'Martini Man' also makes highly selective personal appearances at events in key markets – in Greece it is headline news.

Launch of 'Pop-Art'

To ensure high PR coverage in Spain, Greece and Portugal the advertising agency launched the campaign by literally bringing the ad to life, inviting journalists to a glitzy art gallery. In Portugal, it was held at the Lisbon Expo, and the event stopped traffic. 'Martini Man' was mobbed – and became a live news item!

Campaign results

The campaign was launched in 1995. In 1996, after 14 years of declining sales, Martini sales increased by 500,000 cases in Europe, over one per cent. The only variable was the advertising.

This growth has continued. In 1998 the European sales of Martini were up in 10 of the 15 major markets in Europe. Total European sales are up by 4 per cent; in Greece by 38 per cent; in Portugal by 17 per cent.

Over one million postcards, 50,000 posters and 40,000 sunglasses have been bought as desirable 'collectables' by the 18–30s in Europe. In Spain, 700,000 copies of the CD were sold in three months, reaching no. 5 in the charts. The campaign and the 'Martini Man' are spoofed on comedy shows, and qualitative research notes that the gesture with the lips is being copied at street level.

The campaign launch in Greece generated €114,200 worth of free media publicity and in Portugal, following the re-creation of the ad, 63 per cent of 18–24s across the country knew of the event.

Source: Adapted from the case presentation for the M&M Awards.

Part B: The Global Eurocard/Mastercard 'Priceless' campaign[1]

Background

In the autumn of 1997 McCann-Erickson New York introduced a new advertising campaign on behalf

[1] The advertising agency for this case is Universal McCann Worldwide (henceforth called McCann). The campaign achieved the M&M Award in 2000 for 'Best Campaign in the Financial Services/Consulting Sector'. The author would like to thank Universal McCann Worldwide, London for the advertising material they have provided.

of MasterCard International. The campaign, entitled 'Priceless' (see Plate 22) was launched initially into North America and then into certain Australasian and South American markets.

The campaign registered a strong and instant impact, differentiating MasterCard powerfully not only from key competition (Visa and American Express) but also from its own former image.

During 1998/1999 the process was embarked

upon to introduce 'Priceless' advertising for Eurocard/MasterCard into Europe. The following countries are now running McCann-Erickson-generated advertising for Eurocard/MasterCard:

Germany	Autumn 1998
Switzerland	Spring 1999
Iceland	Spring 1999
Ireland	Summer 1999
Greece	Summer 1999
France	Summer 1999
UK	Autumn 1999
Italy	December 1999
Norway	January 2000
Israel	May 2000
Portugal	May 2000
Czech Republic	May 2000
Hungary	May 2000
Turkey	June 2000
Belgium	June 2000
The Netherlands	June 2000

The European scenario

Whereas success for the campaign had been registered in the homogeneous US market, the marketing scenario in Europe is vastly different. A consortium – Europay International – represents and manages the interests of all European banks that issue Eurocard/MasterCard. Europay International acts as the franchisee for the MasterCard brand in Europe.

All the European countries differ in terms of the relative strengths of Eurocard/MasterCard and its major competitors' card brands, but there is also a very vibrant European debit card sector and cash and cheques are still in frequent use.

Objectives of Eurocard/MasterCard

In every market, the objective was to build brand awareness and saliency improvements, leading to increases in both issuance and frequency and value of usage.

To do this, it was clear that the ad agency (McCann) would have to 'think global, act local'.

Creative strategy and consumer insights

The key element of the creative strategy was to reach a group of individuals in each country who are termed as *Good Revolvers* – people who use their credit cards intelligently and responsibly, using them to achieve good things in their lives for their families, their friends and themselves.

The insight gained was that this *conceptual target* consists of people who wish to lead rich lives, not merely rich lifestyles. They make the same purchases and expend similar amounts of money as Visa or American Express users – but they have a different rationale. More family oriented, less hedonistic. More in line with current values of personal balance and harmony, rather than the materialistic values which applied previously – to one degree or another – across the major West European markets.

Brand footprint

McCann-Erickson uses a strategic tool called Brand Footprint to express the equity and personality of a brand. With data gathered from both qualitative and quantitative research the advertising agency determines the key values of a brand and then translates these values into the dominant desired personality traits.

As a basis for this strategy it was clear that there would have to be a move from working with an under-performing and unsatisfactory *current* Brand Footprint to supporting a *desired* Brand Footprint, which is much more compelling. If communicated correctly this would turn this emotionally neutral brand into a brand that the target audience would 'feel good about using', because it was able to fulfil both their functional and emotional needs.

The *current* Brand Footprint was defined as:

● Eurocard/MasterCard means Everyday, Ordinary, Generic

● Eurocard/MasterCard is Unassuming, Unpretentious, Practical

The *desired* Brand Footprint for European markets was then established as:

● Eurocard/MasterCard means:
  – Everything that matters
  – Real life
  – The best way to pay

● Eurocard/MasterCard is:
  – In touch
  – Genuine
  – Purposeful

The communications concept

The *selling idea* is distilled as:

Eurocard/MasterCard: the best way to pay for everything that matters.

The *creative expression* becomes:

There are some things money can't buy – for everything else there's Eurocard/MasterCard.

The *creative execution* is as follows. The TV commercials have a consistent format – a series of purchases are shown and the actual prices indicated in local or appropriate international currency. An emotionally based moment is described which by inference is even more valuable than anything that money can buy:

'Making him a promise and keeping it: Priceless'
'Passing secret recipes from one generation to another: Priceless'
'The ability to surprise (your partner) again and again: Priceless'
'The first apartment of your own: Priceless'
'Twenty-five years together – some better, some worse: Priceless'

Quality of adaptation and quality of local production

The experience of McCann indicated that they had to be extremely locally sensitive both in the expression of the 'Priceless' moment and in the nature and cost of the actual purchases made.

The bridging mechanism between the functional and emotional expression is very fragile and if any aspect of the mix is inappropriate, the integrity of the communications platform is compromised. Accordingly all markets *without exception* were sensitively researched – covering usage and attitudes of credit cards; local values and the emotional expression thereof; existing international and locally created materials which were rigorously inspected.

Creative material used

A reel of creative material was attached, containing European-generated work, as well as adaptations of non-European material.

The media strategy

McCann planned and bought media in the main (but not all) markets: UK, Ireland, France, Czech Republic, Hungary, Greece.

The 'Priceless' concept can be leveraged across all media, and is now being used to support sponsorships (e.g. Euro 2000), but TV was the major medium selected to launch the campaign into Europe. Unlike print media, TV spots are able to build towards a surprising and rewarding 'Priceless' moment, which adds fundamentally to he overall impact of individual spots and the campaign as a whole.

Airtime was selected in individual markets which would build a highly competitive position for Eurocard/MasterCard. In France the media budget was concentrated into TV in order to achieve a spend leadership in that medium and was deployed in such a way as to reach all age groups within the Conceptual Target. In Switzerland and the UK, cinema was added into the mix – again to reach the all-important younger audience, who are currently in the process of acquiring their first credit card. In Norway, TV was used for the first time ever to support MasterCard in that country.

Results

Content research

Qualitative research in pre- and post-launch periods indicates that the European Conceptual Target for the campaign is very susceptible to the campaign and its content. It has been a campaign that does not encourage reckless expenditure. It is advertising that clearly understands people as individuals and addresses them in an adult and positive manner.

Tracking research

Given that each country introduced 'Priceless' advertising at different times, and given that hitherto each country has used different tracking and reporting methods, there are no constant results. Also in each country Universal McCann has worked from different bases for all measurement criteria.

Some general results can be outlined:

● Advertising awareness has increased compared with previous Eurocard/MasterCard campaigns.

- Advertising awareness has increased compared with Visa.
- Brand awareness and relevance has increased – particularly in France.
- Record daily transactions have been registered in Norway.
- In Germany, the campaign shows positive results – particularly in terms of recognition of the emotional content of the advertising. In addition the brand has been clearly 'modernized'.
- In the UK, there has been a clear strengthening of the emotional brand positioning as well increasing perceptions of breadth of usage of the brand.

Questions

1. Is there a difference between the marketing of the two products, as regards the importance of the cross-cultural environment?

2. Make a comparison of the two cases with respect to advertising standardization and localization.

3. With regard to the implementation of international marketing strategy, how should the organizations of the two companies (behind the products) be organized and motivated in order to follow up the two advertising campaigns?

4. Why is timing so important for the implementation of international advertising strategies?

5. Discuss the measurements for 'success' of the two advertising campaigns.

World market leader in the niche of anatomical models and biological teaching aids

As Otto H. Gies, one of the two presidents at 3B Scientific[1] in Hamburg, drives home after work, he wonders if 3B Scientific can keep up the double-digit growth rates which it has had for the last ten years and which have made 3B Scientific the biggest producer in the world within the special segment of anatomical models and biological teaching aids.

Between 1995 and 1996 the 3B Scientific group (Paul Binhold Lehrmittelfabrik GmbH) 'only' had a 10 per cent increase in sales. At the same time, more and more Chinese 'no name' discount products entered the market. Even though these Chinese products are often bad copies of the 3B Scientific products, it still disturbs Otto H. Gies to hear about customers who buy these 3B Scientific copies in spite of the far better service back-up which customers get from 3B Scientific.

As far as Otto H. Gies can see, the following strategic possibilities exist to lead 3B Scientific into the next millennium as number one in the world:

● To profile 3B Scientific products as global brands to a larger extent, so that customers are able to see and feel the difference between copies and original 3B Scientific products.

● To start production of certain labour-intensive products in China, perhaps in a joint venture with a competitor.

● To establish strong marketing and sales positions in the growth centres of south-east Asia.

Otto H. Gies also doubts if the present international organizational structure of 3B Scientific is geared to meet the sharpened competition in the future.

As Otto H. Gies arrives at his home, he has not yet made up his mind, but plans to address the problem at the next management meeting.

Company profiled

The 3B Scientific group is a family of companies specializing in the manufacture and world-wide marketing of anatomical models and biological teaching aids. The product programme includes the following:

● Skeletons, torsos and human organ models.

● Injection training arms, patient care mannequins and medical simulators.

● Botanical models.

● Zoological models and animal skeletons.

● Anatomical wall charts.

● Anatomical gift models.

Some examples from the product programme are shown in Plate 23.

The 3B Scientific group distributes products world-wide. Its customers include universities, schools, ministries of health and education, hospitals, educational and medical distributors, students and the pharmaceutical industry.

In spring 1995 the Binhold group was enlarged to include a new affiliate, American 3B Scientific, founded in Atlanta, USA, for the purpose of expanding the group's business only in the North American market. Now Nikon 3B Scientific Japan also exists.

Throughout the 1990s the group has succeeded in establishing a new company every two years. Its affiliates in Dresden and Budapest are also operating profitably, making Paul Binhold, the company's 85-year-old founder, very proud of what he has achieved: 'I set up the company and laid the foundations; it is now up to our young people to proceed and expand the business.'

At present, five companies comprise the 3B Scientific group:

● Paul Binhold Lehrmittelfabrik GmbH, Hamburg (headquarters; international sales and logistics: EU/Asia/Africa).

● DHM Lehrmittelfabrik GmbH, Dresden (production, sales and logistics: western Europe).

[1] If you want to know more about 3B Scientific and their products, please visit their home-page at the following Web site: http://www.3bscientific.com.

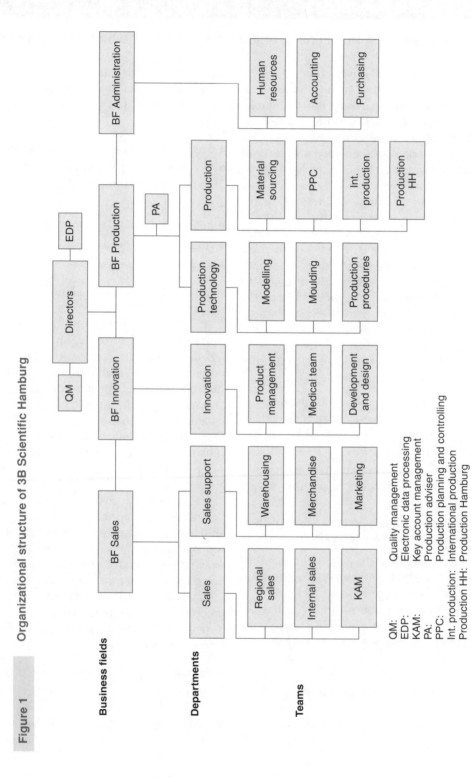

Figure 1   Organizational structure of 3B Scientific Hamburg

● Biocalderoni KFT, Budapest (production and logistics: eastern Europe).

● American 3B Scientific, Atlanta, USA (sales and logistics: North America).

● Nikon 3B Scientific, Nigata, Japan (sales and logistics: Japan).

The volume part of production has already been moved to eastern Europe.

The subsidiaries are either distributing or manufacturing companies. All product improvement and new product development is done in 3B Hamburg headquarters. The 3B Scientific group employs around 350 people, of whom 100 are based at the headquarters in Hamburg.

Roughly 80 per cent of 3B Scientific's sales come from export activities. Consequently, the 3B Scientific product catalogues are available in fifteen languages, including major Asian languages such as Japanese, Chinese, Korean and Turkish. 3B Scientific has a world-wide price guarantee: if a product of comparable quality at a lower price is available, Binhold absorbs the difference. 3B Scientific considers the action a worthwhile way to gather information on competitors' pricing practices from around the globe.

The total sales of the whole group in 1996 were about DM33 million, split by regions as shown in Table 1. The organizational structure of the headquarters in Hamburg is shown in Figure 1. Most of the communication from the subsidiaries to 3B Scientific Hamburg goes directly to the directors, especially Otto H. Gies.

In the sales department (see Figure 1) new customers are taken care of by the regional sales team.

If new customers become loyal 3B customers, they move on to the internal sales department. If customers have been loyal 3B customers for two or three years and are ordering more than DM100,000 of products per year, they move on to the last department where they will be taken care of by a special key account manager. These customers are often big dealers offering broad product programmes to the educational market, with their own catalogues where the products of 3B Scientific can have their own pages. These dealers often cooperate with the key account manager about direct marketing activities, promotional materials and exhibitions.

Now let us look at an example of how 3B Scientific attacks a new market.

Penetrating the Japanese market

At the beginning of the 1990s locally manufactured models were priced 30–40 per cent higher in Japan than equivalent German products, but Japanese wholesalers had shown themselves reluctant to import from Germany. Convinced that 3B Scientific still had the formula for success in Japan too, Otto H. Gies took up the challenge by starting to learn the language and local customs. He then had Japanese editions of the 3B catalogue printed, and embarked on personal sales calls to dealers around the country. He offered lower prices on the German-made models, resulting in bigger profits for dealers and prompting them to pressurize wholesalers to change their mind and import from Germany. The resulting success is an example of 3B Scientific's ability to adapt to the needs of individual markets. Beside printing Japanese-language versions of its sales materials, the company has modified its product to accommodate torsos with Asian facial features (see the 'multicultural torsos' in plate 28).

As Otto H. Gies arrives at work the next morning, he asks for your advice about the following problems.

Questions

1. Make an evaluation of the three growth strategies considered by Otto H. Gies at the start of this case.

2. Until now 3B Scientific has primarily targeted its marketing at the educational market. In recent years it has

Table 1	Distribution of total sales by regions, 1996 (%)
Germany	21
Europe (excl. Germany)	30
North America	25
Asia/Pacific	15
South America	7
Middle East	1
Africa	1
Total	100

developed a number of skeleton gift products (see Plate 23) for the consumer retail market, but without any great success so far.

(a) What are the key success factors for 3B Scientific in the consumer retail market? What argues for and against more focus on 3B's marketing for the consumer retail market?

(b) Make your conclusions on the basis of the above.

3. Is the internal organization at headquarters (Figure 1) an appropriate structure? Discuss alternative ways of structuring the internal organization. Make your conclusions on this basis.

Case V.3 Dandy

Part B: The corporate organizational structure of the Dandy group

The Danish chewing gum producer Dandy has in a few years developed into one of the leading chewing gum suppliers in Europe with brands like STIMOROL and DIROL. The important milestones in the history of Dandy are as follows:

1927:	Production of chewing gum begins.
1946:	First Dandy exports.
1956:	The STIMOROL brand is launched in Denmark.
1978:	Dandy acquires Fertin Laboratories in Sweden.
1979:	First sugar-free STIMOROL flavours are introduced.
1992:	ISO 9001 certification of Dandy head-quarters and subsidiaries.
1993:	DIROL is launched in Russia.
1995:	Market leadership (with STIMOROL and DIROL) in eastern Europe and Russia (read more about this in Case IV.2).

In 1996 the Dandy group employed 1,100 people at its headquarters and 1,500 world-wide. It produced 26,000 tons of chewing gum and had a turnover of DKK1.8 billion. In four years Dandy has more than doubled its turnover and more than quadrupled its profit. The market shares on the European chewing gum market are shown in Table 1.

Table 1 **Market shares in the European chewing gum market (%)**

Producer (nationality)	Total (dragee + sticks)	Dragee segment
Dandy (Denmark)	20	48
Wrigley (USA)	41	33
Warner Lambert (USA)	7	6
Perfetti (Italy)	13	–
Kraft (USA)	9	–
Huktamäki/Leaf (Finland)	5	13
Others	5	–
Total	100	100

The European chewing gum market is moving in the direction of an increased consumption of dragee chewing gum (tablets) at the expense of sticks. Furthermore, since 1985 the consumption of sugar-free chewing gum has increased nearly five-fold, and in the same period the consumption of dental chewing gum has increased by a factor of nearly seven. Outside Europe (and the former Soviet Union, CIS) Dandy has only a sporadic market presence with the exception of South Africa and Taiwan. In Taiwan Dandy has a market share of 20 per cent.

Organizational structure

As the organizational chart in Figure 1 shows, Dandy is basically divided into four business units.

Dandy Chewing Gum A/S

For Dandy Chewing Gum A/S the right idea depends on the right timing. Market trends are monitored constantly and the organization reflects the ambition of meeting changing consumer needs with speed and flexibility. Dandy Chewing Gum A/S develops, manufactures and sells chewing gum and bubble gum world-wide. The products are marketed as branded articles or novelties or under customers' own brands. Activities include the world-wide sale of branded articles like DIROL, Dandy, Dandy Light and Clip & Clap and the sale of STIMOROL in selected markets outside Europe (e.g. South Africa, Taiwan). Dandy Chewing Gum A/S markets its products through a network of distributors and subsidiaries. The products are manufactured in Denmark and at the joint-venture factory in Zimbabwe. Among its activities are thus the establishment and operation of joint-venture factories.

Stimorol Chewing Gum A/S

Stimorol Chewing Gum is the largest of the four business units. It markets the branded article STIMOROL and private labels in the bigger markets

Figure 1   **The international organizational structure of the Dandy group**

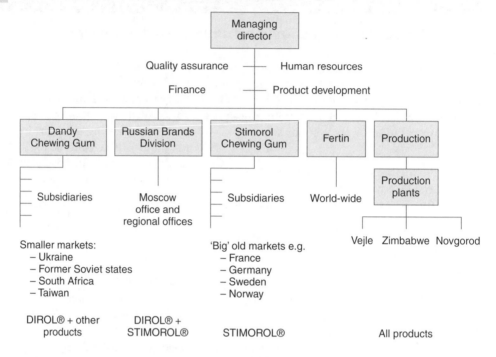

in Europe, either via its own sales subsidiaries or via national distributors. For more than 30 years the STIMOROL brand has had a strong appeal to the young in many countries. In 1990 'The original strong taste' concept was born following European consumer research to determine the core values of the STIMOROL brand.

Russian Brands Division A/S

This is the newest of the four business units. The Russian Brands Division markets DIROL and STIMOROL in Russia through the Dandy RBD Rep. Office in Moscow. Russia is the biggest market of the Dandy group today. Together STIMOROL and DIROL have more than 50 per cent of the chewing gum market in Russia.

Fertin A/S

Fertin A/S is a successful pharmaceutical business unit in the Dandy group. It has specialized in developing, producing and selling medicinal and semi-medicinal products, especially in the form of chewing gum. Fertin A/S produces branded articles such as V6 which are marketed via the company's

own distributors or sales companies in Stimorol Chewing Gum A/S. Furthermore, Fertin A/S manufactures private-label products for other companies in the pharmaceutical industry.

Together with Novartis – the former Ciba-Geigy – Fertin produces the nicotine chewing gum Nicotinell. SmithKline Beecham is a partner in the production of Odol chewing gum, which is a dental chewing gum. Gillette's Oral B chewing gum is also produced by Fertin. Fertin also produces chewing gum with vitamin C for various markets.

Fertin A/S has its own research and development department and carries out the necessary medical documentation. Clinical trials and tests take place in consultation with selected physicians, dentists, hospitals or dental colleges. Fertin has shown that a number of drugs have advantages when using chewing gum as the drug delivery system: for example, in the prevention or cure of mouth and tooth diseases, as medicine for children, or when rapid absorption is required.

Plate 24 is an illustration of Dandy's product programme and the positioning of the brands that Dandy manufactures for others (private labels).

Questions

1. How would you characterize the present international organizational structure of the Dandy group?

2. What are the advantages and disadvantages of the present structure versus alternative structures?

3. Give a proposal for Dandy's product/market strategy till the year 2005.

4. What implications would your proposal in 3 have for Dandy's international organizational structure?

Case V.4 SKF Rolling Bearings

Asia: the great challenge

It is spring 1996. Outside SKF's HQ in Göteborg the grass is sprouting and growing vigorously in the fertile Swedish soil. Inside there is just as much activity. Peter Augustsson, chief executive officer of SKF, has during the last couple of years followed the explosive development taking place in the Far East. Asia has shown the fastest economic growth in the world. The increase in China's gross domestic product exceeded 10 per cent in 1995. In Korea growth was 9 per cent and in Taiwan 7 per cent.

As a consequence of this development, Peter Augustsson and the top management group have decided to hive off the Asian division. However, some problems have arisen from combining an organizational structure based on geography and an organizational structure based on products. At the same time Peter Augustsson has been somewhat in doubt whether it is possible to increase SKF's market share in bearings in the Japanese market from its present level of 1 per cent (see Table 1). The reason for the low market share is, of course, that Japan has some of the world's largest producers of bearings to the car industry. But SKF has been able to take the lead over the Japanese in all other markets, so why not challenge the Japanese manufacturers in their home market?

Background

A basic form of ball bearing existed even in early Roman times. One was discovered in the remains of a ship dating from the reign of the emperor Caligula in AD 40. But the breakthrough did not occur until the nineteenth century, with the invention of the pedal cycle. In order to ease the effort of the rider, the wheels had to rotate easily. This accelerated the development of the ball bearing. In 1907 Sven Wingquist, a bright young Swedish engineer, developed the world's first self-aligning ball bearing. In the same year that the self-aligning ball bearing became a commercial reality, Svenska Kullager Fabriken (SKF) was founded.

Over the next six decades, SKF grew and became the world leader in bearing technology and its applications. In 1926 production of cars was started by a subsidiary of SKF, called AB Volvo. In 1935 AB Volvo became independent of SKF, and it later grew to become one of the major car producers in Europe. Through the 1960s and 1970s SKF was highly centralized and large economies of scale meant that huge quantities of bearings could be sold at competitive prices in the world market. In 1987 SKF's rolling bearing business was restructured into three business areas, each with world-wide responsibility: SKF Bearing

Table 1		The bearings market in 1995: world-wide market shares of top manufacturers							
Europe		**North America**		**Latin America**		**Asia (excl. Japan)**		**Japan**	
Manufacturer	**%**	**Manufacturer**	**%**	**Manufacturer**	**%**	**Manufacturer**	**%**	**Manufacturer**	**%**
SKF (Sweden)	30	Timken (USA)	20	SKF (Sweden)	30	SKF (Sweden)	20	NSK (Japan)	30
INA (Germany)	15	Torrington (USA)	14	FAG (Germany)	20	NSK (Japan)	15	NTN (Japan)	30
FAG (Germany)	10	SKF (Sweden)	12	Timken (USA)	15	NTN (Japan)	15	Other Japanese manufacturers	35
Japanese manufacturers	15	Japanese manufacturers	20	Japanese manufacturers	10	Timken (USA)	10	SKF (Sweden)	1
Others	30	Others	34	Others	25	Others	40	Others	4
Total	100	Total	100	Total	100	Total	100	Total	100

Source: Adapted from Annual Report, 1995, and other SKF material.

Industries, SKF Bearing Services and SKF Specialty Bearings.

Today, operating in some 130 countries, SKF is world leader in the rolling bearing business. Bearings, seals and special steels are SKF's main product areas. In addition the group also manufactures and sells a host of other industrial precision components. The company has some 43,000 employees and more than 80 manufacturing facilities throughout the world. Its international sales network is backed up by about 20,000 distributors and retailers. SKF's major customer areas are the automotive industry, the industrial aftermarket, railways, electrical industry and heavy industry. World-wide availability of SKF products is supported by a technical advisory service. One of the main contributors to SKF's strength is its R & D. The company's R & D strategy is to concentrate research in one high-powered centre in the Netherlands and then complement that centre with product development and testing facilities around the globe.

The SKF organization

During 1995, a new organizational structure was gradually introduced into the group. Originally geographically focused, the group's operations have now been divided into ten divisions (see Figure 1), each with global responsibility for its operations. SKF Asian Bearing Division is an exception, however, since total responsibility for most of the group's bearings operations in Asia has been assigned to this division.

The Asian division has been separated not only because the Asian region is showing rapid growth, but also because it is a very heterogeneous market, with very different cultures. These reasons were

Figure 1   **SKF's organization**

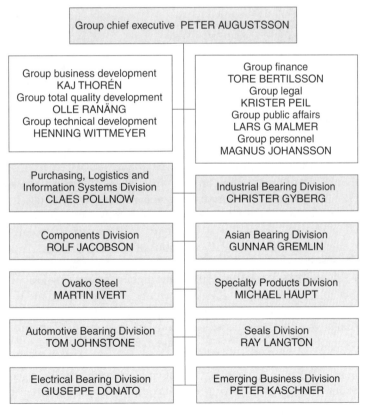

(Source: SKF Annual Report, 1995)

Table 2		SKF sales by application field and geographical area, 1995	
Application field	**%**	**Geographical area**	**%**
Industrial users	29	Europe (excl. Sweden)	56
General machinery	17	Sweden	5
Cars	16	North America	18
Trucks	8	Rest of the world	21
Heavy industry	8		
Electrical industry	6		
End users	6		
Vehicle replacement	5		
Aero-space	3		
Railways	2		
Total	100	Total	100

Source: SKF Annual Report, 1995.

Figure 2	Segmenting customers for rolling bearings

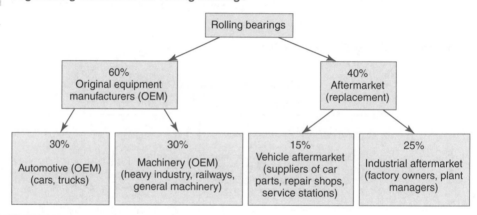

considered sufficiently important for the company to decide that efforts in this region must be managed locally, and that all decisions could then be made very quickly.

The rolling bearings business

Of the total net sales of the SKF Group in 1995 (SEK36.7 billion), the rolling bearings business accounted for 84 per cent (or SEK31.0 billion). Table 2 shows the total sales of bearings classified by application and geographical area.

Plate 30, shows product examples from two application fields: trucks and the electrical industry.

If the world market for bearings is divided into customer segments such as passenger cars, trucks, the aftermarket, etc., SKF holds leading positions within all segments with the exception of electronic motors. In general, its customers can be grouped into different categories as shown in Figure 2 (the percentages in Figure 2 are proportions of SKF sales).

Traditionally, OEM customers have been given the highest priority by SKF because of their high-volume production standards. However, profit margins are low in the OEM sector and SKF is under constant pressure to keep price increases below the rate of inflation.

In the vehicle aftermarket the OEM customers (such as Mercedes, Volkswagen and Ford) may also be competitors through their own spare parts divisions. The specialist suppliers of car parts will typically buy SKF bearings and sell them under their own brand name to distributors. Overall, the three largest companies in the world bearings industry are SKF, NSK Japan and NTN Japan.

A breakthrough for bearings in the Japanese market

At the beginning of July 1996 Peter Augustsson receives a fax from Tom Johnstone, president of the SKF Automotive Division. It reads:

Hi Peter

Good news!

As you already know, I am in Japan at the moment negotiating a contract on our wheel bearings with Suzuki cars. I have succeeded in getting a contract involving about US$1 million annually over a five-year period. We secured an order competing against very strong domestic bearing manufacturers. The order signals the start of a long-term involvement with Suzuki which I believe will benefit both our companies.

Peter, I think this is a definite breakthrough in our efforts to penetrate the Japanese car industry with our products.

Regards

Tom Johnstone

Peter Augustsson is, of course, very pleased on behalf of Tom Johnstone and SKF, but is still a little sceptical about the possibilities of SKF seriously penetrating the Japanese bearings market.

As a consultant you are asked to give an independent assessment of SKF's business possibilities in Asia. You are specifically asked the following questions.

Questions

1. Give an assessment of the new organization's ability to exploit future global business possibilities, especially in Asia. Include an assessment of the relevance of combining a geographic organizational structure and a product/functional organizational structure.

2. How would you assess SKF's possibilities of penetrating the Japanese rolling bearing market? Consider the following:
   (a) Which kind of entry mode and penetration strategy would you advise?
   (b) What is a realistic goal for SKF's market share in bearings in Japan?
   (c) Should SKF use resources in other parts of the world rather than in Japan?

Global marketing research/ decision support system

After studying this appendix you should be able to do the following:

- Explain the importance of having a carefully designed international information system.

- Link global marketing research to the decision-making process.

- Discuss the key problems in gathering and using international market data.

- Distinguish between different research approaches, data sources and data types.

- Understand the relevance of the World Wide Web as an important data source in global marketing research.

A.1 Introduction

The prime function of global marketing is to make and sell what international buyers want, rather than simply selling whatever can be most easily made. Therefore what customers require must be assessed through marketing research and/or through establishing a decision support system, so that the firm can direct its marketing activities more effectively by fulfilling the requirements of the customers.

The term 'marketing research' refers to gathering, analyzing and presenting information related to a well-defined problem. Hence the focus of marketing research is a specific problem or project with a beginning and an end.

Marketing research differs from a decision support system (DSS), which is information gathered and analyzed on a continual basis. In practice, marketing research and DSS are often hard to differentiate, so they will be used interchangeably in this context.

A.2 **Linking global marketing research to the decision-making process**

Global marketing research should be linked to the decision-making process within the firm. The recognition that a situation requires action is the initiating factor in the decision-making process.

Even though most firms recognize the need for domestic marketing research, this need is not fully understood for global marketing activities. Most SMEs conduct no international market research before they enter a foreign market. Often, decisions concerning entry and expansion in overseas markets and the selection and appointment of distributors are made after a subjective assessment of the situation. The research done is usually less rigorous, less formal and less quantitative than in LSEs. Furthermore, once an SME has entered a foreign market, it is likely to discontinue any research of that market. Many business executives therefore appear to view foreign market research as relatively unimportant.

A major reason that firms are reluctant to engage in global marketing research is the lack of sensitivity to cross-cultural customer tastes and preferences. What information should the global marketing research/DSS provide?

Table A.1 summarizes the principal tasks of global marketing research, according to the major decision phases of the global marketing process. As can be seen, both internal (firm-specific) and external (market) data are needed. The role of a firm's internal information system in providing data for marketing decisions is often forgotten.

How the different types of information affect the major decisions have been thoroughly discussed in the different parts and chapters of this book. Besides the split between internal and external data, the two major sources of information are primary data and secondary data:

● *Primary data*. These can be defined as information that is collected first-hand, generated by original research tailor-made to answer specific current research questions. The major advantage of primary data is that the information is specific ('fine grained'), relevant and up to date. The disadvantages of primary data are, however, the high costs and amount of time associated with the collection of this type of data.

● *Secondary data*. These can be defined as information that has already been collected for other purposes and is thus readily available. The major disadvantage is that the data are often more general and 'coarse grained' in nature. The advantages of secondary data are the low costs and amount of time associated with its collection. For those who are unclear on the terminology, secondary research is frequently referred to as 'desk research'.

The two basic forms of research (primary and secondary research) will be discussed in further detail later in this appendix.

If we combine the split of internal/external data with primary/secondary data, it is possible to place data in four categories. In Figure A.1 this approach is used to categorize indicator variables for answering the following marketing questions. Is there

Table A.1	Information for the major global marketing decisions	
	Global marketing decision	**Information needed**
	Deciding whether to internationalize	Assessment of global market opportunities (global demand) for the firm's products Commitment of the management to internationalize Competitiveness of the firm compared to local and international competitors Domestic versus international market opportunities
	Deciding which markets to enter	Ranking of world markets according to market potential of countries/regions Local competition Political risks Trade barriers Cultural/psychic 'distance' to potential market
	Deciding how to enter foreign markets	Nature of the product (standard versus complex product) Size of markets/segments Behaviour of potential intermediaries Behaviour of local competition Transport costs Government requirements
	Designing the global marketing programme	Buyer behaviour Competitive practice Available distribution channels Media and promotional channels
	Implementing and controlling the global marketing programme	Negotiation styles in different cultures Sales by product line, sales force customer type and country/region Contribution margins Marketing expenses per market

a market for the firm's product A in country B? If yes, how large is it and what is the possible market share for the firm to obtain? Note that in Figure A.1 only a limited number of indicator variables are shown.

As a rule, no primary research should be done without first searching for relevant secondary information, and secondary data should be used whenever available and appropriate. Besides, secondary data often help to define problems and research objectives. In most cases, however, secondary sources cannot provide all the information needed and the company must collect primary data.

In Figure A.1 the most difficult and costly kind of data to obtain is probably the strengths–weaknesses profile of the firm (internal and primary data). However, because it compares the profile of the firm with those of its main competitors, this quadrant is a very important indicator of the firm's international competitiveness. The following two sections discuss different forms of secondary research and primary research.

Figure A.1　Categorization of data for assessment of market potential in a country

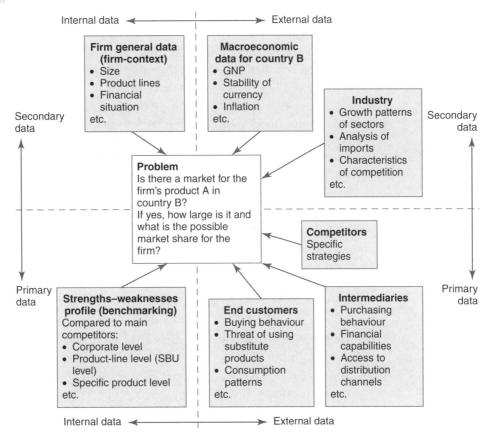

A.3　Secondary research

With many international markets to consider, it is essential that firms begin their market research by seeking and utilizing secondary data.

Advantages of secondary research

Secondary research conducted from the home base is less expensive and less time consuming than research conducted abroad. No contacts have to be made outside the home country, thus keeping commitment to possible future projects at a low level. Research undertaken in the home country about the foreign environment also has the benefit of objectivity. The researcher is not constrained by overseas customs. As a preliminary stage of a market-screening process, secondary research can quickly generate background information to eliminate many countries from the scope of enquiries.

Disadvantages of secondary research

Problems with secondary research are as follows:

- *Non-availability of data*. In many developing countries, secondary data are very scarce. These weak economies have poor statistical services – many do not even carry out a population census. Information on retail and wholesale trade is especially difficult to obtain. In such cases, primary data collection becomes vital.

- *Reliability of data*. Sometimes political considerations may affect the reliability of data. In some developing countries, governments may enhance the information to paint a rosy picture of the economic life in the country. In addition, due to the data collection procedures used, or the personnel who gathered the data, many data lack statistical accuracy. As a practical matter, the following questions should be asked to judge effectively the reliability of data sources (Cateora, 1993, p. 346):

  Who collected the data? Would there be any reason for purposely misrepresenting the facts?
  For what purpose was the data collected?
  How was the data collected (methodology)?
  Are the data internally consistent and logical in the light of known data sources or market factors?

- *Data classification*. In many countries, the data reported are too broadly classified for use at the micro level.

- *Comparability of data*. International marketers often like to compare data from different countries. Unfortunately, the secondary data obtainable from different countries are not readily comparable because national definitions of statistical phenomena differ from one country to another.

Although the possibility of obtaining secondary data has increased dramatically, the international community has grown increasingly sensitive to the issue of data privacy. Readily accessible large-scale databases contain information valuable to marketers but considered privileged by the individuals who have provided the data. The international marketer must therefore also pay careful attention to the privacy laws in different nations and to the possible consumer response to using such data. Neglecting these concerns may result in research backfiring and the corporate position being weakened.

In doing secondary research or building a decision support system, there are many information sources available. Generally, these secondary data sources can be divided into internal and external sources (Figure A.1). The latter can be classified as either international/global or regional/country-based sources.

Internal data sources

Internal company data can be a most fruitful source of information. However, it is often not utilized as fully as it should be.

The global marketing and sales departments are the main points of commercial interaction between an organization and its foreign customers. Consequently, a great deal of information should be available, including the following:

- *Total sales.* Every company keeps a record of its total sales over a defined time period: for example, weekly records, monthly records and so on.
- *Sales by countries.* Sales statistics should be split up by countries. This is partly to measure the progress and competence of the export manager or the salesperson (sometimes to influence earnings because commission may be paid on sales) and partly to measure the degree of market penetration in a particular country.
- *Sales by products.* Very few companies sell only one product. Most companies sell a range of products and keep records for each kind of product or, if the range is large, each product group.
- *Sales volume by market segment.* Such segmentation may be geographical or by type of industry. This will give an indication of segment trends in terms of whether they are static, declining or expanding.
- *Sales volume by type of channel distribution.* Where a company uses several different distribution channels, it is possible to calculate the effectiveness and profitability of each type of channel. Such information allows marketing management to identify and develop promising channel opportunities, and results in more effective channel marketing.
- *Pricing information.* Historical information relating to price adjustments by product allows the organization to establish the effect of price changes on demand.
- *Communication mix information.* This includes historical data on the effects of advertising campaigns, sponsorship and direct mail on sales. Such information can act as a guide to the likely effectiveness of future communication expenditure plans.
- *Sales representatives' records and reports.* Sales representatives should keep a visit card or file on every 'live' customer. In addition, sales representatives often send reports to the sales office on such matters as orders lost to competitors and possible reasons why, as well as on firms that are planning future purchasing decisions. Such information could help to bring improvements in marketing strategy.

External data sources

A very basic method of finding international business information is to begin with a public library or a university library. The Internet (World Wide Web, or www) can help in the search for data sources. The Internet has made available thousands of databases for intelligence research (i.e. research on competitors). In addition, electronic databases carry marketing information ranging from the latest news on product development to new thoughts in the acedemic and trade press and updates in international trade statistics. However, the Internet will not totally replace other sources of secondary data. Cost compared to data quality will still be a factor influencing a company's choice of secondary data sources.

Figure A.2   **Groupings of external secondary data sources**

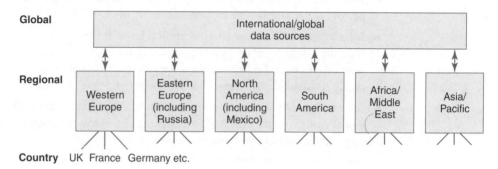

GEOGRAPHIC LEVEL

The external data sources are grouped geographically as shown in Figure A.2. In the rest of this section, Web sites are indicated by **bold type**. These and the other data sources listed are only a fraction of the total number of data sources available.

International/global sources (www addresses)

The links to the international data sources may be reached at **www.booksites.net/hollensen** or **www.sb.sdu.dk/~svend**.

A.4 ▎ Primary research

Qualitative and quantitative research

If a marketer's research questions are not adequately answered by secondary research, it may be necessary to search for additional information in primary data. These data can be collected by qualitative and quantitative research. Quantitative

Figure A.3   **The 'trade-off' in the choice between quantitative and qualitative research**

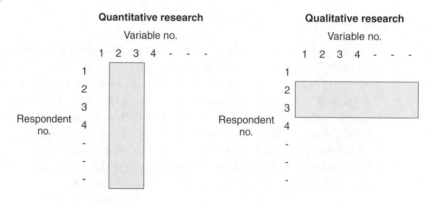

and qualitative techniques can be distinguished by the fact that quantitative techniques involve getting data from a large representative group of respondents.

The objective of qualitative research techniques is to give a holistic view of the research problem, and therefore these techniques must have a large number of variables and few respondents (illustrated in Figure A.3). Choosing between quantitative and qualitative techniques is a question of trading off breadth and depth in the results of the analysis.

Other differences between the two research methodologies are summarized in Table A.2.

Data retrieval and analysis of quantitative respondent data are based on a comparison of data between all respondents. This places heavy demands on the measuring instrument (the questionnaire), which must be well structured (with different answering categories) and tested before the survey takes place. All respondents are given identical stimuli: that is, the same questions. This approach will not usually give any problems, as long as the respondent group is homogeneous. However, if it is a heterogeneous group of respondents, it is possible that the same question will be understood in different ways. This problem becomes especially intensified in cross-cultural surveys.

Table A.2	Quantitative versus qualitative research	
Comparison dimension	**Quantitative research (e.g. a postal questionnaire research)**	**Qualitative research (e.g. a focus group interview or the case method)**
Objective	To quantify the data and generalize the results from the sample to the population of interest	To gain an initial and qualitative understanding of the underlying reasons and motives
Type of research	Descriptive and/or casual	Exploratory
Flexibility in research design	Low (as a result of a standardized and structured questionnaire: one-way communication)	High (as a result of the personal interview, where the interviewer can change questions during the interview: two-way communication)
Sample size	Large	Small
Choice of respondents	Representative sample of the population	Persons with considerable knowledge of the problem (key informants)
Information per respondent	Low	High
Data analysis	Statistical summarization	Subjective, interpretive
Ability to replicate with same result	High	Low
Interviewer requirements	No special skills required	Special skills required (an understanding of the interaction between interviewer and respondent)
Time consumption during the research	*Design phase*: high (formulation of questions must be correct) *Analysis phase*: low (the answers to the questions can be coded)	*Design phase*: low (no 'exact' questions are required before the interview) *Analysis phase*: high (as a result of many 'soft' data)

Data retrieval and analysis of qualitative data, however, are characterized by a high degree of flexibility and adaptation to the individual respondent and his or her special background. Another considerable difference between qualitative and quantitative surveys is the source of data:

● Quantitative techniques are characterized by a certain degree of distance as the construction of the questionnaire, data retrieval and data analysis take place in separate phases. Data retrieval is often done by people who have not had anything to do with the construction of the questionnaire. Here the measuring instrument (the questionnaire) is the critical element in the research process.
● Qualitative techniques are characterized by proximity to the source of data, where data retrieval and analysis are done by the same person: namely, the interviewer. Data retrieval is characterized by interaction between the interviewer and the respondent, where each new question is to a certain degree dependent on the previous question. Here it is the interviewer and his or her competence (or lack of the same) which is the critical element in the research process.

Qualitative techniques imply a less sharp separation between data retrieval and analysis/interpretation, since data retrieval (for example, the next question in a personal interview) will be dependent on the interviewer's interpretation of the previous answer. The researcher's personal experience from field work (data retrieval) is generally a considerable input into the analysis phase.

Triangulation: mixing qualitative and quantitative research methods

Combined use of quantitative and qualitative research methods in the study of the same phenomenon is termed triangulation (Jick, 1979; Denzin, 1978). The triangulation metaphor is from navigation and military strategy, which use multiple reference points to locate an object's exact position. Similarly, market researchers can improve the accuracy and validity of their judgements by collecting both quantitative and qualitative data.

Sometimes it is relevant to use qualitative data collected by, for example, in-depth interview of a few key informants as the explorative input to the construction of the best possible questionnaire for the collection of quantitative data. In this way, triangulation can enrich our understanding of a research question before a structured and formalized questionnaire is designed.

Research design

Figure A.4 shows that designing research for primary data collection calls for a number of decisions on research approaches, contact methods, sampling plan and research instruments. The following pages will look at the various elements of Figure A.4 in further detail.

Research problem/objectives

Companies are increasingly recognizing the need for primary international research. As the extent of a firm's international involvement increases, so does the importance and complexity of its international research. The primary research process should begin with a definition of the research problem and the establishment of specific objectives. The major difficulty here is translating the business problem into a research problem with a set of specific researchable objectives. In this initial stage, researchers often embark on the research process with only a vague grasp of the total problem. Symptoms are often mistaken for causes, and action determined by symptoms may be oriented in the wrong direction.

Research objectives may include obtaining detailed information for better penetrating the market, for designing and fine-tuning the marketing mix, or for monitoring the political climate of a country so that the firm can expand its operation successfully. The better defined the research objective is, the better the researcher will be able to determine the information requirement.

Research approaches

In Figure A.4 three possible research approaches are indicated: observation, surveys and experiments.

Figure A.4   **Primary data collection: research design**

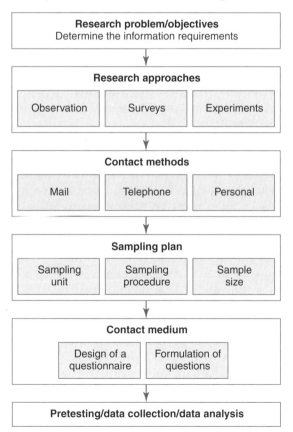

635

Observation

This approach to the generation of primary data is based on watching and some-times recording market-related behaviour. Observational techniques are more suited to investigating what people do than why they do it. Here are some examples of this approach:

● Store checks: a food-products manufacturer sends researchers into supermarkets to find out the prices of competing brands or how much shelf space and display support retailers give its brands. To conduct in-store research in Europe, for example, store checks, photo audits of shelves and store interviews must be scheduled well in advance and need to be preceded by a full round of introduction of the researchers to store management and personnel.

● Mechanical observations are often used to measure TV viewership.

● Cash register scanners can be used to keep track of customer purchases and inventories.

Observational research can obtain information that people are unwilling or unable to provide. In some countries, individuals may be reluctant to discuss personal habits or consumption. In such cases, observation is the only way to obtain the nec-essary information. In contrast, some things are simply not observable, such as feel-ings, attitudes and motives, or private behaviour. Long-term or infrequent behaviour is also difficult to observe. Because of these limitations, researchers often use observation along with other data collection methods.

Experiments

Experiments gather casual information. They involve selecting matched groups of subjects, giving them different treatments, controlling unrelated factors and check-ing for differences in group responses. Thus experimental research tries to explain cause-and-effect relationships.

The most used marketing research application of experiments is in test marketing. This is a research technique in which a product under study is placed on sale in one or more selected localities or areas, and its reception by consumers and the trade is observed, recorded and analyzed. In order to isolate, for example, the sales effects of advertising campaigns, it is necessary to use relatively self-contained marketing areas as test markets.

Performance in these test markets gives some indication of the performance to be expected when the product goes into general distribution. However, experiments are difficult to implement in global marketing research. The researcher faces the task of designing an experiment in which most variables are held constant or are comparable across cultures. To do so represents a major challenge. For example, an experiment that intends to determine a casual effect within the distribution system of one country may be difficult to transfer to another country, where the distribu-tion system is different. As a result, experiments are used only rarely, even though their potential value to the international market researcher is recognized.

Surveys

The survey research method is based on the questioning of respondents and represents, both in volume and in value terms, perhaps the most important method of collecting data. Typically, the questioning is structured: a formal questionnaire is prepared and the questions are asked in a prearranged order. The questions may be asked verbally, in writing or via computer.

Survey research is used for a variety of marketing issues, including the following:

● Customer attitudes.

● Customer buying habits.

● Potential market size.

● Market trends.

Unlike experimental research, survey research is usually aimed at generating descriptive rather than casual data. Unlike observational research, survey research usually involves the respondent.

Because of the importance and diversity of survey research in global marketing, it is on this particular aspect that we now concentrate.

Contact methods

The method of contact chosen is usually a balance between speed, degree of accuracy and costs. In principle, there are three possibilities when choosing a contact method: personal (face-to-face) interviews, telephone interviews and mail surveys. Each method has its own strengths and weaknesses. Table A.3 gives an overview of these.

Mail surveys

These can collect a large amount of data that can be quantified and coded into a computer. A low research budget combined with a widely dispersed population may mean that there is no alternative to the mail survey. However, the major problem is its potentially low response rate.

Telephone interviews

In some ways these are somewhere between personal and mail surveys. They generally have a response rate higher than mail questionnaires, but lower than face-to-face interviews; their cost is usually less than with personal interviews, and they allow a degree of flexibility when interviewing. However, the use of visual aids is not possible and there are limits to the number of questions that can be asked before respondents either terminate the interview or give quick (invalid) answers to speed up the process. The use of computer-aided telephone interviewing (CATI) is growing. Centrally located interviewers read questions from a computer monitor and input answers via the keyboard. Routeing through the questionnaire is computer controlled, helping the process of interviewing. Some research firms set up terminals in shopping centres, where respondents sit down at a terminal, read questions from a screen and type their answers into the computer.

Personal interviews

Personal interviews take two forms – individual and group interviewing. *Individual interviewing* involves talking with people in their homes or offices, in the street, or

Table A.3

Strengths and weaknesses of the three contact methods

Questions/questionnaire	Mail	Telephone	Personal
Flexibility (ability to clarify problems)	Poor	Good	Excellent
Possibility of in-depth information (use of open-ended questions)	Fair	Fair	Excellent
Use of visual aids	Good	Poor	Good
Possibility of a widely dispersed sample	Excellent	Excellent	Fair
Response rates	Poor	Good	Good
Ask sensitive questions (anonymity of respondent is assumed)	Good	Poor	Fair
Control of interviewer effects (no interviewer bias)	Excellent	Fair	Poor
Speed of data collection	Poor	Excellent	Good
Costs	Good	Excellent	Poor

in shopping arcades. The interviewer must gain the cooperation of the respondents. *Group interviewing (focus-group interviewing)* consists of inviting six to ten people to gather for a few hours with a trained moderator to talk about a product, service or organization. The moderator needs objectivity, knowledge of the subject and industry, and some understanding of group and consumer behaviour. The participants are normally paid a small sum for attending.

Personal interviewing is quite flexible and can collect large amounts of information. Trained interviewers can hold a respondent's attention for a long time and can explain difficult questions. They can guide interviews, explore issues and probe as the situation requires. Interviewers can show subjects actual products, advertisements or packages, and observe reactions and behaviour.

The main drawbacks of personal interviewing are the high costs and sampling problems. Group interview studies usually employ small sample sizes to keep time and costs down, but it may be hard to generalize from the results. Because interviewers have more freedom in personal interviews, the problem of interviewer bias is greater.

Thus, there is no 'best' contact method – it all depends on the situation. Sometimes it may even be appropriate to combine the three methods.

Sampling plan

Except in very restricted markets, it is both impractical and too expensive for a researcher to contact all the people who could have some relevance to the research problem. This total number is known statistically as the 'universe' or 'population'. In marketing terms, it comprises the total number of actual and potential users/ customers of a particular product or service.

The population can also be defined in terms of elements and sampling units. Suppose that a lipstick manufacturer wants to assess consumer response to a new line of lipsticks and wants to sample females over fifteen years of age. It may be possible to sample females of this age directly, in which case a sampling unit would be the same as an element. Alternatively, households might be sampled and all females over fifteen in each selected household then interviewed. Here, the sampling unit is the household, and the element is a female over fifteen years old.

What is usually done in practice is to contact a selected group of consumers/customers to be representative of the entire population. The total number of consumers who could be interviewed is known as the 'sample frame', while the number of people who are actually interviewed is known as the 'sample'.

Sampling procedure

There are several kinds of sampling procedure, with probability and non-probability sampling being the two major categories:

- *Probability sampling.* Here it is possible to specify in advance the chance that each element in the population will have of being included in a sample, although there is not necessarily an equal probability for each element. Examples are simple random sampling, systematic sampling, stratified sampling and cluster sampling (see Malhotra (1993) for more information).

- *Non-probability sampling.* Here it is not possible to determine the above-mentioned probability or to estimate the sampling error. These procedures rely on the personal judgement of the researcher. Examples are convenience sampling, quota sampling and snowball sampling (see Malhotra (1993) for more information).

Given the disadvantages of non-probability samples (results are not projectable to the total population, and sampling error cannot be computed), one may wonder why they are used so frequently by marketing researchers. The reasons relate to the inherent advantages of non-probability sampling:

- Non-probability samples cost less than probability samples.
- If accuracy is not critical, non-probability sampling may have considerable appeal.
- Non-probability sampling can be conducted more quickly than probability sampling.
- Non-probability sampling, if executed properly, can produce samples of the population that are reasonably representative (e.g. by use of quota sampling) (Malhotra, 1993, p. 359).

Sample size

Once we have chosen the sampling procedure, the next step is to determine the appropriate sample size. Determining the sample size is a complex decision and involves financial, statistical and managerial considerations. Other things being equal, the larger the sample, the less the sampling error. However, larger samples cost more money, and the resources (money and time) available for a particular research project are always limited.

In addition, though, the cost of larger samples tends to increase on a linear basis, whereas the level of sampling error decreases at a rate only equal to the square root of the relative increase in sample size. For example, if sample size is quadrupled, data collection costs will be quadrupled too, but the level of sampling error will be reduced by only one-half. Among the methods for determining the sample size are the following:

● Traditional statistical techniques (assuming the standard normal distribution).
● Budget available. Although seemingly unscientific, this is a fact of life in a business environment based on the budgeting of financial resources. This approach forces the researcher to consider carefully the value of information in relation to its cost.
● Rules of thumb. The justification for a specified sample size may boil down to a 'gut feeling' that this is an appropriate sample size, or it may be a result of common practice in the particular industry.
● Number of subgroups to be analyzed. Generally speaking, the more subgroups that need to be analyzed, the larger the required total sample size.

In transnational market research, sampling procedures become a rather complicated matter. Ideally, a researcher wants to use the same sampling method for all countries in order to maintain consistency. Sampling desirability, however, often gives way to practicality and flexibility. Sampling procedures may have to vary across countries in order to ensure reasonable comparability of national groups. Thus, the relevance of a sampling method depends on whether it will yield a sample that is representative of a target group in a certain country, and on whether comparable samples can be obtained from similar groups in different countries.

Contact medium/measurement instrument

Designing the questionnaire

A good questionnaire cannot be designed until the precise information requirements are known. It is the vehicle whereby the research objectives are translated into specific questions. The type of information sought, and the type of respondents to be researched, will have a bearing upon the contact method to be used, and this in turn will influence whether the questionnaire is relatively unstructured (with open-ended questions) aimed at depth interviewing, or relatively structured (with closed-ended questions) for 'on the street' interviews.

In cross-cultural studies open-ended questions appear useful because they may help to identify the frame of reference of the respondents. Another issue is the choice between direct and indirect questions. Societies have different degrees of sensitivity to certain questions. Questions related to the income or age of the respondent may be accepted differently in different countries. Thus, the researcher must be sure that the questions are culturally acceptable. This may mean that questions that can be asked directly in some societies will have to be asked indirectly in others.

Formulation (wording) of questions

Once the researcher has decided on specific types of question, the next task is the actual writing of the questions. Four general guidelines are useful to bear in mind during the wording and sequencing of each question:

- *The wording must be clear.* For example, try to avoid two questions in one.
- *Select words so as to avoid biasing the respondent.* For example, try to avoid leading questions.
- *Consider the ability of the respondent to answer the question.* For example, asking respondents about a brand or store that they have never encountered creates a problem. Since respondents may be forgetful, time periods should be relatively short. For example: 'Did you purchase one or more cola(s) within the last week?'
- *Consider the willingness of the respondent to answer the question.* 'Embarrassing' topics that deal with things like borrowing money, sexual activities and criminal records must be dealt with in a careful manner. One technique is to ask the question in the third person or to state that the behaviour or attitude is not unusual prior to asking the question. For example: 'Millions of people suffer from haemorrhoids. Do you or does any member of your family suffer from this problem?'

The impact of language and culture is of particular importance when wording questions. The goal for the global marketing researcher should be to ensure that the potential for misunderstandings and misinterpretations of spoken or written words is minimized. Both language and cultural differences make this issue an extremely sensitive one in the global marketing research process.

In many countries, different languages are spoken in different areas. In Switzerland, German is used in some areas and French and Italian in others. As we have seen, the meaning of words often differs from country to country. For example, in the United States the concept of 'family' generally refers only to the parents and children. In the southern part of Europe, the Middle East and many Latin countries, it may also include grandparents, uncles, aunts, cousins and so forth.

When finally evaluating the questionnaire, the following items should be considered:

- Is a certain question necessary? The phrase 'It would be nice to know' is often heard, but each question should either serve a purpose or be omitted.
- Is the questionnaire too long?
- Will the questions achieve the survey objectives?

Pretesting

No matter how comfortable and experienced the researcher is in international research activities, an instrument should always be pretested. Ideally, such a pretest is carried out with a subset of the population under study, but a pretest should at least be conducted with knowledgeable experts and/or individuals. The pretest should also be conducted in the same mode as the final interview. If the study is to be 'on the street' or in the shopping arcade, then the pretest should be the same.

Even though a pretest may mean time delays and additional cost, the downward risks of poor research are simply too great for this process to be omitted.

Data collection

The global marketing researcher must check that the data are gathered correctly, efficiently and at a reasonable cost. The market researcher has to establish the parameters under which the research is conducted. Without clear instructions the interviews may be conducted in different ways by different interviewers. Therefore, the interviewers have to be instructed about the nature of the study, start and completion time, and sampling methodology. Sometimes a sample interview is included with detailed information on probing and quotas. Spot checks on these administration procedures are vital to ensure reasonable data quality.

Data analysis and interpretation

Once data have been collected, the final steps are the analysis and interpretation of findings in the light of the stated problem. Analyzing data from cross-country studies calls for substantial creativity as well as scepticism. Not only are data often limited, but frequently results are significantly influenced by cultural differences. This suggests that there is a need for properly trained local personnel to function as supervisors and interviewers; alternatively the international market researchers require substantial advice from knowledgeable local research firms, which also can take care of the actual collection of data. Although data in cross-country analysis are often of a qualitative nature, the researcher should, of course, use the best and most appropriate tools available for analysis. On the other hand, international researchers should be cautioned against using overly sophisticated tools for unsophisticated data. Even the best of tools will not improve data quality. The quality of data must be matched with the quality of the research tools.

Problems with using primary research

Non-response

Non-response is the inability to reach selected elements in the sample frame. As a result, opinions of the sample elements who do not respond are not obtained or properly represented. A good sampling method can only identify elements who should be selected; there is no guarantee that such elements will ever be included.

The two main reasons for non-response errors are as follows:

- *Not being at home.* In countries where males are still dominant in the labour force, it may be difficult to contact a head of household at home during working hours. Frequently, only housewives or servants are home during the day.

- *Refusal to respond.* Cultural habits in many countries virtually prohibit communication with a stranger, particularly for women. This is the case in the Middle East, much of the Mediterranean area and throughout most of southeast Asia – in fact, wherever strong traditional societies persist. Moreover, in many societies such matters as preferences for hygienic products and food products are too personal to be shared with an outsider. For example, in many Latin American countries, a woman may feel ashamed to talk with a researcher about her choice of a brand of sanitary towels, or even hair shampoo or perfume. Respondents may also suspect that the interviewers are agents of the government, seeking information for the imposition of additional taxes. Finally, privacy is becoming a big issue in many countries: for example, in Japan the middle class is showing increasing concern about the protection of personal information.

Measurement

The best research design is useless without proper measurements. A measurement method that works satisfactorily in one culture may fail to achieve the intended purpose in another country. Special care must therefore be taken to ensure the reliability and validity of the measurement method.

If we measure the same phenomenon over and over again with the same measurement device and we get similar results, then the method is reliable. There are two types of validity: internal and external.

Internal validity

If a measurement method lacks (internal) validity, it is not measuring what it is supposed to. The concepts of reliability and validity are illustrated in Figure A.5. In the diagram, the bull's eye is what the measurement device is supposed to 'hit'.

Situation 1 shows holes all over the target. It could be due to the use of a bad measurement device. If a measurement instrument is not reliable, there are no circumstances under which it can be valid. However, just because an instrument is reliable, the instrument is not automatically valid. We see this in *situation 2*, where the instrument is reliable but is not measuring what it is supposed to measure. The shooter has a steady eye, but the sights are not adjusted properly. *Situation 3* is the ideal situation for the researcher to be in. The measurement method is both reliable and valid.

| Figure A.5 | Illustrations of possible reliability and validity situations in measurement |

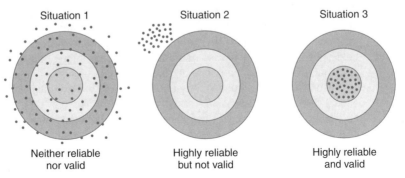

(Source: McDaniel and Gates, 1993, p. 372)

An instrument proven to be reliable and valid in one country may not be so in another culture. The same measurement scales may have different reliabilities in different cultures because of various levels of consumers' product knowledge. Therefore, it may be dangerous simply to compare results in cross-country research. One way to minimize the problem is to adapt measurement scales to local cultures by pretesting measures in each market of interest until they show similar and satisfactory levels of reliability.

External validity

External validity is concerned with the possible generalization of research results to other populations. For example, high external validity exists if research results obtained for a marketing problem in one country will be applicable to a similar marketing problem in another country. If such a relationship exists, it may be relevant to use the analogy method for estimating market demand in different countries. Estimating by analogy assumes, for example, that the demand for a product develops in much the same way in countries that are similar.

Exhibit A.1	Gathering and interpreting information in Asia-Pacific

The Asia-Pacific market has been highlighted as a key market area for this decade, so obtaining reliable information in the region is of crucial importance to companies wishing to develop these markets. However, a recent survey by Lasserre (1993), with results from 167 European marketing and planning executives operating in the Asia-Pacific region, found that only in Japan, Singapore and Hong Kong were companies able easily to access data that were viewed as being of a good quality (see Figure A.6)

Vietnamese data, in particular, are not trusted by researchers. The fact that Vietnam is characterized by an almost total lack of reliable data on virtually every aspect of doing business is confirmed by Dang and Speece (1996). The infrastructure to support marketing research is very bad in Vietnam. For example, telephones are rare and government development plans hope to reach a telephone density of just 3 per cent by the year 2000. As mail is also a very difficult and slow contact method, face-to-face interviews seem to be the only way to learn something about what potential Vietnamese customers think and want.

The most important data sources in Asia-Pacific are the personal sources of companies (primary research, whether from customers, from other business relations, or from their own in-house surveys). The importance of primary research confirms the widely held opinion that business in Asia-Pacific depends more heavily on the network of personal relationships than on analysis of hard data (secondary research).

This pattern is valid from country to country, with the exception of Japan, where secondary data are both accessible and of good quality. The only problem for western firms here seems to be the cost of acquiring it. Government data sources are also important in Singapore. Generally, however, personal contacts and in-house surveys are very important data sources in Asia-Pacific.

Sources: Lasserre (1993); Dang and Speece (1996).

Other types of marketing research

A distinction is made between ad-hoc and continuous research.

Ad-hoc research

An ad-hoc study focuses on a specific marketing problem and collects data at one point in time from one sample of respondents. Examples of ad-hoc studies are usage and attitude surveys, and product and concept tests via custom-designed or multiclient studies. More general marketing problems (e.g. total market estimates for product groups) may be examined by use of Delphi studies.

Custom-designed studies

These are based on the specific needs of the client. The research design is based on the research brief given to the marketing research agency or internal marketing researcher. Because they are tailor-made, such surveys can be expensive.

Multiclient studies

These are a relatively low-cost way for a company to answer specific questions without embarking on its own primary research. There are two types of multiclient study:

● *Independent research studies.* These are carried out totally independently by research companies (e.g. Frost and Sullivan) and then offered for sale.

Figure A.6   **Information base in Asia-Pacific**

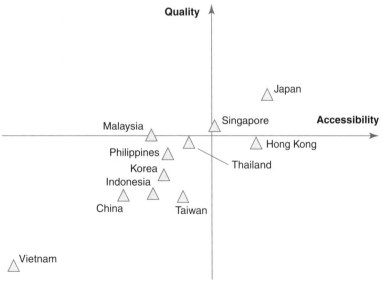

(Source: Lasserre, 1993, p. 57)

● *Omnibus studies.* Here a research agency will target specified segments in a particular foreign market and companies will buy questions in the survey. Consequently, interviews (usually face-to-face or by telephone) may cover many topics. Clients will then receive an analysis of the questions purchased. For omnibus studies to be of use, the researcher must have clearly defined research needs and a corresponding target segment in order to obtain meaningful information.

Delphi studies

This type of research approach clearly aims at qualitative rather than quantitative measures by aggregating the information of a group of experts. It seeks to obtain answers from those who possess particular in-depth expertise instead of seeking the average responses of many with only limited knowledge.

The area of concern may be future developments in the international trading environment or long-term forecasts for market penetration of new products. Typically, 10–30 key informants are selected and asked to identify the major issues in the area of concern. They are also requested to rank their statements according to importance and explain the rationale behind the ranking. Next, the aggregated information is returned to all participants, who are encouraged to state clearly their agreements or disagreements with the various rank orders and comments. Statements can be challenged and then, in another round, participants can respond to the challenges. After several rounds of challenge and response, a reasonably coherent consensus is developed.

One drawback of the technique is that it requires several steps, and therefore months may elapse before the information is obtained. However, the emergence of e-mail may accelerate the process. If done properly, the Delphi method can provide insightful forecast data for the international information system of the firm.

Continuous research (longitudinal designs)

A longitudinal design differs from ad-hoc research in that the sample or panel remains the same over time. In this way, a longitudinal study provides a series of pictures which give an in-depth view of developments taking place. The panel consists of a sample of respondents, who have agreed to provide information at specified intervals over an extended period.

There are two major types of panel:

● *Consumer panels.* These provide information on their purchases over time. For example, a grocery panel would record the brands, pack sizes, prices and stores used for a wide range of supermarket brands. By using the same households over a period of time, measures of brand loyalty and switching can be achieved together with a demographic profile of the type of person or household who buys particular brands.

● *Retailer panels.* By gaining the cooperation of retail outlets (e.g. supermarkets), sales of brands can be measured by laser scanning the bar codes on goods as they pass through the checkout. Although brand loyalty and switching cannot be measured in this way, retail audits can provide accurate assessments of sales achieved by store. A major provider of retail data is the A.C. Nielsen company.

A.6 Summary

The basic objective of the global marketing research function is to provide management with relevant information for more accurate decision making. The objective is the same for both domestic and global marketing. However, global marketing is more complex because of the difficulty of gathering information about multiple different foreign environments.

In this appendix, special attention has been given to the information collection process and the use of marketing information. This coverage is far from being exhaustive, and the reader should consult marketing research textbooks for specific details related to particular research topics.

An international marketer should initiate research by searching first for any relevant secondary data. Typically, a great deal of information is already available, and the researcher needs to know how to identify and locate the international sources of secondary data.

If it is necessary to gather primary data, the international marketer should be aware that it is simply not possible to replicate elsewhere the methodology used in one country. Some adaptation of the research method to different countries is usually necessary.

The firm should set up a decision support system to handle the gathered information efficiently. This system should integrate all information inputs, both internal and external. However, in the final analysis, every international marketer should keep in mind that an information system is no substitute for sound judgement.

Questions for discussion

1. Explore the reasons for using a marketing information system in the international market. What are the main types of information you would expect to use?

2. What are some of the problems that a global marketing manager can expect to encounter when creating a centralized marketing information system? How can these problems be solved?

3. What are the dangers of translating questionnaires (that have been designed for one country) for use in a multicountry study? How would you avoid these dangers?

4. Identify and classify the major groups of factors that must be taken into account when conducting a foreign market assessment.

5. An American manufacturer of shoes is interested in estimating the potential attractiveness of China for its products. Identify and discuss the sources and the types of data that the company will need in order to obtain a preliminary estimate.

6. Identify and discuss the major considerations in deciding whether research should be centralized or decentralized.

7. Distinguish between internal and external validity. What are the implications of external validity for international marketers?

8. Would Tokyo be a good test market for a new brand planned to be marketed world-wide? Why or why not?

9. If you had a contract to do marketing research in Saudi Arabia, what problems would you expect in obtaining primary data?

10. Do demographic variables have universal meanings? Is there a chance that they may be interpreted differently in different cultures?

11. In forecasting sales in international markets, to what extent can the past be used to predict the future?

12. How should the firm decide whether to gather its own intelligence or to buy it from outside?

References

Cateora, P.R. (1993) *International Marketing* (8th edn), Irwin, Homewood, IL.

Dang, T. and Speece, M. (1996) 'Marketing research in Vietnam', *Journal of International Marketing and Marketing Research*, vol. 21, no. 3, pp. 145–61.

Denzin, N.K. (1978) *The Research Act* (2nd edn), McGraw-Hill, New York.

Jick, T.D. (1979) 'Mixing qualitative and quantitive methods: triangulation in action', *Administrative Science Quarterly*, vol. 24, December, pp. 602–11.

Lasserre, P. (1993) 'Gathering and interpreting strategic intelligence in Asia Pacific', *Long Range Planning*, vol. 26, no. 3, pp. 55–66.

McDaniel, C. Jr. and Gates, R. (1993) *Contemporary Marketing Research* (2nd edn), West Publishing Co., Minneapolis, MN.

Malhotra, N.K. (1993) *Marketing Research: An applied orientation*, Prentice Hall, Englewood Cliffs, NJ.

E-commerce glossary

Bandwidth   Indicates the speed at which data are transferred using a particular network medium. It is measured in bits per second (bps).

Banner advertisement   A graphic displayed on a Web page for purposes of brand building or driving traffic to a site.

Bricks-and-mortar   Physical retail stores.

Browser   Program such as Netscape Navigator or Microsoft Internet Explorer, that enables users to view Web pages.

Channel conflicts   A significant threat arising from the introduction of an Internet channel is that while disintermediation gives the opportunity for a company to sell direct and increase the profitability of products it also threaten existing distribution arrangements with existing partners.

Cost per mille (CPM)   Cost per 1,000 ad impressions. An advertising pricing metric that equals the dollar amount paid to reach 1,000 persons in an estimated audience.

Cookies   Bits of information about Web site visitors created by Web sites and stored on client computers.

Cybermediaries   Intermediaries who bring together buyers and sellers or those with particular information or service needs.

Cyberspace   This term was preferred by science fiction writers to indicate the futuristic nature of using the Internet, the prefix 'cyber' indicating a blurring between humans, machines and communications.

Disintermediation   The removal of intermediaries such as distributors or brokers that formerly linked a company to its customer. In particular, disintermediation enables a company to sell direct to the customer by cutting out the middle man.

Domain name   The last part of a URL that includes the organization's unique name followed by a top-level domain name designating the type of organization, such as *.com* for 'commercial' or *.edu* for 'educational'.

E-business   A term describing the use of digital and Internet technologies in the full range of business functions.

Electronic commerce (e-commerce)   Business activities conducted using electronic data transmission via the Internet.

Electronic data exchange (EDI)   The exchange, using digital media, of standardized business document such as purchase orders and invoices between buyers and sellers.

Electronic mail (e-mail)   A message transmitted electronically over the Internet or local area network to one or more receivers.

E-mail ads   Personalized e-mail advertising messages sent to a particular customer usually with a link to the advertiser's Web site.

Extranet   A network system that extends a company's intranet and allows it to connect with the networks of business partners or other designated associates.

Infomediary   An intermediary business whose main source of revenue derives from capturing consumer information and developing detailed profiles of individual customers for use by third parties.

Intermediaries   On-line sites that help bring different parties such as buyers and sellers together.

Internet   The physical network that links computers across the globe. It consists of the infrastructure of network servers and communication links between them.

Intranet   A private information network for company employees that is available only within the company's premises.

IPO   Initial Public Offering. The first sales of stocks to the public.

Market space   A virtual marketplace such as the Internet in which no direct contract occurs between buyers and sellers.

Mass customization   The ability to create tailored marketing messages or products for an individual customer or a group of similar customers yet retain the economies of scale and the capacity of mass marketing or production.

Mass marketing   One-to-many communication between a company and potential customers with limited tailoring of the message.

Meta-site   The prefix 'meta', from the Greek for 'between, with, or after' has come to mean 'going a level above or beyond'. So a meta-site would be a super site with many links, larger and more extensive than a customary Web site.

MP3   A compression format that has revolutionized the way high-quality digital music can be delivered over the Internet.

One-to-many communication model   A model of communications in which one entity communicates with a number of other entities.

One-to-one communication model   A model of communications in which one entity communicates with one other entity.

Portal   A Web site that acts as a gateway to the information on the Internet by providing search engines, directories and other services such as personalized news or free e-mail.

Reverse auction   A type of auction in which sellers bid prices for which they are willing to sell items or services.

Spam   Electronic junk mail.

Transaction costs   The total of all costs incurred by a buyer and seller as they gather information and negotiate a transaction.

Virtual fairs   On-line sites that show new products, technologies, and services to current or potential buyers.

Web addresses (universal resource locators – URLs)   Web addresses refer to particular pages on a Web server, which is hosted by a company or organization. The technical name for Web addresses is uniform or universal resource locators (URLs).

Web application protocol (WAP)   A standard that enables mobile phones to access text from Web sites.

Web server   Computer that holds the pages and images that form a Web site and accepts requests from Web browsers to download them. The Web server is the host for the Web site.

World Wide Web (www)   The subset of Internet computers that connects computers and the contents in a specific way which allows for easy sharing of data using a standard interface.

Index